WEBSTER'S 21ST CENTURY WORLD ATLAS

The Editors of AND Cartographic

BARNES & NOBLE BOOKS
NEW YORK

Contents

4 Key map and legend

6 World flags and statistics

30 World: Political

32 North America: Political

34 Canada

36 United States

38 United States: Northwest

40 United States: Northeast

42 United States: Southeast

44 United States: Southwest

46 Central America
and the Caribbean

48 South America: Political

50 South America: North

52 South America: South

54 Europe: Political

56 Scandinavia

58 Central Europe

Produced by AND Cartographic Publishers Ltd
Alberto House, Hogwood Lane
Finchampstead, Berks, RG40 4RF
United Kingdom

This edition published by Barnes & Noble, Inc.,
by arrangement with AND Cartographic Publishers Ltd.

1999 Barnes & Noble Books

ISBN 0-7607-1658-7 casebound
ISBN 0-7607-1659-5 paperback

Originated by AND Cartographic Publishers Ltd.

Printed and bound in China

99 00 01 02 MC 9 8 7 6 5 4 3 2 1
99 00 01 02 MP 9 8 7 6 5 4 3 2 1

60 Germany
62 Benelux
64 British Isles
66 France
68 Spain and Portugal
70 The Alpine States
72 Italy
74 The Balkans
76 Greece and Western Turkey
78 European Russia
80 Asia: Political
82 Asia: Northwest
84 Asia: Northeast
86 Asia: East
88 Japan and Korea
90 Asia: Southeast
92 Malaysia and Indonesia
94 Asia: South
96 The Middle East
98 Turkey
100 Israel and the Gulf States
102 Africa: Political
104 Africa: Northeast
106 Africa: Northwest
108 Africa: West
110 Africa: Central
112 Africa: Southern
114 Oceania: Political
116 Australia
118 New Zealand
120 Polar Regions
121 Glossary
122 Index

Legend and key map

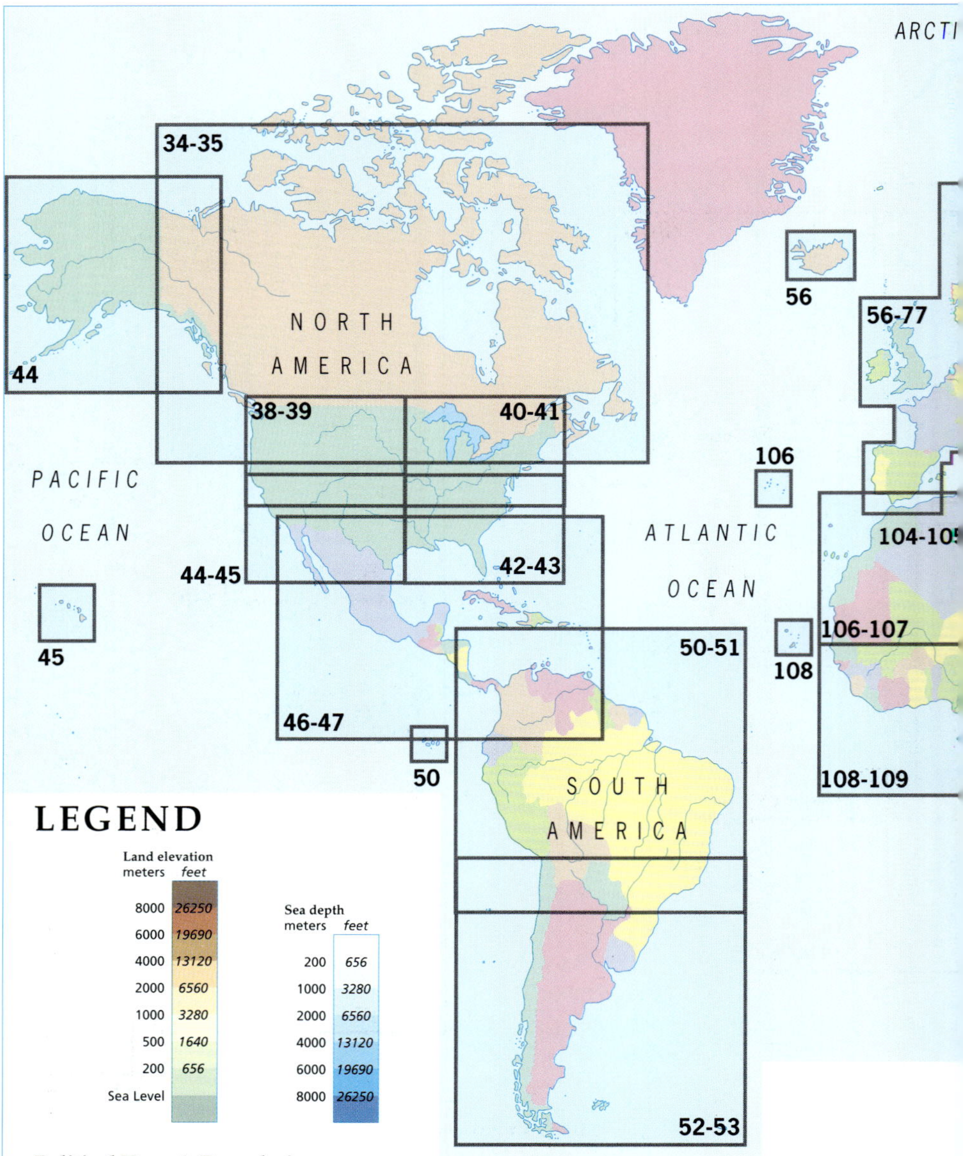

ARCTI
34-35
44
NORTH
AMERICA
38-39
40-41
56
56-77
106
PACIFIC
OCEAN
ATLANTIC
OCEAN
44-45
42-43
104-10
45
50-51
106-107
108
46-47
50
108-109
SOUTH
AMERICA
52-53
LEGEND
Land elevation
meters feet
8000 26250
6000 19690
4000 13120
2000 6560
1000 3280
500 1640
200 656
Sea Level
Sea depth
meters feet
200 656
1000 3280
2000 6560
4000 13120
6000 19690
8000 26250

Political Type & Boundaries

CANADA	country
ONTARIO	state or province
	international boundary
	state or province boundary
	undefined/disputed boundary or ceasefire/demarcation line

Communications

- highway
- main road
- other road or track
- railroad
- international airport

Topographic Features

Mount Ziel 1510	elevation above sea leve in meters
133	elevation below sea leve in meters
Khyber Pass 1080	mountain pass (height in meters)

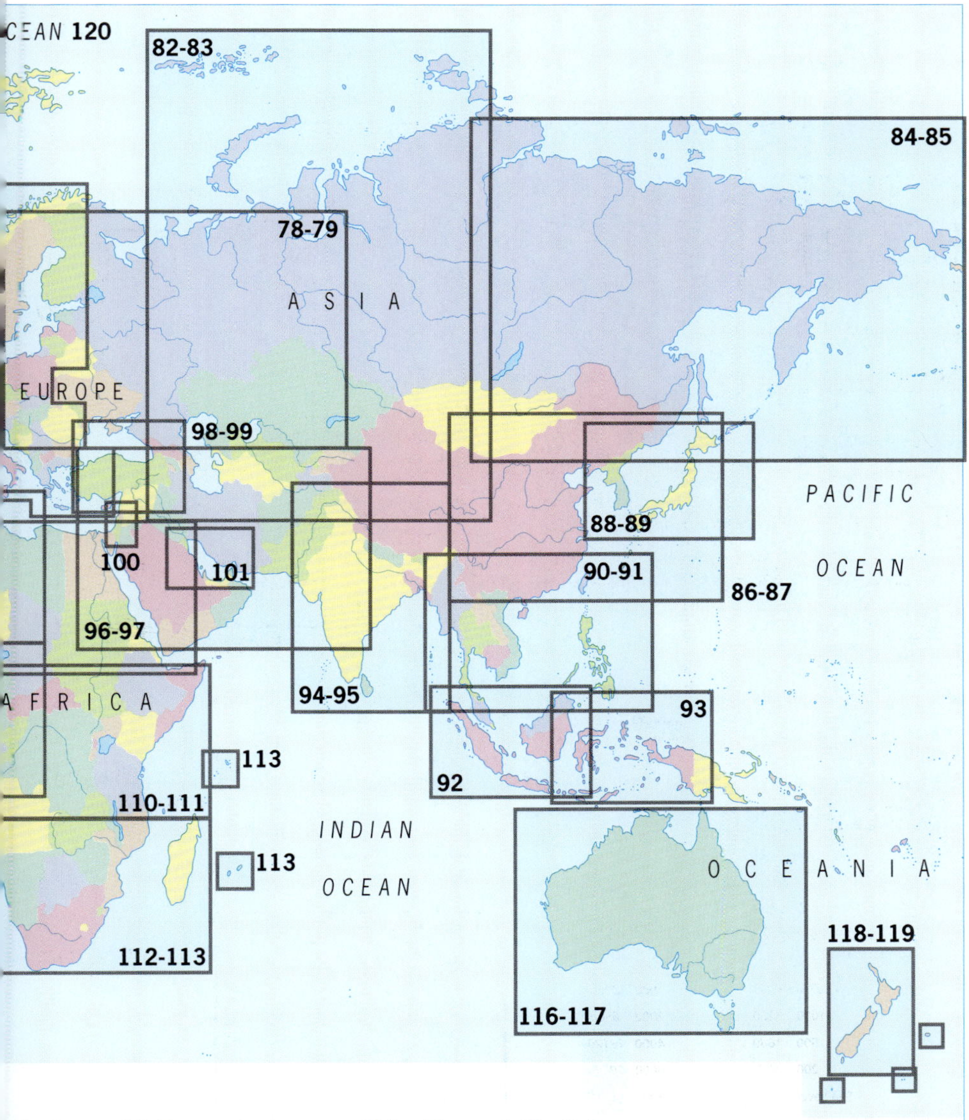
CEAN 120
82-83
84-85
78-79
A S I A
EUROPE
98-99
100
101
96-97
94-95
88-89
90-91
86-87
PACIFIC
OCEAN
93
92
AFRICA
113
110-111
113
INDIAN
OCEAN
112-113
OCEANIA
118-119
116-117

Hydrographic Features

	river, canal
	seasonal river
Niagara Falls, Kariba Dam	waterfall, dam
	lake, seasonal lake
	salt lake, seasonal salt lake
	ice cap or glacier

Cities, Towns & Capitals

CHICAGO	over 3 million
HAMBURG	1 – 3 million
Bulawayo	250 000 – 1 million
Antofogasta	100 000 – 250 000
Ajaccio	25 000 – 100 000
Indian Springs	under 25 000

LONDON	country capital
Columbia	state or province capital
	urban area

Cultural Features

Persepolis	ancient site or ruin
	ancient wall

World Flags and Statistics

National populations: United Nations, Population Division, Dept. of Economic & Social Affairs, 1998

NORTH AND CENTRAL AMERICA

Antigua and Barbuda

Area: 171 sq. mi.
Population: 67,000
Capital: St John's (*pop:* 22,342)
Religions: Protestant, Roman Catholic
Languages: English, Creole
Political system: Constitutional monarchy
Economy: Tourism, fishing
GNP per capita: US$7,380
Currency: East Caribbean dollar

Bahamas, The

Area: 5,358 sq. mi.
Population: 296,000
Capital: Nassau (*pop:* 172,196)
Religions: Protestant, Roman Catholic
Languages: English, Creole
Political system: Constitutional monarchy
Economy: Tourism, banking
GNP per capita: US$11,940
Currency: Bahamian dollar

Barbados

Area: 166 sq. mi.
Population: 268,000
Capital: Bridgetown (*pop:* 108,000)
Religions: Protestant, Roman Catholic
Languages: English, Creole
Political system: Constitutional monarchy
Economy: Sugar, tourism
GNP per capita: US$6,560
Currency: Barbados dollar

Belize

Area: 8,763 sq. mi.
Population: 230,000
Capital: Belmopan (*pop:* 44,087)
Religion: Christian
Languages: English, Spanish, Creole
Political system: Constitutional monarchy
Economy: Agriculture, tourism
GNP per capita: US$2,740
Currency: Belize dollar

Canada

Area: 3,849,674 sq. mi.
Population: 30,563,000
Capital: Ottawa (*pop:* 1,010,288)
Religions: Roman Catholic, Protestant
Languages: English, French
Political system: Constitutional monarchy
Economy: Light industries
GNP per capita: US$19,290
Currency: Canadian dollar

Costa Rica

Area: 19,730 sq. mi.
Population: 3,841,000
Capital: San José (*pop:* 1,186,417)
Religion: Roman Catholic
Languages: Spanish, English, Creole
Political system: Republic
Economy: Agriculture, coffee
GNP per capita: US$2,640
Currency: Costa Rican colón

Cuba

Area: 42,804 sq. mi.
Population: 11,116,000
Capital: Havana (*pop:* 2,175,888)
Religion: Roman Catholic
Languages: Spanish, English
Political System: Republic
Economy: Sugar
GNP per capita: US$1,250
Currency: Cuban peso

Dominica

Area: 290 sq. mi.
Population: 71,000
Capital: Roseau (*pop:* 16,243)
Religions: Roman Catholic, Protestant
Languages: English, Creole
Political system: Republic
Economy: Bananas, tourism
GNP per capita: US$3,120
Currency: East Caribbean dollar

Capital city population figures reflect greater metropolitan areas

Dominican Republic

Area: 18,816 sq. mi.
Population: 8,232,000
Capital: Santo Domingo
(*pop:* 2,134,779)
Religions: Roman Catholic, Protestant
Main language: Spanish
Political system: Republic
Economy: Mining, sugar
GNP per capita: US$1,670
Currency: Dominican Republic peso

Haiti

Area: 10,714 sq. mi.
Population: 7,952,000
Capital: Port-au-Prince
(*pop:* 690,168)
Religions: Roman Catholic, Protestant
Languages: Creole, French
Political system: Republic
Economy: Dependent on foreign aid
GNP per capita: US$330
Currency: Gourde

El Salvador

Area: 8,124 sq. mi.
Population: 6,032,000
Capital: San Salvador
(*pop:* 422,570)
Religions: Roman Catholic, Protestant
Main language: Spanish
Political system: Republic
Economy: Coffee, foreign aid
GNP per capita: US$1,810
Currency: El Salvador colón

Honduras

Area: 43,277 sq. mi.
Population: 6,147,000
Capital: Tegucigalpa
(*pop:* 670,000)
Religions: Roman Catholic, others
Languages: Spanish, English
Political system: Republic
Economy: Bananas, coffee
GNP per capita: US$700
Currency: Lempira

Grenada

Area: 133 sq. mi.
Population: 93,000
Capital: St George's
(*pop:* 4,788)
Religions: Roman Catholic, Protestant
Languages: English, Creole
Political system: Constitutional monarchy
Economy: Spices, cocoa
GNP per capita: US$3,000
Currency: East Caribbean dollar

Jamaica

Area: 4,243 sq. mi.
Population: 2,538,000
Capital: Kingston
(*pop:* 103,962)
Religions: Christian, others
Languages: English, Creole
Political system: Constitutional monarchy
Economy: Bauxite, tourism
GNP per capita: US$1,560
Currency: Jamaican dollar

Guatemala

Area: 42,042 sq. mi.
Population: 10,801,000
Capital: Guatemala City
(*pop:* 1,675,589)
Religion: Christian
Languages: Spanish, Indian languages
Political system: Republic
Economy: Agriculture, sugar
GNP per capita: US$1,500
Currency: Quetzal

Mexico

Area: 756,066 sq. mi.
Population: 95,831,000
Capital: Mexico City
(*pop:* 15,047,685)
Religions: Roman Catholic, Protestant
Languages: Spanish, Indian languages
Political system: Republic
Economy: Oil, cash crops
GNP per capita: US$3,680
Currency: Peso

Nicaragua

Area: 50,193 sq. mi.
Population: 4,807,000
Capital: Managua (*pop:* 608,020)
Religions: Roman Catholic, others
Languages: Spanish, English
Political system: Republic
Economy: coffee, sugar
GNP per capita: US$410
Currency: Córdoba

Panama

Area: 29,157 sq. mi.
Population: 2,767,000
Capital: Panama City (*pop:* 445,902)
Religions: Roman Catholic, others
Languages: Spanish, Creole
Political system: Republic
Economy: Banking, insurance
GNP per capita: US$3,080
Currency: Balboa

St Kitts-Nevis

Area: 101 sq. mi.
Population: 39,000
Capital: Basseterre (*pop:* 14,161)
Religion: Protestant
Languages: English, Creole
Political system: Constitutional monarchy
Economy: Sugar, tourism
GNP per capita: US$6,160
Currency: East Caribbean dollar

St Lucia

Area: 240 sq. mi.
Population: 150,000
Capital: Castries (*pop:* 56,000)
Religions: Roman Catholic, others
Languages: English, Creole
Political system: Constitutional monarchy
Economy: Agriculture
GNP per capita: US$3,620
Currency: East Caribbean dollar

St Vincent and the Grenadines

Area: 150 sq. mi.
Population: 112,000
Capital: Kingstown (*pop:* 33,694)
Religions: Protestant, Roman Catholic
Languages: English, Creole
Political system: Constitutional monarchy
Economy: Agriculture
GNP per capita: US$2,500
Currency: East Caribbean dollar

Trinidad and Tobago

Area: 1,981 sq. mi.
Population: 1,283,000
Capital: Port of Spain (*pop:* 50,878)
Religions: Christian, Hindu, Muslim
Main language: English
Political system: Republic
Economy: Oil, gas
GNP per capita: US$4,230
Currency: Trinidad and Tobago dollar

United States

Area: 3,615,276 sq. mi.
Population: 274,028,000
Capital: Washington DC (*pop:* 7,051,495)
Religions: Protestant, Roman Catholic, Jewish
Languages: English, Spanish
Political system: Republic
Economy: Manufacturing, agriculture
GNP per capita: US$28,740
Currency: US dollar

SOUTH AMERICA

Argentina

Area: 1,073,518 sq. mi.
Population: 36,123,000
Capital: Buenos Aires (*pop:* 10,686,163)
Religions: Roman Catholic, Jewish, others
Languages: Spanish, English
Political system: Republic
Economy: Beef, wheat
GNP per capita: US$8,570
Currency: Peso

Bolivia

Area: 424,165 sq. mi.
Population: 7,957,000
Capital: Sucre (*pop:* 144,994)
Religions: Roman Catholic, others
Languages: Spanish, Quechua, Aymará
Political system: Republic
Economy: Mining, oil
GNP per capita: US$950
Currency: Boliviano

Brazil

Area: 3,300,171 sq. mi.
Population: 165,851,000
Capital: Brasilia (*pop:* 1,601,094)
Religion: Christian
Main language: Portuguese
Political system: Republic
Economy: Mining industry
GNP per capita: US$4,720
Currency: Real

Chile

Area: 292,135 sq. mi.
Population: 14,824,000
Capital: Santiago (*pop:* 5,257,937)
Religions: Roman Catholic, Protestant
Languages: Spanish, Indian languages
Political system: Republic
Economy: Copper, wine
GNP per capita: US$5,020
Currency: Chilean peso

Colombia

Area: 439,737 sq. mi.
Population: 40,803,000
Capital: Bogotá (*pop:* 8,000,000)
Religions: Roman Catholic, others
Languages: Spanish, Indian languages
Political system: Republic
Economy: Coffee, coal
GNP per capita: US$2,280
Currency: Colombian peso

Ecuador

Area: 109,484 sq. mi.
Population: 12,175,000
Capital: Quito (*pop:* 1,387,887)
Religions: Roman Catholic, others
Languages: Spanish, Quechua
Political system: Republic
Economy: Bananas, oil
GNP per capita: US$1,590
Currency: Sucre

Guyana

Area: 83,000 sq. mi.
Population: 850,000
Capital: Georgetown (*pop:* 250,000)
Religions: Christian, Hindu, Muslim
Languages: English, Creole
Political system: Republic
Economy: Bauxite, gold
GNP per capita: US$800
Currency: Guyana dollar

Paraguay

Area: 157,048 sq. mi.
Population: 5,222,000
Capital: Asuncion (*pop:* 718,690)
Religions: Roman Catholic, other
Languages: Spanish, Guaraní
Political system: Republic
Economy: Agriculture, electricity
GNP per capita: US$2,010
Currency: Guaraní

Peru

Area: 496,225 sq. mi.
Population: 24,797,000
Capital: Lima (*pop:* 6,483,901)
Religions: Roman Catholic, others
Languages: Spanish, Quechua, Aymará
Political system: Republic
Economy: Minerals, fishing
GNP per capita: US$2,460
Currency: New Sol

Surinam

Area: 63,037 sq. mi.
Population: 414,000
Capital: Paramaribo
(*pop:* 200,970)
Religions: Christian, Hindu, Muslim
Languages: Dutch, Sranang Tongo, Hindi
Political system: Republic
Economy: Aluminium, bauxite
GNP per capita: US$1,240
Currency: Surinam guilder

Uruguay

Area: 68,500 sq. mi.
Population: 3,289,000
Capital: Montevideo
(*pop:* 1,383,660)
Religions: Roman Catholic, Protestant, Jewish
Main language: Spanish
Political system: Republic
Economy: Agriculture, livestock
GNP per capita: US$6,020
Currency: New Uruguayan peso

Venezuela

Area: 352,145 sq. mi.
Population: 23,242,000
Capital: Caracas (*pop:* 2,784,042)
Religions: Roman Catholic, Protestant
Languages: Spanish, Indian languages
Political system: Republic
Economy: Oil, coal, bauxite
GNP per capita: US$3,450
Currency: Bolívar

EUROPE

Albania

Area: 11,099 sq. mi.
Population: 3,119,000
Capital: Tirana (*pop:* 244,153)
Religions: Muslim, Greek Orthodox
Languages: Albanian, Greek
Political system: Republic
Economy: Oil, gas
GNP per capita: US$750
Currency: Lek

Andorra

Area: 175 sq. mi.
Population: 72,000
Capital: Andorra la Vella
(*pop:* 16,151)
Religions: Roman Catholic, others
Languages: Catalan, French, Spanish
Political system: Constitutional principality
Economy: Tourism, banking, commerce
GNP per capita: US$14,000
Currency: French franc, Spanish peseta

Austria

Area: 32,378 sq. mi.
Population: 8,140,000
Capital: Vienna (*pop:* 1,806,737)
Religions: Roman Catholic, Protestant
Main language: German
Political system: Republic
Economy: Manufacturing industry
GNP per capita: US$27,980
Currency: Schilling

Belarus

Area: 80,155 sq. mi.
Population: 10,315,000
Capital: Minsk
(*pop:* 1,687,400)
Religions: Russian Orthodox, Roman Catholic
Languages: Belarusian, Russian
Political system: Republic
Economy: Food processing
GNP per capita: US$2,150
Currency: Rouble

Belgium

Area: 11,783 sq. mi.
Population: 10,141,000
Capital: Brussels (*pop:* 960,324)
Religions: Roman Catholic, others
Languages: Flemish, French
Political system: Constitutional monarchy
Economy: Steel, glassware
GNP per capita: US$26,490
Currency: Belgian franc

Bosnia-Herzegovina

Area: 19,741 sq. mi.
Population: 3,675,000
Capital: Sarajevo
(*pop:* 415,631)
Religion: Muslim
Languages: Serbo-Croat, Croato-Serb
Political system: Republic
Economy: Manufacturing industry
GNP per capita: US$2,600
Currency: Convertible marka

Bulgaria

Area: 42,823 sq. mi.
Population: 8,336,000
Capital: Sofia (*pop:* 1,188,563)
Religions: Christian, Muslim, Jewish
Languages: Bulgarian, Turkish
Political system: Republic
Economy: Agriculture, wine
GNP per capita: US$1,140
Currency: Lev

Croatia

Area: 34,022 sq. mi.
Population: 4,481,000
Capital: Zagreb
(*pop:* 867,717)
Religions: Roman Catholic, Protestant
Languages: Croato-Serb, Serbo-Croat
Political system: Republic
Economy: Manufacturing
GNP per capita: US$4,610
Currency: Kuna

Czech Republic

Area: 30,450 sq. mi.
Population: 10,282,000
Capital: Prague (*pop:* 1,216,568)
Religions: Roman Catholic,
Protestant
Languages: Czech, Slovak
Political system: Republic
Economy: Heavy industry
GNP per capita: US$5,200
Currency: Koruna

Denmark

Area: 16,639 sq. mi.
Population: 5,270,000
Capital: Copenhagen
(*pop:* 1,353,333)
Religions: Evangelical, Lutheran, others
Main language: Danish
Political system: Constitutional monarchy
Economy: Industry, agriculture
GNP per capita: US$32,500
Currency: Kroner

Estonia

Area: 17,413 sq. mi.
Population: 1,429,000
Capital: Tallinn (*pop:* 447,672)
Religions: Evangelical, Lutheran
Languages: Estonian, Russian
Political system: Republic
Economy: Machinery, shipping
GNP per capita: US$3,330
Currency: Kroon

Finland

Area: 130,559 sq. mi.
Population: 5,154,000
Capital: Helsinki
(*pop:* 1,016,291)
Religions: Evangelical, Lutheran, Greek Orthodox
Languages: Finnish, Swedish
Political system: Republic
Economy: Engineering
GNP per capita: US$24,080
Currency: Markka

France

Area: 212,935 sq. mi.
Population: 58,683,000
Capital: Paris (*pop:* 9,319,367)
Religions: Roman Catholic,
Protestant
Main language: French
Political system: Republic
Economy: Steel, chemicals
GNP per capita: US$26,050
Currency: Franc

Germany

Area: 137,735 sq. mi.
Population: 82,133,000
Capital: Berlin (*pop:* 3,472,009)
Religions: Protestant, Roman Catholic
Main language: German
Political system: Republic
Economy: Cars, engineering
GNP per capita: US$28,260
Currency: Deutsche mark

Greece

Area: 50,949 sq. mi.
Population: 10,600,000
Capital: Athens (*pop:* 3,027,922)
Religions: Greek Orthodox, Muslim
Main language: Greek
Political system: Republic
Economy: Tourism, shipping
GNP per capita: US$12,010
Currency: Drachma

Hungary

Area: 35,920 sq. mi.
Population: 10,116,000
Capital: Budapest (*pop:* 2,002,121)
Religions: Roman Catholic, Protestant
Languages: Magyar, German
Political system: Republic
Economy: Industry, agriculture
GNP per capita: US$4,430
Currency: Forint

Iceland

Area: 39,769 sq. mi.
Population: 276,000
Capital: Reykjavik (*pop:* 153,210)
Religions: Evangelical, Lutheran, others
Languages: Icelandic, Danish
Political system: Republic
Economy: Fishing
GNP per capita: US$27,580
Currency: Icelandic króna

Ireland, Republic of

Area: 27,137 sq. mi.
Population: 3,681,000
Capital: Dublin (*pop:* 952,700)
Religions: Roman Catholic, Protestant
Languages: English, Irish
Political system: Republic
Economy: Agriculture
GNP per capita: US$18,280
Currency: Punt

Italy

Area: 116,320 sq. mi.
Population: 57,369,000
Capital: Rome (*pop:* 2,693,383)
Religions: Roman Catholic, other
Main language: Italian
Political system: Republic
Economy: Industry design, textiles
GNP per capita: US$20,120
Currency: Lira

Latvia

Area: 24,942 sq. mi.
Population: 2,424,000
Capital: Riga (*pop:* 847,976)
Religions: Evangelical, Lutheran, others
Languages: Latvian, Russian
Political system: Republic
Economy: Transport, defence equipment
GNP per capita: US$2,430
Currency: Lats

Liechtenstein

Area: 62 sq. mi.
Population: 32,000
Capital: Vaduz (*pop:* 5,072)
Religions: Roman Catholic, Protestant
Main language: German
Political system: Constitutional monarchy
Economy: Banking, dental products
GNP per capita: US$33,500
Currency: Swiss franc

Lithuania

Area: 25,174 sq. mi.
Population: 3,694,000
Capital: Vilnius
(*pop:* 581,500)
Religions: Roman Catholic, others
Languages: Lithuanian, Russian
Political system: Republic
Economy: Textiles, engineering
GNP per capita: US$2,230
Currency: Litas

Luxembourg

Area: 998 sq. mi.
Population: 422,000
Capital: Luxembourg
(*pop:* 76,446)
Religions: Roman Catholic, others
Languages: Letzebuergesch, French, German
Political system: Constitutional monarchy
Economy: Steel-making
GNP per capita: US$45,440
Currency: Luxembourg franc

Macedonia

Area: 9,928 sq. mi.
Population: 1,999,000
Capital: Skopje
(*pop:* 448,229)
Religions: Christian, Muslim
Languages: Macedonian, Serbo-Croat
Political system: Republic
Economy: Reliant on foreign aid
GNP per capita: US$1,090
Currency: Dinar

Malta

Area: 122 sq. mi.
Population: 384,000
Capital: Valletta (*pop:* 9,144)
Religions: Roman Catholic, Anglican
Languages: Maltesse, English
Political system: Republic
Economy: Tourism
GNP per capita: US$11,000
Currency: Maltese lira

Moldova

Area: 13,012 sq. mi.
Population: 4,378,000
Capital: Chisinau
(*pop:* 667,100)
Religions: Romanian Orthodox, Jewish
Languages: Moldovan, Russian
Political system: Republic
Economy: Wine, tobacco, cotton
GNP per capita: US$540
Currency: Leu

Monaco

Area: 0.4 sq. mi.
Population: 33,000
Capital: Monaco (*pop:* 27,063)
Religions: Roman Catholic, others
Languages: French, Italian
Political system: Constitutional monarchy
Economy: Tourism, gambling
GNP per capita: US$16,000
Currency: French franc

Netherlands

Area: 15,770 sq. mi.
Population: 15,678,000
Capital: Amsterdam
(*pop:* 1,100,764)
Religions: Roman Catholic, Protestant, others
Main language: Dutch
Political system: Constitutional monarchy
Economy: Machinery, chemicals
GNP per capita: US$25,820
Currency: Guilder

Norway

Area: 125,050 sq. mi.
Population: 4,419,000
Capital: Oslo (*pop:* 758,949)
Religions: Evangelical, Lutheran, others
Main language: Norwegian
Political system: Constitutional monarchy
Economy: Oil, gas
GNP per capita: US$36,090
Currency: Krone

Poland

Area: 124,808 sq. mi.
Population: 38,718,000
Capital: Warsaw (*pop:* 1,643,203)
Religions: Roman Catholic, others
Main language: Polish
Political system: Republic
Economy: Heavy industry
GNP per capita: US$3,590
Currency: Zloty

Portugal

Area: 35,514 sq. mi.
Population: 9,869,000
Capital: Lisbon (*pop:* 2,561,225)
Religions: Roman Catholic, Protestant
Main language: Portuguese
Political system: Republic
Economy: Agriculture, wine
GNP per capita: US$10,450
Currency: Escudo

Romania

Area: 92,043 sq. mi.
Population: 22,474,000
Capital: Bucharest (*pop:* 2,060,551)
Religions: Romanian Orthodox, Roman Catholic
Main language: Romanian
Political system: Republic
Economy: Heavy industry
GNP per capita: US$1,420
Currency: Leu

Russia

Area: 6,592,850 sq. mi.
Population: 147,434,000
Capital: Moscow (*pop:* 8,663,142)
Religions: Russian Orthodox, Jewish, Muslim
Main language: Russian
Political system: Republic
Economy: Oil, gas
GNP per capita: US$2,740
Currency: Rouble

San Marino

Area: 24 sq. mi.
Population: 26,000
Capital: San Marino (*pop:* 4,251)
Religions: Roman Catholic, Protestant
Main language: Italian
Political system: Republic
Economy: Tourism, light industry
GNP per capita: US$20,000
Currency: Italian lira

Slovakia

Area: 18,924 sq. mi.
Population: 5,377,000
Capital: Bratislava (*pop:* 451,272)
Religions: Roman Catholic, Protestant
Languages: Slovak, Hungarian, Czech
Political system: Republic
Economy: Heavy industry
GNP per capita: US$3,700
Currency: Koruna

Slovenia

Area: 7,821 sq. mi.
Population: 1,993,000
Capital: Ljubljana (*pop:* 330,000)
Religions: Roman Catholic, Muslim
Languages: Slovene, Hungarian, Italian
Political system: Republic
Economy: Manufacturing, tourism
GNP per capita: US$9,680
Currency: Tolar

Spain

Area: 195,365 sq. mi.
Population: 39,628,000
Capital: Madrid (*pop:* 3,084,673)
Religions: Roman Catholic, others
Languages: Spanish, Basque
Political system: Constitutional monarchy
Economy: Agriculture, industry
GNP per capita: US$14,510
Currency: Peseta

Sweden

Area: 173,732 sq. mi.
Population: 8,875,000
Capital: Stockholm
(*pop:* 1,532,803)
Religions: Evangelical, Lutheran, Roman Catholic
Main language: Swedish
Political system: Constitutional monarchy
Economy: Car industry, electronics
GNP per capita: US$26,220
Currency: Swedish krona

Switzerland

Area: 15,940 sq. mi.
Population: 7,299,000
Capital: Bern (*pop:* 321,932)
Religions: Roman Catholic, Protestant
Languages: German, French, Italian
Political system: Republic
Economy: Banking, tourism
GNP per capita: US$44,430
Currency: Swiss franc

Ukraine

Area: 233,090 sq. mi.
Population: 50,861,000
Capital: Kiev (*pop:* 2,646,100)
Religions: Ukrainian Orthodox, others
Languages: Ukrainian, Russian
Political system: Republic
Economy: Heavy industry
GNP per capita: US$1,040
Currency: Hryvna

United Kingdom

Area: 94,248 sq. mi.
Population: 58,649,000
Capital: London
(*pop:* 6,962,319)
Religions: Protestant, Roman Catholic, others
Main language: English
Political system: Constitutional monarchy
Economy: Financial services, defence
GNP per capita: US$20,710
Currency: Pound

Vatican City

Area: 0.2 sq. mi.
Population: 1,000
Capital: Vatican City (*pop:* 480)
Religion: Roman Catholic
Main language: Italian
Political system: Absolute rule
Economy: Investment
GNP per capita: not available
Currency: Italian lira

Yugoslavia

Area: 39,449 sq. mi.
Population: 10,635,000
Capital: Belgrade
(*pop:* 1,136,786)
Religions: Orthodox Catholic, Muslim
Languages: Serbo-Croat, Albanian, Hungarian
Political system: Republic
Economy: Largely barter
GNP per capita: US$1,400
Currency: New dinar

AFRICA

Algeria

Area: 919,595 sq. mi.
Population: 30,081,000
Capital: Algiers (*pop:* 3,250,000)
Religions: Muslim, Christian
Languages: Arabic, Berber, French
Political system: Republic
Economy: Oil, gas
GNP per capita: US$1,490
Currency: Algerian dinar

Angola

Area: 481,354 sq. mi.
Population: 12,092,000
Capital: Luanda (*pop:* 475,328)
Religions. Roman Catholic, Protestant
Main language: Portuguese
Political system: Republic
Economy: Oil, diamonds
GNP per capita: US$340
Currency: Readjusted kwanza

Benin

Area: 43,484 sq. mi.
Population: 5,781,000
Capital: Porto Novo (*pop:* 179,138)
Religions: Traditional beliefs, Muslim
Languages: French, Fon, Bariba, Yoruba
Political system: Republic
Economy: Subsistence farming
GNP per capita: US$380
Currency: Franc CFA

Botswana

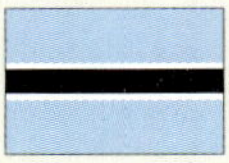

Area: 224,607 sq. mi.
Population: 1,570,000
Capital: Gaborone (*pop:* 133,468)
Religions: Traditional beliefs, Anglican
Languages: Setswana, English
Political system: Republic
Economy: Diamonds, copper
GNP per capita: US$3,260
Currency: Pula

Burkina

Area: 105,792 sq. mi.
Population: 11,305,000
Capital: Ouagadougou (*pop:* 634,479)
Religions: Traditional beliefs, Muslim
Languages: French, Mossi, Fulani, Tuareg
Political system: Republic
Economy: Agriculture
GNP per capita: US$240
Currency: Franc CFA

Burundi

Area: 10,747 sq. mi.
Population: 6,457,000
Capital: Bujumbura (*pop:* 235,440)
Religions: Roman Catholic, traditional beliefs
Languages: Kirundi, French, Kiswahili
Political system: Republic
Economy: Agriculture
GNP per capita: US$180
Currency: Burundi franc

Cameroon

Area: 183,569 sq. mi.
Population: 14,305,000
Capital: Yaoundé (*pop:* 653,670)
Religions: Traditional beliefs, Christian
Languages: French, English
Political system: Republic
Economy: Oil, timber, cocoa
GNP per capita: US$650
Currency: Franc CFA

Cape Verde

Area: 1,557 sq. mi.
Population: 408,000
Capital: Praia (*pop:* 80,000)
Religions: Roman Catholic, Protestant
Languages: Portuguese, Creole
Political system: Republic
Economy: Subsistence farming
GNP per capita: US$1,090
Currency: Escudo

Central African Republic

Area: 240,535 sq. mi.
Population: 3,485,000
Capital: Bangui (*pop:* 473,817)
Religions: Christian, traditional beliefs
Languages: French, Sango
Political system: Republic
Economy: Subsistence farming, gold
GNP per capita: US$320
Currency: Franc CFA

Chad

Area: 495,755 sq. mi.
Population: 7,270,000
Capital: Ndjamena (*pop:* 179,000)
Religions: Muslim, Christian
Languages: French, Arabic, Sara
Political system: Republic
Economy: Subsistence farming
GNP per capita: US$240
Currency: Franc CFA

Comoros

Area: 863 sq. mi.
Population: 658,000
Capital: Moroni (*pop:* 17,267)
Religions: Muslim, Roman Catholic
Languages: French, Arabic, Comoran
Political system: Republic
Economy: Subsistence farming
GNP per capita: US$400
Currency: Comorian franc

Congo

Area: 132,047 sq. mi.
Population: 2,785,000
Capital: Brazzaville
(*pop:* 596,200)
Religions: Roman Catholic, traditional beliefs
Languages: French, Lingala, Kikongo
Political system: Republic
Economy: Oil, sugar, coffee
GNP per capita: US$660
Currency: Franc CFA

Congo, Democratic Republic of

Area: 905,355 sq. mi.
Population: 49,139,000
Capital: Kinshasa
(*pop:* 2,664,309)
Religions: Christian, traditional beliefs
Languages: Swahili, Lingala, French
Political system: Republic
Economy: Minerals
GNP per capita: US$110
Currency: Congolese franc

Djibouti

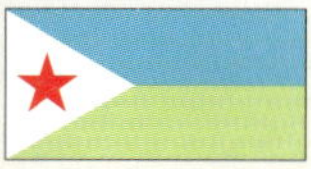

Area: 8,958 sq. mi.
Population: 623,000
Capital: Djibouti
(*pop:* 340,700)
Religions: Christian, others
Languages: Arabic, French, Somali
Political system: Republic
Economy: Sea trade
GNP per capita: US$1,000
Currency: Djibouti franc

Egypt

Area: 386,662 sq. mi.
Population: 65,978,000
Capital: Cairo (*pop:* 13,000,000)
Religions: Muslim, others
Main language: Arabic
Political system: Republic
Economy: Oil, gas
GNP per capita: US$1,180
Currency: Egyptian pound

Equatorial Guinea

Area: 10,831 sq. mi.
Population: 431,000
Capital: Malabo (*pop:* 30,418)
Religions: Roman Catholic, others
Languages: French, Spanish
Political system: Republic
Economy: Timber, cocoa, oil
GNP per capita: US$1,050
Currency: Franc CFA

Eritrea

Area: 45,406 sq. mi.
Population: 3,577,000
Capital: Asmara
(*pop:* 358,100)
Religions: Coptic Christian, Muslim, others
Languages: English, Arabic
Political system: Republic
Economy: Subsistence farming, gold
GNP per capita: US$210
Currency: Nakfa

Ethiopia

Area: 426,373 sq. mi.
Population: 59,649,000
Capital: Addis Ababa
(*pop:* 2,316,400)
Religions: Muslim, Christian
Languages: Amharic, English, Arabic
Political system: Republic
Economy: Subsistence farming
GNP per capita: US$110
Currency: Ethiopian birr

Gabon

Area: 103,347 sq. mi.
Population: 1,167,000
Capital: Libreville (*pop:* 251,000)
Religions: Roman Catholic, Protestant
Languages: French, Fang, Eshira
Political system: Republic
Economy: Oil, timber, cocoa
GNP per capita: US$4,230
Currency: Franc CFA

Gambia, The

Area: 4,361 sq. mi.
Population: 1,229,000
Capital: Banjul (*pop:* 109,986)
Religions: Muslim, Christian
Languages: English, Mandinka, Fula, Wollof
Political system: Republic
Economy: Agriculture, fishing
GNP per capita: US$350
Currency: Dalasi

Ghana

Area: 92,098 sq. mi.
Population: 19,162,000
Capital: Accra (*pop:* 738,498)
Religions: Traditional beliefs, Muslim
Languages: English, Twi, Fanti
Political system: Republic
Economy: Cocoa, timber, gold
GNP per capita: US$370
Currency: Cedi

Guinea

Area: 94,926 sq. mi.
Population: 7,337,000
Capital: Conakry (*pop:* 763,000)
Religions: Muslim, Christian
Languages: French, Susu, Malinké
Political system: Republic
Economy: Cash crops
GNP per capita: US$570
Currency: Guinea franc

Guinea-Bissau

Area: 13,948 sq. mi.
Population: 1,161,000
Capital: Bissau (*pop:* 109,214)
Religions: Traditional beliefs, Muslim
Languages: Portuguese, Creole
Political system: Republic
Economy: Subsistence farming
GNP per capita: US$240
Currency: Franc CFA

Ivory Coast

Area: 124,504 sq. mi.
Population: 14,292,000
Capital: Yamoussoukro (*pop:* 126,191)
Religions: Traditional beliefs, Muslim
Main language: French
Political system: Republic
Economy: Cash crops, timber
GNP per capita: US$690
Currency: Franc CFA

Kenya

Area: 224,081 sq. mi.
Population: 29,008,000
Capital: Nairobi (*pop:* 1,400,000)
Religions: Roman Catholic, Protestant
Languages: Swahili, English
Political system: Republic
Economy: Tourism, tea
GNP per capita: US$330
Currency: Kenya shilling

Lesotho

Area: 11,720 sq. mi.
Population: 2,062,000
Capital: Maseru (*pop:* 288,951)
Religions: Roman Catholic, Protestant
Languages: Sesotho, English
Political system: Constitutional monarchy
Economy: Subsistence farming
GNP per capita: US$670
Currency: Loti

Liberia

Area: 43,000 sq. mi.
Population: 2,666,000
Capital: Monrovia (*pop:* 421,053)
Religions: Traditional beliefs, Muslim
Languages: English, many ethnic languages
Political system: Republic
Economy: Unstable
GNP per capita: US$850
Currency: Liberian dollar

Libya

Area: 679,362 sq. mi.
Population: 5,339,000
Capital: Tripoli (*pop:* 1,000,000)
Religions: Muslim, others
Languages: Arabic, Tuareg
Political system: Republic
Economy: Oil
GNP per capita: US$7,000
Currency: Libyan dinar

Madagascar

Area: 226,658 sq. mi.
Population: 15,057,000
Capital: Antananarivo (*pop:* 377,600)
Religions: Traditional beliefs, Christian
Languages: Malagasy, French
Political system: Republic
Economy: Coffee, vanilla
GNP per capita: US$250
Currency: Franc malgache

Malawi

Area: 45,747 sq. mi.
Population: 10,346,000
Capital: Lilongwe (*pop:* 233,973)
Religions: Protestant, traditional beliefs
Languages: Chichewa, English
Political system: Republic
Economy: Tobacco, tea
GNP per capita: US$220
Currency: Kwacha

Mali

Area: 478,841 sq. mi.
Population: 10,694,000
Capital: Bamako (*pop:* 658,275)
Religions: Muslim, traditional beliefs
Languages: French, Bambara, Fulani
Political system: Republic
Economy: Farming, herding, fishing
GNP per capita: US$260
Currency: Franc CFA

Mauritania

Area: 395,956 sq. mi.
Population: 2,529,000
Capital: Nouakchott (*pop:* 850,000)
Religion: Muslim
Languages: Arabic, French, Pulaar
Political system: Republic
Economy: Agriculture, mining
GNP per capita: US$450
Currency: Ouguiya

Mauritius

Area: 788 sq. mi.
Population: 1,141,000
Capital: Port Louis (*pop:* 144,776)
Religions: Hindu, Roman Catholic, Muslim
Languages: Creole, English, French, Hindi
Political system: Republic
Economy: Sugar, tourism
GNP per capita: US$3,800
Currency: Mauritius rupee

Morocco

Area: 172,414 sq. mi.
Population: 27,377,000
Capital: Rabat (*pop:* 1,220,000)
Religion: Muslim
Languages: Arabic, Berber, French, Spanish
Political system: Constitutional monarchy
Economy: Phosphates, tourism
GNP per capita: US$1,250
Currency: Dirham

Mozambique

Area: 309,496 sq. mi.
Population: 18,880,000
Capital: Maputo (*pop:* 882,601)
Religions: Traditional beliefs, Christian
Main language: Portuguese
Political system: Republic
Economy: Foreign aid
GNP per capita: US$90
Currency: Metical

Namibia

Area: 318,261 sq. mi.
Population: 1,660,000
Capital: Windhoek (*pop:* 147,056)
Religions: Christian, others
Languages: English, Afrikaans, German
Political system: Republic
Economy: Uranium, diamonds
GNP per capita: US$2,220
Currency: Namibian dollar

Niger

Area: 489,191 sq. mi.
Population: 10,078,000
Capital: Niamey (*pop:* 392,169)
Religions: Muslim, traditional beliefs
Languages: French, Hausa, Djerma, Fulani
Political system: Republic
Economy: Uranium
GNP per capita: US$200
Currency: Franc CFA

Nigeria

Area: 356,669 sq. mi.
Population: 106,409,000
Capital: Abuja (*pop:* 378,671)
Religions: Muslim, Christian
Languages: English, Hausa, Yoruba, Ibo
Political system: Republic
Economy: Oil
GNP per capita: US$260
Currency: Naira

Rwanda

R

Area: 10,169 sq. mi.
Population: 6,604,000
Capital: Kigali (*pop:* 156,000)
Religions: Roman Catholic, traditional beliefs
Languages: Kinyarwanda, French, English
Political system: Republic
Economy: Coffee, oil, gas
GNP per capita: US$210
Currency: Rwanda franc

São Tomé and Príncipe

Area: 372 sq. mi.
Population: 141,000
Capital: São Tomé (*pop:* 43,420)
Religions: Roman Catholic, others
Languages: Portuguese, Creole
Political system: Republic
Economy: Cocoa, coffee, palm oil
GNP per capita: US$270
Currency: Dobra

Senegal

Area: 75,955 sq. mi.
Population: 9,003,000
Capital: Dakar (*pop:* 1,641,358)
Religions: Muslim, traditional beliefs
Languages: French, Wolof, Fulani, Serer
Political system: Republic
Economy: Farming, mining
GNP per capita: US$550
Currency: Franc CFA

Seychelles

Area: 176 sq. mi.
Population: 76,000
Capital: Victoria (*pop:* 24,324)
Religions: Roman Catholic, others
Languages: French, English, Creole
Political system: Republic
Economy: Tourism
GNP per capita: US$6,880
Currency: Rupee

Sierra Leone

Area: 27,699 sq. mi.
Population: 4,568,000
Capital: Freetown (*pop:* 469,776)
Religions: Traditional beliefs, Muslim
Languages: English, French, Krio
Political system: Republic
Economy: Subsistence farming
GNP per capita: US$200
Currency: Leone

Swaziland

Area: 6,704 sq. mi.
Population: 952,000
Capital: Mbabane (*pop:* 38,290)
Religions: Protestant, others
Languages: Siswati, English
Political system: Absolute monarchy
Economy: Cash crops, asbestos
GNP per capita: US$1,440
Currency: Lilangeni

Somalia

Area: 246,201 sq. mi.
Population: 9,237,000
Capital: Mogadishu (*pop:* 1,000,000)
Religions: Sunni Muslim, others
Languages: Somali, Arabic, English
Political system: Republic
Economy: Foreign aid
GNP per capita: US$500
Currency: Somali shilling

Tanzania

Area: 341,217 sq. mi.
Population: 32,102,000
Capital: Dodoma (*pop:* 88,474)
Religions: Traditional beliefs, Muslim
Languages: Swahili, English
Political system: Republic
Economy: Agriculture, cash crops
GNP per capita: US$210
Currency: Shilling

South Africa

Area: 471,445 sq. mi.
Population: 39,357,000
Capital: Pretoria (*pop:* 525,583)
Religions: Protestant, Roman Catholic, others
Languages: English, Afrikaans, Zulu, Xhosa
Political system: Republic
Economy: Manufacturing, agriculture
GNP per capita: US$3,400
Currency: Rand

Togo

Area: 21,925 sq. mi.
Population: 4,397,000
Capital: Lomé (*pop:* 366,476)
Religions: Traditional beliefs, Christian
Languages: French, Ewe
Political system: Republic
Economy: Agriculture, coffee
GNP per capita: US$330
Currency: Franc CFA

Sudan

Area: 967,500 sq. mi.
Population: 28,292,000
Capital: Khartoum (*pop:* 924,505)
Religions: Muslim, traditional beliefs
Languages: Arabic, English
Political system: Republic
Economy: Cash crops
GNP per capita: US$280
Currency: Sudanese dinar

Tunisia

Area: 63,170 sq. mi.
Population: 9,335,000
Capital: Tunis (*pop:* 1,394,749)
Religions: Muslim, Christian
Languages: Arabic, French, English
Political system: Republic
Economy: Oil, gas
GNP per capita: US$2,090
Currency: Tunisian dinar

Uganda

Area: 93,065 sq. mi.
Population: 20,554,000
Capital: Kampala (*pop:* 750,000)
Religions: Roman Catholic, Protestant, others
Languages: English, Swahili
Political system: Republic
Economy: Coffee, mining
GNP per capita: US$330
Currency: Uganda shilling

Zambia

Area: 290,587 sq. mi.
Population: 8,781,000
Capital: Lusaka (*pop:* 982,362)
Religions: Christian, traditional beliefs
Languages: English, Nyanja, Tonga, Beruba
Political system: Republic
Economy: Subsistence farming
GNP per capita: US$380
Currency: Kwacha

Zimbabwe

Area: 150,872 sq. mi.
Population: 11,377,000
Capital: Harare (*pop:* 1,189,103)
Religions: Christian, traditional beliefs
Languages: English, Shona, Ndebele
Political system: Republic
Economy: Self-sufficient
GNP per capita: US$750
Currency: Zimbabwe dollar

ASIA

Afghanistan

Area: 251,773 sq. mi.
Population: 21,354,000
Capital: Kabul (*pop:* 1,424,400)
Religions: Sumi, Muslim
Languages: Dari, Pushtu
Political system: Republic
Economy: Agriculture
GNP per capita: US$300
Currency: Afghani

Armenia

Area: 11,506 sq. mi.
Population: 3,536,000
Capital: Yerevan (*pop:* 1,254,000)
Religions: Armenian Apostolic, others
Languages: Armenian, Russian
Political system: Republic
Economy: Mining, agriculture
GNP per capita: US$530
Currency: Dram

Azerbaijan

Area: 33,436 sq. mi.
Population: 7,669,000
Capital: Baku (*pop:* 1,149,000)
Religions: Muslim, Armenian Apostolic
Languages: Azerbaijani, Russian
Political system: Republic
Economy: Oil, gas
GNP per capita: US$510
Currency: Manat

Bahrain

Area: 268 sq. mi.
Population: 595,000
Capital: Manama (*pop:* 140,401)
Religions: Shi'a Muslim, Christian
Languages: Arabic, English
Political system: Constitutional monarchy
Economy: Oil, gas
GNP per capita: US$7,840
Currency: Bahraini dinar

Bangladesh

Area: 55,598 sq. mi.
Population: 124,774,000
Capital: Dhaka (*pop:* 3,397,187)
Religions: Muslim, Hindu
Languages: Bengali, English
Political system: Republic
Economy: Foreign aid, jute
GNP per capita: US$270
Currency: Taka

Bhutan

Area: 18,147 sq. mi.
Population: 2,004,000
Capital: Thimphu (*pop:* 15,000)
Religions: Buddhist, Hindu
Languages: Dzongkha, English
Political system: Absolute monarchy
Economy: Subsistence farming
GNP per capita: US$400
Currency: Ngultrum

Brunei

Area: 2,226 sq. mi.
Population: 315,000
Capital: Bandar Seri Begawan (*pop:* 49,902)
Religions: Muslim, Buddhist, Christian
Languages: Malay, English
Political system: Absolute monarchy
Economy: Oil, gas
GNP per capita: US$14,500
Currency: Brunei dollar

Cambodia

Area: 69,898 sq. mi.
Population: 10,716,000
Capital: Phnom Penh (*pop:* 832,000)
Religions: Buddhist, Muslim
Languages: Khmer, Chinese, Vietnamese
Political system: Constitutional monarchy
Economy: Rubber, timber
GNP per capita: US$300
Currency: Riel

China

Area: 3,705,408 sq. mi.
Population: 1,240,658,000
Capital: Beijing (*pop:* 7,362,426)
Religions: Confucian, Buddhist
Languages: Mandarin Chinese, Cantonese
Political system: Republic
Economy: Agriculture, industry
GNP per capita: US$860
Currency: Yuan

Cyprus

Area: 3,572 sq. mi.
Population: 771,000
Capital: Nicosia (*pop:* 188,800)
Religions: Greek Orthodox, Muslim
Languages: Greek, Turkish
Political system: Republic
Economy: Tourism, shipping
GNP per capita: US$11,500
Currency: Cyprus pound

Georgia

Area: 26,911 sq. mi.
Population: 5,059,000
Capital: Tbilisi (*pop:* 1,268,000)
Religion: Georgian Orthodox
Languages: Georgian, Russian, Armenian
Political system: Republic
Economy: Food processing
GNP per capita: US$840
Currency: Lari

India

Area: 1,269,346 sq. mi.
Population: 982,223,000
Capital: New Delhi (*pop:* 301,297)
Religions: Hindu, Muslim, Christian
Languages: Hindi, English, others
Political system: Republic
Economy: High-tech industry, clothing
GNP per capita: US$390
Currency: Indian rupee

Indonesia

Area: 735,358 sq. mi.
Population: 206,338,000
Capital: Jakarta (*pop:* 9,160,500)
Religions: Muslim, Christian, others
Languages: Bahasa Indonesian, Dutch, English
Political system: Republic
Economy: Timber, minerals
GNP per capita: US$1,110
Currency: Rupiah

Iran

Area: 630,577 sq. mi.
Population: 65,758,000
Capital: Tehran (*pop:* 6,750,043)
Religion: Shi'a Muslim
Languages: Persian, Turkish, Kurdish, Arabic
Political system: Republic
Economy: Oil
GNP per capita: US$1,780
Currency: Rial

Iraq

Area: 169,235 sq. mi.
Population: 21,800,000
Capital: Baghdad (*pop:* 3,841,268)
Religion: Shi'a Muslim
Languages: Arabic, Kurdish, Turkic, Aramaic
Political system: Republic
Economy: Oil, collapsed due to UN sanctions
GNP per capita: US$1,800
Currency: Dinar

Israel

Area: 8,130 sq. mi.
Population: 7,020,000
Capital: Jerusalem (*pop:* 662,700)
Religions: Jewish, Muslim
Languages: Hebrew, Arabic
Political system: Republic
Economy: Industry, agriculture
GNP per capita: US$15,900
Currency: Shekel

Japan

Area: 145,870 sq. mi.
Population: 126,281,000
Capital: Tokyo (*pop:* 11,927,457)
Religions: Shinto, Buddhism
Main language: Japanese
Political system: Constitutional monarchy
Economy: Electronics
GNP per capita: US$37,850
Currency: Yen

Jordan

Area: 37,738 sq. mi.
Population: 6,304,000
Capital: Amman (*pop:* 1,270,000)
Religions: Muslim, Christian
Languages: Arabic, English, French
Political system: Constitutional monarchy
Economy: Phosphates, chemicals
GNP per capita: US$1,570
Currency: Jordanian dinar

Kazakhstan

Area: 1,049,156 sq. mi.
Population: 16,319,000
Capital: Astana (*pop:* 292,000)
Religions: Muslim, Russian Orthodox
Languages: Kazakh, Russian
Political system: Republic
Economy: Gas, oil, coal, uranium
GNP per capita: US$1,340
Currency: Tenge

Kuwait

Area: 6,880 sq. mi.
Population: 1,811,000
Capital: Kuwait (*pop:* 400,000)
Religions: Muslim, Christian
Languages: Arabic, English
Political system: Constitutional monarchy
Economy: Oil, gas
GNP per capita: US$17,390
Currency: Kuwaiti dinar

Kyrgyzstan

Area: 76,641 sq. mi.
Population: 4,643,000
Capital: Bishkek (*pop:* 627,800)
Religions: Muslim, Russian Orthodox
Languages: Kirghiz, Russian
Political system: Republic
Economy: Collective farming, coal
GNP per capita: US$440
Currency: Som

Laos

Area: 91,429 sq. mi.
Population: 5,163,000
Capital: Vientiane (*pop:* 120,000)
Religions: Buddhist, Christian
Languages: Lao, French
Political system: Republic
Economy: Timber, mining
GNP per capita: US$400
Currency: Kip

Lebanon

Area: 4,015 sq. mi.
Population: 3,191,000
Capital: Beirut (*pop:* 1,500,000)
Religions: Muslim, Christian
Languages: Arabic, French, English
Political system: Republic
Economy: Banking, services
GNP per capita: US$3,350
Currency: Lebanese pound

Malaysia

Area: 127,320 sq. mi.
Population: 21,410,000
Capital: Kuala Lumpur (*pop:* 1,145,075)
Religions: Muslim, Buddhist
Languages: Malay, English, Chinese, Tamil
Political system: Constitutional monarchy
Economy: Electronics, cars
GNP per capita: US$4,680
Currency: Malaysian dollar

Maldives

Area: 115 sq. mi.
Population: 271,000
Capital: Male (*pop:* 62,973)
Religion: Sunni Muslim
Main language: Maldivian
Political system: Republic
Economy: Tourism, fishing
GNP per capita: US$1,150
Currency: Rufiyaa

Mongolia

Area: 604,829 sq. mi.
Population: 2,579,000
Capital: Ulan Bator (*pop:* 515,100)
Religions: Buddhist, Muslim
Languages: Mongolian, Kazakh
Political system: Republic
Economy: Agriculture, oil, coal
GNP per capita: US$390
Currency: Tugrik

Myanmar (Burma)

Area: 261,228 sq. mi.
Population: 44,497,000
Capital: Rangoon (*pop:* 2,513,023)
Religions: Buddhist, Muslim
Languages: Burmese, English, Shan, Karen
Political system: Republic
Economy: Teak, rice
GNP per capita: US$1,000
Currency: Kyat

Nepal

Area: 56,827 sq. mi.
Population: 22,847,000
Capital: Kathmandu (*pop:* 419,073)
Religions: Hindu, Buddhist
Main language: Nepali
Political system: Constitutional monarchy
Economy: Agriculture
GNP per capita: US$210
Currency: Nepalese rupee

North Korea

Area: 46,540 sq. mi.
Population: 23,348,000
Capital: Pyongyang (*pop:* 2,000,000)
Religions: Traditional beliefs, Buddhist
Main language: Korean
Political system: Republic, one-party state
Economy: Manufacturing, agriculture
GNP per capita: US$1,000
Currency: Won

Oman

Area: 82,030 sq. mi.
Population: 2,382,000
Capital: Muscat (*pop:* 400,000)
Religions: Ibadi Muslim, Hindu
Languages: Arabic, Qarra, Mahra
Political system: Absolute monarchy
Economy: Oil, gas
GNP per capita: US$4,820
Currency: Rial

Pakistan

Area: 307,374 sq. mi.
Population: 148,166,000
Capital: Islamabad (*pop:* 350,000)
Religions: Sunni Muslim, Hindu
Languages: Punjabi, Urdu, Sindi, Pushto
Political system: Republic
Economy: Cotton, rice, oil
GNP per capita: US$490
Currency: Pakistan rupee

Philippines

Area: 115,831 sq. mi.
Population: 72,944,000
Capital: Manila (*pop:* 8,594,150)
Religions: Roman Catholic, Protestant
Languages: Filipino, English
Political system: Republic
Economy: Agriculture
GNP per capita: US$1,220
Currency: Philippine peso

Qatar

Area: 4,247 sq. mi.
Population: 579,000
Capital: Doha (*pop:* 217,294)
Religions: Sunni Muslim, Hindu
Languages: Arabic, English
Political system: Absolute monarchy
Economy: Oil, gas
GNP per capita: US$11,600
Currency: Qatar riyal

Saudi Arabia

Area: 830,000 sq. mi.
Population: 20,181,000
Capital: Riyadh (*pop:* 1,800,000)
Religions: Sunni Muslim
Languages: Arabic, English
Political system: Absolute monarchy
Economy: Oil, gas
GNP per capita: US$7,040
Currency: Saudi riyal

Singapore

Area: 239 sq. mi.
Population: 3,476,000
Capital: Singapore
Religions: Buddhist, Christian, Muslim
Languages: Malay, Mandarin, Tamil, English
Political system: Republic
Economy: Finance, banking
GNP per capita: US$32,940
Currency: Singapore dollar

South Korea

Area: 38,330 sq. mi.
Population: 46,109,000
Capital: Seoul (*pop:* 10,776,201)
Religions: Mahayana Buddhist, Protestant
Main language: Korean
Political system: Republic
Economy: Ship-building, cars
GNP per capita: US$10,550
Currency: Won

Sri Lanka

Area: 25,332 sq. mi.
Population: 18,455,000
Capital: Colombo (*pop:* 615,000)
Religions: Buddhist, Hindu, Christian
Languages: Sinhala, Tamil, English
Political system: Republic
Economy: Tea, tourism
GNP per capita: US$800
Currency: Sri Lankan rupee

Syria

Area: 71,498 sq. mi.
Population: 15,333,000
Capital: Damascus
(*pop:* 1,549,000)
Religions: Sunni Muslim, Christian
Languages: Arabic, Kurdish, Turkish
Political system: Republic
Economy: Oil
GNP per capita: US$1,150
Currency: Syrian pound

Taiwan

Area: 13,800 sq. mi.
Population: 21,700,000
Capital: Taipei (*pop:* 2,607,010)
Religions: Buddhist, Confucian, Taoist
Languages: Mandarin Chinese, Taiwanese
Political system: Republic
Economy: Manufacturing, electronics
GNP per capita: US$12,000
Currency: New Taiwan dollar

Tajikistan

Area: 55,251 sq. mi.
Population: 6,015,000
Capital: Dushanbe
(*pop:* 602,000)
Religion: Sunni Muslim
Languages: Tajik, Uzbek, Russian
Political system: Republic
Economy: Carpet-making
GNP per capita: US$330
Currency: Tajik rouble

Thailand

Area: 198,115 sq. mi.
Population: 60,300,000
Capital: Bangkok
(*pop:* 5,876,000)
Religions: Buddhist, Muslim
Languages: Thai, Chinese, Khmer, Malay
Political system: Constitutional monarchy
Economy: Manufacturing, rice, rubber
GNP per capita: US$2,800
Currency: Baht

Turkey

Area: 299,158 sq. mi.
Population: 64,479,000
Capital: Ankara (*pop:* 3,103,000)
Religion: Muslim
Main language: Turkish
Political system: Republic
Economy: Textiles, manufacturing
GNP per capita: US$3,130
Currency: Turkish lira

Turkmenistan

Area: 188,456 sq. mi.
Population: 4,309,000
Capital: Ashkhabad
(*pop:* 407,000)
Religion: Muslim
Languages: Turkmenian, Russian, Uzbek
Political system: Republic
Economy: Cotton, gas
GNP per capita: US$630
Currency: Manat

United Arab Emirates

Area: 32,278 sq. mi.
Population: 2,353,000
Capital: Abu Dhabi
(*pop:* 450,000)
Religion: Sunni Muslim
Languages: Arabic, English
Political system: Federation of absolute monarchies
Economy: Oil, gas
GNP per capita: US$17,400
Currency: Dirham

Uzbekistan

Area: 172,742 sq. mi.
Population: 23,574,000
Capital: Tashkent
(*pop:* 2,094,000)
Religions: Muslim
Languages: Uzbek, Russian
Political system: Republic
Economy: Agriculture, oil, gas
GNP per capita: US$1,010
Currency: Sum

Vietnam

Area: 128,066 sq. mi.
Population: 77,562,000
Capital: Hanoi (*pop:* 3,056,146)
Religions: Buddhist, Roman Catholic
Languages: Vietnamese, French, English
Political system: Republic
Economy: Steel, gas, oil
GNP per capita: US$320
Currency: Dông

Yemen

Area: 203,850 sq. mi.
Population: 16,887,000
Capital: San'a (*pop:* 926,595)
Religion: Sunni Muslim
Main language: Arabic
Political system: Republic
Economy: Oil, gas
GNP per capita: US$270
Currency: Riyal

AUSTRALIA AND OCEANIA

Australia

Area: 2,988,902 sq. mi.
Population: 18,520,000
Capital: Canberra (*pop:* 307,100)
Religions: Protestant, Roman Catholic
Main Language: English
Political system: Constitutional monarchy
Economy: Mining, agriculture
GNP per capita: US$20,540
Currency: Australian dollar

Fiji

Area: 7,056 sq. mi.
Population: 796,000
Capital: Suva (*pop:* 141,273)
Religions: Christian, Hindu, Muslim
Languages: Fijian, Hindi
Political system: Republic
Economy: Sugar, gold, timber
GNP per capita: US$2,470
Currency: Fiji dollar

Kiribati

Area: 280 sq. mi.
Population: 81,000
Capital: Bairiki (*pop:* 17,921)
Religions: Roman Catholic, Protestant
Languages: I-Kiribati, English
Political system: Republic
Economy: Coconuts, copra
GNP per capita: US$910
Currency: Australian dollar

Marshall Islands

Area: 70 sq. mi.
Population: 60,000
Capital: Dalap-Uliga-Darrit (*pop:* 20,000)
Religions: Protestant, Roman Catholic
Languages: Marshallese, English
Political system: Republic
Economy: Copra, tuna-fishing
GNP per capita: US$1,770
Currency: US dollar

Micronesia, Federated States of

Area: 271 sq. mi.
Population: 114,000
Capital: Palikir
Religions: Roman Catholic, Protestant
Languages: English, Yapese, Ulithian, Woleaian
Political system: Republic
Economy: Fishing, US aid
GNP per capita: US$1,980
Currency: US dollar

Nauru

Area: 8 sq. mi.
Population: 11,000
Capital: Yaren
Religions: Christian, others
Languages: Nauruan, English
Political system: Republic
Economy: Phosphate
GNP per capita: US$10,000
Currency: Australian dollar

New Zealand

Area: 104,454 sq. mi.
Population: 3,796,000
Capital: Wellington (*pop:* 326,900)
Religions: Protestant, Roman Catholic
Languages: English, Maori
Political system: Constitutional monarchy
Economy: Agriculture, wool
GNP per capita: US$16,480
Currency: New Zealand dollar

Palau

Area: 177 sq. mi.
Population: 19,000
Capital: Koror (*pop:* 10,493)
Religions: Christian, traditional beliefs
Languages: Palauan, English
Political system: Republic
Economy: Coconuts, US aid
GNP per capita: US$2,260
Currency: US dollar

Papua New Guinea

Area: 178,704 sq. mi.
Population: 4,600,000
Capital: Port Moresby (*pop:* 173,500)
Religions: Christian, others
Languages: English, Pidgin English
Political system: Constitutional monarchy
Economy: Gold, copper, oil
GNP per capita: US$940
Currency: Kina

Samoa

Area: 1,093 sq. mi.
Population: 174,000
Capital: Apia (*pop:* 36,000)
Religions: Protestant, Roman Catholic
Languages: Samoan, English
Political system: Constitutional monarchy
Economy: Agriculture, banking
GNP per capita: US$1,150
Currency: Tala

Solomon Islands

Area: 11,157 sq. mi.
Population: 417,000
Capital: Honiara (*pop:* 40,000)
Religions: Christian, others
Main language: English
Political system: Constitutional monarchy
Economy: Palm oil, copra, cocoa
GNP per capita: US$900
Currency: Solomon Islands dollar

Tonga

Area: 288 sq. mi.
Population: 98,000
Capital: Nuku'alofa (*pop:* 29,018)
Religions: Protestant, Roman Catholic
Languages: Tongan, English
Political system: Constitutional monarchy
Economy: Cash crops
GNP per capita: US$1,830
Currency: Pa'anga

Tuvalu

Area: 10 sq. mi.
Population: 11,000
Capital: Fongafale (*pop:* 2,856)
Religions: Protestant, others
Languages: Tuvaluan, English
Political system: Constitutional monarchy
Economy: Fishing, foreign aid
GNP per capita: US$600
Currency: Australian dollar

Vanuatu

Area: 4,706 sq. mi.
Population: 182,000
Capital: Port-Vila (*pop:* 26,100)
Religions: Protestant, Roman Catholic
Languages: Bislama, English, French
Political system: Republic
Economy: Copra, cocoa
GNP per capita: US$1,310
Currency: Vatu

Equatorial Scale 1 : 154 000 000

0 1000 2000 3000 4000 km

0 1000 2000 miles

ARCTIC OCEAN
Ellesmere Island
GREENLAND
(Denmark)
Greenland Sea
Baffin Bay
Victoria Island
Baffin Island
Beaufort Sea
Arctic Circle
ALASKA
(U.S.)
Yukon
Mackenzie
Anchorage
Nuuk (Godthåb)
ICELAND
Reykjavík
Norwegian Sea
Hudson Bay
Bering Sea
Gulf of Alaska
CANADA
ROCKY MOUNTAINS
Edmonton
Calgary
Winnipeg
Vancouver
Lake Superior
Seattle
Missouri
Lake Huron
Ottawa
St Lawrence
Québec
Montréal
Lake Michigan
Toronto
Chicago
Detroit
Denver
New York
Philadelphia
UNITED STATES
Kansas City
Washington D.C.
San Francisco
Los Angeles
San Diego
Phoenix
Dallas
Atlanta
Mississippi
Houston
New Orleans
Rio Grande
Bermuda (U.K.)
ATLANTIC OCEAN
Açores (Portugal)
Madeira (Portugal)
Islas Canarias (Spain)
REPUBLIC OF IRELAND
Dublin
UNITED KINGDOM
London
PORTUGAL
Lisboa
SPAIN
Madrid
ANDORRA
Rabat
Casablanca
MOROCCO
WESTERN SAHARA (Morocco)
MAURITANIA
Nouakchott
Dakar
SEN.
Banjul
THE GAMBIA
Bamako
MALI
Niger
Bissau
GUINEA-BISSAU
GUINEA
Conakry
Freetown
SIERRA LEONE
Monrovia
IVORY COAST
Yamoussoukro
Accra
GHANA
BURKINA
CAPE VERDE
EQUATORIAL
SÃO TOMÉ & PRÍNCIPE
Tropic of Cancer
Monterrey
MEXICO
Gulf of Mexico
THE BAHAMAS
La Habana
CUBA
HAITI
DOMINICAN REP.
Santo Domingo
PUERTO RICO (U.S.)
ANTIGUA & BARBUDA
ST KITTS-NEVIS
DOMINICA
ST LUCIA
ST VINCENT & THE GRENADINES
BARBADOS
GRENADA
JAMAICA
Guadalajara
Ciudad de México
BELIZE
Guatemala
GUATEMALA
HONDURAS
EL SALVADOR
NICARAGUA
Managua
San José
COSTA RICA
Panamá
PANAMA
Caribbean Sea
Caracas
TRINIDAD & TOBAGO
VENEZUELA
Georgetown
GUYANA
SURINAME
FRENCH GUIANA (Fr.)
Bogotá
COLOMBIA
HAWAII (U.S.)
PACIFIC OCEAN
Equator
Islas Galápagos (Ecuador)
Quito
ECUADOR
Iquitos
Amazon
Manaus
Belém
Fortaleza
Recife
BRAZIL
KIRIBATI
PERU
Lima
Salvador
Arequipa
La Paz
BOLIVIA
Sucre
Brasília
French Polynesia
Belo Horizonte
PARAGUAY
Tropic of Capricorn
Asunción
Rio de Janeiro
São Paulo
Curitiba
Pitcairn Is. (U.K.)
Córdoba
Porto Alegre
Santiago
CHILE
ARGENTINA
URUGUAY
Buenos Aires
Montevideo
Falkland Islands (U.K.)
Punta Arenas
South Georgia (U.K.)
South Sandwich Islands (U.K.)
Antarctic Circle
Bellinghausen Sea
Weddell Sea
Ross Sea
150°
120°
90°
60°
30°
0°

World: Political

ARCTIC OCEAN
Zemlya Frantsa-Iosifa
Severnaya Zemlya
Svalbard (Norway)
Barents Sea
Novaya Zemlya
FINLAND
Arkhangel'sk
RUSSIA
Yakutsk
Anadyr'
Arctic Circle
Helsinki
Tallinn
Sankt-Peterburg
EST.
LAT.
Riga
LITH.
Vilnius
Minsk
BELARUS
Moskva
Nizhny Novgorod
Yekaterinburg
Samara
Omsk
Irkutsk
POLAND
Warszawa
UKRAINE
Kyyiv
Kharkiv
MOLDOVA
Budapest
HUNG.
ROMANIA
Bucuresti
Beograd
CRO.
BOS.
YUG.
BULGARIA
Sofiya
MAC.
Tiranë
ALB.
Black Sea
Istanbul
GEORGIA
ARMENIA
AZER.
Baki
Caspian Sea
Volgograd
Volga
Astana
KAZAKHSTAN
Aral Sea
Irtysh
Bishkek
Almaty
KYRGYZSTAN
Tashkent
UZBEKISTAN
TURKMENISTAN
Ashgabat
Dushanbe
TAJIKISTAN
AFGHANISTAN
Kabul
Islamabad
PAKISTAN
GREECE
Athina
TURKEY
Ankara
SYRIA
CYPRUS
LEB.
Dimashq
ISRAEL
Amman
JORDAN
Baghdad
IRAQ
Tehran
IRAN
KUWAIT
BAHRAIN
QATAR
Abu Zabi
U.A.E.
Masqat
OMAN
SAUDI ARABIA
Ar Riyad
Makkah
YEMEN
San'a
Adan
Mediterranean Sea
El Qahira
EGYPT
LIBYA
Red Sea
Nile
ERITREA
Asmara
El Khartum
SUDAN
CHAD
Ndjamena
DJIBOUTI
Adis Abeba
ETHIOPIA
SOMALIA
Muqdisho
CENTRAL AFRICAN REP.
Bangui
UGANDA
KENYA
Nairobi
Kisangani
DEMOCRATIC REPUBLIC OF CONGO
Brazzaville
Kinshasa
Kananga
RW.
BUR.
Lake Victoria
TANZANIA
Dodoma
Dar es Salaam
SEYCHELLES
Moroni
COMOROS
ZAMBIA
Lusaka
MAL.
Lilongwe
Harare
ZIMB.
MOZAMBIQUE
MADAGASCAR
Antananarivo
Réunion (France)
Port Louis
MAURITIUS
BOTSWANA
Gaborone
Maputo
Pretoria
SWAZILAND
LESOTHO
Durban
SOUTH AFRICA
Ürümqi
MONGOLIA
Ulaanbaatar
GOBI DESERT
CHINA
Lanzhou
Beijing
Harbin
Shenyang
Vladivostok
NORTH KOREA
P'yongyang
Soul
SOUTH KOREA
Qingdao
Huang He
Sea of Japan
Sapporo
JAPAN
Tokyo
Osaka
Wuhan
Chang Jiang
Chongqing
Shanghai
East China Sea
T'ai-pei
TAIWAN
Hong Kong
HIMALAYAS
NEPAL
Kathmandu
BHT.
Delhi
New Delhi
Karachi
Ganges
BANG.
Dhaka
Calcutta
INDIA
Mumbai
Hyderabad
Chennai
Arabian Sea
Bay of Bengal
SRI LANKA
Colombo
MALDIVES
MYANMAR (BURMA)
Yangon
LAOS
Viangchan
Ha Noi
VIETNAM
THAILAND
Krung Thep
CAMB.
Phnum Penh
South China Sea
Manila
PHILIPPINES
Cebu
Davao
PALAU
BRUNEI
Bandar Seri Begawan
MALAYSIA
Kuala Lumpur
SINGAPORE
Singapore
Banjarmasin
INDONESIA
Jakarta
Surabaya
PAPUA NEW GUINEA
Port Moresby
Sea of Okhotsk
Petropavlovsk-Kamchatskiy
Bering Sea
PACIFIC OCEAN
Tropic of Cancer
Northern Mariana Islands (U.S.)
MARSHALL ISLANDS
FEDERATED STATES OF MICRONESIA
Equator
NAURU
KIRIBATI
SOLOMON ISLANDS
Honiara
TUVALU
VANUATU
FIJI
Suva
Tropic of Capricorn
INDIAN OCEAN
AUSTRALIA
Perth
Brisbane
Sydney
Canberra
Adelaide
Melbourne
Tasmania
NEW ZEALAND
Auckland
Wellington
Christchurch
Tasman Sea
Chatham Island (N.Z.)
Îles Kerguélen (France)
SOUTHERN OCEAN
Antarctic Circle
ANTARCTICA
London Selected capital cities
Brisbane Other cities
30°
60°
90°
120°
150°
180°
0°
Country Abbreviations
ALB. ALBANIA
AZER. AZERBAIJAN
BANG. BANGLADESH
BEL. BELGIUM
BHT. BHUTAN
BOS. BOSNIA-HERZEGOVINA
BUR. BURUNDI
CAMB. CAMBODIA
CRO. CROATIA
EST. ESTONIA
HUNG. HUNGARY
LAT. LATVIA
LEB. LEBANON
LITH. LITHUANIA
LUX. LUXEMBOURG
MAC. MACEDONIA
MAL. MALAWI
RUS. RUSSIA
RW. RWANDA
SEN. SENEGAL
SL. SLOVENIA
SLOVAK. SLOVAKIA
SWITZ. SWITZERLAND
U.A.E. UNITED ARAB EMIRATES
YUG. YUGOSLAVIA
ZIMB. ZIMBABWE

Scale 1 : 47 600 000

0 500 1000 1500 2000 km

0 500 1000 miles

ARCTIC OCEAN
North Pole
NORWAY
Shetland Is. (U.K.)
Faeroes (Denmark)
ICELAND
Reykjavik
Arctic Circle
Denmark Strait
Greenland Sea
Jan Mayen (Norway)
Svalbard (Spitzbergen) (Norway)
Wandel Sea
GREENLAND (Denmark)
Nuuk (Godthåb)
Cape Farewell
ATLANTIC OCEAN
Labrador Sea
Davis Strait
Baffin Bay
Nares Strait
Ellesmere Island
Queen Elizabeth Islands
Devon Island
Bylot I.
Arctic Bay
Baffin Island
Cumberland Sd
Iqaluit
Cape Dyer
Resolution I.
Cape Chidley
Ungava Bay
Hudson Strait
Péninsule d'Ungava
Foxe Basin
Foxe Pen.
Prince Charles Island
Melville Pen.
Southampton Island
Coats I.
Mansel I.
Hudson Bay
Belcher Islands
James Bay
Parry Islands
Melville Island
Viscount Melville Sound
Somerset Island
Brodeur Pen.
Gulf of Boothia
Boothia Pen.
King William Island
Prince of Wales Island
Victoria Island
Banks Island
Prince Patrick Island
Amundsen Gulf
Bathurst Inlet
Beaufort Sea
Mackenzie Bay
Inuvik
Great Bear Lake
Great Slave Lake
Yellowknife
Baker Lake
Garry Lake
Nueltin Lake
Reindeer Lake
Lake Athabasca
Slave
Peace
Mackenzie
Mackenzie Mts.
CANADA
Cape Churchill
Churchill
Nelson
Thompson
Lake Winnipeg
Lake Winnipegosis
Lake Manitoba
Sandy Lake
Winisk
Lake Nipigon
Lake Superior
Thunder Bay
Winnipeg
Regina
Saskatoon
Saskatchewan
Edmonton
Calgary
Lethbridge
Dawson Creek
Kelowna
Kamloops
Fraser
Vancouver
Victoria
Vancouver I.
Seattle
Spokane
Portland
Columbia
Blue Mts.
ROCKY MOUNTAINS
Coast Mountains
Mt. Roosevelt 2972
Mt. Waddington 4042
Mt. Logan 6050
Whitehorse
Yukon
Juneau
Alexander Archipelago
Prince of Wales I.
Queen Charlotte Islands
Graham I.
Queen Charlotte Sound
Prince Rupert
Gulf of Alaska
Kodiak I.
Anchorage
Mt. McKinley 6194
Alaska Range
Fairbanks
ALASKA (U.S.)
Brooks Range
Point Barrow
Point Hope
Kotzebue Sound
Norton Sound
Bering Strait
Nunivak I.
St. Matthew I.
St. Lawrence I.
Pribilof Is.
Bristol Bay
Aleutian Islands
Fox Islands
Aleutian Trench
Bering Sea
East Siberian Sea
Wrangel I.
International Date Line
Anadyrskiy Zaliv
ASIA
RUSSIA
Cape Harrison
Smallwood Reservoir
Schefferville
Réservoir Manicouagan
Fort George
Akimiski I.
Kapuskasing
Sudbury
Val-d'Or
Chicoutimi
Baie Comeau
St. Lawrence
Québec
MONTRÉAL
Ottawa
Île d'Anticosti
Gulf of St. Lawrence
St.-Pierre-et-Miquelon (France)
Cape Breton I.
Nova Scotia
Halifax
Cape Sable
St. Anthony
Newfoundland
St. John's
Cape Race

North America: Political

ATLANTIC OCEAN
PACIFIC OCEAN
UNITED STATES
MEXICO
SOUTH AMERICA
THE BAHAMAS
CUBA
HAITI
DOMINICAN REPUBLIC
JAMAICA
BELIZE
GUATEMALA
HONDURAS
EL SALVADOR
NICARAGUA
COSTA RICA
PANAMA
Gulf of Mexico
Caribbean Sea
Greater Antilles
Lesser Antilles
Tropic of Cancer
Equator
NEW YORK
PHILADELPHIA
Baltimore
Washington D.C.
Virginia Beach
Raleigh
Charlotte
Savannah
Jacksonville
Atlanta
Miami
Tampa
Cleveland
Cincinnati
Columbus
Knoxville
Nashville
Memphis
DETROIT
CHICAGO
Milwaukee
Indianapolis
St. Louis
Kansas City
Denver
Oklahoma City
Little Rock
Mobile
New Orleans
HOUSTON
SAN ANTONIO
Austin
Corpus Christi
DALLAS
Fort Worth
Abilene
El Paso
Albuquerque
PHOENIX
Tucson
Las Vegas
Salt Lake City
Reno
Sacramento
San Francisco
San Jose
Fresno
LOS ANGELES
SAN DIEGO
Mexicali
Ensenada
Hermosillo
Ciudad Obregón
Ciudad Juárez
La Paz
Matamoros
MONTERREY
Ciudad Madero
León
GUADALAJARA
CIUDAD DE MÉXICO
Veracruz
Acapulco
Mérida
Belmopan
GUATEMALA
San Salvador
Tegucigalpa
Managua
San José
Panamá
LA HABANA (HAVANA)
Santiago de Cuba
Nassau
PORT-AU-PRINCE
SANTO DOMINGO
Kingston
San Juan
Puerto Rico (U.S.)
CARACAS
BARRANQUILLA
MEDELLÍN
BOGOTÁ
CALI
QUITO
GUAYAQUIL
Iquitos
Chiclayo
Bermuda (U.K.)
Islas Galápagos (Galápagos Is.) (Ecuador)
Clipperton Island (France)
Islas Revillagigedo (Mexico)
Middle America Trench
Puerto Rico Trench
Sierra Madre Occidental
Sierra Madre del Sur
Baja California
Golfo de California
Río Grande
Mississippi

Scale 1 : 18 900 000

0 200 400 600 km
0 100 200 300 miles

Beaufort Sea
Gulf of Alaska
ALASKA (U.S.)
Anchorage
Fairbanks
YUKON TERRITORY
Whitehorse
Dawson Creek
Mackenzie Mountains
NORTHWEST TERRITORIES
Great Bear Lake
Great Slave Lake
Yellowknife
Banks Island
Victoria Island
Amundsen Gulf
BRITISH COLUMBIA
Coast Mountains
ROCKY MOUNTAINS
Prince George
Vancouver
Victoria
ALBERTA
Edmonton
Calgary
SASKATCHEWAN
Saskatoon
Regina
MANITOBA
Winnipeg
Lake Winnipeg
Lake Athabasca
Great Plains
UNITED STATES
WASHINGTON
Seattle
OREGON
Portland
IDAHO
MONTANA
WYOMING
NORTH DAKOTA
SOUTH DAKOTA
MINNESOTA
Minneapolis
NEVADA
UTAH
Pacific coast: Queen Charlotte Islands
6059 Mt. Logan
4670 Mt. Fairweather
3954 Mt. Robson

Canada

Baffin Bay
Davis Strait
GREENLAND (Denmark)
Upernavik
Kangersuatsiaq (Prøven)
Upernavik Kujalleq
Ukkusissat
Uummannaq Fjord
Nuussuaq
Ilulissat (Jakobshavn)
Qeqertarsuaq (Disko)
Qeqertarsuup Tunua (Disko Bugt)
Kangaatsiaq
Sisimiut (Holsteinsborg)
Maniitsoq (Sukkertoppen)
Napasoq
Nuuk (Godthåb)
Qeqertarsuatsiaat (Fiskenæsset)
Paamiut (Frederikshåb)
Ivittuut
Nanortalik
Nunarsuit
Tasiilaq (Angmagssalik)
Gyldenløves Fjord
Kong Frederick VI Kyst
Kangeq (Kap Cort Adelaer)
Lindenow Fjord
Uummannarsuaq (Kap Farvel)
Arctic Circle
Jones Sound
Devon Island
Lancaster Sound
Bylot Island
Arctic Bay
Borden Peninsula
Brodeur Peninsula
Pond Inlet
Buchan Gulf
Scott Inlet
Cape Christian
Clyde River
Baffin Island
Home Bay
Boothia
Igloolik
Rowley I.
Hall Beach
Pelly Bay
Melville Peninsula
Parry Bay
Prince Charles Island
Air Force I.
Foxe Basin
Wales I.
Cape Dyer
Nettilling Lake
Cumberland Peninsula
Pangnirtung
Cumberland Sound
Cape Mercy
Cape Dominion
Bowman Bay
Cape Dorchester
Amadjuak Lake
Hall Peninsula
Lemieux Islands
Foxe Peninsula
Iqaluit
Frobisher Bay
Loks Land
Roes Welcome Sound
Southampton Island
Foxe Channel
Cape Dorset
Salisbury I.
Lake Harbour
Resolution Island
Nottingham I.
Hudson Strait
Cap de Nouvelle-France
Chesterfield Inlet
Fisher Strait
Evans Strait
Coats Island
Ivujivik
Salluit
Quaqtaq
Akpatok Island
Cape Chidley
Port Burwell
Mansel Island
Péninsule d'Ungava
Ungava Bay
Kangiqsualujjuaq
George
Hebron
Cod Island
Nutak
1729
LABRADOR SEA
ATLANTIC OCEAN
NEWFOUNDLAND
Ottawa Islands
HUDSON BAY
Lac Payne
Kuujjuaq
Nain
Hopedale
Cape Harrison
Groswater Bay
Rigolet
Cartwright
Inukjuak
Lac Minto
King George Is.
Sleeper Is.
Nastapoka Is.
Lac à l'Eau Claire
Lac Bienville
Schefferville
LABRADOR
Smallwood Reservoir
Churchill
Churchill Falls
Lake Melville
Port Hope Simpson
Battle Harbour
Belle Isle
Cape Bauld
St. Anthony
Strait of Belle Isle
Belcher Islands
Réservoir Caniapiscau
Labrador City
Ashuanipi
Ashuanipi Lake
Petit Mécatina
Long Range Mts
Roddickton
White Bay
Notre Dame Bay
Fogo I.
Bonavista Bay
Gander
St. John's
Fort Severn
Kuujjuarapik
Winisk
Cape Henrietta Maria
Long I.
Rés. de La Grande 4
Rés. de La Grande 2
Rés. de La Grande 3
QUÉBEC
Monts Otish
1021
Deer Lake
Grand Falls
NEWFOUNDLAND
Severn
Winisk
James Bay
Fort George
Réservoir Opinaca
Eastmain
Natashquan
Havre-St-Pierre
Stephenville
Harbour Breton
Trepassey
Cape Race
Fortune Bay
Grand Ban
Big Trout Lake
Ekwan
Attawapiskat
Akimiski Island
Réservoir Manicouagan
Sept-Îles
Île d'Anticosti
Port-Menier
Gulf of St. Lawrence
Cape Ray
Channel-Port aux Basques
St-Pierre et-Miquelon (France)
Cabot Strait
Eastmain
Manouane Lake
Charlton I.
Rupert
Winisk Lake
Albany
Fort Rupert
Moosonee
Baie du Poste
Chute des Passes
Réservoir Pipmuacan
Manicouagan
Péninsule de Gaspé
Matane
Îles de la Madeleine
Lac St. Joseph
Fort Hope
Harricanaw
Lac Evans
Chibougamau
Mistassini
Les Escoumins
St. Lawrence
Rimouski
PRINCE EDWARD ISLAND
Charlottetown
Northumberland Strait
Sydney
Cape Breton Island
Port Hawkesbury
ONTARIO
Missinaibi
Coral
Miquelon
Réservoir Gouin
Lac St-Jean
Chicoutimi
Jonquière
Bathurst
NEW BRUNSWICK
Edmundston
Presque Isle
Moncton
Amherst
Truro
New Glasgow
Sable I.
Lake Nipigon
Armstrong
Nakina
Longlac
Geraldton
Nipigon
Hearst
Kapuskasing
Cochrane
Amos
Senneterre
Baie St. Paul
Montmagny
Houlton
Fredericton
St. John
Bay of Fundy
NOVA SCOTIA
Dartmouth
Halifax
Bridgewater
Marathon
Timmins
Lake Abitibi
Val-d'Or
La Tuque
Québec
Lévis
Thunder Bay
Foleyet
Kirkland Lake
Rouyn
Réservoir Cabonga
Trois Rivières
Jackman
St. Stephen
MAINE
Yarmouth
Shelburne
Cape Sable
Lake Superior
Isle Royale
Copper Harbor
Keweenaw Pen.
Chapleau
Wawa
Cobalt
Mont-Laurier
Sorel
Sherbrooke
North Bay
Ottawa
MONTRÉAL
White Mts.
Mt. Washington 1917
Augusta
Lewiston
Portland
Apostle Is.
Marquette
Sault Ste. Marie
Sudbury
Pembroke
Smiths Falls
Cornwall
Granby
Burlington
Plattsburgh
Ironwood
Manistique
Blind River
Manitoulin I.
Parry Sound
Georgian Bay
Huntsville
Ogdensburg
1629
Montpelier
NEW HAMPSHIRE
Rhinelander
Iron Mountain
Escanaba
MICHIGAN
Tobermory
Orillia
Kingston
Peterborough
Watertown
VERMONT
Concord
Massachusetts Bay
Portsmouth
WISCONSIN
Marinette
Alpena
Lake Huron
Owen Sound
Barrie
Oshawa
Brattleboro
Boston
Wausau
Green Bay
Traverse City
Toronto
Lake Ontario
Utica
Albany
MASS.
Worcester
Cape Cod
Appleton
Oshkosh
Sheboygan
Lake Michigan
Mt. Pleasant
Bay City
Saginaw
Kitchener
Hamilton
London
Rochester
Syracuse
NEW YORK
Catskill Mts. 1295
Springfield
Hartford
CONN.
Providence
New Bedford
RHODE ISLAND
Grand Rapids
Muskegon
Flint
Sarnia
Chatham
St. Catharines
Buffalo
Binghamton
New Haven
Bridgeport
Long I.
Milwaukee
Lansing
DETROIT
Lake Erie
Windsor
Ann Arbor
Erie
Jamestown
Meadville
PENNSYLVANIA
Scranton
Paterson
Newark
NEW YORK

Scale 1 : 21 200 000

0 200 400 600 km

0 100 200 300 miles

BRITISH COLUMBIA
ALBERTA
SASKATCHEWAN
MANITOBA
CANADA
WASHINGTON
OREGON
IDAHO
MONTANA
WYOMING
NORTH DAKOTA
SOUTH DAKOTA
NEBRASKA
NEVADA
UTAH
COLORADO
KANSAS
CALIFORNIA
ARIZONA
NEW MEXICO
TEXAS
OKLA
UNITED
MEXICO
PACIFIC OCEAN
ROCKY MOUNTAINS
Great Plains
Columbia Mountains
Great Basin
Colorado Plateau
Edwards Plateau
Sierra Nevada
Cascade Range
Bitterroot Range
Sierra Madre Occidental
Baja California
Golfo de California
Tropic of Cancer
Calgary
Vancouver
Victoria
Seattle
Tacoma
Olympia
Spokane
Portland
Salem
Eugene
Boise
Helena
Great Falls
Missoula
Billings
Salt Lake City
Ogden
Reno
Carson City
Sacramento
San Francisco
Oakland
San Jose
Fresno
Bakersfield
LOS ANGELES
Long Beach
Santa Ana
SAN DIEGO
Tijuana
Ensenada
Mexicali
Las Vegas
PHOENIX
Mesa
Tucson
Flagstaff
Albuquerque
Santa Fe
El Paso
Ciudad Juárez
Denver
Colorado Springs
Pueblo
Cheyenne
Casper
Rapid City
Pierre
Bismarck
Regina
Amarillo
Lubbock
Oklahoma City
Wichita
Hermosillo
Chihuahua
Ciudad Obregón
Culiacán
Mazatlán
Durango
Torreón
MONTERREY
Saltillo
Reynosa
Aguascalientes
Zacatecas
San Luis Potosí
León
GUADALAJARA
La Paz
Mt. Rainier 4392
Mt. Shasta 4317
Mt. Whitney 4418
Mt. Elbert 4399
Gannett Peak 4202
Kings Peak 4123
Borah Peak 3859
Grand Teton 4190

United States

ONTARIO
QUÉBEC
MINNESOTA
WISCONSIN
MICHIGAN
IOWA
ILLINOIS
INDIANA
OHIO
PENNSYLVANIA
NEW YORK
VERMONT
NEW HAMPSHIRE
MAINE
MASS.
CONN.
R.I.
NEW JERSEY
DELAWARE
MARYLAND
WEST VIRGINIA
VIRGINIA
KENTUCKY
TENNESSEE
NORTH CAROLINA
SOUTH CAROLINA
GEORGIA
FLORIDA
ALABAMA
MISSISSIPPI
LOUISIANA
ARKANSAS
MISSOURI
Appalachian Mountains
ATLANTIC OCEAN
Gulf of Mexico
THE BAHAMAS
CUBA
LA HABANA (HAVANA)
Straits of Florida
Yucatan Channel
Great Bahama Bank
Tropic of Cancer
Lake Superior
Lake Michigan
Lake Huron
Lake Erie
Lake Ontario
Georgian Bay
Thunder Bay
Sault Ste. Marie
Sudbury
Ottawa
MONTRÉAL
Québec
Toronto
Hamilton
Buffalo
DETROIT
CHICAGO
Milwaukee
Minneapolis
St. Paul
Des Moines
Omaha
Kansas City
St. Louis
Indianapolis
Columbus
Cincinnati
Cleveland
Toledo
Pittsburgh
PHILADELPHIA
NEW YORK
Newark
Boston
Providence
Hartford
Albany
Washington D.C.
Baltimore
Richmond
Norfolk
Virginia Beach
Louisville
Nashville
Memphis
Charlotte
Atlanta
Birmingham
Jacksonville
Tampa
Orlando
Miami
New Orleans
Mobile
Little Rock
Tulsa
Savannah
Charleston
Key West
Nassau
Matanzas
Camagüey
Mérida
95° 90° 85° 80° 75° 70°
H J K L M N
1 2 3 4 5 6 7

Scale 1 : 9 900 000

0 100 200 300 km

0 50 100 150 miles

A
B
C
D
125° W
120°
115°
1
2
3
4
45° N
40°
35°
P A C I F I C   O C E A N
BRITISH COLUMBIA
ALBERTA
WASHINGTON
OREGON
IDAHO
NEVADA
CALIFORNIA
UNITED STATES
GREAT BASIN
Vancouver Island
Vancouver
North Vancouver
Squamish
Tofino
Ucluelet
Port Alberni
Nanaimo
Victoria
Duncan
Port Renfrew
Strait of Georgia
Strait of Juan de Fuca
Cape Flattery
Chilliwack
Hope
Princeton
Penticton
Nelson
Trail
Cranbrook
Sparwood
Fort Macleod
Lethbridge
Cardston
Bellingham
3285 Mt. Baker
Ross Lake
Anacortes
Mount Vernon
Rockport
Mazama
Okanogan
Omak
Republic
Colville
Metaline Falls
Priest Lake
Bonners Ferry
Eureka
Elko
Lake McDonald
Browning
West Glacier
Kalispell
Libby
Sandpoint
Pend Oreille Lake
Newport
Forks
2428 Mt. Olympus
Edmonds
Everett
3213 Glacier Peak
Monroe
Lake Chelan
Chelan
Seattle
Bremerton
Queets
Renton
Tacoma
Auburn
Hyak
Leavenworth
Wenatchee
Banks Lake
Wilbur
Franklin D. Roosevelt Lake
Deer Park
Spokane
Coeur d'Alene
Coeur d'Alene Lake
Lookout Pass 1440
Thompson Falls
Flathead Lake
Choteau
Ravalli
Missoula
Hoquiam
Aberdeen
Olympia
4392 Mt. Rainier
Ellensburg
Moses Lake
Sprague
Ritzville
Colfax
Pullman
Potlatch
Raymond
Willapa Bay
Centralia
Chehalis
Packwood
Yakima
Richland
Pasco
Kennewick
Snake
Pomeroy
Dayton
Clarkston
Lewiston
Orofino
Dworshak Reservoir
Clearwater
Clearwater Mountains
Bitterroot Range
Lolo
Deer Lodge
Helena
Townsend
Ilwaco
Astoria
Kelso
Longview
3752 Mt. Adams
Goldendale
Walla Walla
Hermiston
Columbia
Seaside
Rainier
St. Helens
Vancouver
Arlington
Pendleton
Grangeville
Hamilton
Anaconda
Butte
Lost Trail Pass 2132
Pioneer Mountains
Tillamook
Hillsboro
Portland
3427 Mt. Hood
The Dalles
Heppner
La Grande
Enterprise
Riggins
Salmon
Dillon
Ennis
Newberg
Woodburn
Salem
Spray
Baker
New Meadows
Salmon River Mountains
Cascade Reservoir
Challis
Lima
Newport
Albany
Corvallis
Madras
Prineville
John Day
Blue Mountains
Cascade
Weiser
Payette
3859 Borah Peak
3681 Hyndam Peak
Eugene
Springfield
Bend
Coast Range
Cascade Range
Reedsport
La Pine
Burns
Riley
Caldwell
Nampa
Boise
Hailey
Arco
Idaho Falls
Blackfoot
Coos Bay
Coquille
Roseburg
Silver Lake
Summer Lake
Harney Lake
Malheur Lake
Malheur Mountains
Owyhee
Mountain Home
Shoshone
Snake River Plain
Pocatello
Cape Blanco
Port Orford
Crater Lake
Frenchglen
Jordan Valley
Bruneau
American Falls
Rupert
McCammon
Grants Pass
Medford
Chiloquin
Upper Klamath Lake
Valley Falls
Lake Albert
Burns Junction
Twin Falls
Rogue
Ashland
Klamath Falls
Lakeview
Steens Mountains
Brookings
Goose Lake
Denio
McDermitt
Owyhee
Rogerson
Malad City
Crescent City
Klamath
Yreka
Clear Lake Reservoir
Alturas
Upper Lake
Middle Lake
Lower Lake
Black Rock Desert
Contact
Snowville
Tremonton
Brigham City
Logan
Ogden
4317 Mt. Shasta
Weed
Dunsmuir
Clair Engle Lake
Burney
Adin
Great Salt Lake
Great Salt Lake Desert
Wells
Arcata
Eureka
Cape Mendocino
Weaverville
Redding
Shasta Lake
Eagle Lake
Gerlach
Winnemucca
Elko
Humboldt
West Wendover
Layton
Salt Lake City
Chester
Susanville
Honey Lake
Rye Patch Reservoir
Battle Mountain
Lake Almanor
Red Bluff
Pyramid Lake
Lovelock
Lage's
Tooele
Sandy
Orem
Provo
Utah Lake
Cummings
Blairsden
Donner Pass 2160
Reno
Wadsworth
Austin
Eureka
Oroville
Grass Valley
Sparks
Fallon
Carson City
Fort Bragg
Williams
Ukiah
Lakeport
Punta Arena
Yerington
Ely
Delta
Lake Tahoe
South Lake Tahoe
Auburn
Sacramento
Woodland
Walker Lake
Hawthorne
Sevier Lake
Salina
Santa Rosa
Napa
Jackson
Petaluma
Vallejo
Lodi
Bridgeport
Warm Springs
Milford
Beaver
Richfield
Berkeley
Concord
Golden Gate
Oakland
Stockton
Sonora
Mono Lake
Coaldale
Tonopah
San Francisco
Fremont
Modesto
El Portal
Lake Crowley
4342 White Mountain Peak
Goldfield
Pioche
Caliente
Panguitch
Cedar City
Redwood City
Sunnyvale
San Jose
Merced
Bishop
Scotty's Junction
Alamo
Washington
St. George
Mount Carmel
Kanab
Santa Cruz
Monterey Bay
Gilroy
Los Banos
Madera
Clovis
Sierra Nevada
Salinas
Fresno
4418 Mt. Whitney
Owens Lake
Beatty
Indian Springs
Moapa
Hanford
Visalia
Las Vegas
Overton
Lake Mead
Point Sur
Big Sur
King City
Santa Lucia Range
San Joaquin Valley
Tulare
Olancha
Death Valley
Trona
Shoshone
Henderson
Boulder City
Grand Canyon
COLORADO PLATEAU
Delano
Porterville
Isabella Lake
Onyx
Jean
Cambria
Paso Robles
Wasco
Ridgecrest
Johannesburg
Peach Springs
San Luis Obispo
Arroyo Grande
Bakersfield
Searchlight
Kingman
Seligman
Williams
Santa Maria
Wheeler Ridge
Mojave
Baker
Mojave Desert
Bullhead City
Ash Fork
Flagstaff
Lompoc
Point Conception
Santa Barbara
Santa Clarita
Barstow
Ludlow
Needles
Palmdale
Lake Havasu
Lake Havasu City
Bagdad
Prescott
ARIZONA
Santa Cruz Island
San Miguel I.
Santa Rosa I.
Oxnard
Glendale
Pasadena
San Bernardino
Twentynine Palms
Alamo Lake
Mayer
Wickenburg
LOS ANGELES
Anaheim

United States: Northwest

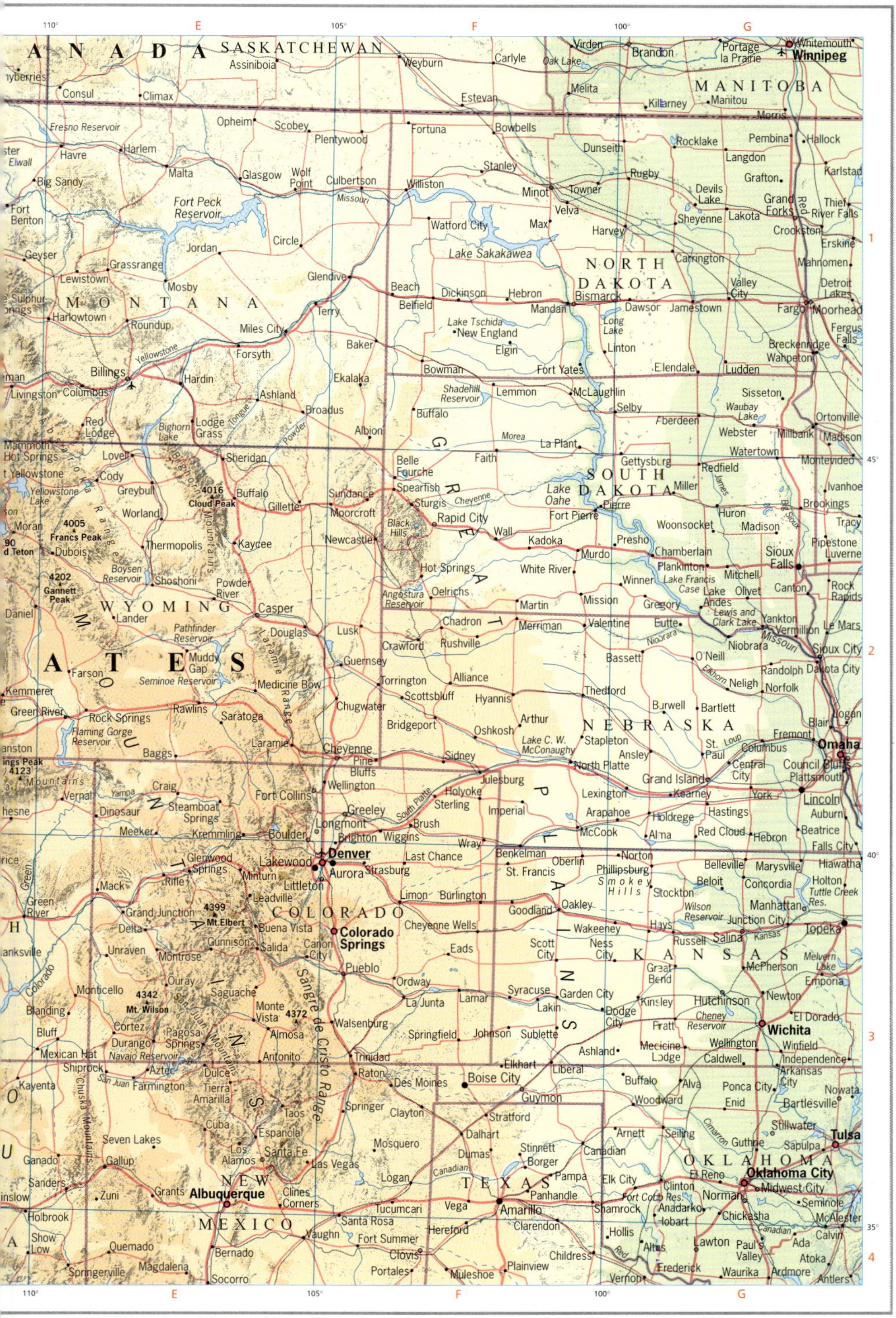

110°
E
105°
F
100°
G
CANADA
SASKATCHEWAN
Assiniboia
Weyburn
Carlyle
Virden
Brandon
Portage la Prairie
Whitemouth
Winnipeg
Oak Lake
Melita
Consul
Climax
Estevan
MANITOBA
Killarney
Manitou
Morris
Eresno Reservoir
Opheim
Scobey
Plentywood
Fortuna
Bowbells
Dunseith
Rocklake
Pembina
Hallock
Havre
Harlem
Langdon
Elwall
Malta
Glasgow
Wolf Point
Culbertson
Missouri
Stanley
Rugby
Grafton
Karlstad
Big Sandy
Williston
Minot
Towner
Devils Lake
Grand Forks
Thief River Falls
Fort Benton
Fort Peck Reservoir
Velva
Sheyenne
Lakota
Red
Crookston
Watford City
Max
Harvey
Erskine
Jordan
Circle
Lake Sakakawea
Carrington
Mahnomen
Geyser
Grassrange
Glendive
NORTH DAKOTA
Lewistown
Mosby
Beach
Dickinson
Hebron
Bismarck
Valley City
Detroit Lakes
MONTANA
Belfield
Mandan
Dawson
Jamestown
Fargo
Moorhead
Harlowtown
Terry
Roundup
Miles City
Lake Tschida
New England
Long Lake
Breckenridge
Fergus Falls
Baker
Elgin
Linton
Wahpeton
Yellowstone
Forsyth
Billings
Hardin
Ekalaka
Bowman
Fort Yates
Elendale
Ludden
Livingston
Columbus
Ashland
Shadehill Reservoir
Lemmon
McLaughlin
Sisseton
Broadus
Buffalo
Selby
Waubay Lake
Ortonville
Red Lodge
Bighorn Lake
Lodge Grass
Tongue
Powder
Albion
Morea
Aberdeen
Webster
Millbank
Madison
Mammoth Hot Springs
Yellowstone
Lovell
Sheridan
La Plant
Watertown
Faith
Gettysburg
Redfield
Montevideo
45°
Cody
Belle Fourche
SOUTH DAKOTA
Miller
Yellowstone Lake
Greybull
4016 Cloud Peak
Buffalo
Sundance
Spearfish
Cheyenne
Lake Oahe
James
Ivanhoe
Worland
Gillette
Moorcroft
Sturgis
Pierre
Huron
Brookings
Moran
4005 Francis Peak
Black Hills
Rapid City
Fort Pierre
Woonsocket
Madison
Big Sioux
Tracy
Teton
Dubois
Thermopolis
Kaycee
Newcastle
Wall
Kadoka
Presho
Pipestone
Luverne
Boysen Reservoir
Murdo
Chamberlain
Sioux Falls
4202 Gannett Peak
Shoshoni
Powder River
Hot Springs
White River
Plankinton
Mitchell
Oelrichs
Winner
Lake Francis Case
Lake Andes
Olivet
Canton
Rock Rapids
WYOMING
Lander
Casper
Angostura Reservoir
Martin
Mission
Gregory
Lewis and Clark Lake
Daniel
Pathfinder Reservoir
Douglas
Lusk
Chadron
Merriman
Valentine
Butte
Yankton
Vermillion
Le Mars
Niobrara
Missouri
Muddy Gap
Laramie Range
Crawford
Rushville
Bassett
O'Neill
Niobrara
Sioux City
2
STATES
Farson
Guernsey
Elkhorn
Randolph
Dakota City
Seminoe Reservoir
Medicine Bow
Torrington
Alliance
Thedford
Neligh
Norfolk
Kemmerer
Scottsbluff
Hyannis
Green River
Rock Springs
Rawlins
Saratoga
Chugwater
Burwell
Bartlett
Logan
Flaming Gorge Reservoir
Bridgeport
Oshkosh
Arthur
NEBRASKA
Blair
Laramie
Lake C. W. McConaughy
Stapleton
Fremont
Omaha
Baggs
Cheyenne
Sidney
Ansley
St. Paul
Loup
Columbus
Kings Peak 4123
Pine Bluffs
North Platte
Central City
Council Bluffs
Plattsmouth
Yampa
Craig
Wellington
Julesburg
Grand Island
Vernal
Fort Collins
Holyoke
Kearney
York
Steamboat Springs
Greeley
Sterling
Lexington
Lincoln
Dinosaur
South Platte
Imperial
Arapahoe
Holdrege
Hastings
Auburn
Meeker
Kremmling
Boulder
Longmont
Brush
Brighton
Wiggins
Wray
McCook
Alma
Red Cloud
Hebron
Beatrice
Glenwood Springs
Denver
Lakewood
Benkelman
Norton
Falls City
40°
Last Chance
Oberlin
Phillipsburg
Belleville
Marysville
Hiawatha
Rifle
Minturn
Aurora
Strasburg
St. Francis
Green
Littleton
Smoky Hills
Beloit
Concordia
Holton
Tuttle Creek Res.
Mack
Leadville
Limon
Burlington
Stockton
Green River
Grand Junction
4399 Mt. Elbert
COLORADO
Goodland
Oakley
Wilson Reservoir
Manhattan
Junction City
Delta
Buena Vista
Colorado Springs
Cheyenne Wells
Wakeeney
Hays
Topeka
Gunnison
Salida
Canon City
Scott City
Ness City
Russell
Salina
Kansas
Unraven
Montrose
Eads
KANSAS
Melvern Lake
Pueblo
Great Bend
McPherson
Emporia
Colorado
Ouray
Sangre de Cristo Range
Ordway
Monticello
4342 Mt. Wilson
Saguache
Syracuse
Garden City
Newton
Blanding
Monte Vista
4372
La Junta
Lamar
Lakin
Kinsley
Hutchinson
El Dorado
Dodge City
Walsenburg
Pratt
Cheney Reservoir
Wichita
Cortez
Pagosa Springs
Alamosa
Bluff
Durango
Springfield
Johnson
Sublette
Wellington
Winfield
3
Mexican Hat
Navajo Reservoir
Antonito
Trinidad
Ashland
Medicine Lodge
Caldwell
Independence
Shiprock
Aztec
Elkhart
Liberal
Arkansas City
Kayenta
San Juan
Farmington
Dulce
Raton
Des Moines
Boise City
Buffalo
Alva
Ponca City
Nowata
Chuska Mountains
Tierra Amarilla
Guymon
Woodward
Enid
Bartlesville
Taos
Springer
Clayton
Stratford
Cimarron
Stillwater
Tulsa
Cuba
Dalhart
Arnett
Seiling
Guthrie
Sapulpa
Seven Lakes
Espanola
Mosquero
Dumas
Stinnett
Canadian
Ganado
Gallup
Los Alamos
Santa Fe
Las Vegas
Borger
OKLAHOMA
Sanders
Canadian
Pampa
Elk City
El Reno
Oklahoma City
Zuni
Grants
Albuquerque
NEW MEXICO
Clines Corners
Logan
TEXAS
Clinton
Midwest City
Panhandle
Fort Cobb Res.
Norman
Seminole
Holbrook
Tucumcari
Vega
Amarillo
Shamrock
Anadarko
Chickasha
Santa Rosa
Clarendon
Hobart
Canadian
McAlester
35°
Show Low
Quemado
Vaughn
Hereford
Hollis
Lawton
Paul's Valley
Ada
Calvin
Bernado
Fort Sumner
Altus
Atoka
4
Springerville
Magdalena
Clovis
Plainview
Childress
Red
Frederick
Waurika
Ardmore
Socorro
Portales
Muleshoe
Vernon
Antlers
110°
E
105°
F
100°
G

Scale 1 : 9 900 000

0 100 200 300 km

0 50 100 150 miles

MANITOBA
MINNESOTA
WISCONSIN
IOWA
ILLINOIS
INDIANA
OHIO
MICHIGAN
KANSAS
MISSOURI
ARKANSAS
OKLAHOMA
KENTUCKY
TENNESSEE
ALABAMA
MISSISSIPPI
GEORGIA
UNITED ST
C A
O N T
Lake Superior
Lake Michigan
Lake Huron
Thunder Bay
Duluth
Minneapolis
St. Paul
Milwaukee
CHICAGO
DETROIT
Toledo
Madison
Des Moines
Omaha
Kansas City
St. Louis
Indianapolis
Cincinnati
Louisville
Nashville
Memphis
Little Rock
Tulsa
Springfield
Lincoln
Grand Rapids
Green Bay
Sioux Falls
Fargo
Peoria
Evansville
Chattanooga
Knoxville
Huntsville
Lexington
Dayton
Columbus
Fort Wayne
South Bend
Lansing
Sault Ste. Marie
Marquette
Rochester
Cedar Rapids
Davenport
Fort Smith

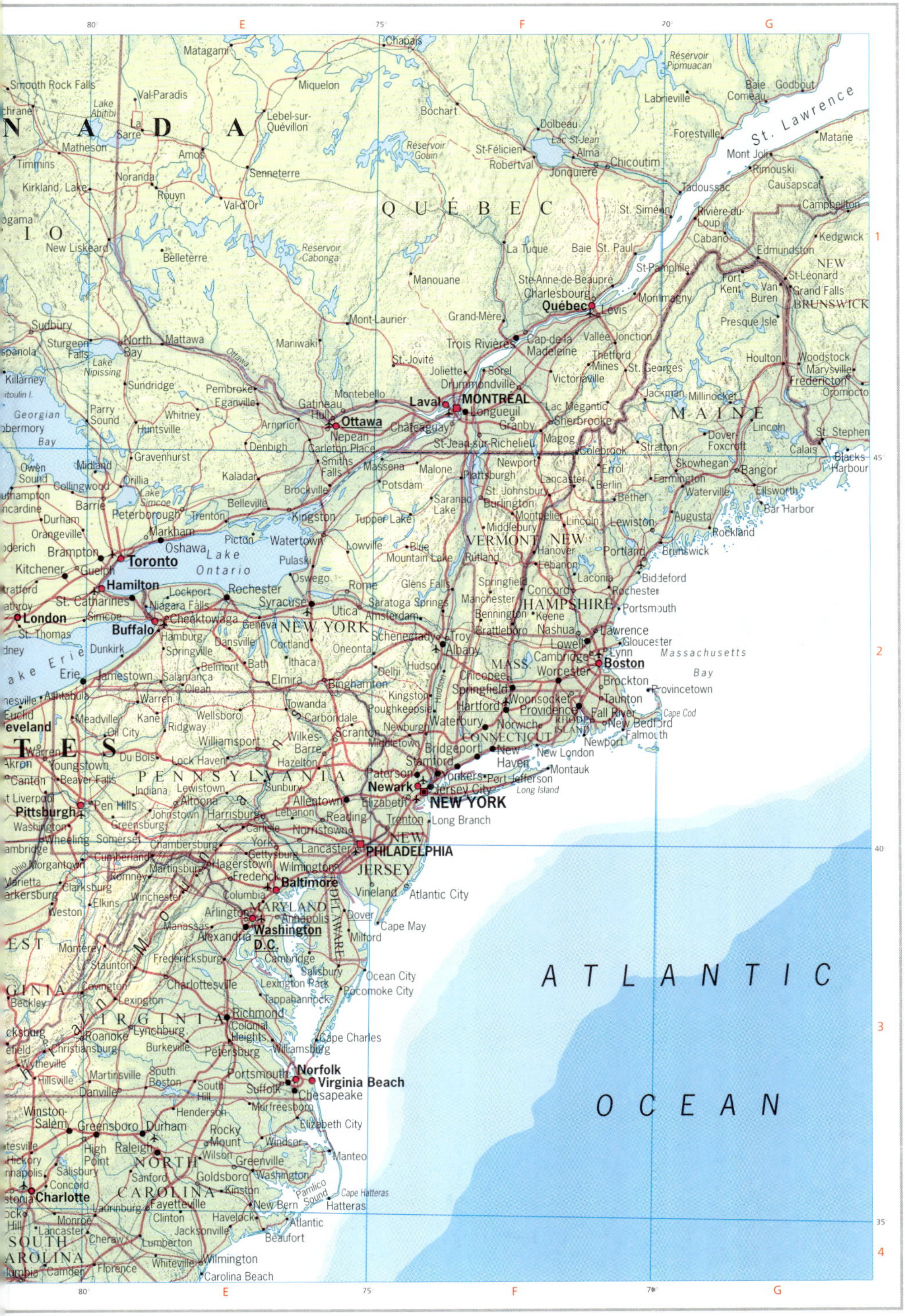

80°
E
75°
F
70°
G
1
2
3
4
45°
40°
35°
Chapais
Matagami
Réservoir Pipmuacan
Smooth Rock Falls
Val-Paradis
Miquelon
Baie Comeau
Godbout
Labrieville
Lake Abitibi
Lebel-sur-Quévillon
Bochart
St. Lawrence
N A D A
La Sarre
Dolbeau
Forestville
Matane
Matheson
Lac St-Jean
Alma
Réservoir Gouin
St-Félicien
Mont Joli
Amos
Timmins
Roberval
Jonquière
Chicoutimi
Rimouski
Noranda
Senneterre
Kirkland Lake
Rouyn
Tadoussac
Causapscal
Val-d'Or
Q U É B E C
St. Siméon
Campbellton
Rivière-du-Loup
I O
Cabano
Kedgwick
Reservoir Cabonga
New Liskeard
La Tuque
Baie St. Paul
Edmundston
Belleterre
St-Pamphile
NEW
Ste-Anne-de-Beaupré
St-Léonard
Manouane
Fort Kent
Van Buren
Charlesbourg
Grand Falls
Montmagny
BRUNSWICK
Québec
Lévis
Mont-Laurier
Grand-Mère
Presque Isle
Sudbury
Mattawa
Vallée Jonction
Sturgeon Falls
North Bay
Maniwaki
Trois Rivières
Cap-de-la-Madeleine
Thetford Mines
Houlton
Woodstock
Lake Nipissing
Ottawa
St. Jovité
St. Georges
Marysville
Killarney
Joliette
Sorel
Victoriaville
Fredericton
Drummondville
Oromocto
Sundridge
Pembroke
Montebello
Millinocket
Georgian Bay
Parry Sound
Eganville
Gatineau
Laval
MONTRÉAL
Jackman
Hull
Longueuil
Lac Mégantic
M A I N E
Whitney
Arnprior
Ottawa
Granby
Sherbrooke
Lincoln
Huntsville
Nepean
Châteauguay
St. Stephen
Denbigh
Carleton Place
St-Jean-sur-Richelieu
Magog
Colebrook
Stratton
Dover-Foxcroft
Calais
Gravenhurst
Smiths Falls
Massena
Malone
Newport
Errol
Skowhegan
Blacks Harbour
Midland
Owen Sound
Orillia
Kaladar
Potsdam
Plattsburgh
Lancaster
Berlin
Farmington
Bangor
Collingwood
Lake Simcoe
Brockville
Saranac Lake
St. Johnsbury
Burlington
Waterville
Ellsworth
Barrie
Belleville
Bethel
Bar Harbor
Peterborough
Trenton
Kingston
Tupper Lake
Montpelier
Lincoln
Lewiston
Augusta
Durham
Orangeville
Markham
Picton
Watertown
Lowville
Middlebury
Rockland
Brampton
Oshawa
Lake Ontario
Pulaski
Blue Mountain Lake
VERMONT
NEW
Hanover
Portland
Brunswick
Toronto
Rutland
Lebanon
Kitchener
Guelph
Oswego
Rome
Glens Falls
Springfield
Laconia
Biddeford
Hamilton
Lockport
Rochester
Manchester
Concord
Rochester
St. Catharines
Niagara Falls
Syracuse
Saratoga Springs
HAMPSHIRE
Portsmouth
Simcoe
Utica
Amsterdam
Bennington
Keene
London
Cheektowaga
Geneva
NEW YORK
Brattleboro
Nashua
Lawrence
St. Thomas
Buffalo
Schenectady
Troy
Lowell
Gloucester
Hamburg
Cortland
Albany
Lynn
Massachusetts Bay
Dunkirk
Dansville
Oneonta
MASS.
Cambridge
Springville
Bath
Ithaca
Hudson
Boston
Lake Erie
Belmont
Delhi
Worcester
Erie
Jamestown
Salamanca
Olean
Elmira
Binghamton
Chicopee
Brockton
Springfield
Provincetown
Ashtabula
Warren
Kingston
Woonsocket
Taunton
Euclid
Towanda
Poughkeepsie
Hartford
Providence
Cape Cod
Meadville
Kane
Wellsboro
Carbondale
Newburgh
Waterbury
Norwich
Fall River
Cleveland
Oil City
Ridgway
Wilkes-Barre
Scranton
Middletown
CONNECTICUT
RHODE ISLAND
New Bedford
Falmouth
Williamsport
Bridgeport
New Haven
Newport
Warren
Du Bois
Lock Haven
Hazelton
Stamford
New London
Akron
Youngstown
Montauk
Canton
Beaver Falls
P E N N S Y L V A N I A
Paterson
Yonkers
Port Jefferson
Indiana
Lewistown
Sunbury
Newark
Jersey City
Long Island
Altoona
Allentown
Elizabeth
NEW YORK
Pittsburgh
Penn Hills
Johnstown
Harrisburg
Lebanon
Reading
Washington
Greensburg
Carlisle
Norristown
Trenton
Long Branch
Wheeling
Somerset
Chambersburg
York
NEW
Cambridge
Lancaster
PHILADELPHIA
Morgantown
Cumberland
Gettysburg
Martinsburg
Hagerstown
Wilmington
JERSEY
Marietta
Romney
Frederick
Parkersburg
Clarksburg
Baltimore
Vineland
Atlantic City
Elkins
Winchester
Columbia
Weston
Arlington
MARYLAND
Manassas
Annapolis
Dover
Cape May
Washington D.C.
Alexandria
DELAWARE
Milford
Monterey
Fredericksburg
Cambridge
Staunton
Salisbury
Ocean City
Charlottesville
A T L A N T I C
Lexington Park
Pocomoke City
Covington
Beckley
Lexington
Tappahannock
Richmond
V I R G I N I A
Colonial Heights
Roanoke
Lynchburg
Cape Charles
Christiansburg
Burkeville
Petersburg
Williamsburg
Wytheville
Norfolk
Martinsville
South Boston
Portsmouth
Virginia Beach
Hillsville
Danville
South Hill
Suffolk
Chesapeake
O C E A N
Henderson
Murfreesboro
Winston-Salem
Greensboro
Durham
Rocky Mount
Elizabeth City
High Point
Raleigh
Windsor
Hickory
N O R T H
Wilson
Greenville
Manteo
Salisbury
Sanford
Goldsboro
Washington
Concord
C A R O L I N A
Kinston
Pamlico Sound
Cape Hatteras
Charlotte
Fayetteville
New Bern
Hatteras
Laurinburg
Clinton
Havelock
Monroe
Atlantic
Lancaster
Jacksonville
Beaufort
SOUTH
Cheraw
Lumberton
CAROLINA
Wilmington
Camden
Florence
Whiteville
Carolina Beach

Scale 1 : 9 900 000

0 100 200 300 km

0 50 100 150 miles

A
B
C
D
1
2
3
4
5
100° W
95°
90°
40° N
35°
30°
25°
100°
NEBRASKA
IOWA
KANSAS
MISSOURI
ILLINOIS
UNITED STATES
OKLAHOMA
ARKANSAS
TEXAS
LOUISIANA
MISSISSIPPI
TENN
ALA
MEXICO
GREAT PLAINS
GULF OF MEXICO
Omaha
Lincoln
Des Moines
Council Bluffs
Topeka
Kansas City
Independence
St. Joseph
St. Louis
Springfield
Wichita
Tulsa
Oklahoma City
Amarillo
Lubbock
Memphis
Little Rock
Shreveport
Fort Worth
Arlington
DALLAS
Waco
Austin
SAN ANTONIO
HOUSTON
Galveston
Beaumont
Baton Rouge
New Orleans
Jackson
Corpus Christi
Laredo
Nuevo Laredo
Brownsville
Matamoros
Reynosa
MONTERREY
San Nicolás de los Garzas
Guadalupe
Saltillo
Monclova
Ciudad Victoria
Piedras Negras
Ciudad Acuña
Del Rio
Abilene
San Angelo
Midland
Big Spring
Tyler
Longview
Texarkana
Lafayette
Pensacola
Mobile
Port Arthur
Mississippi River Delta
Padre Island
Matagorda Island
Sierra Madre Oriental
Tropic of Cancer
Rio Grande
Mississippi

United States: Southeast

85°
E
80°
F
75°
G
1
2
3
4
5
40°
35°
30°
25°
Toledo
Lake Erie
Euclid
Lorain
Cleveland
Parma
Warren
Akron
Youngstown
Fort Wayne
Findlay
Van Wert
Upper Sandusky
Massillon
Canton
Beaver Falls
Lima
Marion
Mansfield
East Liverpool
Pittsburgh
St. Marys
Bellefontaine
Mount Vernon
Urbana
Delaware
Columbus
OHIO
Wheeling
Zanesville
Piqua
Dayton
Springfield
Lancaster
Indianapolis
Greenfield
Rushville
Shelbyville
Middletown
Hamilton
Circleville
Athens
Marietta
Parkersburg
Chillicothe
Hillsboro
Cincinnati
Covington
Ripley
Gallipolis
Portsmouth
Jackson
Weston
Clarksburg
Morgantown
Elkins
WEST VIRGINIA
Charleston
South Charleston
Huntington
Ironton
Ashland
Carrollton
Frankfort
Georgetown
Lexington
Morehead
Winchester
KENTUCKY
Danville
Richmond
Louisa
Beckley
Salyersville
Williamson
Stanford
Campbellsville
Hazard
Jenkins
Bluefield
Manchester
Richlands
Glasgow
Somerset
London
Wytheville
Pineville
Middlesboro
Abingdon
Bristol
Kingsport
Johnson City
Elizabethton
Jefferson City
Morristown
Boone
Knoxville
Hot Springs
Statesville
Hickory
Asheville
Waynesville
Kannapolis
Gastonia
Charlotte
Murphy
Franklin
Athens
Dayton
Cleveland
Spartanburg
Greenville
Seneca
Rock Hill
Lancaster
Dalton
Blairsville
Dahlonega
Anderson
Gainesville
Newberry
SOUTH CAROLINA
Greenwood
Camden
Columbia
Sumter
Saluda
Florence
Conway
Manning
Myrtle Beach
Georgetown
Orangeburg
Augusta
Waynesboro
Allendale
Summerville
North Charleston
Charleston
Mount Pleasant
Beaufort
Hilton Head Island
Savannah
Hinesville
Statesboro
Atlanta
Marietta
Smyrna
Rome
Sandy Springs
Calhoun
Covington
Thomson
East Point
Eatonton
Milledgeville
Macon
Louisville
GEORGIA
La Grange
Talbotton
Perry
Dublin
Columbus
Americus
Vidalia
McRae
Pembroke
Union Springs
Cuthbert
Cordele
Albany
Tifton
Douglas
Jesup
Waycross
Blakely
Moultrie
Bainbridge
Thomasville
Valdosta
Brunswick
Kingsland
Folkston
Fernandina Beach
Jacksonville
Baldwin
Jasper
Live Oak
Lake City
Tallahassee
Perry
Carrabelle
Apalachee Bay
Apalachicola
C. San Blas
Cross City
St. Augustine
Palatka
Gainesville
Bunnell
Williston
Daytona Beach
Crystal River
Ocala
New Smyrna Beach
Leesburg
Sanford
Titusville
Brooksville
Orlando
Cocoa
Cape Canaveral
Spring Hill
Palm Harbor
FLORIDA
Clearwater
Largo
Tampa
Lakeland
Melbourne
Palm Bay
St. Petersburg
Bowling Green
Vero Beach
Bradenton
Sarasota
Sebring
Lake Placid
Fort Pierce
Fort Saint Lucie
Arcadia
Lake Okeechobee
Port Charlotte
Punta Gorda
West Palm Beach
Fort Myers
Belle Glade
Cape Coral
Coral Springs
Delray Beach
Naples
Pompano Beach
Fort Lauderdale
Hollywood
Hialeah
Everglades City
Kendall
Miami
Perrine
Homestead
Flamingo
Key Largo
Islamorada
Big Pine
Key West
Straits of Florida
Cay Sal Bank (The Bahamas)
Bimini Is.
Grand Bahama
West End
Freeport City
Little Abaco
Coopers Town
Marsh Harbour
Great Abaco
N.E. Providence Channel
THE BAHAMAS
Berry Is.
The Bluff
Governor's Harbour
Eleuthera
Nicholls Town
Nassau
New Providence
Andros
Andros Town
Bannerman Town
Arthur's Town
Cat I.
Exuma Sound
Mangrove Cay
Kemp's Bay
Devil's Point
Cockburn Town
San Salvador
Great Exuma
George Town
Rum Cay
Tropic of Cancer
PENNSYLVANIA
Meadville
Oil City
Kane
Ridgway
Du Bois
Lock Haven
Williamsport
Indiana
Altoona
Johnstown
Greensburg
Somerset
Sunbury
Lewistown
Harrisburg
Carlisle
Chambersburg
Cumberland
Hagerstown
Gettysburg
York
Lancaster
Lebanon
Reading
Allentown
Norristown
Wilkes-Barre
Hazleton
Scranton
Carbondale
NEW YORK
Middletown
Newburgh
Waterbury
Hartford
CONNECTICUT
Norwich
Fall River
New Bedford
Newport
Bridgeport
New Haven
New London
Stamford
Yonkers
Port Jefferson
Montauk
Long Island
Paterson
Newark
Jersey City
NEW YORK CITY
Trenton
Long Branch
PHILADELPHIA
NEW JERSEY
Wilmington
Vineland
Atlantic City
Cape May
Baltimore
Columbia
Frederick
Martinsburg
Romney
Winchester
Arlington
Alexandria
Washington D.C.
Annapolis
Dover
DELAWARE
Milford
Cambridge
MARYLAND
Manassas
Fredericksburg
Monterey
Staunton
Salisbury
Ocean City
Lexington Park
Pocomoke City
Tappahannock
Charlottesville
Covington
Lexington
Richmond
Lynchburg
Roanoke
Burkeville
Colonial Heights
Petersburg
Blacksburg
Christiansburg
VIRGINIA
Cape Charles
Martinsville
South Boston
South Hill
Portsmouth
Norfolk
Virginia Beach
Chesapeake
Suffolk
Hillsville
Danville
Roanoke Rapids
Murfreesboro
Winston-Salem
Henderson
Elizabeth City
Windsor
Durham
High Point
Greensboro
Rocky Mount
Manteo
NORTH CAROLINA
Raleigh
Wilson
Greenville
Salisbury
Concord
Sanford
Goldsboro
Washington
Pamlico Sound
Cape Hatteras
Hatteras
Kinston
New Bern
Fayetteville
Monroe
Laurinburg
Clinton
Havelock
Atlantic
Beaufort
Cheraw
Lumberton
Jacksonville
Whiteville
Wilmington
Carolina Beach
Cape Fear
Appalachian Mountains
ATLANTIC OCEAN

Scale 1 : 9 900 000

0 100 200 300 km

0 50 100 150 miles

PACIFIC OCEAN
CALIFORNIA
GREAT BASIN
NEVADA
Sierra Nevada
Coast Range
San Joaquin Valley
Death Valley
Mojave Desert
Red Bluff
Cummings
Blairsden
Oroville
Donner Pass
2160
Reno
Sparks
Wadsworth
Fallon
Pyramid Lake
Lovelock
Austin
Eureka
Ely
Lage's
Fort Bragg
Punta Arena
Ukiah
Williams
Lakeport
Grass Valley
Marysville
Auburn
Woodland
Placerville
Lake Tahoe
Carson City
South Lake Tahoe
Yerington
Walker Lake
Hawthorne
Santa Rosa
Napa
Sacramento
Petaluma
Vallejo
Berkeley
Concord
Stockton
Bridgeport
Mono Lake
Golden Gate
San Francisco
Oakland
Modesto
Sonora
Fremont
Redwood City
Sunnyvale
San Jose
Merced
El Portal
Santa Cruz
Monterey Bay
Salinas
Madera
Clovis
Fresno
Hanford
Visalia
Bishop
Lake Crowley
4342 White Mountain Peak
4418 Mt. Whitney
Owens Lake
Coaldale
Tonopah
Goldfield
Scotty's Junction
Warm Springs
Beatty
Olancha
Point Sur
Big Sur
King City
Tulare
Porterville
Delano
Isabella Lake
Onyx
Trona
Shoshone
Cambria
Paso Robles
Wasco
Bakersfield
Ridgecrest
Johannesburg
San Luis Obispo
Arroyo Grande
Santa Maria
Lompoc
Point Conception
Wheeler Ridge
Mojave
Edwards
Barstow
Santa Barbara
Santa Clarita
Palmdale
Santa Cruz Island
San Miguel I.
Santa Rosa I.
Oxnard
Glendale
Pasadena
San Bernardino
LOS ANGELES
Torrance
Anaheim
Long Beach
Santa Ana
Huntington Beach
Santa Barbara I.
Santa Catalina I.
Gulf of Santa Catalina
San Nicolas I.
San Clemente I.
Oceanside
Escondido
SAN DIEGO
El Cajon
Chula Vista
Tijuana
Mexicali
Ensenada
Twentynine Palms
Indio
Salton Sea
Desert Center
Brawley
El Centro
Yuma
Ludlow
Needles
Lake Havasu
Lake Havasu City
Topock
Blythe
Las Vegas
Henderson
Lake Mead
Boulder City
Jean
Searchlight
Baker
Indian Springs
Moapa
Overton
Alamo
Pioche
Caliente
Washington
St. George
Cedar City
Kanab
Sevier Lake
Milford
Beaver
Richfield
Delta
Gunnison
Salina
Eureka
Mount Pleasant
Utah Lake
Kingman
Bullhead City
Seligman
Ash Fork
Clarkdale
Peach Springs
Bagdad
Alamo Lake
Mayer
Wickenburg
Pioneer
Glendale
Tempe
Gila
Gila Bend
Wellton
Ajo
San Luis Rio Colorado
Sonoyta
Golfo de Santa Clara
Puerto Peñasco
El Sahuaro
Caborca
Golfo de California
Baja California
Angel de la Guarda
Puerto Libertad
Tiburón
San Lorenzo
Rosarito
Punta San Gabriel
Guerrero Negro
Bahía Kino
Colorado
U T
COLO
ARI
PLAT
1
RUSSIA
Chukchi Sea
Arctic Circle
Bering Strait
Kotzebue Sound
Point Hope
Wainwright
Barrow
Point Barrow
Teshekpuk Lake
Harrison Bay
Prudhoe Bay
Beaufort Sea
Kaktovik
Cape Dalhousie
Mackenzie Bay
Tuktoyaktuk
Eskimo Lakes
Paulatuk
Inuvik
Colville Lake
Brooks Range
Noatak
Colville
Kotzebue
Kobuk
Selawik
Big Lake
Old Crow
Richardson Mts
Arctic Red River
Fort McPherson
Great Bear Lake
NORTHWEST TERRITORIES
Norman Wells
Fort Norman
Teller
Seward Peninsula
Deering
Stevens Village
Circle
CANADA
Nome
Koyukuk
Hughes
Huslia
Galena
Ruby
ALASKA (U.S.)
Fairbanks
Eagle
YUKON TERRITORY
Dawson
Mayo
Keno Hill
Selwyn Mts
Mackenzie Mts
Macmillan Pass
Tungsten
Norton Sound
Unalakleet
Kaltag
Nenana
Delta Junction
Tanacross
Tok
Paxson
St. Lawrence Island
Kotlik
McGrath
6194 Mt. McKinley
Alaska Range
Kuskokwim Mts
Beaver Creek
Ross River
Watson Lake
St. Matthew Island
Cape Romanzof
Hooper Bay
Yukon
Aniak
Napamute
Willow
Glennallen
Kluane Lake
Whitehorse
Johnson's Crossing
Lower Post
Nunivak Island
Etolin Strait
Bethel
Anchorage
Mt. Logan 6050
5489
Haines Junction
Teslin
Atlin
BRITISH COLUMBIA
Dease Lake
Bering Sea
Cape Mendenhall
Kipnuk
Kuskokwim Bay
Platinum
3075
Iliamna Volcano
Cook Inlet
Cape Cleare
Cape St. Elias
Yakutat
4670 Mt. Fairweather
Tulsequah
Telegraph Creek
Juneau
Admiralty I.
Pribilof Islands
Cape Newenham
Dillingham
Naknek
Cape Constantine
Bristol Bay
Afognak Island
Kodiak
Kodiak Island
Shelikof Strait
Aleutian Range
Gulf of Alaska
Chichagof I.
Alexander Archipelago
3136 Mt. Ratz
Revillagigedo I.
Ketchikan
Prince of Wales Island
2505 Veniaminof Volcano
Alaska Peninsula
Kupreanof Pt.
Trinity Islands
Aleutian Islands
Unimak I.
Shumagin Islands
Chirikof Island
Islands of the Four Mountains
Umnak I.
Unalaska I.
Fox Islands
PACIFIC OCEAN
Scale 1 : 27 100 000
Dixon Entrance
Graham I.
Masset
Queen Charlotte Islands
Moresby I.
3
Bering Sea
Attu I.
Aleutian Islands
Kiska I.
Amchitka I.
Tanaga I.
Adak I.
Atka I.
Andreanof Islands
Islands of the Four Mountains
PACIFIC OCEAN
2
Mana
1576
Kauai
Puuwai
Niihau
Lihue
PACIFIC OCEAN
Scale 1 : 9 875 000

110°
E
105°
F
100°
G
40°
35°
30°
25°
1
2
3
4
ROCKY MOUNTAINS
COLORADO
KANSAS
GREAT PLAINS
OKLAHOMA
NEW MEXICO
TEXAS
UNITED STATES
MEXICO
Sierra Madre Occidental
Sierra Madre Oriental
Sangre de Cristo Range
Chuska Mountains
Black Range
Smokey Hills
Edwards Plateau
Gulf of Mexico
Tropic of Cancer
Denver
Aurora
Lakewood
Littleton
Boulder
Longmont
Kremmling
Meeker
Minturn
Glenwood Springs
Rifle
Leadville
Grand Junction
4399 Mt. Elbert
Buena Vista
Mack
Price
Green River
Delta
Salida
Canon City
Colorado Springs
Pueblo
Unraven
Montrose
Gunnison
Ouray
Saguache
Hanksville
Monticello
4342 Mt. Wilson
Monte Vista
4372
Blanding
Bluff
Cortez
Pagosa Springs
Navajo Reservoir
Walsenburg
Alamosa
Antonito
Trinidad
La Junta
Ordway
Lamar
Springfield
Strasburg
Last Chance
Limon
Burlington
Cheyenne Wells
Eads
Wray
Benkelman
Oberlin
Norton
St. Francis
Phillipsburg
Stockton
Beloit
Goodland
Oakley
Wakeeney
Hays
Russell
Salina
Scott City
Ness City
Great Bend
Syracuse
Lakin
Garden City
Hutchinson
Kinsley
Pratt
Dodge City
Medicine Lodge
Johnson
Sublette
Ashland
Liberal
Elkhart
Guymon
Boise City
Belleville
Concordia
Marysville
Holton
Manhattan
Topeka
Tuttle Creek Res.
Junction City
Kansas
Melvern Lake
Emporia
McPherson
Newton
El Dorado
Wichita
Cheney Reservoir
Wellington
Winfield
Caldwell
Arkansas City
Independence
Bartlesville
Ponca City
Alva
Enid
Buffalo
Woodward
Nowata
Oologah Lake
Keystone Lake
Stillwater
Sapulpa
Tulsa
Guthrie
Seiling
Arnett
Oklahoma City
Midwest City
El Reno
Clinton
Elk City
Norman
Seminole
McAlester
Chickasha
Anadarko
Hobart
Fort Cobb Res.
Altus
Lawton
Hollis
Paul's Valley
Ada
Calvin
Ardmore
Lake Texoma
Atoka
Antlers
Hugo
Frederick
Waurika
Marietta
Durant
Denison
Sherman
Paris
Gainesville
Wichita Falls
Vernon
Lake Kemp
Seymour
Olney
Bowie
Denton
McKinney
Plano
Garland
Irving
Fort Worth
Arlington
DALLAS
Jacksboro
Haskell
Throckmorton
Anson
Breckenridge
Athens
Ennis
Corsicana
Hillsboro
Stephenville
Cisco
Abilene
Mexia
Palestine
Waco
Brownwood
Coleman
Ballinger
San Angelo
Gatesville
Brady
Eden
Temple
Lampasas
Cameron
Hearne
Georgetown
Bryan
College Station
Lake Buchanan
Lake Travis
Austin
Brenham
Mason
Fredericksburg
Kerrville
San Marcos
Lockhart
New Braunfels
Seguin
Columbus
Rosenburg
SAN ANTONIO
Hondo
Uvalde
Del Rio
Comstock
Langtry
Amistad Reservoir
Ciudad Acuña
Piedras Negras
Eagle Pass
Pearsall
Crystal City
Pleasanton
Yoakum
El Campo
Victoria
Bay City
Kenedy
Port Lavaca
Beeville
George West
Sinton
Matagorda Island
Cotulla
Robstown
Corpus Christi
Alice
Kingsville
Laredo
Nuevo Laredo
Hebbronville
Falfurrias
Padre Island
Zapata
Falcon Lake
Rio Grande City
Laguna Madre
Raymondville
Mercedes
Harlingen
Reynosa
Matamoros
Clayton
Des Moines
Springer
4011 Wheeler Peak
Taos
Tierra Amarilla
Dulce
Aztec
Farmington
Shiprock
Kayenta
Espanola
Santa Fe
Los Alamos
Cuba
Seven Lakes
Las Vegas
Mosquero
Logan
Tucumcari
Clines Corners
Ganado
Gallup
Zuni
Grants
Sanders
Winslow
Holbrook
Albuquerque
Santa Rosa
Vaughn
Clovis
Fort Sumner
Portales
Show Low
Quemado
Bernado
Magdalena
Socorro
Springerville
Alpine
Elephant Butte Reservoir
Carrizozo
Hondo
Roswell
Glenwood
San Carlos Lake
Clifton
Truth or Consequences
Caballo Reservoir
Alamogordo
Artesia
Lake McMillan
Hobbs
Carlsbad
Hayden
Safford
Silver City
Bowie
Lordsburg
Deming
Las Cruces
Tucson
Benson
Columbus
El Paso
Ciudad Juárez
Bisbee
Douglas
Agua Prieta
Nogales
Cananea
Magdalena
Janos
Nuevo Casas Grandes
Lucero
Cumpas
El Sueco
Buenaventura
Mazocahui
Madera
Hermosillo
Sahuaripa
Tónichi
Temóchic
Cuauhtémoc
Chihuahua
Ciudad Delicias
Ciudad Camargo
Empalme
Ciudad Obregón
Sierra Blanca
Van Horn
Pecos
Fort Stockton
Marfa
Marathon
Presidio
Ojinaga
2389 Emory Peak
2896 Picacho del Centinela
Sanderson
Sheffield
Ozona
Rocksprings
McCamey
Rankin
Monahans
Odessa
Midland
Andrews
Seminole
Big Spring
Sweetwater
Sterling City
Twin Buttes Reservoir
Lamesa
Snyder
Post
Tahoka
Brownfield
Plains
Lubbock
Littlefield
Muleshoe
Plainview
Floydada
Dickens
Aspermont
Guthrie
Childress
Paducah
Hereford
Vega
Canyon
Amarillo
Dalhart
Dumas
Stinnett
Borger
Pampa
Panhandle
Shamrock
Canadian
Clarendon
Stratford
La Perla
Nueva Rosita
Múzquiz
Sabinas
Anáhuac
Monclova
Villaldama
Sabinas Hidalgo
San Nicolás de los Garzas
MONTERREY
Guadalupe
Saltillo
Montemorelos
Linares
San Fernando
Villagrán
Presa de las Adjuntas
La Pesca
Soto la Marina
Ciudad Victoria
Doctor Arroyo
Matehuala
Tula
González
Ciudad Mante
Ciudad del Maíz
Ciudad Madero
Tampico
Ciudad Valles
San Luis Potosí
Cerritos
Charcas
Presa de la Boquilla
Jiménez
Hidalgo del Parral
Villa Ocampo
Cuatro Ciénegas
San Pedro de las Colonias
Bermejillo
Gómez Palacio
Torreón
Matamoros
Tepehuanes
Francisco I. Madero
Miguel Auza
El Potosí
Durango
Rio Grande
Sombrerete
Fresnillo
Zacatecas
Valparaíso
Jerez
Salinas
Luis Moya
Villanueva
Acaponeta
Tecuala
Rio Grande
Pecos
Colorado
Canadian
Red
Cimarron
Gila
San Juan
HAWAII (U.S.)
158°
157°
156°
155°
D
E
F
G
22°
21°
20°
19°
Oahu
Kaneohe
Kailua
Honolulu
Kalaupapa
Molokai
Wailuku
Lanai City
Lanai
Paia
3054
Maui
Kahoolawe
Hawi
Honokaa
Hawaii
4205 Mauna Kea
Hilo
Kailua Kona
4169 Mauna Loa
Papa
Kalapana
Naalehu
Ka Lae

Scale 1 : 22 100 000

0 200 400 600 km
0 100 200 300 miles

PACIFIC OCEAN
GULF OF
MEXICO
UNITED STATES
MEXICO
CALIFORNIA
ARIZONA
NEW MEXICO
COLORADO
KANSAS
OKLAHOMA
TEXAS
MISSOURI
ARKANSAS
LOUISIANA
GUATEMALA
EL SALVADOR
LOS ANGELES
SAN DIEGO
PHOENIX
DALLAS
HOUSTON
SAN ANTONIO
MONTERREY
GUADALAJARA
CIUDAD DE MÉXICO
PUEBLA
Las Vegas
Albuquerque
El Paso
Ciudad Juárez
Tucson
Mesa
Tijuana
Mexicali
Ensenada
Oklahoma City
Tulsa
Wichita
Fort Worth
Austin
Corpus Christi
Chihuahua
Hermosillo
Ciudad Obregón
Culiacán
Mazatlán
Durango
Torreón
Saltillo
Guadalupe
Reynosa
Matamoros
Tampico
Aguascalientes
San Luis Potosí
León
Irapuato
Celaya
Querétaro
Morelia
Cuernavaca
Veracruz
Jalapa Enríquez
Acapulco
Villahermosa
Tuxtla Gutiérrez
Mérida
Golfo de California
Baja California
Sierra Madre Occidental
Sierra Madre del Sur
Bahía de Campeche
Tropic of Cancer
Equator
Clipperton I. (France)
Islas Revillagigedo (Mexico)

Central America and the Caribbean

ATLANTIC OCEAN
CARIBBEAN SEA
THE BAHAMAS
CUBA
LA HABANA (HAVANA)
JAMAICA
Kingston
HAITI
PORT-AU-PRINCE
DOMINICAN REPUBLIC
SANTO DOMINGO
San Juan
Puerto Rico (U.S.)
Greater Antilles
Lesser Antilles
Leeward Islands
Windward Islands
Netherlands Antilles
ANTIGUA AND BARBUDA
ST. KITTS-NEVIS
DOMINICA
Roseau
ST. LUCIA
Castries
BARBADOS
Bridgetown
ST. VINCENT & THE GRENADINES
Kingstown
GRENADA
St. George's
TRINIDAD AND TOBAGO
Port of Spain
VENEZUELA
CARACAS
COLOMBIA
BOGOTÁ
MEDELLÍN
CALI
BARRANQUILLA
Cartagena
PANAMA
Panama
COSTA RICA
San José
NICARAGUA
Managua
Tegucigalpa
BRAZIL
Bermuda (U.K.)
Hamilton
Nassau
Miami
Tampa
Jacksonville
Orlando
Atlanta
Charlotte
Norfolk
Virginia Beach
Richmond
Nashville
GEORGIA
FLORIDA
VIRGINIA
NORTH CAROLINA
SOUTH CAROLINA
KENTUCKY
WEST VIRGINIA
MARYLAND
Tropic of Cancer
Equator

Scale 1 : 38 400 000

0 500 1000 1500 km

0 250 500 750 miles

ATLANTIC OCEAN
Caribbean Sea
BRAZIL
VENEZUELA
COLOMBIA
PERU
ECUADOR
GUYANA
SURINAM
FRENCH GUIANA
CUBA
JAMAICA
HAITI
DOMINICAN REP.
THE BAHAMAS
NORTH AMERICA
Mid-Atlantic Ridge
Lesser Antilles
Greater Antilles
Puerto Rico Trench
Tropic of Cancer
Equator
LA HABANA (HAVANA)
Nassau
Kingston
PORT-AU-PRINCE
SANTO DOMINGO
San Juan
CARACAS
BOGOTÁ
QUITO
GUAYAQUIL
LIMA
BARRANQUILLA
MEDELLÍN
CALI
Panamá
San José
Managua
Tegucigalpa
Georgetown
Paramaribo
Cayenne
MANAUS
BELÉM
FORTALEZA
RECIFE
SALVADOR
BRASÍLIA
Natal
João Pessoa
Maceió
Aracaju
Teresina
São Luís
Macapá
Boa Vista
Porto Velho
Rio Branco
Palmas
Cuiabá
Iquitos
Cusco
Callao
Trujillo
Chimbote
Chiclayo
La Paz
Port of Spain
BARBADOS
ST. VINCENT & THE GRENADINES
TRINIDAD AND TOBAGO
GRENADA
ST. LUCIA
DOMINICA
ANTIGUA AND BARBUDA
ST. KITTS-NEVIS
Islas Galápagos (Galapagos Is.) (Ecuador)

ATLANTIC OCEAN
PACIFIC OCEAN
SCOTIA SEA
Drake Passage
ARGENTINA
CHILE
URUGUAY
PARAGUAY
BUENOS AIRES
SANTIAGO
MONTEVIDEO
Asunción
SÃO PAULO
RIO DE JANEIRO
CURITIBA
PORTO ALEGRE
BELO HORIZONTE
CÓRDOBA
Campo Grande
Ribeirão Prêto
Niterói
Vitória
Santos
Florianópolis
Rio Grande
Lagoa dos Patos
La Plata
Río de la Plata
Embalse del Río Negro
Resistencia
San Miguel de Tucumán
Santa Fé
Rosario
Laguna Mar Chiquita
Paraná
Mendoza
Aconcagua 6960
Valparaíso
Talcahuano
Valdivia
Neuquén
Bahía Blanca
Golfo San Matías
Golfo de San Jorge
Pampas
Patagonia
Isla de Chiloé
Archipiélago de los Chonos
Archipiélago de la Reina Adelaida
Punta Arenas
Estrecho de Magallanes
Bahía Grande
Río Gallegos
Isla Grande de Tierra del Fuego
Isla de los Estados
Cabo de Hornos (Cape Horn)
Falkland Is. (U.K.)
Stanley
East Falkland
West Falkland
Scotia Ridge
Shag Rocks (U.K.)
South Georgia (U.K.)
South Orkney Is. (U.K.)
South Shetland Is. (U.K.)
South Sandwich Is. (U.K.)
Traversay Is.
Candlemas I.
Saunders I.
Montague I.
South Sandwich Trench
Meteor Depth 8325
Ilha da Trindade (Brazil)
Ilhas Martin Vaz (Brazil)
Tropic of Capricorn
Islas de los Desventurados (Chile)
Islas Juan Fernández (Chile)
Chile Trench
Nazca Ridge
Ojos del Salado 6908
Sierra de Calalaste
Tarija
Paraguay
A
B
C
D
E
F
G
H
J
K
5
6
7
8
9
10
20°
30°
40°
50°
60°
70°
80°
90°
100°

Scale 1 : 22 100 000

0 200 400 600 km
0 100 200 300 miles

CARIBBEAN SEA
PACIFIC OCEAN
NICARAGUA
COSTA RICA
PANAMA
COLOMBIA
VENEZUELA
ECUADOR
PERU
BOLIVIA
CHILE
ARGENTINA
AMAZONAS
RONDÔNIA
ACRE
San José
Panamá
BARRANQUILLA
Cartagena
Santa Marta
MARACAIBO
CARACAS
Valencia
Maracay
Barquisimeto
Cúcuta
Bucaramanga
MEDELLÍN
Manizales
Pereira
Ibagué
BOGOTÁ
CALI
Pasto
QUITO
GUAYAQUIL
Cuenca
Iquitos
Piura
Chiclayo
Trujillo
Callao
LIMA
Cusco
Arequipa
La Paz
Cochabamba
Santa Cruz
Sucre
Potosí
Oruro
Arica
Iquique
Ciudad Guayana
Ciudad Bolívar
Porto Velho
Rio Branco
Equator
Islas Galápagos (Galapagos Islands) (Ecuador)
Peru-Chile Trench
Nazca Ridge
Lesser Antilles
Kingstown
St. George's
Salar de Uyuni
Lago Titicaca
Copyright AND Cartographic Publishers Ltd.

South America: North

ATLANTIC OCEAN
Equator
F
G
H
J
K
L
55°
50°
45°
40°
35°
10°
5°
0°
15°
20°
1
2
3
4
5
6
7
8
Georgetown
New Amsterdam
Corriverton
Paramaribo
Nieuw Amsterdam
Nieuw Nickerie
Apoera
Albina
Iracoubo
St. Laurent
Kourou
Brokopondo
Cayenne
SURINAM
FRENCH GUIANA
1230 Juliana Top
Oiapoque
Camopi
Cabo Orange
Calçoene
Amapá
Cabo Norte
AMAPÁ
Pôrto Grande
Mouths of the Amazon
Pôrto Santana
Macapá
Meriruma
Arere
Mazagão
Afuá
Chaves
Baia de Marajó
Ilha de Marajó
Salinópolis
Bragança
Viseu
BELÉM
Vigia
Castanhal
Breves
Portel
Cametá
Acará
Baião
Camiranga
Ilha de São Luís
São Luís
Almeirim
Monte Alegre
Prainha
Obidos
Faro
Santarém
Parintins
Itacoatiara
Altamira
Tucuruí
Represa Tucuruí
Jacunda
Pindaré Mirim
Rosário
Itapicuru Mirim
Bacabal
Codó
Camocim
Sobral
Itapipoca
FORTALEZA
Caucaia
Luzilândia
Piripiri
Canindé
Aracati
Campo Maior
Caxias
Timon
Teresina
Pedreiras
MARANHÃO
CEARÁ
Areia Branca
Macau
Mossoró
Cabo de São Roque
RIO GRANDE DO NORTE
Currais Novos
Natal
Guarabira
João Pessoa
Campina Grande
Jaboatão
Olinda
RECIFE
Caruaru
Garanhuns
Palmares
Maceió
Arapiraca
ALAGOAS
SERGIPE
Aracaju
Estância
PERNAMBUCO
PARAÍBA
Sousa
Juazeiro do Norte
Crato
Ouricuri
Petrolina
Juazeiro
Paulo Afonso
Picos
Floriano
Amarante
Oeiras
PIAUÍ
Uruçuí
Canto do Buriti
São Raimundo Nonato
Marabá
Imperatriz
Araguatins
Grajaú
Barra do Corda
Pastos Bons
Pôrto Franco
Carolina
Balsas
Araguaína
Alto Parnaíba
Pedro Afonso
Gilbués
TOCANTINS
Macaúba
Palmas
Pôrto Nacional
Dianópolis
Peixe
Paranã
Barreiras
Ibotirama
Bom Jesus da Lapa
Barra
Xique Xique
Barragem de Sobradinho
Senhor do Bonfim
Jacobina
Irecê
Mundo Novo
Serrinha
Tucano
Esplanada
Alagoinhas
Camacari
SALVADOR
Baia de Todos os Santos
Feira de Santana
Itaberaba
Santo Antônio de Jesus
1850
Jequié
Gandu
Ubaitaba
Ilhéus
Itabuna
Vitória da Conquista
Brumado
Guanambi
BAHIA
Itapetinga
Itapebi
Belmonte
Pôrto Seguro
Prado
Caravelas
Nanuque
Teófilo Otoni
Itambacuri
Governador Valadares
ESPÍRITO SANTO
Linhares
Cariacica
Vitória
Cachoeiro de Itapemirim
Campos
RIO DE JANEIRO
Niterói
Nova Iguaçu
Volta Redonda
Agulhas Negras 2797
Juiz de Fora
Ubá
Muriaé
Manhuaçu
2890 Pico da Bandeira
Ipatinga
Itabira
BELO HORIZONTE
2033 Pico de Itambé
Diamantina
MINAS GERAIS
Mimas Novas
Bocaiúva
Montes Claros
Salinas
Janaúba
Monte Azul
Januária
Manga
Planalto Central
Paracatu
Patos de Minas
Curvelo
Sete Lagoas
Pará de Minas
Divinópolis
Formiga
Lavras
Passos
Três Corações
São Carlos
Ribeirão Prêto
Franca
Barretos
Uberaba
Araxá
Uberlândia
Araguari
Ituiutaba
Limeira
Piracicaba
Bauru
Lins
Araçatuba
SÃO PAULO
São José do Rio Prêto
Andradina
Marília
Assis
Presidente Prudente
Paranavaí
Fernandópolis
Paranaíba
Ribas do Rio Pardo
Campo Grande
MATO GROSSO DO SUL
Aquidauana
Miranda
Corumbá
Jardim
Pôrto Murtinho
Dourados
Ponta Porã
Pedro Juan Caballero
Rio Verde de Mato Grosso
Rio Verde
Jataí
Itumbiara
Ipameri
Piers do Rio
Catalão
Cristalina
Goiânia
Anápolis
BRASÍLIA
DISTRITO FEDERAL
Formosa
Goiás
Ceres
Uruaçu
Niquelândia
Posse
GOIÁS
Porangatu
Aragarças
Iporá
Barra do Garças
Alto Garças
Rondonópolis
Cuiabá
Cáceres
Barra do Bugres
Rosário Oeste
Diamantino
Juruena
MATO GROSSO
Campo de Diauarum
São Félix
Santa Maria das Barreiras
Conceição do Araguaia
São Félix
Araras
PARÁ
BRAZIL
Manuelzinho
Jacareacanga
Barra do São Manuel
Cachimbo
Itaituba
Canumã
Itaituba
Serra dos Carajás
Serra do Cachimbo
Serra do Roncador
Serra Formosa
Serra Tumucumaque
Serra Acari
Serra da Ibiapaba
Serra dos Dois Irmãos
Chapada Diamantina
Serra Geral de Goiás
Planalto do Mato Grosso
Pantanal
Tapajós
Xingu
Tocantins
Araguaia
Amazonas (Amazon)
Parnaíba
São Francisco
Paranaíba
Paraná
I. Fernando de Noronha
Atol das Rocas

Scale 1 : 22 100 000

0 200 400 600 km
0 100 200 300 miles

PACIFIC OCEAN
PERU
BOLIVIA
CHILE
ARGENTINA
PAR
Nazca Ridge
Peru-Chile Trench
Tropic of Capricorn
Islas de los Desventurados (Chile)
San Félix
San Ambrosio
Islas Juan Fernández (Chile)
Isla Robinson Crusoe
Isla Alejandro Selkirk
Cordillera Occidental
Cordillera Oriental
Nazca
Nudo Coropuna 6425
Lomas
Atico
Arequipa
Camana
Mollendo
Ilo
Puno
Juli
Lago Titicaca
La Paz
Guaqui
Nevado Sajama 6542
Tacna
Arica
Corocoro
Oruro
Poopó
Challapata
Cochabamba
Totora
Samaipata
Santa Cruz
Sucre
Potosí
Cabezas
Camiri
Cuya
Iquique
Río Mulatos
Salar de Uyuni
Uyuni
Tupiza
Tarija
Villa Montes
Boyuibe
Lagunillas
Volcán San Pedro 6159
Calama
Tocopilla
María Elena
Punta Angamos
Baquedano
Antofagasta
La Quiaca
Orán
Tartagal
Embarcación
Los Blancos
San Salvador de Jujuy
San Pedro
San Antonio de los Cobres
Salta
Volcán Llullaillaco 6723
Nevados de Cachi 6720
Los Vientos
Santa Catalina
Taltal
Punta Ballena
Volcán Antofalla 6440
Chañaral
Caldera
Copiapó
Ojos del Salado 6908
Paso de San Francisco 4722
6872
Cerro Bonete
Andalgalá
Tinogasta
Catamarca
Tafí Viejo
San Miguel de Tucumán
La Banda
Santiago del Estero
Metán
Monte Quemado
Campo Gallo
Huasco
Cabo Bascuñán
La Serena
Coquimbo
Punta Lengua de Vaca
Ovalle
Combarbalá
Rivadavia
Cerro Las Tórtolas 6332
Majicana 6250
La Rioja
Recreo
Chepes
San José de Jáchal
Cruz del Eje
San Francisco
CÓRDOBA
Cerro Champaqui 2880
Río Cuarto
San Juan
Cerro Mercedario 6770
Paso de la Cumbre 3832
Cerro Aconcagua 6960
Mendoza
San Luis
Mercedes
Cerro Tupungato 6800
Viña del Mar
Valparaíso
SANTIAGO
San Antonio
San Bernardo
Rancagua
San Fernando
Pichilemu
San Rafael
General Alvear
Curicó
Talca
Linares
Cauquenes
San Carlos
Tomé
Talcahuano
Concepción
Punta Lavapié
Lebu
Chillán
Volcán Domuyo 4709
Cerro Nevado 3810
2500
Los Ángeles
Angol
Victoria
Temuco
1884
Paso de Hachado
Neuquén
Gen. Roca
Volcán Lanín 3740
Valdivia
Punta Galera
Osorno
Puerto Montt
Maullín
Ancud
Isla de Chiloé
Minchinmávida 2470
Volcán Corcovado 2300
Golfo de Corcovado
Isla Guafo
Archipiélago de los Chonos
Puerto Aisen
Coihaique
Chile Chico
Cerro San Valentín 4058
Cerro San Lorenzo 3700
Golfo de Penas
Isla Campana
Isla Wellington
Cerro Murallón 3600
Isla Madre de Dios
Isla Contreras
Archipiélago de la Reina Adelaida
Isla Desolación
Isla Santa Inés
Isla Clarence
Isla Londonderry
Isla Hoste
Punta Arenas
Estrecho de Magallanes
Isla Riesco
Isla Grande de Tierra del Fuego
Río Grande
Cerro Yogan 2469
Navarino
Isla Wollaston
Cabo de Hornos (Cape Horn)
Drake Passage
El Turbio
Río Gallegos
Punta Dungeness
Lago Argentino
Bahía Grande
Puerto Santa Cruz
Tres Lagos
Gobernador Gregores
San Julián
Puerto Deseado
Punta Medanosa
Jaramillo
Perito Moreno
Las Heras
Colonia
Golfo de San Jorge
Cabo Tres Puntas
Camarones
Cabo dos Bahías
José de San Martín
Paso de Indios
Las Plumas
Trelew
Rawson
Gastre
Telsen
Ingeniero Jacobacci
Maquinchao
Sierra Colorada
Sierra Grande
Golfo San Matías
Península Valdés
Valcheta
San Antonio Oeste
Río Colorado
Bahía Blanca
Puelches
Puelén
Santa Rosa
General Acha
Realicó
General Pico
Villa Huidobro
Laboulaye
Pergamino
Rosario
Las Varillas
Rafaela
Ceres
Añatuya
Quimilí
Presidencia Roque
Castelli
Sáenz Peña
Resistencia
Villa Montes
Fortín Coronel Eugenio Garay
Mariscal Estigarribia
Filadelfia
Esteros
Las Lomitas
Roboré
Bañados del Izozog
San José de Chiquitos
El Cerro
Montero
Bahía

BRAZIL
GOIÁS
MATO GROSSO DO SUL
MINAS GERAIS
ESPÍRITO SANTO
RIO DE JANEIRO
SÃO PAULO
PARANÁ
SANTA CATARINA
RIO GRANDE DO SUL
URUGUAY
Itumbiara
Ipameri
Patos de Minas
Araguari
Uberlândia
Ituiutaba
Uberaba
Araxá
Paranaíba
Fernandópolis
Rio Verde de Mato Grosso
Pantanal
Taquari
Puerto Suárez
Campo Grande
Ribas do Rio Pardo
Aquidauana
Jardim
Ponta Porã
Dourados
Presidente Prudente
Andradina
Araçatuba
São José do Rio Prêto
Franca
Ribeirão Prêto
Passos
Lins
Marília
Bauru
Assis
Piracicaba
Campinas
Limeira
Sorocaba
SÃO PAULO
Santo André
Santos
São Vicente
Jacupiranga
Londrina
Maringá
Paranavaí
Umuarama
Guaíra
Toledo
Cascavel
Campo Mourão
Castro
Ponta Grossa
CURITIBA
Lapa
Paranaguá
Isla de São Francisco
Joinville
Mafra
Itajaí
Blumenau
Florianópolis
Lajes
Laguna
Tubarão
Criciúma
Caxias do Sul
Novo Hamburgo
Vacaria
Passo Fundo
Erechim
Chapecó
Palmas
União da Vitória
Foz do Iguaçu
Ciudad del Este
Coronel Oviedo
Caaguazú
Asunción
Rosario
Formosa
Encarnación
Posadas
Corrientes
Santa Rosa
Carazinho
Cruz Alta
São Borja
Santiago
Santa Maria
Uruguaiana
Mercedes
Cachoeira do Sul
PORTO ALEGRE
Lagoa dos Patos
Santana do Livramento
Artigas
Rivera
Salto
Tacuarembó
Bagé
Pelotas
Rio Grande
Melo
Paysandú
Lagoa Mirim
Albardão do João Maria
Santa Vitória do Palmar
Durazno
Mercedes
Florida
Minas
Maldonado
MONTEVIDEO
Quilmes
La Plata
Río de la Plata
Bahía Samborombón
Punta Norte
Dolores
Pinamar
Mar del Plata
Necochea
Divinópolis
Formiga
Lavras
Varginha
Serra da Mantiqueira
Juiz de Fora
Pico da Bandeira 2890
Agulhas Negras 2797
Petrópolis
Nova Iguaçu
Duque de Caxias
Niterói
RIO DE JANEIRO
Isla Grande
Isla de São Sebastião
Cabo Frio
Campos
Cabo de São Tomé
Vitória
Cariacica
BELO HORIZONTE
Sete Lagoas
Curvelo
Corinto
Diamantina
Pico de Itambé 2033
Teófilo Otoni
Nanuque
Prado
Caravelas
Itambacuri
Governador Valadares
Ipatinga
Linhares
Serra do Espinhaço
Ilha da Trindade (Brazil)
Ilhas Martin Vaz (Brazil)
Tropic of Capricorn
ATLANTIC OCEAN
Falkland Islands (U.K.)
Stanley
East Falkland
Mt. Adam 700
Mt. Usborne 705
Falkland Sound
Scotia Ridge
Shag Rocks (U.K.)
Cape Alexandra
Grytviken
2934 Mt. Paget
South Georgia (U.K.)
Cape Disappointment
SCOTIA SEA

Scale 1 : 27 700 000

0 250 500 750 1000 km

0 100 200 300 400 500 miles

ICELAND
Reykjavik
Arctic Circle
Norwegian Sea
Faeroes (Denmark)
Rockall
Shetland Is. (U.K.)
Outer Hebrides
Orkney Is.
NORWAY
SWEDEN
Tromsø
Trondheim
Sundsvall
Bergen
Stavanger
Oslo
Stockholm
Vänern
Göteborg
Gotland
Gulf of Bothnia
SCOTLAND
Glasgow
Edinburgh
NORTHERN IRELAND
Belfast
REP. OF IRELAND
Dublin (Baile Átha Cliath)
UNITED KINGDOM
WALES
ENGLAND
Cardiff
BIRMINGHAM
Plymouth
LONDON
North Sea
DENMARK
Århus
København (Copenhagen)
Bornholm
Baltic Sea
ATLANTIC OCEAN
English Channel
Channel Islands
Amsterdam
NETHERLANDS
Bruxelles (Brussels)
BELGIUM
Luxembourg
LUXEMBOURG
HAMBURG
Hannover
BERLIN
GERMANY
Frankfurt
Elbe
Ems
Rhine
Gdańsk
RUSSIA
Kalinin
WARSZAWA (WARSAW)
POLAND
Wisła
Odra (Oder)
(Vistula)
PRAHA (PRAGUE)
CZECH REP.
MÜNCHEN (MUNICH)
Danube
WIEN (VIENNA)
SLOVAKIA
Bratislava
AUSTRIA
HUNGARY
BUDAPEST
LIECHTENSTEIN
Vaduz
Bern
SWITZERLAND
Seine
PARIS
Loire
FRANCE
Strasbourg
Bay of Biscay
Cabo Fisterra
Bordeaux
Lyon
Massif Central
Rhône
4808 Mt. Blanc
Alps
Genova (Genoa)
MILANO (MILAN)
Ljubljana
SLOVENIA
Zagreb
CROATIA
BOSNIA-HERZEGOVINA
Sarajevo
BEOGRAD (BELGRADE)
YUGOSLAVIA
Skopje
MACEDONIA
Tiranë (Tirana)
ALBANIA
GREECE
SAN MARINO
MONACO
Andorra la Vella
ANDORRA
Marseille
Pyrenees
Ebro
PORTUGAL
LISBOA (LISBON)
Tajo
MADRID
SPAIN
Cabo de São Vicente
BARCELONA
Valencia
Islas Baleares (Balearic Islands)
Menorca
Mallorca
Eivissa
Corse (Corsica) (France)
Ajaccio
Sardegna (Sardinia) (Italy)
Cagliari
VATICAN CITY
ROMA (ROME)
ITALY
Appennino
Adriatic Sea
NAPOLI (NAPLES)
Taranto
Tyrrhenian Sea
Kerkyra (Corfu)
Ionian Sea
Palermo
Mte. Etna 3340
Sicilia (Sicily)
Valletta
MALTA
Tunis
Strait of Gibraltar
Gibraltar (U.K.)
Ceuta (Spain)
Melilla (Spain)
RABAT
ALGER (ALGIERS)
Mediterranean Sea
AFRICA
Tarābulus (Tripoli)
Banghāzī

Barents Sea
O. Kolguyev
Vorkuta
Vadsø
Murmansk
Pechora
Ural'skiy Khrebet (Ural Mountains)
Surgut
NOVOSIBIRSK
Ob'
White Sea
Arkhangel'sk
Severnaya Dvina
Irtysh
OMSK
Kama
Onezhskoye Ozero (Lake Onega)
Ladozhskoye Ozero (Lake Ladoga)
PERM'
Kirov
YEKATERINBURG
CHELYABINSK
Astana
Vologda
SANKT-PETERBURG (ST. PETERSBURG)
RUSSIA
Rybinskoye Vdkhr.
KAZAN'
UFA
NIZHNIY NOVGOROD
Volga
Dvina
MOSKVA (MOSCOW)
SAMARA
MINSK
BELARUS
Prypyats'
Don
Khoper
Ural
Aral Sea
KYYIV (KIEV)
KHARKIV
VOLGOGRAD
Donets
UKRAINE
DONETS'K
DNIPROPETROVS'K
Astrakhan'
ROSTOV-NA-DONU
MOLDOVA
Chişinău
Dnipro
Sea of Azov
Aktau
ODESA (ODESSA)
Krym'
Stavropol'
Groznyy
Elbrus 5642
BUCUREŞTI (BUCHAREST)
Sevastopol'
Caucasus
Caspian Sea
Ashgabat (Ashkhabad)
Black Sea
T'BILISI
BAKI (BAKU)
MASHHAD
Burgas
Samsun
YEREVAN
İSTANBUL
Bursa
ANKARA
TEHRĀN (TEHERAN)
İZMIR
Gaziantep
ASIA
Antalya
Rodos (Rhodes) (Greece)
Lefkoşa (Nicosia)
BAGHDĀD
BEYROUTH (BEIRUT)
DIMASHQ (DAMASCUS)
AMMĀN
Al Kuwayt (Kuwait)
Persian Gulf
Yerushalayim (Jerusalem)
EL QÂHIRA (CAIRO)
Nile

Scale 1 : 7 900 000

0 100 200 300 km

0 50 100 150 miles

Barents Sea
NORWEGIAN SEA
Greenland Sea
RUSSIA
KARELIYA
FINLAND
SWEDEN
NORWAY
ICELAND
Lappland
Vatnajökull
Murmansk
Reykjavík
Oulu
Vaasa
Umeå
Luleå
Trondheim
Tromsø
Hammerfest
Akureyri
Arctic Circle
Vesterålen
Lofoten
Hvannadalshnúkur 2119
Kebnekaise 2123
Hekla 1991
Snæfell 1833
Grímsvötn 1719

Scandinavia

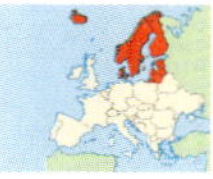

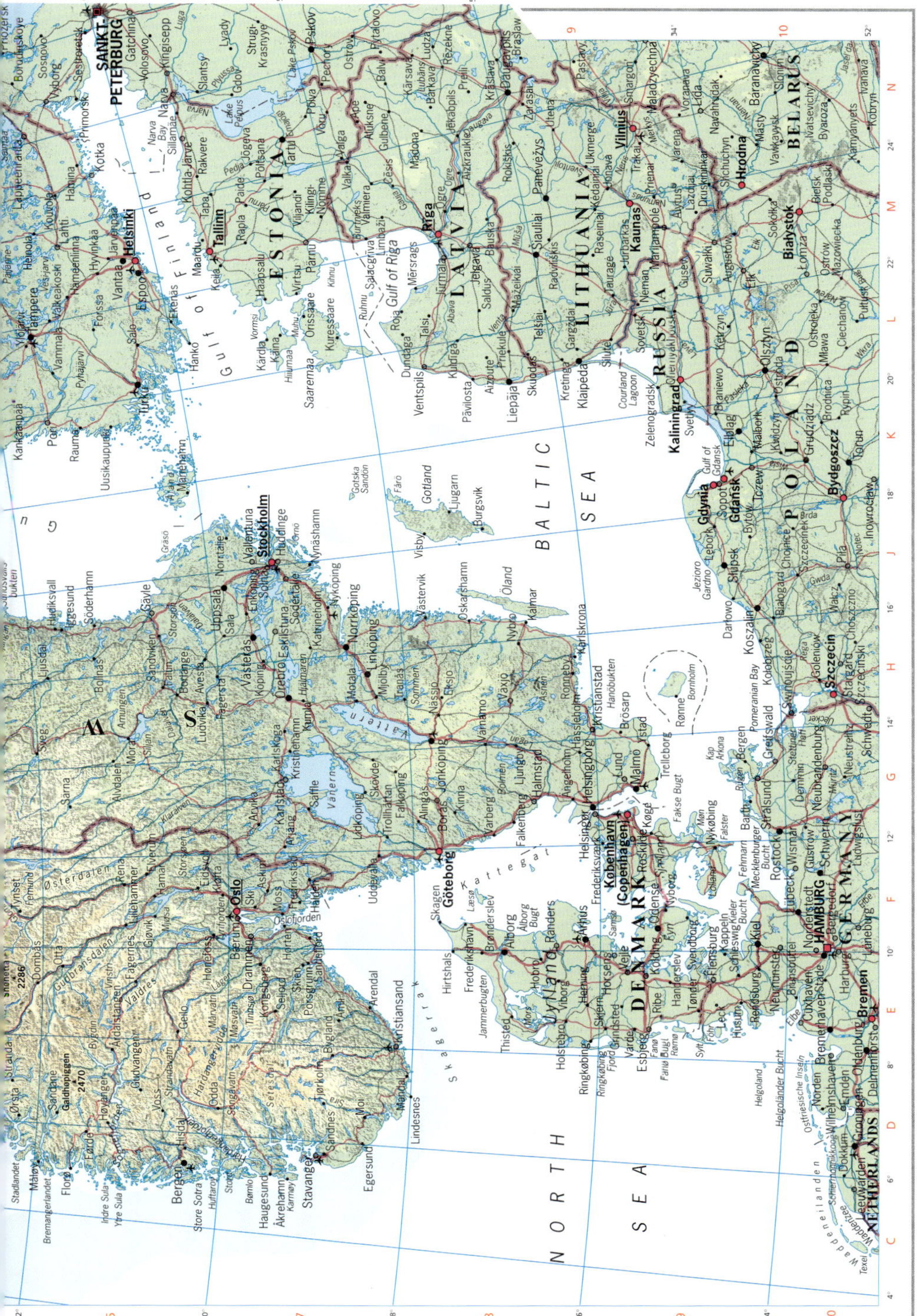
NORTH SEA
BALTIC SEA
Gulf of Finland
Gulf of Riga
Skagerrak
Kattegat
ESTONIA
LATVIA
LITHUANIA
BELARUS
RUSSIA
POLAND
GERMANY
DENMARK
NETHERLANDS
SANKT-PETERBURG
Helsinki
Tallinn
Riga
Vilnius
Kaunas
Kaliningrad
Gdańsk
Gdynia
Stockholm
Göteborg
Oslo
København (Copenhagen)
HAMBURG
Bremen
Bergen
Stavanger
Kristiansand
Malmö
Århus
Uppsala
Norrköping
Linköping
Gotland
Öland
Bornholm
Vänern
Vättern
Bydgoszcz
Szczecin
Białystok
Hrodna
Klaipėda
Liepāja
Ventspils
Daugavpils
Tartu
Pärnu
Turku
Tampere
Pskov
Saaremaa
Hiiumaa
Jylland
Galdhøpiggen 2470

Scale 1 : 4 750 000

0 50 100 150 km

0 25 50 75 miles

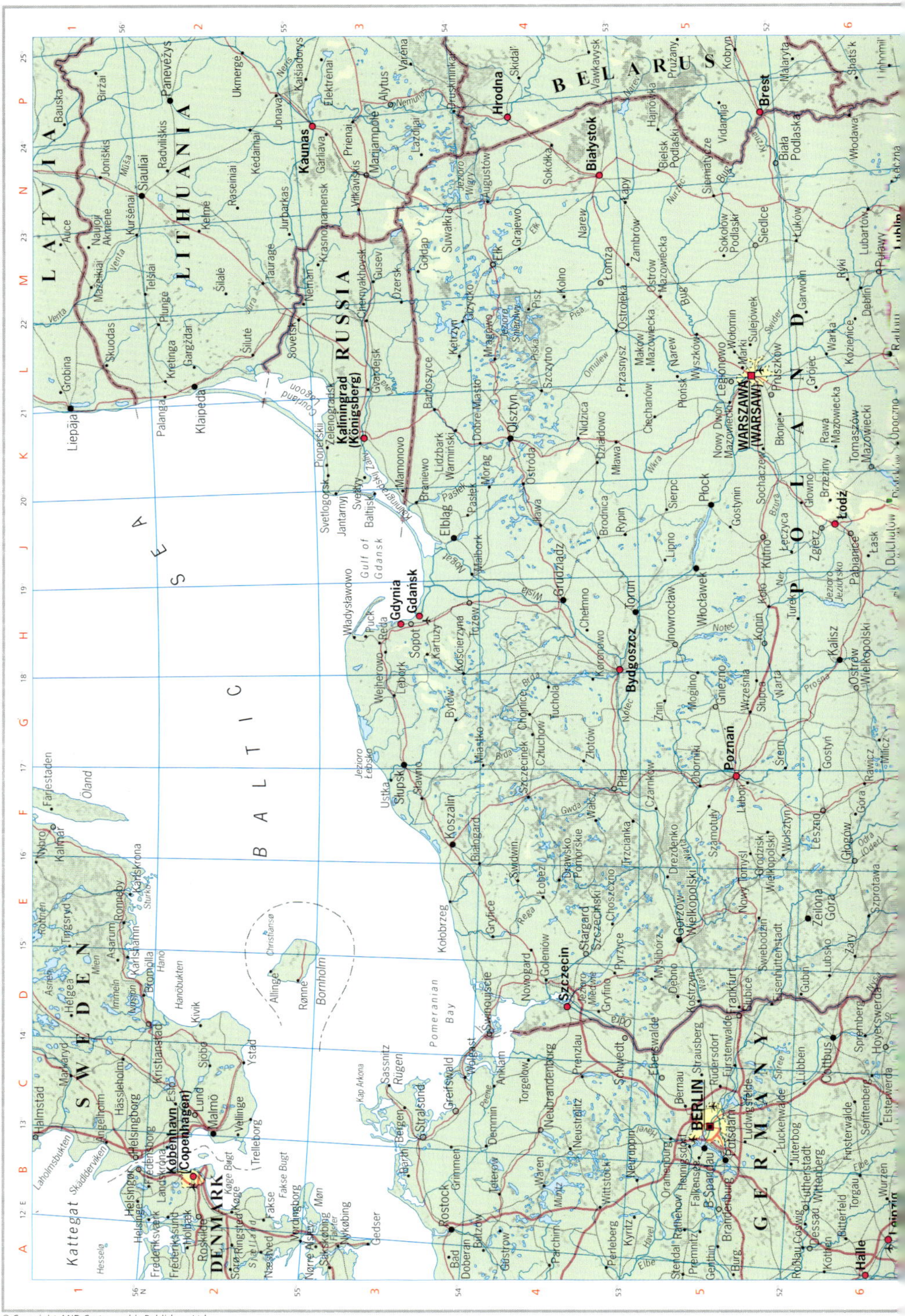
LATVIA
LITHUANIA
BELARUS
RUSSIA
POLAND
GERMANY
SWEDEN
DENMARK
BALTIC SEA
Gulf of Gdansk
Pomeranian Bay
Kattegat
Öland
Bornholm
Rügen
Courland Lagoon
Liepāja
Klaipėda
Šiauliai
Panevėžys
Kaunas
Hrodna
Brest
Białystok
Kaliningrad (Königsberg)
Olsztyn
Gdynia
Gdańsk
Bydgoszcz
Toruń
Poznań
Łódź
WARSZAWA (WARSAW)
Szczecin
BERLIN
Potsdam
Rostock
Halle
København (Copenhagen)
Malmö
Lund
Helsingborg
Karlskrona
Kalmar
Koszalin
Słupsk
Elbląg
Grudziądz
Włocławek
Płock
Kalisz
Frankfurt
Cottbus

Central Europe

CZECH REPUBLIC
SLOVAKIA
HUNGARY
AUSTRIA
UKRAINE
ROMANIA
CROATIA
SLOVENIA
YUGOSLAVIA
ITALY
Carpathian Mountains
PRAHA (PRAGUE)
WIEN (VIENNA)
BUDAPEST
Bratislava
Ljubljana
Zagreb
Kraków
Wrocław (Breslau)
Dresden
Chemnitz
Brno
Ostrava
Katowice
Częstochowa
Sosnowiec
Cluj-Napoca
Timişoara
Debrecen
Miskolc
Košice
Szeged
Pécs
Győr
Graz
Salzburg
Linz
Lviv
Oradea
Kecskemét
Uzhhorod
Plzeň
České Budějovice
Olomouc
Nitra
Žilina
Banská Bystrica
Prešov
Rzeszów
Tarnów
Kielce
Opole
Gliwice
Zabrze
Bielsko-Biała
Szombathely
Székesfehérvár
Veszprém
Nyíregyháza
Subotica
Maribor
Klagenfurt
Villach
Innsbruck
Passau
Udine
Sankt Pölten
Böhmerwald
Danube
2043 Dumbier
2995 Hohe Dachstein
2864 Triglav
1456 Großer Arber
1014 Kékes
Balaton

Scale 1 : 3 550 000

0 50 100 150 km

0 25 50 75 miles

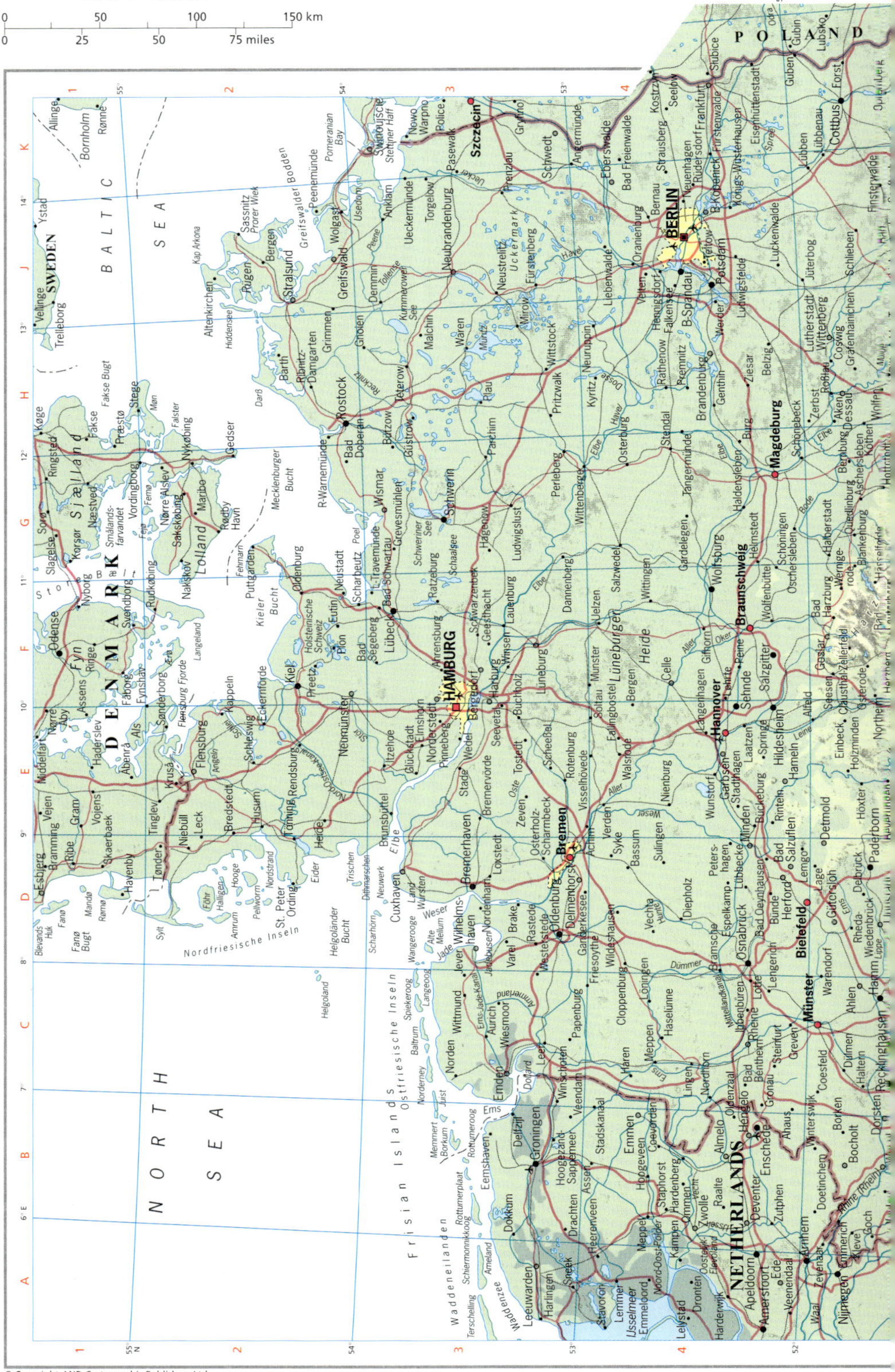
POLAND
DENMARK
SWEDEN
NETHERLANDS
BALTIC SEA
NORTH SEA
Frisian Islands
Nordfriesische Inseln
Ostfriesische Inseln
Waddeneilanden
Waddenzee
Pomeranian Bay
Mecklenburger Bucht
Kieler Bucht
Helgoländer Bucht
Bornholm
Sjælland
Fyn
Lolland
Falster
Møn
Rügen
Usedom
Fehmarn
Lüneburger Heide
BERLIN
HAMBURG
Bremen
Hannover
Braunschweig
Magdeburg
Schwerin
Rostock
Kiel
Lübeck
Szczecin
Potsdam
Münster
Bielefeld
Osnabrück
Oldenburg
Bremerhaven
Cuxhaven
Flensburg
Stralsund
Greifswald
Neubrandenburg
Wolfsburg
Hildesheim
Lüneburg
Celle
Frankfurt
Cottbus
Groningen
Leeuwarden
Enschede
Apeldoorn
Odense
Esbjerg
Elbe
Weser
Ems
Oder
Havel
Spree
Aller
Harz

Germany

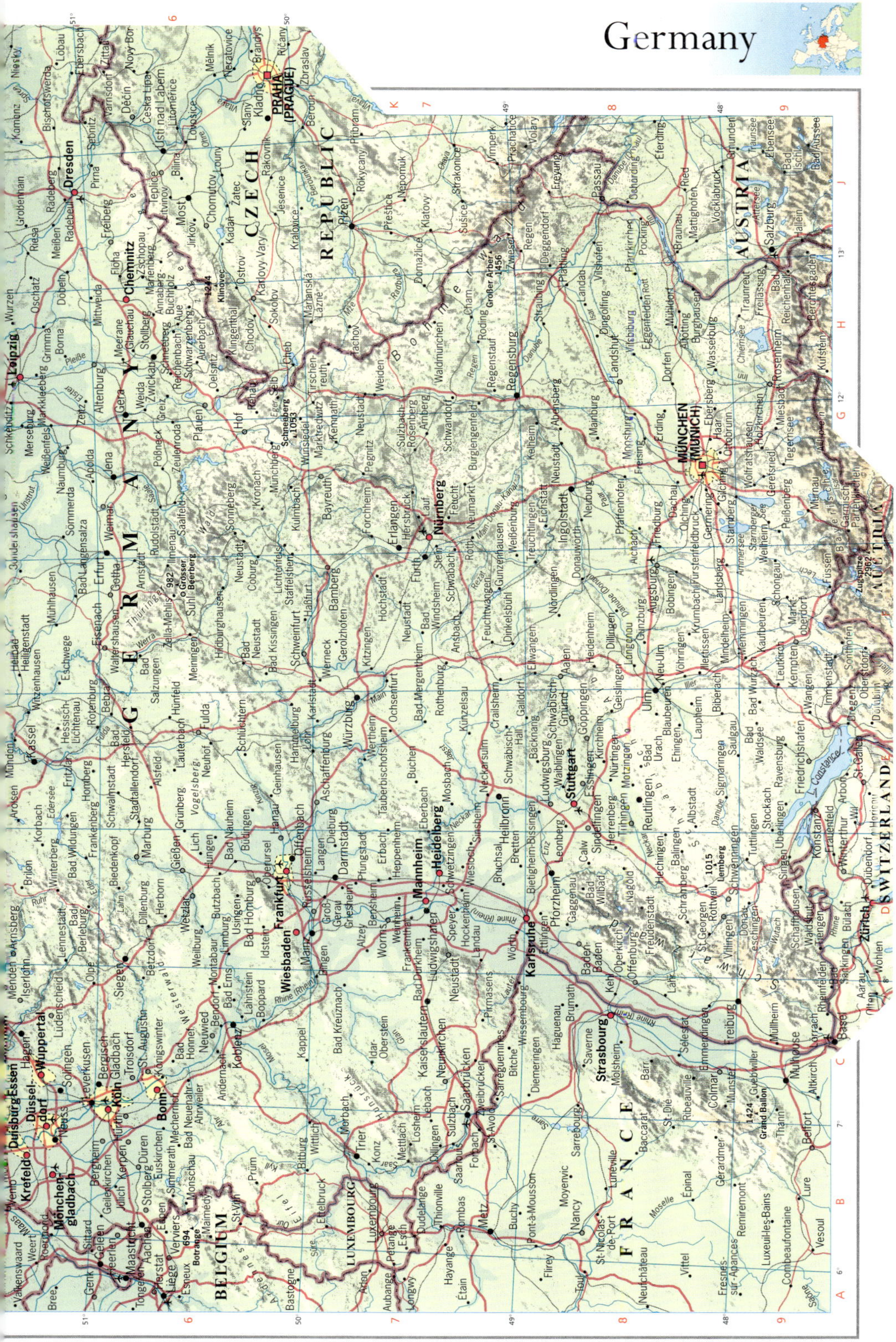
GERMANY
CZECH REPUBLIC
AUSTRIA
SWITZERLAND
FRANCE
BELGIUM
LUXEMBOURG
Berlin
PRAHA (PRAGUE)
Dresden
Leipzig
Chemnitz
MÜNCHEN (MUNICH)
Nürnberg
Regensburg
Stuttgart
Karlsruhe
Mannheim
Heidelberg
Frankfurt
Wiesbaden
Mainz
Offenbach
Darmstadt
Würzburg
Kassel
Köln
Bonn
Düsseldorf
Essen
Duisburg
Wuppertal
Krefeld
Mönchengladbach
Aachen
Koblenz
Trier
Saarbrücken
Strasbourg
Zürich
Basel
Augsburg
Ulm
Ingolstadt
Erfurt
Jena
Gera
Zwickau
Plzeň
Salzburg
Luxembourg
Metz
Nancy
Freiburg
Lake Constance
Rhine (Rhein)
Danube (Donau)
Main
Mosel
Zugspitze 2962

Scale 1 : 3 150 000

0 50 100 150 km

0 25 50 75 miles

UNITED KINGDOM
ENGLAND
NORTH SEA
English Channel
Strait of Dover
South Downs
The Weald
The Wash
The Broads
The Fens
Baie de la Seine
Baie de la Somme
LONDON
BIRMINGHAM
PARIS
Nottingham
Leicester
Coventry
Buxton
Leek
Matlock
Chesterfield
Worksop
Bolsover
Mansfield
Alfreton
East Retford
Newark-on-Trent
Lincoln
Louth
Mablethorpe
Horncastle
Skegness
Sleaford
Derby
Long Eaton
Burton-upon-Trent
Grantham
Boston
Hunstanton
Cromer
Cannock
Loughborough
Melton Mowbray
Oakham
Spalding
King's Lynn
East Dereham
Norwich
Great Yarmouth
Lowestoft
Tamworth
Walsall
Nuneaton
Stamford
Peterborough
Wisbech
March
Bedworth
Market Harborough
Corby
Rugby
Kettering
Huntingdon
Thetford
Diss
Southwold
Redditch
Warwick
Royal Leamington Spa
Wellingborough
Northampton
Newmarket
Bury St. Edmunds
Stowmarket
Aldeburgh
Orford Ness
Stratford
Evesham upon-Avon
Daventry
Towcester
Cambridge
Woodbridge
Ipswich
Banbury
Bedford
Milton Keynes
Letchworth
Royston
Sudbury
Felixstowe
Harwich
Chipping Norton
Leighton Buzzard
Stevenage
Bishop's Stortford
Braintree
Colchester
The Naze
Woodstock
Aylesbury
Luton
Welwyn Garden City
Clacton-on-Sea
Witney
Oxford
Hemel Hempstead
St. Albans
Harlow
Abingdon
High Wycombe
Cheshunt
Chelmsford
Watford
Swindon
Maidenhead
Slough
Brentwood
Foulness
Reading
Basildon
Southend-on-Sea
Newbury
Windsor
Staines
Grays
Thames
Kingston upon Thames
Camberley
Rochester
Herne Bay
Margate
North Foreland
Ramsgate
Basingstoke
Farnborough
Woking
Epsom
Gravesend
Gillingham
Faversham
Canterbury
Andover
Aldershot
Guildford
Sevenoaks
Maidstone
Deal
Salisbury
Reigate
Winchester
Alton
Haslemere
Crawley
Ashford
Dover
Petersfield
Horsham
East Grinstead
Royal Tunbridge Wells
Folkestone
Southampton
Eastleigh
Fareham
Havant
Portsmouth
Chichester
Worthing
Brighton
Lewes
Dungeness
Gosport
Lymington
Cowes
Newport
Ryde
The Solent
Isle of Wight
Bognor Regis
Shoreham
Newhaven
Bexhill
Hastings
Eastbourne
Beachy Head
Zeebrugge
Blankenberge
Oostende
Middelkerke
Nieuwpoort
De Panne
Veurne
Dunkerque
Gravelines
Calais
Diksmuide
Torhout
Tielt
Roeselare
Izegem
Poperinge
Ieper
Kortrijk
Menen
Cap Gris-Nez
Boulogne-sur-Mer
Desvres
St-Omer
Hazebrouck
Bailleul
Tourcoing
Roubaix
Armentières
Lille
Lys
Étaples
Fruges
Béthune
Montreuil
Lens
Berck
Hesdin
Hénin-Beaumont
Avion
St-Pol-sur-Ternoise
Douai
Rue
Arras
St-Valéry-sur-Somme
Doullens
Abbeville
Bapaume
Le Tréport
Somme
Albert
Fauville-en-Caux
Dieppe
Blangy-sur-Bresle
Amiens
Péronne
St-Quentin
Fécamp
Cap d'Antifer
Étretat
Neufchâtel-en-Bray
Tôtes
Roye
Tergnier
Cherbourg
Valognes
Bolbec
Yvetot
Forges-les-Eaux
Marseille-en-Beauvaisis
Breteuil
Montdidier
Noyon
Le Havre
Lillebonne
Seine
Gournay-en-Bray
Beauvais
Rouen
Honfleur
Carentan
St-Étienne-du-Rouvray
Clermont
Compiègne
Aisne
Oise
La Haye-du-Puits
Bayeux
Ouistreham
Caen
Elbeuf
Louviers
Les Andelys
Creil
Senlis
Villers-Cotterêts
Crépy-en-Valois
St-Lô
Lisieux
Méru
Chantilly
Coutances
Villers-Bocage
Bernay
Vernon
Chambly
Pontoise
Château-Thierry
Granville
Falaise
Vimoutiers
Évreux
Conches-en-Ouche
Mantes-la-Jolie
Herblay
St-Denis
Bobigny
Meaux
Villedieu-les-Poêles
Vire
Condé-sur-Noireau
St-Germain-en-Laye
Gacé
Eure
Versailles
Créteil
Coulommiers
Flers
Avranches
Argentan
L'Aigle
Verneuil
Houdan
Trappes
Orsay
Orly
Pontorson
Mortain
Rânes
Dreux
Coulommiers
Courtacon

Benelux

Frisian Islands
Waddeneilanden
Waddenzee
Terschelling
Ameland
Vlieland
Texel
Schiermonnikkoog
Rottumerplaat
Rottumeroog
Memmert
Juist
Borkum
Norden
Aurich
Emden
Eemshaven
Dokkum
Delfzijl
Dollard
Leeuwarden
Harlingen
Groningen
Hoogezand-Sappemeer
Winschoten
Leer
Papenburg
Westerstede
Oldenburg
Delmenhorst
Bremen
Brake
Rastede
Osterholz-Scharmbeck
Achim
Ganderkesee
Syke
Wildeshausen
Bassum
Den Burg
Den Helder
Sneek
Drachten
Assen
Veendam
Stadskanaal
Friesoythe
Cloppenburg
Heerenveen
IJsselmeer
Stavoren
Lemmer
Wieringermeer Polder
Schagen
Bergen
Alkmaar
Enkhuizen
Emmeloord
Noord Oost-Polder
Hoorn
Markermeer
Lelystad
Edam
Marken
Purmerend
Castricum
IJmuiden
Zaanstad
Haarlem
Zandvoort
Amsterdam
Oostelijk-Flevoland
Dronten
Kampen
Zwolle
Meppel
Hoogeveen
Coevorden
Emmen
Haren
Meppen
Löningen
Haselünne
Vechta
Sulingen
Diepholz
Staphorst
Hardenberg
Ommen
Vecht
Lingen
Nordhorn
Dümmer
Bramsche
Espelkamp
Petershagen
Almelo
Oldenzaal
Raalte
Rheine
Ibbenbüren
Osnabrück
Lübbecke
Minden
Bad Oeynhausen
Harderwijk
Bussum
Lisse
Katwijk aan Zee
Noordwijk aan Zee
Hilversum
NETHERLANDS
Apeldoorn
Deventer
Hengelo
Enschede
Bad Bentheim
Gronau
Steinfurt
Lotte
Lengerich
Bünde
Herford
Bad Salzuflen
Lemgo
Leiden
Alphen
Amersfoort
Scheveningen
's-Gravenhage
Wassenaar
Zeist
Ede
Zutphen
Ahaus
Greven
Bielefeld
Lage
Hoek van Holland
Europoort
Delft
Utrecht
Veenendaal
Gouda
Lek
Arnhem
Doetinchem
Winterswijk
Münster
Warendorf
Gütersloh
Detmold
Rotterdam
Schiedam
Voorne
Goeree
Putten
Dordrecht
Overflakkee
Waal
Zevenaar
Nijmegen
Emmerich
Borken
Bocholt
Coesfeld
Dülmen
Ahlen
Rheda-Wiedenbrück
Delbrück
Beckum
Lippe
Paderborn
Lippstadt
Gorinchem
Maas
Oss
's-Hertogenbosch
Kleve
Goch
Xanten
Rhine (Rhein)
Wesel
Haltern
Dorsten
Selm
Lünen
Hamm
Recklinghausen
Unna
Werl
Soest
Büren
Marsberg
Oosterhout
Waalwijk
Tilburg
Oudenbosch
Breda
Roosendaal
Bergen op Zoom
Tholen
Oosterschelde
Goes
Essen
Venray
Helmond
Geldern
Oberhausen
Gelsenkirchen
Bottrop
Herne
Dortmund
Bochum
Witten
Essen
Menden
Arnsberg
Warstein
Brilon
Eindhoven
Deurne
Venlo
Moers
Duisburg
Mülheim
Hagen
Iserlohn
Meschede
Korbach
Turnhout
Valkenswaard
Krefeld
Düsseldorf
Wuppertal
Winterberg
Terneuzen
Hulst
Antwerpen (Antwerp)
Herentals
Lommel
Mol
Weert
Mönchengladbach
Roermond
Neuss
Lüdenscheid
Remscheid
Lennestadt
Bad Berleburg
Frankenberg
St. Niklaas
Lokeren
Gent
Lier
Geel
Bree
Albert Kanaal
Beringen
Grevenbroich
Dormagen
Solingen
Leverkusen
Gummersbach
Olpe
Mechelen
Aalst
Vilvoorde
Aarschot
Diest
Genk
Sittard
Geleen
Heerlen
Bergheim
Geilenkirchen
Jülich
Köln
Bergisch Gladbach
Siegen
Biedenkopf
Marburg
Asse
Leuven
Hasselt
St. Truiden
Tienen
Maastricht
Kerkrade
Eschweiler
Kerpen
Hürth
Troisdorf
Siegburg
GERMANY
Betzdorf
Dillenburg
Herborn
Oudenaarde
Bruxelles (Brussels)
Halle
Enghien
Tongeren
Herstal
Aachen
Stolberg
Düren
Euskirchen
Brühl
Bonn
St. Augustin
Königswinter
Westerwald
Gießen
Wetzlar
Ath
Tubize
Wavre
Waremme
Liège
Eupen
Simmerath
Monschau
Mechernich
Rheinbach
Bad Honnef
Remagen
Weilburg
Soignies
BELGIUM
Nivelles
Gembloux
Seraing
Amay
Verviers
Esneux
Schleiden
Bad Neuenahr-Ahrweiler
Neuwied
Montabaur
Butzbach
Bad Nauheim
Mons
Andenne
Huy
Spa
694
Botrange
Malmedy
Blankenheim
Andernach
Bendorf
Bad Ems
Limburg
Usingen
Binche
La Louvière
Namur
Charleroi
Ourthe
Koblenz
Lahnstein
Boppard
Taunus
Bad Homburg
Oberursel
Idstein
Taunusstein
Frankfurt
Valenciennes
Maubeuge
Jeumont
Thuin
Mettet
Ciney
Dinant
St-Vith
Prüm
Daun
Mosel
Florennes
Marche
Philippeville
Rochefort
Eifel
Wiesbaden
Mainz
Rüsselsheim
Langen
Groß-Gerau
Avesnes-sur-Helpe
Sambre
Givet
ARDENNES
Kyll
Kappel
Fourmies
Couvin
St-Hubert
Bastogne
Bitburg
Wittlich
Bingen
Ingelheim
Darmstadt
Griesheim
Pfungstadt
Hirson
Oise
Revin
Our
Vianden
Sûre
Bad Kreuznach
Bad Sobernheim
Alzey
Bensheim
Heppenheim
Rumigny
Charleville-Mézières
Neufchâteau
Ettelbruck
Schweich
Morbach
Kirchheimbolanden
Marle
LUXEMBOURG
Trier
Konz
Saarburg
Birkenfeld
Idar-Oberstein
Worms
Weinheim
Sedan
Florenville
Semois
Arlon
Glan
Frankenthal
Luxembourg
Aubange
Pétange
Virton
Esch
Montmédy
Mannheim
Bad Dürkheim
Ludwigshafen
Rethel
Tanney
Stenay
Longwy
Dudelange
Mettlach
Losheim
Merzig
Lebach
Landstuhl
Kaiserslautern
Schwetzingen
Speyer
Mazagran
Villerupt
Thionville
Dillingen
Saarlouis
Neunkirchen
Sulzbach
Neustadt
Hockenheim
Germersheim
Fismes
Hayange
Völklingen
Saarbrücken
Forbach
Zweibrücken
Pirmasens
Landau
Dahn
Reims
Verdun
Étain
Rombas
Bruchsal
FRANCE
Suippes
Ste-Menehould
Metz
St-Avold
Sarreguemines
Eitche
Lauter
Wissembourg
Wörth
Karlsruhe
Marne
Épernay
Souilly
Meuse
Châlons-sur-Marne
St-Mihiel
Buchy
Pont-à-Mousson
Diemeringen
Ettlingen
Rastatt
Gaggenau
Champaubert
Haguenau
Moselle
Sarre
Moyenvic
Sarrebourg
Baden-Baden
Bad Wildbad
Brumath
Sézanne
Vitry-le-François
Bar-le-Duc
Commercy
Toul
Nancy
Saverne
Forbach
Rhine (Rhein)

Scale 1 : 4 750 000

0 50 100 150 km

0 25 50 75 miles

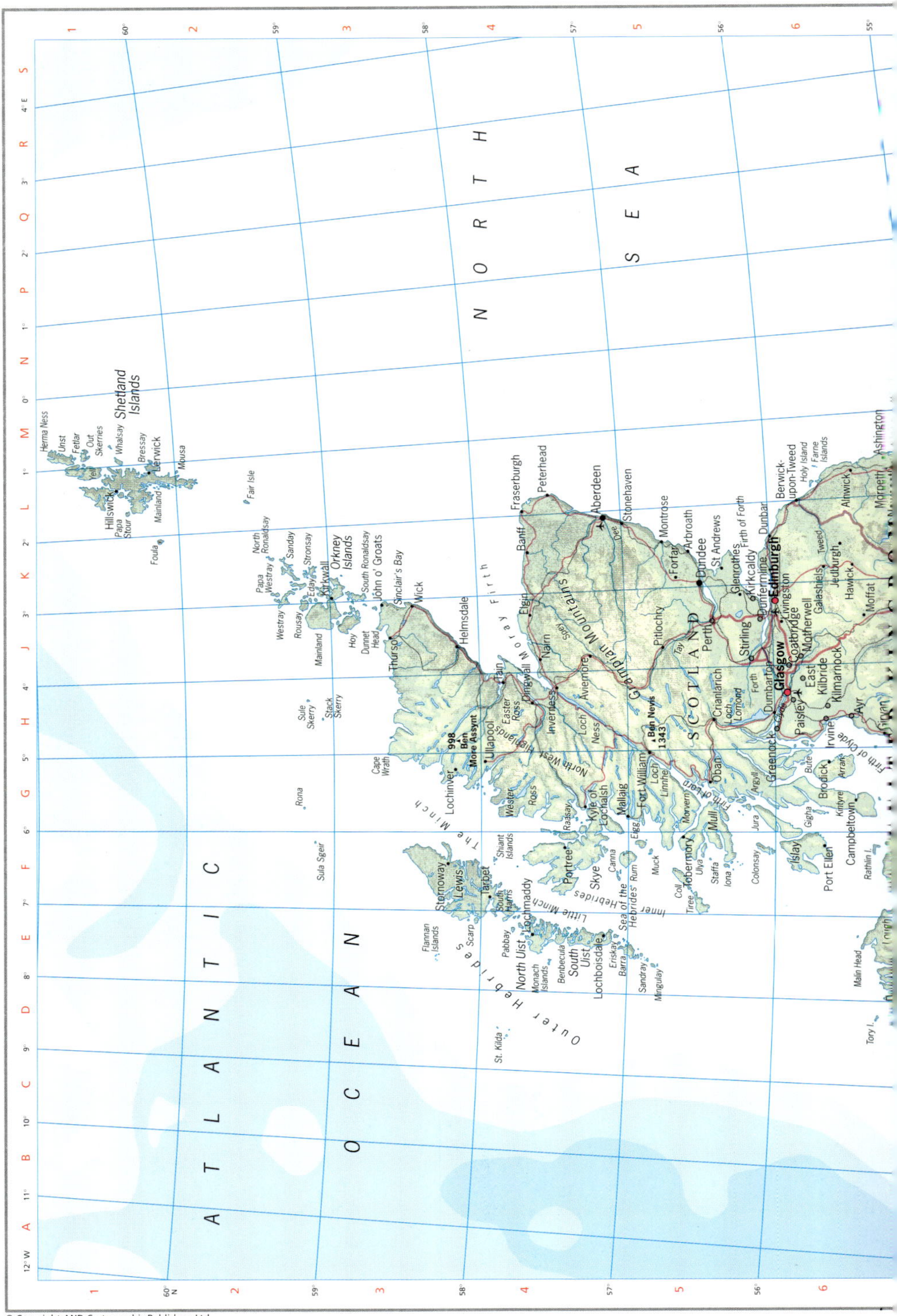

ATLANTIC OCEAN
NORTH SEA
SCOTLAND
Shetland Islands
Herma Ness
Unst
Fetlar
Yell
Out Skerries
Whalsay
Bressay
Lerwick
Mousa
Mainland
Hillswick
Papa Stour
Foula
Fair Isle
North Ronaldsay
Sanday
Stronsay
Papa Westray
Westray
Eday
Rousay
Kirkwall
Orkney Islands
Mainland
Hoy
South Ronaldsay
John o' Groats
Sinclair's Bay
Dunnet Head
Thurso
Wick
Helmsdale
Moray Firth
Sule Skerry
Stack Skerry
Cape Wrath
Rona
Sula Sgeir
Lochinver
998 Ben More Assynt
Ullapool
Tain
Dingwall
Easter Ross
North West Highlands
Wester Ross
Inverness
Nairn
Elgin
Banff
Fraserburgh
Peterhead
Aberdeen
Stonehaven
Dee
Spey
Grampian Mountains
Aviemore
Loch Ness
Ben Nevis 1343
Fort William
Loch Linnhe
Pitlochry
Tay
Perth
Montrose
Arbroath
Forfar
Dundee
St Andrews
Glenrothes
Kirkcaldy
Firth of Forth
Dunfermline
Edinburgh
Livingston
Dunbar
Stirling
Crianlarich
Loch Lomond
Forth
Dumbarton
Glasgow
Coatbridge
Motherwell
East Kilbride
Paisley
Greenock
Clyde
Kilmarnock
Ayr
Irvine
Firth of Clyde
Bute
Arran
Brodick
Kintyre
Campbeltown
Gigha
Islay
Port Ellen
Jura
Argyll
Colonsay
Oban
Firth of Lorn
Mull
Morvern
Tobermory
Ulva
Staffa
Iona
Coll
Tiree
Muck
Eigg
Rum
Canna
Mallaig
Kyle of Lochalsh
Raasay
Portree
Skye
Sea of the Hebrides
Inner Hebrides
Little Minch
The Minch
Shiant Islands
Stornoway
Lewis
Tarbert
South Harris
Scarp
Flannan Islands
Pabbay
North Uist
Lochmaddy
Monach Islands
Benbecula
South Uist
Lochboisdale
Eriskay
Barra
Sandray
Mingulay
Outer Hebrides
St. Kilda
Berwick-upon-Tweed
Holy Island
Farne Islands
Tweed
Galashiels
Jedburgh
Hawick
Moffat
Alnwick
Morpeth
Ashington
Girvan
Rathlin I.
Main Head
Tory I.

British Isles

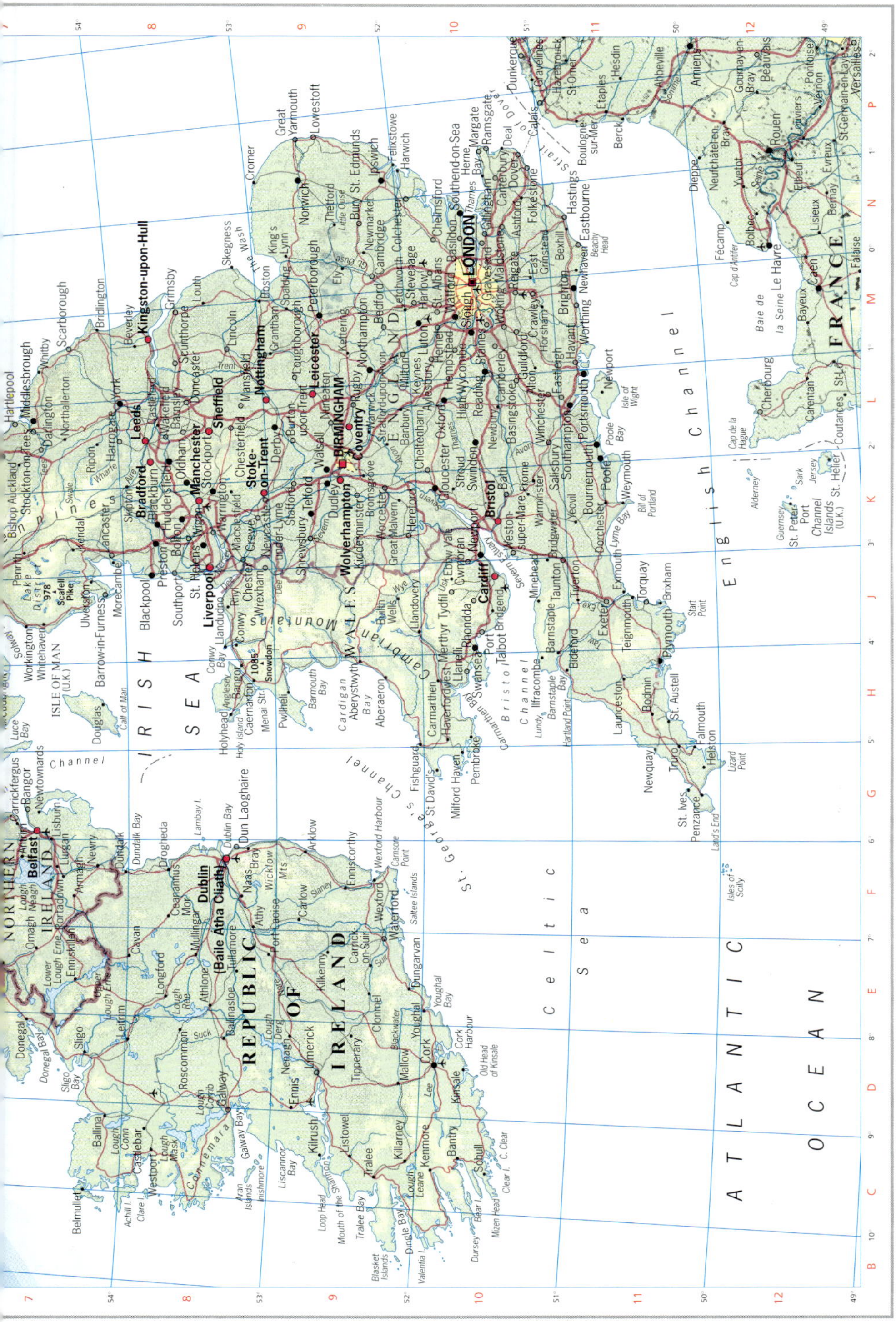

ATLANTIC OCEAN
IRISH SEA
English Channel
Celtic Sea
St. George's Channel
Bristol Channel
Strait of Dover
FRANCE
ENGLAND
WALES
REPUBLIC OF IRELAND
NORTHERN IRELAND
ISLE OF MAN (U.K.)
Channel Islands (U.K.)
LONDON
BIRMINGHAM
Dublin (Baile Átha Cliath)
Belfast
Liverpool
Manchester
Leeds
Sheffield
Bradford
Kingston-upon-Hull
Nottingham
Leicester
Coventry
Wolverhampton
Stoke-on-Trent
Bristol
Cardiff
Swansea
Plymouth
Southampton
Portsmouth
Brighton
Norwich
Ipswich
Cambridge
Oxford
Reading
Cork
Limerick
Galway
Waterford
Le Havre
Rouen
Caen
Cherbourg
Dunkerque
Calais
Boulogne-sur-Mer
Amiens
Isle of Wight
Cambrian Mountains
Snowdon
Scafell Pike
Land's End
Lizard Point
Isles of Scilly

Scale 1 : 4 750 000

0 50 100 150 km
0 25 50 75 miles

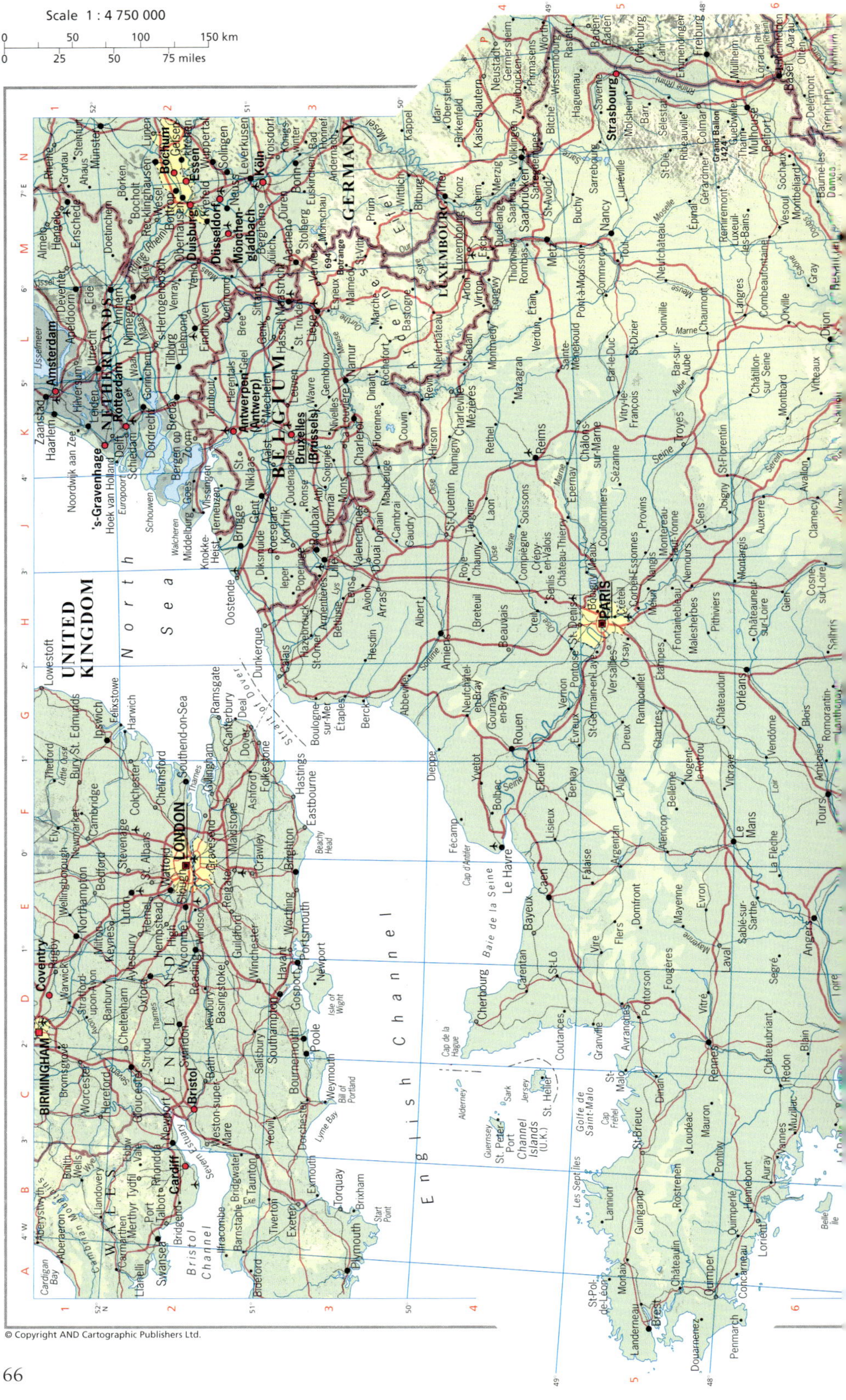
UNITED KINGDOM
NETHERLANDS
BELGIUM
GERMANY
LUXEMBOURG
ENGLAND
WALES
North Sea
English Channel
Bristol Channel
LONDON
PARIS
BIRMINGHAM
Channel Islands (U.K.)

France

FRANCE
SPAIN
ITALY
SWITZERLAND
MONACO
ANDORRA
ATLANTIC OCEAN
Bay of Biscay
MEDITERRANEAN SEA
Golfe du Lion
Massif Central
Plateau du Limousin
PYRENEES
Paris
Bordeaux
Toulouse
Marseille
Lyon
Nice
Montpellier
Limoges
Clermont-Ferrand
Grenoble
Perpignan
Toulon
Nîmes
Avignon
St-Étienne
Poitiers
La Rochelle
Angoulême
Périgueux
Bergerac
Cahors
Rodez
Albi
Carcassonne
Narbonne
Béziers
Pau
Tarbes
Lourdes
Bayonne
Biarritz
Arcachon
Royan
Niort
Châteauroux
Montluçon
Vichy
Roanne
Mâcon
Valence
Orange
Arles
Aix-en-Provence
Cannes
St-Tropez
Annecy
Genève
Lausanne
Chamonix
Mont Blanc 4808
Torino
Cuneo
Bilbao
Donostia (San Sebastián)
Pamplona
Vitoria-Gasteiz
Logroño
Huesca
Zaragoza
Girona
Figueres
Loire
Garonne
Dordogne
Rhône
Gironde
Puy de Dôme 1464
Puy de Sancy 1885
Mont Mézenc 1753
Monte Perdido 3355
Aneto 3404
Mont Pelat 3053
Monte Viso 3841
Gran Paradiso 4061
Monte Rosa 4634
Matterhorn 4478
Île d'Oléron
Île de Ré
Île d'Yeu
Îles d'Hyères
Camargue

Scale 1 : 4 750 000
0 50 100 km
0 25 50 miles
Bay of Biscay
Costa Verde
Cabo Ortegal
Cabo Peñas
Ortigueira
Viveiro
Cervo
Ferrol
A Coruña
As Pontes de García Rodríguez
Ribadeo
Luarca
Avilés
Gijón
Villaviciosa
Santander
Santoña
Laredo
Getxo
Portugalete
Barakaldo
Carballo
Betanzos
Villalba
Tineo
Pola de Siero
Oviedo
Langreo
Llanes
Torrelavega
Camariñas
Ordes
Sta. Comba
Guitiriz
A Fonsagrada
Cangas de Narcea
Mieres
Laviana
Cabanquinta (Aller)
Cabo Fisterra (Cape Finisterre)
Santiago
Melide
Lugo
Lena
Embalse del Ebro
Reinosa
Muros
Noia
Padrón
Teo
Villablino
Cordillera Cantábrica
Porto do Son
Becerreá
Cistierna
Trespaderne
Cabo Corrubedo
A Estrada
Lalín
Sarria
Ebro
Miranda de Ebro
Sta. Eugenia (Ribeira)
Vilagarcía
Monforte de Lemos
Bembibre
Ponferrada
León
Guardo
Sedano
O Grove
Pontevedra
Marín
Carballino
Miño
Sil
Astorga
Briviesca
Cangas
Redondela
Ourense
O Barco (Barco de Valdeorras)
La Bañeza
Sahagún
Burgos
Vigo
Porriño
Ponteareas
Xinzo de Limia
A Gudiña
Villavelayo
Tui
Hortiguela
ATLANTIC OCEAN
Caminha
Verín
Benavente
Palencia
Lerma
Ponte da Barca
Bragança
Villalpando
Viana do Castelo
Chaves
Esla
Emb. de Ricobayo
Aranda de Duero
Barcelos
Braga
Venda Nova
Valladolid
Duero
Póvoa de Varzim
Guimarães
Mirandela
Miranda do Douro
Zamora
Toro
Tordesillas
Peñafiel
Tua
Sabor
Medina de Campo
Matosinhos
Vila do Conde
Vila Real
Porto
Gondomar
Torre de Moncorvo
Fuentesauco
Cerezo de Abajo
Vila Nova de Gaia
Douro
Emb. de Almendra
Espinho
São João de Madeira
Meda
Arévalo
Salamanca
Peñaranda de Bracamonte
Segovia
Lumbrales
Puerto de Navacerrada
Murtosa
Trancoso
Pinhel
Alba
Colmenar Viejo
S. Sebastian de los Reyes
Aveiro
Viseu
Sistema Central
Guarda
Ciudad Rodrigo
Emb. de Sta. Teresa
Ávila
Collado Villalba
Guadalajara
Santa Comba Dão
Serra da Estrela
Sierra de Gata
Alcobendas
Alcalá de Henares
Béjar
MADRID
Alcorcón
Torrejón de Ardoz
Cabo Mondego
Estrela 1993
Covilhã
Emb. de Gabriel y Galán
Móstoles
Getafe
Figueira da Foz
Coimbra
2592 Pico Almanzor
Parla
Valdemoro
Fundão
Tiétar
Talavera de la Reina
Maqueda
Aranjuez
Soure
Pombal
Coria
Plasencia
Ocaña
Leiria
Sertã
Navalmoral de la Mata
Toledo
Merinha Grande
Castelo Branco
Bgem. do Castelo de Bode
Emb. de Alcántara Uno
SPAIN
Nazaré
Tomar
Navahermosa
Entroncamento
Abrantes
Nisa
Peniche
Caldas da Rainha
Cáceres
Trujillo
Madridejos
Cabo Carvoeiro
PORTUGAL
Valencia de Alcántara
Emb. de García Sola
Alcázar de S. Juan
Santarém
Tagus (Tejo)
Portalegre
Ponte de Sor
Albuquerque
Torres Vedras
Miajadas
Navalvillar de Pela
Guadiana
Vila Franca de Xira
Mora
Bgem. do Maranhão
Monforte
Daimiel
Manzanares
Coruche
Elvas
Montijo
Mérida
Don Benito
Abenójar
Ciudad Real
Amadora
Lisboa (Lisbon)
Estoril
Cascais
Badajoz
Emb. de la Serena
Almadén
Valdepeñas
Barreiro
Estremoz
Almada
Almendralejo
Castuera
Puertollano
Setúbal
Évora
Costa do Sol
Villafranca de los Barros
Cabeza del Buey
Cabo de Espichel
Alcácer do Sal
Sierra Morena
Zafra
Peñarroya-Pueblonuevo
Pozoblanco
Villanueva de Córdoba
La Carolina
Portel
Sado
Jerez de los Caballeros
Azuaga
Grândola
Ardila
Moura
Fregenal de la Sierra
Emb. del Bembézar
Bailén
Linares
Ferreira do Alentejo
Beja
Andújar
Sines
Montoro
Baeza
Úbeda
Serpa
Cortegana
Córdoba
Aljustrel
Constantina
Jódar
Jaén
Castro Verde
Guadalquivir
Martos
Odemira
Guadiana
Lora del Río
Palma del Río
Bgem. de Sta. Clara
Valverde del Camino
Montilla
Baena
Alcaudete
Carmona
Écija
Alcoutim
Sevilla
Marchena
Puente-Genil
Lucena
Alcalá la Real
Aljezur
Almonte
Alcalá de Guadaira
Genil
Priego de Córdoba
Cabo de S. Vicente
Portimão
Huelva
Osuna
Rute
Granada
Lagos
Loulé
Tavira
Ayamonte
Dos Hermanas
Archidona
Albufeira
Faro
Olhão
Golfo de Cádiz
Las Cabezas de San Juan
Utrera
Morón de la Frontera
Loja
Sierra Nevada
3482 Mulhacén
Antequera
Lebrija
Olvera
Cordillera
Villamartín
Emb. de Guadalhorce
Vélez-Málaga
Sanlúcar de Barrameda
Arcos de la Frontera
Ronda
Alhaurín el Grande
Motril
Adra
Jerez de la Frontera
Ubrique
Málaga
Nerja
Almuñécar
El Puerto de Sta. María
Puerto Real
Torremolinos
Cádiz
Medina Sidonia
Marbella
Fuengirola
San Fernando
Chiclana de la Frontera
Estepona
Costa del Sol
Vejer de la Frontera
Barbate
San Roque
La Línea
Cabo de Trafalgar
Algeciras
Gibraltar (U.K.)
Tarifa
Strait of Gibraltar
Cap Spartel
Ceuta (Spain)
Isla de Alborán (Spain)
Tanger
El Borj
Cap Negro
Tétouan
Asilah
MOROCCO
Bou Ahmed
A B C D E F G
1 2 3 4 5 6 7 8 9
10° W 9° 8° 7° 6° 5° 4° 3°
44° 43° N 42° 41° 40° 39° 38° 37° 36°

Spain and Portugal

FRANCE
PYRENEES
ANDORRA
Andorra la Vella
Bayonne
Biarritz
Orthez
St-Jean-de-Luz
Irun
Rentería
Donostia (San Sebastián)
Azpeitia
Bergara
Tolosa
Beasain
Alsasua
Estella
Logroño
Calahorra
Arnedo
Tafalla
Pamplona
Roncesvalles
Sangüesa
Emb. de Yesa
Jaca
Sabiñánigo
Oloron-Ste-Marie
St-Palais
Pau
Lourdes
Tarbes
Bagnères-de-Bigorre
St-Gaudens
St-Girons
Muret
Castelnaudary
Carcassonne
Pamiers
Foix
Limoux
Narbonne
Béziers
Agde
Sète
Cap d'Agde
Golfe du Lion
Sigean
Rivesaltes
Perpignan
Ax-les-Thermes
Port-Vendres
Le Perthus
Les Escaldes
La Seu d'Urgell
3355 Monte Perdido
Aneto 3404
Aínsa
Sort
Tremp
Berga
Ripoll
Olot
Figueres
Roses
Banyoles
Girona
Palafrugell
Palamós
Sant Feliu de Guíxols
Lloret de Mar
Costa Brava
Torelló
Manlleu
Vic
Sant Celoni
Granollers
Arenys de Mar
Mataró
Manresa
Terrassa
Sabadell
Badalona
BARCELONA
Sant Boi
El Prat de Llobregat
Gavà
Sitges
Vilafranca del Penedès
Vilanova y la Geltrú
Igualada
Tàrrega
Balaguer
Lleida
Monzón
Barbastro
Huesca
Ejea de los Caballeros
Emb. de la Sotonera
Tudela
Tarazona
Alagón
Sariñena
Zaragoza
El Burgo de Ebro
Fraga
Caspe
Azaila
Montblanc
Valls
Reus
Tarragona
Cambrils
Costa Dorada
Alcañiz
Gandesa
Tortosa
Cabo Tortosa
Amposta
Sant Carlos de la Ràpita
Vinaròs
Benicarló
Morella
Montalbán
Calamocha
Daroca
Calatayud
Medinaceli
Alcolea del Pinar
Molina de Aragón
Monreal del Campo
Soria
Sistema Ibérico
Sierra de Gúdar
Teruel
Cañaveras
Cuenca
Torreblanca
Onda
Castelló de la Plana
Vila-real
Borriana
La Vall d'Uixo
Islas Columbretes
Sagunt
Golfo de Valencia
Burjassot
Paterna
Valencia
Torrent
Utiel
Emb. de Contreras
Motilla del Palancar
Cofrents
Júcar
Carlet
Algemes
Cullera
Alzira
Xàtiva
Gandia
Oliva
Dénia
Xàbia
Cabo de la Nao
Ontinyent
Alcoi
Almansa
Albacete
Chinchilla de Monte-Aragón
La Roda
Yecla
Villena
Elda
Hellín
Jumilla
Benidorm
La Vila Joiosa
Novelda
Aspe
Alicante
Elch
Crevillent
Santa Pola
Costa Blanca
Cieza
Caravaca de la Cruz
Molina de Segura
Orihuela
Torrevieja
Alcantarilla
Murcia
Zarzadilla de Totana
Alhama de Murcia
Lorca
Huércal Overa
Águilas
Golfo de Mazarrón
La Union
Cabo de Palos
Cartagena
Albox
Vera
Carboneras
Níjar
Almería
Golfo de Almería
Cabo de Gata
Islas Baleares (Balearic Islands)
Menorca
Ciutadella
Mahón
Mallorca
Pollença
Cap de Formentor
Sóller
Sa Pobla
Inca
Artà
Manacor
Palma
Sa Dragonera
Llucmajor
Cap de ses Salines
Cabrera
Eivissa (Ibiza)
San Antonio Abad
Formentera
Mediterranean Sea
ALGERIA
ALGER (ALGIERS)
Dellys
Tizi Ouzou
Ain Taya
Bou Ismail
Rouiba
Thenia
Lakhdaria
Larba
Boufarik
Blida
Boghni
Cherchell
Gouraya
Hadjout
Ténès
Bouira
Ain Bessem
Médéa
Beni Slimane
Sour el Ghozlane
Miliana
Khemis Miliana
Bouzghaia
Berrouaghia
Ech Chélif
Chélif
Atlas Mountains
Aïn-Tédélès
Bou Kadir
Bordj Bounaam
Theniet el Had
Ksar el Boukhari
Ain el Hadjel
Bougzoul
Mostaganem
Arzew
Mers el Kébir
Relizane
Gdyel
Oran
Oued Tlélat
Mohammadia
Cap Figalo
El Amria
Sig
Mascara
Hammam Bou Hadjar
Beni Saf
Ain Témouchent

Scale 1 : 3 550 000

0 50 100 150 km

0 25 50 75 miles

A
B
C
D
E
F
6° E
7°
8°
9°
10°
11°
48° N
47°
46°
45°
44°
2
3
4
5
6
7
St-Mihiel
Pont-à-Mousson
Buchy
Bitche
Wörth
Bruchsal
Heilbronn
Schwäbisch Hall
Crailsheim
Gunzenhausen
Dinkelsbühl
Weißenburg
Bar-le-Duc
Flirey
Commercy
Wissembourg
Karlsruhe
Ettlingen
Bretten
Bietigheim-Bissingen
Backnang
Gaildorf
Ellwangen
Treuchtlingen
Nancy
Toul
Sarrebourg
Haguenau
Pforzheim
Ludwigsburg
Waiblingen
Aalen
Nördlingen
Ingolstadt
St-Nicolas-de-Port
Lunéville
Saverne
Brumath
Baden-Baden
Gaggenau
Bad Wilbad
Leonberg
Stuttgart
Esslingen
Schwäbisch-Gmünd
Göppingen
Heidenheim
Donauwörth
Houdelaincourt
Strasbourg
Molsheim
Kehl
Oberkirch
Herrenberg
Böblingen
Kirchheim
Nürtingen
Geislingen
Dillingen
Neufchâteau
Baccarat
Barr
Offenburg
Nagold
Tübingen
Metzingen
Langenau
GERMANY
Châtenois
Moselle
Sélestat
Lahr
Freudenstadt
Reutlingen
Bad Urach
Ulm
Günzburg
Augsburg
Friedberg
Vittel
St-Dié
Ribeauvillé
Rhine (Rhein)
Hechingen
Balingen
Blaubeuren
Neu-Ulm
Vöhringen
Bobingen
Krumbach
Val-de-Meuse
Épinal
Gérardmer
Colmar
Emmendingen
Schramberg
St. Georgen
Rottweil
Albstadt
Ehingen
Laupheim
Illertissen
Fürstenfeldbruck
Fresnes-sur-Apances
Munster
Villingen
Schwenningen
Schwäbische Alb
Biberach
Mindelheim
Landsberg
Langres
Remiremont
Guebwiller
Freiburg
Donaueschingen
Sigmaringen
Saulgau
Memmingen
Ammersee
Luxeuil-les-Bains
Vosges
Schwarzwald
Tuttlingen
Bad Waldsee
Kaufbeuren
Starnberger See
Weilheim
Combeaufontaine
Thann
Mulhouse
Müllheim
Stockach
Bad Wurzach
Leutkirch
Schongau
Champlitte
Lure
Belfort
Altkirch
Lörrach
Waldshut-Tiengen
Singen
Überlingen
Ravensburg
Friedrichshafen
Marktoberdorf
Gray
Saône
Vesoul
Montbéliard
Sochaux
Basel
Rheinfelden
Schaffhausen
Konstanz
L. Constance
Wangen
Kempten
Doubs
Säckingen
Reinach
Bad Zurzach
Rhine (Rhein)
Bülach
Frauenfeld
Arbon
Immenstadt
Füssen
Delémont
Aarau
Zürich
Winterthur
Wil
Sonthofen
Pfach
Olten
Wohlen
Dübendorf
St. Gallen
Bregenz
Dornbirn
Oberstdorf
Besançon
Grenchen
Solothurn
Aare
Herisau
Garmisch-Partenkirchen
Biel
Huttwil
Zuger See
Zug
Rapperswil
Vaduz
Feldkirch
Bludenz
Telfs
Innsbruck
Dole
La Chaux-de-Fonds
Emmen
Walensee
LIECHTENSTEIN
Mouchard
Pontarlier
Neuchâtel
Burgdorf
Luzern
Schwyz
Kappl
Landeck
Poligny
Lac de Neuchâtel
Payerne
Bern
Köniz
SWITZERLAND
Altdorf
Klosters
Pfunds
Champagnole
Yverdon-les-Bains
Fribourg
Thun
Thuner See
Brienzer See
Glarner Alpen
Vorderrhein
Chur
Davos
Lons-le-Saunier
Vallorbe
Bulle
Spiez
Interlaken
St-Laurent-en-Grandvaux
Morges
Lausanne
Vevey
Gstaad
Jungfrau 4158
Airolo
St. Moritz
Ortles 3905
Silandro
St-Claude
Nyon
Lake Geneva (Lac Léman)
Montreux
Berner Alpen
Lepontine
Bormio
Cles
Oyonnax
Thonon-les-Bains
Monthey
Sion
Sierre
Visp
Brig
Formazza
Biasca
Poschiavo
Malè
Ain
Genève
Annemasse
Chiavenna
Sondrio
Cluses
Martigny
Locarno
Bellinzona
Edolo
Rhône
Chamonix
Zermatt
4478 Matterhorn
4634 Monte Rosa
Domodossola
Lugano
Colico
Alpi Orobie
Annecy
Lac d'Annecy
4808 Mont Blanc
Lago Maggiore
Luino
Lago di Como
Lago di Lugano
Lago di Lecco
San Pellegrino Terme
Breno
Riva del Garda
Aix-les-Bains
Ugine
Aosta
Omegna
Verbania
Varese
Como
Lecco
Albino
Darfo
Rovereto
Lac du Bourget
Sées
Varallo
Lago d'Iseo
Chambéry
Isère
Gran Paradiso 4061
Cogne
Borgosesia
Borgomanero
Saronno
Seregno
Monza
Bergamo
Gardone Val Trompia
Schio
Moûtiers
Cossato
Biella
Busto Arsizio
Rho
Treviglio
Brescia
Lago di Garda
Valdagno
Voiron
Orco
Ivrea
Novara
Magenta
MILANO (MILAN)
Arzignano
St-Jean-de-Maurienne
Rivarolo
Vercelli
Lodi
Crema
Villafranca
Verona
Massif des Écrins
Modane
Chivasso
Vigevano
Oglio
Grenoble
Susa
Po
Trino
Garlasco
Pavia
Adda
Chiese
Venaria
Torino (Turin)
Casale Monferrato
Cremona
Mántova
Legnago
Valbonnais
Oulx
Rivoli
Moncalieri
Chieri
Valenza
Stradella
Codogno
Piádena
Ostiglia
Briançon
Pinerolo
Asti
Alessandria
Piacenza
Casalmaggiore
Chauffayer
Carmagnola
Tortona
Voghera
Guastalla
Drac
Monte Viso 3841
Nizza Monferrato
Varzi
Trebbia
Fidenza
Guillestre
Saluzzo
Bra
Alba
Acqui Terme
Novi Ligure
Bobbio
Salsomaggiore Terme
Parma
Carpi
Savigliano
Ovada
Fornovo di Taro
Reggio nell'Emilia
Modena
Gap
St-Paul
Fossano
Tanaro
Bormida
Appennino Tosco-Emiliano
Sassuolo
Serres
St-Vincent-les-Forts
Cuneo
Mondovì
Voltri
Genova (Genoa)
Borgo val di Taro
Bologna
Sisteron
Borgo San Dalmazzo
Savona
Varazze
Vado Ligure
Rapallo
Chiavari
Pontrémoli
Pavullo nel Frignano
Maritime Alps
Finale Ligure
Sestri Levante
Fivizzano
Digne-les-Bains
Guillaumes
Loano
Albenga
Aulla
Sarzana
Carrara
Massa
La Spezia
Lerici
Golfo di Genova
Manosque
Lac de St-Croix
Entrevaux
Alassio
Impéria
Pietrasanta
Camaiore
Pescia
Pistóia
Prato
Castellane
Vence
Monaco
Ventimiglia
San Remo
Forte dei Marmi
Viaréggio
Lucca
Firenze (Florence)
Cagnes-sur-Mer
Grasse
Nice
MONACO
Antibes
Cannes
Pisa
Empoli
Arno
Draguignan
Ligurian Sea
Pontedera
S. Miniato
Greve in Chianti
Brignoles
Fréjus
St-Raphaël
Livorno
Certaldo
Poggibonsi
St-Tropez
Gorgona
Rosignano Solvay
Volterra
San Gimignano
Toulon
Hyères
Marittimo
Cécina
FRANCE
ITALY

The Alpine States

CZECH REPUBLIC
SLOVAKIA
AUSTRIA
HUNGARY
SLOVENIA
CROATIA
BOSNIA-HERZEGOVINA
SAN MARINO
WIEN (VIENNA)
Bratislava
Ljubljana
Zagreb
Venézia (Venice)
Gulf of Venice
Golfo di Trieste
Adriatic Sea
Dinaric Alps
Niedere Tauern
Hohe Tauern
Karnische Alpen
Großglockner 3798
Triglav 2864
Snežnik 1796
Vaganski Vrh 1758
Danube
Drava
Sava
Salzburg
Linz
Graz
Klagenfurt
Innsbruck
Maribor
Trieste
Rijeka
Split
Zadar
Ancona
Rimini
Ravenna
Regensburg
Passau
Győr
Szombathely
Banja Luka
Balaton
Neusiedler See
Istra
Krk
Cres
Lošinj
Pag
Brač

Scale 1 : 4 750 000

0 50 100 150 km

0 25 50 75 miles

AUSTRIA
SWITZERLAND
HUNGARY
SLOVENIA
CROATIA
BOSNIA HERZEGOVINA
SAN MARINO
VATICAN CITY
MONACO
FRANCE
LIECHTENSTEIN
CORSE (CORSICA) (France)
Adriatic Sea
Ligurian Sea
Gulf of Venice
Golfo di Genova
MILANO (MILAN)
Venezia (Venice)
ROMA (ROME)
Torino (Turin)
Genova (Genoa)
Firenze (Florence)
Bologna
Zagreb
Ljubljana
Verona
Trieste
Nice
Bern

Italy

Tyrrhenian Sea
Ionian Sea
MEDITERRANEAN SEA
Golfo di Taranto
Malta Channel
Sicilian Channel
SARDEGNA (SARDINIA) (Italy)
SICILIA (SICILY)
TUNISIA
ALGERIA
MALTA
NAPOLI (NAPLES)
Palermo
Messina
Catánia
Bari
Cagliari
Tunis
Valletta
Sassari
Taranto
Brindisi
Lecce
Foggia
Potenza
Salerno
Cosenza
Catanzaro
Reggio di Calabria
Siracusa
Trapani
Marsala
Agrigento
Enna
Isole Lipari
Isole Égadi
Strait of Bonifacio
Monte Etna 3323
Monte Pollino 2248
Vesuvio 1281
Punta La Marmora 1834
Monte Limbara 1359
Bizerte
Pantelleria (Italy)
Ustica

Scale 1 : 4 750 000

0 50 100 150 km

0 25 50 75 miles

AUSTRIA
SLOVAKIA
HUNGARY
SLOVENIA
CROATIA
BOSNIA-
HERZEGOVINA
YUGOSLAVIA
SRBIJA
(SERBIA)
CRNA GORA
(MONTENEGRO)
KOSOVO
VOJVODINA
ALBANIA
ITALY
MACED
ADRIATIC SEA
WIEN
(VIENNA)
Bratislava
BUDAPEST
Ljubljana
Zagreb
Sarajevo
BEOGRAD
(BELGRADE)
Podgorica
Tiranë
(Tirana)
Skopje
Košice
Miskolc
Debrecen
Szeged
Pécs
Graz
Klagenfurt
Maribor
Rijeka
Trieste
Pula
Split
Dubrovnik
Osijek
Novi Sad
Banja Luka
Mostar
Timişoara
Priština
Bari
Foggia
Balaton
Danube
(Duna)
Drava
Sava
Drina
Triglav
2864
Durmitor
2522
Kékes
1014
Istra
Dugi Otok
Brač
Hvar
Korčula
Mljet
Vis
Pag
Krk
Cres
Lake Scutari
L. Ohrid
L. Prespa
Monte Calvo
1055
Tèrmoli
Manfredonia
Barletta
Molfetta
Monopoli
Durrës
Shkodër
Elbasan
Kragujevac
Niš
Subotica
Zrenjanin
Tuzla
Zenica
Zadar
Šibenik
Karlovac
Sisak
Varaždin
Leoben
St. Pölten
Wels
Steyr
Győr
Székesfehérvár
Kecskemét
Szolnok
Nyíregyháza
Arad
Pančevo
Smederevo
Čačak
Kraljevo
Peć
Prizren
Ohrid
Bitola
Tetovo
14° E
15°
16°
17°
18°
19°
20°
21°
22°
48° N
46°
45°
44°
43°
42°
41°
A
B
C
D
E
F
G
H
J
1
2
3
4
5
6
7
8
9

The Balkans

UKRAINE
MOLDOVA
ROMANIA
BULGARIA
TURKEY
GREECE
BLACK SEA
Carpathian Mountains
Stara Planina
Chişinău
BUCUREŞTI (BUCHAREST)
SOFIYA (SOFIA)
ODESA (ODESSA)
İSTANBUL
Cluj-Napoca
Constanţa
Varna
Plovdiv
Burgas
Braşov
Iaşi
Craiova
Galaţi
Brăila
Ploieşti
Piteşti
Sibiu
Timişoara
Ruse
Pleven
Shumen
Dobrich
Stara Zagora
Sliven
Yambol
Edirne
Kırklareli
Tekirdağ
Chernivtsi
Kolomyya
Mukacheve
Uzhhorod
Bălţi
Tiraspol
Tighina
Cahul
Izmayil
Tulcea
Sulina
Danube (Dunărea)
Mouths of the Danube
Dniester
Prut
Siret
Mureş
Olt
Jiu
Argeş
Ialomiţa
Iskar
Maritsa
Marmara Denizi (Sea of Marmara)
İstanbul Boğazı (Bosporus)
Thrakiko Pelagos
Moldoveanu 2544
Musala 2925
Midzor 2169
Ludogorie
Rhodope Mountains
Yıldız Dağları
Suceava
Botoşani
Piatra-Neamţ
Bacău
Vaslui
Bârlad
Focşani
Buzău
Slobozia
Călăraşi
Giurgiu
Alexandria
Slatina
Târgovişte
Târgu Jiu
Râmnicu Vâlcea
Drobeta-Turnu Severin
Deva
Hunedoara
Alba Iulia
Târgu Mureş
Bistriţa
Baia Mare
Satu Mare
Zalău
Miercurea-Ciuc
Sfântu Gheorghe
Vidin
Lom
Montana
Vratsa
Lovech
Gabrovo
Veliko Tŭrnovo
Razgrad
Silistra
Targovishte
Kardzhali
Khaskovo
Pazardzhik
Blagoevgrad
Kyustendil
Pernik
Smolyan
Kavala
Xanthi
Komotini
Alexandroupoli
Drama
Serres
Kilkis
K L M N O P Q R S T
23° 24° 25° 26° 27° 28° 29° 30°
48° 47° 46° 45° 44° 43° 42° 41°
1 2 3 4 5 6 7 8 9

Scale 1 : 4 750 000

0 50 100 150 km

0 25 50 75 miles

YUGOSLAVIA
CRNA GORA (MONTENEGRO)
SRBIJA (SERBIA)
KOSOVO
MACEDONIA
ALBANIA
BULGARIA
GREECE
Stara Planina
SOFIYA (SOFIA)
Plovdiv
Skopje
Tiranë (Tirana)
Thessaloniki
Athina (Athens)
Podgorica
Priština
Shkodër
Durrës
Elbasan
Vlorë
Korçë
Bitola
Prilep
Ohrid
Kavala
Xanthi
Komotini
Alexandroupoli
Kozani
Larisa
Volos
Lamia
Ioannina
Kerkyra (Corfu)
Patra
Korinthos
Pireas
Tripoli
Kalamata
Sparti
Chalkidiki
Peloponnisos
Thermaikos Kolpos
Kassandreia
Thasos
Samothraki
Limnos
Lesvos (Lesbos)
Chios
Andros
Tinos
Naxos
Paros
Thira
Kyklades (Cyclades)
Aegean Sea
Ionian Sea
Ionioi Nisoi
Kefallonia
Zakynthos
Lefkada
Kythira
Krytiko Pelagos
Steno Antikythiro
MEDITERRANEAN SEA
Chania
Rethymno
Irakleio (Iraklion)
Kriti (Crete)
2911 Olympos
2925 Musala
2457
2456
2033

Greece and Western Turkey

BLACK SEA
MEDITERRANEAN SEA
TURKEY
ANATOLIA
CYPRUS
Varna
Devnya
Provadiya
Aytos
Karnobat
Nos Emine
Nesebur
Pomorie
Burgas
Burgaski Zaliv
Sozopol
Grudovo
Malko Tarnovo
Resovo
Igneada
Kirklareli
Kiyiköy
Pinarhisar
Vize
Babaeski
Saray
Karacaköy
Lüleburgaz
Çerkezköy
Hayrabolu
Çorlu
Muratli
Silivri
İSTANBUL
İstanbul Boğazı (Bosporus)
Şile
Ağva
Kandira
Karasu
Büyükçekmece
Yeşilköy
Büyükada
Tekirdağ
Malkara
Marmara Denizi (Sea of Marmara)
Marmara Adası
Kapıdağı Yarimadası
İmrali Adası
Şarköy
Türkeli Adası
Paşalimanı Adası
Erdek
Bandirma
Gemlik Körfezi
Gemlik
Mudanya
Yalova
Gebze
İzmit
Karamürsel
İznik
İznik Gölü
Sakarya
Geyve
Bilecik
Bursa
İnegöl
Ulubat Gölü
Karacabey
Mustafakemalpaşa
Biga
Gönen
Çan
Susurluk
Balıkesir
Burhaniye
Ayvalik
Savastepe
Bigadiç
Dursunbey
Tavşanli
Kütahya
Bozüyük
Eskişehir
Kaymaz
Sivrihisar
Polatli
ANKARA
Elmadağ
Kirikkale
Yerkov
Balâ
Kirşehir
Mucur
Kulu
Şereflikoçhisar
Tuz Gölü
Cihanbeyli
Gülşehir
Nevşehir
Aksaray
Sultanhanı
Niğde
Bor
Karapinar
Ereğli
Konya
Sarayönü
Kadınhanı
Çumra
Karaman
Zonguldak
Ereğli
Çaycuma
Bartin
Cide
Azdavay
Kastamonu
Safranbolu
Karabük
İnebolu
Kerempe Burnu
Tosya
Akçakoca
Düzce
Bolu
Mudurnu
Köroğlu Tepesi 2400
Köroğlu Dağlari
Gerede
Çerkeş
Kurşunlu
Çankırı
Kizilirmak
Çubuk
Beypazarı
Nallihan
Çerikli
Soma
Kinik
Kirkağaç
Gölcük
Demirci
Simav
Akhisar
Bergama
Dikili
Aliağa
Foça
Manisa
Menemen
Saruhanli
Gölmarmara
Gediz
Salihli
Kula
Uşak
Banaz
Afyon
Emirdağ
Bolvadin
Çay
Akşehir
Sarkikaraağaç
Sandıklı
Eğridir Gölü
Dinar
Keçiborlu
Isparta
Eğirdir
Beyşehir Gölü
Beyşehir
Burdur
Burdur Gölü
Acı Göl
Bucak
Kizilkaya
Seydişehir
Çevizli
Bozkır
Aksek
İZMİR
Karşıyaka
Turgutlu
Kemalpaşa
Alaşehir
Urla
Bayindir
Ödemiş
Seferihisar
Torbali
Tire
Selçuk
Kuşadasi
Germencik
Aydin
Nazilli
Sarayköy
Ortaklar
İncirliova
Söke
Koçarli
Çine
Denizli
2528 Esler Dağ
Kale
Çamiçigölü
Samos
Yenihisar
Yatağan
Milas
Muğla
Boz Dağ 2419
Bodrum
Kara Ada
Gökova Körfezi
Kos
Datça
Marmaris
Dalaman
Köyceğiz
Gölhisar
Korkuteli
Antalya
Serik
Manavgat
Alanya
Elmali
3073
Fethiye
Kemer
Kalkan
Beydağlari
Finike
Kumluca
Yardımcı Burnu
Antalya Körfezi
Megisti (Greece)
Geyik Dağ 2877
Toros Dağlari
Kizilalan
Ermenek
Mut
Karacal T. 2339
Gazipaşa
Anamur
Aydincik
Ovacik
Silifke
Erdemli
İçel (Mersin)
Lipsoi
Dodekanisos (Dodecanese)
Nisyros
Symi
Tilos
Rodos
Rodos (Rhodes)
Lindos
Chalki
Kattavia
Saria
Karpathos
Aigialousa
Keryneia
Lefkosia (Nicosia)
Ammochostos (Famagusta)
C. Arnaoutis
Polis
Troodos
Olympus 1952
Larnaka
Cape Greko
Pafos
Lemesos (Limassol)

Scale 1 : 14 300 000

0 200 400 600 km
0 100 200 300 miles

Norwegian Sea
Barents Sea
NORWAY
SWEDEN
FINLAND
KARELIYA
Kol'skiy Poluostrov
Beloye More (White Sea)
Gulf of Bothnia
Gulf of Finland
BALTIC SEA
Gulf of Riga
ESTONIA
LATVIA
LITHUANIA
RUSSIA
POLAND
BELARUS
UKRAINE
MOLDOVA
ROMANIA
BULGARIA
SLOVAKIA
HUNGARY
Sea of Azov
Black Sea
Krym
Oslo
Stockholm
Helsinki
Tallinn
Riga
Vilnius
Minsk
WARSZAWA (WARSAW)
MOSKVA (MOSCOW)
SANKT-PETERBURG (ST PETERSBURG)
KYYIV (KIEV)
Chişinău
BUCUREŞTI (BUCHAREST)
Trondheim
Uppsala
Västerås
Örebro
Norrköping
Linköping
Jönköping
Göteborg
Gotland
Turku
Tampere
Oulu
Vaasa
Kuopio
Jyväskylä
Lahti
Petrozavodsk
Arkhangel'sk
Severodvinsk
Murmansk
Vologda
Cherepovets
Yaroslavl'
Kostroma
Rybinsk
Tver'
Ivanovo
Vladimir
Dzerzhinsk
NIZHNIY NOVGOROD
Ryazan'
Tula
Kaluga
Bryansk
Orel
Kursk
Lipetsk
Tambov
Voronezh
Belgorod
Smolensk
Vitsyebsk
Mahilyow
Homyel'
Hrodna
Brest
Kaunas
Klaipėda
Liepāja
Daugavpils
Gdańsk
Gdynia
Kaliningrad
Bydgoszcz
Łódź
Białystok
Lublin
Kraków
Katowice
Częstochowa
L'viv
Zhytomyr
Chernihiv
Sumy
KHARKIV
Poltava
Cherkasy
Kirovohrad
Kryvyy Rih
DNIPROPETROVS'K
Dniprodzerzhyns'k
Zaporizhzhya
DONETS'K
Makiyivka
Luhans'k
Mariupol'
Taganrog
ROSTOV-NA-DONU
Novocherkassk
Mykolayiv
ODESA (ODESSA)
Kherson
Simferopol'
Sevastopol'
Kerch
Krasnodar
Stavropol'
VOLGOGRAD
Cluj-Napoca
Constanţa
Galaţi
Brăila
Ploieşti
Pskov
Novgorod
Lake Peipus
Ladozhskoye Ozero (Lake Ladoga)
Onezhskoye Ozero
Vänern
Vättern

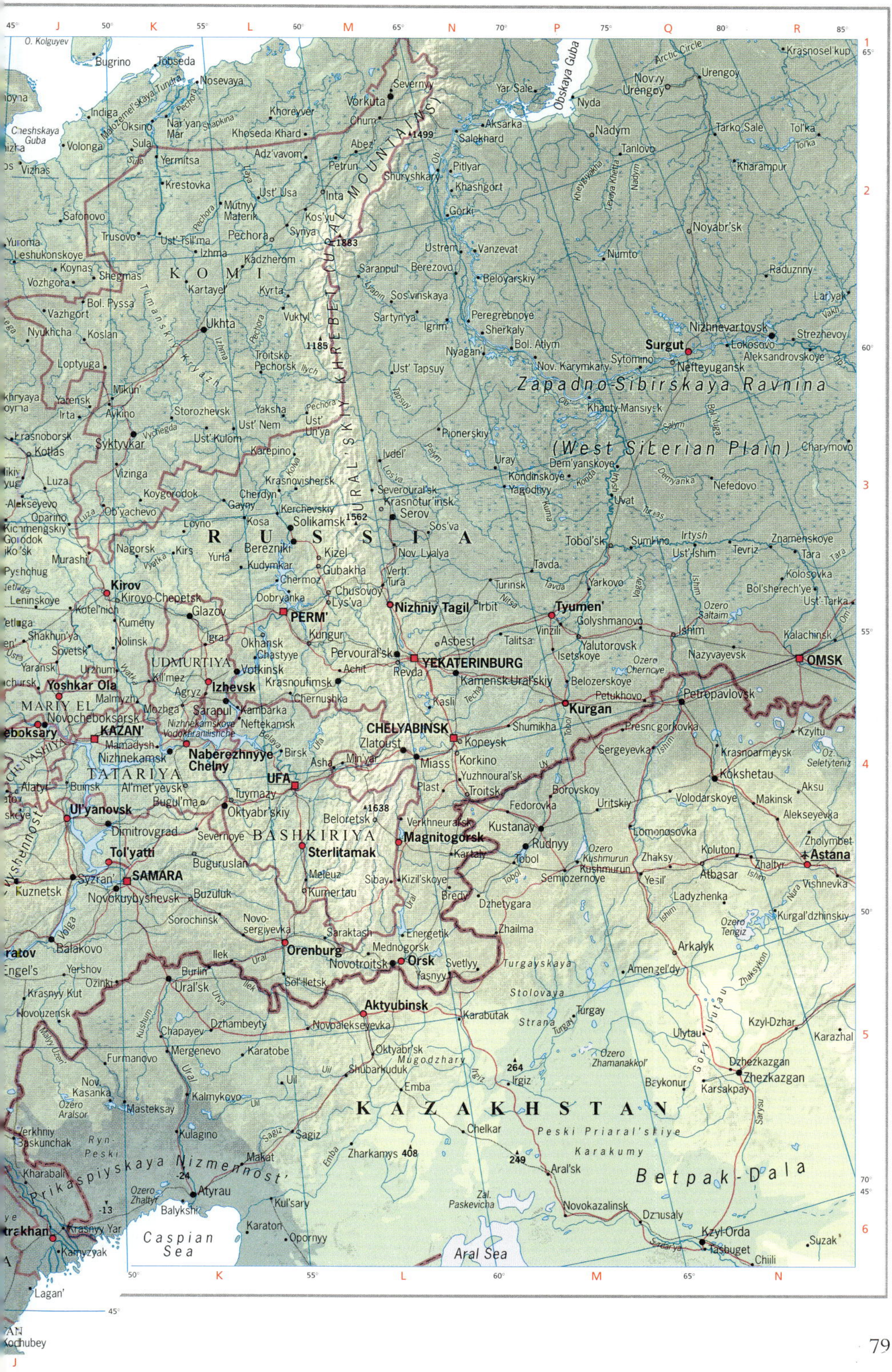

O. Kolguyev
Bugrino
Tobseda
Nosevaya
Indiga
Chëshskaya Guba
Volonga
Nar'yan Mar
Khoreyver
Khoseda Khard
Vorkuta
Severnyy
Yermitsa
Krestovka
Adz'vavom
Petrun
Abez
Chum
Inta
Ust' Usa
Mutnyy Materik
Pechora
Kos'yu
Synya
Kadzherom
Safonovo
Trusovo
Ust'-Tsil'ma
Izhma
Yuroma
Leshukonskoye
Koynas
Shegmas
Vozhgora
K O M I
Kartayel'
Kyrta
Bol. Pyssa
Vazhgort
Nyukhcha
Koslan
Ukhta
Vuktyl'
Loptyuga
Troitsko-Pechorsk
Mikun'
Yarensk
Irta
Aykino
Storozhevsk
Yaksha
Syktyvkar
Ust' Kulom
Ust' Nem
Ust' Un'ya
Krasnoborsk
Kotlas
Vizinga
Karepino
Luza
Koygorodok
Alekseyevo
Ob'yachevo
Oparino
Cherdyn'
Gayny
Krasnovishersk
Kerchevskiy
Solikamsk
Loyno
Kosa
Nagorsk
Kirs
Yurla
Berezniki
Murashi
Kudymkar
Kizel
Gubakha
Chermoz
Chusovoy
Lys'va
Dobryanka
Kirov
Kirovo-Chepetsk
Leninskoye
Kotel'nich
Glazov
PERM'
Kumeny
Kungur
Nolinsk
Shakhun'ya
Sovetsk
Okhansk
Chastyye
Pervoural'sk
Votkinsk
UDMURTIYA
Yaranski
Urzhum
Kil'mez
Achit
Yoshkar Ola
Malmyzh
Agryz
Izhevsk
Krasnoufimsk
Chernushka
MARIY EL
Novocheboksarsk
Mozhga
Sarapul
Kambarka
Neftekamsk
KAZAN'
Mamadysh
Nizhnekamsk
Naberezhnyye Chelny
Birsk
CHUVASHIYA
TATARIYA
Al'met'yevsk
Buinsk
UFA
Asha
Tuymazy
Bugul'ma
Ul'yanovsk
Oktyabr'skiy
Dimitrovgrad
Severnoye
BASHKIRIYA
Beloretsk
Tol'yatti
Sterlitamak
SAMARA
Syzran'
Buguruslan
Meleuz
Kumertau
Kuznetsk
Novokuybyshevsk
Buzuluk
Sorochinsk
Novo-sergiyevka
Balakovo
Orenburg
Engel's
Yershov
Ozinki
Ilek
Burlin
Ural'sk
Sol'-Iletsk
Krasnyy Kut
Novouzensk
Dzhambeyty
Chapayev
Furmanovo
Mergenevo
Karatobe
Kalmykovo
Nov. Kasanka
Masteksay
Ozero Aralsor
Kulagino
Ryn-Peski
Prikaspiyskaya Nizmennost'
Makat
Sagiz
Atyrau
Ozero Zhaltyr
Balykshi
Krasnyy Yar
Kamyzyak
Caspian Sea
Karaton
Opornyy
Kul'sary
Lagan'
URAL'SKIY KHREBET (URAL MOUNTAINS)
1499
1883
1185
1562
1638
R U S S I A
Saranpul
Berezovo
Sos'vinskaya
Sartyn'ya
Igrim
Ust' Tapsuy
Ivdel'
Pionerskiy
Severoural'sk
Krasnotur'insk
Serov
Sos'va
Nov. Lyalya
Verkh. Tura
Nizhniy Tagil
Irbit
Turinsk
Tavda
Asbest
Talitsa
YEKATERINBURG
Revda
Kamensk-Ural'skiy
Kasli
CHELYABINSK
Kopeysk
Zlatoust
Miass
Korkino
Yuzhnoural'sk
Troitsk
Plast
Verkhneural'sk
Magnitogorsk
Kartaly
Sibay
Kizil'skoye
Bredy
Dzhetygara
Zhailma
Energetik
Mednogorsk
Novotroitsk
Orsk
Yasnyy
Svetlyy
Saraktash
Aktyubinsk
Novoalekseyevka
Karabutak
Oktyabr'sk
Mugodzhary
Shubarkuduk
Emba
Zharkamys
408
264
Irgiz
249
Chelkar
Aral'sk
Zal. Paskevicha
Aral Sea
K A Z A K H S T A N
Turgayskaya Stolovaya Strana
Turgay
Peski Priaral'skiye Karakumy
Betpak-Dala
Novokazalinsk
Dzhusaly
Kzyl-Orda
Tasbuget
Chiili
Suzak
Yar-Sale
Obskaya Guba
Nyda
Aksarka
Salekhard
Pitlyar
Khashgort
Shuryshkary
Gorki
Ustrem
Vanzevat
Beloyarskiy
Peregrebnoye
Sherkaly
Nyagan'
Bol. Atlym
Nov. Karymkary
Arctic Circle
Novyy Urengoy
Urengoy
Nadym
Tanlovo
Tarko Sale
Tol'ka
Kharampur
Noyabr'sk
Numto
Raduzhnyy
Lar'yak
Nizhnevartovsk
Surgut
Lokosovo
Strezhevoy
Aleksandrovskoye
Sytomino
Nefteyugansk
Zapadno-Sibirskaya Ravnina
Khanty-Mansiysk
(West Siberian Plain)
Uray
Dem'yanskoye
Kondinskoye
Yagodnyy
Nefedovo
Charymovo
Uvat
Tobol'sk
Sumkino
Ust'-Ishim
Tevriz
Znamenskoye
Tara
Kolosovka
Bol'sherech'ye
Ust'-Tarka
Yarkovo
Tyumen'
Vinzili
Golyshmanovo
Ozero Saltaim
Ishim
Kalachinsk
Yalutorovsk
Isetskoye
Nazyvayevsk
OMSK
Belozerskoye
Petukhovo
Petropavlovsk
Kurgan
Shumikha
Presnogorkovka
Kzyltu
Sergeyevka
Krasnoarmeysk
Kokshetau
Aksu
Borovskoy
Fedorovka
Uritskiy
Volodarskoye
Makinsk
Alekseyevka
Kustanay
Rudnyy
Lomonosovka
Tobol
Ozero Kushmurun
Kushmurun
Semiozernoye
Zhaksy
Koluton
Zhaltyr
Astana
Yesil'
Atbasar
Vishnevka
Ladyzhenka
Kurgal'dzhinskiy
Ozero Tengiz
Arkalyk
Amangel'dy
Kzyl-Dzhar
Karazhal
Ulytau
Ozero Zhamanakkol'
Baykonur
Karsakpay
Dzhezkazgan
Zhezkazgan
Gory Ulutau

Scale 1 : 45 100 000

0 500 1000 1500 2000 km

0 500 1000 miles

ATLANTIC OCEAN
Norwegian Sea
Arctic Circle
North Sea
Barents Sea
ARCTIC
Spitsbergen
Svalbard (Norway)
Zemlya Frantsa-Iosifa (Franz Josef Land)
Nordkapp
Novaya Zemlya
Karskoye More (Kara Sea)
White Sea
Ladozhskoye Ozero
LISBOA (LISBON)
LONDON
Oslo
Amsterdam
Stockholm
MADRID
PARIS
København (Copenhagen)
Helsinki
EUROPE
BERLIN
Arkhangel'sk
SANKT-PETERBURG (ST. PETERSBURG)
ALGER (ALGIERS)
WARSZAWA (WARSAW)
Mediterranean Sea
ROMA (ROME)
MOSKVA (MOSCOW)
KYYIV (KIEV)
TUNIS
NIZHNIY NOVGOROD
Ural'skiy Khrebet (Ural Mountains)
Zapadno-Sibirskaya Ravnina (West Siberian Plain)
Ob'
Yenisey
Tarābulus (Tripoli)
ODESA (ODESSA)
YEKATERINBURG
SAMARA
RUS
Athina (Athens)
Black Sea
ISTANBUL
OMSK
Tropic of Cancer
ANKARA
TURKEY
Caucasus
Volga
Ural
Astana
GEORGIA
T'BILISI
CYPRUS
ARMENIA
YEREVAN
KAZAKHSTAN
Caspian Sea
Aral Sea
Ozero Balkhash (Lake Balkhash)
Altai Mts
BEYROUTH (BEIRUT)
SYRIA
LEBANON
AZER-BAIJAN
EL QÂHIRA (CAIRO)
DIMASHQ (DAMASCUS)
BAKI (BAKU)
ISRAEL
UZBEKISTAN
Yerushalayim
AMMAN
ALMATY
ÜRÜMQI
AFRICA
JORDAN
IRAQ
TURKMENISTAN
TASHKENT
Bishkek
BAGHDĀD
Ashgabat (Ashkhabad)
KYRGYZSTAN
TEHRĀN (TEHERAN)
TAJIKISTAN
Dushanbe
Lake Nasser
KUWAIT
IRAN
K2 8611
Al Kuwayt (Kuwait)
KĀBUL
Hindu Kush
Karakoram
Kunlun Shan
Nile
JIDDAH (JEDDA)
AR RIYĀD (RIYADH)
AFGHANISTAN
Islamabad
Himalaya
Red Sea
Persian Gulf
BAHRAIN
El Khartum (Khartoum)
SAUDI ARABIA
QATAR
Abū Zabī (Abu Dhabi)
PAKISTAN
Indus
Asmara
U.A.E.
Gulf of Oman
DELHI
Mt. Everest 8848
NEPAL
New Delhi
KARACHI
Kathmandu
Rub' al Khālī (Empty Quarter)
Masqat (Muscat)
San'ā
YEMEN
OMAN
Ganges
ĀDĪS ĀBEBA (ADDIS ABABA)
'Adan (Aden)
Djibouti
Gulf of Aden
Arabian Sea
CALCUTTA
MUMBAI (BOMBAY)
INDIA
Suqutrā (Socotra) (Yemen)
Equator
Bay of Bengal
HYDERABAD
MUQDISHO (MOGADISHU)
CHENNAI (MADRAS)
Laccadive Is. (India)
INDIAN OCEAN
SRI LANKA
Colombo
MALDIVES
Male
Mahé Island
Victoria
COMOROS
SEYCHELLES

ALASKA (U.S.)
St. Lawrence I.
Bering Strait
Arctic Circle
O. Vrangelya
Bering Sea
Anadyr'
Aleutian Islands (U.S.)
Aleutian Trench
International Date Line
Tropic of Cancer
Novosibirskiye Ostrova
Vostochno-Sibirskaye More (East Siberian Sea)
More Laptevykh (Laptev Sea)
Khrebet Kolymskiy
Verkhoyanskiy Khrebet
Lena
Yakutsk
Kamchatka
Petropavlovsk-Kamchatskiy
Sea of Okhotsk
Sakhalin
Kuril'skiye Ostrova (Kuril Islands)
Kuril Trench
Stanovoy Khrebet
Amur
Ozero Baykal
PACIFIC OCEAN
Hokkaidō
SAPPORO
HARBIN
Vladivostok
JAPAN
Honshū
Ulaanbaatar
NORTH KOREA
Sea of Japan
TŌKYŌ
3776
Fuji-san
MONGOLIA
SHENYANG
P'YŎNGYANG
SŎUL (SEOUL)
ŌSAKA
Izu-shotō
Japan Trench
BEIJING
Gobi Desert
SOUTH KOREA
Shikoku
Nagasaki
Kyūshū
Ogasawara-shotō (Japan)
Kazan-rettō (Japan)
Wake I. (U.S.)
Huang He
QINGDAO
Yellow Sea
LANZHOU
East China Sea
Amami-Ōshima
Nansei-shotō (Ryukyu Islands)
Okinawa
SHANGHAI
Mariana Trench
Pohnpei
WUHAN
CHONGQING
Chang Jiang
FUZHOU
T'AI-PEI
TAIWAN
Northern Mariana Islands (U.S.)
Guam (U.S.)
Caroline Islands
Challenger Deep
11033
Equator
GUANGZHOU
HONG KONG
Luzon Strait
Luzon
HA NÔI (HANOI)
Mekong
Mt. Pulog
2929
Yap
OCEANIA
Hainan
Viangchan (Vientiane)
LAOS
VIETNAM
South China Sea
PHILIPPINES
MANILA
Samar
Philippine Trench
THAILAND
Mindoro
Cebu
Panay
Negros
Mindanao
Davao
Bismarck Sea
Palawan
Sulu Sea
CAMBODIA
Phnum Penh
Gulf of Thailand
HÔ CHI MINH (SAIGON)
G. Kinabalu
4094
Sabah
Celebes Sea
Halmahera
Biak
Puncak Jaya
5030
New Guinea
Irian Jaya
Bandar Seri Begawan
BRUNEI
MALAYSIA
Sarawak
Selat Makassar
Molucca Sea
Aru
Dolak
Torres Strait
Seram
MEDAN
KUALA LUMPUR
Borneo
Sulawesi (Celebes)
Buru
Banda Sea
Arafura Sea
Tanimbar
SINGAPORE
Sumatera (Sumatra)
Banjarmasin
Buton
Gulf of Carpentaria
Kepulauan Mentawai
INDONESIA
Timor
Java Sea
Flores
Sumba
SURABAYA
Sumbawa
JAKARTA
Jawa (Java)
Bali
Lombok
Timor Sea

Scale 1 : 18 900 000

0 200 400 600 km

0 100 200 300 miles

BARENTS SEA
Karskoye More (Kara Sea)
More Laptevykh (Laptev Sea)
Pechorskoye More
Beloye More (White Sea)
RUSSIA
SAKHA
KOMI
NORWAY
Novaya Zemlya
Severnaya Zemlya
Zemlya Frantsa-Iosifa (Franz Josef Land)
Zapadno-Sibirskaya Ravnina (West Siberian Plain)
Sredne-Sibirskoye Ploskogor'ye
Poluostrov Taymyr
Poluostrov Yamal
Gydanskiy Poluostrov
Kol'skiy Poluostrov
Obskaya Guba
Yeniseyskiy Kryazh
Ural
Arctic Circle
Murmansk
Arkhangel'sk
Severodvinsk
Vorkuta
Noril'sk
Dudinka
Dikson
Salekhard
Nadym
Surgut
Nizhnevartovsk
Khanty-Mansiysk
Syktyvkar
Ukhta
Pechora
Kirov
PERM'
Yoshkar Ola
Cheboksary
Nizhniy Tagil
Bratsk
Tiksi
Khatanga
Ust'-Ilimsk
Ob'
Yenisey
Lena
Pechora
Ostrov Vaygach
Ostrov Kolguyev
Ostrov Belyy
Ostrov Vize
Ostrov Ushakova
Ostrov Oktyabr'skoy Revolyutsii
Ostrov Bol'shevik
Ostrov Komsomolets
Bjørnøya (Bear Island) (Norway)
Zemlya Aleksandry
Zemlya Vil'cheka
Mys Zhelaniya
Gora Kamen 2037
Gora Yenashimskiy Polkan 1104
Nordkapp
Varangerfjorden

Asia: Northwest

KAZAKHSTAN
MONGOLIA
CHINA
UZBEKISTAN
TURKMENISTAN
KYRGYZSTAN
TAJIKISTAN
AFGHANISTAN
PAKISTAN
IRAN
NOVOSIBIRSK
OMSK
CHELYABINSK
SAMARA
UFA
ALMATY
TASHKENT
ÜRÜMQI
Astana
Bishkek
Dushanbe
Ashgabat (Ashkhabad)
MASHHAD
Caspian Sea
Aral Sea
Tarim Pendi
Betpak-Dala
Karakumy
Kyzylkum

Scale 1 : 18 900 000

0 200 400 600 km

0 100 200 300 miles

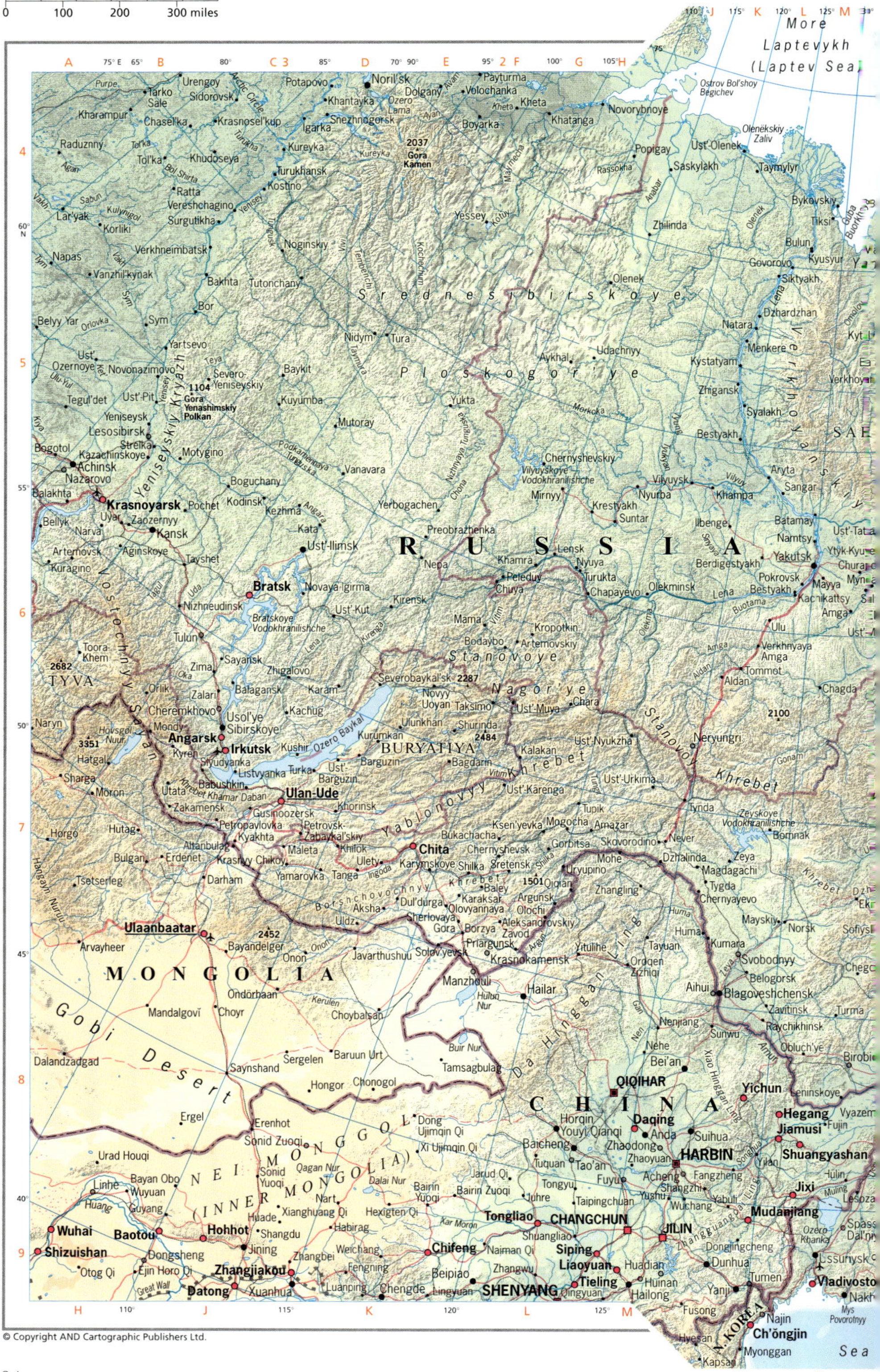

RUSSIA
MONGOLIA
CHINA
TYVA
BURYATIYA
N. KOREA
NEI MONGGOL (INNER MONGOLIA)
Srednesibirskoye Ploskogor'ye
Stanovoye Nagor'ye
Stanovoy Khrebet
Yablonovyy Khrebet
Vostochnyy Sayan
Yeniseyskiy Kryazh
Verkhoyanskiy
Gobi Desert
Da Hinggan Ling
More Laptevykh (Laptev Sea)
Ozero Baykal
Bratskoye Vodokhranilishche
Vilyuyskoye Vodokhranilishche
Zeyskoye Vodokhranilishche
Noril'sk
Dudinka
Khatanga
Tiksi
Krasnoyarsk
Achinsk
Kansk
Bratsk
Ust'-Ilimsk
Angarsk
Irkutsk
Ulan-Ude
Chita
Yakutsk
Mirnyy
Lensk
Neryungri
Blagoveshchensk
Svobodnyy
Ulaanbaatar
Darhan
Choybalsan
Manzhouli
Hailar
Qiqihar
Daqing
Harbin
Jilin
Changchun
Siping
Tieling
Shenyang
Chifeng
Tongliao
Hohhot
Baotou
Wuhai
Shizuishan
Datong
Zhangjiakou
Chengde
Yichun
Hegang
Jiamusi
Shuangyashan
Jixi
Mudanjiang
Vladivostok
Ch'ŏngjin
Great Wall
2037 Gora Kamen
1104 Gora Yenashimskiy Polkan
2682
3351
2452
2287
2484
2100
1501

Asia: Northeast

Ostrov Vrangelya
Vostochno-Sibirskoye More
(East Siberian Sea)
Novosibirskiye Ostrova
(New Siberian Islands)
Chukchi Sea
Bering Strait
Arctic Circle
Diomede Islands
King Island
ALASKA (U.S.)
St. Lawrence Island
St. Matthew Island
Proliv Longa
Vankarem
Enurmino
Uelen
Lavrentiya
Val'karay
Uvargin
Polyarnyy
Mys Shelagskiy
Pevek
Chaunskaya Guba
Mal. Baranikha
Ust' Chaun
Chukotskiy Khrebet
Egvekinot
Zaliv Kresta
Uel'kal
Chukotskiy Poluostrov
Provideniya
Nunligram
Anadyrskiy Zaliv
Ugol'nyye Kopi
Anadyr'
Beringovskiy
Mys Navarin
Ambarchik
Stanovaya
Cherskiy
Kolymskaye
Anyuysk
Chimchememel'
Markovo
Kolymskaya Nizmennost'
Ozero Ozhogino
Ozhogino
Druzhina
Belaya Gora
Srednekolymsk
Bur-Khaybyt
Suordakh
Khonuu
Yukagirskoye Ploskogor'ye
Shcherbakovo
Yugo-Tala
Zyryanka
Dzhigudzhak
Kolymskiy Khrebet
Ayanka
Khatyrka
Bering Sea
Gora Ledyanaya
Achayvayam
Olyutorskiy
Mys Olyutorskiy
Olyutorskiy Zaliv
Tilichiki
Ust'-Penzhino
Mikino
Tylkhoy
Gizhiga
Nayakhan
Gora Pobeda
Khrebet Cherskogo
Ust'-Nera
El'ginskiy
Artyk
Khudzhakh
Seymchan
Omsukchan
Susuman
Debin
Orotukan
Strelka
Pik Aborigen
Talaya
Atka
Tomtor
Khrebet Suntar Khayata
Ust'-omchug
Palatka
Magadan
Talon
Okurchan
Yamsk
Mys Tolstoy
Mys Alevina
Gizhiginskaya Guba
Penzhinskaya Guba
Il'pyrskiy
Ossora
Karaginskiy Zaliv
Ostrov Karaginskiy
Palana
Ugulan
Zaliv Shelikhova
Arka
Okhotsk
Ulya
Mys Erikan
Dzhugdzhur
Ayan
Mys Yuzhnyy
Ust'-Khayryuzovo
Ust'-Sopochnoye
Mys Sivuchiy
Komandorskiye Ostrova
Ostrov Beringa
Ostrov Mednyy
Aleutian Islands (U.S.)
Attu Island
Cape Wrangell
Buldir Island
Agattu Island
Klyuchi
Klyuchevskaya Sopka
Ust'-Kamchatsk
Kamchatskiy Zaliv
KAMCHATKA
Atlasovo
Sredinnyy Khrebet
Mil'kovo
Kronotskiy Zaliv
Petropavlovsk-Kamchatskiy
Shantarskiye Ostrova
Ostrov Bol. Shantar
Mys Elizavety
Poluostrov Shmidta
Sakhalinskiy Zaliv
Okha
Sea of Okhotsk
Oktyabr'skiy
Ozernovskiy
Ostrov Atlasova
Mys Lopatka
Ostrov Shumshu
Ostrov Paramushir
Tugur
Litke
Mago
Bol. Vlas'evo
Nikolayevsk-na-Amure
Takht
Bogorodskoye
Lazarev
Nogliki
De-Kastri
Polinyosipenko
Sofiysk
Komsomol'sk-na-Amure
Gurskoye
Aleksandrov-Sakhalinskiy
Sakhalin
Smirnykh
Poronaysk
Shakhtërsk
Uglegorsk
Zaliv Terpeniya
Mys Terpeniya
Makarov
Vanino
Tatarskiy Proliv
Tomari
Dolinsk
Nel'ma
Chekhov
Kholmsk
Yuzhno-Sakhalinsk
Korsakov
Svetlaya
Zaliv Aniva
Mys Kril'on
Mys Aniva
La Pérouse Strait
Ostrov Onekotan
Ostrov Shiashkotan
Ostrov Rasshua
Ostrov Simushir
Ostrov Urup
Kuril'skiye Ostrova (Kuril Islands)
Ostrov Iturup
Ostrov Kunashir
Shikotan-tō
Habomai-shoto
PACIFIC OCEAN
Rebun-tō
Rishiri-tō
Wakkanai
Shiretoko-misaki
Monbetsu
Asahikawa
Takikawa
Asahi-dake
Kitami
Nemuro
Otaru
Obihiro
Kushiro
SAPPORO
Tomakomai
Hokkaidō
Oshamambe
Muroran
Hiroo
Okushiri-tō
Esan-misaki
Erimo-misaki
Hakodate
Mutsu
Tsugaru Kaikyō
JAPAN

Scale 1 : 15 900 000

0 200 400 600 km

0 100 200 300 miles

MONGOLIA
GOBI DESERT
CHINA
NEI MONGGOL (INNER MONGOLIA)
Altai Mts
Ulaanbaatar (Ulan Bator)
Bayandelger
Ondörhaan
Herlen Gol
Choybalsan
Dzüünbulag
Baruun Urt
Sergelen
Chonogol
Hongor
Dong Ujm
Xi Ujim
Altay
Bayanhongor
Arvayheer
Böön Tsagaan Nuur
Aj Bogd Uul 3802
3772
3951
3590
Mandalgovĭ
Choyr
Sayns hand
Barkol
4925 Karlik Shan
Atlas Bogd 2695
Yandun
Urt
2517
2825
Dalandzadgad
Erenhot
Sonid Zuoqi
Xilinhot
Bairin
Ergel
Gaxun Nur
Saihan Toroi
Ejin Qi
Gongpoquan
Hongliuyuan
Anxi
Qiaowan
Dunhuang
Ruo Shui
Sonid Yuoqi
Qagan Nur
Da'ai Nur
Nart
Xianghuang Qi
Huade
Shangdu
Habirag
Weichang
Fengning
Bayan Obo
Urad Houqi
Wuyuan
Linhe
Guyang
Baotou
Wuchuan
Hohhot
Jining
Zhangbei
Zhangjiakou
Xuanhua
Yanqing
BEIJING (PEKING)
TANGS
Langfang
TIANJIN
Yumen
Jiayuguan
Jinta
6209
Great Wall
Bayan Mod
Dangne Nanshan
4840
Da Qaidam
6194
Qilian Shan
Har Hu
Zhangye
Wuhai
Dongsheng
Qingshuihe
Datong
Hunyuan
Shizuishan
Ejin Horo Qi
Shanyin
3058
Laiyuan
Zhuo Xian
Qilian
Obo
Jinchang
Otog Qi
Yinchuan
Fugu
Baode
Yuanping
Dai Xian
Baoding
Qinghai Hu
Gangca
Datong
Wuwei
Ulan
Menyuan
Gulang
Wuzhong
Yulin
Huang He (Yellow River)
Xinzhou
TAIYUAN
SHIJIAZHUANG
Cangzhou
Xining
Dulan
Qinghai Nanshan
Yongdeng
Gonghe
Zhongning
Suide
Lin Xian
Lishi
Yangquan
Dezhou
Botou
Dong
Zichang
Wubu
Yuci
Fenyang
Nangong
LANZHOU
Jiexiu
Xingtai
Binzhou
Gyaring Hu
Nigoring Hu
Huashixia
Huang He (Yellow River)
Linxia
Guyuan
Qingyang
Yan'an
Handan
Liaocheng
JINAN
Madoi
Xiahe
Jingning
Pingliang
Fu Xian
Linfen
Changzhi
Anyang
Tai'an
5200
Bayan Har Shan
Hancheng
Houma
Jincheng
Hebi
Qufu
Darlag
Xiwu
Tianshui
Wei
Min Xian
Tongchuan
Yuncheng
Xinxiang
Heze
Jining
Yushu
Sêrxü
Baoji
Xianyang
Sanmenxia
Jiaozou
Kaifeng
Zoigê
Feng Xian
Wudu
Weinan
XI'AN
Luoyang
ZHENGZHOU
Shangqui
Xuchang
Huaibei
Shangzhou
Hanzhong
Xiangcheng
Taikeng
Bo Xian
Pingdingshan
Songpan
Wen Xian
Shiquan
Xixia
Neixiang
Luohe
Zhoukou
Suqian
Xi Xiang
Ankang
Guoyang
Barkam
Qamdo
Garzê
Guangyuan
Han Shui
Shiyan
Jun Xian
Nanyang
Zhumadian
Xincai
Fuyang
Bengbu
Jiangyou
Wanyuan
Laohekou
Tongbai
Huaibin
Huainan
Luhuo
Jinsha
Bamda
Dawu
Deyang
Mianyang
Jialing Jiang
Xiangfan
Xinyang
Huangchuan
HEFEI
NANJING
Danba
CHENGDU
Nanchong
Daxian
Suizhou
Guangshui
Lu'an
Chao Xian
Markam
Litang
Kangding
Chang Jiang (Yangtze)
Badong
Jingmen
Yingcheng
Macheng
7514 Gongga Shan
Ya'an
Wanxian
Enshi
Yichang
Tianmen
Xiaogan
Fanchang
Leshan
Neijiang
Fuling
Jiangling
Shashi
WUHAN
Anqing
Dêqên
Zigong
CHONGQING
Mianyang
Huangshi
Xianning
Gongshan
Zhongdian
Jinsha
Yibin
Luzhou
Qijiang
Jinshi
Puqi
Jiujiang
Chang Jiang (Yangtze)
Mianning
Dayong
Yueyang
De'an
Jingdezhen
Weixi
Xichang
Songkan
Changde
Miluo
Xiushui
Yongxiu
Poyang Hu
Boyang
Lijiang
Jishou
Yiyang
NANCHANG
Shangrao
Salween
Bijie
Zunyi
Dukou
Wu
Huaihua
Xiangtan
CHANGSHA
Xinyu
Lushui
Weining
Lengshuijiang
Pingxiang
Yichun
Linchuan
Yongren
Liupanshui
GUIYANG
Shaoyang
Ji'an
Dali
Yuanmou
Anshun
Kaili
Hengyang
Baoshan
Qujing
Guanling
Duyun
Lengshuitan
Taihe
Jiangle
Chuxiong
KUNMING
Beipan
Leiyang
Yun Xian
Xingyi
Zixing
Changting
Nanpan
Guilin
Chenzhou
Ganzhou
Gengma
Lincang
Hechi
Longyan
Tropic of Cancer
Jinggu
Kaiyuan
Bose
Lipu
Pingle
Lian Xian
Shaoguan
Cangyuan
Yanshan
Liuzhou
He Xian
Zhangzhou
Yuanjiang
Gejiu
Funing
Meizhou
Lancang
Simao
Yuan
Amo
Pingguo
Heshan
Wuzhou
Qingyuan
Chaozhou
Jinghong
Binyang
Liu
Shantou
Jingxi
You
Nanning
Zhaoqing
GUANGZHOU
Lai Chau
Lao Cai
Cao Bang
VIETNAM
Cenxi
Foshan
Huizhou
Lufeng
Wuxu
Yu
Xi Jiang
Jiangmen
Dongguan
MYANMAR
Phongsali
LAOS
Tuan Giao
Tuyên Quang
Pingxiang
Qinzhou
Yulin
Zhongshan
Shenzhen
Macau
HONG KONG
Yangjiang
Hepu
Gulf of Tongking
Beihai
Suixi
Maoming
Zhanjiang
A B C D E F
1 2 3 4 5 6
95° E
100°
105°
110°
115°
45° N
40°
35°
30°
25°

Asia: East

SEA OF JAPAN
YELLOW SEA
EAST CHINA SEA
PACIFIC OCEAN
NORTH KOREA
SOUTH KOREA
JAPAN
TAIWAN
HOKKAIDŌ
HONSHŪ
SHIKOKU
KYŪSHŪ
QIQIHAR
Bei'an
Yichun
Hegang
Jiamusi
Suihua
Anda
Daqing
Lanxi
HARBIN
Acheng
Zhaoyuan
Baicheng
Tao'an
Tuquan
Horqin Youyi Qianqi
Da'an
Fuyu
Yushu
Wuchang
Shangzhi
Yabuli
Fangzheng
Jixi
Mudanjiang
Tongyu
Taipingchuan
Jarud Qi
Shulan
JILIN
CHANGCHUN
Jurhe
Tongliao
Shuangliao
Siping
Liaoyuan
Kangping
Faku
Zhangwu
Tieling
Dunhua
Yanji
Antu
Huadian
Huinan
Hailong
Hunjiang
Qingyuan
Fuxin
SHENYANG
FUSHUN
Benxi
Liaoyang
Jinzhou
ANSHAN
Haicheng
Yingkou
Dandong
Sinŭiju
Jinxi
Suizhong
Qinhuangdao
Wafangdian
Zhuanghe
Xinjin
Lüshun
DALIAN
Korea Bay
Yantai
Weihai
Rongcheng
Shandong
Bandao
Weifang
QINGDAO
Jiaonan
Rizhao
Lianyungang
Guanyun
Yancheng
Xinghua
Taizhou
Zhenjiang
Nantong
Changshu
Wuxi
Suzhou
SHANGHAI
Jiaxing
Haining
Yuyao
Zhongze
Shaoxing
NINGBO
Fenghua
Ninghai
Jinhua
Linhai
Huangyan
Lishui
Wenzhou
Fuding
Ningde
Matsu (Taiwan)
FUZHOU
T'ao-yuan
Chi-lung
T'AI-PEI
Hsin-chu
3884
Hsueh-Shan
T'ai-chung
Chang-hua
Chia-i
3950
Yu Shan
T'ai-tung
P'ing-tung
Oluan-pi
Bikin
Lesozavodsk
Ozero Khanka
Spassk-Dal'niy
Grodekovo
Dongjingcheng
Ussuriysk
Partizansk
Nakhodka
Mys Povorotnyy
Vladivostok
Tumen
Rudnaya Pristan'
Svetlaya
Sikhote Alin
Zhangguangcai Ling
Xiao Hinggan Ling
Da Hinggan Ling
Songhua
Muling
Najin
Hyesan
Kilchu
Kapsan
Kimch'aek
Manp'o
Ch'osan
Kanggye
Hamhŭng
Ch'ŏngp'yŏng
Pukch'ŏng
Pakch'ŏn
P'YŎNGYANG
Wŏnsan
Kosŏng
Songnim
Sariwŏn
Namp'o
Haeju
Kaesŏng
Sokch'o
SŎUL (SEOUL)
INCH'ŎN
Anyang
Suwŏn
Ch'ŏngju
Kangnŭng
Tonghae
Ulchin
Andong
TAEJŎN
P'ohang
Kunsan
Chŏnju
KWANGJU
PUSAN
Mokp'o
Sunch'ŏn
Cheju
Cheju do (South Korea)
Ullŭng do
Tok-tō
Korea Strait
Tsushima
Higashi-suidō
Oki-shotō
Dōgo
Zaliv Aniva
Mys Aniva
Mys Kril'on
La Pérouse Strait
Wakkanai
Rebun-tō
Rishiri-tō
Esashi
Monbetsu
Shiretoko-misaki
Ostrov Iturup
Ostrov Kunashir
Shikotan-tō
Abashiri
Haboro
Nayoro
Shibetsu
Asahikawa
2290
Asahi-dake
Kitami
Nemuro
Takikawa
Kushiro
Otaru
SAPPORO
Obihiro
Hiroo
Tomakomai
Erimo-misaki
Oshamambe
Okushiri-tō
Mori
Muroran
Esan-misaki
Esashi
Hakodate
Matsumae
Tsugaru-kaikyō
Mutsu
Aomori
Hachinohe
Hirosaki
Noshiro
Ōdate
Morioka
Akita
Hanamaki
Ichinoseki
Kamaishi
Sakata
Furukawa
Ishinomaki
Shinjō
Yamagata
Sendai
Niigata
Fukushima
Ryōtsu
Sado-shima
Kōriyama
Iwaki
Suzu-misaki
Nanao
Jōetsu
Nagano
Utsunomiya
Mito
Toyama
Kanazawa
Maebashi
Kashima
Matsumoto
Fukui
Kōfu
TŌKYŌ
YOKOHAMA
Tsuruoka
Fuji-san
3776
Gifu
NAGOYA
Shizuoka
Shimoda
Izu-shotō
Miyake-jima
Hachijō-jima
Tottori
KYŌTO
Yonago
Izumo
Chūgoku-sanchi
ŌSAKA
Suzuka
Hamamatsu
Okayama
KŌBE
Matsusaka
Hamada
HIROSHIMA
Takamatsu
Wakayama
Tokushima
Shiono-misaki
Hōfu
Matsuyama
Kōchi
Nakamura
KITA-KYŪSHŪ
Shimonoseki
FUKUOKA
Kurume
Ōita
Sasebo
Isahaya
Kumamoto
Goto-rettō
Fukue-jima
Nagasaki
Nobeoka
Yatsushiro
Miyazaki
Akune
Miyakonojō
Kagoshima
Kanoya
Makurazaki
Ōsumi-shotō
Tanega-shima
Yaku-shima
Amami-Ōshima
Naze
Nansei-shotō (Ryukyu Islands)
Nago
Okinawa
Naha
Sakishima-shotō
Tropic of Cancer
Myōjin
Sumisu-jima
Tori-shima
Sōfu-gan
120°
125°
130°
135°
140°
145°
45°
40°
35°
30°
25°
G
H
J
K
L
M
1
2
3
4
5
6

Scale 1 : 7 900 000

0 100 200 300 km

0 50 100 150 miles

RUSSIA
CHINA
NORTH KOREA
SOUTH KOREA
SEA
JAPAN
Korea Bay
Yellow Sea
East China Sea
Korea Strait
SHIKOKU
KYŪSHŪ
CHANGCHUN
JILIN
SHENYANG
FUSHUN
ANSHAN
Mudanjiang
Jixi
Tongliao
Siping
Liaoyuan
Tieling
Liaoyang
Benxi
Yingkou
Dandong
Wafangdian
Sinŭiju
Hunjiang
Tonghua
Yanji
Vladivostok
Ussuriysk
Nakhodka
Ch'ŏngjin
Kimch'aek
Hamhŭng
Wŏnsan
P'YŎNGYANG
Namp'o
Kaesŏng
SŎUL (SEOUL)
INCH'ŎN
Puch'ŏn
Songnam
Anyang
Suwŏn
Wŏnju
Ch'ŏngju
TAEJŎN
Kunsan
Ch'ŏnju
TAEGU
P'ohang
Ulsan
PUSAN
Masan
KWANGJU
Mokp'o
Sunch'ŏn
Chinju
Yŏsu
Cheju
Cheju do (South Korea)
Ullŭng do
Paekdu San 2750
Mt. Tuun 2487
Ozero Khanka
HIROSHIMA
Fukuyama
Okayama
Kurashiki
Himeji
Akashi
ŌSAKA
KŌBE
KYŌTO
Matsue
Tottori
Takamatsu
Tokushima
Matsuyama
Kōchi
Shimonoseki
KITA-KYŪSHŪ
FUKUOKA
Kurume
Ōita
Nagasaki
Kumamoto
Miyazaki
Kagoshima
Nobeoka
Sasebo
Saga
Tsushima
Iki
Gotō-rettō
Ōsumi-shotō
Yaku-shima
Tanega-shima
Oki-shotō

Japan and Korea

J
138°
K
140°
L
142°
M
144°
N
146°
P
148°
Q
150°
R
1
2
3
4
5
6
7
8
44°
42°
40°
38°
36°
34°
32°
30°
Sea of Okhotsk
Ostrov Iturup
1819
Ostrov Kunashir
Yuzhno Kuril'sk
Shikotan-tō
Shibotsu-jima
Wakkanai
Sōya-misaki
Rebun-tō
Rishiri-tō
Hamatonbetsu
Esashi
Teshio
Otoineppu
Omū
Okoppe
Haboro
Nayoro
Monbetsu
Shiretoko-misaki
Abashiri
Rausu
Shibetsu
Rumoi
Asahikawa
Asahi-dake
2290
Kitami
Shibetsu
Kussharo-ko
Takikawa
Furano
Nemuro
Shakotan-misaki
Ishikari-wan
Otaru
Iwamizawa
Kamoenai
SAPPORO
Ikeda
Akkeshi
Kushiro
Obihiro
Kutchan
Shikotsu-ko
Tomakomai
Oshamambe
Date
HOKKAIDŌ
Setana
Uchiura-wan
Muroran
Monbetsu
Hiroo
Okushiri-tō
Yakumo
Mori
Urakawa
Erimo-misaki
Kamiiso
Esashi
Esan-misaki
Hakodate
Ō-shima
Matsumae
Ōma
Shiriya-zaki
Tsugaru-kaikyō
Mutsu
Kodomari-misaki
Mutsu-wan
Yokohama
Aomori
Noheji
Ajigasawa
Hirosaki
Hachinohe
Henashi-zaki
Ōdate
Ninohoe
Kuji
Noshiro
Fudai
Morioka
Akita
Miyako
Hanamaki
Honjō
Yokote
Kamaishi
Kitakami
2230
Ichinoseki
Kesennuma
Sakata
Shinjō
Tsuruoka
Furukawa
Ishinomaki
Kinka-san
Yamagata
Sendai
Ryōtsu
Sadoga-shima
Shibata
Yonezawa
Niigata
2105
Sōma
Fukushima
Haramachi
Sanjō
Suzu-misaki
Nagaoka
Aizu-wakamatsu
Kōriyama
Kashiwazaki
Tajima
HONSHŪ
Jōetsu
Shirakawa
Nanao
Mikuni-sammyaku
Kuroiso
Iwaki
Nagano
Toyama
Utsunomiya
Hitachi
Kanazawa
Maebashi
Kiryu
Ueda
Oyama
Mito
3180
Takasaki
Matsumoto
Tsuchiura
JAPAN
PACIFIC OCEAN
Okaya
Takayama
Kawagoe
TŌKYŌ
Chōshi
Hachiōji
Funabashi
Kōfu
Chiba
Inubō-zaki
3192
YOKOHAMA
Iida
Fuji-san 3776
KAWASAKI
NAGOYA
3120
Yokosuka
Katsuura
Toyota
Numazu
Sagami-nada
Tateyama
Suzuka
Shizuoka
Nojima-zaki
Fujieda
Shimoda
Matsusaka
Hamamatsu
Omae-saki
Ise
Nii-jima
Izu-shotō
Kōzu-shima
Miyake-jima
Mikura-jima
Hachijō-jima
Aoga-shima
Sumisu-jima
Tori-shima

Scale 1 : 15 900 000

0 200 400 600 km

0 100 200 300 miles

BHUTAN
INDIA
BANGLADESH
MYANMAR (BURMA)
LAOS
THAILAND
CAMBODIA
VIETNAM
CHI
MALAY
INDONESIA
SINGAPORE
Tashigang
Hapoli
Pangin
Zayu
Deqen
Dibrugarh
Tinsukia
Itanagar
Brahmaputra
Jorhat
Barpeta
Nagaon
Golaghat
Goalpara
Guwahati
Shillong
Dimapur
Kohima
Sylhet
Silchar
Imphal
Bhairab Bazar
Agartala
Tropic of Cancer
Comilla
Feni
Aizawl
Karnafuli Reservoir
Rangamati
Kalemyo
Saiha
Haka
CHITTAGONG
Cox's Bazar
Teknaf
Paletwa
3053 Mt. Victoria
Pakokku
Sittwe
Monywa
MANDALAY
Amarapura
Kyaukse
Myingyan
Meiktila
Taunggyi
Chauk
Magwe
Minbu
Taungdwingyi
Ramree Island
Cheduba Island
Sandoway
Kyeintali
Taungup
Pyè
Irrawaddy
Henzada
Letpadan
Pathein
Insein
YANGON (RANGOON)
Bogale
Pegu
Cape Negrais
Mouths of the Irrawaddy
Bay of Bengal
Gulf of Martaban
Preparis North Channel
Preparis Island
Preparis South Channel
Coco Island
Coco Channel
North Andaman
Andaman Islands (India)
Middle Andaman
Ritchie's Archipelago
South Andaman
Duncan Passage
Little Andaman
Andaman Sea
Ten Degree Channel
Car Nicobar
Katchall
Little Nicobar
Nicobar Islands (India)
Great Nicobar
Sabang
Banda Aceh
Lhokseumawe
Bireun
Takengon
Langsa
Meulaboh
SUMATERA (SUMATRA)
3145 Gunung Leuser
MEDAN
INDIAN OCEAN
Sibigo
Simeulue
Sinabang
Danau Toba
Singkilbaru
Barus
Sibolga
Gunungsitoli
Nias
Tebingtinggi
Pematangsiantar
Prapat
Balige
Kotapinang
Dumai
Duri
Tazungdam
Gongshan
Zhongdian
Xichang
Putao
Weixi
Tabong
Maingkwan
Lijiang
Dukou
Chindwin
Myitkyina
Lushui
Salween
Dali
Yongren
Hopin
Baoshan
Bhamo
Katha
Mawlaik
Wandingzhen
Mong Yu
Yun Xian
Lincang
Kalewa
Kanbalu
Mabein
Hsweni
Lashio
Shwebo
Mogok
Gengma
Cangyuan
Jinggu
Mong Yai
Mongkung
Kunhing
Kengtung
Lancang
Simao
Jinghong
Wan Hsa-la
Loikaw
Toungoo
Pasawng
Papun
Thaton
Moulmein
Kawkareik
Ye
Tavoy
Mergui
Mergui Archipelago
Kawthaung
Chiang Rai
Mae Hong Son
Chiang Mai
Mae Sariang
Lampang
Siri Kit Dam
Nan
Uttaradit
Tak
Nam Ping
Phitsanulok
Phichit
Nakhon Sawan
Chainat
Chao Phraya
Sangkhla Buri
Chaiyaphum
Nakhon Ratchasima
Sara Buri
Ayutthaya
KRUNG THEP (BANGKOK)
Rat Buri
Phet Buri
Samut Songkhram
Bight of Bangkok
Pattaya
Rayong
Chanthaburi
Aranyaprathet
Ban Hua Hin
Prachuap Khiri Khan
Bang Saphan Yai
Chumphon
Ranong
Ko Chang
Gulf of Thailand
Ko Samui
Surat Thani
Takua Pa
Phuket
Krabi
Nakhon Si Thammarat
Thung Song
Phatthalung
Trang
Thale Luang
Songkhla
Hat Yai
Pattani
Satun
Yala
Narathiwat
Langkawi
Alor Setar
Sungei Petani
George Town
Pinang
Kota Bharu
Kuala Kerai
Taiping
Gerik
G. Korbu 2182
Kuala Terengganu
Ipoh
Dungun
Kuala Lipis
Malay Peninsula
Kuantan
Bentong
Temerloh
KUALA LUMPUR
Seremban
Segamat
Strait of Malacca
Melaka
Keluang
Muar
Batu Pahat
Johor Bahru
Kunming
Chuxiong
Yuanmou
Qujing
Xingyi
Gejiu
Kaiyuan
Yuanjiang
Yanshan
Funing
Lao Cai
Lai Chau
Phongsali
Louang Namtha
Muang Sing
Muang Xai
Muang Khoua
Tuan Giao
Son La
Viêt Tri
Moc Chau
Xam Nua
Mekong
Louangphrabang
Ban Ban
Xiangkhoang
Viangchan (Vientiane)
Muang Pakxan
Chiang Khan
Nong Khai
Udon Thani
Sakhon Nakhon
Loei
Chum Phae
Khon Kaen
Mukdahan
Savannakhet
Roi Et
Lam Chi
Khemmarat
Ubon Ratchathani
Suwannaphum
Mae Nam Mun
Surin
Det Udom
Pakxé
Attapu
M. Khong
Sisophon
Siĕmréab
Batdâmbâng
Tônlé Sab
Stœng Trêng
Kampong Cham
Krông Kaôh Kong
Phnum Penh
Tay Ninh
Sihanoukville
Dao Phu Quoc
Long Xuyen
Rach Gia
Cân Tho
My Tho
Bac Liêu
Ca Mau
Nam Can
Mouths of the Mekong
Côn Son
HÔ CHI MINH (SAIGON)
Vung Tau
Chon Thanh
Biên Hoa
Bao Lôc
Phan Thiêt
Phan Rang
Da Lat
Cam Ranh
Nha Trang
Ninh Hoa
Buôn Mê Thuôt
Tuy Hoa
Plây Cu
Kon Tum
Virôchey
Qui Nhon
Quang Ngai
Hôi An
Da Năng
Huê
Quang Tri
Dông Hôi
Muang Khammouan
Muang Phin
Khamkeut
Ha Tinh
Vinh
Thanh Hoa
Nam Dinh
HAI PHONG
HA NÔI (HANOI)
Thai Nguyen
Tuyen Quang
Cao Bang
Tien Yen
Hon Gai
Mong Cai
Gulf of Tongking
Pingxiang
Nanning
Qinzhou
Beihai
Hepu
Zhanjiang
Haikou
Dan Xian
Hainan
Dongfang
Tongshi
Sanya
Wuxu
Jingxi
Bose
Heshan
Pingguo
Binyang
Liuzhou
Guilin
Yangshuo
Hechi
Nanpan
Xingyi
Guanling
Duyun
Kaili
GUIYANG
Anshun
Liupanshui
Weining
Bijie
Zunyi
Huaihua
Jishou
Jinsha
Beipan
Kepulauan Natuna
Laut
Natuna Besar
Panarik
Subi Besar
Jemaja
Kepulauan Anambas (Indonesia)
Tanjung Datu
Sambas
Pemangkat
Singkawang
Kuching
25° N
20°
15°
10°
5°
95° E
100°
105°
110°
A
B
C
D
1
2
3
4
5
6

Asia: Southeast

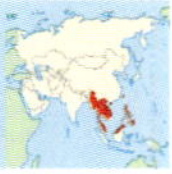

EAST CHINA SEA
Nansei-shotō (Ryukyu Islands)
Nago
Okinawa
Naha
JAPAN
Sakishima-shotō
Tropic of Cancer
Xiangtan
CHANGSHA
Xinyu
Linchuan
Shangrao
Pucheng
Wenzhou
Lianyuan
Lengshuijiang
Yichun
Pingxiang
Fuding
Hengyang
Ji'an
Taihe
Jiangle
Nanping
Ningde
Leiyang
Matsu (Taiwan)
Zixing
Changting
Yong'an
FUZHOU
Chenzhou
Ganzhou
Putian
Longyan
Quanzhou
Chi-lung
T'ao-yuan
T'AI-PEI
Hsin-chu
Shaoguan
Lian Xian
Zhangzhou
Chinmen (Taiwan)
3884
Hsueh-Shan
He Xian
Meizhou
Xiamen
T'ai-chung
Chang-hua
Qingyuan
Chaozhou
Chia-i
3950
Yu Shan
TAIWAN
Wuzhou
Shantou
GUANGZHOU
Huizhou
Lufeng
T'ai-nan
T'ai-tung
Zhaoqing
Dongguan
Shanwei
Jiangmen
Foshan
Shenzhen
KAO-HSIUNG
P'ing-tung
Zhongshan
HONG KONG
Macau
Yangjiang
Oluan-pi
Luzon Strait
Batan Islands
Dongsha Qundao (Pratas) (China)
PACIFIC OCEAN
Balintang Channel
Babuyan Islands
Claveria
San Vicente
Laoag
Aparri
Kabugao
Lal-Lo
Tuguegarao
Vigan
Luzon
Ilagan
Bontoc
San Fernando
Mt. Pulog
2929
Baguio
Santiago
Alaminos
Dagupan
San Carlos
Paracel Islands
Tarlac
Cabanatuan
Angeles
SOUTH CHINA SEA
Polillo Is.
Olongapo
QUEZON CITY
MANILA
Pasig
San Pablo
Daet
Nasugbu
Calauag
Cantanduanes
Virac
Batangas
Lucena
Lopez
Boac
Legaspi
Mamburao
Calapan
Mindoro
2488
Pinamalayan
Mount Baco
Masbate
Maasin
Catarman
Samar
Allen
Calbayog
Mindoro Strait
San Pedro
Catbalogan
Calamian Group
Coron
Nabas
Placer
Kalibo
Roxas
Tacloban
El Nido
Panay
Bogo
Ormoc
Leyte
Iloilo
Bacolod
Sogod
San Jose de Buenavista
Cebu
Libjo
Dinagat
Spratly Islands
Carcar
Talibon
Roxas
Bohol
Dapa
Palawan
Cauayan
Bais
Surigao
Puerto Princesa
Negros
Dumaguete
Butuan
Madrid
Tandag
Quezon
PHILIPPINES
Prosperidad
Dipolog
2560
Cagayan de Oro
Brooke's Point
Manukan
Liloy
Iligan
Malaybalay
Bislig
Sulu Sea
Balabac
Pagadian
Mindanao
Tagum
Sibuco
Cotabato
Davao
Balabac Strait
Zamboanga
Moro Gulf
2954
Mt. Apo
Mati
Kudat
Isabela
Tacurong
Polomolok
Cape San Agustin
Langkon
Kota Belud
4094
Basilan
Palimbang
General Santos
G. Kinabalu
Ranau
Jolo
Pangutaran Group
Glan
Kota Kinabalu
Sandakan
Sarangani Is.
SIA
Beaufort
SABAH
Tungku
Tawitawi
Lahad Datu
Kepulauan Nanusa
Bandar Seri Begawan
Bongao
Sulu Archipelago
Seria
Semporna
Kepulauan Karkaralong
Kalabakan
Kepulauan Talaud
BRUNEI
Gunung Mulu
2371
Tawau
Celebes Sea
Bareo
Sangir
INDONESIA
Tarakan
Kepulauan Sangir
Morotai
Bintulu
Belaga
Tanjungselor
2499
Molucca Sea
Daruba
Sibu
SARAWAK
Tanjungredeb
Sarikei
Kapit
INDONESIA
KALIMANTAN
2988
Muarawahau
Sangkulirang
E
F
G
H
J
115°
120°
125°
130°
25°
20°
15°
10°
5°
1
2
3
4
5
6

Scale 1 : 15 900 000

0 200 400 600 km
0 100 200 300 miles

THAILAND
MALAYSIA
SINGAPORE
BRUNEI
PHILIPPINES
INDONESIA
South China Sea
Sulu Sea
Celebes Sea
Java Sea
Flores Sea
INDIAN OCEAN
Strait of Malacca
Selat Makassar
Selat Karimata
Malay Peninsula
SUMATERA
BORNEO
KALIMANTAN
SARAWAK
SABAH
JAWA (JAVA)
Sulawesi (Celebes)
KUALA LUMPUR
SINGAPORE
JAKARTA
BANDUNG
SEMARANG
SURABAYA
PALEMBANG
MEDAN
Bandar Seri Begawan
Kota Kinabalu
Sandakan
Ipoh
George Town
Kuala Terengganu
Kuantan
Johor Bahru
Padang
Pekanbaru
Jambi
Bengkulu
Tanjungkarang Telukbetung
Banda Aceh
Pontianak
Kuching
Banjarmasin
Balikpapan
Samarinda
Ujung Pandang
Yogyakarta
Surakarta
Malang
Denpasar
Mataram

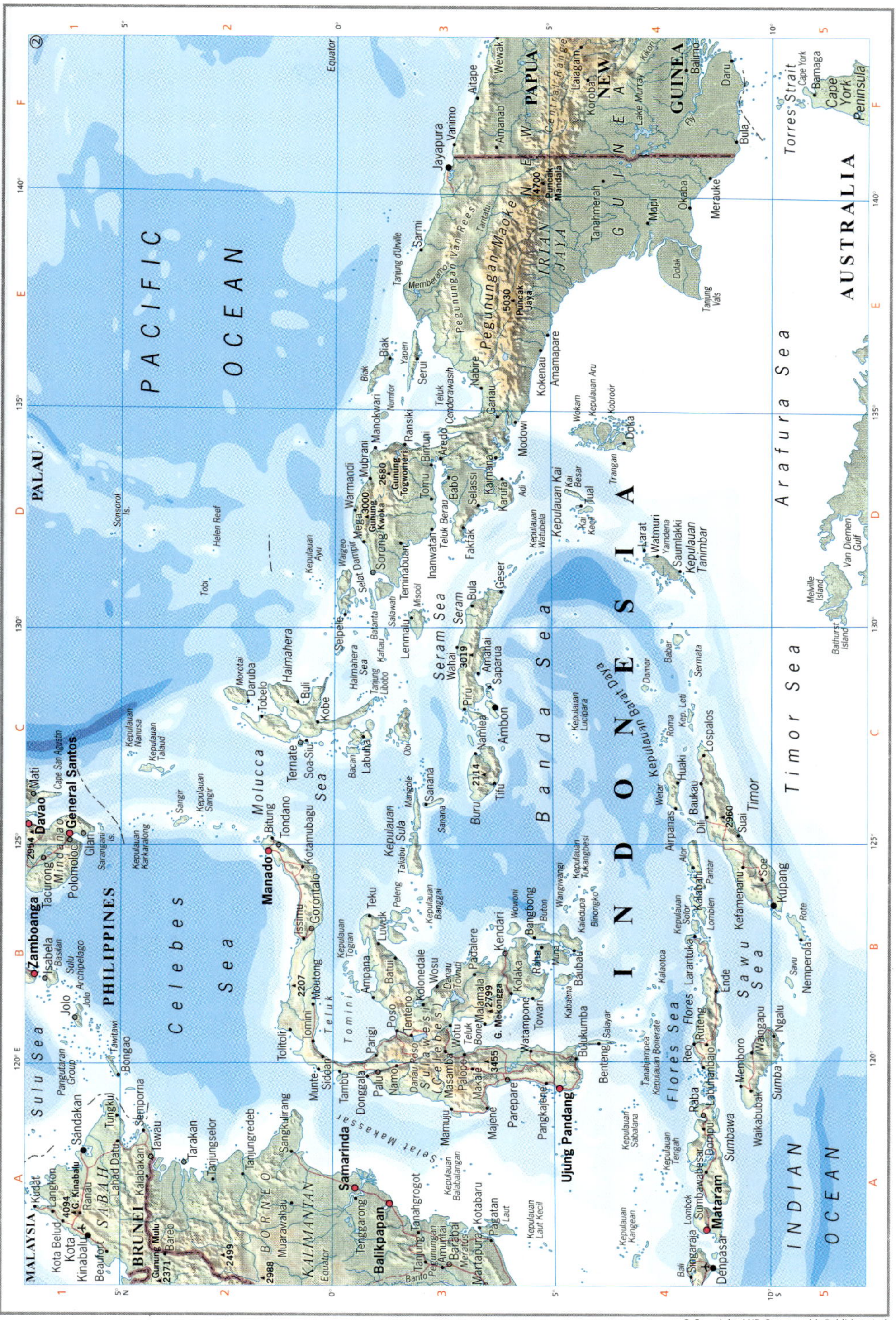

PACIFIC OCEAN
INDIAN OCEAN
Sulu Sea
Celebes Sea
Molucca Sea
Halmahera Sea
Seram Sea
Banda Sea
Flores Sea
Sawu Sea
Timor Sea
Arafura Sea
Torres Strait
Selat Makassar
Teluk Tomini
Teluk Cenderawasih
Equator
MALAYSIA
BRUNEI
PHILIPPINES
PALAU
INDONESIA
AUSTRALIA
PAPUA NEW GUINEA
SABAH
BORNEO
KALIMANTAN
IRIAN JAYA
NEW GUINEA
Sulawesi (Celebes)
Mindanao
Halmahera
Seram
Buru
Timor
Sumba
Sumbawa
Flores
Lombok
Bali
Pegunungan Maoke
Pegunungan Van Rees
Central Range
Cape York Peninsula
Kota Kinabalu
Sandakan
Tawau
Samarinda
Balikpapan
Banjarmasin
Ujung Pandang
Kendari
Manado
Gorontalo
Palu
Ternate
Sorong
Manokwari
Biak
Jayapura
Vanimo
Wewak
Merauke
Daru
Ambon
Kupang
Dili
Mataram
Denpasar
Zamboanga
Davao
General Santos
Jolo
Puncak Jaya 5030
Puncak Mandala 4700
G. Kinabalu 4094

Scale 1 : 15 900 000

0 200 400 600 km

0 100 200 300 miles

CHINA
Xizang Gaoyuan
(Plateau of Tibet)
Kunlun Shan
Hoh Xil Shan
Gangdisê Shan
HIMALAYA
NEPAL
BHUTAN
BANGLADESH
MYANMAR
(BURMA)
INDIA
PAKISTAN
AFGHANISTAN
JAMMU & KASHMIR
Karakoram
Thar Desert
Mouths of the Ganges
Tropic of Cancer
KABUL
Islamabad
LAHORE
DELHI
New Delhi
KATHMANDU
Thimphu
DHAKA
CALCUTTA
Lhasa
MANDALAY
CHITTAGONG
Mount Everest 8848
K2 8611

Asia: South

BAY OF BENGAL
ARABIAN SEA
INDIAN OCEAN
Coromandel Coast
Malabar Coast
Laccadive Islands
MALDIVES
SRI LANKA
Andaman Islands (India)
Nicobar Islands (India)
Ten Degree Channel
Nine Degree Channel
Eight Degree Channel
One and Half Degree Channel
Duncan Passage
Coco Channel
Preparis North Channel
Preparis South Channel
Mouths of the Irrawaddy
Mouths of the Krishna
Gulf of Mannar
Palk Strait
Cape Comorin
Dondra Head
Point Pedro
Equator
HYDERABAD
BANGALORE
CHENNAI (MADRAS)
MADURAI
COIMBATORE
VISHAKHAPATNAM
Vijayawada
Warangal
Guntur
Nellore
Pondicherry
Salem
Erode
Tiruchchirappalli
Tirunelveli
Tuticorin
Thiruvananthapuram (Trivandrum)
Kochi (Cochin)
Kozhikode (Calicut)
Mangalore
Mysore
Hubli
Kolhapur
Sangli
Solapur
Gulbarga
Bellary
Kurnool
Davangere
Vellore
Rajahmundry
Kakinada
Colombo
Kandy
Jaffna
Trincomalee
Galle
Matara
Male
Pathein
Bogale
Henzada

Scale 1 : 17 400 000

0 200 400 600 km

0 100 200 300 miles

Black Sea
Caspian Sea
Mediterranean Sea
Persian Gulf
Red Sea
Gulf of Aden
TURKEY
GEORGIA
ARMENIA
AZERBAIJAN
RUSSIA
SYRIA
LEBANON
ISRAEL
JORDAN
CYPRUS
IRAQ
KUWAIT
SAUDI ARABIA
BAHRAIN
QATAR
YEMEN
EGYPT
SUDAN
ERITREA
ETHIOPIA
DJIBOUTI
SOMALIA
ISTANBUL
ANKARA
T'BILISI
YEREVAN
BAKI (BAKU)
TEHRAN
BAGHDĀD
DIMASHQ (DAMASCUS)
BEYROUTH (BEIRUT)
Lefkosia (Nicosia)
Yerushalayim (Jerusalem)
'AMMĀN
EL QÂHIRA (CAIRO)
AR RIYĀD (RIYADH)
Al Kuwayt (Kuwait)
Al Manāmah
Ad Dawhah (Doha)
San'ā
Asmara
El Khartum (Khartoum)
Djibouti
Makkah (Mecca)
Al Madīnah (Medina)
JIDDAH (JEDDA)
'Adan (Aden)
HALAB (ALEPPO)
Tel Aviv-Yafo
EL ISKANDARÎYA (ALEXANDRIA)
Bādiyat ash Shām (Syrian Desert)
An Nafud
Ad Dahnā
Rub' al Khālī (Empty Quarter)
Nubian Desert
Sinai
Tropic of Cancer
Lake Nasser
Anadolu Dağları
Euphrates
Tigris
Nile

UZBEKISTAN
TURKMENISTAN
AFGHANISTAN
PAKISTAN
TAJIKISTAN
KYRGYZSTAN
CHINA
INDIA
IRAN
OMAN
JAMMU &
KASHMIR
TASHKENT
Namagan
Andizhan
Osh
Fergana
Samarkand
Bukhara
Dushanbe
Karshi
Termez
Navoi
Nukus
Urgench
Dashkhovuz
Ashgabat
(Ashkhabad)
Mary
MASHHAD
Neyshābūr
Herāt
Mazar-e Sharif
KABUL
Kandahār
Ghazni
Peshawar
Islamabad
Rawalpindi
Srinagar
LAHORE
FAISALABAD
Multan
Quetta
Sukkur
Hyderabad
KARACHI
Gwadar
Zāhedān
Kermān
Bandar-e Abbās
Sharjah
Abu Zabī
(Abu Dhabi)
Masqat
(Muscat)
Amritsar
LUDHIANA
Chandigarh
DELHI
New Delhi
Agra
JAIPUR
Jodhpur
Bikanar
Ajmer
Kota
Udaipur
AHMADABAD
VADODARA
SURAT
INDORE
Ujjain
Rajkot
Jamnagar
Bhavnagar
Porbandar
MUMBAI (BOMBAY)
KALYAN
PUNE
Nasik
Aurangābād
Kolhapur
Hubli
Kashi
Hotan
Karakumy
Peski
Kavir
Dasht-e Lut
Thar Desert
Hindu Kush
Gulf of Oman
Strait of Hormuz
Mouths of the Indus
ARABIAN
SEA
Tropic of Cancer

Scale 1 : 7 900 000

0 100 200 300 km

0 50 100 150 km

A B C D E F G
1 2 3 4 5 6 7
26° E 28° 30° 32° 34° 36°
44° N
42°
40°
38°
36°
34°
ROMANIA
BUCUREŞTI (BUCHAREST)
Urziceni
Slobozia
Ialomiţa
Danube
Babadag
Lacul Razim
Lacul Sinoie
Hârşova
Cernavodă
Medgidia
Constanţa
Mangalia
Fetesti
Călăraşi
Olteniţa
Titu
Bolintin Vale
Videle
Alexandria
Giurgiu
Zimnicea
Tutrakan
Silistra
Ruse
Tervel
Byala
Razgrad
Dobrich
Popovo
Novi Pazar
Balchik
Targovishte
Shumen
Veliko Turnovo
Provadiya
Varna
Nos Kaliakra
Trjavna
BULGARIA
Nova Zagora
Sliven
Aytos
Nesebur
Nos Emine
Stara Zagora
Yambol
Burgas
Pomorie
Burgaski Zaliv
Grudovo
Sozopol
Elkhovo
Malko Turnovo
Kharmanli
Rezovo
Edirne
Yildiz Dağlari
İğneada
Kirklareli
Kıyıköy
Babaeski
Saray
Karacaköy
İstanbul Boğazi (Bosporus)
Uzunköprü
Lüleburgaz
Evros
Hayrabolu
Çorlu
Silivri
İpsala
Malkara
Tekirdağ
Keşan
Yeşilköy
İSTANBUL
Şarköy
Marmara Denizi
Marmara Adası
Gelibolu
Erdek
Bandirma
Gebze
İzmit
Yalova
Gemlik
İznik
İznik Gölü
Çanakkale
Bursa
İnegöl
Ezine
Edremit
Balikesir
Lesvos
Ayvalik
Mytilini
Bergama
Plomari
Akhisar
Aliağa
Manisa
İZMIR
Salihli
Samos
Fournoi
Söke
Aydin
Milas
Leros
Kalymnos
Bodrum
Muğla
Gökova Körfezi
Kos
Nisyros
Datça
Marmaris
Dalaman
Tilos
Symi
Rodos
Fethiye
GREECE
Chalki
Lindos
Saria
Karpathos
Kattavia
Kasos
Megisti (Greece)
BLACK SEA
Yevpatoriya
Krym'
Simferopol'
UKRAINE
Kerch
Feodosiya
Sevastopol'
Sudak
Alushta
Balaklava
Yalta
Alupka
Anap
İnce Burun
Sinop
Cide
İnebolu
Ayancık
Bartın
Zonguldak
Kastamonu
Alaçam
Bafra Burun
Bafra
Samsun
Ereğli
Karasu
Safranbolu
Karrabük
Boyabat
Vezirköprü
Çarşamba
Düzce
Osmancık
Havza
Sakarya
Bolu
Gerede
Kurşunlu
Merzifon
Taşova
2400
Köroğlu Dağları
Çankiri
Amasya
Kizilirmak
Çorum
Turhal
Sakarya
Beypazari
Kalecik
Tokat
Eskişehir
ANKARA
Çerikli
Tavşanli
Kirikkale
Sorgun
Yildizeli
Kütahya
Bâlâ
Yerköy
Yozgat
Polatli
Simav
Sivrihisar
Kirşehir
Sarıkaya
Şarkişla
ANATOLIA
Kulu
Uşak
Emirdağ
Şereflikoçhisar
TURKEY
Afyon
Bünyan
Tuz Gölü
Cihanbeyli
Sandikli
Nevşehir
Kayseri
Pinarbaşi
Dinar
Eğridir Gölü
Akşehir
Aksaray
Yeşilhisar
Saimbeyli
Göksun
Denizli
Isparta
Burdur
Beyşehir
Beyşehir Gölü
Konya
Niğde
Bucak
2288
Ulukişla
Ereğli
Seyhan
Kahraman Maraş
Korkuteli
Bozkir
Kozan
Kadirli
Antalya
Karaman
Osmaniye
Serik
Elmali
Manavgat
Toros Dağlari
Tarsus
ADANA
Antalya Körfezi
Finike
Kumluca
Alanya
Mut
İçel (Mersin)
Karataş
İskenderun
Ermenek
Silifke
Kirikhan
Anamur
Antakya
Yayladaği
C. Apostolos Andreas
Aigialousa
Keryneia
Al Lādhiqīyah
Idlib
HALAB (ALEPPO)
C. Arnaoutis
Lefkosia (Nicosia)
Ammochostos (Famagusta)
Polis
Olympus
Troodos 1952
Baniyas
Hamāh
Pafos
C. Greko
Larnaka
Lemesos (Limassol)
CYPRUS
Tartūs
Tall Kalakh
Hims (Homs)
Al Hamīdīyah
Trâblous (Tripoli)
Halba
3087
Qornet es Saouda
2464
2659
MEDITERRANEAN SEA
BEYROUTH (BEIRUT)
2628
Zahlé
Tal'at Mūsá
An Nabk
LEBANON
Saïda
Qaraaoun
Soûr
Qatanā
Dūmā
DIMASHQ (DAMASCUS)

Turkey

RUSSIA
GEORGIA
ARMENIA
AZERBAIJAN
AZER.
IRAN
IRAQ
MESOPOTAMIA
CASPIAN
SEA
KALMYKIYA
ADYGEYA
KARACHAYEVO-CHERKESIYA
KABARDINO-BALKARIYA
SEVERNAYA OSETIYA
INGUSHETIYA
CHECHNYA
DAGESTAN
Krasnodar
Stavropol'
Armavir
Nevinnomyssk
Budennovsk
Neftekumsk
Kislovodsk
Pyatigorsk
Cherkessk
Maykop
Sochi
Sokhumi
Nal'chik
Vladikavkaz
Groznyy
Makhachkala
Kaspiysk
Derbent
Elbrus
Kazbek
Diklosmta
Kut'aisi
Batumi
Gori
T'BILISI
Rust'avi
Gyumri
Vanadzor
Hrazdan
Sevana Lich
YEREVAN
Mt. Ararat 5165
Gäncä
Mingäçevir
Sumqayıt
BAKI (BAKU)
Kür
Araz
Naxçıvan
Lankäran
Ardabil
TABRIZ
Orumiyeh
Maragheh
Zanjan
Rasht
Trabzon
Rize
Giresun
Ordu
Gumushane
Bayburt
Erzurum
Erzincan
Kars
Ağri
Van Gölü
Van
Tatvan
Bitlis
Muş
Bingöl
Elazığ
Malatya
Diyarbakır
Batman
Siirt
Mardin
Şanlıurfa
Adıyaman
Hakkari
Cizre
Al Qamishli
Al Hasakah
Ar Raqqah
Dayr az Zawr
Al Mawsil
Arbil
As Sulaymaniyah
Kirkuk
Tikrit
Samarra'
Ba'qubah
BAGHDAD
Ar Ramadi
Euphrates
Tigris
Kermanshah
Sanandaj
Bādiyat ash Shām (Syrian Desert)

Israel

Scale 1 : 3 900 000

0 50 100 150 km

0 25 50 75 miles

A
B
C
D
E
1
2
3
4
5
6
7
34° E
35°
36°
37°
38°
35° N
34°
33°
32°
31°
30°
CYPRUS
Lapithos
Akanthou
Keryneia
Lefkosia (Nicosia)
Lefkonikon
Trikomon
C. Eleaia
Ammochostos Bay
Mesaoria Plain
Ceasefire line
Ammochostos (Famagusta)
Paralimni
Aya Napa
C. Greko
Dhekelia
Larnaka
Vasilikos
Lemesos (Limassol)
MEDITERRANEAN
SEA
LEBANON
BEYROUTH (BEIRUT)
Jablah
Bāniyās
Al Qadmūs
Masyāf
Hamāh
Khān Shaykhūn
Khirbat Isrīyah
As Sa'ān
Salamīyah
1385
Jabal an Nuşayrīyah
Ţarţūs
Burj Şāfītā
Ar Rastan
Hims (Homs)
Tall Kalakh
Al Hamīdīyah
Bahrat Hims
Furqlus
Tiyās
Trâblous (Tripoli)
Halba
2216
Zgharta
3087
Qornet es Saouda
Hermel
Batroûn
Jbail
Joûnié
Qartaba
Ba'albek
Tal 'at Mūsá
2659
An Nabk
Al Qaryatayn
Bi'r Bazīrī
Yabrūd
2628
Jebel Liban
Jebel esh Sharqi
SYRIA
Aley
Zahlé
Jayrūd
Al Quţayfah
Sab' Abār
Az Zabadānī
Dūmā
Dumayr
Saïda
Jezzine
DIMASHQ (DAMASCUS)
Marjayoûn
Mt. Hermon
2814
Qaţanā
Soûr
Qiryat Shemona
Burāq
Al Qunayţirah
Nahariyya
As Sanamayn
Zefat
GOLAN HEIGHTS
'Akko
Karmi'el
Qiryat Motzkin
Sea of Galilee
Izra'
Shahbā'
Ghadīr Minqār
Hefa (Haifa)
Teverya
Qiryat Ata
1735
Nazareth
Irbid
As Suwaydā'
Jabal ad Durūz
Zikhron Ya'aqov
Afula
Dar'ā
Buşrá ash Shām
Hadera
Bet She'an
Husn
Ramtha
Şalkhad
Bādiyat ash Shām
(Syrian Desert)
Jenin
'Ajlūn
1247
Mafraq
1234
Netanya
Jarash
Tulkarm
Nablus
Jordan
Zarqā'
Tel Aviv-Yafo
Petah Tiqwa
Salt
Suweilih
WEST BANK
Er Ruseifa
Rishon le Ziyyon
Ramla
Ramallah
'AMMĀN
Sahāb
Rehovot
Yerushalayim (Jerusalem)
Jericho
El Azraq
Suweima
Na'ūr
ISRAEL
Mādabā
1010
Ashqelon
Qiryat Gat
Bethlehem
Gaza
Dab'a
GAZA STRIP
Sederot
Hebron
Dead Sea
Dhībān
Al Hadīthah
Khān Yūnis
Ofaqim
An Nabk
Mazra
Rafah
Arad
Qaţrāna
Sabkhet el Bardawīl
Be'er Sheva
Newe Zohar
Karak
El 'Arīsh
Revivim
Sedom
JORDAN
Dīmona
Safi
Wādī as Sirhān
Negev
Abu Aweigila
Qezi'ot
Sede Boqer
Tafila
Hāsā
Bāyir
En Hazeva
G. Halāl
892
J. el Atā'ita
1641
Jurf ed Darāwīsh
1082
Jebel Ithrīyat
Mizpe Ramon
Shaubak
Unayzah
Bir Gifgâfa
1000
1006
Bir Hasana
1615
1094
G. Yi'allaq
Har Saggi
Beer Menuha
Wādī Mūsā
EGYPT
Jebel Mubrak
1727
Ma'ān
El Jafr
SINAI
Gharandal
Naqb Ashtar
Nakhl
El Kuntilla
Jebel el Batrā
1555
Yotvata
SAUDI ARABIA
El Thamad
Gebel el Tîh
1030
J. Bāqir
1592
Ram
Elat
J. Ram
1754
At Tubayq
1080
Rās el Nafas
'Aqaba
Ar Ramlah
Gulf of Aqaba
1520
Al Mudawwara
1224
Ath Thāyat

Scale 1 : 7 900 000

0 100 200 300 km

0 50 100 150 km

The Gulf States

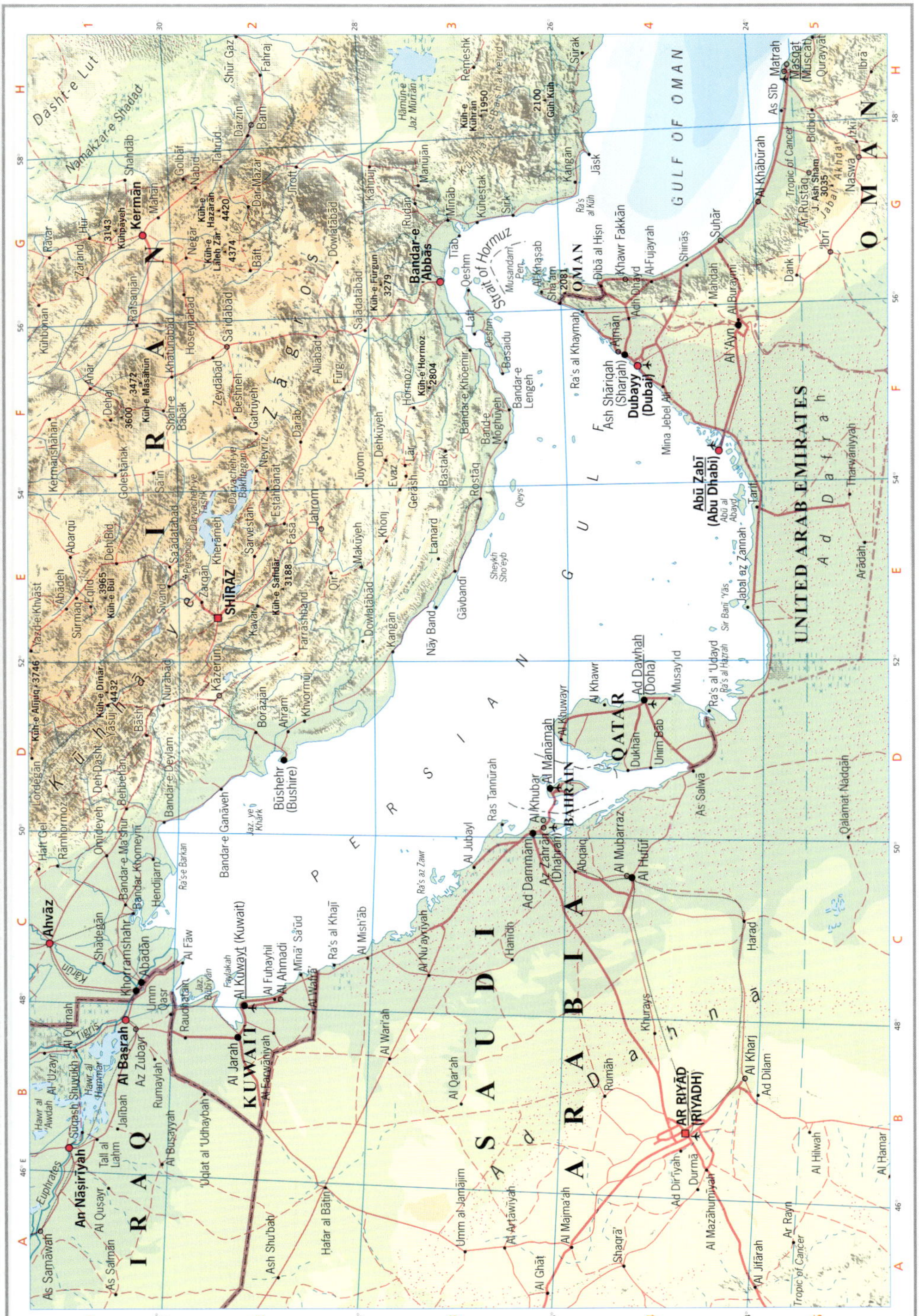

IRAN
IRAQ
KUWAIT
SAUDI ARABIA
BAHRAIN
QATAR
UNITED ARAB EMIRATES
OMAN
PERSIAN GULF
GULF OF OMAN
Strait of Hormuz
Zāgros
Ad Dahnā
Ad Dafrah
Dasht-e Lut
Tropic of Cancer
Euphrates
Tigris
Shīrāz
Kermān
Bandar-e 'Abbās
Būshehr (Bushire)
Ahvāz
Ābādān
Khorramshahr
Al Başrah
An Nāşirīyah
Al Kuwayt (Kuwait)
Al Jahrah
Ad Dammām
Al Khubar
Az Zahrān (Dhahran)
Al Hufūf
Ar Riyāḑ (Riyadh)
Al Manāmah
Ad Dawḩah (Doha)
Abū Ẓabī (Abu Dhabi)
Dubayy (Dubai)
Ash Shāriqah (Sharjah)
Ra's al Khaymah
Al 'Ayn
Şuḩār
Masqaţ (Muscat)
Maţraḩ

Scale 1 : 41 100 000

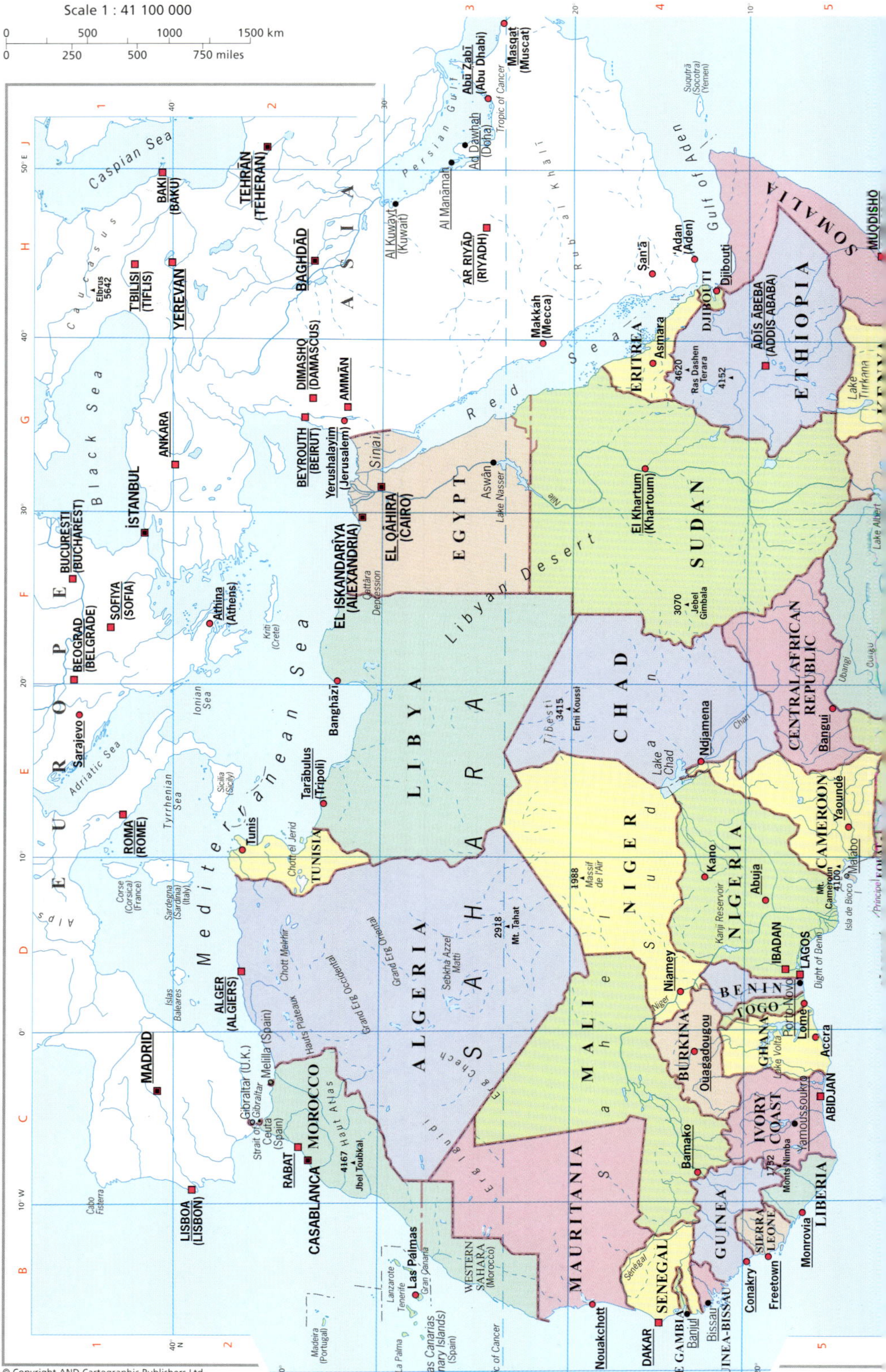

0 500 1000 1500 km
0 250 500 750 miles
EUROPE
ASIA
SAHARA
Caspian Sea
Black Sea
Mediterranean Sea
Red Sea
Persian Gulf
Gulf of Aden
Libyan Desert
Rub' al Khali
Sahel
LISBOA (LISBON)
MADRID
ALGER (ALGIERS)
RABAT
CASABLANCA
ROMA (ROME)
Tunis
Tarābulus (Tripoli)
Banghāzī
BEOGRAD (BELGRADE)
BUCUREŞTI (BUCHAREST)
SOFIYA (SOFIA)
Sarajevo
Athína (Athens)
İSTANBUL
ANKARA
T'BILISI (TIFLIS)
YEREVAN
BAKI (BAKU)
TEHRĀN (TEHERAN)
BAGHDĀD
DIMASHQ (DAMASCUS)
'AMMĀN
BEYROUTH (BEIRUT)
Yerushalayim (Jerusalem)
EL ISKANDARĪYA (ALEXANDRIA)
EL QĀHIRA (CAIRO)
Aswân
Lake Nasser
Al Kuwayt (Kuwait)
Al Manāmah
Ad Dawḩah (Doha)
Abū Ẓabī (Abu Dhabi)
Masqaṭ (Muscat)
AR RIYĀD (RIYADH)
Makkah (Mecca)
Şan'ā
'Adan (Aden)
Tropic of Cancer
MOROCCO
ALGERIA
TUNISIA
LIBYA
EGYPT
SUDAN
CHAD
NIGER
MALI
MAURITANIA
WESTERN SAHARA (Morocco)
SENEGAL
THE GAMBIA
GUINEA-BISSAU
GUINEA
SIERRA LEONE
LIBERIA
IVORY COAST
BURKINA
GHANA
TOGO
BENIN
NIGERIA
CAMEROON
CENTRAL AFRICAN REPUBLIC
ERITREA
DJIBOUTI
ETHIOPIA
SOMALIA
El Khartum (Khartoum)
Asmara
ĀDĪS ĀBEBA (ADDIS ABABA)
Djibouti
MUQDISHO
Ndjamena
Bangui
Yaoundé
Malabo
Abuja
Kano
IBADAN
LAGOS
Porto-Novo
Lomé
Accra
Ouagadougou
Niamey
Bamako
ABIDJAN
Yamoussoukro
Monrovia
Freetown
Conakry
Bissau
Banjul
DAKAR
Nouakchott
Las Palmas
Islas Canarias (Canary Islands) (Spain)
Madeira (Portugal)
Gibraltar (U.K.)
Melilla (Spain)
Ceuta (Spain)
Jbel Toubkal 4167
Elbrus 5642
Mt. Tahat 2918
Emi Koussi 3415
Jebel Gimbala 3070
Ras Dashen Terara 4620
Mt. Cameroun 4100
Lake Chad
Lake Turkana

Africa: Political

INDIAN OCEAN
ATLANTIC OCEAN
REPUBLIC OF CONGO
KINSHASA
Kananga
Brazzaville
GABON
CABINDA (Angola)
LUANDA
ANGOLA
NAMIBIA
Windhoek
Walvis Bay
Namib Desert
Brandberg 2574
Etosha Pan
BOTSWANA
Gaborone
Kalahari Desert
Makgadikgadi
Okavango Delta
ZAMBIA
Lusaka
Ndola
Lubumbashi
ZIMBABWE
HARARE
Bulawayo
Lake Kariba
MALAWI
Lilongwe
Mt. Mulanje
MOZAMBIQUE
MAPUTO
Beira
Mozambique Channel
SWAZILAND
Mbabane
SOUTH AFRICA
Pretoria
Johannesburg
DURBAN
Port Elizabeth
CAPE TOWN
Cape of Good Hope
Cape Agulhas
St. Helena Bay
LESOTHO
Maseru
Drakensberg
TANZANIA
DAR ES SALAAM
Dodoma
Lake Tanganyika
Lake Nyasa
Lake Mweru
Lake Kivu
BURUNDI
Bujumbura
RWANDA
Kigali
Lake Victoria
NAIROBI
Mombasa
Mt. Kilimanjaro
5895
Pemba I.
Zanzibar I.
COMOROS
Njazidja
Mayotte (France)
Glorieuses (France)
Juan de Nova (France)
MADAGASCAR
ANTANANARIVO
Tanjona Bobaomby
Tanjona Vohimena
SEYCHELLES
Seychelles Is.
Amirante Is.
Coetivy I.
Agalega Is. (Mauritius)
Cosmoledo Group
Tropic of Capricorn
Zambezi
Limpopo
Orange
Vaal
Cunene
Cuanza
Kwango
Kasai
Ascension (U.K.)
St. Helena (U.K.)
Tristan da Cunha (U.K.)
Gough I. (U.K.)
Prince Edward Island (South Africa)
Îles Crozet (France)
Annobón (Pagalu) (Equatorial Guinea)

Scale 1 : 15 900 000

0 200 400 600 km

0 100 200 300 miles

TUNISIA
Tarābulus (Tripoli)
Zuwārah
Az Zāwīyah
Al Khums
Zlītan
Remada
Bori Jenein
Nālūt
Jādū
Gharyān
Mişrātah
Mizdah
Banī Walīd
Abu Qarin
Khalīj Surt
Surt
Al Baydā'
Ra's al Hilāl
Darnah
Al Marj
Banghāzī
Al Jabal al Akhdar
Qamīnis
Tubruq
Mediterra
Ra's al Muraysah
Salûm
Sidi Barrani
Matrûh
EL IS
(ALE
Bordj Messaouda
Ghadāmis
Daraj
Al Qaryāt
Abū Nujaym
As Sidrah
Ajdābiyā
Wādī al Fārigh
Wādī al Hamīm
Libyan Plateau
Qattara Depression
-133
ALGERIA
Al Hammādah al Hamrā'
Ash Shuwayrif
Hūn
Waddān
Marādah
Al Jaghbūb
Awjilah
Siwa
In Aménas
Zillah
Bi'r Zaltan
Great Sand Sea
Calanscio Sand Sea
As Sarīr
Idhān Awbārī
Adīrī
Birāk
Al Harūj al Aswad
Illizi
Sabhā
Awbārī
Ummal Arānib
Tmassah
LIBYA
Tassili-n'-Ajjer
Murzūq
Tarāghin
Waw al Kabīr
Ghāt
Tāzirbū
Djanet
Al Qatrūn
Idhān Murzūq
Ramlat Rabyānah
Libyan Desert
Tropic of Cancer
Abu Ballâs 465
Sarīr Tibestī
Gilf Kebir Plateau
Plateau du Djado
Toummo
Ténéré du Tafassasset
Djado
Bardai
3265 Pic Toussidé
3376 Tarso Emissi
1893 Jebel Uweinat
Séguédine
Zouar
Tibesti
3415 Emi Koussi
Ténéré
Bilma
Grand Erg de Bilma
SAHARA
Borkou
Dépression du Mourdi
Arbre du Ténéré
Faya
Erg du Ténéré
NIGER
Fada
Bodélé
Massif Ennedi
Oum-Chalouba
Nédély
Koufey
Bahr el Ghazal
Manga
Nguigmi
Lake Chad
Mao
CHAD
SU
Maïné Soroa
Moussoro
Abéché
Kutum
Kebkabiya
El Fasher
Umm Keddada
Nguru
Baga
Ati
Hadejia
Gashua
Geidam
Ngoura
Lac Fitri
Oum-Hadjer
El Geneina
Marra Plateau
3070 Jebel Gimbala
Mongonu
Azare
Potiskum
Maiduguri
Ndjamena
Mongo
En Nahu
Damaturu
Bitkine
Nyala
El Odaiya
Darazo
Dumboa
Massif de Guéra
Abou Déia
NIGERIA
Mokolo
Mélfi
Ed Da'en
Gombe
Biu
Maroua
Chari
Am Timan
Rahad el Berdi
El Muglad
Kumo
Gombi
Bongor
Bousso
Numan
Guider
Figuil
Fianga
Birao
Kendégué
Jalingo
Yola
Garoua
Léré
Pala
Kelo
Lai
Koumra
Sarh
Ganye
Tchamba
Lac de Lagdo
Nyamlell
2049 Hossére Vokre
Moundou
Ndélé
CENTRAL
Beli
CAMEROON
Baibokoum
Ouadda
Tignère
Ngaoundéré
Koum
Paoua
Batangafo
AFRICAN REPUBLIC
Wau

LEBANON
Saida
Sour
SYRIA
As Suwaydā'
Hefa (Haifa)
ISRAEL
Tel Aviv-Yafo
Yerushalayim (Jerusalem)
Gaza
Irbid
Zarqā'
'AMMĀN
Dead Sea
Negev
JORDAN
Ma'ān
Būr Sa'īd (Port Said)
Dumyât
Kafr el Sheikh
El Mansûra
Tanta
Damanhûr
Alamein
Benha
Ismâ'ilîya
Suez Canal
EL QÂHIRA (CAIRO)
Giza Pyramids
EL GIZA
El Suweis (Suez)
Helwan
Sinai
Elat
'Aqaba
El Faiyûm
Beni Suef
Benî Mazâr
El Minya
Ras Ghârib
2637 Gebel Katherina
Gulf of Aqaba
Khalig el Suweis
Sharm el Sheikh
Mallawi
Abnûb
Asyût
Hurghada
Dubā
Akhmîm
Sohâg
Bûr Safâga
Quseir
Girga
Qena
Qus
Valley of the Kings
Luxor
El Khârga
Isna
Idfu
Bârîs
Kom Ombo
Aswân
Aswân Dam
Lake Nasser
Abu Simbel
Wadi Halfa
Akasha
Nubian Desert
Delgo
Kerma
Dongola
Abu Hamed
Merowe
Ed Debba
Berber
Atbara
Shendi
Nile (Bahr el Nil)
Umm Durman (Omdurman)
El Khartum Bahri
El Khartum (Khartoum)
Wad Medani
Ed Dueim
Gedaref
Sennar
Singa
Kosti
Rabak
El Obeid
Umm Ruwaba
Bahr el Abiad (White Nile)
Bahr el Azraq (Blue Nile)
Ed Damazin
Er Renk
Roseires Reservoir
Kadugli
Melut
Kurmuk
Tonga
Malakal
Bahr el Ghazal
Nasir
Duk Faiwil
Marsa Alam
Râs Banâs
Red Sea
ADMINISTERED BY SUDAN
Halaib
Bur Sudan (Port Sudan)
Suakin
Sinkat
Haiya
Tokar
Kassala
Khashm el Girba
2780
Algena
ERITREA
Akordat
Keren
Massawa
Teseney
Barentu
Asmara
Adi Ugri
Om Hajer
Himora
Aksum
Adigrat
Ādīgrat
Āsela
Mek'ele
Dahlak Archipelago
Dehalak Desēt
T'i'o
Subcule 1280
Ed
Assab
Bab al Mandab
Gallabat
Metema
Gonder
Dabat
4620 Ras Dashen Terara
T'ana Hāyk'
Bahir Dar
Debre Tabor
4193 Ābune Yosēf
4231 Guna Terara
Mot'a
Dese
4152 Birhan
4000 Abuye Meda
Gewanē
Mayçh'ew
Guba
Burē
Āsosa
Abay Wenz
Debre Markos
Mendī
Fichē
Nek'emtē
Hāgere Hiywet
3357 Dendi
ĀDĪS ĀBEBA (ADDIS ABABA)
Nazrēt
Tulu Welel 3302
Gīmbī
Gambēla
Gorē
Āgaro
Giyon
Āsela
3359 Mai Gudo
Negele
K'ech'a Terara 4193
Goba
Ginir
ETHIOPIA
DJIBOUTI
Tendaho
Dikhil
Yoboki
Ras Bir
Tadjoura
Djibouti
Saylac
Dirē Dawa
Hārer
Mī'ēso
Ar Rutba
Bādiyat ash Sham (Syrian Desert)
Turayf
Al Qurayyāt
Al Jālamīd
'Ar'ar
Al 'Uwayqīlah
Al Jawf
Rafhā'
An Nafud
Tabūk
Al Humaydah
Taymā'
Ḩā'il
Jabal Shammar
Al Ḩijāz
Al Wajh
Umm Lajj
Ash Shurayf
Yanbu'al Bahr
Al Madīnah (Medina)
Rābigh
Qadīmah
Usfān
Makkah (Mecca)
JIDDAH (JEDDA)
Ras Abu Shagara
At Tā'if
Al Līth
'Asīr
Al Qunfudhah
Qal'at Bīshah
Abhā
Jīzān
Jazā'ir Farasān
SAUDI ARABIA
Buraydah
'Unayzah
Rumāh
AR RIYĀD (RIYADH)
Ad Dawādimī
'Afīf
Ḩalabān
Zalim
Al Kharj
Harad
Tropic of Cancer
Laylā
As Sulayyil
Ad Dahnā
Ḩafar al Bāţin
Al Jubayl
Karbalā'
Al Ḩillah
Al Kūt
IRAQ
An Nukhayb
An Najaf
As Samāwah
Euphrates
Tigris
An Nāşirīyah
Al 'Ashurīyah
As Salmān
Al Başrah
Al Buşayyah
Dezfūl
Al 'Amārah
Masjed Soleymān
IRAN
Ahvāz
Bandar-e Ma'shur
Khorramshahr
Ābādān
Jazīrat Būbīyān
KUWAIT
Al Kuwayt (Kuwait)
Al Wafrā'
Persian Gulf
Zahrān
Najrān
Şad'ah
Ḩūth
Harad
Sharūrah
Wuday'ah
Zamakh
Mar'ib
Shabwah
As Zaydīyah
Şan'ā'
3760 Jabal an Nabī Shu'ayb
YEMEN
Al Ḩudaydah
Bayt al Faqīh
Dhamār
2514 Jabal Thamar
Lawdar
Ḩabbān
Ibb
Ta'izz
Al Mukhā
At Turbah
Zinjibār
'Adan (Aden)
Gulf of Aden
Maydh
Ceerigaabo
Berbera
Cabdul Qaadir
Booraama
Hargeysa
Burco
Caynabo
SOMALIA
Haud
Degeh Bur
Werdēr
K'ebrī Dehar
Geladī

Scale 1 : 15 900 000

0 200 400 600 km

0 100 200 300 miles

ATLANTIC OCEAN
AÇORES (AZORES) (Portugal)
Corvo
Flores
São Jorge
Faial
Pico
Terceira
São Miguel
Ponta Delgada
Santa Maria
Porto Santo
Funchal
MADEIRA (Portugal)
ISLAS CANARIAS (CANARY ISLANDS) (Spain)
La Palma
Santa Cruz de Tenerife
Gomera
Tenerife
Hierro
3710 Pico de Teide
Las Palmas
Gran Canaria
Lanzarote
Arrecife
Puerto del Rosario
Fuerteventura
Tropic of Cancer
Cádiz
Strait of
Tanger
Asilah
Larache
Ouezzane
Kénitra
RABAT
CASABLANCA
El Jadida
Khemisset
Meknès
Ras Beddouza
Safi
Settat
Khouribga
Oued Zem
Benguerir
Beni Mellal
Essaouira
Chichaoua
El Kelaâ des Srarhna
Marrakech
Cap Rhir
Agadir
Taroudannt
4167 Jbel Toubkal
4071 Irhil M'Goun
3737 Jbel Ayachi
Haut Atlas
Ouarzazate
Tazenakht
Er Rachidia
Tiznit
Anti-Atlas
Akka
Tata
Zagora
Bou Izakarn
Tan-Tan
Cap Juby
Tarfaya
El Aaiún
Boujdour
Hammada du Drâa
Tindouf
Sebkha de Tindouf
Es Semara
Galtat Zemmour
Bir Mogrein
'Aïn Ben Tili
Erg Iguidi
Bordj Flye Sante Marie
Ad Dakhla
Punta Sarga
WESTERN SAHARA (Morocco)
Sebkha Oum el Drouss Telli
Fdérik
Zouérat
Nouâdhibou
Râs Nouâdhibou
Tichla
Sebkhet de Chemchâm
Ile Tidra
Cap Timiris
Atâr
Ouadâne
Akjoujt
Sebkhet Te-n-Dghâmcha
Taoudenni
Erg Chech
SAHARA
Nouakchott
MAURITANIA
Boutilimit
Tidjikdja
Moudjéria
Tîchît
Rosso
Saint Louis
Dagana
Aleg
Bogué
Louga
Kébémer
DAKAR
Cap Vert
Tivaouane
Thiès
Linguère
Kaédi
Aoukâr
Kiffa
'Ayoûn el 'Atroûs
Oualâta
Touba
Matam
Mbour
Diourbel
SENEGAL
Sénégal
Kankossa
Néma
Joal-Fadiout
Kaolack
Banjul
Kaffrine
Bakel
Brikama
THE GAMBIA
Georgetown
Kidira
Kayes
Nioro
Kaarta
Diéma
Nara
Tambacounda
Cabo Roxo
Bignona
Kolda
Basse Santa Su
Ziguinchor
Vélingara
Bamboul
Bafoulabé
Bissau
GUINEA-BISSAU
Koundâra
Kédougou
Orango
Arquipélago dos Bijagós
Satadougou
Kita
Lac de Manantali
Gaoual
Boké
Labé
Fouta Djallon
GUINEA
Dinguiraye
Cap Verga
Mamou
Dabola
Kindia
Conakry
Dubréka
Kankan
Siguiri
Faranah
Kabala
SIERRA LEONE
Freetown
Port Loko
Makeni
Kissidougou
Kati
Bamako
Mandingue
Lac de Sélingue
Bougouni
Sikasso
Koutiala
Ségou
Niger
San
Sokolo
MALI
Araouane
Azaouâd
Lac Faguibine
Goundam
Tombouctou
Niger
Bamba
Bourem
Niafounké
Lac Débo
Lac Do
Douentza
Hombori
Mopti
Gao
Ansongo
Labbezenga
Djibo
Dori
Tougan
Yako
Kaya
BURKINA
Ouagadougou
Dédougou
Koudougou
Black Volta
Boromo
Koupéla
Bobo Dioulasso
Diébougou
Tenkodogo
Fada Ngourma
MOROCCO

Africa: Northwest

MEDITERRANEAN SEA
SPAIN
Málaga
Almería
Gibraltar
Al Hoceima
Melilla (Spain)
Nador
Ghazaouet
Tlemcen
Oujda
Jerada
MOROCCO
Tendrara
Bouârfa
Figuig
Oran
Mostaganem
Mascara
Relizane
Sidi Bel Abbès
Saïda
Tiaret
Frenda
Ténès
Khemis Miliana
Ech Chélif
ALGER (ALGIERS)
Blida
Tizi Ouzou
Bouira
Bordj Bou Arréridj
Bejaïa
Skikda
Mila
Guelma
Annaba
Cap de Fer
Sétif
Constantine
Aïn Oussera
M'Sila
Bou Saâda
Chott el Hodna
Batna
Aïn Beïda
Khenchela
Djelfa
Messaad
Laghouat
Hauts Plateaux
Atlas Saharien
Aïn Sefra
Brézina
Benoud
Biskra
Négrine
Chott Melrhir
Djamâa
Touggourt
Ghardaïa
El Oued
Ouargla
Béni Abbès
Grand Erg Occidental
Sebkha de Timimoun
Timimoun
El Goléa
Grand Erg Oriental
Bordj Messaouda
Ghadāmis
Adrar
Plateau du Tademaït
Hassi Bel Guebbour
Bordj Omar Driss
ALGERIA
Reggane
Sebkha Mekerrhane
Sebkha Azzel Matti
In Salah
Tanezrouft
Arak
Mehiet
In Ekker
Illizi
Tassili-n'-Ajjer
Djanet
In Aménas
Hoggar
2918 Mont Tahat
2306 Mont Serkout
Tamanrasset
Bordj Mokhtar
Tessalit
Adrar des Ifôghas
Aguelhok
Kidal
Tassili du Hoggar
Assamakka
MALI
Talak
Vallée de l'Azaouagh
Ménaka
Tillabéri
Gothèye
Niamey
Dogondoutchi
Dosso
Baléyara
Bagaroua
Birnin Konni
Tahoua
Tchin Tabaradene
Bani-Bangou
Arlit
1988 Adrar Tamgak
Massif de l'Aïr
2022 Monts Bagzane
Ténéré
Arbre du Ténéré
Agadez
Falaise de Tiguidit
NIGER
Aderbissinat
Dakoro
Gangara
Tanout
Madaoua
Maradi
Zinder
Katsina
Sokoto
Argungu
NIGERIA
SARDEGNA (SARDINIA) (Italy)
Cagliari
Bizerte
Tunis
Cap Bon
Béja
Jendouba
Hammam Lif
Nabeul
Golfe de Hammamet
Sousse
Kasserine
Tébessa
Kairouan
TUNISIA
Ksour Essaf
Sfax
Îles Kerkenah
Gafsa
Tozeur
Chott el Jerid
Nefta
Golfe de Gabès
Gabès
Houmt Souk
Île de Jerba
Matmata
Medenine
Pantelleria (Italy)
Lampedusa (Italy)
MALTA
ITALY
Cosenza
Catanzaro
Isole Lipari
Palermo
Messina
Reggio di Calabria
SICILIA (Sicily)
Mte. Etna 3323
Catánia
Siracusa
Tarābulus (Tripoli)
Az Zāwiyah
Tarhūnah
Al Khums
Zlītan
Misrātah
Remada
Nālūt
Jādū
Gharyān
Mizdah
Banī Walīd
Abu Qarin
Khalīj Surt
Surt
Bordj Jenein
Daraj
Al Qaryāt
Abū Nujaym
As Sidrah
Al Hammādah al Hamrā
Ash Shuwayrif
Hūn
Waddān
LIBYA
Zillah
Idhān Awbārī
Adīrī
Birāk
Sabhā
Awbārī
Al Harūj al Aswad
Tmassah
Ummal Arānib
Murzūq
Tarāghin
Wāw al Kabīr
Ghāt
Al Qatrūn
Idhān Murzūq
Sarīr Tibesti
Tropic of Cancer
Toummo
Plateau du Djado
Djado
Ténéré du Tafassasset
Séguédine
Bardai
3265 Pic Toussidé
3376 Tarso Emissi
Zouar
Tibesti
3415 Emi Koussi
Bilma
Grand Erg de Bilma
Erg du Ténéré
Borkou
Faya
Bodélé
CHAD
Nédéley
Manga
Koufey
Nguigmi
Lake Chad
Mao
Bahr el Ghazāl
E F G H J
0° 5° 10° 15° E
40° 35° 30° 25° 20° 15°
1 2 3 4 5 6

Scale 1 : 15 900 000

0 200 400 600 km

0 100 200 300 miles

MAURITANIA
SENEGAL
THE GAMBIA
GUINEA-BISSAU
GUINEA
SIERRA LEONE
LIBERIA
IVORY COAST
MALI
BURKINA
GHANA
SAHARA
ATLANTIC OCEAN
Gulf of
Equator
DAKAR
Cap Vert
Saint Louis
Louga
Kébémer
Tivaouane
Thiès
Mbour
Joal-Fadiout
Kaolack
Kaffrine
Diourbel
Touba
Linguère
Matam
Bakel
Kidira
Tambacounda
Kolda
Vélingara
Kédougou
Ziguinchor
Bignona
Cabo Roxo
Banjul
Brikama
Georgetown
Bissau
Orango
Arquipélago dos Bijagós
Rosso
Bogué
Dagana
Aleg
Kaédi
Boutilimit
Moudjéria
Kiffa
Kankossa
Ayoûn el Atroûs
Néma
Oualâta
Aoukâr
Nioro du Sahel
Nara
Diéma
Kayes
Bafoulabé
Kaarta
Bambouk
Sénégal
Didiéni
Kita
Lac de Manantali
Satadougou
Koundara
Fouta Djallon
Labé
Dinguiraye
Siguiri
Kankan
Dabola
Mamou
Faranah
Kindia
Boké
Cap Verga
Dubréka
Conakry
Kabala
Makeni
Koidu
Port Loko
Freetown
Bo
Kenema
Bonthe
Sherbro Island
Zimmi
Kissidougou
Guéckédou
Beyla
Voinjama
Nzérékoré
1752 Monts Nimba
Gbarnga
Ganta
Monrovia
Kakata
Buchanan
Greenville
Zwedru
Gbaaka
Cape Palmas
Tabou
Toulepleu
Guiglo
Man
Touba
Odienné
Korhogo
Ferkessédougou
Ouangolodougou
Katiola
Bouaké
Lac de Kossou
Daloa
Yamoussoukro
Issia
Gagnoa
Divo
Soubré
San-Pédro
Sassandra
Abengourou
Aboisso
Bandama
Comoé
Bondoukou
ABIDJAN
Bamako
Kati
Niger
Koutiala
Bougouni
Lac de Sélingue
Sikasso
Ségou
Sokolo
San
Mopti
Tombouctou
Lac Faguibine
Goundam
Niafounké
Lac Do
Hombori
Lac Débo
Douentza
Bamba
Bourem
Gao
Djibo
Dori
Tougan
Yako
Kaya
Ouagadougou
Koudougou
Dédougou
Boromo
Black Volta
Bobo Dioulasso
Diébougou
Léo
Tenkodogo
Navrongo
Bawku
Bolgatanga
Lawra
Wa
Tamale
White Volta
Bole
Kintampo
Techiman
Lake Volta
Sunyani
Kumasi
Obuasi
Dunkwa
Oda
Koforidua
Accra
Tema
Cape Coast
Sekondi
Takoradi
Cape Three Points
Ascension (U.K.)
A
B
C
D
1
2
3
4
5
6
15° W
10°
5°
0°
15° N
10°
5°
0°
Ponta do Sol
Santo Antão
Mindelo
São Vicente
São Nicolau
Sal
Pedra Lume
Boa Vista
Curral Velho
ATLANTIC OCEAN
São Tiago
Maio
Porto Inglês
Fogo
Praia
São Filipe
25° W
CAPE VERDE

Scale 1 : 15 900 000

0 200 400 600 km

0 100 200 300 miles

CHAD
CENTRAL AFRICAN REPUBLIC
DEMOCRATIC REPUBLIC OF CONGO
CONGO
CAMEROON
GABON
NIGERIA
SUDAN
RWANDA
BURUNDI
ANGOLA
ZAMBIA
ATLANTIC OCEAN
Massif Abou Déia
Mélfi
du Guéra
Am Timan
Mokolo
Maroua
Bongor
Bousso
Kendégué
Guider
Fianga
Figuil
Léré
Pala
Lai
Kélo
Koumra
Sarh
Lac de Lagdo
Moundou
Doba
Goré
Baibokoum
Ngaoundéré
Paoua
Koum
Bocaranga
Batangafo
Kaga Bandoro
Bossangoa
Bozoum
Bouar
Garoua Boulai
Baoro
Carnot
Bossambélé
Damara
Sibut
Ippy
Bria
Bambari
Ndélé
Ouadda
Kotto
Birao
Rahad el Berdi
Ed Da'ein
Babanusa
El Muglad
Kadugli
Nyamlell
Bahr el Ghazal
Tonga
Wau
Tonj
Rumbek
Bahr el Jebel (Mountain Nile)
Djéma
Obo
Tambura
Maridi
Amadi
Lanya
Yambio
Yei
Bertoua
Berbérati
Gamboula
Bangui
Zongo
Bosobolo
Kouango
Alindao
Bangassou
Mbomou
Rafai
Zémio
Mobaye
Mobayi-Mbongo
Yakoma
Monga
Bondo
Ango
Uele
Yokadouma
Nola
Libenge
Gemena
Businga
Kungu
Dongo
Akula
Lisala
Jandongi
Aketi
Rubi
Buta
Bumba
Bambesa
Poko
Niangara
Dungu
Isiro
Watsa
Faradje
Arua
Mungbere
Wamba
Mahagi
Aburo
2437
Lake Albert
Bunia
Dja
Sembé
Ouésso
Dongou
Imese
Impfondo
Makanza
Epéna
Sangha
Ubangi
Congo
Bongandanga
Basankusu
Wenga
Bolomba
Mbandaka
Djolu
Basoko
Yangambi
Kisangani
Banalia
Lindi
Ituri
Bomili
Nia-Nia
Irumu
Mambasa
Bafwasende
Beni
5110
Mount Stanley
Fort Portal
Katonga
Butembo
Lubero
Lake Edward
Mbarara
Masaka
Kamande
Mékambo
Equator
Makoua
Owando
Ewo
Obouya
Okoyo
Gamboma
Bolobo
Djambala
Ngo
Plateaux Batéké
Kasai
Busira
Boende
Tshuapa
Bokatola
Bokungu
Lac Tumba
Luilaka
Lomela
Opala
Lomami
Lubutu
Muhulu
Lowa
Ikela
Monkoto
Inongo
Lac Mai-Ndombe
Kutu
Lomela
Punia
Mount Karisimbi 4510
Goma
Gisenyi
Lake Kivu
Kigali
Kabale
Bukoba
Bukavu
Butare
Ngara
Kalima
Shabunda
Ulindi
Kamituga
Bujumbura
Gitega
Muyinga
Kibondo
Kindu
Kama
Uvira
3303
Bururi
Rutana
Fizi
Makamba
Kasulu
Kigoma
Uvinza
Ujiji
Bandundu
Dekese
Kole
Lodja
Sankuru
Kibombo
Kasongo
Luama
Brazzaville
KINSHASA
Kwilu
Ilebo
Bena Dibele
Lubefu
Luozi
Mayamba
Kenge
Masi-Manimba
Mweka
Mabanza-Ngungu
Inkisi-Kisantu
Kikwit
Idiofa
Lulua
Lusambo
Banana
Boma
Matadi
Songololo
Popokabaka
Gungu
Luebo
Lubao
Kongolo
Kananga
Mbuji-Mayi
Kalemie
Lukuni
M'banza Congo
Maquela do Zombo
Quimbele
Kwango
Tshikapa
Gandajika
Kabalo
Nyunzu
Lake Tanganyika
Great Rift Valley
Mwene-Ditu
Kabongo
N'zeto
Kahemba
Chitato
Luiza
Moba
Manono
Kaniama
Lomami
Luvua
Negage
Lurema
Cuilo
Cuango
Kapanga
Kasai
Lubilash
Miloro
Sumbawanga
Caxito
LUANDA
Capenda-Camulemba
Chicapa
Kamina
Pweto
Lake Mweru Wantipa
Lac Upemba
Mbala
Lucala
Cuanza
Malanje
Sandoa
Lake Mweru
Kilwa
Mporokoso
Saurimo
Lubudi
Kawambwa
Quibala
Cacola
Kasaji
Lac Nzilo
Lufira
Kasenga
Porto Amboim
Muconda
Luau
Dilolo
Kolwezi
Guba
Tenke
Lac de Retenue de la Lufira
Mwenda
Sumbe
Waku-Kungo
Caianda
Likasi
Mansa
Nsombo
Lake Bangweulu
Andulo
Luena
Lovua
Mwinilunga
Lubumbashi
Mingi
Camacupa
Sachanga
Lobito
Bailundo
Benguela
Kuito
Cuemba
Lucusse
Lumbala Kaquengue
West Lunga
Solwezi
Chingola
Mufulira
Mukuku
Huambo
Chavuma
Zambezi
Kitwe
Luanshya
Ndola
Cubal
Chitembo
Cangamba
Lutembo
Manyinga
Kabompo
Kasempa
Serenje
Lucira
Caluquembe
Caconda
Luangwa
A
B
C
D
1
2
3
4
5
6
15° E
20°
25°
30°
10° N
5°
0°
10° S

Africa: Central

ETHIOPIA
SOMALIA
KENYA
DJIBOUTI
YEMEN
ERITREA
MOZAMBIQUE
MALAWI
MADAGASCAR
COMOROS
SEYCHELLES
INDIAN OCEAN
Gulf of Aden
ĀDĪS ĀBEBA
(ADDIS ABABA)
NAIROBI
MUQDISHO
(MOGADISHU)
DAR ES SALAAM
Djibouti
'Adan
(Aden)
Hargeysa
Dodoma
Lilongwe
Moroni
Mombasa
Kismaayo
Marka
Zanzibar
Dirē Dawa
Hārer
Berbera
Bender Qaasim
Garoowe
Gaalkacyo
Hobyo
Beledweyne
Baydhabo
Jawhar
Kisumu
Kampala
Nakuru
Arusha
Moshi
Tanga
Malindi
Lamu
Mtwara
Lindi
Kilwa Masoko
Morogoro
Mbeya
Tabora
Lake Turkana
Lake Victoria
Lake Nyasa
Lake Natron
Lake Eyasi
Lake Manyara
Lake Rukwa
Ogaden
Haud
Guban
Masai Steppe
Pemba Island
Zanzibar Island
Mafia Island
Pate Island
Aldabra Group
Cosmoledo Group
Astove Island
Assumption Island
Farquhar Group
Îles Glorieuses (France)
Mayotte (France)
Mamoudzou
Mutsamudu
Njazidja
Nzwani
Mwali
Antsiranana
Nosy Be
Ambanja
Massif du Tsaratanana
Mt Kilimanjaro 5895
Kirinyaga (Mt Kenya) 5199
Mount Elgon 4321
Ras Dashen
Equator
Webi Shabeelle
Jubba
Tana
Galana
Rufiji
Ruvuma
Wabē Shebelē Wenz
Genalē Wenz
Abay Wenz
Omo Wenz
UNDER KENYAN ADMINISTRATION

Scale 1 : 15 900 000

0 200 400 600 km

0 100 200 300 miles

A
B
C
D
15° E
20°
25°
30°
10° S
15°
20°
25°
30°
35°
1
2
3
4
5
6
DEMOCRATIC REPUBLIC OF CONGO
ANGOLA
ZAMBIA
ZIMBABWE
BOTSWANA
NAMIBIA
SOUTH AFRICA
LESOTHO
ATLANTIC OCEAN
Kalahari Desert
Namib Desert
Huila Plateau
Serra da Chela
Tropic of Capricorn
Great Karoo
Little Karoo
Makgadikgadi
Okavango Delta
Etosha Pan
Lake Kariba
Lake Mweru
Lucala
Malanje
Capenda-Camulemba
Saurimo
Sandoa
Kilwa
Lubudi
Kawambwa
Cuanza
Cacola
Muconda
Luau
Dilolo
Kasaji
Lac Nzilo
Kasenga
Mwenda
Kolwezi
Tenke
Likasi
Minga
Mansa
Lubumbashi
Caianda
Lôvua
Mwinilunga
Solwezi
Mufulira
Chingola
Kitwe
Ndola
Luanshya
Kasempa
Manyinga
Kabompo
Kapiri Mposhi
Kabwe
Porto Amboim
Quibala
Sumbe
Waku-Kungo
Andulo
Luena
Camacupa
Bailundo
Sachanga
Cuemba
Lucusse
Lumbala Kaquengue
Lobito
Benguela
Kuito
Huambo
Chitembo
Chavuma
Zambezi
Cubal
Lucira
Caluquembe
Caconda
Lutembo
Cangamba
Lukulu
Kuvango
Menongue
Kaoma
Mumbwa
Lubango
Luampa
Lusaka
Namibe
Chiume
Mongu
Cuito Cuanavale
Tombua
Punta Albina
Caiundo
Kafue
Namwala
Mavinga
Senanga
Cahama
Mulobezi
Kariba
Humbe
Choma
Chinhoyi
Foz do Cunene
Ondjiva
Sesheke
Kazungula
Livingstone
Cuangar
Ruacana
Ondangwa
Rundu
Bagani
Kongola
Hwange
Victoria Falls
Chegutu
Opuwo
Mohembo
Cape Fria
Seronga
Kwekwe
Sesfontein
Tsumeb
Gweru
Grootfontein
Tsumkwe
Maun
Masvingo
Bulawayo
Outjo
Sehithwa
Nata
Zvishavane
Otjiwarongo
Plumtree
Gwanda
2574
Brandberg
Orapa
Francistown
Omaruru
Lake Xau
Mwenezi
Okahandja
Ghanzi
Selebi-Phikwe
Karibib
Windhoek
Gobabis
Mamuno
Serowe
Swakopmund
Walvis Bay
Rehoboth
Mahalapye
Alldays
Kang
Ellisras
NORTHERN PROVINCE
Pietersburg
Arandis
Tshane
Molepolole
Mochudi
Thabazimbi
Gaborone
Mariental
Nylstroom
Maltahöhe
Kanye
Lobatse
Sun City
Pretoria
Mamelodi
Mmabatho
Vorstershoop
GAUTENG
MPUMALANGA
Johannesburg
Soweto
Springs
Tshabong
NORTH WEST
Lüderitz
Vanderbijlpark
Vereeniging
Aus
Keetmanshoop
Seeheim
Bokspits
Vryburg
Klerksdorp
Bloemhof
Kuruman
Kroonstadt
Karasburg
Postmasburg
Warrenton
Welkom
Bethlehem
FREE STATE
Alexander Bay
Upington
Kimberley
Mont aux Sources 3299
Vioolsdrif
Douglas
Maseru
Port Nolloth
Pofadder
Kenhardt
Bloemfontein
3095
Thaba Putsoa
Pietermaritzburg
Springbok
NORTHERN CAPE
Prieska
Jagersfontein
Mafeteng
Brandvlei
Britstown
De Aar
Colesberg
Aliwal North
Kokstad
Carnarvon
Calvinia
Victoria West
Elliot
Umtata
Vanrhynsdorp
Middelburg
Fraserburg
Queenstown
Port St. Johns
St. Helena Bay
Sutherland
Beaufort West
Graaff-Reinet
Cradock
EASTERN CAPE
Cape Columbine
Vrendenburg
Aberdeen
King William's Town
Piketberg
Fort Beaufort
East London
Malmesbury
Touws River
Laingsburg
Willowmore
Worcester
WESTERN CAPE
Oudtshoorn
Uitenhage
CAPE TOWN
Paarl
Port Elizabeth
Khayelitsha
Strand
Riversdale
George
Knysna
Mosselbaai
Cape of Good Hope
Bredasdorp
Cape St. Francis
Cape Agulhas
Kunene
Cunene
Cubango
Cuito
Cuando
Zambezi
Okavango
Eiseb
Fish
Orange
Molopo
Vaal
Limpopo
Shashe
Kraai
Sondags
Doring
Chicapa
West Lunga

TANZANIA
MALAWI
MOZAMBIQUE
MADAGASCAR
COMOROS
SEYCHELLES
MAURITIUS
INDIAN OCEAN
Mozambique Channel
Lake Nyasa
Lilongwe
Blantyre
Zomba
Mount Mulanje
Monte Namuli
Lake Chilwa
Lago de Cahora Bassa
Tete
Beira
Chimoio
Mutare
Quelimane
Chinde
Pebane
Moma
Angoche
Nampula
Nacala
Moçambique
Cuamba
Lichinga
Pemba
Montepuez
Mocímboa da Praia
Quionga
Cabo Delgado
Mtwara
Lindi
Newala
Masasi
Songea
Njombe
Lukumburu
Liwale
Nyamtumbo
Tunduru
Mbamba Bay
Livingstonia
Karonga
Chitipa
Mzuzu
Mzimba
Nkhotakota
Salima
Dedza
Mangochi
Mandimba
Ruvuma
Rovuma
Zambezi
Lugenda
Lurio
Inhambane
Massinga
Xai-Xai
Chókwè
Chibuto
Maputo
Ponta Khehuene
Bela Vista
Mkuze
Lake St. Lucia
Empangeni
Limpopo
Save
Nova Mambone
Ilha do Bazaruto
Mapinhane
Chigubo
Mabalane
Chicualacuala
Espungebera
Ponta Zavora
Moroni
Njazidja
Mutsamudu
Nzwani
Mwali
Mamoudzou
Mayotte (France)
Îles Glorieuses (France)
Aldabra Group
Assumption Island
Cosmoledo Group
Astove Island
Farquhar Group
Antsiranana
Ambilobe
Nosy Be
Iharaña
Sambava
Andapa
Antalaha
Maroantsetra
Tsaratanana
Massif du Tsaratanana
2876
Bealanana
Analalava
Mahajanga
Soalala
Tanjona Vilanandro
Besalampy
Ambato Boeny
Maevatanana
Mahavavy
Ikopa
Betsiboka
Juan de Nova (France)
Morafenobe
Maintirano
Nosy Barren
Antsalova
Beravina
Tsiroanomandidy
ANTANANARIVO
2643
Tsiafajavona
Moramanga
Toamasina
Ambatondrazaka
Fenoarivo Atsinanana
Soanierana-Ivongo
Antongila
Tanjona Masoala
Nosy Boraha
Vatomandry
Mahanoro
Marolambo
Nosy-Varika
Mananjary
Ifanadiana
Fianarantsoa
Ambositra
Antsirabe
Fandriana
Miandrivazo
Belo Tsiribihina
Morondava
Malaimbandy
Mandabe
Manja
Morombe
Mangoky
Tanjona Ankaboa
Ankazoabo
Sakaraha
Toliara
Onilahy
Betioky
Ampanihy
Bekily
Betroka
Ihosy
Manakara
Vohipeno
Farafangana
Vangaindrano
Manantenina
Tôlañaro
Ambovombe
Tanjona Vohimena
Tropic of Capricorn
Bassas da India (France)
Île Europa (France)
Praslin I.
Silhouette I.
Victoria
Mahé Island
Amirante Is.
Coëtivy I.
Port Louis
St-Denis
Réunion (France)
Aldabra Group
Assumption Island
Cosmoledo Group
Astove Island
St. Pierre I.
Providence
Farquhar Group
Agalega Islands (Mauritius)

Scale 1 : 55 500 000

0 500 1000 1500 2000 km

0 250 500 750 1000 miles

BEIJING (PEKING)
P'YŎNGYANG
SŎUL (SEOUL)
Sea of Japan
Honshū
3776 Fuji-san
TŌKYŌ
QINGDAO
ŌSAKA
Huang He
Yellow Sea
Shikoku
Nagasaki
Kyūshū
A S I A
Izu-shotō
Japan Trench
SHANGHAI
East China Sea
Nansei-shotō
Ogasawara-shotō (Japan)
Kazan-rettō (Japan)
FUZHOU
T'AI-PEI
Tropic of Cancer
HONG KONG
Luzon Strait
Pagan
Northern Mariana Islands (U.S.)
Wake I. (U.S.)
Mt. Pulog 2929
Luzon
Saipan
Rota
Guam (U.S.)
Mariana Trench
MARSHALL ISLANDS
Taongi
Enewetak
Bikini
Ratak Chain
Ralik Chain
South China Sea
MANILA
11033 Challenger Deep
M I C R O N E S I A
Mindoro
Samar
FEDERATED STATES OF MICRONESIA
Caroline Islands
Chuuk
Pohnpei
Palikir
Dalap-Uliga-Darrit
Majuro
Panay
Cebu
Yap
Palawan
Negros
Philippine Trench
Mindanao
Palau
Koror
Kosrae
Butaritari
Sulu Sea
Davao
Tinaca Point
PALAU
Nomoi Is.
4094 Gunong Kinabalu
Tarawa
Bairiki
Celebes Sea
M E L A N E S I A
Gilbert Islands
Halmahera
Yaren
NAURU
Banaba
Borneo
Biak
Admiralty Is.
New Hanover
Molucca Sea
Bismarck Sea
New Ireland
Nukumanu Is.
Equator
Sulawesi (Celebes)
Macassar Strait
5030 Puncak Jaya
Bougainville Island
Choiseul
SOLOMON ISLANDS
TUVALU
Ellice Islands
Fongafale
Banjarmasin
Buru
Seram
New Guinea
Central Range 4509
PAPUA NEW GUINEA
Mt. Victoria 4073
New Britain
Santa Isabel
Malaita
Buton
Aru
Banda Sea
New Georgia I.
Honiara
Greater Sunda Is.
Tanimbar
Dolak
Port Moresby
Louisiade Archipelago
Guadalcanal
Santa Cruz Is.
Lombok
Sumbawa
SURABAYA
Bali
Flores
Arafura Sea
Torres Strait
Cape York
San Cristóbal
Rotuma
Jawa (Java)
Sumba
Timor
Melville I.
Cape Arnhem
Groote Eylandt
Coral Sea
VANUATU
Espiritu Santo
Timor Sea
Joseph Bonaparte Gulf
Darwin
Gulf of Carpentaria
Malakula
Bonaparte Archipelago
Great Barrier Reef
Coral Sea Islands Territory
Îles Chesterfield
Port-Vila
Éfaté
Viti Levu
INDIAN OCEAN
1612 Bartle Frere
Nouvelle Calédonie (France)
Loyalty Is.
Maré
Hunter I.
Nouméa
Great Sandy Desert
Great Dividing Range
Capricorn Group
A U S T R A L I A
Barrow I.
Lake Mackay
Macdonnell Ranges
Great Artesian Basin
Sandy Cape
Fraser I.
North West Basin
Tropic of Capricorn
Shark Bay
867 Uluru (Ayers Rock)
Lake Eyre
BRISBANE
Cape Byron
Norfolk I. (Australia)
Cape Inscription
Great Victoria Desert
Lord Howe I. (Australia)
Flinders Ranges
Darling
Ball's Pyramid
SYDNEY
North Cape
PERTH
Cape Naturaliste
Canberra
Murray
Auckland
Cape Carnot
ADELAIDE
Australian Alps
North Island
Archipelago of the Recherche
Great Australian Bight
Kangaroo I.
Cape Howe
MELBOURNE
Tasman Sea
NEW ZEALAND
Bass Strait
King I.
Flinders I.
Cape Farewell
Wellington
Tasmania
1617 Mt. Ossa
Hobart
South East Cape
South Island
3754 Mt. Cook
Christchurch
West Cape
Bounty
Southwest Cape
Stewart I.
Antipodes

Oceania: Political

NORTH AMERICA
LOS ANGELES
SAN DIEGO
Guadalupe (Mexico)
HAWAII (U.S.)
Hawaiian Islands
Laysan I.
Necker I.
Kauai
Oahu
Honolulu
Maui
Hawaii
PACIFIC
OCEAN
Tropic of Cancer
Johnston I. (U.S.)
N. W. Christmas Island Ridge
Is. Revillagigedo (Mexico)
Palmyra I. (U.S.)
Tabuaeran
Line Islands
Kiritimati
Howland (U.S.)
Baker (U.S.)
Jarvis (U.S.)
Phoenix Islands
Rawaki
Birnie
Orona
Manra
KIRIBATI
Malden I.
Starbuck I.
Equator
POLYNESIA
Atafu
Nukunonu
Tokelau (New Zealand)
Tongareva
Swains I.
Danger Is.
Nassau
Manihiki
Vostok I.
Caroline I.
Nuku Hiva
Hiva Oa
Marquesas Islands
SAMOA
Savaii
Apia
Upolu
American Samoa
Tutuila
Suvorov I.
Flint I.
Îles Désappointement
Rose I.
Cook Islands (New Zealand)
Motu One
Îles Palliser
Archipel des Tuamotu
Pukapuka
Raroia
Tafahi
TONGA
Tonga Islands
Tonga Trench
Niue (New Zealand)
Palmerston I.
Aitutaki
Arch. de la Société
Tahiti
Hao
Îles Duc de Gloucester
French Polynesia
Rarotonga
Mangaia
Îles Maria
Rurutu
Tubuai
Raevavae
Tubuai Islands
Mururoa
Groupe Actéon
Morane
Gambier Is.
Mangareva
Oeno
Henderson I.
Pitcairn Is. (U.K.)
Ducie I.
Ata
Horizon Depth 10882
Tropic of Capricorn
Rapa
Marotiri
Kermadec Trench
Easter I. (Chile)
South West Pacific Basin

Scale 1 : 18 900 000

0 200 400 600 km
0 100 200 300 miles

INDONESIA
Sumba
Bondokodi
Waingapu
Sawu Sea
Ngalu
Savu
Rote
Timor
Kupang
Timor Sea
Arafura
Melville Island
Bathurst Island
Clarence Strait
Beagle Gulf
Darwin
Van Diemen Gulf
Adelaide River
Pine Creek
Katherine
Mataranka
Joseph Bonaparte Gulf
Cape Scott
Wingate Mountains
Cape Londonderry
Bonaparte Archipelago
Port Warrender
Seringapatam Reef
Scott Reef
Sandy I.
INDIAN OCEAN
Wyndham
Drysdale River
Timber Creek
Lake Argyle Tourist Village
Lake Argyle
Daly Waters
Collier Bay
Sunday Strait
Cape Lévêque
Lombadina
King Sound
Derby
Mount Ord 936
Kimberley Plateau
Halls Creek
Newcastle Waters
Kalkaring
Inverway
Rowley Shoals
Broome
Fitzroy Crossing
Tanami Desert
Tanami
Sandfire Flat Roadhouse
Port Hedland
Great Sandy Desert
Percival Lakes
Gregory Lake
The Granites
Lake Wills
Lake White
Monte Bello Is.
Barrow I.
Roebourne
Lake Mackay
Yuendumu
North West Cape
Exmouth
Hamersley Range
Mount Bruce 1235
Wittenoom
Tom Price
1251 Mount Meharry
Newman
Lake Dora
AUSTRALIA
Lake Macdonald
Mount Liebig 1524
Mount Ziel 1510
Macdonnell Ranges
North West Basin
Gibson Desert
Lake Disappointment
Lake Hopkins
Lake Neale
Lake Amadeus
Tropic of Capricorn
Minilya Roadhouse
1106 Mount Augustus
Lake Macleod
910 Mount Essendon
WESTERN AUSTRALIA
Uluru (Ayers Rock) 867
Kulgera
Carnarvon
Landor
Lake Carnegie
Mount Aloysius 1085
Musgrave Ranges
1440 Mount Woodroffe
Shark Bay
Cape Inscription
Dirk Hartog I.
Useless Loop
Denham
Overlander Roadhouse
Wiluna
Nannine
Great Victoria Desert
SOUTH AUSTRALIA
Yeo Lake
Neale Junction
Lake Austin
Leinster
Mount Magnet
Rason Lake
Leonora
Lake Carey
Lake Maurice
Mullewa
Lake Barlee
Geraldton
Payne's Find
Menzies
Nullarbor Plain
Wubin
Lake Moore
Deakin
Badgingarra
Pithara
Bindi Bindi
Coolgardie
Kalgoorlie
Rawlinna
Eucla
Head of Bight
Goomalling
Southern Cross
Lake Lefroy
Northam
Merredin
Twilight Cove
PERTH
Cunderdin
Norseman
Fremantle
Mandurah
Lake Dundas
Point Culver
Israelite Bay
Bunbury
Williams
Lake Grace
Ravensthorpe
Geographe Bay
Cape Naturaliste
Esperance
Cape Arid
Manjimup
Boxwood Hill
Esperance Bay
Archipelago of the Recherche
Cape Leeuwin
Augusta
Cranbrook
Cheyne Bay
Walpole
Albany
Point d'Entrecasteaux
Denmark
Great Australian Bight
INDIAN OCEAN

Australia

PAPUA NEW GUINEA
Port Moresby
Alotau
D'Entrecasteaux Islands
Louisiade Archipelago
CORAL SEA ISLANDS
CORAL SEA
TERRITORY (Australia)
Osprey Reef
Shark Reef
Bougainville Reef
Holmes Reefs
Diane Bank
Willis Group
Herald Cays
Magdelaine Cays
Diamond Islets
Flinders Reefs
Turtle I.
Tregosse Islets
Malay Reef
PACIFIC OCEAN
Swain Reefs
Capricorn Group
Cato I.
Tropic of Capricorn
Lord Howe I.
Ball's Pyramid
TASMAN SEA
GREAT BARRIER REEF
Mulgrave I.
Moa (Banks Island)
Torres Strait
Prince of Wales Island
Cape York
Bamaga
Somerset
Cape Grenville
Duifken Point
Weipa
Cape York Peninsula
Cape Direction
Albatross Bay
Aurukun
Princess Charlotte Bay
Cape Melville
Silver Plains
Cape Flattery
Cape Wessel
Wessel Islands
Cape Arnhem
Nhulunbuy
Nangalala
Bickerton Island
Groote Eylandt
Numbulwar
Gulf of Carpentaria
Sir Edward Pellew Group
Borroloola
Wellesley Islands
Mornington I.
Bentinck I.
Kowanyama
Laura
Cooktown
Dunbar
Cape Crawford
Karumba
Burketown
Normanton
Port Douglas
Mareeba
Cairns
1612 Mount Bartle Frere
Innisfail
Mount Garnet
Lorraine
Barkly Tableland
Ingham
Halifax Bay
Greenvale
Mutarnee
Townsville
Ayr
Bowen
The Whitsundays
Proserpine
Repulse Bay
Camooweal
Mount Isa
Lake Nash
Richmond
McKinlay
Charters Towers
Mount Douglas
Mackay
Sarina
Nebo
Broad Sound
Clairview
Townshend I.
QUEENSLAND
GREAT DIVIDING RANGE
Winton
Tobermorey
Boulia
Muttaburra
Clermont
Great Artesian Basin
Yeppoon
Rockhampton
Curtis I.
Gladstone
Barcaldine
Jericho
Emerald
Springsure
Simpson Desert
Jundah
Tambo
Banana
Bundaberg
Sandy Cape
Birdsville
Betoota
Windorah
Lake Yamma Yamma
Augathella
Taroom
Eidsvold
Hervey Bay
Fraser I.
Maryborough
Lake Eyre Basin
Sturt Stony Desert
Charleville
Gayndah
Roma
Gympie
Oodnadatta
Quilpie
Muckadilla
Miles
Kingaroy
Caloundra
Tirari Desert
Lake Eyre North
Thargomindah
Grey Range
Saint George
Moonie
Dalby
Moreton I.
BRISBANE
North Stradbroke I.
Toowoomba
Beenleigh
Mount Roberts 1387
Surfers Paradise
Gold Coast
Cunnamulla
Dirranbandi
Bungunya
Goondiwindi
Boggabilla
Casino
Cape Byron
Ballina
Coober Pedy
Lake Eyre South
Hungerford
Tibboburra
Lake Blanche
Enngonia
Marree
Lake Callabonna
Wanaaring
Moree
Tenterfield
Glenn Innes
Bourke
Brewarrina
Leigh Creek
Lake Frome
Walgett
Grafton
Round Mountain 1608
Flinders Ranges
Glendambo
Lake Torrens
White Cliffs
Louth
Narrabri
Armidale
Coffs Harbour
Pimba
Darling
Coolabah
Gunnedah
Lake Gairdner
Hawker
Broken Hill
Wilcannia
NEW SOUTH WALES
Nyngan
Coonabarabran
Tamworth
Black Sugarloaf 1494
Quirindi
Port Macquarie
Gawler Ranges
Port Augusta
Whyalla
Orroroo
Gilgandra
Dubbo
Taree
Kyancutta
Eyre Peninsula
Port Pirie
Ivanhoe
Condobolin
Singleton
Cowell
Burra
Murray River
Pooncarie
Roto
Orange
1274
Cessnock
Newcastle
Lincoln
Morgan
Wentworth
Goolgowi
Marsden
Bathurst
Lithgow
Spencer Gulf
Gawler
Renmark
Katoomba
ADELAIDE
Murray Bridge
Balranald
Hay
Cowra
1204
Cootamundra
SYDNEY
Cape Carnot
Inneston
Investigator Strait
Victor Harbor
Tailem Bend
Ouyen
Swan Hill
Narrandera
Wollongong
Wagga Wagga
Canberra
Nowra
Cape Borda
Kingscote
Kangaroo I.
Hopetoun
Deniliquin
Finley
Tumut
Big Desert
Albury
A.C.T.
Bordertown
Batemans Bay
Lacepede Bay
Cape Jaffa
Robe
Little Desert
VICTORIA
Shepparton
Horsham
GREAT DIVIDING RANGE
2230 Mount Kosciuszko
Cooma
Seymour
Mount Bogong
Omeo
1986
Bombala
Hamilton
Ballarat
Yea
Eden
Mount Gambier
Portland
Cape Nelson
Geelong
MELBOURNE
Morwell
Bairnsdale
Cape Howe
Warrnambool
Korumburra
Sale
Apollo Bay
Walkerville
Port Albert
Wilson's Promontory
South East Point
King Island
Currie
Bass Strait
Flinders I.
Furneaux Group
Whitemark
Cape Barren I.
Cape Grim
Stanley
Banks Strait
Burnie
George Town
TASMANIA
Devonport
Launceston
1617 Mount Ossa
Queenstown
Swansea
Cape Forestier
Lake Gordon
Hobart
Port Arthur
Dover
Storm Bay
South West Cape
South East Cape
A.C.T. = Australian Capital Territory

Scale 1 : 6 350 000

0 100 200 km

0 50 100 miles

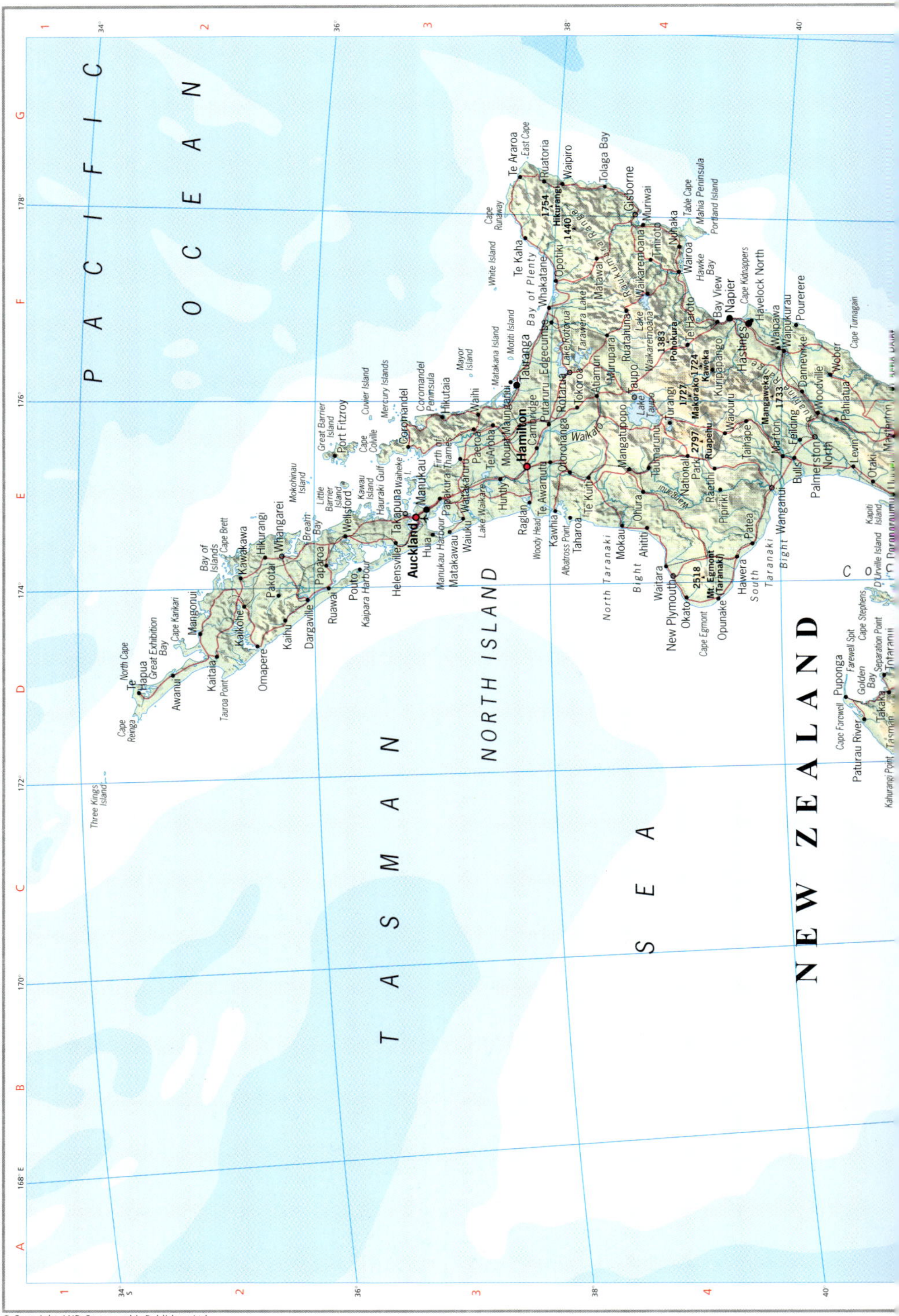

P A C I F I C
O C E A N
T A S M A N
S E A
NORTH ISLAND
NEW ZEALAND
North Taranaki Bight
South Taranaki Bight
Bay of Plenty
Cape Reinga
North Cape
Three Kings Island
Te Hapua
Great Exhibition Bay
Cape Karikari
Awanui
Kaitaia
Tauroa Point
Mangonui
Kaikohe
Kawakawa
Bay of Islands
Cape Brett
Omapere
Kaihu
Hikurangi
Whangarei
Pakotai
Dargaville
Paparoa
Ruawai
Pouto
Kaipara Harbour
Bream Bay
Mokohinau Island
Little Barrier Island
Great Barrier Island
Port Fitzroy
Cuvier Island
Mercury Islands
Wellsford
Helensville
Takapuna
Waiheke I.
Auckland
Manukau
Huia
Manukau Harbour
Matakawau
Papakura
Waiuku
Hauraki Gulf
Firth of Thames
Thames
Coromandel
Coromandel Peninsula
Whitianga
Waihi
Paeroa
Te Aroha
Huntly
Mount Maunganui
Tauranga
Hamilton
Cambridge
Raglan
Te Awamutu
Kawhia
Albatross Point
Taharoa
Te Kuiti
Mokau
Ohura
Waitara
New Plymouth
Okato
Cape Egmont
Mt. Egmont (Taranaki)
2518
Opunake
Hawera
Patea
Wanganui
Taihape
Waiouru
Ruapehu
2797
Raetihi
Pipiriki
National Park
Taumarunui
Turangi
Lake Taupo
Taupo
Rotorua
Lake Rotorua
Tarawera Lake
Putaruru
Tokoroa
Atiamuri
Mangakino
Whakatane
Opotiki
Te Kaha
Cape Runaway
White Island
Motiti Island
Matakana Island
Mayor Island
Te Araroa
East Cape
Ruatoria
Hikurangi
1754
Waipiro
Tolaga Bay
Gisborne
Muriwai
Tiniroto
Nuhaka
Wairoa
Table Cape
Mahia Peninsula
Portland Island
Hawke Bay
Napier
Bay View
Te Haroto
Hastings
Havelock North
Cape Kidnappers
Waipawa
Waipukurau
Porangahau
Dannevirke
Woodville
Pahiatua
Feilding
Palmerston North
Bulls
Marton
Levin
Otaki
Kapiti Island
Cape Turnagain
Murupara
Ruatahuna
Lake Waikaremoana
Waikaremoana
Kaweka
Makorako 1724
1727
1383
Pohokura
Mangaweka
1733
Kuripapango
Cape Farewell
Farewell Spit
Puponga
Golden Bay
Paturau River
Takaka
Separation Point
Cape Stephens
D'Urville Island
Kahurangi Point
Tasman

New Zealand

PACIFIC OCEAN
SOUTH ISLAND
Canterbury Bight
Foveaux Strait
Chatham Islands (New Zealand)
Chatham I.
The Sisters
Western Reef
Petre Bay
Hanson Bay
Waitangi
287
Pitt Strait
Pitt I.
Pyramid I.
Antipodes Islands (New Zealand)
366
Campbell Island (New Zealand)
569
Auckland Island (New Zealand)
Enderby Island
Adams Island
South West Cape
668
Wellington
983
Mt. Ross
Cape Palliser
Ngawihi
Cape Campbell
Blenheim
Ward
Clarence
Kaikoura
Tapuaenuku
2885
Mt. Richmond
1760
Mt. Owen
1875
Richmond
Howard Junction
Saint Arnaud
Murchison
Westport
Seddonville
Cape Foulwind
Charleston
Inangahua
1532
Reefton
Runanga
Greymouth
Kumara
Hokitika
Ahaura
Mt. Travers
2338
Springs Junction
Hanmer Springs
Dillon Cone
2174
Waiau
Parnassus
Culverden
Waipara
Mt. Murchison
2400
Lake Coleridge
Oxford
Rangiora
Pegasus Bay
Christchurch
Lyttelton
Banks Peninsula
Akaroa
Sheffield
Rolleston
Leeston
Mount Hutt
Ashburton
Canterbury Plains
Mt. Arrowsmith
2795
2330
Mount Somers
Geraldine
Temuka
Timaru
Fairlie
Lake Tekapo
Lake Pukaki
Mount Cook
Mt. Cook
3754
Harihari
Franz Josef Glacier
Abut Head
Lake Paringa
Haast
Jackson Head
Mt. Huxley
2499
2423
Mt. Brewster
2355
Mt. Alba
Mt. Aspiring
3027
Makarora
Lake Ohau
Omarama
Twizel
Cave
Lake Benmore
Kurow
Waimate
Oamaru
Herbert
Hampden
Palmerston
Otago Peninsula
Cape Saunders
Dunedin
Mosgiel
Milton
Balclutha
Nugget Point
Owaka
Waikawa
Clarks Junction
Kyeburn
Becks
Omakau
Alexandra
Roxburgh
Lawrence
Clinton
Edendale
Mokoreta
Fortrose
Tarras
Luggate
Lake Wanaka
Wanaka
Cromwell
Lake Wakatipu
Queenstown
2819
Milford Sound
Moffat Peak
2085
Jane Peak
2035
Te Anau
Lake Te Anau
Mt. Donald
1612
1628
Lake Manapouri
Lake Hauroko
Lake Poteriteri
1722
Mossburn
Waikaia
Lumsden
Gore
Mataura
Monowai
Ohai
Clifden
Winton
Riverton
Invercargill
Bluff
Te Waewae Bay
Waewae Bay
Puysegur Point
Cape Providence
Resolution Island
Secretary Island
Solander Island
Ruapuke Island
Stewart Island
Mt. Anglem
980
750
Mason Bay
Southwest Cape

Polar Regions

Scale 1 : 69 500 000

0 500 1000 1500 2000 km

0 250 500 750 1000 miles

RUSSIA
Arctic Circle
Lena
Yenisey
Amur
Ural'skiy Khrebet (Ural Mountains)
Volga
MOSKVA (MOSCOW)
UKRAINE
KYYIV (KIEV)
BELARUS
LITHUANIA
LATVIA
ESTONIA
POLAND
Kuril'skiye Ostrova
Sakhalin
Sea of Okhotsk
Arkhangel'sk
Ladozhskoye Ozero (Lake Ladoga)
Karskoye More (Kara Sea)
Novaya Zemlya
Murmansk
Helsinki
FINLAND
Baltic Sea
Gulf of Bothnia
Stockholm
SWEDEN
GERMANY
DENMARK
Oslo
NORWAY
Klyuchevskaya Sopka
4750
Zaliv Shelikhova
More Laptevykh (Laptev Sea)
Severnaya Zemlya
Barents Sea
Zemlya Frantsa-Iosifa (Franz Josef Land) (Russia)
Nordkapp
Komandorskiye Ostrova
Novosibirskiye Ostrova (New Siberia Islands)
Vostochno-Sibirskoye More (East Siberian Sea)
Nordaustlandet
Bjørnøya (Norway)
Spitsbergen
Svalbard (Norway)
Attu Island
Bering Sea
Arctic Ocean
North Pole
Norwegian Sea
North Sea
UNITED KINGDOM
International Dateline
O. Vrangelya
Anadyrskiy Zaliv
Chukchi Sea
Greenland Sea
Jan Mayen (Norway)
Dublin (Baile Átha Cliath)
REP. OF IRELAND
St. Lawrence I.
Bering Strait
Aleutian Islands
Norton Sound
Nunivak I.
Limit of Pack Ice
Ellesmere I.
Denmark Strait
ICELAND
Reykjavík
Bristol Bay
Yukon
ALASKA (U.S.)
Brooks Range
Mt. McKinley
6194
Beaufort Sea
Sverdrup Is.
Queen Elizabeth Islands
Melville I.
GREENLAND (Denmark)
3700
Gunnbjørns Fjeld
Anchorage
Banks I.
Baffin Bay
Limit of Drift Ice
Kodiak I.
Gulf of Alaska
Mt. Logan
6059
Victoria I.
Baffin Island
Davis Strait
Nuuk (Godthåb)
Mackenzie
Mackenzie Mountains
Great Bear Lake
ATLANTIC OCEAN
PACIFIC OCEAN
Alexander Archipelago
CANADA
Foxe Basin
Queen Charlotte Islands
Coast Mountains
Great Slave Lake
Hudson Bay
Hudson Strait
Labrador Sea

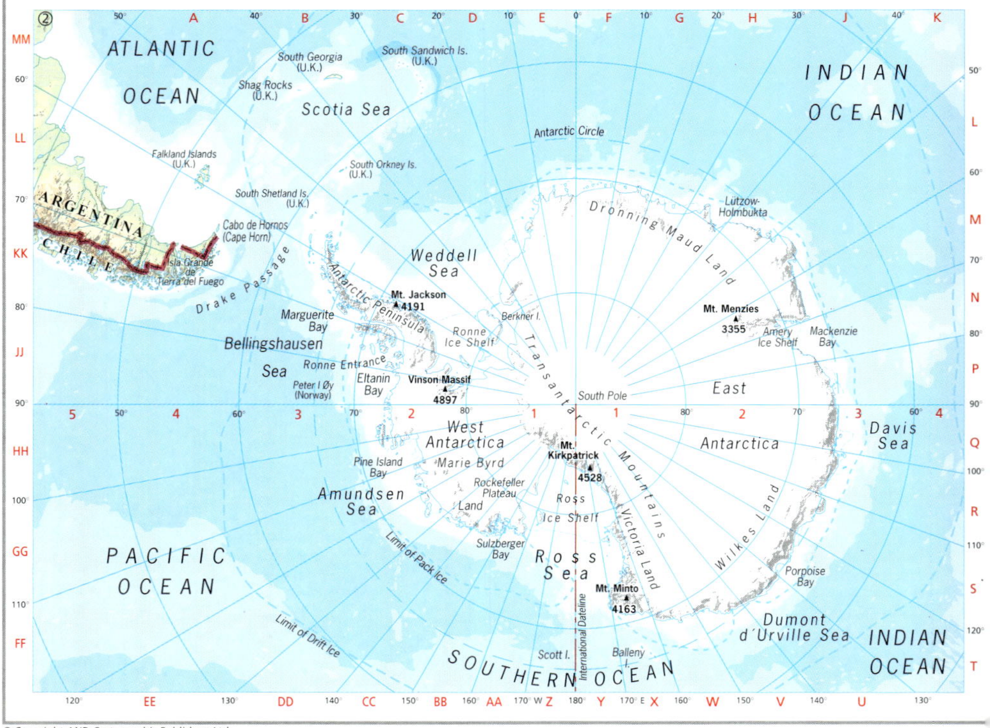

ATLANTIC OCEAN
South Georgia (U.K.)
South Sandwich Is. (U.K.)
Shag Rocks (U.K.)
Scotia Sea
INDIAN OCEAN
Antarctic Circle
Falkland Islands (U.K.)
South Orkney Is. (U.K.)
South Shetland Is. (U.K.)
Lutzow-Holmbukta
ARGENTINA
CHILE
Cabo de Hornos (Cape Horn)
Dronning Maud Land
Isla Grande de Tierra del Fuego
Weddell Sea
Drake Passage
Antarctic Peninsula
Mt. Jackson
4191
Marguerite Bay
Berkner I.
Mt. Menzies
3355
Amery Ice Shelf
Mackenzie Bay
Ronne Ice Shelf
Bellingshausen Sea
Ronne Entrance
Transantarctic Mountains
Peter I Øy (Norway)
Eltanin Bay
Vinson Massif
4897
South Pole
East Antarctica
West Antarctica
Davis Sea
Mt. Kirkpatrick
4528
Pine Island Bay
Marie Byrd Land
Rockefeller Plateau
Amundsen Sea
Ross Ice Shelf
Victoria Land
Wilkes Land
Limit of Pack Ice
Sulzberger Bay
PACIFIC OCEAN
Ross Sea
Porpoise Bay
Mt. Minto
4163
International Dateline
Limit of Drift Ice
Dumont d'Urville Sea
INDIAN OCEAN
Scott I.
Balleny I.
SOUTHERN OCEAN

Glossary

This is a glossary of the geographical terms used in this atlas. The first column shows the local spelling, the second the language of origin, and the third the English translation.

A

açude	Portuguese	reservoir
adası	Turkish	island
akra	Greek	peninsula
alpen	German	mountains
alpes	French	mountains
alpi	Italian	mountains
älven	Swedish	river
archipiélago	Spanish	archipelago
arquipélago	Portuguese	archipelago

B

bab	Arabic	strait
bahía	Spanish	bay
bahir, bahr	Arabic	bay, lake, river
baía	Portuguese	bay
baie	French	bay
baja	Spanish	lower
bandar	Arabic, Somalian, Malay, Persian	harbour, port
baraji	Turkish	dam
barragem	Portuguese	reservoir
ben	Gaelic	mountain
Berg(e)	German	mountain(s)
boğazı	Turkish	strait
Bucht	German	bay
buḩayrat	Arabic	lake
burnu, burun	Turkish	cape

C

cabo	Spanish	cape
canal	French, Spanish	canal, channel
canale	Italian	canal, channel
cerro	Spanish	mountain
chott	Arabic	marsh, salt lake
co	Tibetan	lake
collines	French	hills
cordillera	Spanish	range

D

dağ(ı)	Turkish	mountain
dağlar(ı)	Turkish	mountains
danau	Indonesian	lake
daryacheh	Persian	lake
dasht	Persian	desert
djebel	Arabic	mountain(s)
-do	Korean	island

E

embalse	Spanish	reservoir
erg	Arabic	sandy desert
estrecho	Spanish	strait

F

feng	Chinese	mountain
-fjördur	Icelandic	fjord
-flói	Icelandic	bay

G

Gebirge	German	range
golfe	French	bay, gulf
golfo	Italian, Portuguese, Spanish	bay, gulf
göl, gölü	Turkish	lake
gora	Russian	mountain
gory	Russian	mountains
gunong	Malay	mountain
gunung	Indonesian	mountain

H

hai	Chinese	lake, sea
hāmūn	Persian	lake, marsh
hawr	Arabic	lake
hu	Chinese	lake, reservoir

I

île(s)	French	island(s)
ilha(s)	Portuguese	island(s)
isla(s)	Spanish	island(s)

J

jabal	Arabic	mountain(s)
-järvi	Finnish	lake
jaza'īr	Arabic	islands
jazīrat	Arabic	island
jbel	Arabic	mountain
jebel	Arabic	mountain
jezero	Serbo-Croatian	lake
jezioro	Polish	lake
jiang	Chinese	river
-jima	Japanese	island
-joki	Finnish	river
-jökull	Icelandic	glacier

K

kepulauan	Indonesian	islands
khrebet	Russian	mountain range
-ko	Japanese	lake
kolpos	Greek	bay, gulf
körfezi	Turkish	bay, gulf
kryazh	Russian	ridge
kūh(ha)	Persian	mountain(s)

L

lac	French	lake
lacul	Romanian	lake
lago	Italian, Portuguese, Spanish	lake
lagoa	Portuguese	lagoon
laguna	Spanish	lagoon, lake
limni	Greek	lake
ling	Chinese	mountain(s), peak
liqeni	Albanian	lake
loch, lough	Gaelic	lake

M

massif	French	mountains
-meer	Dutch	lake, sea
mont	French	mount
monte	Italian, Portuguese, Spanish	mount
montes	Portuguese, Spanish	mountains
monts	French	mountains
muntii	Romanian	mountains
mys	Russian	cape

N

nafud	Arabic	desert
nevado	Spanish	snow-capped mountain
nuruu	Mongolian	mountains
nuur	Mongolian	lake

O

ostrov(a)	Russian	island(s)
ozero	Russian	lake

P

pegunungan	Indonesian	mountains
pelagos	Greek	sea
pendi	Chinese	basin
pesky	Russian	sandy desert
pic	French	peak
pico	Portuguese, Spanish	peak
planalto	Portuguese	plateau
planina	Bulgarian	mountains
poluostrov	Russian	peninsula
puerto	Spanish	harbour, port
puncak	Indonesian	peak
punta	Italian, Spanish	point
puy	French	peak

Q

qundao	Chinese	archipelago

R

ras, râs, ra's	Arabic	cape
represa	Portuguese	dam, reservoir
-rettō	Japanese	archipelago
rio	Portuguese	river
río	Spanish	river

S

sahra	Arabic	desert
salar	Spanish	salt flat
-san	Japanese, Korean	mountain
-sanmaek	Korean	mountains
sebkha	Arabic	salt flat
sebkhet	Arabic	salt marsh
See	German	lake
serra	Portuguese	range
severnaya, severo-	Russian	northern
shan	Chinese	mountain(s)
-shima	Japanese	island
-shotō	Japanese	islands
sierra	Spanish	range

T

tanjona	Malagasy	cape
tanjung	Indonesian	cape
teluk	Indonesian	bay, gulf
ténéré	Berber	desert
-tō	Japanese	island

V

vârful	Romanian	mountain
-vesi	Finnish	lake
vodokhranilishche	Russian	reservoir
volcán	Spanish	volcano

W

wādī	Arabic	watercourse
Wald	German	forest

Z

-zaki	Japanese	cape
zaliv	Russian	bay, gulf

Index

How to use the index

This is an alphabetically arranged index of the places and features that can be found on the maps in this atlas. Each name is generally indexed to the largest scale map on which it appears. If that map covers a double page, the name will always be indexed by the left-hand page number.

Names composed of two or more words are alphabetized as if they were one word.

All names appear in full in the index, except for 'St.' and 'Ste.', which although abbreviated, are indexed as though spelled in full.

Where two or more places have the same name, they can be distinguished from each other by the country or province name which immediately follows the entry. These names are indexed in the alphabetical order of the country or province.

Alternative names, such as English translations, can also be found in the index and are cross-referenced to the map form by the '=' sign. In these cases the names also appear in brackets on the maps.

Settlements are indexed to the position of the symbol, all other features are indexed to the position of the name on the map.

Abbreviations used in this index are explained in the list opposite.

Finding a name on the map

Each index entry contains the name, followed by a page reference and a grid reference. All entries except settlements also contain a symbol indicating the feature type (for example, ocean, river):

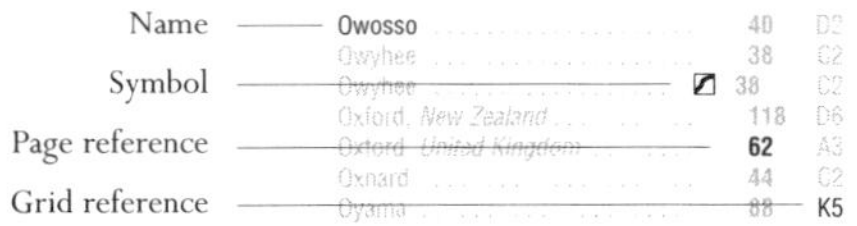

Name
Symbol
Page reference
Grid reference
Owosso 40 D2
Owyhee 38 C2
Owyhee 38 C2
Oxford, New Zealand 118 D6
Oxford, United Kingdom 62 A3
Oxnard 44 C2
Oyama 88 K5

The grid reference locates a place or feature within a rectangle formed by the network of lines of longitude and latitude. A name can be found by referring to the red letters and numbers placed around the maps. First find the letter, which appears along the top and bottom of the map, and then the number, down the sides. The name will be found within the rectangle uniquely defined by that letter and number. A number in brackets preceding the grid reference indicates that the name is to be found within an inset map.

Abbreviations

Ak.	Alaska	*N.D.*	North Dakota
Al.	Alabama	*Nebr.*	Nebraska
Ariz.	Arizona	*Nev.*	Nevada
Ark.	Arkansas	*Nfld.*	Newfoundland
B.C.	British Columbia	*N.H.*	New Hampshire
Calif.	California	*N. Ire.*	Northern Ireland
Colo.	Colorado	*N.J.*	New Jersey
Conn.	Connecticut	*N. Mex.*	New Mexico
Del.	Delaware	*N.W.T.*	Northwest Territories
Dem. Rep. of Congo	Democratic Republic of Congo	*N.Y.*	New York
Eng.	England	*Oh.*	Ohio
Fla.	Florida	*Okla.*	Oklahoma
Ga.	Georgia	*Ont.*	Ontario
Ia.	Iowa	*Oreg.*	Oregon
Id.	Idaho	*Orkney Is.*	Orkney Islands
Ill.	Illinois	*Pa.*	Pennsylvania
Ind.	Indiana	*R.G.S.*	Rio Grande do Sul
Kans.	Kansas	*R.I.*	Rhode Island
Ky.	Kentucky	*S.C.*	South Carolina
La.	Louisiana	*Scot.*	Scotland
Man.	Manitoba	*S.D.*	South Dakota
Mass.	Massachusetts	*Shetland Is.*	Shetland Islands
Md.	Maryland	*Tenn.*	Tennessee
Me.	Maine	*Tex.*	Texas
M.G.	Mato Grosso	*Ut.*	Utah
Mich.	Michigan	*Va.*	Virginia
Minn.	Minnesota	*Vt.*	Vermont
Miss.	Mississippi	*Wash.*	Washington
Mo.	Missouri	*Wis.*	Wisconsin
Mont.	Montana	*W. Va.*	West Virginia
N.B.	New Brunswick	*Wyo.*	Wyoming
N.C.	North Carolina	*Y.T.*	Yukon Territory

Symbols

This is a list of all the symbols used in the index to distinguish between different features. Any entry which has no symbol is a settlement.

- Country name
- State or province name
- Country capital
- State or province capital
- Mountain, volcano, peak
- Mountain range
- Physical region or feature
- River, canal
- Lake, salt lake
- Gulf, strait, bay
- Sea, ocean
- Cape, point
- Island or island group, rocky or coral reef
- Place of interest
- Historic region

A

Aachen 62 J4
Aalen 60 F8
Aalst 62 G4
Aarau 70 D3
Aare 70 C3
Aarschot 62 G4
Aba 108 F3
Abādān 101 C1
Ābādeh 101 E1
Abadla 106 E2
Abaji 108 F3
Abakaliki 108 F3
Abakan 82 S7
Abancay 50 C6
Abano Terme 70 G5
Abarqū 101 E1
Abashiri 88 N1
Abava 56 M8
Ābaya Hāyk' 110 F2
Abay Wenz 104 G5
Abbeville, *France* 62 D4
Abbeville, *United States* 42 C4
Abd al Kūrī 96 F7
Abéché 104 D5
Abengourou 108 D3
Abenójar 68 F6
Åbenrå 60 E1
Abensberg 60 G8
Abeokuta 108 E3
Aberaeron 64 H9
Aberdeen, *South Africa* 112 C6
Aberdeen, *United Kingdom* 64 K4
Aberdeen, *Miss., United States* 42 D3
Aberdeen, *S.D., United States* 38 G1
Aberdeen, *Wash., United States* 38 B1
Aberdeen Lake 34 M4
Aberystwyth 64 H9
Abez' 78 M1
Abhā 104 H4
Abhar 98 N5
Abidjan 108 D3
Abilene 44 G2
Abiline 32 M6
Abingdon, *United Kingdom* 62 A3
Abingdon, *United States* 42 E2
Abnûb 104 F2
Aboisso 108 D3
Abomey 108 E3
Abong Mbang 108 G4
Abou Déia 104 C5
Abqaiq 101 C4
Abrantes 68 B5
Absaroka Range 38 E1
Abū al Abayḑ 101 E4
Abu Aweigîla 100 B6
Abu Ballâs 104 E3
Abu Dhabi = Abū Ẓabī 101 F4
Abu Hamed 104 F4
Abuja 108 F3
Ābune Yosēf 104 G5
Abū Nujaym 104 C1
Abu Qarin 104 C1
Aburo 110 E3
Abu Simbel 104 F3
Abut Head 118 B6
Abuye Meda 110 F1
Abū Ẓabī 101 F4
Abv Nujaym 106 J2
Acaponeta 36 E7
Acapulco 46 E5
Acará 50 H4
Acarigua 50 D2
Accra 108 D3
Achaguas 46 L7
Achayvayam 84 W4
Acheng 86 H1
Achenkirch 70 G3
Achen See 70 G3
Achill Island 64 B8
Achim 60 E3
Achinsk 82 S6
Achit 78 L3
Aci Göl 76 M7
A Cihanbeyli 76 Q6
Acireale 72 K11
Acklins Island 46 K4
Aconcagua 48 D7
Açores 106 (1)B2
A Coruña 68 B1
Acqui Terme 70 D6
Acre 50 C5
Acri 72 L9
Ada 58 K12
Ada 42 B3
Adak Island 44 (3)C1
Adam 96 G5
Adams Island 118 (2)B1
'Adan 96 E7
Adana 98 F5
Adda 70 E5
Ad Dafrah 101 E5
Ad Dahnā 101 B3
Ad Dakhla 106 B4
Ad Dammām 101 D3
Ad Dawādimī 96 D5
Ad Dawḩah 101 D4
Ad Dilam 101 B5
Ad Dir'īyah 101 B4
Addis Ababa = Ādīs Ābeba 110 F2
Ad Dīwānīyah 96 D3
Adel 40 B2
Adelaide 116 G6
Adelaide Peninsula 34 M3
Adelaide River 116 F2
Aden = Adan 96 E7
Aderbissinat 108 F1
Adh Dhayd 101 F4
Adi 92 (2)D3
Adige 70 G5
Adīgrat 104 G5
Adilabad 94 C5
Adin 38 B2
Adīrī 104 B2
Ādīs Ābeba 110 F2
Adi Ugri 104 G5
Adıyaman 96 C2
Adjud 74 Q3
Adler 98 H2
Admiralty Island 34 E5
Admiralty Islands 114 E6
Adoni 94 C5
Adour 66 F10
Adra 68 H8
Adrano 72 J11
Adrar 106 E3
Adrar des Ifôghas 106 F5
Adrar Tamgak 106 G5
Adria 70 H5
Adriatic Sea 72 H4
Adycha 84 P3
Adygeya 98 J1
Adygeysk 98 H1
Adz'vavom 78 L1
Aegean Sea 76 H5
A Estrada 68 B2
Afghanistan 96 H3
'Afīf 104 H3
Afikpo 108 F3
Afognak Island 44 (1)G4
A Fonsagrada 68 C1
Afragóla 72 J8
'Afrīn 98 G5
Afuá 50 G4
'Afula 100 C4
Afyon 76 N6
Agadez 106 G5
Agadir 106 D2
Agadyr' 82 N8
Agalega Islands 102 J7
Agan 84 B4
Āgaro 110 F2
Agartala 94 F4
Agathonisi 76 J7
Agattu Island 84 W6
Agde 66 J10
Agen 66 F9
Ağin 98 H4
Aginskoye 82 S6
Agios Efstratios 76 H5
Agios Georgios 76 F7
Agios Nikolaos 76 H9
Agnita 74 M4
Agra 94 C3
Agrakhanskiy Poluostrov 98 M2
Agri 72 L8
Ağri 98 K4
Agrigento 72 H11
Agrinio 76 D6
Agrópoli 72 K8
Agryz 78 K3
Agua Prieta 44 E2
Aguascalientes 46 D4
A Gudiña 68 C2
Aguelhok 106 F5
Águilas 68 J7
Agulhas Negras 50 H8
Ağva 76 M3
Ahar 98 M4
Ahaura 118 C6
Ahaus 62 K2
Ahititi 118 E4
Ahlen 62 K3
Ahmadabad 94 B4
Ahmadnagar 94 B5
Ahmadpur East 94 B3
Ahr 60 B6
Ahram 101 D2
Ahrensburg 60 F3
Ahvāz 96 E3
Aichach 60 G8
Aigialousa 98 F6
Aigina 76 F7
Aigio 76 E6
Aigosthena 76 F6
Aihui 84 M6
Aim 84 N5
Ain 66 L7
Aïn Beïda 106 G1
'Aïn Ben Tili 106 D3
Aïn Bessem 68 P8
Aïn el Hadjel 68 P9
Ain Oussera 106 F1
Ainsa 68 L2
Aïn Sefra 106 E2
Ain Taya 68 P8
Aïn-Tédélès 68 L8
Aïn Témouchent 68 J9
Airão 50 E4
Aire 64 L8
Air Force Island 34 S3
Airolo 70 D4
Airpanas 92 (2)C4
Aisne 62 F5
Aitape 92 (2)F3
Aitkin 40 B1
Aitutaki 114 K7
Aiud 74 L3
Aix-en-Provence 66 L10
Aix-les-Bains 66 L8
Aizawl 94 F4
Aizkraukle 56 N8
Aizpute 56 L8
Aizu-wakamatsu 88 K5
Ajaccio 72 C7
Aj Bogd Uul 86 B2
Ajdābiyā 104 D1
Ajigasawa 88 L3
Ajka 58 G10
Ajlun 100 C4
Ajmān 101 F4
Ajmer 94 B3
Ajo 44 D2
Akanthou 100 A1
Akaroa 118 D6
Akasha 104 F3
Akashi 88 H6
Akbalyk 82 P8
Akçakale 98 H5
Akçakoca 76 P3
Aken 60 H5
Aketi 110 C3
Akhalk'alak'i 98 K3
Akhisar 76 K6
Akhmîm 104 F2
Akhty 98 M3
Akimiski Island 34 Q6
Akita 88 L4
Akjoujt 106 C5
Akka 106 D3
Akkajaure 56 J3
Akkeshi 88 N2
'Akko 100 C4
Akmeqit 96 L2
Aknanes 56 (1)B2
Akobo 110 E2
Akola 94 C4
Akonolinga 108 G4
Akordat 104 G4
Akpatok Island 34 T4
Akqi 82 P9
Akra Drepano 76 G5
Akra Sounio 76 F7
Akra Spatha 76 F9
Akra Trypiti 76 G9
Åkrehamn 56 C7
Akron 40 D2
Aksaray 98 E4
Aksarka 82 M4
Akşehir 76 P6
Akseki 76 P7
Aksha 84 J6
Akshiy 82 P9
Aksu 82 Q9
Aksuat 82 Q8
Āksum 104 G5
Aktau, *Kazakhstan* 54 K3
Aktau, *Kazakhstan* 82 N7
Aktogay 82 N8
Aktogay 82 P8
Aktuma 82 M8
Aktyubinsk 78 L4
Akula 110 C3
Akune 88 F8
Akure 108 F3
Akureyri 56 (1)E2
Akwanga 108 F3
Alabama 42 D3
Alaçam 98 F3
Alagoas 50 K5
Alagoinhas 50 K6
Alagón 68 J3
Al Ahmadi 101 C2
Al 'Amārah 96 E3
Alaminos 90 F3
Alamo 38 C3
Alamogordo 44 E2
Alamo Lake 44 D2
Åland 56 K6
Alanya 98 E5
Alappuzha 94 C7
Al Arţāwīyah 96 E4
Alaşehir 76 L6
Al 'Ashurīyah 104 H1
Alaska 44 (1)F2
Alaska Peninsula 44 (1)E4
Alaska Range 44 (1)G3
Alassio 70 D6
Alatri 72 H7
Alatyr' 78 J4
Alaverdı 98 L3
Alavus 56 M5
Alaykuu 82 N9
Al 'Ayn 101 F4
Alazeya 84 S2
Alba, *Italy* 70 D6
Alba, *Spain* 68 E4
Albacete 68 J5
Alba Iulia 74 L3
Albania 76 B3
Albany 34 Q6
Albany, *Australia* 116 C6
Albany, *Ga., United States* 42 E3
Albany, *Ky., United States* 42 E2
Albany, *N.Y., United States* 40 F2
Albany, *Oreg., United States* 38 B2
Albardão do João Maria 52 L4
Al Başrah 96 E3
Albatross Bay 116 H2
Albatross Point 118 E4
Al Baydā' 104 D1
Albenga 70 D6
Albert 62 E4
Alberta 34 H6
Albertirsa 58 J10
Albert Kanaal 62 G3
Albert Lea 40 B2
Albert Nile 110 E3
Albertville 66 M8
Albi 66 H10
Albina 50 G2
Albino 70 E5
Albion 38 F1
Ålborg 56 E8
Ålborg Bugt 56 F8
Albox 68 H7
Albstadt 60 E8
Albufeira 68 B7
Āl Bū Kamāl 98 J6
Albuquerque 44 E1
Al Buraymī 96 G5
Alburquerque 68 D5
Albury 116 J7
Al Buşayyah 101 B1
Alcácer do Sal 68 B6
Alcala de Guadaira 68 E7
Alcala de Henares 68 G4
Alcalá la Real 68 G7
Alcamo 72 G11
Alcañiz 68 K3
Alcantarilla 68 J7
Alcaraz 68 H6
Alcaudete 68 F7
Alcazar de San Juan 68 G5
Alcobendas 68 G4
Alcoi 68 K6
Alcolea del Pinar 68 H3
Alcorcón 68 G4
Alcoutim 68 C7
Aldabra Group 112 (2)A2
Aldan 84 M5
Aldan 84 N5
Aldeburgh 62 D2
Alderney 66 C4
Aldershot 62 B3
Aleg 106 C5
Aleksandrov-Sakhalinskiy 84 Q6
Aleksandrovskiy Zavod 84 K6
Aleksandrovskoye 78 Q2
Alekseyevka 82 N7
Aleksinac 74 J6
Alençon 66 F5
Aleppo = Ḩalab 98 G5
Aléria 72 D6
Alès 66 K9
Aleşd 58 M10
Alessándria 70 D6
Ålesund 56 D5

Aleutian Islands 44 (3)B1
Aleutian Range 44 (1)F4
Aleutian Trench 80 W5
Alexander Archipelago 44 (1)K4
Alexander Bay 112 B5
Alexander City 42 D3
Alexandra 118 B7
Alexandreia 76 E4
Alexandria = El Iskandarîya, *Egypt* 104 E1
Alexandria, *Romania* 74 N6
Alexandria, *La., United States* 42 C3
Alexandria, *Minn., United States* 40 A1
Alexandria, *Va., United States* 40 E3
Alexandroupoli 76 H4
Alexis Creek 34 G6
'Āley 100 C3
Aley 82 Q7
Aleysk 82 Q7
Al Farwānīyah 101 B2
Al Fāw 101 C2
Alfeld 60 E5
Alföld 74 H2
Alfonsine 70 H6
Alfreton 62 A1
Al Fuḩayḩil 101 C2
Al-Fujayrah 101 G4
Algeciras 68 E8
Algemes 68 K5
Algena 104 G4
Alger 106 F1
Algeria 106 E3
Al Ghāţ 101 A3
Al Ghayḑah 96 F6
Alghero 72 C8
Algiers = Alger 106 F1
Algona 40 B2
Al Hadīthah 100 E5
Alhama de Murcia 68 J7
Al Ḩamar 101 B5
Al Ḩamīdīyah 100 C2
Al Ḩammādah al Ḩamrā' 106 G3
Al Harūj al Aswad 104 C2
Al Ḩasakah 98 J5
Alhaurmín el Grande 68 F8
Al Ḩijāz 104 G2
Al Ḩillah 96 D3
Al Ḩilwah 101 B5
Al Hoceima 106 E1
Al Ḩudaydah 104 H5
Al Hufūf 101 C4
Al Ḩumayḑah 96 C4
Aliabad 101 F2
Aliağa 76 J6
Aliakmonas 76 E4
Āli Bayramlı 98 N4
Alicante 68 K6
Alice 42 B4
Alice Springs 116 F4
Alicudi 72 J10
Aligarh 94 C3
Alindao 110 C2
Alingås 56 G8
Alisos 44 D2
Aliwal North 112 D6
Al Jabal al Akhḑar 104 D1
Al Jaghbūb 104 D2
Al Jālamīd 104 G1
Al Jarah 101 B2
Al Jawf 104 G2
Aljezur 68 B7
Al Jifārah 101 A5
Al Jubayl 101 C3
Aljustrel 68 B7
Al Kāmil 96 G5
Al Khābūrah 101 G5
Al Kharj 101 B4
Al Khaşab 101 G3
Al Khawr 101 D4
Al Khubar 101 D3
Al Khums 106 H2
Al Khuwayr 101 D3
Alkmaar 62 G2
Al Kūt 96 E3
Al Kuwayt 101 C2
Al Lādhiqīyah 98 F6
Allahabad 94 D3
Allakh-Yun' 84 P4
Alldays 112 D4
Allen 90 G4
Allendale 42 E3
Allentown 40 E2
Aller 60 E4
Aller = Cabañquinta 68 E1
Alliance 38 F2
Allier 66 J8
Allinge 58 D2
Al Lith 104 H3
Alma, *Canada* 40 F1
Alma, *Nebr., United States* 38 G2
Alma, *Wis., United States* 40 B2
Almada 68 A6
Almadén 68 F6
Al Madīnah 104 G3
Al Majma'ah 96 E4
Almalyk 82 M9
Al Manāmah 101 D3
Almansa 68 J6
Al Marj 104 D1
Almaty 82 P9
Al Mawşil 98 K5
Al Mazāhumīyah 101 B4
Almazán 68 H3
Almeirim 50 G4
Almelo 62 J2
Almendralejo 68 D6
Almería 68 H8
Al'met'yevsk 82 J7
Almiros 76 E5
Al Mish'āb 101 C2
Almonte 68 D7
Almora 94 C3
Almosa 38 E3
Al Mubarraz 101 C4
Al Mudawwara 100 D7
Al Mukallā 96 E7
Al Mukhā 104 H5
Almuñécar 68 G8
Al Muqdādīyah 98 L7
Al Nu'ayrīyah 101 C3
Alnwick 64 L6
Alonnisos 76 F5
Alor 92 (2)B4
Alor Setar 90 C5
Alotau 116 K2
Alpena 40 D1
Alphen 62 G2
Alpi Lepontine 70 D4
Alpine 44 E2
Alpi Orobie 70 E4
Alps 70 B5
Al Qadmūs 100 D1
Al Qāmishlī 98 J5
Al Qar'ah 101 B3
Al Qaryāt 104 B1
Al Qaryatayn 100 E2
Al Qaţrūn 104 B3
Al Qunayţirah 100 C3
Al Qunfudhah 104 H4
Al Qurayyāt 104 G1
Al Qurnah 101 B1
Al Quşayr 101 A1
Al Quţayfah 100 D3
Als 60 E1
Alsask 34 K6
Alsasua 68 H2
Alsfeld 60 E6
Altaelva 56 M2
Altai Mountains 86 A1
Altamira 50 G4
Altamura 72 L8
Altanbulag 84 H6
Altay 82 R7
Altay, *China* 82 R8
Altay, *Mongolia* 86 B1
Altdorf 70 D4
Alte Mellum 60 D3
Altenburg 60 H6
Altenkirchen 60 J2
Altkirch 70 C3
Alto Garças 50 G7
Alto Molócuè 112 F3
Alton, *United Kingdom* 62 B3
Alton, *United States* 40 B3
Altoona 40 E2
Alto Parnaíba 50 H5
Altötting 70 H2
Altun Shan 82 S10
Alturas 38 B2
Altus 42 B3
Al 'Ubaylah 96 F5
Alūksne 56 P8
Alupka 98 E1
Alushta 98 F1
Al 'Uwayqīlah 104 H1
Al 'Uzayr 101 B1
Alva 42 B2
Alvarães 50 E4
Älvdalen 56 H6
Älvsbyn 56 L4
Al Wafrā' 101 B2
Al Wajh 104 G2
Alwar 94 C3
Al Wari'ah 101 B3
Alytus 58 P3
Alzey 60 D7
Alzira 68 K5
Amadi 110 E2
Amādīyah 98 K5
Amadjuak Lake 34 S4
Amadora 68 A6
Amahai 92 (2)C3
Amakusa-Shimo-shima 88 E7
Amaliada 76 D7
Amalner 94 C4
Amamapare 92 (2)E3
Amami-Ōshima 80 S7
Amanab 92 (2)F3
Amándola 72 H6
Amantéa 72 L9
Amapá 50 G3
Amapá 50 G3
Amarante 50 J5
Amarapura 90 B2
Amarillo 44 F1
Amasya 98 F3
Amay 62 H4
Amazar 84 L6
Amazon = Amazonas 48 F4
Amazonas 50 D4
Amazonas 50 E4
Ambala 94 C2
Ambanjā 112 H2
Ambarchik 84 U3
Ambato 50 B4
Ambato Boeny 112 H3
Ambatondrazaka 112 H3
Amberg 60 G7
Ambikapur 94 D4
Ambilobe 112 H2
Amboise 66 G6
Ambon 92 (2)C3
Ambositra 112 H4
Ambovombe 112 H5
Amchitka Island 44 (3)B1
Amderma 82 L4
Amdo 94 F2
Ameland 62 H1
Amengel'dy 82 M7
American Falls 38 D2
American Samoa 114 J7
Americus 42 E3
Amersfoort 62 H2
Amery 34 N5
Amery Ice Shelf 120 (2)M2
Ames 40 B2
Amfilochia 76 D6
Amfissa 76 E6
Amga 84 L5
Amga 84 N4
Amgun' 84 P6
Amherst 34 U7
Amiens 62 E5
Amirante Islands 112 (2)B2
Amistad Reservoir 44 F3
Amlekhganj 94 D3
Åmli 56 E7
'Ammān 100 C5
Ammerland 62 K1
Ammersee 70 F2
Ammochostos 98 E6
Ammochostos Bay 100 A1
Amo 90 C2
Amol 96 F2
Amorgos 76 H8
Amos 40 E1
Ampana 92 (2)B3
Ampanihy 112 G4
Amparai 94 D7
Ampezzo 70 H4
Amposta 68 L4
Amrān 96 D6
Amravati 94 C4
Amritsar 94 B2
Amroha 94 C3
Amrum 60 D2
Amsterdam, *Netherlands* 62 G2
Amsterdam, *United States* 40 F2
Amstetten 70 K2
Am Timan 104 D5
Amudar'ya 82 L9
Amundsen Gulf 34 G2
Amundsen Sea 120 (2)GG3
Amungen 56 H6
Amuntai 92 (1)F3
Amur 84 P6
Amursk 84 P6
Amvrakikos Kolpos 76 C6
Anabar 84 J2
Anaconda 38 D1
Anacortes 38 B1
Anadarko 38 G3
Anadolu Dağları 98 H3
Anadyr' 84 X4
Anadyrskaya Nizmennost' 84 X3
Anadyrskiy Zaliv 84 Y3
Anafi 76 H8
'Ānah 98 J6
Anaheim 44 C2
Anáhuac 44 F3
Analalava 112 H2
Anamur 98 B5
Anan 88 H7
Anantapur 94 C6
Anan'yiv 74 T2
Anapa 98 G1
Anápolis 50 H7
Anār 101 F1
Anārak 96 E3
Anardara 96 H3
Anatolia 76 M6
Añatuya 52 J4
Anchorage 44 (1)H3
Ancona 72 H5
Ancud 52 G7
Anda 86 H1
Andalgalá 52 H4
Åndalsnes 56 D5
Andalusia 42 D3
Andaman Islands 90 A4
Andaman Sea 90 A4
Andapa 112 H2
Andarāb 96 J2
Andenne 62 H4
Andernach 62 K4
Anderson 34 F3
Anderson 42 E
Andes 48 D5
Andfjorden 56 J2
Andipsara 76 H6
Andizhan 82 N9
Andkhvoy 96 J2
Andoas 50 B4
Andong 88 E
Andorra 68 L2
Andorra la Vella 68 M2
Andover 62 A
Andøya 56 H2
Andradina 52 L
Andreanof Islands 44 (3)C
Andrews 44 F
Andria 72 L
Andros 76 G
Andros, *Greece* 76 G
Andros, *The Bahamas* 42 F
Andros Town 42 F
Androtl 94 B
Andrychów 58 J
Andûjar 68 F
Andulo 112 B
Aneto 68 L
Angara 84 G
Angarsk 84 G
Ånge 56 H
Angel de la Guarda 44 D
Angeles 90 G
Ängelholm 56 G
Angeln 60 E
Angermünde 60 K
Angern 70 M
Angers 66 E6
Anglesey 64 H8
Angmagssalik = Tasiilaq 34 Z
Ango 110 D
Angoche 112 F
Angol 52 G6
Angola 102 E
Angola 40 D
Angostura Reservoir 38 F
Angoulême 66 F8
Angren 82 M
Anguilla 46 M
Aniak 44 (1)F
Anina 74 J
Anıyaman 98 H
Ankang 86 D
Ankara 98 E
Ankazoabo 112 G
Anklam 60 J
Ankpa 108 F
Ånn 56 G
Anna 78 H
Annaba 106 G
Annaberg-Buchholz 60 H6
An Nabk, *Saudi Arabia* 100 E
An Nabk, *Syria* 100 D
An Nafud 104 G
An Nāirīyah 96 E
An Najaf 96 D
Annapolis 40 E
Annapurna 94 D
Ann Arbor 40 D
An Nāşirīyah 104 J
Annecy 70 B
Annemasse 70 B
Anniston 42 D
Annobón 108 F
Annonay 66 K
An Nukhayb 96 D
Anqing 86 F
Ansbach 60 F
Anshan 88 B

Anshun 86 D5
Ansley 38 G2
Anson 42 B3
Ansongo 106 F5
Antakya 98 G5
Antalaha 112 J2
Antalya 76 N8
Antalya Körfezi 76 N8
Antananarivo 112 H3
Antarctic Peninsula 120 (2)LL3
Antequera 68 F7
Anti-Atlas 106 D3
Antibes 70 C7
Antigo 40 C1
Antigua 46 M5
Antigua and Barbuda 46 M5
Antikythira 76 F9
Antiparos 76 G7
Antipaxoi 76 C5
Antipayuta 82 P4
Antipodes Islands 118 (3)A1
Antlers 42 B3
Antofagasta 52 G3
Antonito 38 E3
Antrim 64 F7
Antropovo 78 H3
Antsalova 112 G3
Antsirabe 112 H3
Antsirañana 112 H2
Antu 88 E2
Antwerp = Antwerpen 62 G3
Antwerpen 62 G3
Anuradhapura 94 D7
Anxi 86 B2
Anyang, *China* 86 E3
Anyang, *South Korea* 88 D5
Anyuysk 84 U3
Anzhero-Sudzhensk 82 R6
Anzio 72 G7
Aoga-shima 88 K7
Aomori 88 L3
Aosta 70 C5
Aoukâr 106 C5
Aoukoukar 108 C1
Apalachee Bay 42 E4
Apalachicola 42 D4
Aparri 90 G3
Apatin 74 F4
Apatity 78 F1
Ape 56 P8
Apeldoorn 62 H2
Api 94 D2
Apia 114 J7
Apoera 50 F2
Apolda 60 G5
Apollo Bay 116 H7
Aporé 50 G7
Apostle Islands 40 B1
Apoteri 50 F3
Appalachian Mountains 42 E3
Appennino 72 G5
Appennino Abruzzese 72 H6
Appennino Calabro 72 K10
Appennino Lucano 72 K8
Appennino Tosco-Emiliano 70 E6
Appennino Umbro-Marchigiano 72 H6
Appleton 40 C2
Aprília 72 G7
Apure 50 D2
Apurimac 50 C6
Āqā 96 H3
'Aqaba 100 C7
Aquidauana 50 F8
Ara 94 D3
Arabian Sea 96 H6
Aracaju 50 K6
Aracati 50 K4
Araçatuba 50 G8
Aracuca 46 L7
Arad 74 J3
Arādah 96 F5
Arafura Sea 92 (2)D5
Aragarças 50 G7
Araguaia 48 F4
Araguaina 50 H5
Araguari 50 H7
Araguatins 50 H5
Arāk 96 E3
Arak 106 F3
Aral Sea 82 K8
Aral'sk 78 M5
Aranda de Duero 68 G3
Aranđjelovac 74 H5
Aran Island 64 D6
Aran Islands 64 B8
Aranjuez 68 G4
Aranos 112 B4
Aranyaprathet 90 C4
Araouane 106 E5
Arapahoe 38 G2
Arapiraca 50 K5
'Ar'ar 96 D3
Araras 50 G5
Ararat 98 L4
Arauca 50 D2
Araxá 50 H7
Araz 98 L4
Arbīl 98 K5
Arbon 70 E3
Arbre du Ténéré 106 G5
Arbroath 64 K5
Arcachon 66 D9
Arcadia 42 E4
Arcata 38 B2
Archidona 68 F7
Archipelago of the Recherche 116 D6
Archipel de la Société 114 L7
Archipel des Tuamotu 114 M7
Archipiélago de Camagüey 46 J4
Archipiélago de la Reina Adelaida 52 F9
Archipiélago de los Chonos 52 F7
Arco 38 D2
Arcos de la Frontera 68 E8
Arctic Bay 34 P2
Arctic Ocean 120 (1)A1
Arctic Red River 34 E3
Arda 76 H3
Ardabīl 98 N4
Ardahan 98 K3
Årdalstangen 56 D6
Ardas 76 J3
Ardatov 78 J4
Ardennes 62 G4
Ardestān 96 F3
Ardila 68 C6
Ardmore 36 G5
Aredo 92 (2)D3
Areia Branca 50 K5
Arendal 56 E7
Arenys de Mar 68 N3
Arequipa 50 C7
Arere 50 G4
Arévalo 68 F3
Arezzo 72 F5
Argan 82 R9
Argenta 70 G6
Argentan 62 B6
Argentina 52 H6
Argenton-sur-Creuse 66 G7
Argeş 74 N5
Argolikos Kolpos 76 E7
Argos 76 E7
Argos Orestiko 76 D4
Argostoli 76 C6
Argun' 84 K6
Argungu 108 E2
Argunsk 84 L6
Argyll 64 G5
Århus 56 F8
Ariano Irpino 72 K7
Ari Atoll 94 B8
Arica 50 C7
Ariège 66 G11
Arihge 68 M2
Arinos 50 F6
Aripuanã 50 E5
Aripuanã 50 E5
Ariquemes 50 E5
Arizona 44 D2
Arjäng 56 G7
Arka 84 Q5
Arkadak 78 H4
Arkadelphia 42 C3
Arkalyk 82 M7
Arkansas 42 C3
Arkansas 42 C3
Arkansas City 42 B2
Arkhalts'ikhe 98 K3
Arkhangel'sk 78 H2
Arkhipelag Nordenshel'da 82 R2
Arklow 64 F9
Arkoudi 76 C6
Arles 66 K10
Arlington, *Oreg., United States* 38 B1
Arlington, *Tex., United States* 42 B3
Arlington, *Va., United States* 40 E3
Arlit 106 G5
Arlon 62 H4
Armagh 64 F7
Armavir 98 J1
Armenia 98 K3
Armenia 50 B3
Armentières 62 E4
Armidale 116 K6
Armstrong 34 P6
Armyans'k 78 F5
Arnedo 68 H2
Arnett 42 B2
Arnhem 62 H3
Arnhem Land 116 F2
Arno 70 F7
Arnøy 56 G3
Arnøya 56 L1
Arnprior 40 E1
Arnsberg 62 L3
Arnstadt 60 F6
Arolsen 60 E5
Arorae 114 H6
Arquipélago dos Bijagós 108 A2
Ar Ramādī 96 D3
Ar Ramlah 100 C7
Arran 64 G6
Ar Raqqah 98 H6
Arras 62 E4
Arrasate 68 H1
Ar Rastan 100 D2
Ar Rawḑah 96 E7
Ar Rayn 101 A5
Arrecife 106 C3
Ar Riyāḑ 96 E5
Arrow Lake 38 C1
Arroyo Grande 44 B1
Ar Ruşāfah 98 H6
Ar Rustāq 96 G5
Ar Ruţba 96 D3
Ar Ruways 96 F5
Årsandøy 56 G4
Arsiè 70 G5
Arta, *Greece* 76 C5
Arta, *Mallorca* 68 P5
Artem 88 G2
Artemovsk 82 S7
Artemovskiy 84 K5
Artesia 44 F2
Arthur 38 F2
Arthur's Town 42 F5
Artigas 52 K5
Artillery Lake 34 J4
Artsyz 74 S4
Artux 82 F10
Artvin 98 J3
Artyk 84 Q4
Aru 114 D6
Arua 110 E3
Aruba 46 K6
Arumã 50 E4
Arusha 110 F4
Arvayheer 86 C1
Arviat 34 N4
Arvidsjaur 56 K4
Arvika 56 G7
Ary 82 Y3
Aryta 84 M4
Arzamas 78 H3
Arzew 68 K9
Arzignano 70 G5
Asahi-dake 88 M2
Asahikawa 88 M2
Āsalē 104 G5
Asansol 94 E4
Asarum 58 D1
Asbest 78 M3
Ascension 102 B6
Ascensión 50 E7
Aschaffenburg 60 E7
Aschersleben 60 G5
Áscoli Piceno 72 H6
Āsela 110 F2
Åsele 56 J4
Asenovgrad 76 G3
Asha 78 L3
Ashburton 118 C6
Asherton 42 B4
Asheville 40 D3
Ashford 62 C3
Ash Fork 44 D1
Ashgabat 96 G2
Ashington 64 L6
Ashizuri-misaki 88 G7
Ashkhabad = Ashgabat 96 G2
Ashland, *Kans., United States* 38 G3
Ashland, *Ky., United States* 40 D3
Ashland, *Mont., United States* 38 E1
Ashland, *Oreg., United States* 38 B2
Ashland, *Wis., United States* 40 B1
Ashqelon 100 B5
Ash Shadādah 98 J5
Ash Shāriqah 101 F4
Ash Shiḩr 96 E7
Ash Shu'bah 101 A2
Ash Shurayf 104 G2
Ash Shuwayrif 106 H3
Ashtabula 40 D2
Ashuanipi 34 T6
Ashuanipi Lake 34 T6
Āsika 94 D5
Asilah 106 D1
Asinara 72 C7
Asino 82 R6
Asīr 104 H3
Aşkale 98 J4
Askim 56 F7
Askot 94 D3
Asmara 104 G4
Åsnen 56 H8
Aso 70 J7
Āsosa 110 E1
Aspang Markt 70 M3
Aspe 68 K6
Aspermont 44 F2
As Pontes de Garcia Rodriguez 68 C1
As Sa'an 100 E1
Assab 104 H5
As Şalīf 96 D6
As Salmān 96 E3
As Salwā 101 D4
Assamakka 106 G5
As Samāwah 104 J1
Aş Şanamayn 100 D3
As Sarīr 104 D2
Asse 62 G4
Assen 62 J2
Assens 60 E1
As Sīb 101 H5
As Sidrah 104 C1
Assiniboia 34 K7
Assiniboine 34 M7
Assis 52 L3
Assisi 72 G5
As Sukhnah 98 H6
As Sulaymānīyah 98 L6
As Sulayyil 96 E5
Assumption Island 110 H5
As Suwaydā' 100 D4
As Suwayh 96 G5
Astakida 76 J9
Astana 82 N7
Astara 96 E2
Asti 70 D6
Astorga 68 D2
Astoria 38 B1
Astove Island 110 H6
Astrakhan' 78 J5
Astypalaia 76 J8
Asunción 52 K4
Aswân 104 F3
Aswân Dam 104 F3
Asyût 104 F2
As Zaydīyah 104 H4
Ata 114 J8
Atafu 114 J6
Atakpamé 108 E3
Atâr 106 C4
Atasu 82 N8
Atbara 104 F4
Atbasar 78 N4
Atchison 42 B2
Aterno 72 H6
Ath 62 F4
Athabasca 34 J5
Athens = Athina 76 F7
Athens, *Al., United States* 42 D3
Athens, *Ga., United States* 42 E3
Athens, *Oh., United States* 42 E2
Athens, *Tenn., United States* 42 E2
Athens, *Tex., United States* 42 B3
Athina 76 F7
Athlone 64 E8
Ath Thāyat 100 D7
Athy 64 F8
Ati 104 C5
Atiamuri 118 F4
Atico 50 C7
Atikokan 40 B1
Atka 84 S4
Atka Island 44 (3)C1
Atlanta 42 E3
Atlantic, *Ia., United States* 42 B1
Atlantic, *N.C., United States* 42 F3
Atlantic City 40 F3
Atlantic Ocean 64 C2
Atlantic Ocean 102 C7
Atlas Bogd 86 B2
Atlas Mountains 68 N9
Atlasovo 84 T5
Atlas Saharien 106 E2
Atlin 34 E5
Atmakur 94 C5
Atmore 42 D3

Atoka 42 B3
Atokos 76 C6
Atol das Rocas 50 L4
Aṭ Ṭā'if 96 D5
Attapu 90 D4
Attawapiskat 34 Q6
Attersee 70 J3
Attica 40 C2
Attu Island 44 (3)A1
Attu Island 120 (1)KK4
At Turbah 104 H5
Atyrau 78 K5
Aubagne 66 L10
Aubange 62 H5
Aube 66 K5
Aubenas 66 K9
Aubry Lake 34 F3
Auburn, *Al.*,
United States 42 D3
Auburn, *Calif.*,
United States 38 B3
Auburn, *Nebr.*,
United States 38 G2
Auburn, *Wash.*,
United States 38 B1
Aubusson 66 H8
Auce 58 M1
Auch 66 F10
Auchi 108 F3
Auckland 118 E3
Auckland Island 118 (2)B1
Aude 66 H10
Aue 60 H6
Auerbach 60 H6
Augathella 116 J5
Augsburg 70 F2
Augusta, *Australia* 116 C6
Augusta, *Italy* 72 K11
Augusta, *Ga.*,
United States 42 E3
Augusta, *Me.*,
United States 40 G2
Augustów 58 M4
Aulla 70 E6
Aurangābād 94 C5
Auray 66 C6
Aurich 62 K1
Aurillac 66 H9
Aurora, *Colo.*,
United States 38 F3
Aurora, *Ill.*,
United States 40 C2
Aurora, *Mo.*,
United States 42 C2
Aurukun 116 H2
Aus 112 B5
Auschwitz = Oświęcim 58 J7
Austin, *Minn.*,
United States 40 B2
Austin, *Nev.*,
United States 38 C3
Austin, *Tex.*,
United States 42 B3
Australia 116 E4
Australian Alps 114 E9
Australian Capital
Territory 116 J7
Austria 70 J3
Autun 66 K7
Auxerre 66 J6
Avallon 66 J6
Avam 84 E2
Āvārsin 98 M4
Aveiro 68 B4
Avellino 72 J8
Averøya 56 D5
Avesnes-sur-Helpe 62 F4
Avesta 56 J6
Avezzano 72 H6
Aviemore 64 J4
Avignon 66 K10
Ávila 68 F4
Avilés 68 E1
Avion 62 E4
Avola 72 K12
Avon, *United Kingdom* 62 A2
Avon, *United Kingdom* 62 A3
Avranches 66 D5
Avrig 74 M4
Awaji-shima 88 H6
Awanui 118 D2
Awat 82 Q9
Awatere 118 D5
Awbārī 104 B2
Awjilah 104 D2
Awka 108 F3
Ax-les-Thermes 66 G11
Ayacucho 50 C6
Ayaguz 82 Q8
Ayakkuduk 82 M9
Ayamonte 68 C7
Ayan 84 E3
Ayan 84 P5
Aya Napa 100 A2
Ayancık 98 F3
Ayanka 84 V4
Ayaviri 50 C6
Aydin 98 B5
Aydıncık 76 R8
Ayers Rock = Uluru 116 F5
Aykhal 84 J3
Aykino 82 H5
Aylesbury 62 B3
Aylmer Lake 34 K4
Aynī 96 J2
Aynī 82 M10
Ayn 'Īsá 98 H5
Ayoûn el 'Atroûs 106 D5
Ayr, *Australia* 116 J3
Ayr, *United Kingdom* 64 H6
Aytos 74 Q7
Ayutthaya 90 C4
Ayvalik 76 J5
Azaila 68 K3
Azaouâd 106 E5
Āzarān 98 M5
Azare 108 G2
A'zāz 98 G5
Azdavay 76 R3
Azerbaijan 98 M3
Azogues 50 B4
Azores = Açores 106 (1)B2
Azov 78 G5
Azpeitia 68 H1
Azrou 106 D2
Aztec 38 E3
Azuaga 68 E6
Azul 52 K6
Az Zabadānī 100 D3
Aẓ Ẓahrān 101 D3
Az Zāwīyah 104 B1
Az Zubayr 101 B1

B

Ba'albek 100 D2
Baardheere 110 G3
Babadag 74 R5
Babaeski 76 K3
Bāb al Mandab 96 D7
Babanusa 110 D1
Babar 92 (2)C4
Babayevo 78 G3
Babayurt 98 M2
Babo 92 (2)D3
Bābol 96 F2
Babruysk 78 E4
Babura 108 F2
Babushkin 84 H6
Babuyan Islands 90 G3
Bacabal 50 J4
Bacan 92 (2)C3
Bacău 74 P3
Baccarat 70 B2
Bachu 96 L2
Back 34 M3
Bačka Palanka 74 G4
Bačka Topola 74 G4
Backnang 70 E2
Bac Liêu 90 D5
Bacolod 90 G4
Badajós 50 H4
Badajoz 68 D6
Bad al Milḩ 98 K7
Badalona 68 N3
Bad Ausee 70 J3
Bad Bentheim 62 K2
Bad Berleburg 60 D5
Bad Doberan 60 G2
Bad Dürkheim 60 D7
Bad Ems 62 K4
Baden 58 F9
Baden-Baden 70 D2
Bad Freienwalde 60 K4
Badgastein 70 J3
Badgingarra 116 C6
Bad Harzburg 60 F5
Bad Hersfeld 60 E6
Bad Homburg 60 D6
Bad Honnef 62 K4
Badin 94 A4
Bad Ischl 70 J3
Bādiyat ash Shām 100 D4
Bad Kissingen 60 F6
Bad Kreuznach 62 K5
Bad Langensalza 60 F5
Bad Lauterberg 60 F5
Bad Liebenwerda 60 J5
Bad Mergentheim 60 E7
Bad Nauheim 60 D6
Bad Neuenahr-Ahrweiler 62 K4
Bad Neustadt 60 F6
Bad Oeynhausen 60 D4
Badong 86 E4
Bad Reichenhall 70 H3
Bad Säckingen 60 C9
Bad Salzuflen 60 D4
Bad Salzungen 60 F6
Bad Schwartau 60 F3
Bad Segeberg 60 F3
Bad Sobernheim 62 K5
Bad Urach 70 E2
Bad Vöslau 74 D2
Bad Waldsee 70 E3
Bad Wilbad 70 D2
Bad Wildungen 60 E5
Bad Windsheim 60 F7
Bad Wurzach 70 E3
Baena 68 F7
Bærum 56 F7
Baeza 68 G6
Baffin Bay 32 J2
Baffin Island 34 R2
Bafia 108 G4
Bafoulabé 108 B2
Bafoussam 108 G3
Bāfq 96 G3
Bafra 98 F3
Bafra Burun 98 G3
Bāft 101 G2
Bafwasende 110 D3
Baga 104 B5
Bagani 112 C3
Bagaroua 108 E2
Bagdad 44 D2
Bagdarin 84 J6
Bagé 52 L5
Baggs 38 E2
Baghdād 96 D3
Bagheria 72 H10
Baghlān 96 J2
Bagnères-de-Bigorre 66 F10
Bagno di Romagna 70 G7
Bagnols-sur-Cèze 66 K9
Baguio 90 G3
Bagun Datuk 92 (1)C2
Baharampur 94 E4
Bahawalnagar 94 B3
Bahawalpur 94 B3
Bahçe 98 G5
Bahia 50 J6
Bahía Blanca 52 J6
Bahía Blanca 52 J6
Bahía de Banderas 46 C4
Bahía de Campeche 46 F4
Bahía de Manta 50 A4
Bahía de Petacalco 46 D5
Bahía de Pisco 50 B6
Bahía de Santa Elena 50 A4
Bahía de Sechura 50 A5
Bahía Grande 52 H9
Bahia Kino 36 D6
Bahia Kino 46 B3
Bahía Negra 52 K3
Bahía Samborombón 52 K6
Bahir Dar 104 G5
Bahraich 94 D3
Bahrain 101 D4
Baḩrat Ḩimş 100 D2
Bahr el Abiad 104 F5
Bahr el Azraq 104 F5
Bahr el Ghazal 104 C5
Bahr el Ghazal 110 D2
Bahr el Jebel 110 E2
Bahr el Nîl = Nile 104 F4
Baía de Marajó 50 H4
Baía de Todos os Santos 50 K6
Baía do Bengo 108 E6
Baia Mare 74 L2
Baião 50 H4
Baia Sprie 74 L2
Baïbokoum 110 B2
Baicheng, *China* 82 Q9
Baicheng, *China* 86 G1
Baie Comeau 40 G1
Baie de la Seine 62 B5
Baie de la Somme 62 D4
Baie du Poste 34 S6
Baie St. Paul 40 F1
Baiji 98 K6
Baile Átha Cliath = Dublin 64 F8
Bailén 68 G6
Bailleul 62 E4
Bailundo 112 B2
Bainbridge 42 E3
Bairiki 114 H5
Bairin Yuoqi 86 F2
Bairin Zuoqi 86 F2
Bairnsdale 116 J7
Bais 90 G5
Baja 74 F3
Baja California 36 C5
Bakchar 82 Q6
Bakel 108 B2
Baker 114 J5
Baker, *Calif.*,
United States 38 C3
Baker, *Mont.*,
United States 38 H1
Baker, *Oreg.*,
United States 38 C2
Baker Lake 34 M4
Baker Lake 34 M4
Bakersfield 44 C1
Bakhta 84 D4
Baki 96 E1
Bakkafjörđur 56 (1)F1
Bakkaflói 56 (1)F1
Baku = Baki 96 E1
Balâ 98 E4
Balabac 90 F5
Balabac Strait 90 F5
Balagansk 84 G5
Balaghat 94 D4
Balaguer 68 L3
Balakhta 82 S6
Balaklava 98 E
Balakovo 78 J
Bālā Morghāb 82 L1
Bălan 74 N
Balāngīr 94 D
Balashov 78 H
Balassagyarmat 74 G
Balaton 74 E
Balatonfüred 74 E
Balatonlelle 74 E
Balchik 98 C
Balclutha 118 B
Bald Knob 40 B
Baldwin 42 E
Balearic Islands =
Islas Baleares 68 N
Bāleshwar 94 E
Baley 84 K
Baléyara 108 E
Balguntay 82 R
Bali 92 (1)F
Balige 92 (1)B
Balıkesir 76 K
Balikpapan 92 (1)F
Balimo 92 (2)F4
Balingen 70 D2
Balintang Channel 90 G3
Balkhash 82 N8
Ballarat 116 H7
Balleny Island 120 (2)Y3
Ballina, *Australia* 116 K5
Ballina,
Republic of Ireland 64 C7
Ballinasloe 64 D8
Ballinger 44 G2
Ball's Pyramid 116 L6
Ballymena 64 F7
Balmazújváros 74 J2
Balotra 94 B3
Balranald 116 H6
Balş 74 M5
Balsas 46 D5
Balsas 50 H5
Balta 74 S2
Bălţi 74 Q2
Baltic Sea 56 J8
Baltijsk 58 J3
Baltimore 40 E3
Baltrum 60 C3
Balvi 56 P8
Balykchy 82 P9
Balykshi 78 K5
Bam 96 G4
Bamaga 116 H2
Bamako 108 C2
Bamba 106 E5
Bambari 110 C2
Bamberg 60 F7
Bambesa 110 D3
Bambouk 106 C6
Bambouk Kaarta 108 B2
Bamda 86 B4
Bamenda 108 G3
Bāmīān 96 J3
Banaba 114 G6
Bañados del Izozog 50 E7
Banalia 110 D3
Banana, *Australia* 116 K4
Banana,
Dem. Rep. of Congo 110 A5
Banaz 76 M6
Ban Ban 90 C3
Banbury 64 L9
Banda 94 D3
Banda Aceh 90 B5
Bandama 108 C3
Bandar-e 'Abbās 101 G3
Bandar-e Anzalī 96 E2
Bandar-e Deylam 101 D1
Bandar-e Ganāveh 101 D2
Bandar-e Khoemir 101 F3

Bandar-e Lengeh	101	F3
Bandar-e Ma'shur	101	C1
Bandar-e Torkeman	96	F2
Bandar Khomeynī	101	C1
Bandar Seri Begawan	92	(1)E2
Banda Sea	92	(2)C3
Band-e Moghūyeh	101	F3
Bandirma	76	K4
Bandundu	110	B4
Bandung	92	(1)D4
Băneasa	74	Q5
Bāneh	98	L6
Banff, *Canada*	34	H6
Banff, *United Kingdom*	64	K4
Bangalore	94	C6
Bangangté	108	G3
Bangassou	110	C3
Bangbong	92	(2)B3
Banggi	92	(1)F1
Banghāzī	104	D1
Bangka	92	(1)D3
Bangkok = Krung Thep	90	C4
Bangladesh	94	E4
Bangor, *N.Ire., United Kingdom*	64	G7
Bangor, *Wales, United Kingdom*	64	H8
Bangor, *United States*	40	G2
Bang Saphan Yai	90	B4
Bangui	110	B3
Ban Hat Yai	90	C5
Ban Hua Hin	90	B4
Bani-Bangou	108	E1
Banī Walīd	106	H2
Bāniyās	98	F6
Banja Luka	74	E5
Banjarmasin	92	(1)E3
Banjul	108	A2
Ban Khemmarat	90	D3
Banks Island = Moa, *Australia*	116	H2
Banks Island, *B.C., Canada*	34	E6
Banks Island, *N.W.T., Canada*	34	G2
Banks Lake	38	C1
Banks Peninsula	118	D6
Banks Strait	116	J8
Bannerman Town	42	F5
Bannu	94	B2
Bánovce	58	H9
Banská	58	J9
Banská Štiavnica	58	H9
Bansko	76	F3
Bantry	64	C10
Banyo	108	G3
Banyoles	68	N2
Banyuwangi	92	(1)E4
Baode	86	E3
Baoding	86	F3
Baoji	86	D4
Bao Lôc	90	D4
Baoro	110	B2
Baoshan	90	B1
Baotou	86	E2
Baoying	86	F4
Bapaume	62	E4
Ba'qūbah	96	D3
Baquedano	52	H3
Bar	74	G7
Barabai	92	(1)F3
Baraboo	40	C2
Barakaldo	68	H1
Baramati	94	B5
Baramula	94	B2
Baran	94	C3
Baranavichy	78	E4
Baraolt	74	N3
Barbados	50	F1
Barbastro	68	L2
Barbate	68	E8
Barbuda	46	M5
Barcaldine	116	J4
Barcău	74	K2
Barcellona Pozzo di Gotto	72	K10
Barcelona, *Spain*	68	N3
Barcelona, *Venezuela*	46	M6
Barcelos, *Brazil*	50	E4
Barcelos, *Spain*	68	B3
Barco de Valdeorras = O Barco	68	D2
Barcs	74	E4
Bārdā	98	M3
Bardai	104	C3
Barddhamān	94	E4
Bardejov	58	L8
Bareilly	94	C3
Barents Sea	82	E3
Barentu	104	G4
Bareo	92	(1)F2
Barga	94	D2
Bargaal	110	J1
Barguzin	84	H6
Bar Harbor	40	G2
Bari	72	L7
Barikot	94	B1
Barinas	50	C2
Bârîs	104	F3
Barisal	94	F4
Barito	92	(2)A3
Barkam	86	C4
Barkava	56	P8
Barkly Tableland	116	F3
Barkol	82	S9
Bârlad	74	Q3
Bârlad	74	Q3
Bar-le-Duc	62	H6
Barletta	72	L7
Barmer	94	B3
Barmouth Bay	64	H9
Barnaul	82	Q7
Barnsley	64	L8
Barnstaple	64	H10
Barnstaple Bay	64	H10
Barpeta	94	F3
Barquisimeto	50	D1
Barr	70	C2
Barra, *Brazil*	50	J6
Barra, *United Kingdom*	64	E4
Barracão do Barreto	50	G5
Barra do Bugres	50	F7
Barra do Corda	50	H5
Barra do Garças	50	G7
Barra do São Manuel	50	G5
Barragem de Santa Clara	68	B7
Barragem de Sobradinho	50	J5
Barragem do Castelo de Bode	68	B5
Barragem do Maranhão	68	C6
Barranca, *Peru*	50	B4
Barranca, *Peru*	50	B6
Barranquilla	46	K6
Barreiras	50	H6
Barreiro	68	A6
Barretos	50	H8
Barrie	40	E2
Barron	40	B1
Barrow	44	(1)F1
Barrow-in-Furness	64	J7
Barrow Island	116	B4
Barrow Strait	34	N2
Barshatas	82	P8
Barsi	94	C5
Barstow	44	C2
Bar-sur-Aube	66	K5
Barth	60	H2
Bartın	98	E3
Bartle Frere	114	E7
Bartlesville	42	B2
Bartlett	38	G2
Bartoszyce	58	K3
Barus	92	(1)B2
Baruun Urt	86	E1
Barwani	94	B4
Barysaw	78	E4
Basaidu	101	F3
Basankusu	110	B3
Basarabeasca	74	R3
Basarabi	74	R5
Basca	72	C2
Basel	70	C3
Bashkiriya	78	K4
Bāsht	101	D1
Basilan	92	(2)B1
Basildon	62	C3
Basiluzzo	72	K10
Basingstoke	64	L10
Başkale	98	K4
Basoko	110	C3
Bassano	36	D1
Bassano del Grappa	70	G5
Bassar	108	E3
Bassas da India	112	F4
Basse Santa Su	106	C6
Basse Terre	46	M5
Bassett	38	G2
Bass Strait	116	H7
Bassum	60	D4
Bastak	101	F3
Bastānābād	98	M5
Basti	94	D3
Bastia	72	D6
Bastogne	62	H4
Bastrop, *La., United States*	42	C3
Bastrop, *Tex., United States*	42	B3
Bata	108	F4
Batagay	84	N3
Batak	76	G3
Batamay	84	M4
Batangas	90	G4
Batan Islands	90	G2
Batanta	92	(2)C3
Batemans Bay	116	K7
Batesville	42	D3
Bath, *United Kingdom*	64	K10
Bath, *United States*	40	E2
Bathinda	94	B2
Bathurst, *Australia*	116	J6
Bathurst, *Canada*	34	T7
Bathurst Inlet	34	K3
Bathurst Island, *Australia*	116	E2
Bathurst Island, *Canada*	34	M1
Batman	96	D2
Batna	106	G1
Baton Rouge	42	C3
Bátonyterenye	74	G2
Batroûn	100	C2
Battipaglia	72	J8
Battle	34	J6
Battle Creek	40	C2
Battle Harbour	34	V6
Battle Mountain	38	C2
Batu	110	F2
Batui	92	(2)E3
Bat'umi	98	J3
Batu Pahat	92	(1)C2
Baturino	82	F6
Baubau	92	(2)E4
Bauchi	108	F2
Baudette	40	B1
Baukau	92	(2)C4
Baume-les-Dames	66	M6
Bauru	52	M3
Bauska	56	N8
Bautzen	58	D6
Bawean	92	(1)E4
Bawiti	104	E2
Bawku	108	D2
Bayamo	46	J4
Bayanaul	82	P7
Bayandelger	84	H7
Bayan Har Shan	86	B4
Bayanhongor	86	C1
Bayan Mod	86	C2
Bayan Obo	86	D2
Bayansumküre	82	Q9
Bayburt	98	J3
Bay City, *Mich., United States*	40	D2
Bay City, *Tex., United States*	42	B4
Baydhabo	110	G3
Bayerische Alpen	70	G3
Bayeux	62	B5
Bayfield	40	B1
Bayindir	76	K6
Bāyir	100	D6
Baykit	82	T5
Baykonur	82	M8
Bay Minette	42	D3
Bay of Bengal	94	E5
Bay of Biscay	66	C9
Bay of Fundy	34	T8
Bay of Islands	118	E2
Bay of Plenty	118	F3
Bayonne	66	D10
Bayramaly	96	H2
Bayramiç	76	J5
Bayreuth	60	G7
Baysun	96	J2
Bayt al Faqīh	104	H5
Bay View	118	F4
Baza	68	H7
Bazas	66	E9
Bazdar	96	J4
Beach	38	F1
Beachy Head	62	C4
Beagle Gulf	116	E2
Bealanana	112	H2
Bear Island	64	B10
Bear Island = Bjørnøya	82	B3
Bear Lake	38	D2
Beasain	68	H1
Beas de Segura	68	H6
Beatrice	42	B1
Beatty	44	C1
Beaufort, *Malaysia*	92	(1)F1
Beaufort, *N.C., United States*	42	F3
Beaufort, *S.C., United States*	42	E3
Beaufort Sea	32	Q2
Beaufort West	112	C6
Beaumont	42	C3
Beaune	66	K6
Beauvais	62	E5
Beaver	38	D3
Beaver Creek	44	(1)J3
Beaver Dam	40	C3
Beaver Falls	40	D2
Beawar	94	B3
Beazley	52	H5
Bebra	60	E6
Bečej	74	H4
Béchar	106	E2
Beckley	42	E2
Becks	118	B7
Beckum	62	L3
Beclean	74	M2
Bedford, *United Kingdom*	64	M9
Bedford, *United States*	42	D2
Bedworth	62	A2
Beenleigh	116	K5
Beer Menuha	100	C6
Be'ér Sheva'	100	B5
Beeville	42	B4
Behbehān	101	D1
Bei'an	84	M7
Beihai	90	D2
Beijing	86	F3
Beipan	86	D5
Beipiao	86	G2
Beira	112	E3
Beirut = Beyrouth	100	C3
Beiuş	74	K3
Beizhen	88	A3
Béja	106	G1
Bejaïa	106	G1
Béjar	68	E4
Bekdash	96	F1
Békés	58	L11
Békéscsaba	74	J3
Bekily	112	H4
Bela	96	J4
Bela Crkva	74	J5
Belaga	92	(1)E2
Belarus	54	G2
Bela Vista	112	E5
Belaya	78	K3
Belaya Gora	84	R3
Bełchatów	58	J6
Belcher Islands	34	Q5
Beledweyne	110	H3
Belém	50	H4
Belen	46	C2
Belfast	64	G7
Belfield	38	F1
Belfort	70	E3
Belgazyn	82	T7
Belgium	62	G4
Belgorod	78	G4
Belgrade = Beograd	74	H5
Beli	108	G3
Belice	72	H11
Beli Manastir	74	F4
Belinyu	92	(1)D3
Belitung	92	(1)D3
Belize	46	G5
Belize	46	G5
Bellac	66	G7
Bella Coola	34	F6
Bellary	94	C5
Bellefontaine	40	D2
Belle Fourche	38	F2
Belle Glade	42	E4
Belle Île	66	B6
Belle Isle	34	V6
Bellême	66	F5
Belleterre	40	E1
Belleville, *Canada*	40	E2
Belleville, *United States*	42	B2
Bellingham	38	B1
Bellingshausen Sea	120	(2)JJ4
Bellinzona	70	E4
Bello	50	B2
Belluno	70	H4
Bellyk	84	E6
Belmont	40	E2
Belmonte, *Brazil*	50	K7
Belmonte, *Spain*	68	H5
Belmopan	46	G5
Belmullet	64	B7
Belogorsk	84	M6
Belogradchik	74	K6
Belo Horizonte	50	J7
Beloit, *Kans., United States*	42	B2
Beloit, *Wis., United States*	40	C2
Belomorsk	78	F2
Belorechensk	98	H1
Beloretsk	78	L4
Belo Tsiribihina	112	G3
Belovo	82	R7
Beloyarskiy	82	M5
Beloye More	78	G1
Belozersk	78	G2
Belozerskoye	78	N3
Belye Vody	82	M9
Belyy Yar	82	Q6
Belzig	60	H4
Bembibre	68	D2
Bemidji	40	A1
Bena Dibele	110	C4
Benavente	68	E3
Benbecula	64	E4

Bend 38 B2
Bender-Bayla 110 J2
Bender Qaasim 110 H1
Bendorf 62 K4
Bene 112 E3
Benešov 58 D8
Benevento 72 J7
Bengbu 86 F4
Bengkulu 92 (1)C3
Benguela 112 A2
Benguerir 106 D2
Benha 104 F1
Beni 110 D3
Beni 50 D6
Beni Abbès 106 E2
Benicarló 68 L4
Benidorm 68 K6
Benī Mazâr 104 F2
Beni Mellal 106 D2
Benin 108 E2
Benin City 108 F3
Beni Saf 68 J9
Beni Slimane 68 P8
Beni Suef 104 F2
Benito Juaréz 52 K6
Benjamin Constant 50 D4
Benkelman 38 F2
Benkovac 70 L6
Ben More Assynt 64 H3
Ben Nevis 64 H5
Bennington 40 F2
Benoud 106 F2
Bensheim 60 D7
Benson, *Ariz.*, *United States* 44 D2
Benson, *Minn.*, *United States* 36 G2
Benteng 92 (2)B4
Bentinck Island 116 G3
Bentonville 42 C2
Bentung 92 (1)C2
Benue 108 G3
Benxi 86 G2
Beograd 74 H5
Bepazarı 98 D3
Berat 76 B4
Beravina 112 H3
Berber 104 F4
Berbera 104 H5
Berbérati 110 B3
Berchtesgaden 70 J3
Berck 62 D4
Berdigestyakh 84 M4
Berdyans'k 78 G5
Berdychiv 78 E5
Bereeda 110 J1
Berehove 74 K1
Bererreá 68 C2
Berettyóújfalu 74 J2
Berettys 58 L10
Bereznik 78 H2
Berezniki 78 L3
Berezovo 78 N2
Berezovyy 84 P6
Berga 68 M2
Bergama 76 K5
Bérgamo 70 E5
Bergara 68 H1
Bergedorf 60 F3
Bergen, *Netherlands* 62 G2
Bergen, *Norway* 56 C6
Bergen, *Germany* 60 J2
Bergen, *Germany* 60 E4
Bergen op Zoom 62 G3
Bergerac 66 F9
Bergheim 62 J4
Bergisch Gladbach 60 C6
Bergsfjordhalvøya 56 L1
Beringen 62 H3
Beringovskiy 84 X4
Bering Sea 44 (1)C4
Bering Strait 44 (1)C2
Berkeley 44 B1
Berkner Island 120 (2)A2
Berkovitsa 74 L6
Berlin, *Germany* 60 J4
Berlin, *United States* 40 F2
Bermejillo 44 F3
Bermejo 52 K4
Bermeo 68 H1
Bermuda 32 H6
Bern 70 C4
Bernado 44 E2
Bernau 60 J4
Bernay 62 C5
Bernburg 60 G5
Berner Alpen 70 C4
Beroun 58 D8
Berounka 60 J7
Berovo 76 E3
Berrouaghia 68 N8
Berry Islands 42 F4
Bertoua 108 G4
Bertram 40 D1
Beruni 82 L9
Berwick-upon-Tweed 64 L6
Besalampy 112 G3
Besançon 66 M6
Beshneh 101 F2
Bessemer 42 D3
Bestamak 82 P8
Bestuzhevo 78 H2
Bestyakh, *Russia* 84 L3
Bestyakh, *Russia* 84 M4
Betanzos 68 B1
Bětdâmbâng 90 C4
Bethany 40 B2
Bethel, *Ak.*, *United States* 44 (1)E3
Bethel, *Pa.*, *United States* 40 F2
Bethlehem, *Israel* 100 C5
Bethlehem, *South Africa* 112 D5
Béthune 62 E4
Betioky 112 G4
Betoota 116 H5
Betpak-Dala 82 M8
Betroka 112 H4
Bet-She'an 100 C4
Bettiah 94 D3
Betul 94 C4
Betzdorf 60 C6
Beulah 40 C2
Beverley 64 M8
Beverungen 60 E5
Bexhill 62 C4
Bey Dağlari 76 M8
Beyla 108 C3
Beyneu 82 J8
Beypazarı 76 P4
Beyrouth 100 C3
Beyşehir 76 P7
Beyşehir Gölü 76 P7
Bezhetsk 78 G3
Béziers 66 J10
Bhadgaon 94 E3
Bhadrakh 94 E4
Bhadravati 94 C6
Bhagalpur 94 E3
Bhairab Bazar 94 F4
Bhakkar 94 B2
Bhamo 90 B2
Bharuch 94 B4
Bhatpara 94 E4
Bhavnagar 94 B4
Bhawanipatna 94 D5
Bhilai 94 D4
Bhilwara 94 B3
Bhīmavaram 94 D5
Bhind 94 C3
Bhiwandi 94 B5
Bhopal 94 C4
Bhubaneshwar 94 E4
Bhuj 94 A4
Bhusawal 94 C4
Bhutan 94 E3
Biak 92 (2)E3
Biak 92 (2)E3
Biała 58 K8
Biała Podlaska 58 N5
Białogard 58 F3
Białystok 58 N4
Biarritz 66 D10
Biasca 70 D4
Bibbiena 70 G7
Biberach 70 E2
Bicaz 74 P3
Bickerton Island 116 G2
Bicske 74 F2
Bida 108 F3
Bidar 94 C5
Bidbid 101 H5
Biddeford 40 F2
Bideford 64 H10
Biedenkopf 60 D6
Biel 70 C3
Bielefeld 60 D4
Biella 70 D5
Bielsko-Biała 58 J8
Bielsk Podlaski 58 N5
Biên Hoa 90 D4
Bietigheim-Bissingen 70 E2
Big 34 G2
Biga 76 K4
Bigadiç 76 L5
Big Desert 116 H7
Big Falls 40 B1
Bighorn 36 E2
Bighorn Lake 38 E1
Bighorn Mountains 38 E2
Bight of Bangkok 90 C4
Bight of Benin 108 E3
Bight of Biafra 108 F4
Big Lake 44 (1)H2
Bignona 106 B6
Big Pine 42 E5
Big Rapids 40 C2
Big River 34 K6
Big Sandy 38 D1
Big Sioux 38 G2
Big Spring 44 F2
Big Sur 44 B1
Big Trout Lake 34 P6
Bihać 70 L6
Bijapur 94 C5
Bījār 98 M6
Bijeljina 74 G5
Bijelo Polje 74 G6
Bijie 86 D5
Bikanar 94 B3
Bikin 84 N7
Bikini 114 G4
Bilaspur 94 D4
Biläsuvar 98 N4
Bila Tserkva 78 F5
Bilbao 68 H1
Bileća 74 F7
Bilecik 76 M4
Bilečko Jezero 74 F7
Biled 74 H4
Biłgoraj 58 M7
Bilhorod-Dnistrovs'kyy 78 F5
Bílina 60 J6
Billings 38 D1
Bill of Portland 64 K11
Bilma 104 B4
Biloxi 42 D3
Bimini Islands 42 F4
Binche 62 G4
Bindi Bindi 116 C6
Bindura 112 E3
Bingen 60 C7
Binghamton 40 E2
Bingöl 98 J4
Binongko 92 (2)B4
Bintulu 92 (1)E2
Bintuni 92 (2)D3
Binyang 90 D2
Binzhou 86 F3
Biograd 70 L7
Birāk 106 H3
Birao 104 D5
Biratnagar 94 E3
Bi'r Bazīrī 100 E2
Birdsville 116 G5
Bireun 92 (1)B1
Bîr Gifgâfa 100 A6
Birhan 104 G5
Bîr Hasana 100 A6
Bīrjand 96 G3
Birkenfeld 62 K5
Birmingham, *United Kingdom* 64 L9
Birmingham, *United States* 42 D3
Bîr Mogreïn 106 C3
Birnie 114 J6
Birnin-Gwari 108 F2
Birnin Kebbi 108 E2
Birnin Konni 108 F2
Birnin Kudu 108 F2
Birobidzhan 84 N7
Birsk 78 L3
Biržai 58 P1
Bi'r Zalţan 104 C2
Bisbee 44 E2
Biscéglie 72 L7
Bischofshofen 70 J3
Bischofswerda 58 D6
Biševo 72 L6
Bishkek 82 N9
Bishop 38 C3
Bishop Auckland 64 L7
Bishop's Stortford 62 C3
Biskra 106 G2
Bislig 90 H5
Bismarck 36 F2
Bismarck Sea 114 E6
Bissau 106 B6
Bistcho Lake 34 H5
Bistriţa 74 M2
Bistriţa 74 P3
Bitburg 62 J5
Bitche 60 C7
Bitkine 104 C5
Bitlis 98 K4
Bitola 76 D3
Bitonto 72 L7
Bitterfeld 60 H5
Bitterroot Range 38 C1
Bitti 72 D8
Bitung 92 (2)C2
Biu 108 G2
Biwa-ko 88 H6
Bixby 40 B3
Biyāvra 94 C4
Biysk 82
Bizerte 106
Bjelovar 74
Bjørnøya 82
B-Köpenick 60
Blackburn 64
Blackfoot 38
Blackfoot Reservoir 38
Black Hills 38
Blackpool 64
Black Range 44
Black River Falls 40
Black Rock Desert 38
Blacksburg 40
Black Sea 98
Blacks Harbour 40
Black Sugarloaf 116
Black Volta 108
Blackwater 64
Blagny-sur-Bresle 62
Blagodarnyy 98
Blagoevgrad 76
Blagoveshchenka 82
Blagoveshchensk 84
Blain 66
Blair 40
Blairsden 38
Blairsville 42
Blaj 74
Blakely 42
Blanco 50
Blanding 44
Blankenberge 62
Blankenburg 60
Blankenheim 62
Blantyre 112
Blasket Islands 64
Blaubeuren 70
Blaye-et-Sainte-Luce 66
Bled 70
Blenheim 118
Blevands Huk 60
Blida 106
Blind River 36
Bloemfontein 112
Bloemhof 112
Blois 66
Blönduós 56
Błonie 58
Bloomfield 42
Bloomington, *Ill.*, *United States* 40
Bloomington, *Ind.*, *United States* 40
Bludenz 70
Blue Earth 40
Bluefield 40
Bluefields 46
Blue Mountain Lake 40
Blue Mountains 38
Blue Nile = Bahr el Azraq 104
Bluenose Lake 34
Bluff, *New Zealand* 118
Bluff, *United States* 44
Blumenau 52
Blythe 44
Blytheville 42
Bo 108
Boac 90
Boa Vista, *Brazil* 50
Boa Vista, *Cape Verde Islands* 108
Bobbili 94
Bòbbio 70
Bobigny 62
Bobingen 70
Böblingen 70
Bobo Dioulasso 108
Bobr 58
Bobrov 78
Bôca do Acre 50
Boca Grande 46
Boca Grande 48
Bocaiúva 50
Bocaranga 110
Bochart 40
Bochnia 58
Bocholt 60
Bochum 60
Bodaybo 84
Bode 60
Bodélé 104
Boden 56
Bodham 94
Bodmin 64
Bodø 56
Bodrog 58
Bodrum 76
Boe 38
Boende 110
Bogale 90
Bogalusa 42

Boggabilla 116 K5
Boghni 68 P8
Bognor Regis 62 B4
Bogo 90 G4
Bogor 92 (1)D4
Bogorodskoye 84 Q6
Bogotá 50 C3
Bogotol 82 R6
Bogra 94 E4
Boguchany 84 F5
Bogué 106 C5
Bo Hai 86 F3
Bohmerwald 60 H7
Bohol 90 G5
Bohumin 58 H8
Boiaçu 50 E4
Boise 38 C2
Boise City 44 F1
Bojnūrd 82 K10
Bokatola 110 B4
Boké 108 B2
Bokspits 112 C5
Bokungu 110 C4
Bolbec 62 C5
Bole, *China* 82 Q9
Bole, *Ghana* 108 D3
Bolechiv 58 N8
Bolesławiec 58 E6
Bolgatanga 108 D2
Bolhrad 74 R4
Bolintin-Vale 74 N5
Bolivar 40 B3
Bolivia 50 D7
Bollène 66 K9
Bollnäs 56 J6
Bolmen 56 G8
Bolnisi 98 L3
Bolobo 108 H5
Bologna 70 G6
Bolognesi 50 C5
Bolomba 108 H4
Bolotnoye 82 Q6
Bol'shaya Pyssa 78 J2
Bol'sherech'ye 78 P3
Bol'shezemel'skaya
Tundra 82 J4
Bol Shirta 84 C4
Bolshoy Atlym 78 N2
Bol'shoy Osinovaya 84 W3
Bol'shoy Vlas'evo 84 Q6
Bolshoy Yuga 78 P2
Bolsover 62 A1
Bolton 64 K8
Bolu 98 D3
Bolvadin 76 P6
Bolzano = Bozen 70 G4
Boma 108 G6
Bombala 116 J7
Bombay = Mumbai 94 B5
Bomili 110 D3
Bom Jesus da Lapa 50 J6
Bømlo 56 C7
Bomnak 84 M6
Bonāb 98 M5
Bonaparte Archipelago 116 B2
Bonavista Bay 34 W7
Bondeno 70 G6
Bondo 110 C3
Bondokodi 116 C1
Bondoukou 108 D3
Bondowoso 92 (1)E4
Bongandanga 110 C3
Bongao 92 (2)A1
Bongor 108 H2
Bonifacio 72 D7
Bonn 60 C6
Bonners Ferry 38 C1
Bonorva 72 C8
Bonthe 108 B3
Bontoc 90 G3
Bonyhád 74 F3
Boone 40 D3
Boonville 42 C2
Boorama 110 G2
Boosaaso 96 E7
Boothia Peninsula 34 M2
Booué 108 G5
Boppard 60 C6
Bor, *Russia* 84 D4
Bor, *Sudan* 110 E2
Bor, *Turkey* 76 S7
Bor, *Yugoslavia* 74 K5
Borah Peak 38 C3
Borås 56 G8
Borāzjān 101 D2
Bordeaux 66 E9
Borden Peninsula 34 Q2
Border Town 116 H7
Bordj Bou Arréridj 106 F1
Bordj Bounaam 68 M9
Bordj Flye Sante Marie 106 E3
Bordj Messaouda 106 G2
Bordj Mokhtar 106 F4
Bordj Omar Driss 106 G3
Borgarnes 56 (1)C2
Borger 44 F1
Borgomanero 70 D5
Borgo San Dalmazzo 70 C6
Borgo San Lorenzo 70 G7
Borgosésia 70 D5
Borgo Val di Taro 70 E6
Bori Jenein 106 H2
Borislav 58 N8
Borisoglebsk 78 H4
Borjomi 98 K3
Borken 62 J3
Borkou 104 C4
Borkum 62 J1
Borlänge 56 H6
Bórmida 70 D6
Bormio 70 F4
Borna 60 H5
Borneo 92 (1)E3
Bornholm 56 H9
Borodino 82 R5
Borodinskoye 56 Q6
Boromo 108 D2
Borovichi 78 F3
Borovskoy 78 M4
Borriana 68 K5
Borroloola 116 G3
Borşa 74 M2
Borshchiv 74 P1
Borshchovochnyy
Khrebet 84 J7
Borđeyri 56 (1)C2
Borūjerd 96 E3
Borzya 84 K6
Bosa 72 C8
Bosanska Dubica 74 D4
Bosanska Gradiška 74 E4
Bosanska Kostajnica 70 M5
Bosanska Krupa 74 D5
Bosanski Brod 74 F4
Bosanski Novi 74 D4
Bosanski Petrovac 74 D5
Bosansko Grahovo 70 M6
Boşca 74 J4
Bose 90 D2
Bosilegrad 74 K7
Boskovice 58 F8
Bosna 74 F5
Bosnia-Herzegovina 74 E5
Bosobolo 110 B3
Bosporus = İstanbul
Boğazı 76 M3
Bosporus 96 A1
Bossambélé 110 B2
Bossangoa 110 B2
Bossier City 42 C3
Bosten Hu 82 R9
Boston, *United Kingdom* 64 M9
Boston, *United States* 40 F2
Botevgrad 74 L7
Botlikh 96 E1
Botna 74 R3
Botoşani 74 P2
Botou 86 F3
Botrange 62 J4
Botswana 112 C4
Bottrop 62 J3
Bou Ahmed 68 F9
Bouaké 108 C3
Bouar 110 B2
Bouârfa 106 E2
Boufarik 68 N8
Bougainville Island 114 F6
Bougainville Reef 116 J3
Bougouni 108 C2
Bougzoul 68 N9
Bouira 106 F1
Bou Ismaïl 68 N8
Bou Izakarn 106 D3
Boujdour 106 C3
Bou Kadir 68 M8
Boulder 38 E2
Boulder City 44 D1
Boulia 116 G4
Boulogne-sur-Mer 62 D4
Bounty Islands 114 H10
Bourem 106 E5
Bourg-de-Piage 66 L9
Bourg-en-Bresse 66 L7
Bourges 66 H6
Bourgoin-Jallieu 66 L8
Bourke 116 J6
Bournemouth 64 L11
Bou Saâda 106 F1
Bousso 104 C5
Boussu 62 F4
Boutilimit 106 C5
Bouzghaïa 68 M8
Bowbells 38 F1
Bowen 116 J4
Bowie, *Ariz.*,
United States 44 E2
Bowie, *Tex.*,
United States 44 G2
Bowkan 98 M5
Bowling Green, *Fla.*,
United States 42 E4
Bowling Green, *Ky.*,
United States 42 D2
Bowling Green, *Mo.*,
United States 42 C2
Bowman 38 F1
Bowman Bay 34 R3
Bo Xian 86 F4
Boxwood Hill 116 C6
Boyabat 98 F3
Boyang 86 F5
Boyarka 84 F2
Boysen Reservoir 38 E2
Boyuibe 52 J3
Bozcaada 76 H5
Boz Dağ 76 M7
Bozeman 38 D1
Bozen 70 G4
Bozkır 76 Q7
Bozoum 110 B2
Bozüyük 76 N5
Bra 70 C6
Brač 74 D6
Bracciano 72 G6
Bräcke 56 H5
Brad 74 K3
Brádano 72 L8
Bradford 64 L8
Brady 42 B3
Braga 68 B3
Bragança, *Brazil* 50 H4
Bragança, *Portugal* 68 D3
Brahmapur 94 D5
Brahmaputra 94 F3
Brăila 74 Q4
Brainerd 40 B1
Braintree 62 C3
Brake 60 D3
Bramming 60 D1
Brampton 40 E2
Bramsche 60 D4
Branco 50 E3
Brandberg 112 A4
Brandenburg 60 H4
Brandenton 42 E4
Brandon 34 M7
Brandvlei 112 C5
Brandýs 58 D7
Braniewo 58 J3
Brasileia 50 D6
Brasília 50 H7
Braslaw 56 P9
Braşov 74 N4
Bratislava 58 G9
Bratsk 84 G5
Bratskoye
Vodokhranilishche 84 G5
Brattleboro 40 F2
Braţul 74 R4
Braunau 70 J2
Braunschweig 60 F4
Brawley 44 C2
Bray 64 F8
Brazil 48 F4
Brazzaville 110 B4
Brčko 74 F5
Brda 58 G4
Bream Bay 118 E2
Breckenridge 44 G2
Břeclav 58 F9
Breda 62 G3
Bredasdorp 112 C6
Bredstedt 60 E2
Bredy 78 M4
Bree 62 H3
Bregenz 70 E3
Breiđafjörđur 56 (1)A2
Bremangerlandet 56 B6
Bremen, *Germany* 60 D3
Bremen, *United States* 42 D3
Bremerhaven 60 D3
Bremerton 38 B1
Bremervörde 60 E3
Brenham 42 B3
Brennero 70 G4
Breno 70 F5
Brentwood 62 C3
Bréscia 70 F5
Breslau = Wrocław 58 G6
Bressanone = Brixen 72 F2
Bressay 64 M1
Bressuire 66 E7
Brest, *Belarus* 78 D4
Brest, *France* 66 A5
Breteuil 62 E5
Bretten 60 D7
Breves 50 G4
Brewarrina 116 J5
Brewton 42 D3
Brežice 74 C4
Brézina 106 F2
Brezno 58 J9
Bria 110 C2
Briançon 70 B5
Briceni 74 Q1
Bridgend 64 J10
Bridgeport, *Calif.*,
United States 44 C1
Bridgeport, *Conn.*,
United States 40 F2
Bridgeport, *Nebr.*,
United States 38 F2
Bridgetown 50 F1
Bridgewater 34 U8
Bridgwater 64 J10
Bridlington 64 M7
Brienzer See 70 D4
Brig 70 C4
Brigham City 38 D2
Brighton, *United Kingdom* 62 B4
Brighton, *United States* 38 F3
Brignoles 70 B7
Brikama 108 A2
Brilon 60 D5
Bríndisi 72 M8
Brinkley 42 C3
Brisbane 116 K5
Bristol, *United Kingdom* 64 K10
Bristol, *United States* 42 E2
Bristol Bay 44 (1)E4
Bristol Channel 64 H10
British Columbia 34 F5
Britstown 112 C6
Brive-la-Gaillarde 66 G8
Briviesca 68 G2
Brixen 70 G4
Brixham 64 J11
Brlik 82 N9
Brno 58 F8
Broad Sound 116 J4
Broadus 38 E1
Brockton 40 F2
Brockville 40 E2
Brod 74 J9
Brodeur Peninsula 34 P2
Brodick 64 G6
Brodnica 58 J4
Broken Arrow 46 E1
Broken Bow 42 C3
Broken Hill 116 H6
Brokopondo 50 F2
Bromölla 58 D1
Bromsgrove 64 K9
Brønderslev 56 E8
Brooke's Point 90 F5
Brookhaven 36 H5
Brookhaven 42 C3
Brookhaven 46 F2
Brookings, *Oreg.*,
United States 38 B2
Brookings, *S.D.*,
United States 38 G2
Brooks 34 J6
Brooks Range 44 (1)F2
Brooksville 42 E4
Broome 116 D3
Brösarp 56 H9
Brovary 78 F4
Brownfield 44 F2
Browning 38 D1
Brownsville, *Tenn.*,
United States 42 D2
Brownsville, *Tex.*,
United States 42 B4
Brownwood 42 B3
Bruchsal 60 D7
Bruck, *Austria* 70 L3
Bruck, *Austria* 70 M2
Bruck an der Mur 74 C2
Brugge 62 F3
Brühl 62 J4
Bruint 94 G3
Brumado 50 J6
Brumath 70 C2
Bruneau 38 C2
Bruneck 70 G4
Brunei 92 (1)E2
Brunflo 56 H5
Brunico = Bruneck 72 F2
Brunsbüttel 60 E3
Brunswick, *Ga.*,
United States 42 E3
Brunswick, *Me.*,
United States 40 G2
Bruntal 58 G8
Brush 38 F2
Brussels = Bruxelles 62 G4
Bruxelles 62 G4

Bryan 42 B3
Bryanka 82 S6
Bryansk 78 F4
Brzeg 58 G7
Brzeg Dolny 58 F6
Brzeziny 58 J6
B-Spandau 58 C5
Bubi 112 E4
Bucak 98 D5
Bucaramanga 50 C2
Buchanan 108 B3
Buchan Gulf 34 S2
Bucharest = București 74 P5
Buchen 60 E7
Buchholz 60 E3
Buchy 66 M5
Bückeburg 60 E4
București 74 P5
Budapest 74 G2
Budennovsk 98 L1
Büdingen 60 E6
Budrio 70 G6
Buenaventura, *Colombia* 50 B3
Buenaventura, *Mexico* 44 E3
Buena Vista 38 E3
Buenos Aires 52 K5
Buffalo, *Okla.*,
United States 42 B2
Buffalo, *N.Y.*,
United States 40 E2
Buffalo, *S.D.*,
United States 38 F1
Buffalo, *Tex.*,
United States 42 B3
Buffalo, *Wyo.*,
United States 38 E2
Buffalo Lake 34 J4
Buffalo Narrows 34 K5
Buftea 74 N5
Bug 58 L5
Bugojno 74 E5
Bugrino 82 H4
Bugul'ma 78 K4
Buguruslan 78 K4
Buḩayrat al Asad 98 H5
Buḩayrat ath Tharthār 98 K6
Buhuși 74 P3
Builth Wells 64 J9
Buinsk 78 J3
Buir Nur 86 F1
Bujanovac 74 J7
Buje 70 J5
Bujumbura 110 D4
Bukachacha 84 K6
Bukavu 110 D4
Bukhara 96 H2
Bukkittinggi 92 (1)C3
Bukoba 110 E4
Bula, *Indonesia* 92 (2)D3
Bula, *Papua New Guinea* 92 (2)F4
Bülach 70 D3
Bulawayo 112 D4
Buldir Island 84 X6
Bulgan 84 G7
Bulgaria 74 M7
Buli 92 (2)C2
Bulle 70 C4
Bullhead City 44 D1
Bulls 118 E5
Bulukumba 92 (2)B4
Bulun 84 M2
Bumba 110 C3
Bumbești Jiu 74 L4
Buna 110 F3
Bunbury 116 C6
Buncrana 64 E6
Bunda 110 E4
Bundaberg 116 K4
Bünde 60 D4
Bungunya 116 J5
Bunia 110 E3
Bunkie 42 C3
Bunnell 42 E4
Bünyan 98 F4
Buôn Mê Thuôt 90 D4
Buotama 84 M4
Bura 110 F4
Buran 82 R8
Buranj 94 D2
Burao 110 H2
Burāq 100 D3
Buraydah 96 D4
Burco 104 J6
Burdur 98 D5
Burdur Gölü 76 N7
Burē 104 G5
Büren 62 L3
Burg 60 G4
Burgas 74 Q7
Burgaski Zaliv 74 Q7
Burgdorf 70 C3
Burghausen 70 H2
Burglengenfeld 60 H7
Burgos 68 G2
Burgsvik 56 K8
Burhaniye 76 K5
Burhanpur 94 C4
Burjassot 68 K5
Burj Şāfitā 100 D2
Burketown 116 G3
Burkeville 40 E3
Bur-Khaybyt 84 P3
Burkina 108 D2
Burlin 78 K4
Burlington, *Colo.*,
United States 44 F1
Burlington, *Ia.*,
United States 40 B2
Burlington, *Vt.*,
United States 40 F2
Burma = Myanmar 90 B2
Burnet 42 B3
Burney 38 B2
Burnie 116 J8
Burns 38 C2
Burns Junction 38 C2
Burns Lake 34 F6
Burqin 82 R8
Burra 116 G6
Burrel 76 C3
Bursa 76 M4
Bûr Safâga 104 F2
Bûr Sa'îd 104 F1
Bur Sudan 104 G4
Burtnieks 56 N8
Burton-upon-Trent 64 L9
Buru 92 (2)C3
Burundi 110 D4
Bururi 110 D4
Burwell 38 G2
Buryatiya 84 J6
Bury St. Edmunds 62 C2
Būshehr 101 D2
Bushire = Būshehr 101 D2
Businga 110 C3
Busira 110 C4
Buşrá ash Shām 100 D4
Bussum 62 H2
Busto Arsizio 70 D5
Buta 110 C3
Butare 110 D4
Butaritari 114 H5
Bute 64 G6
Butembo 110 D3
Buđardalur 56 (1)C2
Buton 92 (2)B3
Butte, *Mont.*,
United States 38 D1
Butte, *Nebr.*,
United States 38 G2
Butuan 90 H5
Butwal 94 D3
Butzbach 60 D6
Bützow 60 G3
Buulobarde 110 H3
Buxton 62 A1
Buy 78 H3
Buynaksk 98 M2
Büyükada 76 L4
Büyükçekmece 76 L4
Buzai Gumbad 96 K2
Buzançais 66 G7
Buzău 74 P4
Buzău 74 Q4
Buzuluk 78 K4
Byala 74 N6
Byala Slatina 74 L6
Byam Martin Island 34 L2
Byaroza 56 N10
Bydgoszcz 58 H4
Bygdin 56 D6
Bygland 56 D7
Bykovskiy 84 M2
Bylot Island 34 R2
Byskeälven 56 L4
Bystřice 58 G8
Bystrzyca Kłodzka 58 F7
Bytatay 84 N3
Bytča 58 H8
Bytom 58 H7
Bytów 58 G3
Bzura 58 J5

C

Caaguazú 52 K4
Caballococha 50 C5
Caballo Reservoir 44 E2
Cabanatuan 90 G3
Cabano 40 G1
Cabañaquinta 68 E1
Cabdul Qaadir 104 H5
Cabeza del Buey 68 E6
Cabezas 50 E7
Cabimas 50 C1
Cabinda 108 G6
Cabinda 108 G6
Cabo Bascuñán 52 G4
Cabo Beata 46 K5
Cabo Camarón 46 G5
Cabo Carvoeiro 68 A5
Cabo Catoche 46 G4
Cabo Corrientes,
Colombia 50 B2
Cabo Corrientes, *Mexico* 46 C4
Cabo Corrubedo 68 A2
Cabo Cruz 46 J5
Cabo de Espichel 68 A6
Cabo de Gata 68 H8
Cabo de Hornos 52 H10
Cabo de la Nao 68 L6
Cabo Delgado 112 G2
Cabo de Palos 68 K7
Cabo de São Roque 50 K5
Cabo de Sao Tomé 52 N3
Cabo de São Vicente 68 A7
Cabo de Trafalgar 68 D8
Cabo dos Bahías 52 H8
Cabo Fisterra 68 A2
Cabo Frio 52 N3
Cabo Gracias á Dios 46 H6
Cabo Mondego 68 A4
Cabo Norte 50 H3
Cabo Orange 50 G3
Cabo Ortegal 68 B1
Cabo Peñas 68 E1
Caborca 44 D2
Cabo Rojo 46 E4
Cabo Roxo 108 A2
Cabo San Diego 52 H9
Cabo San Francisco de
Paula 52 H8
Cabo San Juan 108 F4
Cabo San Lucas 36 D7
Cabo Santa Elena 46 J7
Cabo Tortosa 68 L4
Cabo Tres Puntas 52 H8
Cabot Strait 34 U7
Cabrera 68 N5
Čačak 74 H6
Cáceres, *Brazil* 50 F7
Cáceres, *Spain* 68 D5
Cachimbo 50 G5
Cachoeira do Sul 52 L4
Cachoeiro de Itapemirim 50 J8
Cacola 112 B2
Caconda 112 B2
Čadca 58 H8
Cadillac, *Mich.*,
United States 40 C2
Cadillac, *Mont.*,
United States 36 E2
Cádiz 68 D8
Caen 62 B5
Caernarfon 64 H8
Cagayan de Oro 90 G5
Cagli 70 H7
Cagliari 72 D9
Cagnes-sur-Mer 70 C7
Caguas 46 L5
Cahama 112 A3
Cahors 66 G9
Cahuapanas 50 B5
Cahul 74 R4
Caia 112 F3
Caianda 112 C2
Caicos Islands 46 K4
Cairns 116 J3
Cairo = El Qâhira 104 F1
Cairo 42 D2
Caiundo 112 B3
Cajamarca 50 B5
Čakovec 74 D3
Calabar 108 F3
Calabozo 50 D2
Calafat 74 K6
Calahorra 68 J2
Calais 62 D4
Calama 52 H3
Calamar 50 C3
Calamian Group 90 F4
Calamocha 68 J4
Călan 74 L4
Calanscio Sand Sea 104 D2
Calapan 90 G4
Călărași, *Moldova* 74 R2
Călărași, *Romania* 74 Q5
Calatafim 72 G11
Calatayud 68 J3
Calauag 90 G4
Calbayog 90 G4
Calçoene 50 G3
Calcutta 94 E4
Caldas da Rainha 68 A5
Caldera 52 G4
Caldwell, *Id.*,
United States 38 C2
Caldwell, *Kans.*,
United States 42 E2
Calf of Man 64 F7
Calgary 34 J6
Calhoun 42 E3
Calhoun City 42 C3
Calhoun Falls 42 E3
Cali 50 E3
Calicut = Kozhikode 94 C6
Caliente 38 C3
California 36 E4
Calilabad 98 M4
Callao 50 B6
Caloundra 116 K5
Caltagirone 72 J11
Caltanissetta 72 J11
Caluquembe 112 A2
Caluula 110 J1
Calvi 72 C6
Calvin 42 B3
Calvinia 112 B6
Calw 70 D2
Camaçari 50 K6
Camacupa 112 B2
Camagüey 46 J4
Camaiore 70 F7
Camana 50 C7
Camargue 66 K1
Camariñas 68 A1
Camarones 52 H7
Ca Mau 90 D5
Camberley 64 M1
Cambodia 90 C4
Cambrai 62 F4
Cambria 38 B3
Cambrian Mountains 64 H1
Cambridge, *New Zealand* 118 E3
Cambridge,
United Kingdom 64 N
Cambridge, *Md.*,
United States 40 E
Cambridge, *Mass.*,
United States 40 F
Cambridge, *Oh.*,
United States 40 D
Cambridge Bay 34 K
Cambrils 68 M
Camden, *Ark.*,
United States 42 C
Camden, *S.C.*,
United States 42 E
Cameron, *La.*,
United States 42 C
Cameron, *Mo.*,
United States 42 C
Cameron, *Tex.*,
United States 42 B
Cameroon 108 G
Cametá 50 H
Çamiçigölü 76 K
Caminha 68 B
Camiranga 50 H
Camocim 50 J
Camooweal 116 G3
Camopi 50 G3
Campbell Island 118 (2)C2
Campbell River 34 F7
Campbellsville 40 C3
Campbellton 40 G1
Campbeltown 64 G6
Campeche 46 F5
Câmpeni 74 L3
Câmpia Turzii 74 L3
Câmpina 74 N4
Campina Grande 50 L5
Campinas 52 M3
Campobasso 72 J7
Campo de Criptana 68 G5
Campo de Diauarum 50 G6
Campo Gallo 52 J4
Campo Grande 52 L3
Campo Maior 50 J4
Campo Mourão 52 L3
Campos 52 N3
Câmpulung 74 N4
Câmpulung Moldovenesc 74 N2
Cam Ranh 90 D4
Çan 76 K4
Canada 32 M4
Canadian 44 F1
Canadian 44 F1
Çanakkale 76 J4
Çanakkale Boğazı 76 J4
Canal de Panamá 46 J7
Cananea 44 D2
Canary Islands =
Islas Canarias 102 A3
Canary Islands =
Islas Canarias 106 B3
Cañaveras 68 H4

Canberra	116	J7
Cancún	46	G4
Çandarli Körfezi	76	J6
Candelaro	74	C8
Candlemas Island	48	J9
Cangamba	112	B2
Cangas	68	B2
Cangas de Narcea	68	D1
Cangyuan	90	B2
Cangzhou	86	F3
Canicatti	72	H11
Canindé	50	K4
Çankiri	98	E3
Canna	64	F4
Cannanore	94	B6
Cannanore	94	C6
Cannes	70	C7
Cannock	62	A2
Canon City	44	E1
Cantanduanes	90	G4
Canterbury	62	D3
Canterbury Bight	118	C7
Canterbury Plains	118	C6
Cân Tho	90	D5
Canto do Buriti	50	J5
Canton, *Miss.*, *United States*	42	D3
Canton, *Oh.*, *United States*	42	E1
Canton, *S.D.*, *United States*	38	G2
Canumã	50	F4
Canumã	50	F5
Canutama	50	E5
Canyon	44	F1
Canyon Ferry Lake	38	D1
Cao Bǎng	90	D2
Caorle	70	H5
Cap Blanc	72	D11
Cap Bon	106	H1
Cap Corse	72	D5
Cap d'Agde	66	J10
Cap d'Antifer	62	C5
Cap de Fer	106	G1
Cap de Formentor	68	P5
Cap de la Hague	66	D4
Cap-de-la-Madeleine	40	F1
Cap de Nouvelle-France	34	S4
Cap de ses Salines	68	P5
Cap des Trois Fourches	68	H9
Cape Agulhas	112	C6
Cape Alexandra	52	P9
Cape Andreas	96	B2
Cape Apostolos Andreas	98	F6
Cape Arid	116	D6
Cape Arnaoutis	98	D6
Cape Arnhem	116	G2
Cape Barren Island	116	J8
Cape Bauld	34	V6
Cape Blanco	38	B2
Cape Borda	116	G7
Cape Breton Island	34	U7
Cape Brett	118	E2
Cape Byron	116	K5
Cape Campbell	118	E5
Cape Canaveral	42	E4
Cape Canaveral	42	E4
Cape Carnot	116	F6
Cape Charles	40	E3
Cape Chidley	34	U4
Cape Christian	34	T2
Cape Churchill	34	N5
Cape Clear	64	C10
Cape Cleare	44	(1)H4
Cape Coast	108	D3
Cape Cod	40	G2
Cape Columbine	112	B6
Cape Colville	118	E3
Cape Comorin	94	C7
Cape Constantine	44	(1)E4
Cape Coral	42	E4
Cape Crawford	116	G3
Cape Croker	116	F2
Cape Dalhousie	44	(1)L1
Cape Direction	116	H2
Cape Disappointment	52	P9
Cape Dominion	34	R3
Cape Dorchester	34	Q3
Cape Dorset	34	R4
Cape Dyer	34	U3
Cape Egmont	118	D4
Cape Eleaia	100	B1
Cape Farewell, *Greenland*	32	F4
Cape Farewell, *New Zealand*	118	D5
Cape Fear	42	F3
Cape Finisterre = Cabo Fisterra	68	A2
Cape Flattery, *Australia*	116	J2
Cape Flattery, *United States*	38	A1
Cape Forestier	116	J8
Cape Foulwind	118	C5
Cape Fria	112	A3
Cape Girardeau	40	C3
Cape Greko	98	F6
Cape Grenville	116	H2
Cape Grim	116	H8
Cape Harrison	34	V6
Cape Hatteras	42	F2
Cape Henrietta Maria	34	Q5
Cape Horn = Cabo de Hornos	52	H10
Cape Howe	116	K7
Cape Inscription	116	B5
Cape Jaffa	116	G7
Cape Karikari	118	D2
Cape Kellett	34	F2
Cape Kidnappers	118	F4
Cape Leeuwin	116	B6
Cape Lévêque	116	D3
Cape Londonderry	116	E2
Cape Lookout	46	J2
Cape May	40	F3
Cape Melville	116	H2
Cape Mendenhall	44	(1)D4
Cape Mendocino	38	A2
Cape Mercy	34	U4
Cape Meredith	52	J9
Cape Naturaliste	116	B6
Capenda-Camulemba	112	B1
Cape Negrais	90	A3
Cape Nelson	116	H7
Cape Newenham	44	(1)E4
Cape of Good Hope	112	B6
Cape Palliser	118	E5
Cape Palmas	108	C4
Cape Parry	34	G2
Cape Providence	118	A8
Cape Race	32	G5
Cape Ray	34	V7
Cape Reinga	118	D2
Cape Romanzof	44	(1)D3
Cape Runaway	118	G3
Cape Sable	34	T8
Cape St. Elias	44	(1)J4
Cape St. Francis	112	C6
Cape San Agustin	90	H5
Cape San Blas	42	D4
Cape Saunders	118	C7
Cape Scott	116	E1
Cape Stephens	118	D5
Cape Terawhiti	118	E5
Cape Three Points	108	D4
Cape Town	112	B6
Cape Turnagain	118	F5
Cape Verde	108	(1)B2
Cape Wessel	116	G2
Cape Wrangell	84	W6
Cape Wrath	64	G3
Cape York	116	H2
Cape York Peninsula	116	H2
Cap Figalo	68	J9
Cap Fréhel	66	C5
Cap Gris-Nez	62	D4
Cap-Haïtien	46	K5
Cap Juby	106	C3
Cap Lopez	108	F5
Cap Negro	68	E9
Capo Carbonara	72	D10
Capo Colonna	72	M9
Capo Gallo	72	H10
Capo Granitola	72	G11
Capo Murro di Porco	72	K11
Capo Palinuro	72	J8
Capo Passero	72	K12
Capo Santa Maria di Leuca	72	N9
Capo San Vito	72	G10
Capo Spartivento	72	C10
Capo Vaticano	72	K10
Capraia	72	D5
Cap Rhir	106	C2
Capri	72	J8
Capricorn Group	116	K4
Cap Rosa	72	C11
Cap Serrat	72	D11
Cap Spartel	68	E9
Cap Timiris	106	B5
Capua	72	J7
Cap Verga	108	B2
Cap Vert	108	A2
Caquetá	50	C4
Caracal	74	M5
Caracarai	50	E3
Caracas	50	D1
Caransebeş	74	K4
Carauari	50	D4
Caravaca de la Cruz	68	J6
Caravelas	50	K7
Carazinho	52	L4
Carballiño	68	B2
Carballo	68	B1
Carbondale, *Ill.*, *United States*	42	D2
Carbondale, *Pa.*, *United States*	42	F1
Carboneras	68	J7
Carbónia	72	C9
Carcar	90	G4
Carcassonne	66	H10
Cardiff	64	J10
Cardigan Bay	64	H9
Cardston	38	D1
Carei	74	K2
Carentan	66	D4
Cariacica	52	N3
Cariati	72	L9
Caribbean Sea	46	J6
Carlet	68	K5
Carleton Place	40	E1
Carlisle, *United Kingdom*	64	K7
Carlisle, *United States*	40	E2
Carlow	64	F9
Carlsbad	44	F2
Carlyle	38	F1
Carmacks	34	D4
Carmagnola	70	C6
Carmarthen	64	H10
Carmarthen Bay	64	G10
Carmaux	66	H9
Carmen	46	B3
Carmona	68	E7
Carnarvon, *Australia*	116	B4
Carnarvon, *South Africa*	112	C6
Car Nicobar	94	F7
Carnot	110	B2
Carnsore Point	64	F9
Carolina	50	H5
Carolina Beach	42	F3
Caroline Island	114	L6
Caroline Islands	114	E5
Carpathian Mountains	58	J8
Carpatii Meridionali	74	K4
Carpentras	66	L9
Carpi	70	F6
Carrabelle	42	E4
Carrara	70	F6
Carrickfergus	64	G7
Carrick-on-Suir	64	E9
Carrington	38	G1
Carrizozo	44	E2
Carroll	40	B2
Carrollton, *Ky.*, *United States*	40	D3
Carrollton, *Mo.*, *United States*	42	C1
Çarşamba	98	G3
Carson City	38	C3
Cartagena, *Colombia*	50	B1
Cartagena, *Spain*	68	K7
Carthage	42	C3
Cartwright	34	V6
Caruarú	50	K5
Carúpano	50	E1
Casablanca	106	D2
Casa Grande	44	D2
Casale Monferrato	70	D5
Casalmaggiore	70	F6
Casarano	72	N9
Cascade, *Id.*, *United States*	38	C2
Cascade, *Mont.*, *United States*	38	C1
Cascade Range	38	B2
Cascade Reservoir	38	C2
Cascais	68	A6
Cascavel	52	L3
Caserta	72	J7
Cashel	112	E3
Casino	116	K5
Casma	70	M5
Caspe	68	K3
Casper	38	E2
Caspian Sea	54	J3
Cassiar	34	F5
Cassino	72	H7
Castanhal	50	H4
Castelbuono	72	J11
Castel di Sangro	72	J7
Castellammare del Golio	72	G10
Castellane	70	B7
Castellaneta	72	L8
Castelli	52	J4
Castelló de la Plana	68	K5
Castelnaudary	66	G10
Castelo Branco	68	C5
Castelsarrasin	66	G10
Castelvetrano	72	G11
Castets	66	D10
Castiglion Fiorentino	70	G7
Castlebar	64	C8
Castleford	64	L8
Castle Point	118	F5
Castres	66	H10
Castricum	62	G2
Castries	46	M6
Castro	52	M3
Castro Verde	68	B7
Castrovíllari	72	L9
Castuera	68	E6
Catamarca	52	H4
Catandica	112	E3
Catánia	72	K11
Catanzaro	72	L10
Catanzaro Marina	72	L10
Catarman	90	G4
Catbalogan	90	H4
Cat Island	42	F5
Cat Lake	34	N6
Cato Island	116	L4
Catriló	52	L6
Catskill Mountains	36	M3
Cattólica	70	H7
Cauayan	90	G5
Cauca	50	C2
Caucaia	50	K4
Caucasia	50	B2
Caucasus	98	K2
Caudry	62	F4
Cauquenes	52	G6
Caura	50	E2
Causapscal	40	G1
Căuşeni	74	S3
Cavaillon	66	L10
Cavalese	70	G4
Cavan	64	E8
Cavárzere	70	H5
Cave	118	C7
Cavinas	50	D6
Cavtat	74	F7
Caxias	50	J4
Caxias do Sul	52	L4
Caxito	108	G6
Çay	76	P6
Cayce	42	E3
Çaycuma	76	Q3
Cayenne	50	G3
Cayman Islands	46	H5
Caynabo	110	H2
Cayos Miskitos	46	H6
Cay Sal Bank	42	E5
Cazorla	68	H7
Ceanannus Mor	64	F8
Ceará	50	J4
Cebu	90	G4
Cebu	90	G4
Cécina	70	F7
Cedar City	38	D3
Cedar Falls	40	B2
Cedar Lake	34	L6
Cedar Rapids	40	B2
Cedros	36	C6
Ceduna	116	F6
Ceerigaabo	110	H1
Cefalù	72	L10
Cegléd	74	G2
Celaya	46	D4
Celebes = Sulawesi	92	(2)A3
Celebes Sea	92	(2)B2
Celje	74	C3
Celldömölk	74	E2
Celle	60	F4
Celtic Sea	64	E10
Centerville	40	B2
Cento	70	G6
Central African Republic	110	C2
Central City	38	G2
Centralia, *Ill.*, *United States*	40	C3
Centralia, *Wash.*, *United States*	38	B1
Central Range	92	(2)F3
Central Siberian Plateau = Srednesibirskoye Ploskogor'ye	80	N2
Cenxi	90	E2
Ceres, *Argentina*	52	J4
Ceres, *Brazil*	50	H7
Cerezo de Abajo	68	G3
Cerignola	72	K7
Çerikli	98	E4
Çerkes	76	Q4
Çerkezköy	76	K3
Cernavodă	74	R5
Cero Champaqui	52	J5
Cerralvo	36	E7
Cërrik	76	C3
Cerritos	44	F4
Cerro Aconcagua	52	G5
Cerro Bonete	52	H4
Cerro de la Encantada	36	C5
Cerro de Pasco	50	B6
Cerro Huehuento	46	C4
Cerro Las Tórtolas	52	H5
Cerro Marahuaca	50	D3
Cerro Mercedario	52	G5
Cerro Murallón	52	G8
Cerro Nevado	52	H6

Cerro Pena Nevade 46 D4
Cerro San Lorenzo 52 G8
Cerro San Valentín 52 G8
Cerros de Bala 50 D6
Cerro Tres Picos 52 J6
Cerro Tupungato 52 H5
Cerro Yaví 50 D2
Cerro Yogan 52 H9
Certaldo 70 G7
Cervaro 72 K7
Cervia 70 H6
Cervionne 72 D6
Cervo 68 C1
Cesena 70 H6
Cesenático 70 H6
Cēsis 56 N8
Česka Lípa 60 K6
České Budějovice 70 K2
Český Krumlov 70 K2
Çeşme 76 J6
Česna 70 M5
Cessano 70 J7
Cessnock 116 K6
Cetate 74 L5
Cetinje 74 F7
Cetraro 72 K9
Ceuta 106 D1
Cevizli 76 P7
Chachapoyas 50 B5
Chaco Boreal 52 K3
Chad 104 C5
Chadan 82 S7
Chadron 38 F2
Chagai 96 H4
Chagda 84 N5
Chaghcharān 96 J3
Chagyl 96 G1
Chāh Bahār 96 H4
Chāībāsa 94 E4
Chainat 90 C3
Chaiyaphum 90 C3
Chalais 66 F8
Chalhuanca 50 C6
Chalinze 110 F5
Chalki 76 K8
Chalkida 76 F6
Chalkidiki 76 F4
Challans 66 D7
Challapata 50 D7
Challenger Deep 114 E4
Challis 38 D2
Châlons-sur-Marne 62 G6
Chalon-sur-Saône 66 K7
Cham 60 H7
Chama 112 E2
Chamba 94 C2
Chambal 94 C3
Chamberlain 38 G2
Chambersburg 40 E3
Chambéry 70 A5
Chambly 62 E5
Chamonix 70 B5
Champagnole 70 A4
Champaign 40 C2
Champaubert 62 F6
Champlitte 70 A3
Chañaral 52 G4
Chandalar 34 B3
Chandeleur Islands 46 G3
Chandigarh 94 C2
Chandler 44 D2
Chandrapur 94 C5
Changane 112 E4
Changara 112 E3
Changchun 88 C2
Changde 86 E5
Chang-hua 86 G6
Chang Jiang 86 D4
Changsha 86 E5
Changshu 86 G4
Changting 86 F5
Changzhi 86 E3
Changzhou 86 F4
Chania 76 G9
Channel Islands, *United Kingdom* 64 K12
Channel Islands, *United States* 36 C5
Channel-Port aux Basques 34 V7
Chanthaburi 90 C4
Chantilly 62 E5
Chanute 42 B2
Chao Phraya 90 C4
Chaouèn 106 D1
Chao Xian 86 F4
Chaoyang 86 G2
Chaozhou 86 F6
Chapada Diamantina 50 J6
Chapais 40 F1
Chapayev 78 K4
Chapayevo 84 K4
Chapayevskoye 82 N7
Chapecó 52 L4
Chapleau 40 D1
Chapra 94 D3
Chara 84 K5
Charcas 44 F4
Chard 34 J5
Chardara 96 J1
Chardzhev 96 H2
Chari 104 C5
Chārīkār 96 J2
Charleroi 62 G4
Charlesbourg 40 F1
Charleston, *New Zealand* 118 C5
Charleston, *S.C., United States* 42 F3
Charleston, *W.Va., United States* 42 E2
Charlestown 42 D2
Charleville 116 J5
Charleville-Mézières 62 G5
Charlevoix 40 C1
Charlotte, *Mich., United States* 40 D2
Charlotte, *N.C., United States* 42 E2
Charlottesville 42 F2
Charlottetown 34 U7
Charlton Island 34 Q6
Charsk 82 Q8
Charters Towers 116 J4
Chartres 66 G5
Charymovo 78 Q3
Chasel'ka 84 C3
Chastyye 78 K3
Châteaguay 40 F1
Châteaubriant 66 D6
Châteaudun 66 G5
Châteaulin 66 A5
Châteauneuf-sur-Loire 66 H6
Châteauroux 66 G7
Château-Thierry 62 F5
Châtellerault 66 F7
Châtenois 70 A2
Chatham 40 D2
Chatham Island 118 (1)B1
Chatham Islands 118 (1)B1
Châtillon-sur Seine 66 K6
Chattanooga 36 J4
Chauffayer 70 B6
Chauk 94 F4
Chaumont 66 L5
Chaunskaya Guba 84 V3
Chauny 62 F5
Chaves, *Brazil* 50 G4
Chaves, *Portugal* 68 C3
Chavuma 112 C2
Cheb 60 H6
Cheboksary 78 J3
Chechnya 98 L2
Cheduba Island 94 F5
Cheektowaga 40 E2
Chegdomyn 84 N6
Chegutu 112 E3
Chehalis 38 B1
Cheju 88 D7
Cheju do 88 D7
Chekhov 84 Q7
Chelan 38 C1
Cheleken 96 F2
Chélif 68 L8
Chelkar 82 K8
Chełm 58 N6
Chełmno 58 H4
Chelmsford 62 C3
Cheltenham 64 L10
Chelyabinsk 78 M3
Chelyuskin 82 U2
Chemnitz 60 H6
Chenab 94 B2
Cheney Reservoir 42 B2
Chengde 86 F2
Chengdu 86 C4
Chengshan Jiao 88 B5
Chennai 94 D6
Chenzhou 86 E5
Chepes 52 H5
Cher 66 G6
Cheraw 42 F3
Cherbaniani Reef 94 B6
Cherbourg 66 D4
Cherchell 68 N8
Cherdyn 78 L2
Cheremkhovo 84 G6
Cherepovets 78 G3
Cherkasy 78 F5
Cherkessk 98 K1
Chermoz 78 L3
Chernihiv 78 F4
Chernivtsi 78 E5
Chernushka 78 L3
Chernyakhovsk 58 L3
Chernyayevo 84 M6
Chernyshevsk 84 K6
Chernyshevskiy 84 J4
Chernyye Zemli 78 J5
Cherokee 40 A2
Cherskiy 84 U3
Cherven Bryag 74 M6
Červonohrad 78 D4
Chesapeake 42 F2
Cheshskaya Guba 78 J1
Cheshunt 62 C3
Chester, *United Kingdom* 64 K8
Chester, *Calif., United States* 38 B2
Chester, *Mont., United States* 38 D1
Chesterfield 64 L8
Chesterfield Inlet 34 N4
Chetumal 46 G5
Chetwynd 34 G5
Ch'ew Bahir 110 F3
Cheyenne 38 F2
Cheyenne 38 F2
Cheyenne Wells 44 F1
Cheyne Bay 116 C6
Chhatarpur 94 C4
Chhindwara 94 C4
Chhuka 94 E3
Chia-i 86 G6
Chiang Khan 90 C3
Chiang-Mai 90 B3
Chiang Rai 90 B3
Chiavari 70 E6
Chiavenna 70 E4
Chiba 88 L6
Chibougamau 34 S6
Chibuto 112 E4
Chicago 40 C2
Chicapa 110 C5
Chichagof Island 44 (1)K4
Chichaoua 106 D2
Chichester 62 B4
Chickasha 42 B3
Chiclana de la Frontera 68 D8
Chiclayo 50 B5
Chico 52 H8
Chicopee 40 F2
Chicoutimi 34 S7
Chicualacuala 112 E4
Chiemsee 70 H3
Chieri 70 C5
Chiese 70 F5
Chieti 72 J6
Chifeng 86 F2
Chiganak 82 N8
Chigubo 112 E4
Chihuahua 44 E3
Chiili 82 M9
Chikwa 112 E2
Chilas 94 B1
Childress 44 F2
Chile 48 D8
Chile Chico 52 G8
Chilik 82 P9
Chilika Lake 94 D4
Chillán 52 G6
Chillicothe, *Mo., United States* 40 B3
Chillicothe, *Oh., United States* 40 D3
Chilliwack 38 B1
Chiloquin 38 B2
Chilpancingo 46 E5
Chi-lung 86 G5
Chimbay 82 K9
Chimborazo 50 B4
Chimbote 50 B5
Chimchememel' 84 V3
Chimec 74 J1
Chimoio 112 E3
China 80 N6
Chincha Alta 50 B6
Chincilla de Monte-Aragón 68 J6
Chinde 112 F3
Chin do 88 C6
Chindwin 90 A2
Chingola 112 D2
Chinhoyi 112 E3
Chiniot 94 B2
Chinju 88 E6
Chinmen 90 F2
Chinnur 94 C5
Chióggia 70 H5
Chios 76 H6
Chios 76 J6
Chipata 112 E2
Chippewa Falls 40 B2
Chipping Norton 62 A3
Chirchik 82 M9
Chirikof Island 44 (1)F5
Chiromo 112 F3
Chirpan 76 H2
Chirripo 46 H7
Chişinău 74 R2
Chişineu-Criş 74 J3
Chita 84 J5
Chitato 110 C5
Chitembo 112 B2
Chitipa 110 E5
Chitradurga 94 C5
Chitral 94 B
Chitré 46 H7
Chittagong 94 F
Chittaurgarh 94 B
Chittoor 94 C5
Chitungwiza 112 E3
Chiume 112 C3
Chivasso 70 C
Chizha 78 H
Chodov 60 H
Choiseul 114 F
Chojnice 58 G
Chokurdakh 84 R
Chókwé 112 E
Cholet 66 E
Choma 112 D
Chomutov 58 C
Chona 84 H
Chonan 88 D
Chone 50 A
Ch'ŏngjin 88 E
Ch'ŏngju 88 D
Chŏngp'yŏng 88 D
Chongqing 80 P
Chŏngŭp 88 D
Ch'ŏnju 88 D
Chonogol 86 F
Chon Thanh 90 D
Chop 58 M
Chornobyl' 78 F
Chornomors'ke 78 F
Ch'osan 88 C
Chōshi 88 L
Choszczno 58 E
Choteau 38 D
Chott el Hodna 106 F
Chott el Jerid 106 G
Chott Melrhir 106 G
Choybalsan 84 J
Choyr 86 D
Chre 66 H
Christchurch 118 D
Christiansburg 40 D
Christiansø 58 E
Christmas Island 92 (1)D
Chrudim 58 E
Chrysi 76 H1
Chu 82 N
Chubut 52 H7
Chugach Mountains 34 B4
Chūgoku-sanchi 86 J3
Chugwater 38 F2
Chukchi Sea 44 (1)C2
Chukotskiy Khrebet 84 W3
Chukotskiy Poluostrov 84 Z3
Chula Vista 44 C2
Chulucanas 50 A5
Chulym 82 R6
Chum 78 M1
Chumikan 84 P6
Chum Phae 90 C3
Chumphon 90 B4
Ch'unch'ŏn 88 D
Chunchura 94 E4
Chundzha 82 P9
Ch'ungju 88 D5
Chur 70 E4
Churapcha 84 N4
Churchill 34 N5
Churchill, *Man., Canada* 34 M5
Churchill, *Nfld., Canada* 34 U6
Churchill Falls 34 U6
Churchill Peak 34 F5
Churu 94 B3
Chuska Mountains 44 E1
Chusovoy 78 L3
Chute des Passes 34 S7
Chuuk 114 F5
Chuvashiya 78 J3
Chuxiong 90 C2
Chuya 84 J5
Ciadîr-Lunga 74 R3
Cide 98 E3
Ciechanów 58 K5
Ciego de Avila 46 J4
Cienfuegos 46 H4
Cieza 68 J6
Cihanbeyli 98 E4
Cijulang 92 (1)D4
Cilacap 92 (1)D4
Cili 86 E5
Cimarron 42 B2
Cimişlia 74 R3
Cîmpeni 58 N11

Cinca 68 L3
Cincinnati 40 D3
Çine 76 L7
Ciney 62 H4
Cintalapa 46 F5
Circle, *Ak., United States* 44 (1)J2
Circle, *Mont., United States* 38 E1
Circleville 40 D3
Cirebon 92 (1)D4
Cirò Marina 72 M9
Cisco 42 B3
Cistierna 68 E2
Citronelle 42 D3
Cittadella 70 G5
Città di Castello 70 H7
Ciucea 74 K3
Ciudad Acuña 44 F3
Ciudad Bolívar 50 E2
Ciudad Camargo 44 E3
Ciudad del Carmen 46 F5
Ciudad del Este 52 L4
Ciudad Delicias 44 E3
Ciudad del Maíz 44 G4
Ciudad de México 46 E5
Ciudad de Valles 46 E4
Ciudad Guayana 50 E2
Ciudad Juárez 44 E2
Ciudad Madero 44 G4
Ciudad Mante 46 E4
Ciudad Obregón 46 C3
Ciudad Real 68 G6
Ciudad-Rodrigo 68 D4
Ciudad Valles 44 G4
Ciudad Victoria 36 G7
Ciutadella 68 P4
Cividale del Friuli 70 J4
Cívita Castellana 72 G6
Civitanova Marche 72 H5
Civitavécchia 72 F6
Cizre 98 K5
Clacton-on-Sea 62 D3
Clair Engle Lake 38 B2
Clairview 116 J4
Clamecy 66 J6
Clare Island 64 B8
Clarence 118 D6
Clarence Strait 116 E2
Clarendon 44 F2
Clarkdale 44 D2
Clarksburg 42 E2
Clarksdale 42 C3
Clarks Junction 118 C7
Clarkston 38 C1
Clarksville, *Ark., United States* 42 C2
Clarksville, *Tenn., United States* 42 D2
Claro 50 G7
Clausthal-Zellerfeld 60 F5
Claveria 90 G3
Clayton 44 F1
Clear Island 64 C10
Clear Lake 40 B2
Clear Lake Reservoir 38 B2
Clearwater 38 C1
Clearwater 42 E4
Clearwater Mountains 38 C1
Cleburne 42 B3
Clermont, *Australia* 116 J4
Clermont, *France* 62 E5
Clermont-Ferrand 66 J8
Cles 70 F4
Cleveland, *Oh., United States* 40 D2
Cleveland, *Tenn., United States* 42 E2
Cleveland, *Tex., United States* 42 B3
Clifden 118 A7
Clifton 44 E2
Climax 38 E1
Clines Corners 44 E2
Clinton, *Canada* 34 G6
Clinton, *New Zealand* 118 B8
Clinton, *Ark., United States* 40 B3
Clinton, *Ia., United States* 36 H3
Clinton, *Miss., United States* 42 C3
Clinton, *Mo., United States* 40 B3
Clinton, *N.C., United States* 42 F3
Clinton, *Okla., United States* 42 B2
Clipperton Island 46 C6
Clonmel 64 E9
Cloppenburg 60 D4
Cloquet 40 B1
Cloud Peak 38 E2
Clovis, *Calif., United States* 38 C3
Clovis, *N.Mex., United States* 44 F2
Cluj-Napoca 74 L3
Cluny 66 K7
Cluses 70 B4
Clyde 64 H6
Clyde River 34 T2
Coaldale 38 C3
Coalville 38 C2
Coari 50 E4
Coast Mountains 34 E5
Coast Range 38 B3
Coatbridge 64 J6
Coats Island 34 Q4
Coatzacoalcos 46 F5
Cobalt 34 R7
Cobán 46 F5
Cobija 50 D6
Cobourg 36 L3
Cobourg Peninsula 116 F2
Cóbuè 112 E2
Coburg 60 F6
Cochabamba 50 D7
Cochin = Kochi 94 C7
Cochrane 40 D1
Cockburn Town 42 G5
Coco 46 H6
Cocoa 42 E4
Cocobeach 108 F4
Coco Channel 90 A4
Coco Island 90 A4
Codajás 50 E4
Codigoro 70 H6
Cod Island 34 U5
Codlea 74 N4
Codó 50 J4
Codogno 70 E5
Codroipo 70 J5
Cody 38 E2
Coesfeld 60 C5
Coëtivy Island 102 J6
Coeur d'Alene 38 C1
Coeur d'Alene Lake 38 C1
Coevorden 62 J2
Coffs Harbour 116 K6
Cofrents 68 J5
Cognac 66 E8
Cogne 70 C5
Coiba 48 C3
Coihaique 52 G8
Coimbatore 94 C6
Coimbra 68 B4
Colchester 62 C3
Colebrook 40 F1
Coleman 42 B3
Coleraine 64 F6
Colesberg 112 D6
Colfax 38 C1
Colibaşi 74 M5
Colico 70 E4
Coll 64 F5
Collado-Villalba 68 F4
College Station 42 B3
Collier Bay 116 D3
Collingwood 40 E2
Collins 42 D3
Colmar 70 C2
Colmenar Viejo 68 G4
Colombia 50 C3
Colombo 94 C7
Colonia Las Heras 52 H8
Colonial Heights 40 E3
Colonsay 64 F5
Colorado 38 E3
Colorado, *Colo., United States* 44 E1
Colorado, *Tex., United States* 44 G2
Colorado Plateau 44 D1
Colorado Springs 38 F3
Columbia 38 C1
Columbia, *La., United States* 42 C3
Columbia, *Md., United States* 42 F2
Columbia, *Mo., United States* 42 C2
Columbia, *S.C., United States* 42 E3
Columbia, *Tenn., United States* 42 D2
Columbia Mountains 34 G6
Columbus, *Ga., United States* 42 E3
Columbus, *Ind., United States* 42 D2
Columbus, *Miss., United States* 42 D3
Columbus, *Mont., United States* 38 E1
Columbus, *Nebr., United States* 38 G2
Columbus, *N.Mex., United States* 44 E2
Columbus, *Oh., United States* 42 E1
Columbus, *Tex., United States* 42 B4
Colville 44 (1)G2
Colville Lake 44 (1)M2
Comacchio 70 H6
Comăneşti 74 P3
Comarnic 74 N4
Combarbalá 52 G5
Combeaufontaine 66 M6
Comilla 90 A2
Comino = Kemmuna 72 J12
Commentry 66 H7
Commercy 62 H6
Como 70 E5
Comoé 108 D3
Comondú 36 D6
Comoros 112 G2
Compiègne 62 E5
Comrat 74 R3
Comstock 44 F3
Conakry 108 B3
Concarneau 66 B6
Conceição do Araguaia 50 H5
Concepción, *Bolivia* 50 E7
Concepción, *Chile* 52 G6
Conches-en-Ouche 62 C6
Conchos 46 C3
Concord, *Calif., United States* 44 B1
Concord, *N.H., United States* 40 F2
Concord, *N.C., United States* 42 E2
Concordia, *Argentina* 52 K5
Concordia, *United States* 42 B2
Condé-sur-Noireau 62 B6
Condobolin 116 J6
Condom 66 F10
Conegliano 70 H5
Conggar 94 F3
Congo 102 E6
Congo 108 G5
Connecticut 40 F2
Connemara 64 C8
Conrad 38 D1
Côn Son 90 D5
Constanţa 98 C1
Constantina 68 E7
Constantine 106 G1
Consul 38 E1
Contact 38 D2
Contamana 50 B5
Contwoyto Lake 34 J3
Convay 42 F3
Conway 42 C2
Conwy 64 J8
Conwy Bay 64 H8
Coober Pedy 116 F5
Cookeville 40 C3
Cook Inlet 44 (1)G4
Cook Islands 114 K7
Cook Strait 118 E5
Cooktown 116 J3
Coolabah 116 J6
Coolgardie 116 D6
Cooma 116 J7
Coonabarabran 116 J6
Coon Rapids 40 B1
Coopers Town 42 F4
Coorabie 116 F6
Coos Bay 38 B2
Cootamundra 116 J6
Copenhagen = København 56 G9
Copiapó 52 G4
Copper Harbor 40 C1
Côqen 94 E2
Coquille 38 B2
Coquimbo 52 G4
Corabia 74 M6
Coral 36 K1
Coral Sea 116 K2
Coral Sea Islands Territory 114 F7
Coral Sea Islands Territory 116 J2
Coral Springs 42 E4
Corantijn 50 F3
Corbeil-Essonnes 66 H5
Corbigny 66 J6
Corby 62 B2
Cordele 42 E3
Cordillera Cantábrica 68 D2
Cordillera Central 48 E5
Cordillera del Condor 50 B5
Cordillera de Mérida 48 D3
Cordillera de Oliva 52 G4
Cordillera Isabella 46 G6
Cordillera Occidental 48 E5
Cordillera Oriental 48 D5
Cordillera Penibética 68 F8
Cordillera Vilcabamba 50 C6
Córdoba, *Argentina* 52 J5
Córdoba, *Spain* 68 F7
Corfu = Kerkyra 76 B5
Coria 68 D5
Corigliano 72 L9
Corinth 42 D3
Corinto 50 H7
Cork 64 D10
Cork Harbour 64 D10
Corleone 72 H11
Çorlu 76 K3
Corn Islands 48 C2
Cornwall 36 M2
Cornwallis Island 34 M2
Coro 50 D1
Corocoro 50 D7
Coromandel 118 E3
Coromandel Coast 94 D6
Coromandel Peninsula 118 E3
Coron 90 G4
Coronation Gulf 34 J3
Coronel Oviedo 52 K4
Coronel Pringles 52 J6
Coronel Suárez 52 J6
Corpus Christi 42 B4
Corrientes 52 K4
Corrigan 42 C3
Corriverton 50 F2
Corse 72 D6
Corsica = Corse 72 D6
Corsicana 42 B3
Corte 72 D6
Cortegana 68 D7
Cortez 44 E1
Cortina d'Ampezzo 70 H4
Cortland 40 E2
Cortona 72 F5
Coruche 68 B6
Çorum 98 F3
Corumbá 50 F7
Corvallis 38 B2
Corvo 106 (1)A2
Cosenza 72 L9
Cosmoledo Group 112 (2)A2
Cosne-sur-Loire 66 H6
Cossato 70 D5
Costa Blanca 68 K7
Costa Brava 68 P3
Costa del Sol 68 F8
Costa de Mosquitos 46 H6
Costa Dorada 68 M4
Costa do Sol 68 A6
Costa Rica 46 G7
Costa Smeralda 72 D7
Costa Verde 68 D1
Costeşti 74 M5
Coswig 60 H5
Cotabato 90 G5
Cotonou 108 E3
Cottage Grove 38 B2
Cottbus 58 D6
Cotulla 42 B4
Couhe 66 F7
Coulommiers 62 F6
Council Bluffs 38 F2
Courland Lagoon 58 L2
Courtacon 62 F6
Courtenay 36 B2
Coushatta 42 C3
Coutances 66 D4
Couvin 62 G4
Covasna 74 P4
Coventry 64 L9
Covilhã 68 C4
Covington, *Ga., United States* 42 E3
Covington, *Ky., United States* 42 E2
Covington, *Va., United States* 40 D3
Cowell 116 G6
Cowes 62 A4
Cowra 116 J6
Çox's Bazar 94 F4
Cradock 112 D6
Craig 38 E2
Crailsheim 60 F7
Craiova 74 L5
Cranbrook, *Australia* 116 C6
Cranbrook, *United States* 36 C2
Crater Lake 38 B2
Crato 50 K5
Crawford 38 F2
Crawfordsville 40 C2
Crawley 62 B3
Cree Lake 34 K5
Creil 62 E5
Crema 70 E5
Cremona 70 F5

Crépy-en-Valois 62 E5
Cres 70 K6
Cres 70 K6
Crescent City 38 B2
Crest 66 L9
Creston 40 B2
Crestview 36 J5
Crestview 46 G2
Crete = Kriti 76 H10
Créteil 62 E6
Creuse 66 G7
Crevillent 68 K6
Crewe 64 K8
Crianlarich 64 H5
Criciúma 52 M4
Cristalina 50 H7
Cristóbal Colón 32 J8
Crna Gora 74 F7
Croatia 74 C4
Crockett 42 B3
Croker Island 116 F2
Cromer 64 P9
Cromwell 118 B7
Crooked Island 46 K4
Crookston 36 G2
Cross City 42 E3
Cross Lake 34 M6
Crossville 40 C3
Crotone 72 M9
Crowley 42 C3
Crowrest Pass 36 D2
Crown Point 40 C2
Cruz Alta 52 L4
Cruz del Eje 52 J5
Cruzeiro do Sul 50 C5
Crvenka 74 G4
Crystal City 42 B4
Crystal Falls 40 C1
Crystal River 42 E4
Crystal Springs 42 C3
Csorna 74 E2
Csurgó 70 N4
Cuamba 112 F2
Cuando 112 C3
Cuangar 112 B3
Cuango 110 B5
Cuanza 110 B5
Cuatro Ciénegas 44 F3
Cuauhtémoc 44 E3
Cuba 38 E3
Cuba 46 H4
Cubal 110 A6
Cubali 112 A2
Cubango 112 B3
Çubuk 76 R4
Cucuí 50 D3
Cúcuta 50 C2
Cuddalore 94 C6
Cuddapah 94 C6
Cuemba 112 B2
Cuenca, *Ecuador* 50 B4
Cuenca, *Spain* 68 H4
Cuernavaca 46 E5
Cuero 42 B4
Cuiabá 50 F7
Cuilo 110 B5
Cuito 112 B3
Cuito Cuanavale 112 B3
Culbertson 38 E1
Culfa 98 L4
Culiacán 46 C4
Cullera 68 K5
Cullman 42 D3
Culpepper 50 (1)A1
Culuene 50 G6
Culverden 118 D6
Cumaná 50 E1
Cumberland 40 E3
Cumberland Peninsula 34 T3
Cumberland Sound 34 T3
Cummings 38 B3
Cumpas 44 E2
Çumra 76 Q7
Cunderdin 116 C6
Cunene 112 A3
Cuneo 70 C6
Cunnamulla 116 J5
Čuprija 74 J6
Cure 66 J6
Curicó 52 G5
Curitiba 52 M4
Currais Novos 50 K5
Curral Velho 108 (1)B1
Currie 116 H7
Curtea de Argeş 74 M4
Curtici 74 J3
Curtis Island 116 K4
Curuá 50 G5
Curup 92 (1)C3
Curuzú Cuatiá 52 K4
Curvelo 50 J7
Cusco 50 C6
Cuthbert 42 E3
Cutro 72 L9
Cuttack 94 E4
Cuvier Island 118 E3
Cuxhaven 60 D3
Cuya 50 C7
Cuyuni 50 F2
Cwmbran 64 J10
Cyclades = Kyklades 76 G7
Cypress Hills 36 D2
Cyprus 98 E6
Czarnków 58 F5
Czech Republic 58 C8
Częstochowa 58 J7
Człuchow 58 G4

D

Da'an 86 G1
Daaquam 40 F1
Dab'a 100 D5
Dabas 74 G2
Dabat 104 G5
Dabola 108 B2
Dąbrowa Górńicza 58 J7
Dăbuleni 74 M6
Dachau 70 G2
Daet 90 G4
Dagana 106 B5
Dagestan 98 M2
Dagupan 90 G3
Da Hinggan Ling 86 G1
Dahlak Archipelago 104 H4
Dahlonega 42 E3
Dahn 62 K5
Dahod 94 B4
Dahongliutan 96 L2
Dahūk 98 K5
Daimiel 68 G5
Dai Xian 86 E3
Dakar 108 A2
Dakoro 108 F2
Dakota City 38 G2
Dakovica 74 H7
Dakovo 74 F4
Dalai Nur 86 F2
Dalälven 56 H6
Dalaman 98 C5
Dalandzadgad 86 C2
Dalap-Uliga-Darrit 114 H5
Da Lat 90 D4
Dalbandin 96 H4
Dalby 116 K5
Dalgān 96 G4
Dalhart 44 F1
Dalhousie 94 C2
Dali 90 C1
Dalian 86 G3
Dalizi 88 D3
Dallas 42 B3
Daloa 108 C3
Dalry 64 H6
Dāltenganj 94 D4
Dalton 42 E3
Dalvík 56 (1)D2
Daly Waters 116 F3
Daman 94 B4
Damanhûr 104 F1
Damar 92 (2)C4
Damara 108 H3
Damasak 108 G2
Damascus = Dimashq 100 D3
Damaturu 108 G2
Damoh 94 C4
Damqawt 96 F6
Danau Poso 92 (2)A3
Danau Toba 92 (1)B2
Danau Towuti 92 (2)B3
Danba 86 C4
Dandeldhura 94 D3
Dandong 88 C3
Da Něng 90 D3
Dangara 96 J2
Danger Islands 114 K7
Danghe Nanshan 86 B3
Daniel 38 D1
Danilov 78 H3
Dank 101 G5
Dankov 78 G4
Dannenberg 60 G3
Dannevirke 118 F5
Dansville 40 E2
Danube 54 F3
Danville, *Ill.*, *United States* 42 D1
Danville, *Ky.*, *United States* 42 E2
Danville, *Va.*, *United States* 42 F2
Dan Xian 90 D3
Dao Phu Quôc 90 C4
Dapa 90 H5
Dapaong 108 E2
Da Qaidam 86 B3
Daqing 84 M7
Dar'ā 100 D4
Dārāb 101 F2
Darabani 74 P1
Daraj 104 B1
Darazo 108 G2
Darbhanga 94 E3
Dardanelles = Çanakkale Boğazı 76 J4
Darende 98 G4
Dar es Salaam 110 F5
Darfo 70 F5
Dargaville 118 D2
Darham 84 H7
Darjeeling 94 E3
Darling 116 H6
Darlington 64 L7
Darłowo 56 J9
Dărmăneşti 74 P3
Dar Mazār 101 G2
Darmstadt 60 D7
Darnah 104 D1
Darnley Bay 34 G3
Daroca 68 J3
Darß 60 H2
Dartmouth 34 U8
Daru 92 (2)F4
Daruba 92 (2)C2
Daruvar 70 N5
Darvaza 82 K9
Darwin 116 F2
Daryacheh-ye Bakhtegan 101 E2
Daryācheh-ye Orūmīyeh 98 L5
Daryacheh-ye Tashk 101 E2
Dārzīn 101 H2
Dashkhovuz 82 K9
Dasht-e Kavir 96 F3
Dasht-e Lut 101 H1
Datça 76 K8
Datça 98 B5
Date 88 L2
Datong 86 C3
Datong 86 E2
Daugava 78 E3
Daugavpils 78 E3
Daun 62 J4
Dauphin 34 M6
Dausa 94 C3
Dăvăci 98 N3
Davangere 94 C6
Davao 90 H5
Davenport 40 B2
Daventry 62 A2
David 46 H7
Davis Sea 120 (2)Q3
Davis Strait 34 V3
Davlekanovo 82 J7
Davos 70 E4
Dawa 86 G2
Dawqah 96 F6
Dawson 44 (1)K3
Dawson Creek, *B.C.*, *Canada* 34 G5
Dawson Creek, *Y.T.*, *Canada* 34 D4
Dawu 86 C4
Dax 66 D10
Daxian 86 D4
Dayong 86 E5
Dayr az Zawr 98 J6
Dayton, *Oh.*, *United States* 40 D3
Dayton, *Tenn.*, *United States* 40 C3
Dayton, *Tex.*, *United States* 42 C4
Dayton, *Wash.*, *United States* 38 C1
Daytona Beach 42 E4
De Aar 112 C6
Dead Sea 100 C5
Deakin 116 E6
Deal 62 D3
De'an 86 F5
Deán Funes 52 J5
Dease Lake 44 (1)M4
Dease Strait 34 J3
Death Valley 38 C3
Deba Habe 108 G2
Debar 76 C3
Dębica 58 L7
Debin 84 S4
Dęblin 58 L6
Dębno 58 D5
Debre Birhan 110 F2
Debrecen 74 J2
Debre Markos 104 G5
Debre Tabor 104 G5
Decatur, *Al.*, *United States* 40 C4
Decatur, *Ill.*, *United States* 40 C3
Decazeville 66 H9
Deccan 94 C5
Děčín 58 D7
Decize 66 J7
Decorah 40 B2
Dedoplis 98 M3
Dédougou 108 D2
Dedza 112 E2
Deering 44 (1)E2
Deer Lake 34 V7
Deer Lodge 38 D1
Deer Park 38 C1
Dee, *Scot.*, *United Kingdom* 64 K4
Dee, *Wales*, *United Kingdom* 64 J9
De Funiak Springs 42 D3
Degeh Bur 110 G2
Deggendorf 70 J2
Dehaj 101 F1
Dehalak Desēt 96 D6
Deh Bid 101 E1
Deh-Dasht 101 D1
Dehkūyeh 101 F3
Dehlonān 96 E3
Dehra 96 L3
Dehra Dun 94 C2
Dehri 94 D4
Deh Shū 96 H3
Deinze 62 F4
Dej 74 L2
De Kalb 42 C3
De-Kastri 84 Q6
Dekese 110 C4
Delano 44 C1
Delaware 40 D2
Delaware 42 F2
Delbrück 60 D5
Delémont 70 C3
Delfoi 76 E6
Delft 62 G2
Delfzijl 62 J1
Delgo 104 F3
Delhi, *India* 94 C3
Delhi, *United States* 40 F2
Delitzsch 60 H5
Dellys 68 P8
Delmenhorst 60 D3
Delnice 70 K5
Delray Beach 42 E4
Del Rio 44 F3
Delta, *Colo.*, *United States* 38 E3
Delta, *Ut.*, *United States* 38 D3
Delta del Orinoco 50 E2
Delta Junction 44 (1)H3
Deming 44 E2
Demirci 76 L5
Demmin 60 J3
Democratic Republic of Congo 110 C4
Demopolis 42 D3
Demyanka 78 P3
Dem'yanskoye 78 N3
Denain 62 F4
Denau 96 J2
Denbigh 40 E1
Den Burg 62 G1
Dender 62 F4
Dendi 110 F2
Denham 116 B5
Den Helder 62 G2
Dénia 68 L6
Deniliquin 116 H7
Denio 38 C2
Denison, *Ia.*, *United States* 40 A2
Denison, *Tex.*, *United States* 42 B3
Denizli 98 C5
Denmark 54 E2
Denmark 116 C6
Denmark Strait 32 D3
Denpasar 92 (1)E4
Denton 44 G2
D'Entrecasteaux Islands 116 K1
Denver 38 F3
Deogarh, *India* 94 B3
Deogarh, *India* 94 D4
Deoghar 94 E4
De Panne 62 E3
Depok 92 (1)D4
Dépression du Mourdi 104 D4
Deputatskiy 84 P3
Dêqên 90 B1
Dera Ghazi Khan 96 K3
Dera Ismail Khan 96 K3
Derbent 96 E1
Derby, *Australia* 116 D3

Derby, *United Kingdom*	64	L9
De Ridder	42	C3
Dermott	42	C3
Derventa	74	E5
Desē	104	G5
Deseado	52	H8
Deseado	52	H8
Desert Center	44	C2
Des Moines, *Ia., United States*	36	H3
Des Moines, *N.Mex., United States*	44	F1
Desna	78	F4
Dessau	60	H5
Desvres	62	D4
Deta	74	J4
Detmold	60	D5
Detroit	36	K3
Detroit Lakes	40	A1
Det Udom	90	C4
Detva	58	J9
Deurne	62	H3
Deva	74	K4
Deventer	62	J2
Devil's Lake	34	L7
Devils Lake	38	G1
Devil's Point	42	F5
Devnya	74	Q6
Devon Island	34	P1
Devonport	116	J8
Dewas	94	C4
Deyang	86	C4
Deyhuk	96	G3
Dezfūl	96	E3
Dezhou	86	F3
Dhahran = Az Ẓahrān	101	D3
Dhaka	94	F4
Dhamār	104	H5
Dhamtri	94	D4
Dhanbad	94	E4
Dhar	94	C4
Dhārwād	94	B5
Dhaulagiri	94	D3
Dhekelia	100	A2
Dhībān	100	C5
Dhoraji	94	B4
Dhule	94	B4
Dhulian	94	E4
Dhuudo	110	J2
Dia	76	H9
Diamantina	50	H7
Diamantino	50	F6
Diamond Islets	116	K3
Diane Bank	116	J3
Dianópolis	50	H6
Dibā al Ḥiṣn	101	G4
Dibbiena	72	F5
Dibrugarh	94	F3
Dickens	44	F2
Dickinson	38	F1
Dickson	42	D2
Didiéni	108	C2
Didymoteicho	76	J3
Die	66	L9
Diébougou	108	D2
Dieburg	60	D7
Diéma	108	C2
Diemel	60	E5
Diemeringen	60	C8
Diepholz	60	D4
Dieppe	62	D5
Diest	62	H4
Diffa	108	G2
Digne-les-Bains	70	B6
Digoin	66	J7
Dijon	66	L6
Dikhil	104	H5
Dikili	76	J5
Diklosmta	98	L2
Diksmuide	62	E3
Dikson	82	Q3
Dikwa	108	G2
Dīla	110	F2
Dili	92	(2)C4
Dilijan	98	L3
Dillenburg	60	D6
Dillingen, *Germany*	60	F8
Dillingen, *Germany*	60	B7
Dillingham	44	(1)F4
Dillion	36	D2
Dillon	38	D1
Dillon Cone	118	D6
Dilolo	112	C2
Dimapur	94	F3
Dimashq	100	D3
Dimitrovgrad, *Bulgaria*	74	N7
Dimitrovgrad, *Russia*	78	J4
Dimitrovgrad, *Yugoslavia*	74	K7
Dīmona	100	C5
Dinagat	90	H4
Dinajpur	94	E3
Dinan	66	C5
Dinant	62	G4
Dinar	98	D4
Dinaric Alps	70	L6
Dindigul	94	C6
Dindori	94	D4
Dingle Bay	64	B9
Dingolfing	70	H2
Dinguiraye	108	B2
Dingwall	64	H4
Dinkelsbühl	60	F7
Dinosaur	38	E2
Diomede Islands	84	AA3
Dioriga Kointhou	76	F7
Diourbel	106	B6
Dipolog	90	G5
Dir	94	B1
Dirē Dawa	110	G2
Dirk Hartog Island	116	B5
Dirranbandi	116	J5
Disko = Qeqertarsuatsiaq	34	V2
Disko Bugt = Qeqertarsuup Tunua	34	V3
Diss	62	D2
Distrito Federal	50	H7
Dithmarschen	60	D2
Dīvāndarreh	98	M6
Divinópolis	52	N3
Divo	108	C3
Divriği	98	H4
Dixon	40	C2
Dixon Entrance	44	(1)L5
Diyarbakır	98	J5
Dja	108	G4
Djado	106	H4
Djamâa	106	G2
Djambala	108	G5
Djanet	106	G4
Djelfa	106	F2
Djéma	110	D2
Djibo	108	D2
Djibouti	104	H5
Djibouti	104	H5
Djolu	110	C3
Djougou	108	E3
Djúpivogur	56	(1)F2
Dnieper	78	F5
Dniester	74	Q1
Dnipro	54	H3
Dniprodzerzhyns'k	78	F5
Dnipropetrovs'k	78	F5
Dnister	54	G3
Dno	78	E3
Doba, *Chad*	110	B2
Doba, *China*	94	E2
Döbeln	60	J5
Doboj	74	F5
Dobre Miasto	58	K4
Dobrich	74	Q6
Dobryanka	78	L3
Doctor Arroyo	44	F4
Dodecanese = Dodekanisos	76	J8
Dodge City	38	F3
Dodoma	110	F5
Doetinchem	62	J3
Doğanşehir	98	G4
Dōgo	88	G3
Dogondoutchi	108	E2
Doha = Ad Dawḩah	101	D4
Doka	92	(2)D4
Dokkum	60	B3
Dolak	92	(2)E4
Dolbeau	40	F1
Dole	70	A3
Dolgany	84	E2
Dolinsk	84	Q7
Dollard	60	C3
Dolný Kubrín	58	J8
Dolomiti	70	G4
Dolo Odo	110	G3
Dolores	52	K6
Dolphin and Union Strait	34	H3
Domar	94	D2
Domažlice	60	H7
Dombås	56	E5
Dombóvár	74	F3
Domfront	66	E5
Dominica	48	E2
Dominican Republic	48	D1
Domodóssola	70	D4
Domokos	76	E5
Dompu	92	(2)A4
Domžale	70	K4
Don	54	H2
Donau = Danube	70	H2
Donaueschingen	70	D3
Donauwörth	60	F8
Don Benito	68	E6
Doncaster	64	L8
Dondra Head	94	D7
Donegal	64	D7
Donegal Bay	64	D7
Donets	54	H3
Donets'k	78	G5
Dongco	94	D2
Dongfang	90	D3
Donggala	92	(2)A3
Donggou	88	C4
Dongguan	90	E2
Dông Hôi	90	D3
Dongjingcheng	88	E1
Donglük	82	R10
Dongning	88	F2
Dongo	108	H4
Dongola	104	F4
Dongou	108	H4
Dongsha Qundao	90	F2
Dongsheng	86	E3
Dong Ujimqin Qi	86	F1
Dongying	86	F3
Doniphan	42	C2
Donji Vakuf	70	N6
Donner Pass	38	B3
Donostia	68	J1
Donousa	76	H7
Dora	70	C5
Dorchester	64	K11
Dordrecht	62	G3
Dorfen	70	H2
Dori	108	D2
Doring	112	B6
Dorion	40	C1
Dormagen	62	J3
Dornbirn	70	E3
Dorog	58	H10
Dorohoi	74	P2
Döröö Nuur	82	S8
Dorsten	62	J3
Dortmund	60	C5
Dos Hermanas	68	E7
Dosse	60	H4
Dosso	108	E2
Dothan	42	D3
Douai	62	F4
Douala	108	F4
Douarnenez	66	A5
Doubs	70	B3
Douentza	108	C2
Douglas, *South Africa*	112	C5
Douglas, *United Kingdom*	64	H7
Douglas, *Ariz., United States*	44	E2
Douglas, *Ga., United States*	42	E3
Douglas, *Wyo., United States*	38	E2
Doullens	62	E4
Dourados	52	L3
Douro	68	B3
Dover, *United Kingdom*	62	D3
Dover, *United States*	42	F2
Dover, *Australia*	116	J8
Dover-Foxcroft	40	G1
Dowlatābād, *Iran*	101	E2
Dowlatābād, *Iran*	101	G2
Dowshī	96	J2
Drac	70	B6
Drachten	62	J1
Dragan	56	H4
Drăgănești-Olt	74	M5
Drăgășani	74	M5
Draguignan	70	B7
Drakensberg	112	D6
Drake Passage	52	G10
Drama	76	G3
Drammen	56	F7
Drasenhofen	70	M2
Drau	70	J4
Drava	74	E4
Dravograd	72	K2
Drawsko Pomorskie	58	E4
Dresden	60	J5
Dreux	62	D6
Drezdenko	58	E5
Drina	74	G5
Driva	56	E5
Drniš	74	D6
Drobeta-Turnu Severin	74	K5
Drochia	74	Q1
Drogheda	64	F8
Drohobych	58	N8
Drôme	66	K9
Dronne	66	F8
Dronning Maud Land	120	(2)F2
Dronten	62	H2
Drummondville	40	F1
Druskininkai	56	M9
Druzhina	84	Q3
Drvar	74	D5
Dryanovo	74	N7
Dryden	36	H2
Drysdale River	116	E3
Dschang	108	G3
Ḑubā	104	G2
Dubai = Dubayy	101	F4
Dubăsari	74	S2
Dubawnt Lake	34	L4
Dubayy	101	F4
Dubbo	116	J6
Dübendorf	70	D3
Dublin, *Republic of Ireland*	64	F8
Dublin, *United States*	42	E3
Dublin Bay	64	F8
Dubna	78	G3
Dubnica	58	H9
Du Bois	40	E2
Dubois, *Id., United States*	38	D2
Dubois, *Wyo., United States*	38	E2
Dubovskoye	78	H5
Dubreka	108	B3
Dubrovnik	74	F7
Dubuque	40	B2
Duchesne	38	D2
Ducie Island	114	P8
Dudelange	62	J5
Duderstadt	60	F5
Dudinka	82	R4
Dudley	64	K9
Duero	68	F3
Dugi Otok	74	B6
Duifken Point	116	H2
Duisburg	62	J3
Duiveland	62	F3
Duk Faiwil	110	E2
Dukhān	101	D4
Dukla	58	L8
Dukou	86	C5
Dulan	86	B3
Dulce	44	E1
Dulce	52	J4
Dul'Durga	84	J6
Dullewala	94	B2
Dülmen	60	C5
Dulovo	74	Q6
Duluth	40	B1
Dūmā	100	D3
Dumaguete	90	G5
Dumai	92	(1)C2
Dumas, *Ark., United States*	42	C3
Dumas, *Tex., United States*	38	F3
Ḑumayr	100	D3
Dumbarton	64	H5
Ďumbier	58	J9
Dumboa	108	G2
Dumfries	64	J6
Dümmer	60	D4
Dumont d'Urville Sea	120	(2)U3
Dumyât	104	F1
Duna = Danube	74	E2
Dunaj = Danube	58	G10
Dunajská Streda	74	E2
Dunakeszi	74	G2
Dunărea = Danube	74	K5
Dunaújváros	74	F3
Dunav = Danube	74	J5
Dunayivtsi	78	E5
Dunbar, *Australia*	116	H3
Dunbar, *United Kingdom*	64	K6
Duncan	38	B1
Duncan Passage	90	A4
Dundaga	56	M8
Dundalk	64	F7
Dundalk Bay	64	F8
Dundee, *South Africa*	112	E5
Dundee, *United Kingdom*	64	K5
Dunedin	118	C7
Dunfermline	64	J5
Dungarvan	64	E9
Dungeness	62	C4
Dungu	110	D3
Dungun	90	C6
Dunhua	88	E2
Dunhuang	86	A2
Dunkerque	62	E3
Dunkirk	40	E2
Dunkwa	108	D3
Dun Laoghaire	64	F8
Dunnet Head	64	J3
Dunseith	38	G1
Dunsmuir	38	B2
Duque de Caxias	52	N3
Du Quoin	42	D2
Durance	66	L10
Durango, *Mexico*	44	F4
Durango, *Spain*	68	H1
Durango, *United States*	38	E3
Durant	42	B3
Durazno	52	K5
Durban	112	E5
Düren	62	J4

Durgapur 94 E4
Durham, *Canada* 40 D2
Durham, *United Kingdom* 64 L7
Durham, *United States* 42 F2
Duri 92 (1)C2
Durmā 101 B4
Durmanec 74 C3
Durmitor 74 G6
Durrës 76 B3
Dursey 64 B10
Dursunbey 76 L5
D'Urville Island 118 D5
Dushanbe 96 J2
Düsseldorf 62 J3
Duvno 70 N7
Duyun 86 D5
Düzce 76 P4
Dvina 54 H2
Dvinskaya Guba 78 G1
Dwarka 94 A4
Dworshak Reservoir 38 C1
Dyat'kovo 78 F4
Dyersburg 42 D2
Dyje 70 M2
Dzavhan 82 S8
Dzerzhinsk 78 H3
Dzhalinda 84 L6
Dzhambeyty 78 K4
Dzhankoy 78 F5
Dzhardzhan 84 L3
Dzharkurgan 96 J2
Dzhetygara 78 M4
Dzhezkazgan 78 N5
Dzhigudzhak 84 T4
Dzhizak 82 M9
Dzhusaly 78 M5
Działdowo 58 K4
Dzüünbulag 86 F1

E

Eads 38 F3
Eagle 44 (1)J3
Eagle Lake 38 B2
Eagle Pass 44 F3
East Antarctica 120 (2)P2
Eastbourne 62 C4
East Cape 118 G3
East China Sea 86 H4
East Dereham 62 C2
Easter Island 114 Q8
Eastern Cape 112 D6
Eastern Ghats 94 C6
Easter Ross 64 H4
East Falkland 52 K9
East Grinstead 62 C3
East Kilbride 64 H6
Eastleigh 62 A4
East Liverpool 42 E1
East London 112 D6
Eastmain 34 R6
Eastmain 34 S6
East Point 42 E3
East Retford 62 B1
East St. Louis 40 B3
East Siberian Sea =
Vostochno-
Sibirskoye More 84 U2
Eatonton 42 E3
Eau Claire 40 B2
Ebbw Vale 64 J10
Ebensee 70 J3
Eberbach 60 D7
Ebersbach 58 D6
Ebersberg 70 G2
Eberswalde 60 J4
Ebinur Hu 82 Q9
Éboli 72 K8
Ebolowa 108 G4
Ebro 68 K3
Eceabat 76 J4
Ech Chélif 106 F1
Echinos 76 G3
Echo Bay 34 H3
Écija 68 E7
Eckernförde 60 E2
Ecuador 50 B4
Ed 104 H5
Edam 62 H2
Eday 64 K2
Ed Da'ein 104 E5
Ed Damazin 104 F5
Ed Debba 104 F4
Ed Dueim 104 F5
Ede, *Netherlands* 62 H2
Ede, *Nigeria* 108 E3
Edéa 108 G4
Edelény 58 K9
Eden, *Australia* 116 J7
Eden, *United States* 44 G2
Edendale 118 B8
Eder 60 D5
Edersee 60 E5
Edessa 76 E4
Edgecumbe 118 F3
Edinburgh 64 J6
Edineţ 74 Q1
Edirne 76 J3
Edmonds 38 B1
Edmonton 34 J6
Edmundson 36 N2
Edmundston 40 G1
Edolo 70 F4
Edremit 76 J5
Edremit Körfezi 76 H5
Edwards 44 C2
Edwards Plateau 44 F2
Eemshaven 62 J1
Éfaté 114 G7
Eferding 58 D9
Effingham 42 D2
Eganville 40 E1
Eger 60 G6
Eger 74 H2
Egersund 56 D7
Eggenfelden 70 H2
Egilsstaðir 56 (1)F2
Eğridir 76 N7
Eğridir Gölü 76 N6
Egvekinot 84 Y3
Egypt 104 E2
Ehingen 70 E2
Eibar 68 H1
Eichstätt 70 G2
Eider 60 D2
Eidsvold 116 K5
Eidsvoll 56 F6
Eifel 62 J4
Eigg 64 F5
Eight Degree Channel 94 B7
Eilenburg 60 H5
Einbeck 60 E5
Eindhoven 62 H3
Eirunepé 50 D5
Eiseb 112 C4
Eisenach 60 F6
Eisenerz 70 K3
Eisenhüttenstadt 58 D5
Eisenstadt 70 M3
Eisleben 60 G5
Eivissa 68 M5
Eivissa 68 M6
Ejea de los Caballeros 68 J2
Ejido Insurgentes 36 D6
Ejin Horo Qi 86 D3
Ejin Qi 86 C2
Ejmiadzin 98 L3
Ekalaka 38 F1
Ekenäs 56 M7
Ekibastuz 82 P7
Ekimchan 84 N6
Ekonda 82 V4
Eksjo 56 H8
Ekwan 34 Q6
El Aaiún 106 C3
Elafonisos 76 E8
El 'Alamein 104 E1
El Amria 68 J9
El 'Arîsh 100 A5
Elat 100 B7
Elazığ 98 H4
El Azraq 100 D5
Elba 72 E6
El Banco 50 C2
Elbasan 76 C3
El Baúl 50 D2
Elbe 60 F3
Elbeuf 62 D5
Elbistan 98 G4
Elbląg 58 J3
El Borj 68 E9
Elbow 36 E1
Elbrus 98 K2
El Burgo de Ebro 68 K3
El Burgo de Osma 68 G3
El Cajon 44 C2
El Callao 50 E2
El Campo 42 B4
El Centro 44 C2
El Cerro 50 E7
Elch 68 K6
Elda 68 K6
El'dikan 84 P4
Eldorado 52 L4
El Dorado, *Mexico* 36 E7
El Dorado, *Ark.,*
United States 42 C3
El Dorado, *Kans.,*
United States 42 B2
El Dorado, *Venezuela* 50 E2
Eldoret 110 F3
Elefsína 76 F6
Elektrėnai 58 P3
El Encanto 50 C4
Elephant Butte Reservoir 44 E2
Eleuthera 36 L6
El Fahs 72 D12
El Faiyûm 104 F2
El Fasher 104 E5
El Geneina 104 D5
Elgin, *United Kingdom* 64 J4
Elgin, *Ill., United States* 40 C2
Elgin, *N.D., United States* 38 F1
El'ginskiy 84 Q4
El Gîza 104 F1
El Goléa 106 F2
El Iskandarîya 104 E1
Elista 78 H5
Elizabeth 40 F2
Elizabeth City 42 F2
Elizabethton 42 E2
El Jadida 106 D2
El Jafr 100 D6
El Jafr 100 D6
Ełk 58 M4
Ełk 58 M4
El Kala 72 C12
Elk City 44 G1
El Kef 72 C12
El Kelaâ des Srarhna 106 D2
El Khârga 104 F2
Elkhart, *Ind.,*
United States 40 C2
Elkhart, *Kans.,*
United States 42 A2
El Khartum 104 F4
El Khartum Bahri 104 F4
Elkhorn 38 G2
Elkhorn 40 C2
Elkhovo 76 J2
Elkins 40 E3
Elko, *Canada* 38 C1
Elko, *United States* 38 C2
Elk River 40 B1
El Kuntilla 100 B7
Ellendale 36 G2
Ellensburg 38 B1
Ellesmere Island 32 K1
Ellice Islands 114 H6
Elliot 112 D6
Ellis 34 J8
Ellisras 112 D4
Elliston 116 F6
Ellsworth 40 G2
Ellwangen 70 F2
Elmadağ 76 R5
Elmali 76 M8
El Mansûra 104 F1
El Minya 104 F2
Elmira 40 E2
Elmshorn 60 E3
El Muglad 104 E5
El Nido 90 F4
El Obeid 104 F5
El Odaiya 104 E5
El Oued 106 G2
El Paso 44 E2
El Portal 44 C1
El Potosi 44 F4
El Prat de Llobregat 68 N3
El Puerto de Santa María 68 D8
El Qâhira 104 F1
El Reno 42 B2
El Sahuaro 44 D2
El Salvador 46 F6
Elster 60 H5
Elsterwerda 60 J5
El Sueco 44 E3
El Suweis 104 F2
Eltanin Bay 120 (2)JJ2
El Tarf 72 C12
El Thamad 100 B7
El Tigre 50 E2
El Turbio 52 G9
Eluru 94 D5
Elvas 68 C6
Elverum 56 F6
Elvira 50 C5
El Wak 110 G3
Ely, *United Kingdom* 64 N9
Ely, *United States* 38 D3
Emajõgi 56 P7
Emämrüd 96 F2
Emba 78 L5
Emba 78 L5
Embalse de Alarcon 68 H5
Embalse de Alcántara Uno 68 D5
Embalse de Almendra 68 D3
Embalse de Contreras 68 J5
Embalse de Gabriel y
Galán 68 D4
Embalse de Garcia Sola 68 E5
Embalse de Guadalhorce 68 F8
Embalse de Guadalmena 68 G6
Embalse de Guri 50 E2
Embalse de la Serena 68 E6
Embalse de la Sotonera 68 K2
Embalse del Bembézar 68 E6
Embalse del Ebro 68 G1
Embalse del Río Negro 48 F7
Embalse de Negratmn 68 G7
Embalse de Ricobayo 68 E3
Embalse de Santa Teresa 68 E4
Embalse de Yesa 68 J2
Embalse Toekomstig 50 F3
Embarcación 52 J3
Emden 60 C3
Emerald 116 J4
Emi Koussi 104 C4
Emin 82 Q8
Emirdağ 76 P5
Emmeloord 62 H2
Emmen 62 J2
Emmendingen 70 C2
Emmerich 62 J3
Emory Peak 44 F3
Empalme 44 D3
Empangeni 112 E5
Empoli 70 F7
Emporia 42 B2
Empty Quarter =
Rub' al Khālī 96 E6
Ems 62 J1
Ems-Jade-Kanal 60 C3
Enafors 78 B2
Encarnación 52 K4
Encs 74 J1
Ende 92 (2)B4
Enderby Island 118 (2)B1
Energetik 78 L4
Enewetak 114 F4
Enez 76 J4
Enfida 72 E12
Engel's 78 J4
Enggano 92 (1)C4
Enghien 62 G4
England 64 L9
English Channel 64 J12
Engozero 56 S4
'En Hazeva 100 C6
Enid 42 B2
Enkhuizen 62 H2
Enköping 56 J7
Enna 72 J11
En Nahud 104 E5
Enngonia 116 J5
Ennis,
Republic of Ireland 64 D9
Ennis, *United States* 38 D1
Enniscorthy 64 F9
Enniskillen 64 E7
Enns 70 K2
Enns 70 K3
Enschede 62 J2
Ensenada 44 C2
Enshi 86 D4
Entebbe 110 E3
Enterprise 38 C1
Entrevaux 70 B7
Entroncamento 68 B5
Enugu 108 F3
Enurmino 84 Z3
Envira 50 C5
Enz 70 D2
Enza 70 F6
Epanomi 76 E4
Epéna 110 B3
Épernay 66 J4
Épinal 70 B2
Epsom 62 B3
Eqlīd 101 E1
Equatorial Guinea 108 F4
Erbach 60 D7
Erçek 98 K4
Erciş 98 K4
Ercolano 72 J8
Érd 74 F2
Erdek 76 K4
Erdemli 76 S8
Erdenet 84 G7
Erding 70 G2
Erechim 52 L4
Ereğli, *Turkey* 98 D3
Ereğli, *Turkey* 98 F5
Ereikoussa 76 B5
Erenhot 86 E2
Erfurt 60 G6
Ergani 98 H4
Erg Chech 106 D4
Erg du Ténéré 106 H5
Ergel 86 D2
Erg Iguidi 106 D3
Erie 40 D2
Erimo-misaki 88 M3
Eriskay 64 E4
Eritrea 104 G4
Erlangen 60 G7

Ermenek 98 E5
Ermoupoli 76 G7
Erode 94 C6
Er Rachidia 106 E2
Er Renk 110 E1
Errol 40 F2
Er Ruseifa 100 D4
Ersekë 76 C4
Erskine 40 A1
Ertai 82 S8
Ertix 82 R8
Erzgebirge 60 H6
Erzin 82 S7
Erzincan 98 H4
Erzurum 98 J4
Esan-misaki 88 L3
Esashi, *Japan* 88 L3
Esashi, *Japan* 88 M1
Esbjerg 56 E9
Escanaba 40 C1
Escárcega 46 F5
Esch 62 J5
Eschwege 60 F5
Eschweiler 62 J4
Escondido 44 C2
Eséka 108 G4
Eşfahān 96 F3
Eskifjöður 56 (1)G2
Eskilstuna 56 J7
Eskimo Lakes 44 (1)L2
Eskişehir 98 D4
Esla 68 E3
Eslāmābād e Gharb 98 M6
Eslamshahr 96 F2
Esler Dağ 76 M7
Eslö 58 C2
Esmeraldas 50 B3
Esneux 62 H4
Espalion 66 H9
Espanola, *Canada* 40 D1
Espanola, *United States* 38 E3
Espelkamp 60 D4
Esperance 116 D6
Esperance Bay 116 D6
Espinho 68 B4
Espírito Santo 50 J7
Espíritu Santo 114 G7
Esplanada 50 K6
Espoo 56 N6
Espungebera 112 E4
Essaouira 106 D2
Es Semara 106 C3
Essen, *Belgium* 62 G3
Essen, *Germany* 62 K3
Essequibo 50 F2
Esslingen 70 E2
Eşţahbānāt 101 F2
Este 70 G5
Estella 68 H2
Estepona 68 E8
Esteros 52 J3
Estevan 36 F2
Estonia 56 M7
Estoril 68 A6
Estrecho de Le Maire 52 H10
Estrecho de Magallanes 52 G9
Estrela 68 C4
Estremoz 68 C6
Estuário do Rio Amazonaz 50 H3
Esztergom 74 F2
Étain 62 H5
Étampes 66 H5
Étang de Berre 66 L10
Étaples 62 D4
Etawah 94 C3
Ethiopia 102 G5
Etolin Strait 44 (1)D3
Etosha Pan 112 B3
Étretat 62 C5
Ettelbruck 60 B7
Ettlingen 60 D8
Eucla 116 E6
Euclid 40 D2
Eufala 42 D3
Eufaula Lake 42 B2
Eugene 38 B2
Eupen 60 B6
Euphrates = Firat 98 H4
Euphrates 96 D3
Eure 62 D6
Eureka, *Calif., United States* 38 B2
Eureka, *Mont., United States* 38 C1
Eureka, *Nev., United States* 44 C1
Eureka, *Ut., United States* 38 D3
Europoort 62 F3
Euskirchen 60 B6
Eutin 60 F2
Eutsuk Lake 34 F6
Evans Strait 34 Q4
Evanston, *Ill., United States* 40 C2
Evanston, *Wyo., United States* 38 D2
Evansville 42 D2
Evaz 101 F3
Everett 38 B1
Everglades City 42 E4
Evergreen 42 D3
Evesham 62 A2
Évora 68 C6
Évreux 62 D5
Evron 66 E5
Evros 76 J3
Evvoia 76 F6
Ewo 108 G5
Exaltación 50 D6
Exe 64 J11
Exeter 64 J11
Exmouth, *Australia* 116 B4
Exmouth, *United Kingdom* 64 J11
Exuma Sound 36 L7
Eyl 110 H2
Eyre Peninsula 116 G2
Ezine 76 J5

F

Faadippolu Atoll 94 B8
Fåborg 60 F1
Fabriano 70 H7
Fada 104 D4
Fada Ngourma 108 E2
Faenza 70 G6
Færingehavn = Kangerluarsoruseq 34 W4
Faeroes 54 D1
Făgăraş 74 M4
Fagernes 56 E6
Fagersta 56 H6
Fagurhólsmýri 56 (1)E3
Fahraj 101 H2
Faial 106 (1)B2
Fairbanks 44 (1)H3
Fair Isle 64 L2
Fairlie 118 C7
Fairmont 40 B2
Faisalabad 94 B2
Faith 38 F1
Faizabad 94 D3
Fakfak 92 (2)D3
Fakse 60 H1
Fakse Bugt 56 G9
Faku 86 G2
Falaise 62 B6
Falaise de Tiguidit 106 G5
Falconara Maríttima 70 J7
Falcon Lake 42 B4
Fălesţi 74 Q2
Falfurrias 42 B4
Falkenberg 56 G8
Falkensee 60 J4
Falkland Islands 52 K9
Falkland Sound 52 J9
Falköping 56 G7
Fallingbostel 60 E4
Fallon 38 C3
Fall River 40 F2
Falls City 36 G3
Falmouth, *United Kingdom* 64 G11
Falmouth, *United States* 40 F2
Falster 60 H2
Fălticeni 74 P2
Falun 56 H6
Famagusta = Ammochostos 100 A1
Fanchang 86 F4
Fandriana 112 H4
Fangzheng 86 H1
Fannūj 96 G4
Fanø 60 D1
Fano 70 J7
Fanø Bugt 60 D1
Faradje 110 D3
Farafangana 112 H4
Farāh 96 H3
Farah Rud 96 H3
Faranah 108 B2
Fareham 62 A4
Farewell Spit 118 D5
Fargo 36 G2
Faribault 40 B2
Faridabad 94 C3
Farihy Alaotra 112 H3
Färjestaden 58 F1
Farmington, *Me., United States* 40 F2
Farmington, *N.Mex., United States* 44 E1
Farnborough 62 B3
Farne Islands 64 L6
Fårö 56 K8
Faro, *Brazil* 50 F4
Faro, *Portugal* 68 C7
Farquhar Group 112 (2)B3
Farrāshband 101 E2
Farson 38 E2
Fasā 101 E2
Fasano 72 M8
Fategarh 94 C3
Fatehpur 94 D3
Făurei 74 Q4
Fauske 56 H3
Fauville-en-Caux 62 C5
Favara 72 H11
Faversham 62 C3
Favignana 72 G11
Faxaflói 56 (1)B2
Faya 104 C4
Fayette 42 D3
Fayetteville, *Ark., United States* 42 C2
Fayetteville, *N.C., United States* 40 E3
Fayetteville, *Tenn., United States* 42 D2
Faylakah 101 C2
Fdérik 106 C4
Featherston 118 E5
Fécamp 62 C5
Federated States of Micronesia 114 E5
Fedorovka 78 M4
Fehmarn 60 G2
Feijó 50 C5
Feilding 118 E5
Feira de Santana 50 K6
Feistritz 70 L3
Fejø 60 G2
Feldbach 70 L4
Feldkirch 70 E3
Feldkirchen 70 K4
Felidu Atoll 94 B8
Felixstowe 62 D3
Feltre 70 G4
Femø 60 G2
Femund 56 F5
Fengcheng 88 C3
Fenghua 86 G5
Fengning 86 F2
Feng Xian 86 D4
Feni 94 F4
Fenyang 86 E3
Feodosiya 98 F1
Fergana 96 K1
Fergus Falls 36 G2
Ferkessédougou 108 C3
Ferlach 70 K4
Fermo 72 H5
Fernandina Beach 42 E3
Fernandópolis 52 L3
Ferrara 70 G6
Ferreira do Alentejo 68 B7
Ferrol 68 B1
Ferry Lake 42 C2
Fès 106 E2
Festus 40 B3
Feteşti 74 Q5
Fethiye 76 M8
Fetisovo 96 F1
Fetlar 64 M1
Feucht 60 G7
Feuchtwangen 60 F7
Feyzābād 96 K2
Fianarantsoa 112 H4
Fianga 110 B2
Fiche 110 F2
Fidenza 70 F6
Fieni 74 N4
Fier 76 B4
Figeac 66 G9
Figline Valdarno 70 G7
Figueira da Foz 68 B4
Figueres 68 N2
Figuig 106 E2
Figuil 108 G3
Fiji 114 H8
Filadélfia 52 J3
Fil'akovo 58 J9
Filiaşi 74 L5
Filicudi 72 J10
Finale Ligure 70 D6
Findlay 40 D2
Fingoè 112 E3
Finike 76 N8
Finland 56 P3
Finlay 34 F5
Finley 116 J7
Finnsnes 56 K2
Finsterwalde 60 J5
Firat 98 H4
Firenze 70 G7
Firminy 66 K8
Firozabad 94 C3
Firozpur 94 B2
Firth of Clyde 64 G6
Firth of Forth 64 K5
Firth of Lorn 64 G5
Firth of Thames 118 E3
Fish 112 B5
Fisher Strait 34 Q4
Fishguard 64 H9
Fiskenæsset = Qeqertarsuatsiaat 34 W4
Fismes 62 F5
Fitzroy Crossing 116 E3
Fivizzano 70 F6
Fizi 110 D4
Flaming Gorge Reservoir 38 E2
Flamingo 42 E4
Flannan Islands 64 E3
Flåsjön 56 H4
Flateyri 56 (1)B1
Flathead Lake 38 D1
Flensburg 60 E2
Flensburg Fjorde 60 E2
Flers 62 B6
Flinders Island 116 J7
Flinders Ranges 116 G6
Flinders Reefs 116 J3
Flin Flon 34 L6
Flint 40 D2
Flint Island 114 L7
Flirey 70 A2
Flöha 60 J6
Florac 66 J9
Florence = Firenze, *Italy* 70 G7
Florence, *Al., United States* 42 D3
Florence, *S.C., United States* 42 F3
Florencia 50 B3
Florennes 62 G4
Florenville 62 H5
Flores, *Azores* 106 (1)A2
Flores, *Indonesia* 92 (2)B4
Flores Sea 92 (2)A4
Floreşti 74 R2
Floriano 50 J5
Florianópolis 52 M4
Florida 42 E4
Florida 52 K5
Florida Keys 32 K7
Florina 76 D4
Florissant 40 B3
Florø 56 C6
Floydada 44 F2
Flumendosa 72 D9
Fly 92 (2)F4
Foča 74 F6
Foça 76 J6
Focşani 74 Q4
Fóggia 72 K7
Fogo 108 (1)B1
Fogo Island 34 W7
Fohnsdorf 70 K3
Föhr 60 D2
Foix 66 G11
Folegandros 76 G8
Foleyet 40 D1
Foligno 72 G6
Folkestone 62 D3
Folkston 42 E3
Follónica 72 E6
Fond du Lac 40 C2
Fondi 72 H7
Fongafale 114 H6
Fontainebleau 66 H5
Fonte Boa 50 D4
Fontenay-le-Comte 66 E7
Fontur 56 (1)F1
Fonyód 72 M2
Forbach, *France* 62 J5
Forbach, *Germany* 62 L6
Forchheim 60 G7
Førde 56 C6
Fordyce 42 C3
Forest, *Canada* 40 D2
Forest, *United States* 42 D3
Forestville 40 G1
Forfar 64 K5
Forges-les-Eaux 62 D5
Forks 38 B1
Forli 70 H6
Formazza 70 D4
Formentera 68 M6
Fórmia 72 H7
Formiga 52 M3
Formosa, *Brazil* 50 H7
Formosa, *Paraguay* 52 K4
Fornovo di Taro 70 F6

Forssa 56 M6
Forst 60 K5
Forsyth 38 E1
Fort Abbas 94 B3
Fortaleza 50 K4
Fort Bayne 40 C4
Fort Beaufort 112 D6
Fort Benton 38 D1
Fort Bragg 44 B1
Fort Chipewyan 34 J5
Fort Cobb Reservoir 42 B2
Fort Collins 38 E2
Fort-de-France 46 M6
Fort Dodge 40 B2
Forte dei Marmi 70 F7
Fort Frances 40 B1
Fort George 34 R6
Fort Gibson Lake 42 B2
Fort Good Hope 34 F3
Forth 64 H5
Fort Hope 34 P6
Fortín Coronel Eugenio Garay 52 J3
Fort Kent 40 G1
Fort Lauderdale 42 E4
Fort Liard 34 G4
Fort Mackay 34 J5
Fort Macleod 38 D1
Fort McMurray 34 J5
Fort McPherson 44 (1)L2
Fort Munro 96 J4
Fort Myers 42 E4
Fort Nelson 34 G5
Fort Norman 44 (1)M3
Fort Payne 42 D3
Fort Peck Reservoir 38 E1
Fort Pierce 42 E4
Fort Pierre 38 F2
Fort Portal 110 E3
Fort Providence 34 H4
Fortrose 118 B8
Fort Rupert 34 R6
Fort St. John 34 G5
Fort Saint Lucie 42 E4
Fort Scott 42 C2
Fort Severn 34 P5
Fort Shevchenko 82 J9
Fort Simpson 34 G4
Fort Smith, *Canada* 34 J4
Fort Smith, *United States* 42 C2
Fort Stockton 44 F2
Fort Summer 44 F2
Fortuna 38 F1
Fortune Bay 34 V7
Fort Vermilion 34 H5
Fort Wayne 42 D1
Fort William 64 G5
Fort Worth 42 B3
Fort Yates 38 F1
Foshan 90 E2
Fosna 56 F5
Fossano 70 C6
Fossombrone 70 H7
Fougamou 108 G5
Fougères 66 D5
Foula 64 K1
Foulness 62 C3
Foumban 108 G3
Fourmies 62 G4
Fournoi 76 J7
Fouta Djallon 108 B2
Foveaux Strait 118 A8
Foxe Basin 34 R3
Foxe Channel 34 R4
Foxe Peninsula 34 R4
Fox Islands 44 (1)D5
Foz do Cunene 112 A3
Foz do Iguaçu 52 L4
Fraga 68 L3
Franca 52 M3
Francavilla 72 M8
Francavilla al Mare 72 J6
France 66 G7
Franceville 108 G5
Francisco I. Madero 44 F4
Francistown 112 D4
Francs Peak 38 E2
Frankenberg 60 D5
Frankenthal 60 D7
Frankfort, *Ind.*, *United States* 42 D1
Frankfort, *Ky.*, *United States* 42 E2
Frankfurt, *Germany* 60 K4
Frankfurt, *Germany* 60 D6
Franklin, *N.C.*, *United States* 40 D3
Franklin, *Tenn.*, *United States* 40 C3
Franklin Bay 34 F2
Franklin D. Roosevelt Lake 38 C1
Franklin Mountains 34 F3
Franklin Strait 34 M2
Franz Josef Glacier 118 C6
Franz Josef Land = Zemlya Frantsa-Iosifa 82 J2
Fraser 34 G6
Fraserburg 112 C6
Fraserburgh 64 L4
Fraser Island 116 K5
Frater 40 D1
Frauenfeld 70 D3
Fredensborg 58 B2
Frederick, *Md.*, *United States* 40 E3
Frederick, *Okla.*, *United States* 42 B3
Fredericksburg, *Tex.*, *United States* 42 B3
Fredericksburg, *Va.*, *United States* 40 E3
Fredericktown 40 B3
Fredericton 34 T7
Frederikshåb = Paamiut 34 X4
Frederikshavn 56 F8
Frederikssund 58 B2
Frederiksværk 56 G9
Fredrikstad 56 F7
Freeport, *Ill.*, *United States* 40 C2
Freeport, *Tex.*, *United States* 42 B4
Freeport City 42 F4
Freer 42 B4
Free State 112 D5
Freetown 108 B3
Fregenal de la Sierre 68 D6
Freiberg 60 J6
Freiburg 70 C3
Freilassing 70 H3
Freising 70 G2
Freistadt 70 K2
Fréjus 66 M10
Fremantle 116 C6
Fremont, *Calif.*, *United States* 44 B1
Fremont, *Nebr.*, *United States* 36 G3
Frenchglen 38 C2
French Guiana 50 G3
French Polynesia 114 L7
Frenda 106 F1
Fresnes-sur-Apances 70 A3
Fresnillo 46 D4
Fresno 44 C1
Fresno Reservoir 38 E1
Freudenstadt 70 D2
Freyung 60 J8
Frias 52 H4
Fribourg 70 C4
Friedburg 70 G2
Friedrichshafen 70 E3
Friesach 70 K4
Friesoythe 60 C3
Frisian Islands 62 H1
Fritzlar 60 E5
Frobisher Bay 34 T4
Frolovo 78 H5
Frome 64 K10
Frontera 46 F5
Frontignan 66 J10
Frosinone 72 H7
Frøya 56 D5
Fruges 62 E4
Frýdek Místek 58 H8
Fudai 88 L4
Fuding 86 G5
Fuengirola 68 F8
Fuentesauco 68 E3
Fuerteventura 106 C3
Fugu 86 E3
Fuhai 82 R8
Fujieda 88 K6
Fujin 84 N7
Fuji-san 88 K6
Fukuchiyama 88 H6
Fukue 88 E7
Fukue-jima 88 E7
Fukui 88 J5
Fukuoka 88 F7
Fukushima 88 L5
Fukuyama 88 G6
Fulda 60 E6
Fulda 60 E6
Fuling 86 D5
Fulton 42 D2
Funabashi 88 L6
Funafuti 114 H6
Funchal 106 B2
Fundão 68 C4
Funing 90 D2
Funtua 108 F2
Furano 88 M2
Fürg 101 F2
Furmanovka 82 N9
Furmanovo 78 J5
Furneaux Group 116 J8
Furqlus 100 E2
Fürstenberg 60 J3
Fürstenfeldbruck 70 G2
Fürstenwalde 60 K4
Fürth 60 F7
Furukawa 88 L4
Fushun 88 B3
Fusong 88 D2
Füssen 70 F3
Futog 74 G4
Fuxhou 86 F5
Fu Xian 86 D3
Fuxin 86 G2
Fuyang 86 F4
Fuyu 86 G1
Fuyun 82 R8
Fuzhou 90 F1
Fyn 60 F1
Fynshav 60 F2

G

Gaalkacyo 110 H2
Gabès 106 H2
Gabon 108 G5
Gaborone 112 D4
Gabrovo 74 N7
Gacé 62 C6
Gacko 74 F6
Gäddede 56 H4
Gadsden 42 D3
Găeşti 74 N5
Gaeta 72 H7
Gafsa 106 G2
Gaggenau 70 D2
Gagnoa 108 C3
Gagra 98 J2
Gaildorf 70 E2
Gaillac 66 G10
Gainesville, *Fla.*, *United States* 42 E4
Gainesville, *Ga.*, *United States* 42 E3
Gainesville, *Mo.*, *United States* 42 C2
Gainesville, *Tex.*, *United States* 42 B3
Gai Xian 88 B3
Gala 94 E3
Galana 110 F4
Galanta 70 N2
Galapagos Islands = Islas Galápagos 50 (1)B1
Galashiels 64 K6
Galaţi 74 R4
Galdhøpiggen 56 D6
Galena 44 (1)F3
Galesburg 40 B2
Galich 78 H3
Gallabat 104 G5
Galle 94 D7
Gallipoli 72 N8
Gallipolis 42 E2
Gällivare 56 L3
Gallup 44 E1
Galtat Zemmour 106 C3
Galveston Bay 36 G6
Galway 64 C8
Galway Bay 64 C8
Gambēla 110 E2
Gambier Islands 114 N8
Gamboma 110 B4
Gamboula 110 B3
Gan 84 L7
Ganado 44 E1
Găncă 98 M3
Gandajika 110 C5
Gander 34 W7
Ganderkesee 60 D3
Gandesa 68 L3
Gāndhīdhām 94 B4
Gandhinagar 94 B4
Gandia 68 K6
Gandu 50 K6
Ganganagar 94 B3
Gangara 108 F2
Gangdise Shan 94 D2
Ganges 66 J10
Ganges 94 E3
Gangi 72 J11
Gangtok 94 E3
Gannett Peak 38 E2
Ganta 108 C3
Ganye 108 G3
Ganzhou 86 E5
Gao 106 E5
Gaoual 106 C
Gap 70 B6
Garanhuns 50 K
Garbsen 60 E
Gardelegen 60 G
Garden City 38 F
Gardēz 96 J
Gardone Val Trómpia 70 F
Gargždai 58 L
Gariau 92 (2)D
Garissa 110 F
Garland 42 B
Garlasco 70 D
Garliava 58 N
Garmisch-Partenkirchen 70 G
Garnett 42 B
Garonne 66 E
Garoowe 110 H
Garoua 108 G
Garoua Boulaï 108 G
Garry Lake 34 L
Garut 92 (1)D
Garwolin 58 L
Gary 36 J
Garyarsa 94 D
Garzê 86 B
Gasan Kuli 96 F
Gasht 96 H
Gashua 108 G
Gastonia 42 E
Gastre 52 H
Gatchina 78 F
Gateshead 64 L
Gatesville 42 B
Gatineau 40 E
Gatrūyeh 101 F
Gauja 56 N8
Gaula 56 F5
Gauteng 112 D5
Gava 68 N3
Gāvbandī 101 E3
Gavdos 76 G10
Gävle 56 J6
Gawler 116 G6
Gawler Ranges 116 G6
Gaxun Nur 86 C2
Gaya, *India* 94 E4
Gaya, *Niger* 108 E2
Gaylord 40 D1
Gayndah 116 K5
Gayny 78 K2
Gaza 100 B5
Gaz-Achak 82 L9
Gazandzhyk 82 K10
Gaza Strip 100 B5
Gaziantep 98 G5
Gazipaşa 76 Q8
Gazli 82 L9
Gbaaka 108 C3
Gbarnga 108 C3
Gdańsk 58 H3
Gdov 56 P7
Gdyel 68 K9
Gdynia 58 H3
Gebel el Tîh 100 A7
Gebel Halâl 100 A6
Gebel Katherina 104 F2
Gebel Yi'allaq 100 A6
Gebze 76 M4
Gedaref 104 G5
Gediz 76 K6
Gediz 76 M6
Gedser 60 G2
Geel 62 H3
Geelong 116 H7
Geesthacht 60 F3
Gê'gvai 94 D2
Geidam 108 G2
Geilenkirchen 62 J4
Geilo 56 E6
Geinhausen 60 E6
Geislingen 70 E2
Geita 110 E4
Gejiu 90 C2
Gela 72 J11
Geladī 110 H2
Geldern 62 J3
Geleen 62 H4
Gelendzhik 98 H1
Gelibolu 76 J4
Gelibolu Yarimadasi 76 J4
Gelsenkirchen 62 K3
Gembloux 62 G4
Gembu 108 G3
Gemena 110 B3
Gemlik 76 M4
Gemlik Körfezi 76 L4
Gemona del Friuli 70 J4
Genalē Wenz 110 G2
General Acha 52 J6
General Alvear 52 H6
General Pico 52 J6

General Pinedo 52 J4
General Roca 52 H6
General Santos 90 H5
Geneva 40 E2
Genève 70 B4
Gengma 90 B2
Genil 68 F7
Genk 62 H4
Genoa = Genova 70 D6
Genova 70 D6
Gent 62 F3
Genteng 92 (1)D4
Genthin 60 H4
Geographe Bay 116 B6
George 112 C6
George 34 T5
George Town, *Australia* 116 J8
George Town, *Malaysia* 92 (1)C1
George Town,
United States 42 F5
Georgetown, *Gambia* 108 B2
Georgetown, *Guyana* 50 F2
Georgetown, *Ky.*,
United States 42 E2
Georgetown, *S.C.*,
United States 42 F3
Georgetown, *Tex.*,
United States 42 B3
George West 42 B4
Georgia 98 K2
Georgia 42 E3
Georgian Bay 40 D1
Gera 60 H6
Geraldine 118 C7
Geraldton, *Australia* 116 B5
Geraldton, *Canada* 36 J2
Gérardmer 70 B2
Gerāsh 101 F3
Gerede 98 E3
Gerefsried 70 G3
Gereshk 96 H3
Gérgal 68 H7
Gerik 90 C5
Gerlach 38 C2
Germantown 40 C3
Germany 60 E6
Germencik 76 K7
Germering 70 G2
Germersheim 62 L5
Gernika 68 H1
Gerolzhofen 60 F7
Gërzë 94 D2
Geser 92 (2)D3
Getafe 68 G4
Gettysburg 38 F2
Getxo 68 H1
Geugnon 66 K7
Gevaş 98 K4
Gevgelija 76 E3
Gewanē 104 H5
Geyik Dağ 76 Q8
Geyser 38 D1
Geyve 76 N4
Ghadāmis 106 G2
Ghadīr Minqār 100 E3
Ghana 108 D3
Ghanzi 112 C4
Gharandal 100 C6
Ghardaïa 106 F2
Gharo 96 J5
Gharyān 106 H2
Ghāt 104 B2
Ghazaouet 106 E1
Ghaziabad 94 C3
Ghazipur 94 D3
Ghazn 96 J3
Gheorgheni 74 N3
Gherla 74 L2
Ghizar 94 B1
Ghotāru 94 B3
Giannitsa 76 E4
Giannutri 72 F6
Giarre 72 K11
Gibraltar 68 E8
Gibson Desert 116 D4
Gideån 56 K5
Gien 66 H6
Gießen 60 D6
Gifhorn 60 F4
Gifu 88 J6
Gigha 64 G6
Giglio 72 E6
Gijón 68 E1
Gila 44 E2
Gila Bend 44 D2
Gilan Garb 98 L6
Gilazi 98 N3
Gilbert Islands 114 H5
Gilbués 50 H5
Gilching 70 G2
Gilf Kebir Plateau 104 E3
Gilgandra 116 J6
Gilgit 96 K2
Gilgit 94 B1
Gillam 34 N5
Gillette 38 E2
Gillingham 62 C3
Gills Rock 40 C1
Gilroy 38 B3
Gīmbī 110 F2
Gimli 34 M6
Gimol'skoe Ozero 56 R5
Gīnīr 110 G2
Giôia del Colle 72 L8
Gióia Tauro 72 K10
Gioura 76 F5
Giresun 98 H3
Girga 104 F2
Girona 68 N3
Gironde 66 E8
Girvan 64 H6
Gisborne 118 G4
Gisenyi 110 D4
Gitega 110 D4
Giurgiu 74 N6
Givet 62 G4
Givors 66 K8
Giyon 110 F2
Gizhiga 84 U4
Gizhiginskaya Guba 84 T4
Giżycko 58 L3
Gjiri i Vlorës 76 B4
Gjirokaster 76 C4
Gjøvik 56 F6
Glacier Peak 38 B1
Gladstone 116 K4
Glamoč 74 D5
Glan 60 C7
Glan 92 (2)C1
Glarner Alpen 70 D4
Glasgow, *United Kingdom* 64 H6
Glasgow, *Ky.*,
United States 40 C3
Glasgow, *Mont.*,
United States 38 E1
Glauchau 60 H6
Glazov 82 J6
Gleisdorf 70 L3
Glendale, *Ariz.*,
United States 44 D2
Glendale, *Calif.*,
United States 44 C2
Glendambo 116 G6
Glendive 38 F1
Glennallen 44 (1)H3
Glenn Innes 116 K5
Glenrothes 64 J5
Glens Falls 40 F2
Glenwood, *Ark.*,
United States 40 B4
Glenwood, *Minn.*,
United States 40 A1
Glenwood, *N.Mex.*,
United States 44 E2
Glenwood Springs 38 E3
Glidden 40 B1
Glina 70 M5
Gliwice 58 H7
Głogów 58 F6
Glomfjord 56 H3
Glomma 56 F5
Glorieuses 102 H7
Gloucester,
United Kingdom 64 K10
Gloucester, *United States* 40 F2
Głowno 58 J6
Głuchołazy 58 G7
Glückstadt 60 E3
Gmünd, *Austria* 70 J4
Gmünd, *Austria* 70 L2
Gmunden 70 J3
Gniezno 58 G5
Gnjilane 76 D2
Gnoien 60 H3
Goalpara 94 F3
Goba 110 F2
Gobabis 112 B4
Gobernador Gregores 52 G8
Gobi Desert 86 C2
Gobustan 96 E1
Goch 62 J3
Godbout 40 G1
Godē 110 G2
Goderich 40 D2
Godhra 94 B4
Gödöllő 74 G2
Gods Lake 34 N6
Godthåb = Nuuk 34 W4
Goeree 62 F3
Goes 62 F3
Gogama 40 D1
Goiânia 50 H7
Goiás 50 G6
Goiás 50 G7
Gökçeada 76 H4
Gökova Körfezi 76 K8
Göksun 98 G5
Golaghat 94 F3
Golan Heights 100 C3
Golbāf 101 G2
Gölbasi 98 G5
Gol'chikha 82 C3
Gölcük 76 K5
Gołdap 58 M3
Gold Coast 116 K5
Golden Bay 118 D5
Goldendale 38 E1
Golden Gate 44 B1
Goldfield 38 C3
Goldsboro 40 E3
Göle 98 K3
Goleniów 58 D4
Golestānak 101 F1
Golfe d'Ajaccio 72 C7
Golfe de Gabès 106 H2
Golfe de Hammamet 106 H1
Golfe de Porto 72 C6
Golfe de Sagone 72 C6
Golfe de Saint-Malo 66 C5
Golfe de Tunis 72 E11
Golfe de Valinco 72 C7
Golfe du Lion 66 J10
Golfo de Almería 68 H8
Golfo de Batabanó 46 H4
Golfo de Cádiz 68 C7
Golfo de California 46 B3
Golfo de Chiriquí 46 H7
Golfo de Corcovado 52 F7
Golfo de Cupica 50 B2
Golfo de Fonseca 46 G6
Golfo de Guayaquil 50 A4
Golfo de Honduras 46 G5
Golfo del Darién 50 B2
Golfo dell' Asinara 72 C7
Golfo de los Mosquitos 50 A2
Golfo de Mazarrón 68 J7
Golfo de Morrosquillo 50 B1
Golfo de Panamá 46 J7
Golfo de Penas 52 F8
Golfo de San Jorge 52 H8
Golfo de Santa Clara 44 D2
Golfo de Tehuantepec 46 E5
Golfo de València 68 L5
Golfo de Venezuela 50 C1
Golfo di Augusta 72 K11
Golfo di Catánia 72 K11
Golfo di Gaeta 72 H7
Golfo di Gela 72 J11
Golfo di Genova 72 C4
Golfo di Manfredonia 72 L7
Golfo di Ólbia 72 D8
Golfo di Oristano 72 C9
Golfo di Orosei 72 D8
Golfo di Palmas 72 C10
Golfo di Policastro 72 K9
Golfo di Salerno 72 J8
Golfo di Sant'Eufemia 72 K10
Golfo di Squillace 72 L10
Golfo di Taranto 72 L8
Golfo di Trieste 70 J5
Golfo San Matías 52 J6
Gölhisar 76 M8
Golin Baixing 88 A1
Gölköy 98 G3
Gölmarmara 76 K6
Golyshmanovo 82 M6
Goma 110 D4
Gombe 108 G2
Gombi 108 G2
Gomera 106 B3
Gómez Palacio 44 F3
Gonam 84 M5
Gonbad-e Kavus 96 G2
Gonda 94 D3
Gonder 104 G5
Gondia 94 D4
Gondomar 68 B3
Gönen 76 K4
Gongga Shan 86 C5
Gonghe 86 C3
Gongliu 82 Q9
Gongpoquan 86 B2
Gongshan 90 B1
Gonzáles 36 G7
Gonzales 42 B4
Gonzalez 44 G4
Goodland 38 F3
Goolgowi 116 J6
Goomalling 116 C6
Goondiwindi 116 K5
Goose Lake 38 B2
Göppingen 70 E2
Góra 58 F6
Gora Bazardyuzi 98 M3
Gora Kamen 82 S4
Gorakhpur 94 D3
Gora Ledyanaya 84 W4
Gora Pobeda 84 R4
Gora Yenashimskiy
Polkan 82 S6
Goražde 74 F6
Gorbitsa 84 K6
Goré 108 H3
Gorē 110 F2
Gore 118 B8
Gorgān 96 F2
Gorgona 70 E7
Gori 98 L2
Gorinchem 62 H3
Goris 98 M4
Gorizia 70 J5
Gorki 78 N1
Gorlice 58 L8
Görlitz 58 D6
Gorna Oryakhovitsa 74 N6
Gornji Milanovac 74 H5
Gorno-Altaysk 82 R7
Gorno Oryakhovitsa 76 H1
Gorodets 78 H3
Gorontalo 92 (2)B2
Goryachiy Klyuch 98 H1
Gory Belukha 82 R8
Gory Ulutau 78 N5
Gorzów Wielkopolski 58 E5
Goslar 60 F5
Gospić 72 K4
Gosport 66 D3
Gostivar 76 C3
Gostyń 58 G6
Gostynin 58 J5
Göteborg 56 F8
Gotha 60 F6
Gothèye 108 E2
Gotland 56 K8
Gotō-rettō 88 E7
Gotse Delchev 76 F3
Gotska Sandön 56 K7
Göttingen 60 E5
Gouda 62 G2
Gough Island 102 B10
Goundam 106 E5
Gouraya 68 M8
Gourdon 66 G9
Gournay-en-Bray 62 D5
Governador Valadares 50 J7
Governor's Harbour 42 F4
Govorovo 84 M3
Gowārān 96 J4
Goya 52 K4
Gozha Co 94 D1
Gozo = Gwardex 72 J12
Graaff-Reinet 112 C6
Grabovica 74 K5
Gračac 70 L6
Gračanica 74 F5
Gradačac 74 F5
Gräfenhainichen 60 H5
Grafton, *Australia* 116 K5
Grafton, *United States* 38 G1
Graham Island 44 (1)L5
Grajaú 50 H5
Grajewo 58 M4
Gram 60 E1
Grampian Mountains 64 H5
Granada, *Nicaragua* 46 G6
Granada, *Spain* 68 G7
Granby 40 F1
Gran Canaria 106 B3
Grand Bahama 42 F4
Grand Ballon 66 N6
Grand Bank 34 V7
Grand Canyon 38 D3
Grande, *Bolivia* 50 E7
Grande, *Brazil* 50 J6
Grande Cache 34 H6
Grande Prairie 34 H5
Grand Erg de Bilma 106 H5
Grand Erg Occidental 106 E3
Grand Erg Oriental 106 F3
Grand Falls, *N.B.*, *Canada* 40 G1
Grand Falls, *Nfld.*,
Canada 34 V7
Grand Forks, *Canada* 36 C2
Grand Forks,
United States 38 G1
Grand Haven 40 C2
Grand Island 38 G2
Grand Junction 38 E3
Grand Marais, *Mich.*,
United States 40 C1
Grand Marais, *Minn.*,
United States 40 B1
Grand-Mère 40 F1
Grândola 68 B6
Grand Portage 40 C1
Grand Rapids, *Canada* 34 M6
Grand Rapids, *Mich.*,
United States 40 C2

Grand Rapids, *Minn.*, *United States* 40 B1
Grand Teton 38 D2
Grangeville 38 C1
Granite Falls 40 A2
Granollers 68 N3
Gran Paradiso 70 C5
Grantham 64 M9
Grants 44 E1
Grants Pass 38 B2
Granville 66 D5
Granville Lake 34 M5
Gräsö 56 K6
Grasse 70 B7
Grassrange 38 E1
Grass Valley 38 B3
Graulhet 66 G10
Gravelines 62 E3
Gravenhurst 40 E2
Gravesend 62 C3
Gravina in Puglia 72 L8
Gray 66 L6
Grayling 40 D2
Grays 62 C3
Grays Lake 38 D2
Grayville 40 C3
Graz 70 L3
Great Abaco 42 F4
Great Artesian Basin 116 H4
Great Australian Bight 116 E6
Great Bahama Bank 46 J4
Great Barrier Island 118 E3
Great Barrier Reef 116 J2
Great Basin 38 C3
Great Bear Lake 44 (1)M2
Great Bend 44 G1
Great Dividing Range 116 J4
Greater Antilles 46 J5
Greater Sunda Islands 114 B6
Great Exhibition Bay 118 D2
Great Exuma 36 L7
Great Falls 38 D1
Great Inagua 46 K4
Great Karoo 112 C6
Great Malvern 64 K9
Great Nicobar 94 F7
Great Ouse 64 N9
Great Plains 38 F2
Great Rift Valley 110 E5
Great Salt Lake 38 D2
Great Salt Lake Desert 38 D2
Great Sand Sea 104 D2
Great Sandy Desert 116 D4
Great Slave Lake 32 N3
Great Victoria Desert 116 E5
Great Wall 86 C3
Great Yarmouth 64 P9
Greece 76 D5
Greeley 38 F2
Green 38 D3
Green Bay 40 C2
Greenfield 42 D2
Greenland 32 G2
Greenland Sea 32 B2
Greenock 64 H6
Green River, *Wyo.*, *United States* 38 E2
Green River, *Ut.*, *United States* 38 D3
Greensboro 42 F2
Greensburg, *Ind.*, *United States* 42 D2
Greensburg, *Pa.*, *United States* 40 E2
Greenvale 116 J3
Green Valley 46 B2
Greenville, *Liberia* 108 C3
Greenville, *Al.*, *United States* 42 D3
Greenville, *Fla.*, *United States* 42 E3
Greenville, *Miss.*, *United States* 42 C3
Greenville, *N.C.*, *United States* 40 E3
Greenville, *S.C.*, *United States* 42 E3
Greenwood, *Miss.*, *United States* 42 C3
Greenwood, *S.C.*, *United States* 42 E3
Gregory 38 G2
Gregory Lake 116 E4
Greifswald 60 J2
Greifswalder Bodden 60 J2
Greiz 60 H6
Grenada 36 J5
Grenada 50 E1
Grenchen 70 C3
Grenoble 66 L8
Gretna 42 C4
Greve in Chianti 70 G7
Greven 62 K2
Grevena 76 D4
Grevenbroich 62 J3
Grevesmühlen 60 G3
Greybull 38 E2
Greymouth 118 C6
Grey Range 116 H5
Griesheim 60 D7
Grieskirchen 70 J2
Grigoriopol 74 S2
Grimma 60 H5
Grimmen 60 J2
Grimsby 64 M8
Grimsey 56 (1)D1
Grimsstaðir 56 (1)E2
Grímsvötn 56 (1)E2
Grindsted 56 E9
Grobina 58 L1
Gröbming 70 J3
Grodekovo 86 J2
Grodzisk Wielkopolski 58 F5
Grójec 58 K6
Gronau 60 C4
Groningen 60 B3
Groote Eylandt 116 G2
Grootfontein 112 B3
Großenhain 60 J5
Großer Arber 60 J7
Grosser Beerberg 60 F6
Grosseto 72 F6
Groß-Gerau 60 D7
Großglockner 70 H3
Groswater Bay 34 V6
Grottaglie 72 M8
Groupe Actéon 114 N8
Grove Hill 42 D3
Groznyy 98 L2
Grubišno Polje 74 E4
Grudovo 76 K2
Grudziądz 58 H4
Grünberg 60 D6
Gryazi 78 G4
Gryazovets 78 H3
Gryfice 58 E4
Gryfino 60 K3
Grytøya 56 J2
Grytviken 52 P9
Gstaad 70 C4
Guadalajara, *Mexico* 46 D4
Guadalajara, *Spain* 68 G4
Guadalcanal 114 F7
Guadalquivir 68 E7
Guadalupe 46 A3
Guadalupe 46 E3
Guadeloupe 48 E2
Guadiana 68 C7
Guadix 68 G7
Guaíra 52 L3
Guajará Mirim 50 D6
Guam 114 E4
Guanambi 50 J6
Guanare 50 D2
Guane 46 H4
Guangshui 86 E4
Guangyuan 86 D4
Guangzhou 90 E2
Guanipa 50 E2
Guanling 86 D5
Guantánamo 46 J4
Guanyun 86 F4
Guaporé 50 E6
Guaqui 50 D7
Guarabira 50 K5
Guarda 68 C4
Guardo 68 F2
Guasave 36 E6
Guastalla 70 F6
Guatemala 46 F5
Guatemala 46 F6
Guaviare 50 D3
Guayaquil 50 B4
Guayaramerín 50 D6
Guaymas 44 D3
Guba, *Democratic Republic of Congo* 110 D6
Guba, *Ethiopia* 104 G5
Guba Buorkhaya 84 N2
Gubakha 78 L3
Guban 110 G2
Gubbi 94 C6
Gúbbio 70 H7
Guben 60 K5
Gubin 58 D6
Gudaut'a 98 J2
Gudbransdalen 56 E6
Gudermes 98 M2
Gudvangen 56 D6
Guebwiller 60 C9
Guéckédou 108 B3
Guelma 106 G1
Guelph 40 D2
Guéret 66 B7
Guernsey 66 C4
Guernsey 38 F2
Guerrero Negro 44 D3
Gugë 110 F2
Gūh Kūh 96 G4
Guiana 46 L7
Guiana Highlands 50 F3
Guider 108 G3
Guiglo 108 C3
Guildford 64 M10
Guilianova 72 H6
Guilin 90 E1
Guillaumes 70 B6
Guillestre 70 B6
Guimarães 68 B3
Guinea 108 B2
Guinea-Bissau 108 A2
Güines 46 H4
Guingamp 66 B5
Güiria 50 E1
Guise 62 F5
Guitiriz 68 C1
Guiyang 86 D5
Gujranwala 94 B2
Gujrat 94 B2
Gulang 86 C3
Gulbarga 94 C5
Gulbene 56 P8
Gulf of Aden 96 E7
Gulf of Alaska 44 (1)H4
Gulf of Aqaba 96 B4
Gulf of Boothia 34 N2
Gulf of Bothnia 56 K6
Gulf of Carpentaria 116 G2
Gulf of Finland 56 M7
Gulf of Gdansk 58 J3
Gulf of Guinea 108 D4
Gulf of Mannar 94 C7
Gulf of Martaban 90 B3
Gulf of Mexico 46 F3
Gulf of Oman 101 G4
Gulf of Riga 56 M8
Gulf of St. Lawrence 34 U7
Gulf of Santa Catalina 44 C2
Gulf of Thailand 90 C4
Gulf of Tongking 90 D3
Gulf of Venice 70 H5
Gulfport 42 D3
Gulistan 82 M9
Gülşehir 76 S6
Gulu 110 E3
Gülübovo 76 H2
Gumdag 96 F2
Gumel 108 F2
Gumla 94 D4
Gummersbach 62 K3
Gummi 108 F2
Gümüşhane 98 H3
Guna 94 C4
Guna Terara 104 G5
Gungu 110 B5
Gunib 98 M2
Gunnbjørns Fjeld 120 (1)U2
Gunnedah 116 K6
Gunnison, *Colo.*, *United States* 38 E3
Gunnison, *Ut.*, *United States* 38 D3
Gunong Kinabalu 92 (1)F1
Guntakal 94 C5
Guntur 94 D5
Gunung Kerinci 92 (1)C3
Gunung Korbu 92 (1)C2
Gunung Kwoka 92 (2)D3
Gunung Leuser 92 (1)B2
Gunung Mekongga 92 (2)B3
Gunung Mulu 92 (1)E2
Gunung Pangrango 92 (1)D4
Gunungsitoli 92 (1)B2
Gunung Togwomeri 92 (2)D3
Günzburg 70 F2
Gunzenhausen 60 F7
Guoyang 86 F4
Gura Humorului 74 N2
Gurk 70 K4
Gurskoye 84 P6
Gürün 98 G4
Gurupi 50 H4
Gusau 108 F2
Gusev 58 M3
Gushgy 96 H2
Gusinoozersk 84 H6
Gúspini 72 C9
Güssing 70 M3
Güstrow 58 B4
Gütersloh 60 D5
Guthrie, *Okla.*, *United States* 38 G3
Guthrie, *Tex.*, *United States* 44 F2
Gutsuo 94 E3
Guttenberg 40 B2
Guwahati 94 F3
Guyana 50 F2
Guyang 86 E2
Guymon 44 F1
Guyuan 86 D3
Guzar 96 J2
Gvardejsk 58 L3
Gwadar 96 H4
Gwalior 94 C3
Gwanda 112 D4
Gwardex 72 J12
Gwda 58 F4
Gweebarra Bay 64 C7
Gweru 112 D3
Gyangzê 94 E3
Gyaring Hu 86 B4
Gyaros 76 G7
Gyda 82 P3
Gydanskiy Poluostrov 82 P3
Gyirong 94 E3
Gyldenløues Fjord 34 Y4
Gympie 116 K5
Gyomaendrőd 74 H3
Gyöngyös 74 G2
Győr 74 E2
Gypsumville 34 M6
Gytheio 76 E8
Gyula 74 J3
Gyumri 98 K3
Gyzylarbat 96 G2

H

Haapajärvi 56 N3
Haapsalu 56 M7
Haar 70 G3
Haarlem 62 G3
Haast 118 B3
Habahe 82 R8
Habarūt 96 F6
Habaswein 110 F3
Habbān 96 E7
Habbānīyah 98 K7
Habirag 86 F2
Habomai-Shoto 84 R8
Haboro 88 L1
Hachijō-jima 88 K7
Hachinohe 88 L3
Hachiōji 88 K6
Hadadong 82 Q9
Haddunmahti Atoll 94 B8
Hadejia 108 F2
Hadejia 108 G2
Hadera 100 B4
Haderslev 60 E1
Ḩaḑhramaut 96 E6
Hadilik 82 R10
Hadjout 68 N8
Haeju 88 C4
Haenam 88 D6
Ḩafar al Bāţin 101 A2
Hafnarfjördur 56 (1)C2
Haft Gel 101 C1
Hagen 62 K3
Hagenow 60 G3
Hāgere Hiywet 110 F2
Hagerstown 40 E3
Haguenau 62 K6
Haicheng 88 B3
Haifa = Ḥefa 100 B4
Haikou 90 E3
Hā'il 96 D4
Hailar 84 K7
Hailey 38 D2
Hailong 88 C2
Hailuoto 56 N4
Hainan 90 D3
Haines Junction 44 (1)K3
Haining 86 G4
Hai Phong 90 D2
Haiti 46 K5
Haiya 104 G4
Hajdúböszörmény 74 J2
Hajdúhadház 58 L10
Hajdúnánás 58 L10
Hajdúszoboszló 58 L10
Hajipur 94 E3
Hajmah 96 G6
Hajnówka 58 N5
Haka 94 F4
Hakkâri 98 K5
Hakodate 88 L3
Ḩalab 98 G5
Ḩalabān 104 H3
Ḩalabja 98 L6
Halaib 104 G3
Halba 100 D2
Halberstadt 60 G5
Halden 56 F7
Haldensleben 60 G4
Halifax 34 U8

Halifax Bay	116	J3
Hall	70	G3
Hall Beach	34	Q3
Halle	62	G4
Hallein	70	J3
Halligen	60	D2
Hallock	38	G1
Hall Peninsula	34	T4
Halls Creek	116	E3
Halmahera	92	(2)C2
Halmahera Sea	92	(2)C3
Halmstad	58	B1
Haltern	62	K3
Hamada	88	G6
Hamadān	96	E3
Hamāh	98	G6
Hamamatsu	88	J6
Hamar	56	F6
Hamarøy	56	H2
Hamatonbetsu	88	M1
Hambantota	94	D7
Hamburg, *Germany*	60	E3
Hamburg, *Ark., United States*	42	C3
Hamburg, *N.Y., United States*	40	E2
Hämeenlinna	56	N6
Hameln	60	E4
Hamersley Range	116	C4
Hamhŭng	88	D3
Hami	82	S9
Hamilton, *Australia*	116	H7
Hamilton, *Bermuda*	46	M2
Hamilton, *Canada*	40	E2
Hamilton, *New Zealand*	118	E3
Hamilton, *Al., United States*	42	D3
Hamilton, *Mont., United States*	38	D1
Hamilton, *Oh., United States*	40	D3
Hamina	56	P6
Hamirpur	94	D3
Hamm	60	C5
Hammada du Drâa	106	D3
Hammam Bou Hadjar	68	K9
Hammamet	72	E12
Hammam Lif	106	H1
Hammelburg	60	E6
Hammerfest	56	M1
Hammer Springs	118	D6
Hampden	118	C7
Hāmūn-e Jaz Mūrīān	101	H3
Hanamaki	88	L4
Hanau	60	D6
Hânceşti	74	R3
Hancheng	86	E3
Hancock	40	C1
Handan	86	E3
Handeni	110	F5
Handerslev	56	E9
Handlová	58	H9
Hanford	44	C1
Hangayn Nuruu	82	T8
Hangu	86	F3
Hangzhou	86	F4
Hanīdh	101	C3
Hanko	56	M7
Hanksville	38	D3
Hanna	34	K6
Hannibal	42	C2
Hannover	60	E4
Hanö	58	D2
Hanöbukten	58	D2
Ha Nôi	90	D2
Hanoi = Ha Nôi	90	D2
Hanover	40	F2
Han Shui	86	D4
Hanson Bay	118	(1)B1
Hanumangarh	94	B3
Hanzhong	86	D4
Hao	114	M7
Hāora	94	E4
Haparanda	56	N4
Hāpoli	94	F3
Hapur	94	C3
Ḩaraḑ, *Saudi Arabia*	96	E5
Ḩaraḑ, *Yemen*	104	H4
Haramachi	88	L5
Harare	112	E3
Harbin	86	H1
Harbour Breton	34	V7
Harburg	60	F3
Hardangerfjorden	56	C7
Hardangervidda	56	D6
Hardenberg	62	J2
Harderwijk	62	H2
Hardin	38	E1
Hardy	42	C2
Haren	62	K2
Härer	110	G2
Hargeysa	110	G2
Har Hu	86	B3
Haridwar	94	C3
Harihari	118	C6
Harima-nada	88	H6
Hari Rud	96	H3
Harlan	40	A2
Hărlău	74	P2
Harlem	38	E1
Harlingen, *Netherlands*	62	H1
Harlingen, *United States*	42	B4
Harlow	64	N10
Harlowtown	38	E1
Harney Basin	36	B3
Harney Lake	38	C2
Härnösand	56	J5
Har Nuur	82	S8
Haro	68	H2
Harricanaw	34	R6
HHarrisburg, *Ill., United States*	40	C3
Harrisburg, *Pa., United States*	42	F1
Harrison	40	B3
Harrison Bay	44	(1)G1
Harrisville	40	D2
Harrogate	64	L8
Har Saggi	100	B6
Harsin	98	M6
Hârşova	74	Q5
Harstad	56	J2
Hartberg	70	L3
Hartford	40	F2
Hartland Point	64	H10
Hartlepool	64	L7
Har Us Nuur	82	S8
Harvey	38	G1
Harwich	62	D3
Harz	60	F5
Hāsā	100	C6
Haselünne	60	C4
Hashtpar	98	N5
Hāsik	96	G6
Haskell	42	B3
Haslemere	62	B3
Hassan	94	C6
Hasselfelde	60	F5
Hasselt	62	H4
Haßfurt	60	F6
Hassi Bel Guebbour	106	G3
Hässleholm	56	G8
Hastings, *New Zealand*	118	F4
Hastings, *United Kingdom*	62	C4
Hastings, *Minn., United States*	40	B2
Hastings, *Nebr., United States*	38	G2
Haţeg	74	K4
Hatgal	84	G6
Ha Tinh	90	D3
Hatteras	42	F2
Hattiesburg	42	D3
Hatvan	74	G2
Haud	104	H6
Haud Ogadēn	110	G2/H2
Haugesund	56	C7
Hauraki Gulf	118	E3
Haut Atlas	106	D2
Hauts Plateaux	106	E2
Havana	42	C1
Havana = La Habana	46	H4
Havant	64	M11
Havel	58	C5
Havelock, *New Zealand*	118	D5
Havelock, *United States*	42	F3
Havelock North	118	F4
Havenby	60	D1
Haverfordwest	64	H10
Havlíčkův Brod	58	E8
Havre	38	E1
Havre-St-Pierre	34	U6
Havrylivtsi	74	P1
Havza	98	F3
Hawaii	44	(2)E2
Hawaii	44	(2)E4
Hawaiian Islands	114	J3
Hawera	118	E4
Hawi	44	(2)F3
Hawick	64	K6
Hawke Bay	118	F4
Hawker	116	G6
Hawr al'Awdah	101	B1
Hawr al Ḩammar	101	B1
Hawthorne	38	C3
Hay	116	H6
Hay	34	H5
Hayange	62	J5
Haydarābad	98	L5
Hayden	44	D2
Hayrabolu	76	K3
Hay River	34	H4
Hays	42	B2
Hazard	40	D3
Hazāribāg	94	E4
Hazebrouck	62	E4
Hazelton, *Canada*	34	F5
Hazelton, *United States*	40	E2
Head of Bight	116	F6
Hearne	42	E3
Hearst	40	D1
Hebbronville	44	G3
Hebgen Lake	38	D2
Hebi	86	E3
Hebron, *Canada*	34	U5
Hebron, *Israel*	100	C5
Hebron, *Nebr., United States*	38	G2
Hebron, *N.D., United States*	38	F1
Hecate Strait	34	E6
Hechi	90	D2
Hechingen	70	D2
Hede	56	G5
Heerenveen	62	H2
Heerlen	62	J4
Hefa	100	B4
Hefei	86	F4
Hegang	86	J1
Hegura-jima	88	J5
Hegyfalu	70	M3
Heide	60	E2
Heidelberg	60	D7
Heidenheim	70	F2
Heilbad Heiligenstadt	60	F5
Heilbronn	60	E7
Heimaey	56	(1)C3
Heinola	56	N6
Hejing	82	R9
Hekla	56	(1)D3
Helagsfjället	56	G5
Helena, *Ark., United States*	42	C3
Helena, *Mont., United States*	38	D1
Helen Reef	92	(2)D2
Helensville	118	E3
Helgea	58	D1
Helgoland	60	C2
Helgoländer Bucht	60	D2
Hellín	68	J6
Helmand	96	H3
Helmond	62	H3
Helmsdale	64	J3
Helmstedt	60	G4
Helodrano Antongila	112	H3
Helong	88	E2
Helsingborg	56	G8
Helsinge	58	B1
Helsingør	56	G8
Helsinki	56	N6
Helston	64	G11
Helwan	104	F2
Hemel Hempstead	64	M10
Henashi-zaki	88	K3
Henderson, *Ky., United States*	40	C3
Henderson, *Nev., United States*	38	D3
Henderson, *N.C., United States*	42	F2
Henderson Island	114	P8
Hendersonville	40	C3
Hendijarn	101	C1
Hengelo	62	J2
Hengyang	86	E5
Henichesk	78	F5
Hénin-Beaumont	62	E4
Hennebont	66	B6
Hennigsdorf	60	J4
Henryetta	40	A3
Henzada	90	B3
Heppenheim	60	D7
Heppner	38	C1
Hepu	90	D2
Héradsflói	56	(1)F2
Herald Cays	116	J3
Herāt	96	H3
Herbert	118	C7
Herborn	60	D6
Herceg-Novi	74	F7
Hereford, *United Kingdom*	64	K9
Hereford, *United States*	46	D2
Herentals	62	G3
Herford	60	D4
Herisau	70	E3
Herlen Gol	86	E1
Hermagor	70	J4
Herma Ness	64	M1
Hermel	100	D2
Hermiston	38	C1
Hermosillo	36	D6
Hernád	58	L9
Herne	60	C5
Herne Bay	62	D3
Herning	56	E8
Herrenberg	70	D2
Hersbruck	60	G7
Herstat	62	H4
Hertlay	62	E6
Hervey Bay	116	K5
Herzberg	60	F5
Hesdin	62	E4
Heshan	90	D2
Hesselø	58	A1
Hessisch-Lichtenau	60	E5
Hettstedt Lutherstadt	60	G5
Heves	58	K10
He Xian	90	E2
Hexigten Qi	86	F2
Heze	86	F3
Hialeah	42	E4
Hiawatha	42	B2
Hibbing	40	B1
Hickory	40	D3
Hidaka-sammyaku	88	M2
Hidalgo del Parral	46	C3
Hiddensee	60	H2
Hierro	106	B3
Higashi-suidō	88	E7
High Point	40	E3
High Wycombe	62	B3
Hiiumaa	56	M7
Hikurangi	118	E2
Hikurangi	118	G3
Hikutaia	118	E3
Hildburghausen	60	F6
Hildesheim	60	E4
Hillsboro, *Oh., United States*	42	E2
Hillsboro, *Oreg., United States*	38	E1
Hillsboro, *Tex., United States*	44	G2
Hillsville	40	E3
Hillswick	64	L1
Hilo	44	(2)F4
Hilton Head Island	42	E3
Hilva	98	H5
Hilversum	62	H2
Himalayas	80	L6
Himarë	76	B4
Himatnagar	94	B4
Himeji	88	H6
Himora	104	G5
Ḩimş	100	D2
Hindu Kush	94	A1
Hindupur	94	C6
Hinesville	42	E3
Hingoli	94	C5
Hinnøya	56	H2
Hiroo	88	M2
Hirosaki	88	L3
Hiroshima	88	G6
Hirson	62	G5
Hirtshals	56	E8
Hisar	94	C3
Hisdal	56	C6
Hispaniola	48	D2
Hitachi	88	L5
Hitoyoshi	88	F7
Hitra	56	D5
Hiuchi-nada	88	G6
Hiva Oa	114	M6
Hjälmaren	56	H7
Hjalmar Lake	34	K4
Hjelmsøya	56	M1
Hlinsko	58	E8
Hlohovec	70	N2
Hlyboka	74	N1
Hlybokaye	78	E3
Ho	108	E3
Hobart, *Australia*	116	J8
Hobart, *United States*	44	G1
Hobbs	44	F2
Hobro	56	E8
Hobyo	110	H3
Hô Chi Minh	90	D4
Höchstadt	60	F7
Hockenheim	60	D7
Hódmezóvásárhely	74	H3
Hodonin	58	G9
Hoek van Holland	62	G3
Hoeryŏng	88	E2
Hof	60	G6
Hofgeismar	60	E5
Höfn	56	(1)F2
Hofsjökull	56	(1)D2
Hōfu	88	F6
Hohe	70	H3
Hohe Dachstein	58	C10
Hohe Tauern	72	G1
Hohhot	86	E2
Hoh Xil Shan	94	E1
Hôi An	90	D3
Hoima	110	E3
Hokitika	118	C6

Hokkaidō 88 N2
Holbæk 58 A2
Holbrook 44 D2
Holdrege 38 G2
Holguín 46 J4
Holíč 70 N2
Hollabrunn 70 M2
Holland 40 C2
Hollis 44 G2
Hollywood 42 E4
Holman 34 H2
Hólmavík 56 (1)C2
Holmes Reefs 116 J3
Holstebro 56 E8
Holsteinische Schweiz 60 F2
Holsteinsborg = Sisimiut 34 W3
Holton 42 B2
Holyhead 64 H8
Holy Island, *Eng.*, *United Kingdom* 64 L6
Holy Island, *Wales*, *United Kingdom* 64 H8
Holyoke 38 F2
Holzkirchen 70 G3
Holzminden 60 E5
Homa Bay 110 E4
Homberg 60 E5
Hombori 106 E5
Home Bay 34 T3
Homestead 42 E4
Homewood 42 D3
Homs = Ḩimş 100 D2
Homyel' 78 F4
Hondo, *N.Mex.*, *United States* 44 E2
Hondo, *Tex.*, *United States* 44 G3
Honduras 46 G6
Hønefoss 56 F6
Honey Lake 38 B2
Honfleur 62 C5
Hon Gai 90 D2
Hong Kong 90 E2
Hongliuyuan 86 B2
Hongor 86 E1
Honiara 114 F6
Honjō 88 K4
Honokaa 44 (2)F3
Honolulu 44 (2)D2
Honshū 88 L5
Hooge 60 D2
Hoogeveen 62 J2
Hoogezand-Sappemeer 62 J1
Hooper Bay 44 (1)D3
Hoorn 62 H2
Hoorn Islands 114 H7
Hopa 98 J3
Hope, *Canada* 38 B1
Hope, *Ak.*, *United States* 34 B4
Hope, *Ark.*, *United States* 42 C3
Hopedale 34 U5
Hopetoun 116 H7
Hopin 94 G4
Hopkinsville 40 C3
Hoquiam 38 B1
Horadiz 98 M4
Horasan 98 K3
Horgo 84 F7
Horizon Depth 114 D8
Hormak 96 H4
Hormoz 101 F3
Horn 70 L2
Hornavan 56 J3
Horncastle 62 B1
Horodenka 74 N1
Horodok 58 N8
Horqin Youyi Qianqi 84 L7
Horsens 56 E9
Horsham, *Australia* 116 H7
Horsham, *United Kingdom* 62 B3
Horten 56 F7
Hortiguela 68 G2
Horton 44 (1)N2
Ḩoseynābād 101 G2
Hoshab 96 H4
Hoshangabad 94 C4
Hospet 94 C5
Hosséré Vokre 108 G3
Hotan 82 Q10
Hotan 82 Q10
Hot Springs, *Ark.*, *United States* 40 B4
Hot Springs, *N.C.*, *United States* 40 D3
Hottah Lake 34 H3
Houdan 62 D6
Houdelaincourt 70 A2
Houghton 40 C1
Houlton 40 G1
Houma, *China* 86 E3
Houma, *United States* 36 H6
Houmt Souk 106 H2
Houston 36 G6
Hovd 82 S8
Hövsgöl Nuur 84 F6
Howard Junction 118 C5
Howland 114 J5
Hoxie 42 C2
Höxter 60 E5
Hoxud 82 R9
Hoy 64 J3
Høyanger 56 D6
Hoyerswerda 60 K5
Hradeç Králové 58 E7
Hranice 58 G8
Hrazdan 98 L3
Hrodna 58 N4
Hron 58 H9
Hrubieszów 58 N7
Hsin-chu 90 G2
Hsueh-Shan 90 G2
Hsweni 90 B2
Huacho 50 B6
Huade 86 E2
Huadian 88 D2
Huaibei 86 F4
Huaibin 86 F4
Huaihua 86 D5
Huainan 86 F4
Huaiyin 86 F4
Huaki 92 (2)C4
Huallaga 50 B5
Huambo 112 B2
Huancayelica 50 B6
Huancayo 50 B6
Huang 84 H3
Huangchuan 86 F4
Huang He 86 F3
Huangshan 86 F5
Huangshi 86 F4
Huang Xian 86 G3
Huangyan 86 G5
Huanren 88 C3
Huanuco 50 B5
Huaráz 50 B5
Huarmey 50 B6
Huasco 52 G4
Huashixia 86 B3
Huatabampo 36 E6
Hubli 94 C5
Huch'ang 88 D3
Huddersfield 64 L8
Huddinge 56 K7
Hudiksvall 56 J6
Hudson 40 F2
Hudson 40 F2
Hudson Bay 34 L6
Hudson Bay 34 P5
Hudson Strait 34 S4
Huê 90 D3
Huelva 68 D7
Huercal Overa 68 J7
Huesca 68 K2
Huéscar 68 H7
Huftaroy 56 C6
Hugo 42 B3
Hugo Lake 42 B3
Huia 118 E3
Huich'ŏn 88 D3
Huila Plateau 112 A3
Huinan 88 C2
Huinca Renancó 52 J5
Huizhou 90 E2
Hulin 84 N7
Hull 40 E1
Hulst 62 G3
Hulun Nur 84 K7
Huma 84 M6
Huma 84 M6
Humaitá 50 E5
Humbe 112 A3
Humboldt 34 L6
Humboldt 38 C2
Hümedān 96 G4
Humenné 58 L9
Humphrey 38 D2
Humpolec 58 E8
Hūn 104 C2
Húnaflói 56 (1)C2
Hunchun 88 F2
Hunedoara 74 K4
Hünfeld 60 E6
Hungary 74 F3
Hungen 60 D6
Hungerford 116 H5
Hüngnam 88 D4
Hunjiang 88 D3
Hunsrück 60 B7
Hunstanton 62 C2
Hunte 60 D4
Hunter Island 114 H8
Huntingburg 42 D2
Huntingdon, *United Kingdom* 62 B2
Huntingdon, *United States* 42 E2
Huntington 42 D1
Huntington Beach 44 C2
Huntly 118 E3
Huntsville, *Canada* 40 E1
Huntsville, *Al.*, *United States* 42 D3
Huntsville, *Tex.*, *United States* 46 E2
Hunyuan 86 E3
Ḩūr 101 G1
Hurdiyo 110 J1
Hurghada 104 F2
Huron 38 G2
Hürth 62 J4
Húsavík 56 (1)E1
Huşi 74 R3
Huslia 44 (1)F2
Husn 100 C4
Husum 60 E2
Hutag 84 G7
Hutanopan 92 (1)B2
Hutchinson 44 G1
Ḩūth 104 H4
Huttwil 70 C3
Huvadu Atoll 94 B8
Huy 62 H4
Huzou 86 G4
Hvannadalshnúkur 56 (1)E2
Hvar 74 D6
Hvar 74 D6
Hvolsvöllur 56 (1)C3
Hwange 112 D3
Hyak 38 B1
Hyannis 38 F2
Hyderabad, *India* 94 C5
Hyderabad, *Pakistan* 96 J4
Hyères 66 M10
Hyesan 88 E3
Hyndam Peak 38 D2
Hyūga 88 F7
Hyvinkää 56 N6

I

Iaco 50 D6
Ialomiţa 74 P5
Ianca 74 Q4
Iaşi 74 Q2
Ibadan 108 E3
Ibagué 50 B3
Ibar 74 H6
Ibb 104 H5
Ibbenbüren 60 C4
Iberia 50 C5
Ibiza = Eivissa 68 M5
Ibiza = Eivissa 68 M6
Ibotirama 50 J6
Ibrā' 96 G5
'Ibrī 101 G5
Ica 50 B6
İçel 98 F5
Iceland 54 C1
Ichalkaranji 94 B5
Ichinoseki 88 L4
Idabel 42 C3
Ida Grove 40 A2
Idah 108 F3
Idaho 38 D2
Idaho Falls 38 D2
Idar-Oberstein 60 C7
Idfu 104 F3
Idhān Awbārī 106 H3
Idhan Murzūq 106 H4
Idiofa 110 C4
Idlib 98 G6
Idstein 60 D6
Ieper 62 E4
Ierapetra 76 H9
Ifanadiana 112 H4
Ife 108 E3
Igarka 82 R4
Iggesund 56 J6
Igizyar 96 L2
Iglésias 72 C9
Igloolik 34 Q3
Ignace 40 B1
İğneada 76 K3
Igoumenitsa 76 C5
Igra 78 K3
Igrim 78 M2
Igualada 68 M3
Iguatu 50 K5
Ilharaña 112 H2
Ihosy 112 H4
Ihtiman 76 F2
Iida 88 J6
Iim 70 E2
Iisalmi 56 P5
Iiulissat 34 W3
Ijebu Ode 108 E3
IJmuiden 62 G2
IJssel 62 J2
IJsselmeer 62 H2
Ikaria 76 J7
Ikeda 88 M2
Ikela 110 C4
Ikhtiman 74 L7
Iki 88 E7
Ikire 108 E3
Ikom 108 F3
Ikopa 112 H3
Ikorodu 108 E3
Ilagan 90 G3
Īlām 96 E3
Iława 58 J4
Ilbenge 84 L4
Ilebo 110 C4
Île d'Anticosti 34 U7
Île de Jerba 106 H2
Île de la Gonâve 46 K5
Île de Noirmoutier 66 C7
Île de Ré 66 D7
Île d'Oléron 66 D8
Île d'Yeu 66 C7
Île Europa 112 G4
Ilek 78 K4
Ilek 78 K4
Île Plane 72 E11
Îles Cani 72 D11
Îles Chesterfield 114 F7
Îles Crozet 102 J10
Îles de la Madeleine 34 U7
Îles Désappointement 114 M7
Îles d'Hyères 66 M11
Îles Duc de Gloucester 114 M7
Îles Glorieuses 112 H2
Ilesha 108 E3
Îles Kerkenah 106 H2
Îles Maria 114 L8
Îles Palliser 114 M7
Île Tidra 106 B5
Île Zembra 72 E11
Ilfracombe 64 H10
Ilha da Trindade 48 H6
Ilha de Marajó 50 H4
Ilha de São Luís 50 J4
Ilha do Bazaruto 112 F4
Ilha Fernando de Noronha 50 L5
Ilha Grande de Gurupa 50 G4
Ilhas Martin Vaz 52 Q3
Ilhéus 50 K6
Iliamna Volcano 44 (1)G3
Iligan 90 G5
Ilkal 94 C5
Iller 70 F3
Illertissen 70 F2
Illichivs'k 74 T3
Illinois 36 H3
Illinois 40 C3
Illizi 106 G3
Ilmenau 60 F6
Ilo 50 C7
Iloilo 90 G4
Ilorin 108 E3
Ilovlya 78 H5
Il'pyrskiy 84 U4
Ilwaco 38 B1
Ilych 78 L2
Imabari 88 G6
Imatra 56 Q6
Imeni-Babushkina 82 G6
Imeni Polinyosipenko 84 P6
Imese 110 B3
Imī 110 G2
İmişli 98 N4
Immeln 58 D1
Immenstadt 70 F3
Ímola 70 G6
Imotski 74 E6
Imperatriz 50 H5
Impéria 70 D7
Imperial 38 F2
Impfondo 110 B3
Imphal 94 F4
Imrali Adası 76 L4
Imroz 76 H4
Inambari 50 C6
In Aménas 106 G3
Inangahua 118 C5
Inanwatan 92 (2)D3
Iñapari 50 D6
Inarijärvi 56 P2
Inca 68 N5
İnce Burun 98 F2
Inch'ŏn 88 D5
Incirliova 76 K7
Indalsälven 56 H5

Independence, *Kans.*, *United States*	42	B2
Independence, *Mo.*, *United States*	40	B3
India	94	C4
Indiana	36	J3
Indiana	40	E2
Indianapolis	42	D2
Indian Ocean	94	D8
Indianola	40	B2
Indian Springs	38	C3
Indiga	78	J1
Indio	44	C2
Indonesia	92	(1)D3
Indore	94	C4
Indramayu	92	(1)D4
Indre	66	G6
Indre Sula	56	C6
Indus	96	K3
İnebolu	98	E3
İnecik	76	K4
İnegöl	98	C3
In Ekker	106	G4
Ineu	74	J3
Ingelheim	62	L5
Ingeniero Jacobacci	52	H7
Ingham	116	J3
Ingoda	84	J6
Ingolstadt	70	G2
Ingrāj Bāzār	94	E3
Ingushetiya	98	L2
Inhambane	112	F4
Inírida	50	D3
Inishmore	64	B8
Inkisi-Kisantu	108	H6
Inn	70	H2
Inner Hebrides	64	F5
Inner Mongolia = Nei Monggol	86	E2
Inneston	116	G7
Innisfail	116	J3
Innsbruck	70	G3
Inongo	110	B4
Inowrocław	58	H5
In Salah	106	F3
Insein	90	B3
Inta	82	K4
Interlaken	70	C4
International Falls	40	B1
Intsy	78	H1
Inubō-zaki	88	L6
Inukjuak	34	R5
Inuvik	44	(1)L2
Invercargill	118	B8
Inverness	64	H4
Inverway	116	E3
Investigator Group	116	F6
Investigator Strait	116	G7
Inya	82	R7
Inya	84	R4
Ioannina	76	C5
Iokanga	82	F4
Iola	42	B2
Iona	64	F5
Ionian Sea	76	B6
Ionioi Nisoi	76	B5
Ios	76	H8
Iowa	36	H3
Iowa City	40	B2
Iowa Falls	40	B2
Ipameri	50	H7
Ipatinga	52	N2
Ipatovo	78	H5
Ipiales	50	B3
Ipiaú	50	K6
Ipoh	92	(1)C2
Iporá	50	G7
Ippy	110	C2
Ipsala	76	J4
Ipswich	64	P9
Iqaluit	34	T4
Iquique	52	G3
Iquitos	50	C4
Iracoubo	50	G2
Irakleia	76	F3
Irakleia	76	H8
Irakleio	76	H9
Iraklion = Irakleio	54	G4
Iran	96	F3
Irānshahr	96	H4
Irapuato	46	D4
Iraq	96	D3
Irbid	100	C4
Irbit	78	M3
Irecê	50	J6
Irgiz	78	M5
Irgiz	78	M5
Irhil M'Goun	106	D2
Irian Jaya	92	(2)E3
Iringa	110	F5
Iriri	50	G4
Irish Sea	64	G8
Irkutsk	84	G6
Iron Mountain	40	C1
Ironton	42	E2
Ironwood	40	B1
Irrawaddy	94	F5
Irshava	74	L1
Irta	78	J2
Irtysh	78	P3
Irtyshsk	82	P7
Irumu	110	D3
Irún	68	J1
Irvine	64	H6
Irving	44	G2
Isabela	92	(2)B1
Isabella	40	B1
Isabella Lake	44	C1
Ísafjarđardjúp	56	(1)A1
Ísafjörđur	56	(1)B1
Isahaya	86	J4
Isar	70	G3
Ischia	72	H8
Ise	88	J6
Isel	70	H4
Isère	70	B5
Iserlohn	62	K3
Isérnia	72	J7
Isetskoye	78	N3
Iseyin	108	E3
Isfana	96	J2
Ishikari-wan	88	L2
Ishim	78	N3
Ishim	78	N4
Ishinomaki	88	L4
Ishkoshim	96	K2
Isiolo	110	F3
Isiro	110	D3
Iskăr	74	M6
İskenderun	98	G5
Iskitim	82	Q7
Isla Alejandro Selkirk	52	E5
Isla Campana	52	F8
Isla Clarence	52	G9
Isla Clarión	46	B5
Isla Coiba	46	H7
Isla Contreras	52	F9
Isla de Alborán	68	G9
Isla de Bioco	108	F4
Isla de Chiloé	52	G7
Isla de Coco	46	G7
Isla de Cozumel	46	G4
Isla de la Juventud	46	H4
Isla de los Estados	52	J9
Isla de Malpelo	50	A3
Isla de Margarita	50	E1
Isla de Providencia	46	H6
Isla de San Andrés	46	H6
Isla de São Francisco	52	M4
Isla de São Sebastião	52	M3
Isla Desolación	52	F9
Isla Española	50	(1)B2
Isla Fernandina	50	(1)A2
Isla Gorgona	50	B3
Isla Grande	52	N3
Isla Grande de Tierra del Fuego	52	H9
Isla Guafo	52	F7
Isla Hoste	52	G10
Isla Isabela	50	(1)A2
Isla La Tortuga	50	D1
Isla Londonderry	52	G9
Islamabad	94	B2
Isla Madre de Dios	52	F8/9
Isla Marchena	50	(1)A1
Islamgarh	94	B3
Islamorada	42	E5
Isla Navarino	52	H10
Island Lake	34	M6
Islands of the Four Mountains	44	(1)C5
Isla Pinta	50	(1)A1
Isla Puná	50	A4
Isla Riesco	52	G9
Isla Robinson Crusoe	52	E5
Isla San Benedicto	46	B5
Isla San Cristóbal	50	(1)B2
Isla San Salvador	50	(1)A2
Isla Santa Cruz	50	(1)A2
Isla Santa Inés	52	F9
Isla Santa María	50	(1)A2
Islas Baleares	68	N5
Islas Canarias	102	A3
Islas Canarias	106	B3
Islas Columbretes	68	L5
Islas de la Bahía	46	G5
Islas de los Desventurados	52	E4
Islas Galápagos	50	(1)B1
Islas Juan Fernández	52	E5
Islas Los Roques	50	D1
Islas Marías	46	C4
Isla Socorro	46	B5
Islas Revillagigedo	46	B5
Islas Wollaston	52	H10
Isla Wellington	52	F8
Islay	64	F6
Isle	66	F8
Isle of Man	64	H7
Isle of Wight	64	L11
Isle Royale	40	C1
Isles of Scilly	64	F12
Ismâ'ilîya	104	F1
İsmayıllı	98	N3
Isna	104	F2
Isoka	112	E2
Isola delle Correnti	72	J12
Isola di Capo Rizzuto	72	M10
Isola di Pantelleria	72	G12
Isole Égadi	72	F11
Isole Lipari	72	J10
Isole Ponziane	72	H8
Isole Trémiti	72	K6
Iso-Vietonen	56	N3
Isparta	76	N7
Íspica	72	J12
Israel	100	B5
Israelite Bay	116	D6
Issia	108	C3
Issimu	92	(2)B2
Issoire	66	J8
Issoudun	66	H7
İstanbul	98	C3
İstanbul Boğazı	98	C3
Istiaia	76	F6
Istmo de Tehauntepec	46	F5
Istra	70	J5
Istres	66	K10
Itaberaba	50	J6
Itabira	50	J7
Itabuna	50	K6
Itacoatiara	50	F4
Itaituba	50	F4
Itajaí	52	M4
Italy	72	E4
Itambacuri	50	J7
Itanagar	94	F3
Itapebi	50	K7
Itapetinga	50	J7
Itapicuru	50	K6
Itapicuru Mirim	50	J4
Itapipoca	50	K4
Itarsi	94	C4
Ithaca	40	E2
Ithaki	76	C6
Ithaki	76	C6
Itiquira	50	F/G7
Ituí	50	C5
Ituiutaba	50	H7
Itumbiara	50	H7
Ituni	50	F2
Ituri	110	D3
Ituxi	50	E5
Itzehoe	60	E3
Ivalo	56	P2
Ivanava	56	N10
Ivangrad	74	G7
Ivanhoe, *Australia*	116	H6
Ivanhoe, *United States*	40	A2
Ivano-Frankivs'k	78	D5
Ivanovo	78	H3
Ivatsevichy	56	N10
Ivdel'	78	M2
Ivittuut	34	X4
Ivory Coast	108	C3
Ivosjön	58	D1
Ivrea	70	C5
Ivujivik	34	R4
Iwaki	88	L5
Iwamizawa	88	L2
Iwo	108	E3
Iyo-nadā	88	G7
Izberbash	98	M2
Izegem	62	F4
Izhevsk	78	K3
Izhma	78	K1
Izhma	78	K2
Izk	96	G5
Izkī	101	G5
Izmayil	74	R4
İzmir	98	B4
İzmir Körfezi	76	J6
İzmit	98	C3
İznik	98	C3
İznik Gölü	98	C3
Izola	70	J5
Izra'	100	D4
Izuhara	88	E6
Izumo	88	G6
Izu-shotō	88	K6

J

Jabal ad Durūz	100	D4
Jabal Akhḍar	101	G5
Jabal al Nuşayrīyah	100	D1
Jabal an Nabī Shu'ayb	104	H4
Jabal Ash Sham	101	G5
Jabal aẓ Ẓannah	101	E4
Jabalpur	94	C4
Jabal Shammar	104	G2
Jabal Thamar	104	J5
Jabiru	116	F2
Jablah	100	C1
Jablonec	58	E7
Jablunkov	58	H8
Jaboatão	50	K5
Jaca	68	K2
Jacareacanga	50	G5
Jackman	40	F1
Jacksboro	42	B3
Jackson, *Calif.*, *United States*	38	B3
Jackson, *Minn.*, *United States*	40	B2
Jackson, *Miss.*, *United States*	42	C3
Jackson, *Oh.*, *United States*	42	E2
Jackson, *Tenn.*, *United States*	42	D2
Jackson Head	118	B6
Jackson Lake	38	D2
Jacksonville, *Fla.*, *United States*	42	E3
Jacksonville, *Ill.*, *United States*	40	B3
Jacksonville, *N.C.*, *United States*	42	F3
Jacksonville, *Tex.*, *United States*	42	B3
Jacmel	46	K5
Jacobabad	94	A3
Jacobina	50	J6
Jacunda	50	H4
Jacupiranga	52	M3
Jade	60	D3
Jadebusen	60	D3
Jādū	106	H2
Jaén	68	G7
Jaen	50	B5
Jaffna	94	D7
Jagdalpur	94	D5
Jagersfontein	112	D5
Jaggang	94	C2
Jagst	60	E7
Jahrom	101	E2
Jaipur	94	C3
Jaisalmer	94	B3
Jajce	74	E5
Jakarta	92	(1)D4
Jakobshavn = Ilulissat	34	W3
Jakobstad	56	M5
Jalālābād	94	B2
Jalandhar	94	C2
Jalapa Enriquez	46	E5
Jalgaon	94	C4
Jalībah	101	B1
Jalingo	108	G3
Jalna	94	C5
Jalón	68	J3
Jalpaiguri	94	E3
Jalūlā	98	L6
Jamaica	46	H5
Jamalpur	94	E3
Jambi	92	(1)C3
James	38	G2
James Bay	34	Q6
Jamestown, *N.Y.*, *United States*	40	E2
Jamestown, *N.D.*, *United States*	38	G1
Jammerbugten	56	E8
Jammu	94	B2
Jammu and Kashmir	94	C2
Jamnagar	94	B4
Jämsä	56	N6
Jamshedpur	94	E4
Janakpur	94	E3
Janaúba	50	J7
Jandaq	96	F3
Jandongi	110	C3
Jane Peak	118	B7
Janesville	40	C2
Jan Mayen	32	C2
Janos	44	E2
Jánossomorja	70	N3
Janów Lubelski	58	M7
Jantarnyj	58	J3
Januária	50	J7
Jaora	94	C4
Japan	88	L5
Japan Trench	114	E2
Japurá	50	D4
Jarābulus	98	H5
Jaramillo	52	H8
Jarash	100	C4

Jardim 52 K3
Jarosław 58 M7
Järpen 56 G5
Jarud Qi 86 G2
Järvenpää 56 N6
Jarvis 114 K6
Jasel'da 56 N10
Jäsk 101 G4
Jason Islands 52 J9
Jasper, *Al., United States* 42 D3
Jasper, *Fla., United States* 42 E3
Jasper, *Tex., United States* 42 C3
Jastrebarsko 70 L5
Jászberény 74 G2
Jataí 50 G7
Jatapu 50 F4
Jaunpur 94 D3
Java = Jawa 92 (1)E4
Javarthushuu 84 J7
Java Sea 92 (1)E4
Javoriv 58 N8
Jawa 92 (1)E4
Jawhar 110 H3
Jayapura 92 (2)F3
Jayrūd 100 D3
Jaza'īr Farasān 104 H4
Jazīrat Būbīyān 101 C2
Jazīrat-ye Khārk 101 D2
Jbail 100 C2
Jbel Ayachi 106 E2
Jbel Bou Naceur 106 E2
Jbel Toubkal 106 D2
Jean 38 C3
Jebba 108 E3
Jebel Bāqir 100 C7
Jebel el Atā'ita 100 C6
Jebel el Batrā 100 C7
Jebel-esh Sharqi 100 C3
Jebel Gimbala 104 D5
Jebel Ithrīyat 100 D6
Jebel Liban 100 C3
Jebel Mubrak 100 C6
Jebel Ram 100 C7
Jebel Uweinat 104 E3
Jedburgh 64 K6
Jedda = Jiddah 96 C5
Jedeida 72 D12
Jędrzejów 58 K7
Jefferson 40 B2
Jefferson City, *Mo., United States* 40 B3
Jefferson City, *Tenn., United States* 42 E2
Jeffersonville 40 C3
Jega 108 E2
Jēkabpils 56 N8
Jelgava 56 M8
Jemaja 92 (1)D2
Jena 60 G6
Jendouba 106 G1
Jenin 100 C4
Jenkins 40 D3
Jequié 50 J6
Jequitinhonha 50 J7
Jerada 106 E2
Jeremoabo 50 K6
Jerez 44 F4
Jerez de la Frontera 68 D8
Jerez de los Caballeros 68 D6
Jericho, *Australia* 116 J4
Jericho, *Israel* 100 C5
Jersey 66 C4
Jersey City 42 G1
Jerusalem = Yerushalayim 100 C5
Jesenice 74 B3
Jesenik 58 G7
Jesi 70 J7
Jésolo 70 H5
Jessore 94 E4
Jesup 42 E3
Jeumont 62 G4
Jever 60 C3
Jeypore 94 D5
Jezioro 58 D4
Jezioro Gardno 56 J9
Jezioro Jeziorsko 58 H6
Jezioro Łebsko 58 F3
Jezioro Śniardwy 58 L4
Jezioro Wigry 58 N2
Jezzine 100 C3
Jhang Maghiana 94 B2
Jhansi 94 C3
Jharsuguda 94 D4
Jhelum 94 B2
Jialing Jiang 86 D4
Jiamusi 86 J1
Ji'an 86 E5
Jiangle 86 F5
Jiangling 86 E4
Jiangmen 86 E6
Jiangyou 86 C4
Jiaonan 86 F3
Jiaozou 86 E3
Jiaxing 86 G4
Jiayuguan 86 B3
Jibou 74 L2
Jičín 58 E7
Jiddah 96 C5
Jiesjavrre 56 N2
Jiexiu 86 E3
Jihlava 58 E8
Jijia 74 Q2
Jijiga 110 G2
Jilib 110 G3
Jilin 88 D2
Jima 110 F2
Jimbolia 74 H4
Jiménez 44 F3
Jimsar 82 R9
Jinan 86 F3
Jinapo Hu 88 E2
Jinchang 86 C3
Jincheng 86 E3
Jindřichův Hradec 58 E8
Jingdezhen 86 F5
Jinggu 86 C6
Jinghe 82 Q9
Jinghong 86 C6
Jingmen 86 E4
Jingning 86 D3
Jingxi 86 D6
Jinhua 86 F5
Jining, *China* 86 E2
Jining, *China* 86 F3
Jinja 110 E3
Jinka 110 F2
Jinsha 86 C5
Jinshi 86 E5
Jinta 86 B2
Jinxi 86 G2
Jinzhou 86 G2
Jirgatol 96 K2
Jirkov 60 J6
Jīroft 101 G2
Jirriiban 110 H2
Jishou 86 D5
Jiu 74 L4
Jiujiang 86 F5
Jiwani 96 H4
Jixi 88 F1
Jīzān 104 H4
Jizera 58 D7
J. J. Castelli 50 D4
Joal-Fadiout 106 B6
João Pessoa 50 L5
Jódar 68 G7
Jodhpur 94 B3
Joensuu 78 E2
Jōetsu 88 K5
Jõgeva 56 P7
Johannesburg, *South Africa* 112 D5
Johannesburg, *United States* 44 C1
John Day 38 C2
John o' Groats 64 J3
John Redmond Reservoir 42 B2
Johnson 42 A2
Johnson City 40 D3
Johnson's Crossing 44 (1)L3
Johnston Island 114 J4
Johnstown 40 E2
Johor Bahru 92 (1)C2
Joigny 66 J5
Joinville, *Brazil* 52 M4
Joinville, *France* 66 L5
Jokkmokk 56 K3
Jökulsa á Fjöllum 56 (1)E1
Jolfa 98 L4
Joliet 36 J3
Joliette 40 F1
Jolo 92 (2)B1
Jolo 92 (2)B1
Jonava 58 P2
Jonesboro 40 B3
Jones Sound 34 P1
Jonesville 42 C3
Jonglei Canal 110 E2
Jongunjärvi 56 P4
Joniškis 58 M1
Jönköping 56 H8
Jonquière 40 F1
Joplin 42 C2
Jordan 100 D5
Jordan 38 E1
Jordan Valley 38 C2
Jorhat 94 F3
Jörn 56 L4
Jos 108 F3
José de San Martin 52 G7
Joseph Bonaparte Gulf 116 E2
Joûnié 100 C2
Juan de Nova 112 G3
Juàzeiro 50 J5
Juàzeiro do Norte 50 K5
Juba 110 E3
Jubba 110 G3
Júcar 68 J5
Juchitán 46 F5
Judenburg 70 K3
Juhre 84 L8
Juist 60 B3
Juiz de Fora 52 N3
Julesburg 38 F2
Juli 50 C7
Juliaca 50 C7
Juliana Top 50 F3
Jülich 62 J4
Jumilla 68 J6
Jumla 94 D3
Junagadh 94 B4
Junction 42 B3
Junction City 42 B2
Jundah 116 H4
Juneau 44 (1)L4
Jungfrau 70 C4
Junggar Pendi 82 R8
Jun Xian 86 E4
Jūra 58 M2
Jura 64 G5
Jura 70 B4
Jurbarkas 58 M2
Jurf ed Darāwīsh 100 C6
Jurhe 86 G2
Jūrmala 56 M8
Jūrmala 78 D3
Juruá 50 D4
Juruena 50 F5
Juruena 50 F6
Justo Daract 52 H5
Jutaí 50 D5
Jüterbog 60 J5
Juwain 96 H3
Ju Xian 86 F3
Jüymand 96 G3
Jüyom 101 F2
Juzur al Halaniyat 96 G6
Jylland 56 E8
Jyvädskylä 78 E2
Jyväskylä 56 N5

K

K2 94 C1
Kaakhka 96 G2
Kaamanen 56 P2
Kaaresuvanto 56 M2
Kaarta 106 C6
Kabaena 92 (2)B4
Kabakly 96 H2
Kabala 108 B3
Kabale 110 E4
Kabalo 110 D5
Kabardino-Balkariya 98 K2
Kabompo 112 C2
Kabongo 110 D5
Kabugao 90 G3
Kābul 96 J3
Kabwe 112 D2
Kachikattsy 84 M4
Kachug 84 H6
Kadama 94 B6
Kadañ 58 C7
Kadinhanı 76 Q6
Kadirli 98 G5
Kadoka 38 F2
Kadoma 112 D3
Kadugli 104 E5
Kaduna 108 F2
Kadzherom 78 L2
Kaédi 106 C5
Kaesŏng 88 D5
Kafanchan 108 F3
Kaffrine 108 A2
Kafiau 92 (2)C3
Kåfjord 56 N1
Kafr el Sheikh 104 F1
Kafue 112 D3
Kaga 88 J5
Kaga Bandoro 110 B2
Kagoshima 88 F8
Kahemba 110 B5
Kahnūj 101 G3
Kahraman Maraş 98 G5
Kahurangi Point 118 C5
Kaiama 108 E3
Kai Besar 92 (2)D4
Kaifeng 86 E4
Kaihu 118 D2
Kaihua 86 F5
Kai Kecil 92 (2)D4
Kaikohe 118
Kaikoura 118
Kaili 86
Kailua 44 (2)
Kailua Kona 44 (2)
Kaimana 92 (2)
Kāina 56
Kainji Reservoir 108
Kaipara Harbour 118
Kairouan 106
Kaiserslautern 60
Kaišiadorys 58
Kaitaia 118
Kaiyuan 90
Kajaani 56
Kakamega 110
Kakata 108
Kakhovs'ke Vodoskhovyshche 78
Käkināda 94
Kaktovik 44 (1)
Kalabagh 94
Kalabahi 92 (2)
Kalabakan 92 (1)
Kalach 78
Kalachinsk 78
Kalach-na-Donu 78
Kaladar 40
Ka Lae 44 (2)
Kalahari Desert 112
Kalajoki 56
Kalakan 84
Kalam 94
Kalamata 76
Kalamazoo 40
Kalampaka 76
Kalaotoa 92 (2)
Kalapana 44 (2)
Kalaupapa 44 (2)
Kalavryta 76
Kale 76
Kalecik 98
Kaledupa 92 (2)
Kalemie 110
Kalemyo 94
Kalevala 56
Kalewa 94
Kalgoorlie 116
Kalianda 92 (1)
Kalibo 90
Kalima 110
Kalimantan 92 (1)
Kaliningrad 58
Kaliningradskij Zaliv 58
Kalispell 38
Kalisz 58
Kalixälven 56
Kalkan 76
Kalkaring 116
Kalkaska 40
Kallavesi 56
Kallsjön 56
Kalmar 56
Kalmykiya 98
Kalmykovo 78
Kalocsa 74
Kalol 94
Kalpakio 76
Kalpeni 94
Kaltag 44 (1)
Kaluga 78
Kalyan 94
Kalymnos 76
Kalymnos 76
Kama 54
Kama 110
Kamaishi 88
Kamande 110
Kamango 82
Kambarka 78
Kambo Ho 88
Kamchatka 84
Kamchatskiy Zaliv 84
Kamenica 76
Kamenka, *Russia* 78
Kamenka, *Russia* 78
Kamen'-na-Obi 82
Kamen'-Rybolov 88
Kamensk-Shakhtinskiy 78
Kamensk-Ural'skiy 78
Kamenz 58
Kamet 94
Kamiiso 88
Kamina 110
Kamituga 110
Kamiyaku 88
Kamloops 34
Kamoenai 88
Kampala 110
Kampen 62
Kampong Cham 90
Kam"yanets'-Podil's'kyy 78

amyanyets 56 M10
amyshin 78 J4
amyzyak 78 J5
anab 44 D1
ananga 110 C5
anazawa 88 J5
anbalu 94 G4
anchipuram 94 C6
andahār 96 J3
andalaksha 56 S3
andalakshskiy Zaliv 78 F1
andi 108 E2
andira 76 N3
andy 94 D7
ane 40 E2
aneohe 44 (2)D2
ang 112 C4
angaatsiaq 34 W3
angal 98 G4
angān, *Iran* 101 E3
angān, *Iran* 101 G4
angaroo Island 116 G7
angchenjunga 94 E3
angding 86 C4
angeq 34 Y4
angerluarsoruseq 34 W4
angersuatsiaq 34 W2
angetet 110 F3
angiqsualujjuaq 34 T5
angmar 94 E3
angnüng 88 E5
ango 108 G4
angping 86 G2
aniama 110 C5
anji Reservoir 102 D4
anjiža 74 H3
ankaanpää 56 M6
ankakee 40 C2
ankan 108 C2
ankossa 106 C5
annapolis 42 E2
ano 108 F2
anoya 88 F8
anpur 94 D3
ansas 42 A2
ansas 42 B2
ansas City, *Kans., United States* 42 C2
ansas City, *Mo., United States* 42 C2
ansk 82 T6
anta 110 F2
antchari 108 E2
antemirovka 78 G5
anye 112 C4
ao-Hsiung 86 G6
aolack 106 B6
aoma 112 C2
apanga 110 C5
ap Arkona 58 C3
apchagay 82 P9
Kap Cort Adelaer = Kangeq 34 Y4
Kap Farvel = Uummannarsuaq 34 Y5
Kapfenberg 70 L3
Kapidağı Yarimadası 76 K4
Kapiri Mposhi 112 D2
Kapit 92 (1)E2
Kapiti Island 118 E5
Kaplice 70 K2
Kapoeta 110 E3
Kaposvár 74 E3
Kappel 60 C6
Kappeln 60 E2
Kappl 70 F3
Kapsan 88 E3
Kapuskasing 36 K2
Kapuvár 74 E2
Kara 82 M4
Kara, *Russia* 82 M4
Kara, *Togo* 108 E3
Kara Ada 76 K8
Kara-Balta 82 N9
Karabekaul 96 H2
Kara-Bogaz-Gol 96 F1
Karabutak 78 M5
Karacabey 76 L4
Karacaköy 76 L3
Karacal Tepe 76 Q8
Karachayevo-Cherkesiya 98 J2
Karachayevsk 98 J2
Karachi 96 J5
Karaganda 82 N8
Karaginskiy Zaliv 84 V5
Karaj 96 F2
Karak 100 C5
Kara-Kala 96 G2
Kara-Köl 82 N9
Karakol 82 P9
Karakoram 80 L6
Karaksar 84 K6
Karam 84 H5
Karaman 98 E5
Karamay 82 R8
Karamea 118 D5
Karamea Bight 118 C5
Karamürsel 76 M4
Karaoy 82 N8
Karapınar 76 R7
Kara-Say 82 P9
Karasburg 112 B5
Kara Sea = Karskoye More 82 L3
Karasu 98 D3
Karasuk 82 P7
Karasuk 82 P7
Karatal 82 P8
Karataş 98 F5
Karatobe 78 K5
Karaton 78 K5
Karatsu 88 E7
Karazhal 78 P5
Karbalā' 96 D3
Karcag 74 H2
Karditsa 76 D5
Kärdla 56 M7
Kareliya 56 R4
Karepino 78 L2
Karesuando 56 M2
Kargalinskaya 98 M2
Kargasok 82 Q6
Kargat 82 P6
Kargil 94 C2
Kargopol' 78 G2
Kariba 112 D3
Kariba Dam 112 D3
Karibib 112 B4
Karimata 92 (1)D3
Karimnagar 94 C5
Karkaralinsk 82 P8
Karkinits'ka Zatoka 78 F5
Karlik Shan 86 A2
Karlovac 74 C4
Karlovasi 76 J7
Karlovo 76 G2
Karlovy Vary 60 H6
Karlshamn 58 D1
Karlskoga 56 H7
Karlskrona 56 H8
Karlsruhe 60 D8
Karlstad, *Norway* 56 G7
Karlstad, *United States* 40 A1
Karlstadt 60 E7
Karmala 94 C5
Karmi'el 100 C4
Karmøy 56 C7
Karnafuli Reservoir 94 F4
Karnal 94 C3
Karnische Alpen 70 H4
Karnobat 76 J2
Karodi 96 J4
Karonga 110 E5
Karpathos 76 K9
Karpathos 76 K9
Karpenisi 76 D6
Karpogory 78 H2
Karrabük 98 E3
Kars 98 K3
Karsakpay 78 N5
Kārsava 56 P8
Karshi 96 J2
Karskoye More 82 L3
Karslyaka 76 K6
Karstula 56 N5
Kartaly 78 M4
Kartayel' 78 K2
Kartuzy 58 H3
Karufa 92 (2)D3
Karumba 116 H3
Karur 94 C6
Karvina 58 H8
Karwar 94 B6
Karystos 76 G6
Kasai 110 B4
Kasaji 112 C2
Kasama 112 E2
Kasansay 82 N9
Kasba Lake 34 L4
Kasempa 112 D2
Kasenga 112 D2
Kāshān 96 F3
Kashi 96 L2
Kashima 86 L3
Kashiwazaki 88 K5
Kāshmar 96 G2
Kashmor 96 J4
Kasimov 78 H4
Kasli 78 M3
Kasongo 110 D4
Kasos 76 K9
Kaspi 98 L3
Kaspiysk 98 M2
Kassala 104 G4
Kassandreia 76 F4
Kassel 60 E5
Kasserine 106 G1
Kastamonu 98 E3
Kastelli 76 F9
Kastoria 76 D4
Kasulu 110 E4
Kasumkent 98 N3
Kasur 94 B2
Kata 84 G5
Katchall 94 F7
Katerini 76 E4
Katete 112 E2
Katha 94 G4
Katherine 116 F2
Kathiawar 96 K5
Kathmandu 94 E3
Kati 108 C2
Katihar 94 E3
Katiola 108 C3
Kato Nevrokopi 76 F3
Katonga 110 E3
Katoomba 116 K6
Katowice 58 J7
Katrineholm 56 J7
Katsina 108 F2
Katsina-Ala 108 F3
Katsuura 88 L6
Kattakurgan 96 J2
Kattavia 76 K9
Kattegat 56 F8
Katun' 82 R7
Katwijkaan Zee 62 G2
Kauai 44 (2)B1
Kaufbeuren 70 F3
Kauhajoki 56 M5
Kaunas 58 N3
Kauno 58 P3
Kaunus 54 G2
Kaura Namoda 108 F2
Kavadarci 76 D3
Kavajë 76 B3
Kavala 76 G4
Kavār 101 E2
Kavaratti 94 B6
Kavarna 74 R6
Kawagoe 88 K6
Kawakawa 118 E2
Kawambwa 110 D5
Kawasaki 88 K6
Kawau Island 118 E3
Kaweka 118 F4
Kawhia 118 E4
Kawkareik 90 B3
Kawthaung 90 B4
Kaya 108 D2
Kayak 82 U3
Kaycee 38 E2
Kayenta 44 D1
Kayes 108 B2
Kaymaz 76 P5
Kaynar 82 P8
Kayseri 98 F4
Kazachinskoye 84 E5
Kazach'ye 84 P2
Kazakdar'ya 82 K9
Kazakhstan 82 L8
Kazan' 78 J3
Kazan 34 M4
Kazanlŭk 76 H2
Kazan-rettō 114 E3
Kazbek 98 L2
Kāzerūn 101 D2
Kazincbarcika 74 H1
Kazungula 112 D3
Kea 76 G7
Kearney 36 G3
Keban Barajı 98 H4
Kébémèr 106 B5
Kebkabiya 104 D5
Kebnekajse 56 K3
K'ebrī Dehar 110 G2
K'ech'a Terara 110 F2
Keçiborlu 76 N7
Kecskemet 74 G3
Kėdainiai 58 N2
Kedgwick 40 G1
Kédougou 108 B2
Kędzierzyn-Koźle 58 H7
Keele 44 (1)M3
Keene 40 F2
Keetmanshoop 112 B5
Keewatin 40 B1
Kefallonia 76 C6
Kefamenanu 92 (2)B4
Keflavík 56 (1)B2
Kegen' 82 P9
Keg River 34 H5
Kehl 70 C2
Keila 56 N7
Keitele 56 N5
Kékes 74 H2
Kelai Thiladhunmathee Atoll 94 B7
Kelheim 70 G2
Kelibia 72 F12
Kelkit 98 G3
Kelmë 58 M2
Kélo 108 H3
Kelowna 34 H7
Kelso 38 B1
Keluang 92 (1)C2
Kem' 78 F2
Kemalpaşa 76 K6
Kemasik 92 (1)C2
Kemer, *Turkey* 76 M8
Kemer, *Turkey* 76 N8
Kemerovo 82 R6
Kemi 56 N4
Kemijärvi 56 P3
Kemijärvi 56 P3
Kemijoki 56 P3
Kemmerer 38 D3
Kemmuna 72 J12
Kemnath 60 G7
Kemp's Bay 42 F5
Kempten 70 F3
Kendal 64 K7
Kendall 42 E4
Kendari 92 (2)B3
Kendawangan 92 (1)E3
Kendégué 108 H2
Kendujhargarh 94 E4
Kenedy 42 B4
Kenema 108 B3
Keneurgench 96 G1
Kenge 110 B4
Kengtung 90 B2
Kenhardt 112 C5
Kénitra 106 D2
Kenmore 64 C10
Kennett 42 D2
Kennewick 38 C1
Keno Hill 44 (1)K3
Kenora 36 H2
Kenosha 40 C2
Kentau 82 M9
Kentucky 36 J4
Kentwood 42 C3
Kenya 102 G5
Keokuk 40 B2
Kępno 58 H6
Kepulauan Anambas 92 (1)D2
Kepulauan Aru 92 (2)E4
Kepulauan Ayu 92 (2)D2
Kepulauan Balabalangan 92 (1)F3
Kepulauan Banggai 92 (2)B3
Kepulauan Barat Daya 92 (2)C4
Kepulauan Batu 92 (1)B3
Kepulauan Bonerate 92 (2)A4
Kepulauan Kai 92 (2)D4
Kepulauan Kangean 92 (1)F4
Kepulauan Karimunjawa 92 (1)D4
Kepulauan Karkaralong 92 (2)B2
Kepulauan Laut Kecil 92 (1)F3
Kepulauan Leti 92 (2)C4
Kepulauan Lingga 92 (1)C2
Kepulauan Lucipara 92 (2)C4
Kepulauan Mentawai 92 (1)B3
Kepulauan Nanusa 92 (2)C2
Kepulauan Natuna 92 (1)D2
Kepulauan Riau 92 (1)C2
Kepulauan Sabalana 92 (1)F4
Kepulauan Sangir 92 (2)C2
Kepulauan Solor 92 (2)B4
Kepulauan Sula 92 (2)B3
Kepulauan Talaud 92 (2)C2
Kepulauan Tanimbar 92 (2)D4
Kepulauan Tengah 92 (1)F4
Kepulauan Togian 92 (2)B3
Kepulauan Tukangbesi 92 (2)B4
Kepulauan Watubela 92 (2)D3
Kerch 98 G1
Kerchevskiy 78 L3
Kerempe Burnu 76 R2
Keren 104 G4
Kericho 110 F4
Kerio 110 F3
Kerki 96 J2
Kerkrade 62 J4
Kerkyra 76 B5
Kerkyra 76 B5
Kerma 104 F4
Kermadec Islands 114 H8
Kermadec Trench 114 J9
Kermān 101 G1
Kermānshāh 96 E3
Kermānshāhān 101 F1
Keros 76 H8
Kerpen 62 J4
Kerrville 42 B3
Kerulen 84 J7
Keryneia 98 E6
Keşan 76 J4

Kesennuma 88 L4
Keşiş Dağları 96 C2
Keszthely 74 E3
Keta 108 E3
Ketapang 92 (1)D3
Ketchikan 44 (1)L4
Kétou 108 E3
Kętrzyn 58 L3
Kettering 64 M9
Kettle Falls 36 C2
Kewanee 40 C2
Keweenaw Peninsula 40 C1
Key Largo 42 E4
Keystone Lake 42 B2
Key West 42 E5
Kezhma 84 G5
Kežmarok 58 K8
Khabarovsk 84 P7
Khadyzhensk 98 H1
Khakasiya 82 R7
Khairwāra 94 B4
Khalīg el Suweis 104 F2
Khalīj Surt 104 C1
Khalūf 96 G5
Khamis Mushay 96 D6
Khamkkeut 90 C3
Khampa 84 L4
Khamrà 84 J4
Khān al Baghdādī 98 K7
Khandagayty 82 S7
Khandwa 94 C4
Khanewal 94 B2
Khannya 82 X4
Khanpur 94 B3
Khān Shaykhūn 100 D1
Khantau 82 N9
Khantayka 84 D3
Khanty-Mansiysk 78 N2
Khān Yūnis 100 B5
Khapalu 94 C1
Kharabali 78 J5
Kharagpur 94 E4
Kharampur 84 B4
Kharan 96 J4
Khargon 94 C4
Kharkiv 78 G5
Kharlu 56 R6
Kharmanli 76 H3
Kharnmam 94 D5
Kharovsk 78 H3
Khartoum = El Khartum 104 F4
Khasavyurt 98 M2
Khāsh 96 H4
Khashgort 78 N1
Khashm el Girba 104 G4
Khashuri 98 K3
Khaskovo 76 H3
Khatanga 84 G2
Khātūnābād 101 F1
Khatyrka 84 X4
Khavda 96 J5
Khawr Fakkān 101 G4
Khaydarken 96 K2
Khayelitsha 112 B6
Khemis Miliana 106 F1
Khemisset 106 D2
Khenchela 106 G1
Kherāmeh 101 E2
Kherson 78 F5
Kheta 82 T3
Kheta 82 T3
Kheygiyakha 78 P2
Khilok 84 J6
Khirbat Isrīyah 100 E1
Khīyāv 98 M4
Khmel'nyts'kyy 78 E5
Khodā Afarīn 98 M4
Kholmsk 84 Q7
Khonj 101 E3
Khon Kaen 90 C3
Khonuu 84 Q3
Khoper 78 H4
Khor 84 P7
Khor 84 P7
Khoreyver 78 L1
Khorinsk 84 H6
Khorramābād 96 E3
Khorramshahr 101 C1
Khorugh 96 K2
Khoseda Khard 78 L1
Khouribga 106 D2
Khrebet Cherskogo 84 P3
Khrebet Dzhagdy 84 N6
Khrebet Dzhugdzhur 84 N5
Khrebet Khamar Daban 84 G6
Khrebet Kolymskiy 80 U3
Khrebet Kopet Dag 96 G2
Khrebet Suntar Khayata 84 P4
Khrebet Tarbagatay 82 Q8
Khroma 84 Q2
Khudoseya 84 C3
Khudzhakh 84 R4

Khujand 96 J1
Khulna 94 E4
Khurayş 101 B4
Khushab 94 B2
Khust 74 L1
Khuzdar 96 J4
Khvormūj 101 D2
Khvoy 98 L4
Khyber Pass 96 K3
Kibaya 110 F4
Kibombo 110 D4
Kibondo 110 E4
Kibre Mengist 110 F2
Kičevo 76 C3
Kichmengskiy Gorodok 78 J3
Kicking Horse Pass 34 H6
Kidal 106 F5
Kidderminster 64 K9
Kidira 108 B2
Kiel 60 F2
Kielce 58 K7
Kieler Bucht 60 F2
Kiev = Kyyiv 78 F4
Kiffa 106 C5
Kigali 110 E4
Kigoma 110 D4
Kihnu 56 M7
Kıkıköy 76 L3
Kikinda 74 H4
Kikori 92 (2)F4
Kikwit 110 B5
Kilchu 88 E3
Kilifi 110 F4
Kilindoni 110 F5
Kilingi-Nõmme 56 N7
Kilis 98 G5
Kiliya 74 S4
Kilkenny 64 E9
Kilkis 76 E4
Killarney, *Canada* 40 D1
Killarney, *Republic of Ireland* 64 C9
Kilmarnock 64 H6
Kil'mez 78 K3
Kilosa 110 F5
Kilrush 64 C9
Kilttan 94 B6
Kilwa 110 D5
Kilwa Masoko 110 F5
Kimberley 112 C5
Kimberley Plateau 116 E3
Kimch'aek 88 E3
Kimolos 76 G8
Kimongo 108 G5
Kimry 78 G3
Kincardine 40 D2
Kinder 42 C3
Kindia 108 B2
Kindu 110 D4
Kineshma 78 H3
Kingaroy 116 K5
King City 38 B3
King George Islands 34 R5
Kingisepp 56 Q7
King Island, *Australia* 116 H7
King Island, *Canada* 84 AA3
Kingman 44 D1
Kingri 96 J3
Kingscote 116 G7
Kingsland 42 E3
King's Lynn 64 N9
King Sound 116 D3
Kings Peak 38 D2
Kingsport 42 E2
Kingston, *Canada* 40 E2
Kingston, *Jamaica* 46 J5
Kingston, *United States* 40 F2
Kingston-upon-Hull 64 M8
Kingston upon Thames 62 B3
Kingstown 50 E1
Kingsville 42 B4
Kingville 46 E3
King William Island 34 M3
King William's Town 112 D6
Kinik 76 K5
Kinka-san 88 L4
Kinna 56 G8
Kinsale 64 D10
Kinshasa 110 B4
Kinsley 42 B2
Kinston 40 E3
Kintampo 108 D3
Kintyre 64 G6
Kinyeti 110 E3
Kinzig 60 E6
Kipini 110 G4
Kipnuk 44 (1)E3
Kirchheim 70 E2
Kirchheimbolanden 62 L5
Kircudbright 64 H7
Kirenga 84 H5
Kirensk 84 H5

Kiribati 114 J6
Kırıkhan 98 G5
Kırıkkale 98 E4
Kirillov 78 G3
Kirinyaga 110 F4
Kirishi 78 F3
Kiritimati 114 L5
Kirkağaç 76 K5
Kirk Bulāg Dāgh 96 E2
Kirkcaldy 64 J5
Kirkjubæjarklaustur 56 (1)E3
Kirkland Lake 40 D1
Kırklareli 76 K3
Kirkūk 98 L6
Kirkwall 64 K3
Kirov, *Kyrgyzstan* 82 N9
Kirov, *Russia* 78 F4
Kirov, *Russia* 78 J3
Kirovohrad 78 F5
Kiroyo-Chepetsk 78 K3
Kirs 78 K3
Kirsanov 78 H4
Kırşehir 98 F4
Kiruna 56 L3
Kiryū 88 K5
Kisangani 110 D3
Kisbér 74 E2
Kiselevsk 82 R7
Kishanganj 94 E3
Kishi 108 E3
Kishiwada 88 H6
Kishtwar 94 C2
Kisii 110 E4
Kiska Island 44 (3)B1
Kiskőrös 74 G3
Kiskunfélegyháza 74 G3
Kiskunhalas 74 G3
Kiskunmajsa 74 G3
Kislovodsk 98 K2
Kismaayo 110 G4
Kissidougou 108 B3
Kisumu 110 E4
Kisvárda 74 K1
Kita 108 C2
Kitakami 88 L4
Kita-Kyūshū 86 H4
Kita-Kyūshū 88 F7
Kitami 88 M2
Kitchener 40 D2
Kitgum 110 E3
Kitimat 34 F6
Kittilä 56 N3
Kitunda 110 E5
Kitwe 112 D2
Kitzingen 60 F7
Kiuruvesi 56 P5
Kivijärvi 56 N5
Kivik 58 D2
Kiya 84 D5
Kıyıköy 98 C3
Kizel 78 L3
Kizilalan 76 R8
Kızılırmak 98 F3
Kızılkaya 76 N7
Kizil'skoye 78 L4
Kızıltepe 98 J5
Kizlyar 98 M2
Kizlyarskiy Zaliv 98 M1
Kladanj 74 F5
Kladno 58 D7
Klagenfurt 70 K4
Klaipėda 56 L9
Klamath 38 B2
Klamath 38 B2
Klamath Falls 38 B2
Klarälven 56 G6
Klatovy 60 J7
Klaus 70 K3
Klerksdorp 112 D5
Kleve 60 B5
Klin 78 G3
Klingenthal 60 H6
Klínovec 60 H6
Klintsy 78 F4
Ključ 70 M6
Kłobuck 58 H7
Kłodzko 58 F7
Kløfta 56 F6
Klosterneuburg 70 M2
Klosters 70 E4
Kluane 34 D4
Kluane Lake 44 (1)J3
Kluczbork 58 H7
Klyuchevskaya Sopka 84 U5
Klyuchi 84 U5
Knezha 74 M6
Knin 74 D5
Knittelfeld 74 B2
Knjaževac 74 K6
Knokke-Heist 62 F3
Knoxville 40 D3
Knysna 112 C6

Koba 92
Kōbe 88
Kobe 92
København 56
Koblenz 60
Kobo 94
Kobroör 92
Kobryn 58
Kobuk 44
Kobuk 44
Kočani 76
Koçarli 76
Kočevje 74
Ko Chang 90
Kochechum 84
Kochi 94
Kōchi 88
Kochkor 82
Kochki 82
Kochubey 98
Kodiak 44
Kodiak Island 44
Kodino 78
Kodinsk 84
Kodomari-misaki 88
Kodyma 74
Köflach 74
Kōfu 88
Køge 58
Køge Bugt 58
Kohat 94
Kohima 94
Koh-i-Qaisir 96
Koh-i-Sangan 96
Kohtla-Järve 56
Koidu 108
Koitere 56
Kokenau 92
Kokkola 56
Kokomo 42
Kokpekty 82
Kokshetau 78
Kokstad 112
Kolaka 92
Kolar 94
Kolari 56
Kolašin 74
Kolda 108
Kolding 56
Kole 110
Kolhapur 94
Kolin 58
Kollam 94
Köln 60
Kolno 58
Koło 58
Kołobrzeg 58
Kologriv 78
Kolomna 78
Kolomyya 74
Kolonedale 92
Kolosovka 78
Kolpashevo 82
Kolpos Agiou Orous 76
Kolpos Kassandras 76
Kolpos Murampelou 76
Kolskijzaliv 56
Kolskiy Poluostrov 78
Kolumadulu Atoll 94
Koluton 78
Kolva 78
Kolwezi 112
Kolyma 84
Kolymskaya Nizmennost' 84
Kolymskaye 84
Komandorskiye Ostrova 84
Komárno 74
Komárom 74
Komatsu 88
Komi 78
Komló 74
Kom Ombo 104
Komotini 76
Komsa 82
Komsomol'skiy 78
Komsomol'sk-na-Amure 84
Konārka 94
Konda 78
Kondagaon 94
Kondinskoye 78
Kondoa 110
Kondopoga 78
Kondrat'yeva 82
Kondūz 96
Kong Frederick VI Kyst 34
Kongi 82
Kongola 112
Kongolo 110
Kongsberg 56
Kongur Shan 82
Königsberg = Kaliningrad 58

Königswinter 60 C6
Königs-Wusterhausen 60 J4
Konin 58 H5
Konispol 76 C5
Konitsa 76 C4
Köniz 70 C4
Konjic 74 E6
Konosha 78 H2
Konotop 78 F4
Konstanz 70 E3
Konstinbrod 74 L7
Kontagora 108 F2
Kon Tum 90 D4
Konya 98 E5
Konz 60 B7
Kootenai 38 C1
Kootenay Lake 36 C2
Kópasker 56 (1)E1
Kópavogur 56 (1)C2
Koper 70 J5
Kopeysk 78 M3
Köping 56 J7
Koplik 74 G7
Koprivnica 74 D3
Korba, *India* 94 D4
Korba, *Tunisia* 72 E12
Korbach 60 D5
Korçë 76 C4
Korčula 74 D7
Korea Bay 88 B4
Korea Strait 88 E6
Korhogo 108 C3
Korinthiakos Kolpos 76 E6
Korinthos 76 E7
Kōriyama 88 L5
Korkino 78 M4
Korkuteli 98 D5
Korla 82 R9
Korliki 84 C4
Körmend 74 D2
Kornat 74 C6
Koroba 92 (2)F4
Köroğlu Dağları 76 Q4
Köroğlu Tepesi 76 P4
Korogwe 110 F5
Koronowo 58 G4
Koror 114 D5
Korosten' 78 E4
Korsakov 84 Q7
Korsør 60 G1
Kortrijk 62 F4
Korumburra 116 J7
Koryakskiy Khrebet 84 V4
Koryazhma 82 H5
Kos 76 K8
Kos 76 K8
Kosa 78 L3
Ko Samui 90 C5
Kościerzyna 58 H3
Kosciusko 42 D3
Kosh Agach 82 R8
Koshoba 96 F1
Košice 58 L9
Koslan 78 J2
Kosŏng 88 E4
Kosovo 76 C2
Kosovska Mitrovica 76 C2
Kosrae 114 G5
Kostajnica 70 M5
Kostenets 76 F2
Kosti 104 F5
Kostino 84 D3
Kostomuksha 56 R4
Kostroma 78 H3
Kostrzyn 58 D5
Kos'yu 78 L1
Koszalin 58 F3
Kőszeg 74 D2
Kota 94 C3
Kotaagung 92 (1)C4
Kotabaru 92 (1)F3
Kota Belud 92 (1)F1
Kota Bharu 92 (1)C1
Kotabumi 92 (1)C3
Kota Kinabalu 92 (1)F1
Kotamubagu 92 (2)B2
Kotapinang 92 (1)B2
Kotel'nich 78 J3
Kotel'nikovo 78 H5
Köthen 60 G5
Kotido 110 E3
Kotka 56 P6
Kotlas 78 J2
Kotlik 44 (1)E3
Kotor Varoš 74 E5
Kotov'sk 78 E5
Kottagudem 94 D5
Kotte 94 D7
Kotto 110 C2
Kotuy 84 G3
Kotzebue 44 (1)E2
Kotzebue Sound 44 (1)D2
Kouango 108 H3
Koudougou 108 D2
Koufey 108 G2
Koulamoutou 108 G5
Koum 108 G3
Koumra 108 H3
Koundâra 108 B2
Koupéla 106 C6
Kourou 50 G2
Koutiala 108 C2
Kouvola 78 E2
Kovdor 56 R3
Kovel' 78 D4
Kovin 74 H5
Kovrov 78 H3
Kowanyama 116 H3
Köyceğiz 76 L8
Koygorodok 78 K2
Koykuk 44 (1)E3
Koynas 78 J2
Koyukuk 44 (1)F2
Kozan 98 F5
Kozani 76 D4
Kozheynikovo 82 W3
Kozhikode 94 C6
Kozienice 58 L6
Kozloduy 74 L6
Kōzu-shima 88 K6
Kpalimé 108 E3
Kraai 112 D6
Krabi 90 B5
Kradeljevo 72 M5
Kragujevac 74 H5
Kraków 58 J7
Kraljeviča 70 K5
Kraljevo 74 H6
Kralovice 58 C8
Kramators'k 78 G5
Kramfors 56 J5
Kranj 74 B3
Krapina 72 K2
Krapinske Toplice 70 L4
Krasino 82 J3
Krāslava 56 P9
Kraśnik 58 M7
Krasnoarmeysk 78 N4
Krasnoborsk 78 J2
Krasnodar 78 G5
Krasnohrad 78 G5
Krasnokamensk 84 K6
Krasnosel'kup 84 C3
Krasnotur'insk 78 M3
Krasnoufimsk 78 L3
Krasnovishersk 78 L2
Krasnoyarsk 84 E5
Krasnoyarskoye
Vodokhranilishche 82 S6
Krasnoznamensk 58 M3
Krasnystaw 58 N7
Krasnyy Chikoy 84 H6
Krasnyy Kut 78 J4
Krasnyy Yar 78 J5
Kratovo 76 E2
Kraynovka 98 M2
Krefeld 62 J3
Kremenchuk 78 F5
Kremmling 38 E2
Krems 70 L2
Kremsmünster 70 K2
Krestovka 78 K1
Krestyakh 84 K4
Kretinga 58 L2
Kribi 108 F4
Krichim 76 G2
Krishna 94 C5
Krishnagiri 94 C6
Kristiansand 56 E7
Kristianstad 56 H8
Kristiansund 56 D5
Kristinehamn 56 H7
Kristinestad 56 L5
Kriti 76 H10
Kriva Palanka 76 E2
Križevci 74 D3
Krk 70 K5
Krk 70 K5
Kroměříž 58 G8
Kronach 60 G6
Krŏng Kaôh Kŏng 90 C4
Kronotskiy Zaliv 84 U6
Kroonstadt 112 D5
Kroper 72 H3
Kropotkin 78 H5
Krosno 58 L8
Krško 70 L5
Krugë 76 B3
Krui 92 (1)C4
Krumbach 70 F2
Krung Thep 90 C4
Kruså 60 E2
Kruševac 74 J6
Krychaw 78 F4
Krym' 98 E1
Krymsk 98 H1
Krynica 58 L8
Krytiko Pelagos 76 G9
Kryve Ozero 74 T2
Kryvyy Rih 78 F5
Krzna 58 N5
Ksar el Boukhari 68 N9
Ksen'yevka 84 K6
Ksour Essaf 106 H1
Kuala Kerai 92 (1)C1
Kuala Lipis 92 (1)C2
Kuala Lumpur 92 (1)C2
Kuala Terengganu 92 (1)C1
Kuandian 88 C3
Kuantan 92 (1)C2
Kuçadasi 76 K7
Kučevo 74 J5
Kuching 92 (1)E2
Kucovë 76 B4
Kudat 92 (1)F1
Kudus 92 (1)E4
Kudymkar 78 K3
Kufstein 70 H3
Kugmallit Bay 34 E2
Kūhbonān 101 G1
Kūhdasht 98 M7
Kūh-e Alījuq 101 D1
Kūh-e Bābā 96 J3
Kūh-e Būl 101 E1
Kūh-e Dīnār 101 D1
Kūh-e Fūrgun 101 G3
Kūh-e Hazārān 101 G2
Kūh-e Hormoz 101 F3
Kūh-e Kalat 96 G3
Kūh-e Kūhrān 101 H3
Kūh-e Lāleh Zār 101 G2
Kūh-e Masāhūn 101 F1
Kūh-e Safidār 101 E2
Kuh-e Sahand 98 M5
Kūhestak 101 G3
Kūh-e Taftān 96 H4
Kūhhā-ye Bashākerd 101 G3
Kūhhā-ye Zāgros 101 D1
Kuhmo 56 Q4
Kūhpāyeh 101 G1
Kuito 112 B2
Kuji 88 L3
Kukës 74 H7
Kukhtuy 84 Q4
Kukinaga 88 F8
Kula 74 K6
Kulagino 78 K5
Kulandy 82 K8
Kuldīga 56 L8
Kulgera 116 F5
Kulmbach 60 G6
Külob 96 J2
Kul'sary 78 K5
Kultsjön 56 H4
Kulu 98 E4
Kulunda 82 P7
Kulynigol 84 C4
Kuma 78 N3
Kumamoto 88 F7
Kumanovo 74 J7
Kumara, *New Zealand* 118 C6
Kumara, *Russia* 84 M6
Kumasi 108 D3
Kumba 108 F4
Kumbakonam 94 C6
Kumeny 78 K3
Kumertau 78 L4
Kumla 56 H7
Kumluca 76 N8
Kummerower See 60 H3
Kumo 108 G3
Kumta 94 B6
Kumukh 98 M2
Kunene 112 A3
Kungrad 82 K9
Kungu 110 B3
Kungur 78 L3
Kunhing 90 B2
Kunlun Shan 94 D1
Kunming 86 C6
Kunsan 88 D6
Kunszetmarton 58 K11
Künzelsau 60 E7
Kuolayarvi 56 Q3
Kuopio 78 E2
Kupang 116 B2
Kupino 82 P7
Kupreanof Point 44 (1)F4
Kup"yans'k 78 G5
Kuqa 82 Q9
Kür 98 M3
Kura 96 E2
Kuragino 84 E6
Kurashiki 88 G6
Kurasia 94 D4
Kurchum 82 Q8
Kürdämir 98 N3
Kurduvadi 94 C5
Kŭrdzhali 76 H3
Kure 88 G6
Kure Island 114 J3
Kuressaare 56 M7
Kureyka 84 D3
Kureyka 84 E3
Kurgal'dzhinskiy 82 N7
Kurgan 78 N3
Kurikka 56 M5
Kuril Islands = Kuril'skiye
Ostrova 84 S7
Kuril'skiye Ostrova 84 S7
Kuril Trench 80 V5
Kuripapango 118 F4
Kurmuk 104 F5
Kurnool 94 C5
Kuroiso 88 K5
Kurow 118 C7
Kuršėnai 58 M1
Kursk 78 G4
Kuršumlija 74 J6
Kurşunlu 98 E3
Kuruman 112 C5
Kurume 88 F7
Kurumkan 84 J6
Kushikino 88 F8
Kushimoto 88 H7
Kushir 84 H6
Kushiro 88 M2
Kushmurun 78 N4
Kushum 78 K4
Kuskokwim Bay 44 (1)E4
Kuskokwim Mountains 44 (1)F3
Kussharo-ko 88 N2
Kustanay 78 M4
Kütahya 98 C4
K'ut'aisi 98 K2
Kutan 98 M1
Kutchan 88 L2
Kutina 74 D4
Kutno 58 J5
Kutu 108 H5
Kutum 104 D5
Kuujjua 34 J2
Kuujjuaq 34 T5
Kuujjuarapik 34 R5
Kuusamo 78 E1
Kuvango 112 B2
Kuwait 101 B2
Kuwait = Al Kuwayt 101 C2
Kuya 78 H1
Kuybyshev 82 P6
Kuygan 82 N8
Kuytun 82 R9
Kuyumba 84 F4
Kuznetsk 78 J4
Kuzomen' 78 G1
Kvaløya, *Norway* 56 M1
Kvaløya, *Norway* 56 J2
Kvalynsk 82 H7
Kwale 110 F4
Kwangju 88 D6
Kwango 110 B5
Kwazulu Natal 112 E5
Kwekwe 112 D3
Kwidzyn 56 K10
Kwilu 108 H5
Kyakhta 84 H6
Kyancutta 116 G6
Kyaukse 94 G4
Kyeburn 118 C7
Kyeintali 94 F5
Kyjov 70 N2
Kyklades 76 G7
Kyle of Lochalsh 64 G4
Kyll 62 J4
Kyllini 76 D7
Kymi 76 G6
Kyŏngju 88 E6
Kyōto 88 H6
Kyparissia 76 D7
Kyperissiakos Kolpos 76 C7
Kyra Panagia 76 G5
Kyren 84 G6
Kyrgyzstan 82 N9
Kyritz 60 H4
Kyrta 78 L2
Kyshtovka 82 P6
Kystatyam 84 L3
Kytalyktakh 84 N3
Kythira 76 E8
Kythira 76 F8
Kythnos 76 G7
Kyūshū 88 F7
Kyūshū-sanchi 88 F7
Kyustendil 76 E2
Kyusyur 84 M2
Kyyiv 78 F4
Kyzyl 82 S7
Kzyl-Dzhar 78 N5

Kzyl-Orda 78 N6
Kzyltu 82 N7

L

Laascaanood 110 H2
Laatzen 60 E4
Laba 108 F2
La Banda 52 J4
La Bañeza 68 E2
La Baule 66 C6
Labbezenga 106 F5
Labe 58 E7
Labé 108 B2
Labin 70 K5
Labinsk 98 J1
Laboulaye 52 J5
Labrador 34 U6
Labrador City 34 T6
Labrador Sea 34 V4
Lábrea 50 E5
Labrieville 40 G1
Labuha 92 (2)C3
Labuhanbajo 92 (2)A4
Labytnangi 82 M4
Laç 74 G8
Lac à l'Eau Claire 34 R5
Lacanau 66 D8
La Carolina 68 G6
Lac Bienville 34 S5
Lac Brochet 34 L5
Laccadive Islands 94 B6
Lac d'Annecy 70 B5
Lac de Bizerte 72 D11
Lac Débo 106 E5
Lac de Kossou 108 C3
Lac de Lagdo 108 G3
Lac de Manantali 108 C2
Lac de Mbakaou 108 G3
Lac de Neuchâtel 70 B4
Lac de Retenue de la Lufira 110 D6
Lac de St-Croix 70 B7
Lac des Bois 34 G3
Lac de Sélingue 108 C2
Lac Do 106 E5
Lac du Bourget 70 A5
Lacedónia 72 K7
Lacepede Bay 116 G7
Lac Evans 34 R6
Lac Faguibine 106 E5
Lac Fitri 104 C5
La Charité-sur-Loire 66 J6
La Chaux-de-Fonds 70 B3
La Chorrera 50 C4
Lac Ichkeul 72 D11
La Ciotat 66 L10
Lac La Biche 34 J6
Lac La Martre 34 H4
Lac Léman = Lake Geneva 70 B4
Lac Mai-Ndombe 110 B4
Lac-Mégantic 40 F1
Lac Minto 34 R5
Lac Nzilo 110 D6
Lac Onangué 108 F5
Láconi 72 D9
Laconia 40 F2
Lac Payne 34 S5
La Crosse 40 B2
La Cruz 36 E7
Lac St-Jean 40 F1
Lac St. Joseph 34 N6
Lac Seul 34 N6
Lac Tumba 110 B4
Lacul Brateş 74 Q4
Lacul Razim 74 R5
Lacul Sinoie 74 R5
Lac Upemba 110 D5
La Dorada 50 C2
Ladozhskoye Ozero 78 F2
Ladysmith, *South Africa* 112 D5
Ladysmith, *United States* 40 B1
Ladyzhenka 78 N4
La Esmeralda 50 D3
Læsø 56 F8
Lafayette, *Ind., United States* 40 C2
Lafayette, *La., United States* 42 C3
Lafia 108 F3
Lafiagi 108 F3
La Flèche 66 E6
Lafnitz 70 M3
Laft 101 F3
Lagan 56 G8
Lagan' 78 J5
Lage 62 L3
Lågen 56 E6
Lage's 38 D2
Laghouat 106 F2
Lagkadas 76 F4
Lagoa dos Patos 52 L5
Lagoa Mirim 52 L5
Lago Argentino 52 G9
Lago de Cahora Bassa 112 E3
Lago del Coghinas 72 C8
Lago del Flumendosa 72 D9
Lago de Maracaibo 50 C2
Lago de Nicaragua 46 G6
Lago de Poopó 50 D7
Lago di Caine 70 D5
Lago di Como 70 E4
Lago di Garda 70 F5
Lago di Lecco 70 E5
Lago di Lugano 70 E5
Lago d'Iseo 70 E5
Lago di Verano 72 K7
Lago Maggiore 70 D5
Lago Omodeo 72 C8
Lago Rogaguado 50 D6
Lagos, *Nigeria* 108 E3
Lagos, *Portugal* 68 B7
Lago Titicaca 50 D7
Lago Trasimeno 72 G5
La Goulette 72 E12
La Grand-Combe 66 K9
La Grande 38 C1
La Grange 42 E3
La Gran Sabana 50 E2
Laguna 52 M4
Laguna de Caratasca 46 H5
Laguna Madre 42 B4
Laguna Mar Chiquita 48 E7
Lagunillas 50 E7
La Habana 46 H4
Lahad Datu 90 F5
Lahat 92 (1)C3
La Haye-du-Puits 62 A5
Lāhījān 96 F2
Lahn 62 L4
Lahnstein 62 K4
Laholmsbukten 58 B1
Lahore 94 B2
Lahr 70 C2
Lahti 56 N6
Laï 110 B2
Laiagam 92 (2)F4
Lai Chau 90 C2
L'Aigle 62 C6
Laihia 56 M5
Laingsburg 112 C6
Laiwu 86 F3
Laiyuan 86 E3
Lajanurpekhi 98 K2
Lajes 52 L4
Lajosmizse 58 J10
La Junta 38 F3
Lake Abbe 110 G1
Lake Abitibi 40 E1
Lake Albert, *Democratic Republic of Congo/Uganda* 110 D3
Lake Albert, *United States* 38 B2
Lake Almanor 38 B2
Lake Amadeus 116 F4
Lake Andes 38 G2
Lake Argyle 116 E3
Lake Argyle Tourist Village 116 E3
Lake Athabasca 34 K5
Lake Austin 116 C5
Lake Balkhash = Ozero Balkhash 80 L5
Lake Bangweulu 112 E2
Lake Barlee 116 C5
Lake Benmore 118 C7
Lake Blanche 116 H5
Lake Buchanan 44 G2
Lake Callabonna 116 H5
Lake Carey 116 D5
Lake Carnegie 116 D5
Lake Chad 104 B5
Lake Charles 42 C3
Lake Chelan 38 B1
Lake Chilwa 112 F3
Lake City 42 E3
Lake Claire 34 J5
Lake Coleridge 118 C6
Lake Constance 70 E3
Lake Crowley 38 C3
Lake C. W. McConaughy 38 F2
Lake Diefenbaker 34 K6
Lake Disappointment 116 D4
Lake District 64 J7
Lake Dojran 76 E3
Lake Dora 116 D4
Lake Dundas 116 B6
Lake Edward 110 D4
Lake Elwall 38 D1
Lake Erie 40 D2
Lake Eyasi 110 E4
Lake Eyre 114 D8
Lake Eyre Basin 116 G5
Lake Eyre North 116 G5
Lake Eyre South 116 G5
Lake Francis Case 38 G2
Lake Frome 116 H6
Lake Gairdner 116 G6
Lake Geneva 70 B4
Lake Gordon 116 H8
Lake Grace 116 C6
Lake Harbour 34 T4
Lake Hauroko 118 A7
Lake Havasu 44 C2
Lake Havasu City 44 D2
Lake Hopkins 116 E4
Lake Hudson 42 B2
Lake Huron 40 D1
Lake Jackson 42 B4
Lake Kariba 112 D3
Lake Kemp 42 B2
Lake Kerkinitis 74 L8
Lake Kivu 110 D4
Lake Kyoga 110 E3
Lake Ladoga = Ladozhskoye Ozero 78 F2
Lakeland 42 E4
Lake Lefroy 116 D6
Lake Louis 34 H6
Lake Macdonald 116 E4
Lake Mackay 116 E4
Lake Macleod 116 B4
Lake Manapouri 118 A7
Lake Manitoba 34 M6
Lake Manyara 110 F4
Lake Maurice 116 F5
Lake McDonald 38 D1
Lake McMillan 44 F2
Lake Mead 38 D3
Lake Melville 34 U6
Lake Michigan 40 C2
Lake Moore 116 C5
Lake Murray 92 (2)F4
Lake Mweru 110 D5
Lake Mweru Wantipa 110 E5
Lake Nash 116 G4
Lake Nasser 104 F3
Lake Natron 110 F4
Lake Neale 116 E4
Lake Nipigon 34 P6/7
Lake Nipissing 40 E1
Lake Nyasa 112 E2
Lake Oahe 38 F2
Lake of the Woods 40 B1
Lake Ohau 118 B7
Lake Ohrid 76 C4
Lake Okeechobee 42 E4
Lake Onega = Onezhskoye Ozero 54 H1
Lake Ontario 40 E2
Lake O' The Cherokees 40 B3
Lake O' The Pines 42 C3
Lake Paringa 118 B6
Lake Peipus 56 P7
Lake Placid 42 E4
Lakeport 38 B3
Lake Poteriteri 118 A8
Lake Powell 38 D3
Lake Prespa 76 D4
Lake Providence 42 C3
Lake Pskov 56 P7
Lake Pukaki 118 C7
Lake Rotorua 118 F4
Lake Rukwa 110 E5
Lake St. Lucia 112 E5
Lake Sakakawea 38 F1
Lake Scutari 74 G7
Lake Simcoe 40 E2
Lake Superior 40 C1
Lake Tahoe 38 B3
Lake Tanganyika 110 D5
Lake Taupo 118 E4
Lake Te Anau 118 A7
Lake Tekapo 118 C6
Lake Tekapo 118 C6
Lake Texoma 42 B3
Lake Torrens 116 G6
Lake Travis 44 G2
Lake Tschida 38 F1
Lake Turkana 110 F3
Lake Victoria 110 E4
Lakeview 38 B2
Lake Volta 108 D3
Lake Waikare 118 E3
Lake Waikaremoana 118 F4
Lake Wakatipu 118 B7
Lake Wanaka 118 B7
Lake White 116 E4
Lake Wills 116 E4
Lake Winnipeg 34 M6
Lake Winnipegosis 34 L6
Lakewood 38 E3
Lake Woods 116 F3
Lake Xau 112 C4
Lake Yamma Yamma 116 H5
Lakhdaria 68 P8
Lakhimpur 94 D3
Lakhpat 94 A4
Lakin 42 A2
Lakki 94 B2
Lakonikos Kolpos 76 E8
Lakota 38 G1
Lalín 68 B2
La Línea 68 E8
Lalitpur 94 C4
Lal-Lo 90 G3
La Loche 34 K5
La Louvière 62 G4
La Maddalena 72 D7
Lamar, *Colo., United States* 44 F1
Lamar, *Mo., United States* 42 C2
Lamard 101 E3
La Marsa 72 E12
Lambaréné 108 G5
Lambay Island 64 G8
Lam Chi 90 C3
Lamesa 44 F2
Lamia 76 E6
Lamone 70 G6
Lampang 90 B3
Lampasas 44 G2
Lampedusa 106 H
Lamu 110 G4
Lanai 44 (2)D3
Lanai City 44 (2)E3
Lancang 90 B2
Lancaster, *United Kingdom* 64 K7
Lancaster, *Mo., United States* 40 B2
Lancaster, *N.H., United States* 40 F2
Lancaster, *Oh., United States* 40 D3
Lancaster, *Pa., United States* 40 E2
Lancaster, *S.C., United States* 42 E3
Lancaster Sound 34 Q2
Lanciano 72 J6
Landau, *Germany* 62 L5
Landau, *Germany* 70 H2
Landeck 70 F3
Lander 38 E2
Landerneau 66 A5
Landor 116 C5
Landsberg 70 F2
Land's End 64 F11
Landshut 70 H2
Landskrona 58 B2
Landstuhl 62 K5
Land Wursten 60 D3
La'nga Co 94 D2
Langarūd 98 N5
Langdon 38 G1
Langeland 60 F1
Langen 62 L5
Langenau 70 F2
Langenhagen 60 E
Langeoog 60 C
Langfang 86 F
Langjökull 56 (1)C2
Langkawi 90 B5
Langkon 90 F5
Langon 66 E9
Langøya 56 H2
Langreo 68 E1
Langres 70 A3
Langsa 90 B6
Langtry 44 F3
Langvatnet 56 G3
Länkäran 98 N4
Lannion 66 B5
L'Anse 40 C1
Lansing 40 D2
Lanxi 86 H1
Lanya 110 E2
Lanzarote 106 C3
Lanzhou 86 C3
Laoag 90 G3
Lao Cai 90 C2
Laohekou 86 E4
Laon 62 F5
La Oroya 50 B6
Laos 90 C3
Laotougou 88 E2
Lapa 52 M4
La Palma 106 B3
La Palma 46 J7
La Paragua 50 E2
La Paz, *Argentina* 52 K5
La Paz, *Bolivia* 50 D7
La Paz, *Mexico* 46 B4
La Pedrera 50 D4

La Perla 44 F3
La Pérouse Strait 86 L1
La Pesca 42 B5
La Pine 38 B2
Lapithos 100 A1
La Plant 38 F1
La Plata 52 K5
Lappajärvi 56 M5
Lappeenranta 56 Q6
Lappland 56 M2
Laptev Sea = More Laptevykh 84 L1
Lapua 56 M5
Łapy 58 M5
La Quiaca 52 H3
L'Aquila 72 H6
Lār 101 F3
Larache 106 D1
Laramie 38 E2
Laramie Range 38 E2
Larantuka 92 (2)B4
Larat 92 (2)D4
Larba 68 P8
Laredo, *Spain* 68 G1
Laredo, *United States* 44 G3
Largo 42 E4
L'Ariana 72 E12
La Rioja 52 H4
Larisa 76 E5
Larkana 96 J4
Larnaka 100 A2
Larne 64 G7
La Rochelle 66 D7
La Roche-sur-Yon 66 D7
La Roda 68 H5
La Romana 46 L5
La Ronge 34 K5
Lar'yak 82 Q5
La Sarre 40 E1
Las Cabezas de San Juan 68 E7
Las Cruces 44 E2
La Serena 52 G4
La Seu d'Urgell 68 M2
La Seyne-sur-Mer 66 L10
Lashio 90 B2
Lashkar Gāh 96 H3
Łask 58 J6
Las Lomitas 52 J3
La Solana 68 G6
Las Palmas 106 B3
La Spézia 70 E6
Las Plumas 52 H7
Last Chance 38 F3
Lastoursville 108 G5
Lastovo 74 D7
Las Varas 36 E7
Las Varillas 52 J5
Las Vegas, *Nev., United States* 38 C3
Las Vegas, *N.Mex., United States* 44 E1
La Teste 66 D9
Latina 72 G7
Latisana 70 J5
La Toma 52 H5
La Tuque 40 F1
Latur 94 C5
Latvia 56 M8
Lauchhammer 60 J5
Lauenburg 60 F3
Lauf 60 G7
Lau Group 114 J7
Launceston, *Australia* 116 J8
Launceston, *United Kingdom* 64 H11
La Union 68 K7
Laupheim 70 E2
Laura 116 H3
Laurel 42 D3
Lauria 72 K8
Laurinburg 42 F3
Lausanne 70 B4
Laut, *Indonesia* 92 (1)F3
Laut, *Malaysia* 92 (1)D2
Lauter 62 K5
Lauterbach 60 E6
Lava 58 L3
Laval, *Canada* 40 F1
Laval, *France* 66 E5
La Vall de Uixo 68 K5
Lavant 70 K4
La Vega 46 K5
Laviana 68 E1
La Vila Joiosa 68 K6
Lavras 52 N3
Lavrentiya 84 Z3
Lavrio 76 G7
Lawdar 104 J5
Lawra 108 D2
Lawrence, *New Zealand* 118 B7
Lawrence, *Kans., United States* 40 A3
Lawrence, *Mass., United States* 40 F2
Lawrenceville 42 D2
Lawton 42 B3
Laya 78 L1
Laylā 104 J3
Laysan Island 114 J3
Layton 38 D2
Lazarev 84 Q6
Lázaro Cárdenas 46 D5
Lazdijai 58 N3
Lazo 84 P3
Leadville 38 E3
Leamington 40 D2
Leavenworth, *Kans., United States* 40 A3
Leavenworth, *Wash., United States* 38 B1
Lebach 62 J5
Lebanon 100 C3
Lebanon, *Mo., United States* 40 B3
Lebanon, *N.H., United States* 40 F2
Lebanon, *Pa., United States* 40 E2
Lebanon, *Tenn., United States* 40 C3
Lebel-sur-Quévillon 40 E1
Lębork 58 G3
Lebrija 68 D8
Lebu Victoria 52 G6
Lecce 72 N8
Lecco 70 E5
Lech 70 F3
Leck 60 D2
Le Creusot 66 K7
Łeczna 58 M6
Łęczyca 58 J5
Ledmozero 56 R4
Lee 64 D10
Leech Lake 40 B1
Leeds 64 L8
Leek 62 A1
Leer 62 K1
Leesburg 42 E4
Leeston 118 D6
Leesville 42 C3
Leeuwarden 62 H1
Leeward Islands 46 M5
Lefkada 76 C6
Lefkada 76 C6
Lefkimmi 76 C5
Lefkonikon 100 A1
Lefkosia 76 R9
Legaspi 90 G4
Legionowo 58 K5
Legnago 70 G5
Legnica 58 F6
Leh 94 C2
Le Havre 62 C5
Lehrte 60 F4
Leiah 94 B2
Leibnitz 70 L4
Leicester 62 A2
Leiden 62 G2
Leie 62 F4
Leigh Creek 116 G6
Leighton Buzzard 62 B3
Leine 60 E4
Leinster 116 D5
Leipzig 60 H5
Leiria 68 B5
Leitrim 64 D8
Leiyang 86 E5
Lek 62 G3
Lelystad 62 H2
Le Mans 66 F6
Le Mars 40 A2
Lemberg 60 D8
Lemesos 76 Q10
Lemgo 62 L2
Lemieux Islands 34 U4
Lemmer 62 H2
Lemmon 38 F1
Le Muret 66 E9
Lena 68 E1
Lena 84 L4
Lendinare 70 G5
Lengerich 62 K2
Lengshuijiang 86 E5
Lengshuitan 86 E5
Leninsk-Kuznetskiy 82 R7
Leninskoye 78 J3
Lenmalu 92 (2)D3
Lenne 62 K3
Lennestadt 62 L3
Lens 62 E4
Lensk 84 K4
Lenti 70 M4
Lentini 72 J11
Léo 108 D2
Leoben 70 L3
León, *Mexico* 46 D4
León, *Nicaragua* 46 G6
León, *Spain* 68 E2
Leonberg 70 E2
Leonforte 72 J11
Leonidi 76 E7
Leonora 116 D5
Le Perthus 66 H11
Lepsy 82 P8
Le Puy 66 J8
Léré 108 G3
Lérici 70 E6
Lerik 98 N4
Lerma 68 G2
Leros 76 J7
Lerwick 64 L1
Lešak 74 H6
Les Andelys 62 D5
Lesatima 110 F4
Lesbos = Lesvos 76 H5
Les Escaldes 66 G11
Les Escoumins 34 T7
Leshan 86 C5
Les Herbiers 66 D7
Leshukonskoye 78 J2
Leskovac 74 J7
Lesosibirsk 82 S6
Lesotho 112 D5
Lesozavodsk 88 G1
Les Sables-d'Olonne 66 D7
Les Sept Îles 66 B5
Lesser Antilles 46 L6
Lesser Slave Lake 34 J5
Lesvos 76 H5
Leszno 58 F6
Letaba 112 E4
Letchworth 62 B3
Letenye 70 M4
Lethbridge 38 D1
Lethem 50 F3
Leticia 50 D4
Letpadan 90 B3
Le Tréport 62 D4
Letterkenny 64 E7
Leutkirch 70 F3
Leuven 62 G4
Leuze 62 F4
Levadeia 76 E6
Lévanzo 72 G10
Levashi 98 M2
Levaya Khetta 78 P2
Leverkusen 62 J3
Levice 58 H9
Levico Terme 70 G4
Levin 118 E5
Lévis 40 F1
Levitha 76 J7
Levoča 58 K9
Levski 74 N6
Lewes 62 C4
Lewis 64 F3
Lewis and Clark Lake 38 G2
Lewis Range 34 J7
Lewiston, *Id., United States* 38 C1
Lewiston, *Me., United States* 40 F2
Lewistown, *Mont., United States* 38 E1
Lewistown, *Pa., United States* 40 E2
Lexington, *Ky., United States* 40 D3
Lexington, *Nebr., United States* 38 G2
Lexington, *Va., United States* 40 E3
Lexington Park 42 F2
Leyte 90 G4
Lezhë 74 G8
Lhari 94 F2
Lhasa 94 F3
Lhazê 94 E3
Lhokseumawe 90 B5
Lian Xian 90 E2
Lianyuan 90 E1
Lianyungang 86 F4
Liaocheng 86 F3
Liao He 88 B3
Liaoyang 88 B3
Liaoyuan 88 C2
Liard 34 F5
Liard River 34 F5
Libby 38 C1
Libenge 110 B3
Liberal 42 A2
Liberec 58 E7
Liberia 108 B3
Liberia 46 G6
Liberty 42 C1
Libjo 90 H4
Libourne 66 E9
Libreville 108 F4
Libya 104 C2
Libyan Desert 104 D2
Libyan Plateau 104 E1
Licata 72 H11
Lich 60 D6
Lichinga 112 F2
Lichtenfels 60 G6
Lida 56 N10
Lidköping 56 G7
Lido di Óstia 72 G7
Lidzbark Warmiński 58 K3
Liebenwalde 60 J4
Liechtenstein 70 E3
Liège 62 H4
Lieksa 56 R5
Lienz 70 H4
Liepāja 58 L1
Lier 62 G3
Liezen 70 K3
Lifford 64 E7
Lignières 66 H7
Ligueil 66 F6
Ligurian Sea 70 D7
Lihue 44 B2
Lijiang 90 C1
Likasi 110 D6
Lilienfeld 70 L2
Lille 62 F4
Lillebonne 62 C5
Lillehammer 56 F6
Lillerto 70 G3
Lilongwe 112 E2
Liloy 90 G5
Lima, *Peru* 50 B6
Lima, *Mont., United States* 38 D2
Lima, *Oh., United States* 40 D2
Limanowa 58 K8
Limassol = Lemesos 76 Q10
Limbaži 56 N8
Limburg 62 L4
Limeira 52 M3
Limerick 64 D9
Limingen 56 G4
Limni Kastorias 76 C4
Limni Kerkinitis 76 E3
Limni Koronia 76 F4
Limni Trichonida 76 D6
Limni Vegoritis 76 D4
Limni Volvi 76 F4
Limnos 76 H5
Limoges 66 G8
Limon 38 F3
Limón 46 H7
Limoux 66 H10
Limpopo 112 D4
Linares, *Chile* 52 G6
Linares, *Mexico* 44 G4
Linares, *Spain* 68 G6
Lincang 90 C2
Linchuan 86 F5
Lincoln, *United Kingdom* 62 B1
Lincoln, *Ill., United States* 40 C2
Lincoln, *Me., United States* 40 G1
Lincoln, *Nebr., United States* 38 G2
Lincoln, *N.H., United States* 40 F2
Lindenow Fjord 34 Y4
Lindesnes 56 D8
Lindi 110 D3
Lindi 110 F6
Lindos 76 L8
Line Islands 114 L5
Linfen 86 E3
Lingen 62 K2
Lingga 92 (1)C3
Lingshui 90 D3
Linguère 108 A1
Lingyuan 86 F2
Linhal 86 G5
Linhares 50 J7
Linhe 86 D2
Linjiang 88 D3
Linköping 56 H7
Linkou 88 F1
Linosa 72 G13
Lins 52 M3
Linton 38 F1
Linxia 86 C3
Lin Xian 86 E3
Linyi 86 F3
Linz 70 K2
Liobomil' 58 P6
Lipari 72 J10
Lipari 72 J10
Lipcani 74 P1

Lipetsk 78 G4
Lipin Bor 78 G2
Lipno 58 J5
Lipova 74 J3
Lippe 62 L3
Lippstadt 62 L3
Lipsoi 76 J7
Liptovský-Mikuláš 58 J8
Lipu 90 E2
Liqeni i Fierzës 74 H7
Liqeni Komanit 74 G7
Lira 110 E3
Liri 72 H7
Lisala 110 C3
Lisboa 68 A6
Lisbon = Lisboa 68 A6
Lisburn 64 G7
Liscannor Bay 64 C9
Lishi 86 E3
Lishui 86 F5
Lisieux 62 C5
Liski 78 G4
L'Isle-sur-la-Sorgue 66 L10
Lisse 62 G2
Lištica 72 M5
Listowel 64 C9
Listvyanka 84 H6
Litang 86 C5
Litani 50 G3
Litava 58 F8
Litchfield, *Ill.*, *United States* 40 C3
Litchfield, *Minn.*, *United States* 40 B1
Lithgow 116 K6
Lithuania 56 L9
Litke 84 Q6
Litomerice 60 K6
Litomyši 58 F8
Litovel 58 G8
Litovko 84 P7
Little Abaco 42 F4
Little Andaman 94 F6
Little Barrier Island 118 E3
Little Current 40 D1
Little Desert 116 H7
Little Falls 40 B1
Littlefield 44 F2
Little Inagua 46 K4
Little Karoo 112 C6
Little Minch 64 E4
Little Nicobar 94 F7
Little Ouse 62 C2
Little Rock 42 C3
Littleton 38 E3
Litvinov 60 J6
Liupanshui 86 C5
Liuzhou 86 D6
Live Oak 42 E3
Liverpool 64 K8
Liverpool Bay 34 F2
Livingston, *United Kingdom* 64 J6
Livingston, *United States* 38 D1
Livingstone 112 D3
Livingstonia 112 E2
Livno 74 E6
Livny 78 G4
Livonia 40 D2
Livorno 70 F7
Liwale 110 F5
Lizard Point 64 G12
Ljubljana 70 K4
Ljugarn 56 K8
Ljungan 56 J5
Ljungby 56 G8
Ljusdal 56 J6
Ljusnan 78 C2
Llandovery 64 J9
Llandudno 64 J8
Llanelli 64 H10
Llanes 68 F1
Llanos 50 C2
Lleida 68 L3
Lli 82 P9
Lloret de Mar 68 N3
Llucmajor 68 N5
Loano 70 D6
Lobatse 112 D5
Löbau 60 K5
Łobez 58 E4
Lobito 112 A2
Locarno 70 D4
Lochboisdale 64 E4
Lochinver 64 G3
Loch Linnhe 64 G5
Loch Lomond 64 H5
Lochmaddy 64 E4
Loch Ness 64 H4
Lockhart 42 B4
Lock Haven 40 E2
Lockport 40 E2
Locri 72 L10
Lodève 66 J10
Lodeynoye 78 F2
Lodge Grass 38 E1
Lodi, *Italy* 70 E5
Lodi, *United States* 38 B3
Lodja 110 C4
Lodwar 110 F3
Łódź 58 J6
Loei 90 C3
Lofoten 56 G3
Logan, *Ia.*, *United States* 40 A2
Logan, *N.Mex.*, *United States* 44 F1
Logan, *Ut.*, *United States* 38 D2
Logansport 40 C2
Logatec 70 K5
Logroño 68 H2
Lohiniva 56 N3
Lohr 60 E7
Loikaw 90 B3
Loir 66 F6
Loire 66 D6
Loja, *Ecuador* 50 B4
Loja, *Spain* 68 F7
Lokan tekojärvi 56 P3
Lokeren 62 F3
Lokichar 110 F3
Lokichokio 110 E3
Lokoja 108 F3
Lokosovo 78 P2
Loks Land 34 U4
Lolland 60 G2
Lollondo 110 F4
Lolo 38 D1
Lom 74 L6
Lomami 110 C4
Lomas 50 C7
Lomas de Zamora 52 K5
Lombadina 116 D3
Lomblen 92 (2)B4
Lombok 92 (1)F4
Lomé 108 E3
Lomela 110 C4
Lomela 110 C4
Lommel 62 H3
Lomonosovka 78 N4
Lompoc 44 B2
Łomża 58 M4
London, *Canada* 40 D2
London, *United Kingdom* 62 B3
London, *United States* 42 E2
Londonderry 64 E6
Londrina 52 L3
Longarone 70 H4
Long Bay 46 J2
Long Beach 44 C2
Long Branch 40 F2
Long Eaton 62 A2
Longford 64 E8
Long Island, *Canada* 34 Q5
Long Island, *United States* 40 F2
Longlac 34 P7
Long Lake 38 F1
Longmont 38 E2
Long Prairie 40 B1
Long Range Mountains 34 V6
Longueuil 40 F1
Longview, *Tex.*, *United States* 42 C3
Longview, *Wash.*, *United States* 38 B1
Longwy 62 H5
Long Xuyên 90 D4
Longyan 90 F1
Löningen 62 K2
Lönsdalen 56 H3
Lons-le-Saunier 70 A4
Lookout Pass 38 C1
Loop Head 64 B9
Lopez 90 G4
Lop Nur 82 S9
Lopphavet 56 L1
Loptyuga 78 J2
Lora del Rio 68 E7
Lorain 40 D2
Loralai 94 A2
Lorca 68 J7
Lordegān 101 D1
Lord Howe Island 116 L6
Lordsburg 44 E2
Loreto 46 B3
Lorient 66 B6
Lörrach 70 C3
Lorraine 116 G3
Los Alamos 44 E1
Los Angeles, *Chile* 52 G6
Los Angeles, *United States* 44 C2
Los Banos 38 B3
Los Blancos 52 J3
Losheim 62 J5
Lošinj 70 K6
Los Mochis 46 C3
Lospalos 92 (2)C4
Los Telares 52 J4
Los Teques 50 D1
Lost Trail Pass 38 D1
Los'va 78 M2
Los Vientos 52 H3
Lotta 56 Q2
Lotte 62 K2
Louang Namtha 90 C2
Louangphrabang 90 C3
Loubomo 108 G5
Loudéac 66 C5
Louga 108 A1
Loughborough 62 A2
Lough Conn 64 C7
Lough Corrib 64 C8
Lough Derg 64 D8
Lough Foyle 64 E6
Lough Leane 64 C9
Lough Mask 64 C8
Lough Neagh 64 F7
Lough Ree 64 E8
Louhans 66 L7
Louisa 40 D3
Louisiade Archipelago 116 K2
Louisiana 42 C3
Louis Trichardt 112 D4
Louisville, *Ga.*, *United States* 42 E3
Louisville, *Ky.*, *United States* 42 D2
Louisville, *Miss.*, *United States* 42 D3
Loukhi 56 S3
Loulé 68 C7
Louny 60 J6
Loup 38 G2
Lourdes 66 E10
Louth, *Australia* 116 J6
Louth, *United Kingdom* 62 C1
Loutra Aidipsou 76 F6
Louviers 62 D5
Lovech 74 M6
Lovell 38 E2
Lovelock 38 C2
Lovosice 60 K6
Lovran 70 K5
Lôvua 112 C2
Lowa 110 D4
Lowell 40 F2
Lower Hutt 118 E5
Lower Lake 38 B2
Lower Lough Erne 64 E7
Lower Post 34 F5
Lowestoft 62 D2
Lowville 40 F2
Loxstedt 60 D3
Loyalty Islands 114 G8
Loyno 78 K3
Loznica 74 G5
L-Travemünde 60 F3
Luama 110 D4
Luampa 112 C3
Lu'an 86 F4
Luanda 110 A5
Luangwa 112 E2
Luangwa 112 E3
Luanping 86 F2
Luanshya 112 D2
Luarca 68 D1
Luau 112 C2
Lubaczów 58 N7
Lubań 58 E6
Lubango 112 A2
Lubāns 56 P8
Lubao 110 D5
Lubartów 58 M6
Lübbecke 62 L2
Lübben 60 J5
Lübbenau 60 J5
Lubbock 44 F2
Lübeck 60 F3
Lubefu 110 C4
Lubero 110 D4
Lubilash 110 C5
Lubin 58 F6
Lublin 58 M6
Lubliniec 58 H7
Lubny 78 F4
Luboń 58 F5
Lubsko 58 D6
Lubudi 110 D5
Lubuklinggau 92 (1)C3
Lubumbashi 110 D6
Lubutu 110 D4
Lucala 110 B5
Lucca 70 F7
Luce Bay 64 H7
Lucedale 42 D3
Lucena, *Philippines* 90 G4
Lucena, *Spain* 68 F7
Lučenec 58 J
Lucera 72 K
Lucero 44 E
Lucira 112 A
Luckenwalde 60 J4
Lucknow 94 D
Luçon 66 D
Lucusse 112 C
Ludden 38 G
Lüdenscheid 62 K
Lüderitz 112 B5
Ludhiana 94 C
Ludington 40 C
Ludlow 44 C
Ludogori 74 P
Luduş 74 M
Ludvika 56 H
Ludwigsburg 70 E
Ludwigsfelde 60 J4
Ludwigshafen 62 L5
Ludwigslust 60 G
Ludza 56 P
Luebo 110 C5
Luena 112 B
Lufeng 90 F
Lufira 110 D
Lufkin 42 C
Luga 56 Q
Luga 78 E
Lugano 70 D4
Lugela 112 F
Lugenda 112 F
Luggate 118 B
Lugo 70 G
Lugoj 74 J4
Lugovoy 82 N
Lugu 94 D
Luhans'k 78 G5
Luhuo 86 C4
Lui 90 E
Luilaka 110 B4
Luino 70 D4
Luis Moya 44 F4
Luiza 110 C5
Lukavac 74 F5
Lukovit 74 M
Łuków 58 M
Lukulu 112 C
Lukumburu 110 F5
Lukuni 110 B5
Luleå 56 M4
Lüleburgaz 76 K
Lulua 110 D5
Lumbala Kaquengue 112 C
Lumberton 42 F
Lumbrales 68 D4
Lumimba 112 E
Lumsden 118 B
Lund 58 C
Lundazi 112 E
Lundy 64 H10
Lüneburg 60 F
Lüneburger Heide 60 F4
Lunel 66 K10
Lünen 62 K
Lunéville 70 B
Lungau 70 J
Luntai 82 Q9
Luohe 86 E4
Luoyang 86 E4
Luozi 110 A4
Lupeni 74 L4
Lūrā Shīrīn 98 L5
Lure 70 B
Luremo 110 B5
Lurgan 64 F
Lurio 112 F
Lusaka 112 D
Lusambo 110 C5
Lushnjë 76 B4
Lushui 86 B5
Lüshun 86 G
Lusk 38 F
Lutembo 112 C
Lutherstadt Wittenberg 60 H5
Luton 62 B
Luts'k 78 E4
Lutto 56 P
Lützow-Holmbukta 120 (2)J
Luverne 40 A
Luvua 110 D5
Luwuk 92 (2)B
Luxembourg 62 H5
Luxembourg 62 J5
Luxeuil-les-Bains 70 B
Luxor 104 F
Luza 78 J
Luza 78 J
Luzern 70 D
Luzhou 86 D5

Luzilândia 50 J4
Luznice 70 K1
Luzon 90 G3
Luzon Strait 90 G2
Luzy 66 J7
L'viv 58 N8
Lyady 56 Q7
Lyapin 78 M2
Lycksele 78 C2
Lydenburg 112 E5
Lyme Bay 64 K11
Lymington 62 A4
Lynchburg 40 E3
Lynn 40 F2
Lynn Lake 34 L5
Lynx Lake 34 K4
Lyon 66 K8
Lys 62 E4
Lys'va 78 L3
Lysychans'k 78 G5
Lyttelton 118 D6

M

Maalosmadulu Atoll 94 B7
Ma'ān 100 C6
Maardu 56 N7
Ma'arrat an Nu'mān 98 G6
Maas 62 J3
Maasin 90 G4
Maastricht 62 H4
Mabalane 112 E4
Mabanza-Ngungu 108 G6
Mabein 90 B2
Mablethorpe 62 C1
Macapá 50 G3
Macas 50 B4
Macassar Strait 114 B6
Macau 90 E2
Macau 90 E2
Macau 50 K5
Macaúba 50 G6
Macclesfield 64 K8
Macdonnell Ranges 116 F4
Macedonia 76 C3
Maceió 50 K5
Macerata 70 J7
Machakos 110 F4
Machala 50 B4
Macheng 86 F4
Machilipatnam 94 D5
Machiques 50 C1
Macia 112 E4
Măcin 74 R4
Mack 44 E1
Mackay 116 J4
Mackay Lake 34 J4
Mackenzie 34 G4
Mackenzie Bay 34 D3
Mackenzie Mountains 34 E3
Mackinaw City 40 D1
Macmillan 34 E4
Macmillan Pass 34 F4
Macomb 40 B2
Macomer 72 C8
Macon, *Ga.*, *United States* 42 E3
Macon, *Mo.*, *United States* 42 C2
Mâcon 66 K7
Macuje 50 C3
Mādabā 100 C5
Madagascar 112 H3
Madan 74 M8
Madaoua 108 F2
Madeira 106 B2
Madeira 50 E5
Maden 98 H4
Madera 44 E3
Madikeri 94 C6
Madison 40 C2
Madison, *Ind.*, *United States* 40 C3
Madison, *Minn.*, *United States* 40 A1
Madison, *S.D.*, *United States* 38 G2
Madisonville 40 C3
Madiun 92 (1)E4
Mado Gashi 110 F3
Madoi 86 B4
Madona 56 P8
Madras = Chennai, *India* 94 D6
Madras, *United States* 38 B2
Madre de Dios 50 C6
Madrid, *Philippines* 90 H5
Madrid, *Spain* 68 G4
Madridejos 68 G5
Madura 92 (1)E4
Madurai 94 C6
Maebashi 88 K5
Mae Hong Son 90 B3
Mae Nam Mun 90 C3
Mae Sariang 90 B3
Maevatanana 112 H3
Mafeteng 112 D5
Maffighofen 70 J2
Mafia Island 110 G5
Mafra 52 M4
Mafraq 100 D4
Magadan 84 S5
Magadi 110 F4
Magdagachi 84 M6
Magdalena 50 C2
Magdalena, *Bolivia* 50 E6
Magdalena, *Mexico* 44 D2
Magdalena, *United States* 44 E2
Magdeburg 60 G4
Magdelaine Cays 116 K3
Magelang 92 (1)E4
Magenta 70 D5
Magerøya 56 N1
Maglaj 74 F5
Máglie 72 N8
Magnitogorsk 78 L4
Magnolia 42 C3
Mago 84 P6
Magog 40 F1
Magu 110 E4
Magwe 90 A2
Mahābād 98 L5
Mahagi 110 E3
Mahajamba 112 H3
Mahajanga 112 H3
Mahalapye 112 D4
Mahān 101 G1
Mahanadi 94 D4
Mahanoro 112 H3
Mahasamund 94 D4
Mahavavy 112 H3
Mahbubnagar 94 D5
Mahḍah 101 G4
Mahé Island 112 (2)C1
Mahenge 110 F5
Mahesāna 94 B4
Mahia Peninsula 118 F4
Mahilyow 78 F4
Mahnomen 40 A1
Mahón 68 Q5
Mahuva 96 K5
Maicao 50 C1
Maidenhead 62 B3
Maidstone 62 C3
Maiduguri 108 G2
Mai Gudo 110 F2
Maímédy 60 B6
Main 60 E7
Mainburg 70 G2
Main-Donau-Kanal 60 G7
Maine 40 G1
Maïné Soroa 108 G2
Maingkwan 90 B1
Mainland, *Orkney Is.*, *United Kingdom* 64 J2
Mainland, *Shetland Is.*, *United Kingdom* 64 L1
Maintirano 112 G3
Mainz 60 D6
Maio 108 (1)B1
Majene 92 (2)A3
Majicana 52 H4
Majuro 114 H5
Makale 92 (2)A3
Makamba 110 D4
Makanza 110 B3
Makarora 118 B7
Makarov 84 Q7
Makarska 74 E6
Makar'yev 78 H3
Makat 78 K5
Makeni 108 B3
Makgadikgadi 112 C4
Makhachkala 98 M2
Makhorovka 82 M7
Makindu 110 F4
Makinsk 78 P4
Makiyivka 78 G5
Makkah 104 G3
Makó 74 H3
Makokou 108 G4
Makongolosi 110 E5
Makorako 118 F4
Makoua 108 H4
Maków Mazowiecka 58 L5
Makran 96 G4
Makronisi 76 G7
Mākū 98 L4
Makumbako 110 E5
Makurazaki 88 F8
Makurdi 108 F3
Makūyeh 101 E2
Makuyuni 110 F4
Malabar Coast 94 B6
Malabo 108 F4
Malack 58 F9
Malacky 70 M2
Malad City 38 D2
Maladzyechna 78 E4
Málaga 68 F8
Malaimbandy 112 H4
Malaita 114 G6
Malakal 110 E2
Malakula 114 G7
Malamala 92 (2)B3
Malang 92 (1)E4
Malanje 110 B5
Malanville 108 E2
Malaryta 58 P6
Malatya 98 H4
Malaut 94 B2
Mālavi 98 M7
Malawi 112 E2
Malaya Baranikha 84 V3
Malaya Vishera 78 F3
Malaybalay 90 H5
Malāyer 96 E3
Malay Peninsula 90 C6
Malay Reef 116 J3
Malaysia 92 (1)C2
Malbork 58 J3
Malchin, *Germany* 60 H3
Malchin, *Mongolia* 82 S8
Malden Island 114 L6
Maldives 94 B8
Maldonado 52 L5
Malé 70 F4
Male 94 B8
Male Atoll 94 B8
Malegaon 94 B4
Malé Karpaty 70 N2
Malesherbes 66 H5
Maleta 84 H6
Malheur 38 C2
Malheur Lake 38 C2
Mali 106 E5
Malindi 110 G4
Malin Head 64 E6
Malkara 76 J4
Malko Tŭrnovo 74 Q8
Mallaig 64 G4
Mallawi 104 F2
Mallorca 68 P5
Mallow 64 D9
Malmédy 62 J4
Malmesbury 112 B6
Malmö 58 C2
Malmyzh 78 K3
Malone 40 F2
Måløy 56 C6
Malozemel'skaya Tundra 78 K1
Målselv 56 K2
Malta 72 J13
Malta 38 E1
Malta Channel 72 J12
Maltahöhe 112 B4
Malvern 40 B4
Malý Dunaj 70 N2
Malyy Uzen' 78 J4
Mama 84 J5
Mamadysh 78 K3
Mambasa 110 D3
Mamburao 90 G4
Mamelodi 112 D5
Mammoth Hot Springs 38 D2
Mamonovo 58 J3
Mamoré 50 D6
Mamou 108 B2
Mamoudzou 112 H2
Mamuju 92 (2)A3
Ma'mūl 96 G6
Mamuno 112 C4
Man 108 C3
Mana 44 (2)A1
Manacapuru 50 E4
Manacor 68 P5
Manado 92 (2)B2
Managua 46 G6
Manakara 112 H4
Manali 94 C2
Mananara 112 H4
Mananara Avaratra 112 H3
Mananjary 112 H4
Manantenina 112 H4
Manassas 40 E3
Manaus 50 E4
Manavgat 76 P8
Manbij 98 G5
Manchester, *United Kingdom* 64 K8
Manchester, *Ia.*, *United States* 40 B2
Manchester, *Ky.*, *United States* 40 D3
Manchester, *Tenn.*, *United States* 40 C3
Manchester, *Vt.*, *United States* 40 F2
Mand 96 H4
Mandabe 112 G4
Mandal 56 D7
Mandalay 90 B2
Mandalgovĭ 86 D1
Mandan 38 F1
Mandera 110 G3
Mandi 94 C2
Mandi Burewala 94 B2
Mandimba 112 F2
Manding 106 D6
Mandla 94 D4
Mandø 60 D1
Mandsaur 94 C4
Mandurah 116 C6
Mandúria 72 M8
Mandvi 94 A4
Mandya 94 C6
Manfredonia 72 K7
Manga 108 G2
Manga 50 J6
Mangaia 114 K8
Mangalia 74 R6
Mangalore 94 E6
Mangareva 114 N8
Mangatupopo 118 E4
Mangaweka 118 F4
Manggar 92 (1)D3
Mangit 96 H1
Mangnai 82 S10
Mango 108 E2
Mangoky 112 G4
Mangole 92 (2)C3
Mangonui 118 D2
Mangrove Cay 42 F5
Manhad 94 B5
Manhattan 42 B2
Manhuaçu 50 J8
Mania 112 H3
Maniamba 112 F2
Manicoré 50 E5
Manicouagan 34 T6
Manihiki 114 K7
Maniitsoq 34 W3
Manila 90 G4
Manisa 76 K6
Manistee 40 C2
Manistique 40 C1
Manitoba 34 M6
Manitou 38 G1
Manitoulin Island 40 D1
Manitouwadge 40 C1
Manitowoc 40 C2
Maniwaki 40 E1
Manizales 50 B2
Manja 112 G4
Manjimup 116 C6
Mankato 40 B2
Manley Hot Springs 34 A4
Mannleu 68 N3
Manna 92 (1)C3
Mannheim 62 L5
Manning, *Canada* 34 H5
Manning, *United States* 42 E3
Manokwari 92 (2)D3
Manono 110 D5
Manosque 66 L10
Manouane 40 F1
Manouane Lake 34 S6
Manp'o 88 D3
Manra 114 J6
Manresa 68 M3
Mansa 112 D2
Mansel Island 34 Q4
Mansfield, *United Kingdom* 62 A1
Mansfield, *La.*, *United States* 42 C3
Mansfield, *Oh.*, *United States* 40 D2
Manta 50 A4
Manteo 42 F2
Mantes-la-Jolie 62 D5
Mántova 70 F5
Manturovo 78 H3
Manú 50 C6
Manuelzinho 50 G5
Manūjān 101 G3
Manukan 90 G5
Manukau 118 E3
Manukau Harbour 118 E3
Manyberries 38 D1
Manyinga 112 C2
Manyoni 110 E5
Manzanares 68 G5
Manzanillo 46 J4
Manzhouli 84 K7
Manzini 112 E5

Mao 104 C5
Maoming 90 E2
Mapam Yumco 94 D2
Mapi 92 (2)E4
Mapinhane 112 F4
Maple Creek 36 E2
Mapuera 50 E4
Maputo 112 E5
Maqueda 68 F4
Maquela do Zombo 110 B5
Maquinchao 52 H7
Maquoketa 40 B2
Maraba 50 H5
Maracaibo 50 C1
Maracay 50 D1
Marādah 104 C2
Maradi 108 F2
Marāgheh 98 M5
Maralal 110 F3
Marand 98 L4
Maranhão 50 H5
Marañón 50 B4
Mărășești 74 Q4
Marathon, *Canada* 40 C1
Marathon, *United States* 44 F2
Marbella 68 F8
Marburg 62 L4
Marcal 70 N3
Marcali 70 N4
March 62 C2
Marche 62 H4
Marchena 68 E7
Mardan 94 B2
Mar del Plata 52 K6
Mardin 98 J5
Maré 114 G8
Mareeba 116 J3
Marettimo 72 F11
Marfa 44 F2
Margate 62 D3
Margherita di Savoia 72 L7
Marghita 74 K2
Margilan 96 K1
Marguerite Bay 120 (2)KK3
María Elena 52 H3
Marianas Trench 114 E4
Marianna 42 D3
Márianská Lázně 60 H7
Mariazell 70 L3
Mar'ib 104 J4
Maribo 60 G2
Maribor 70 L4
Maridi 110 D2
Marie Byrd Land 120 (2)FF2
Marie Galante 46 M5
Mariehamn 56 K6
Marienberg 60 J6
Mariental 112 B4
Marietta 42 E2
Marietta, *Oh.*, *United States* 40 D3
Marietta, *Okla.*, *United States* 42 B3
Mariinsk 82 R6
Marijampolė 58 N3
Marília 52 M3
Marín 68 B2
Marinette 40 C1
Maringá 52 L3
Marino 72 G7
Marion, *Ill.*, *United States* 40 C3
Marion, *Ind.*, *United States* 40 C2
Marion, *Oh.*, *United States* 40 D2
Maripa 50 D2
Mariscal Estigarribia 52 J3
Maritime Alps 70 C6
Marittimo 70 F7
Mariupol' 78 G5
Marīvān 98 M6
Mariy El 78 J3
Marjayoûn 100 C3
Marka 110 G3
Markam 86 B5
Markaryd 58 C1
Marked Tree 42 C2
Marken 62 H2
Markermeer 62 H2
Market Harborough 62 B2
Markham 40 E2
Marki 58 L5
Markit 82 P10
Markkleeberg 60 H5
Markovo 84 W4
Marktoberdorf 70 F3
Marktredwitz 60 H7
Marla 116 F5
Marle 62 F5
Marmande 66 F9
Marmara Adası 76 K4
Marmara Denizi 76 L4
Marmaris 76 L8
Marmolada 70 G4
Marne 62 F5
Maroansetra 112 H3
Marolambo 112 H4
Maroni 50 G3
Marotiri 114 M8
Maroua 108 G2
Marquesas Islands 114 M6
Marquette 40 C1
Marradi 70 G6
Marrakech 106 D2
Marra Plateau 104 D5
Marree 116 G5
Marrupa 112 F2
Marsa Alam 104 F2
Marsabit 110 F3
Marsala 72 G11
Marsberg 62 L3
Marsden 116 J6
Marseille 66 L10
Marseille-en-Beauvaisis 62 D5
Marshall, *Ill.*, *United States* 42 D2
Marshall, *Tex.*, *United States* 42 C3
Marshall Islands 114 G4
Marshalltown 40 B2
Marsh Harbour 42 F4
Marsh Island 42 C4
Martapura, *Indonesia* 92 (1)C3
Martapura, *Indonesia* 92 (1)E3
Martigny 70 C4
Martigues 66 L10
Martin, *Slovakia* 58 H8
Martin, *United States* 38 F2
Martina Franca 72 M8
Martinborough 118 E5
Martinique 46 M6
Martinsburg 40 E3
Martinsville, *Ind.*, *United States* 40 C3
Martinsville, *Va.*, *United States* 40 E3
Marton 118 E5
Martos 68 G7
Maruchak 96 H2
Mårvatn 56 E6
Mary 96 H2
Maryborough 116 K5
Maryland 40 E3
Marysville, *Canada* 40 G1
Marysville, *Calif.*, *United States* 44 B1
Marysville, *Kans.*, *United States* 42 B2
Maryville 40 B2
Masai Steppe 110 F4
Masaka 110 E4
Masalembu Besar 92 (1)E4
Masallı 98 N4
Masamba 92 (2)B3
Masan 88 E6
Masasi 110 F6
Masbate 90 G4
Masbate 90 G4
Mascara 106 F1
Maseru 112 D5
Mashhad 96 G2
Masi-Manimba 110 B4
Masindi 110 E3
Maşīrah 96 G5
Masjed Soleymān 96 E3
Maskanah 98 H5
Mason 42 B3
Mason Bay 118 A8
Mason City 40 B2
Masqaţ 101 H5
Massa 70 F6
Massachusetts 40 F2
Massachusetts Bay 40 G2
Massafra 72 M8
Massa Marittima 72 E5
Massawa 104 G4
Massena 40 F2
Masset 34 E6
Massif Central 66 H8
Massif de Guéra 104 C5
Massif de l'Aïr 106 G5
Massif des Écrins 70 B5
Massif du Chaillu 108 G5
Massif du Tsaratanana 112 H2
Massif Ennedi 104 D4
Massillon 40 D2
Massinga 112 F4
Masteksay 78 K5
Masterton 118 E5
Mastung 96 J4
Masty 56 N10
Masuda 88 F6
Masuguru 112 F2
Masvingo 112 E4
Maşyāf 100 D1
Matadi 110 A5
Matagami 40 E1
Matagorda Island 42 B4
Matakana Island 118 F3
Matakawau 118 E3
Matale 94 D7
Matam 108 B1
Matamoros, *Mexico* 44 F3
Matamoros, *Mexico* 44 G3
Matane 40 G1
Matanzas 36 K7
Matara 94 D7
Mataram 92 (1)F4
Mataranka 116 F3
Mataró 68 N3
Mataura 118 B8
Matawai 118 F4
Matehuala 44 F4
Matera 72 L8
Mátészalka 74 K2
Mateur 72 D11
Matheson 40 D1
Mathraki 76 B5
Mathura 94 C3
Mati 90 H5
Matlock 62 A1
Matmata 106 G2
Mato Grosso 50 F6
Mato Grosso 50 F6
Mato Grosso do Sul 50 F7
Matosinhos 68 B3
Maţraḩ 101 H5
Matrei 70 H4
Matrûh 104 E1
Matsiatra 112 H4
Matsu 86 G5
Matsue 88 G6
Matsumae 88 L3
Matsumoto 88 J5
Matsusaka 88 J6
Matsuyama 88 G7
Mattawa 40 E1
Matterhorn 70 C5
Matthews Ridge 50 E2
Mattighofen 60 J8
Mattoon 40 C3
Maturín 50 E2
Maubeuge 62 F4
Maui 44 (2)F3
Maullín 52 G7
Maun 70 K6
Maun 112 C3
Mauna Kea 44 (2)F4
Mauna Loa 44 (2)F4
Mauritania 106 C5
Mauritius 112 (1)B2
Mauron 66 C5
Mauthen 70 H4
Mavinga 112 C3
Mawlaik 90 A2
Max 38 F1
Maya 84 P5
Maya 92 (1)D3
Mayaguana 46 K4
Mayagüez 46 L5
Mayamba 110 B4
Maych'ew 104 G5
Maydh 110 H1
Mayenne 66 E5
Mayenne 66 E5
Mayer 44 D2
Maykamys 82 P8
Maykop 98 J1
Mayly-Say 96 K1
Maymecha 84 G3
Mayn 84 W4
Mayo 34 D4
Mayor Island 118 F3
Mayotte 112 H2
Mayrhofen 70 G3
Mayskiy 84 M6
Mayumba 108 G5
Mayya 84 N4
Mazagão 50 G4
Mazagran 66 K4
Mazama 38 B1
Mazamet 66 H10
Mazar 82 P10
Mazara del Vallo 72 G11
Mazār-e Sharīf 96 J2
Mazatlán 46 C4
Mažeikiai 58 M1
Mazocahui 44 D3
Mazomora 110 F5
Mazra 100 C5
Mazyr 78 E4
Mazzarino 72 J11
Mbabane 112 E5
Mbala 110 E5
Mbale 110 E3
Mbalmayo 108 G4
Mbamba Bay 112 E2
Mbandaka 110 B3
Mbanga 108 F4
M'banza Congo 110 A5
Mbarara 110 E4
Mbeya 110 E5
Mbomou 110 C3
Mbour 108 A2
Mbuji-Mayi 110 C5
Mbuyuni 110 F5
McAlester 42 B3
McBride 34 G6
McCamey 44 F2
McCammon 38 D2
McClintock 34 N5
McClintock Channel 34 L2
McComb 42 C3
McCook 38 F2
McDermitt 38 C2
McGehee 42 C3
McGrath 44 (1)F3
McKinlay 116 H4
McKinney 42 B3
McLaughlin 38 F1
McLennan 34 H5
McMinnville 40 C3
McPherson 42 B2
McRae 42 E3
Meadow Lake 34 K3
Meadville 40 D3
Meander River 34 H3
Meaux 62 E3
Mecca = Makkah 104 G3
Mechelen 62 G3
Mechernich 62 J4
Mecidiye 76 J4
Mecklenburger Bucht 60 G2
Mecula 112 F2
Meda 68 C4
Medak 94 C5
Medan 92 (1)B2
Médéa 68 N[illegible]
Medellín 50 B2
Medenine 106 H2
Medford 38 B2
Medgidia 74 R5
Mediaş 74 M3
Medicine Bow 38 E2
Medicine Hat 34 J7
Medicine Lodge 42 B2
Medina = Al Madīnah 104 G5
Medinaceli 68 H3
Medina de Campo 68 F3
Medina Sidonia 68 E8
Mediterranean Sea 54 E4
Mednogorsk 78 L4
Medveditsa 78 H4
Medvezh'vyegorsk 78 F2
Meeker 38 E2
Meerane 60 H6
Meerut 94 C3
Mega 92 (2)D3
Megalopoli 76 E7
Meganisi 76 C6
Megara 76 F6
Megisti 76 M8
Mehrān 98 M7
Mehriz 96 F3
Meiktila 90 B2
Meiningen 60 F6
Meißen 60 J5
Meizhou 90 F2
Mejez El Bab 72 D12
Mékambo 108 G4
Mek'elē 104 G5
Meknès 106 D2
Mekong 90 D4
Melaka 92 (1)C2
Melanesia 114 F5
Melbourne, *Australia* 116 H7
Melbourne, *United States* 42 E4
Melchor de Mencos 46 G5
Meldrum Bay 40 D1
Meleuz 78 L4
Mélfi 104 C5
Melfi 72 K8
Melfort 34 L6
Melide 68 B2
Melilla 68 H9
Melita 38 F1
Melitopol' 78 G5
Melk 70 L2
Melkosopochnik 82 N8
Mělník 60 K6
Melo 52 L5
Melton Mowbray 62 B2
Melun 66 H5
Melut 104 F5
Melvern Lake 42 B2
Melville 34 L6
Melville Island, *Australia* 116 F2

Melville Island, *Canada*	32	N2
Melville Peninsula	34	P3
Memberamo	92	(2)E3
Memboro	92	(2)A4
Memmert	62	J1
Memmingen	70	F3
Mempawah	92	(1)D2
Memphis, *Mo., United States*	40	B2
Memphis, *Tenn., United States*	40	C3
Mena	42	C3
Menai Strait	64	H8
Ménaka	106	F5
Mendawai	92	(1)E3
Mende	66	J9
Menden	62	K3
Mendī	110	F2
Mendoza	52	H5
Menemen	76	K6
Menen	62	F4
Menfi	72	G11
Menggala	92	(1)D3
Meniet	106	F4
Menkere	84	L3
Menominee	40	C1
Menomonee Falls	40	C2
Menongue	112	B2
Menorca	68	Q4
Mentok	92	(1)D3
Menyuan	86	C3
Menzel Bourguiba	72	D11
Menzel Bouzelfa	72	E12
Menzel Temime	72	E12
Menzies	116	D5
Meppel	62	J2
Meppen	62	K2
Meran Merano	70	G4
Merauke	92	(2)F4
Mercato Saraceno	70	H7
Merced	38	B3
Mercedes, *Argentina*	52	H5
Mercedes, *Argentina*	52	K4
Mercedes, *United States*	42	B4
Mercedes, *Uruguay*	52	K5
Mercury Islands	118	E3
Mergenevo	78	K5
Mergui	90	B4
Mergui Archipelago	90	B4
Mérida, *Mexico*	46	G4
Mérida, *Spain*	68	D6
Mérida, *Venezuela*	46	K7
Meridian	42	D3
Merinha Grande	68	B5
Meriruma	50	G3
Merke	82	N9
Merkys	56	N9
Merowe	104	F4
Merredin	116	C6
Merrill	40	C1
Merriman	38	F2
Merritt	34	G6
Merseburg	60	H5
Mers el Kébir	68	K9
Mersey	64	J8
Mersin = İcel	76	S8
Mērsrags	56	M8
Merthyr Tydfil	64	J10
Méru	62	E5
Meru	110	F3
Merzifon	98	F3
Merzig	62	J5
Mesa	44	D2
Mesa de Yambi	50	C3
Mesagne	72	M8
Meschede	62	L3
Mesõaria Plain	100	A1
Mesolongi	76	D6
Mesopotamia	98	K6
Messaad	106	F2
Messina, *Italy*	72	K10
Messina, *South Africa*	112	D4
Messini	76	E7
Messiniakos Kolpos	76	D8
Mestre	70	H5
Meta	50	C2
Metairie	42	C4
Metaline Falls	38	C1
Metán	52	J4
Metangula	112	E2
Metema	104	G5
Meteor Depth	48	J9
Metković	74	E6
Metlika	70	L5
Metsovo	76	D5
Mettet	62	G4
Mettlach	62	J5
Metz	62	J5
Metzingen	70	E2
Meulaboh	90	B6
Meuse	62	G4
Mexia	42	B3
Mexicali	44	C2
Mexican Hat	44	E1
Mexico	40	B3
Mexico	46	D4
Meymaneh	96	H2
Mezdra	74	L6
Mezen'	78	H1
Mezenskaya Guba	78	H1
Mezhdurechensk	82	R7
Mezőberény	74	J3
Mezőkövesd	74	H2
Mezőtúr	74	H2
Mfuwe	112	E2
Miajadas	68	E5
Miami, *Fla., United States*	42	E4
Miami, *Okla., United States*	42	C2
Miandowāb	98	M5
Miandrivazo	112	H3
Mīāneh	98	M5
Miangyang	86	E4
Mianning	86	C5
Mianwali	94	B2
Mianyang	86	C4
Miaodao Qundao	86	G3
Miao'ergou	82	Q8
Miass	78	M4
Miastko	58	G4
Michalovce	58	L9
Michigan	40	C1
Michipicoten Island	40	C1
Michurinsk	78	H4
Micronesia	114	F4
Mid-Atlantic Ridge	48	G1
Middelburg, *Netherlands*	62	F3
Middelburg, *South Africa*	112	D6
Middelfart	60	E1
Middelkerke	62	E3
Middle America Trench	32	L8
Middle Andaman	90	A4
Middlebury	40	F2
Middle Lake	38	C2
Middlesboro	40	D3
Middlesbrough	64	L7
Middletown, *N.Y., United States*	40	F2
Middletown, *Oh., United States*	40	D3
Midland, *Canada*	40	E2
Midland, *Mich., United States*	40	D2
Midland, *Tex., United States*	44	F2
Midway Islands	114	J3
Midwest City	42	B2
Midzor	74	K6
Miechów	58	K7
Mielan	66	F10
Mielec	58	L7
Miembwe	110	F5
Mien	58	D1
Miercurea-Ciuc	74	N3
Mieres	68	E1
Miesbach	70	G3
Mī'ēso	110	G2
Miging	94	F3
Miguel Auza	44	F4
Mikhaylovka	78	H4
Mikhaylovskiy	82	P7
Mikino	84	U4
Mikkeli	56	P6
Mikulov	70	M2
Mikun'	78	K2
Mikuni-sammyaku	88	K5
Mikura-jima	88	K7
Mila	106	G1
Milaca	40	B1
Miladhunmadulu Atoll	94	B7
Milan = Milano, *Italy*	70	E5
Milan, *United States*	42	D2
Milano	70	E5
Milas	76	K7
Milazzo	72	K10
Miles	116	K5
Miles City	38	E1
Milford, *Del., United States*	40	E3
Milford, *Ut., United States*	38	D3
Milford Haven	64	G10
Milford Sound	118	A7
Miliana	68	N8
Milicz	58	G6
Milk	34	J7
Mil'kovo	84	T6
Millau	66	J9
Millbank	38	G1
Milledgeville	42	E3
Miller	38	G2
Millerovo	78	H5
Millington	40	C3
Millinocket	40	G1
Miloro	110	E5
Milos	76	G8
Milton, *New Zealand*	118	B8
Milton, *United States*	42	D3
Milton Keynes	62	B2
Miluo	86	E5
Milwaukee	40	C2
Mily	82	L8
Mimizan-Plage	66	D9
Mīnāb	101	G3
Mina Jebel Ali	101	F4
Minas	52	K5
Mīnā' Sa'ūd	101	C2
Minas Gerais	50	H7
Minas Novas	50	J7
Minatitián	46	F5
Minbu	90	A2
Minchinmávida	52	G7
Mincivan	98	M4
Mindanao	90	G5
Mindelheim	70	F2
Mindelo	108	(1)B1
Minden	62	L2
Mindoro	90	G4
Mindoro Strait	90	G4
Minehead	64	J10
Mineola	42	B3
Mineral'nyye Vody	98	K1
Minerva Reefs	114	J8
Minfeng	82	Q10
Minga	110	D6
Mingäçevir	98	M3
Mingäçevir Su Anbarı	98	M3
Mingulay	64	D5
Minicoy	94	B7
Minilya Roadhouse	116	B4
Minna	108	F3
Minneapolis	40	B2
Minnesota	40	A1
Minnesota	40	A2
Miño	68	C2
Minot	38	F1
Minsk	78	E4
Minturn	38	E3
Minusinsk	82	S7
Min Xian	86	C4
Min'yar	78	L3
Miquelon	40	E1
Miraflores	50	C3
Miramas	66	K10
Mirambeau	66	E8
Miranda	50	F8
Miranda de Ebro	68	H2
Miranda do Douro	68	D3
Mirandela	68	C3
Mirbāt	96	F6
Mīrjāveh	96	H4
Mirnyy	84	J4
Mirow	60	H3
Mirpur Khas	94	A3
Mirtoö Pelagos	76	F7
Mirzapur	94	D3
Miskolc	74	H1
Misoöl	92	(2)D3
Mişrātah	104	C1
Missinaibi	34	Q6
Missinipe	34	L5
Mission	38	F2
Mississippi	42	C3
Mississippi	42	D2
Mississippi River Delta	42	D4
Missoula	38	D1
Missouri	38	F1
Missouri	40	B3
Missouri City	42	B4
Mistassibi	34	S7
Mistelbach	70	M2
Mitchell	38	G2
Mithankot	96	K4
Mithaylov	78	G4
Mithymna	76	J5
Mito	88	L5
Mits'iwa	96	C6
Mittellandkanal	62	K2
Mittersill	70	H3
Mittweida	60	H6
Mitú	50	C3
Mitzic	108	G4
Miyake-jima	88	K6
Miyako	88	L4
Miyakonojō	88	F8
Miyazaki	88	F8
Miyoshi	88	G6
Mīzan Teferī	110	F2
Mizdah	106	H2
Mizen Head	64	B10
Mizhhir"ya	74	L1
Mizil	74	P4
Mizpe Ramon	100	B6
Mjölby	56	H7
Mjøsa	56	F6
Mkuze	112	E5
Mladá Boleslav	58	D7
Mladenovac	74	H5
Mława	58	K4
Mljet	74	E7
Mmabatho	112	D5
Moa	116	H2
Moanda	108	G5
Moapa	38	D3
Moba	110	D5
Mobaye	110	C3
Mobayi-Mbongo	110	C3
Moberly	40	B3
Mobile	42	D3
Moçambique	112	G3
Môc Châu	90	C2
Mochudi	112	D4
Mocímboa da Praia	112	G2
Mocuba	112	F3
Modane	70	B5
Módena	70	F6
Modesto	38	B3
Módica	72	J12
Mödling	70	M2
Modowi	92	(2)D3
Modriča	74	F5
Moenkopi	44	D1
Moers	62	J3
Moffat	64	J6
Moffat Peak	118	B7
Mogadishu = Muqdisho	110	H3
Mogilno	58	G5
Mogocha	84	K6
Mogochin	82	Q6
Mogok	90	B2
Mohács	74	F4
Mohammadia	68	L9
Mohe	84	L6
Mohembo	112	C3
Mohoro	110	F5
Mohyliv-Podil's'kyy	74	Q1
Moi	56	D7
Moincêr	94	D2
Moineşti	74	P3
Mo i Rana	56	H3
Moissac	66	G9
Mojave	44	C1
Mojave Desert	44	C2
Mokau	118	E4
Mokohinau Island	118	E2
Mokolo	108	G2
Mokoreta	118	B8
Mokp'o	88	D6
Mol	62	H3
Mola di Bari	72	M7
Molat	70	K6
Molde	56	D5
Moldova	74	P2
Moldova	74	R2
Moldova Nouă	74	J5
Molepolole	112	C4
Molfetta	72	L7
Molina de Aragón	68	J4
Molina de Segura	68	J6
Moline	40	B2
Möll	70	J4
Mollendo	50	C7
Molokai	44	(2)D2
Molopo	112	C5
Molsheim	70	C2
Molucca Sea	92	(2)C2
Moma	112	F3
Mombasa	110	G4
Momchilgrad	74	N8
Møn	60	H2
Monach Islands	64	E4
Monaco	70	C7
Monaco	70	C7
Monahans	44	F2
Mona Passage	46	L5
Monbetsu, *Japan*	88	M1
Monbetsu, *Japan*	88	M2
Moncalieri	70	C5
Monchegorsk	56	S3
Mönchengladbach	62	J3
Monclova	44	F3
Moncton	34	U7
Mondovi	70	C6
Mondragone	72	H7
Mondy	84	G6
Monfalcone	70	J5
Monforte	68	C5
Monforte de Lemos	68	C2
Monfredónia	72	K7
Monga	110	C3
Mongkung	90	B2
Mongo	104	C5
Mongolia	86	B2
Mongonu	108	G2
Mongora	94	B2
Mongu	112	C3
Mong Yai	90	B2
Mong Yu	90	B2

Monkoto 110 C4
Monmouth 40 B2
Mono 108 E3
Mono Lake 38 C3
Monopoli 72 M8
Monor 58 J10
Monowai 118 A7
Monreal del Campo 68 J4
Monreale 72 H10
Monroe, *La.*, *United States* 42 C3
Monroe, *Mich.*, *United States* 40 D2
Monroe, *N.C.*, *United States* 42 E3
Monroe, *Wash.*, *United States* 38 B1
Monroe City 42 C2
Monrovia 108 B3
Mons 62 F4
Monschau 62 J4
Monsélice 70 G5
Montabaur 62 K4
Montague Island 48 J9
Montalbán 68 K4
Montana 74 L6
Montana 38 E1
Montargis 66 H6
Montauban 66 G10
Montauk 40 F2
Mont aux Sources 112 D5
Montbard 66 K6
Montbéliard 70 B3
Montblanc 68 M3
Mont Blanc 70 B5
Montbrison 66 K8
Mont Cameroun 108 F4
Montceau-les-Mines 66 K7
Mont-de-Marsan 66 E10
Montdidier 62 E5
Monte Alegre 50 G4
Monte Azul 50 J7
Montebello 40 F1
Monte Bello Islands 116 B4
Montebelluna 70 H5
Monte Calvo 72 K7
Monte Cinto 72 C6
Montecristo 72 E6
Monte Etna 72 J11
Montefiascone 72 G6
Montego Bay 46 J5
Montélimar 66 K9
Monte Limbara 72 D8
Monte Lindo 52 K4
Montemorelos 42 B4
Monte Namuli 112 F3
Montenegro = Crna Gora 74 F7
Monte Perdino 68 L2
Monte Pollino 72 L9
Montepuez 112 F2
Montepulciano 72 F5
Monte Quemado 52 J4
Montereau-faut-Yonne 66 H5
Monterey 40 E3
Monterey Bay 38 B3
Montería 50 B2
Montero 50 E7
Monte Rosa 70 C5
Monterotondo 72 G6
Monterrey 44 F3
Monte Sant'Angelo 72 K7
Montes Claros 50 J7
Montesilvano Marina 72 J6
Montevarchi 70 G7
Montevideo, *United States* 40 A1
Montevideo, *Uruguay* 52 K5
Monte Viso 70 C6
Monte Vista 44 E1
Montgomery 42 D3
Monthey 70 B4
Monticello 38 E3
Montijo 68 D6
Montilla 68 F7
Mont Joli 40 G1
Mont-Laurier 40 E1
Montluçon 66 H7
Montmagny 40 F1
Montmedy 62 H5
Mont Mézenc 66 K9
Montone 70 G6
Montoro 68 F6
Mont Pelat 66 M9
Montpelier, *Id.*, *United States* 38 D2
Montpelier, *Vt.*, *United States* 40 F2
Montpellier 66 J10
Montréal 40 F1
Montreuil 62 D4
Montreux 70 B4
Montrose, *United Kingdom* 64 K5
Montrose, *United States* 38 E3
Monts Bagzane 106 G5
Mont Serkout 106 G4
Montserrat 46 M5
Monts Nimba 108 C3
Monts Otish 34 S6
Mont Tahat 106 G4
Monywa 90 A2
Monza 70 E5
Monzón 68 L3
Moonie 116 K5
Moorcroft 38 F2
Moorhead 40 A1
Moosburg 70 G1
Moose Jaw 34 K6
Moose Lake 34 M6
Moosomin 34 L6
Moosonee 34 Q6
Mopti 106 E6
Moqor 96 J3
Mór 74 F2
Mora 56 H6
Móra 68 B6
Moradabad 94 C3
Morafenobe 112 G3
Morag 58 J4
Moramanga 112 H3
Moran 38 D2
Morane 114 N8
Moratuwa 94 D7
Morava 58 G8
Moravské Budějovice 70 L1
Morawhanna 50 F2
Moray Firth 64 J4
Morbach 62 K5
Morbi 94 B4
Mordoviya 78 H4
Moreau 38 F1
Morecambe 64 K7
Moree 116 J5
Morehead 40 D3
More Laptevykh 84 L1
Morelia 46 D5
Morella 68 K4
Moresby Island 44 (1)L5
Moreton Island 116 K5
Morez 66 M7
Morgan 116 G6
Morgan City 42 C4
Morgantown 40 D3
Morges 70 B4
Mori 88 L2
Morioka 88 L4
Morkoka 84 J4
Morlaix 66 B5
Mornington Island 116 G3
Morocco 102 C2
Morogoro 110 F5
Moro Gulf 90 G5
Morombe 112 G4
Mörön 84 G7
Morondava 112 G4
Morón de la Frontera 68 E7
Moroni 112 G2
Moron Us He 94 F2
Morotai 92 (2)C2
Moroto 110 E3
Morpeth 64 L6
Morris 38 G1
Morristown 42 E2
Mors 56 E8
Morshansk 78 H4
Mortain 62 B6
Morteros 52 J5
Morvern 64 G5
Morwell 116 J7
Mosbach 60 E7
Mosby 38 D1
Moscow = Moskva 78 G3
Mosel 62 K4
Moselle 62 G6
Moses Lake 38 C1
Mosgiel 118 C7
Moshi 110 F4
Mosjøen 56 G4
Moskenesøy 56 F3
Moskva 78 G3
Mosonmagyaróvár 70 N3
Mosquero 44 F1
Moss 56 F7
Mossburn 118 B7
Mosselbaai 112 C6
Mossoró 50 K5
Most 60 J6
Mostaganem 68 L9
Mostar 74 E6
Móstoles 68 G4
Møsvatn 56 E7
Mot'a 104 G5
Motala 56 H7
Motherwell 64 J6
Motihari 94 D3
Motilla del Palancar 68 J5
Motiti Island 118 F3
Motril 68 G8
Motru 74 K5
Motu One 114 L7
Motygino 82 S6
Mouchard 70 A4
Moudjéria 106 C5
Moudros 76 H5
Mouila 108 G5
Moulins 66 J7
Moulmein 90 B3
Moultrie 42 E3
Moundou 104 C6
Mount Adam 52 J9
Mount Adams 38 B1
Mountain Grove 40 B3
Mountain Home 40 B3
Mountain Nile = Bahr el Jebel 110 E2
Mount Alba 118 B7
Mount Aloysius 116 E5
Mount Anglem 118 A8
Mount Apo 90 H5
Mount Ararat 98 L4
Mount Arrowsmith 118 C6
Mount Aspiring 118 B7
Mount Assiniboine 34 H6
Mount Augustus 116 C4
Mount Baco 90 G3
Mount Baker 38 B1
Mount Bartle Frere 116 J3
Mount Bogong 116 J7
Mount Brewster 118 B7
Mount Bruce 116 C4
Mount Cameroun 102 D5
Mount Carmel 38 D3
Mount Columbia 34 H6
Mount Cook 118 C6
Mount Cook 118 C6
Mount Donald 118 A7
Mount Douglas 116 J4
Mount Egmont 118 E4
Mount Elbert 38 E3
Mount Elgon 110 E3
Mount Essendon 116 D4
Mount Evelyn 116 F2
Mount Everest 94 E3
Mount Fairweather 34 D5
Mount Gambier 116 H7
Mount Garnet 116 J3
Mount Hermon 100 C3
Mount Hood 38 B1
Mount Hutt 118 C6
Mount Huxley 118 B7
Mount Isa 116 G4
Mount Jackson 120 (2)MM2
Mount Karisimbi 110 D4
Mount Kendall 118 D5
Mount Kenya = Kirinyaga 110 F4
Mount Kilimanjaro 110 F4
Mount Kirkpatrick 120 (2)AA1
Mount Kosciuszko 116 J7
Mount Liebig 116 F4
Mount Lloyd George 34 G5
Mount Logan 34 C4
Mount Magnet 116 C5
Mount Maunganui 118 F3
Mount McKinley 44 (1)G3
Mount Meharry 116 C4
Mount Menzies 120 (2)L2
Mount Minto 120 (2)Y2
Mount Mulanje 112 F3
Mount Murchison 118 C6
Mount Nyiru 110 F3
Mount Olympus 38 B1
Mount Ord 116 E3
Mount Ossa 116 J8
Mount Owen 118 D5
Mount Paget 52 P9
Mount Pleasant, *Ia.*, *United States* 40 B2
Mount Pleasant, *Mich.*, *United States* 40 D2
Mount Pleasant, *S.C.*, *United States* 42 F3
Mount Pleasant, *Tex.*, *United States* 42 B3
Mount Pleasant, *Ut.*, *United States* 38 D3
Mount Pulog 90 G3
Mount Rainier 38 B1
Mount Ratz 34 E5
Mount Richmond 118 D5
Mount Roberts 116 K5
Mount Robson 34 H6
Mount Roosevelt 34 F5
Mount Roraima 50 E2
Mount Ross 118 E5
Mount Shasta 38 B2
Mount Somers 118 C6
Mount Stanley 110 D3
Mount Tahat 102 D3
Mount Travers 118 D6
Mount Tuun 88 D3
Mount Usborne 52 K9
Mount Vernon, *Al.*, *United States* 42 D3
Mount Vernon, *Ill.*, *United States* 40 C3
Mount Vernon, *Oh.*, *United States* 40 D2
Mount Vernon, *Wash.*, *United States* 38 B1
Mount Victoria, *Myanmar* 90 A2
Mount Victoria, *Papua New Guinea* 114 E6
Mount Waddington 34 F6
Mount Washington 34 S8
Mount Whitney 38 C3
Mount Wilson 38 E3
Mount Woodroffe 116 F5
Mount Ziel 116 F4
Moura 68 C6
Mousa 64 L2
Moussoro 104 C5
Moutamba 108 G5
Mouth of the Shannon 64 B9
Mouths of the Amazon 48 G3
Mouths of the Danube 74 S4
Mouths of the Ganges 94 E4
Mouths of the Indus 96 J5
Mouths of the Irrawaddy 90 A3
Mouths of the Krishna 94 D5
Mouths of the Mekong 90 D5
Mouths of the Niger 108 F4
Moûtiers 70 B5
Moutong 92 (2)B2
Moyale 110 F3
Moyen Atlas 106 D2
Moyenvic 62 J6
Moyeroo 82 U4
Moyynty 82 N8
Mozambique 112 E3
Mozambique Channel 112 F4
Mozdok 98 L2
Mozhga 78 K3
Mozirje 70 K4
Mpanda 110 E5
Mpika 112 E2
Mporokoso 110 E5
Mpumalanga 112 D5
Mrągowo 58 L4
Mrkonjić-Grad 70 N6
M'Sila 106 F1
Mtsensk 78 G4
Mtwara 110 G6
Muang Khammouan 90 C3
Muang Không 90 D4
Muang Khôngxédôn 90 D3
Muang Khoua 90 C2
Muang Pakxan 90 C3
Muang Phin 90 D3
Muang Sing 90 C2
Muang Xai 90 C2
Muar 92 (1)C2
Muarabungo 92 (1)C3
Muarawahau 92 (1)F2
Mubarek 82 M10
Mubende 110 E3
Mubrani 92 (2)D3
Muck 64 F5
Muckadilla 116 J5
Muconda 110 C6
Mucur 76 S5
Mudanjiang 88 E1
Mudanya 76 L4
Muddy Gap 38 E2
Mudurnu 76 P4
Mufulira 112 D2
Mughshin 96 F6
Muğla 76 L7
Mugodzhary 78 L5
Mühldorf 70 H2
Mühlhausen 60 F5
Muhos 56 N4
Muhu 56 M7
Muhulu 110 D4
Mukacheve 58 M9
Mukdahan 90 C3
Mukry 96 J2
Mukuku 112 D2
Mulaku Atoll 94 B8
Mulde 60 H5
Muleshoe 44 F2
Mulgrave Island 116 H2
Mulhacén 68 G7
Mülheim 62 J3
Mulhouse 70 C3
Muling 88 G1
Mull 64 G5

Mullaittivu 94 D7
Mullewa 116 C5
Müllheim 70 C3
Mullingar 64 E8
Mulobezi 112 D3
Multan 96 K3
Mumbai 94 B5
Mumbwa 112 D2
Muna 92 (2)B4
Münchberg 60 G6
München 70 G2
Münden 60 E5
Mundo Novo 50 J6
Mungbere 110 D3
Munger 94 E3
Munich = München 70 G2
Münster 62 K3
Munster, *France* 70 C2
Munster, *Germany* 60 F4
Munte 92 (2)A2
Muojärvi 56 Q4
Muonio 56 M3
Muqdisho 110 H3
Mur 70 L4
Muradiye 98 K4
Murang'a 110 F4
Murashi 78 J3
Murat 98 K4
Muratlı 76 K3
Murchison 118 D5
Murcia 68 J7
Murdo 38 F2
Mureş 74 J3
Muret 66 G10
Murfreesboro, *N.C., United States* 42 F2
Murfreesboro, *Tenn., United States* 42 D2
Murghob 96 K2
Muriaé 50 J8
Müritz 60 H3
Muriwai 118 F4
Murmansk 56 S2
Murnau 70 G3
Murom 78 H3
Muroran 88 L2
Muros 68 A2
Muroto 88 H7
Murphy 42 E2
Murray 116 H6
Murray 40 C3
Murray Bridge 116 G7
Murray River Basin 116 H6
Murska Sobota 70 M4
Murter 70 L7
Murtosa 68 B4
Murud 94 B5
Murupara 118 F4
Mururoa 114 M8
Murwara 94 D4
Murzūq 106 H3
Mürzzuschlag 70 L3
Muş 98 J4
Mūša 58 N1
Musala 76 F2
Musandam Peninsula 101 G3
Musay'īd 101 D4
Muscat = Masqaţ 101 H5
Musgrave Ranges 116 E5
Mushin 108 E3
Muskegon 40 C2
Muskogee 42 B2
Musoma 110 E4
Mustafakemalpaşa 76 L4
Mut, *Egypt* 104 E2
Mut, *Turkey* 76 R8
Mutare 112 E3
Mutarnee 116 J3
Mutnyy Materik 78 L1
Mutoray 82 U5
Mutsamudu 112 G2
Mutsu 88 L3
Mutsu-wan 88 L3
Muttaburra 116 H4
Muyezerskiy 56 R5
Muyinga 110 E4
Muynak 82 K9
Muzaffarnagar 94 C3
Muzaffarpur 94 E3
Muzillac 66 C6
Múzquiz 44 F3
Muztagata 82 N10
Mwali 112 G2
Mwanza 110 E4
Mweka 110 C4
Mwenda 110 D6
Mwene-Ditu 110 C5
Mwenezi 112 E4
Mwenezi 112 E4
Mwinilunga 112 C2
Myanmar 90 B2
Myingyan 90 B2
Myitkyina 90 B1
Myjava 70 N2
Myjava 70 N2
Mykolayiv 58 N8
Mykonos 76 H7
Mymensingh 94 F4
Mynbulak 82 L9
Myndagayy 84 N4
Myōjin 86 K4
Myonggan 88 E3
Myrdalsjökull 56 (1)D3
Myrina 76 H5
Myrtle Beach 42 F3
Mys Alevina 84 S5
Mys Aniva 86 L1
Mys Buorkhaya 84 N2
Mys Dezhneva 84 Z3
Mys Elizavety 84 Q6
Mys Enkan 84 P5
Mys Govena 84 V5
Mys Kanin Nos 78 H1
Mys Kekurskij 56 S2
Mys Kril'on 86 L1
Myślenice 58 J8
Myślibórz 58 D5
Mys Lopatka, *Russia* 84 T6
Mys Lopatka, *Russia* 84 S2
Mys Navarin 84 X4
Mys Olyutorskiy 84 W5
Mysore 94 C6
Mys Peschanyy 82 J9
Mys Povorotnyy 88 G2
Mys Prubiynyy 78 F5
Mys Shelagskiy 84 V2
Mys Sivuchiy 84 U5
Mys Terpeniya 84 Q7
Mys Tolstoy 84 T5
Mys Yuzhnyy 84 T5
Mys Zhelaniya 82 M2
Myszksw 58 J7
My Tho 90 D4
Mytilini 76 J5
Mývatn 56 (1)E2
Mže 60 H7
Mzimba 112 E2
Mzuzu 112 E2

N

Naalehu 44 (2)F4
Naas 64 F8
Nabas 90 G4
Naberezhnyye Chelny 78 K3
Nabeul 72 E12
Nabīd 101 G2
Nabire 92 (2)E3
Nablus 100 C4
Nacala 112 G2
Náchod 58 F7
Nacogdoches 42 C3
Nadiad 94 B4
Nador 106 E2
Nadvirna 74 M1
Nadym 78 P1
Nadym 78 P2
Næstved 60 G1
Nafpaktos 76 D6
Nafplio 76 E7
Nagano 88 K5
Nagaoka 88 K5
Nagaon 94 F3
Nagarzê 94 F3
Nagasaki 88 E7
Nagaur 94 B3
Nagercoil 94 C7
Nago 86 H5
Nagold 60 D8
Nagorsk 78 K3
Nagoya 88 J6
Nagpur 94 C4
Nagqu 94 F2
Nagyatád 70 N4
Nagykállš 74 J2
Nagykanizsa 70 N4
Nagykáta 58 J10
Nagykörös 74 G2
Naha 86 H5
Nahanni 34 G4
Nahanni Butte 34 G4
Nahr en Nile = Nile 104 F2
Naiman Qi 86 G2
Nain 34 U5
Nairn 64 J4
Nairobi 110 F4
Naivasha 110 F4
Naizishan 88 D2
Najafābād 96 F3
Nájera 68 H2
Najibabad 94 C3
Najin 88 F2
Najrān 104 H4
Nakamura 88 G7
Nakatsu 88 F7
Nakhl 100 A7
Nakhodka, *Russia* 82 P4
Nakhodka, *Russia* 88 G2
Nakhon Ratchasima 90 C3
Nakhon Sawan 90 B3
Nakhon Si Thammarat 90 B5
Nakina 34 P6
Naknek 44 (1)F4
Nakonde 110 E5
Nakskov 60 G2
Nakten 56 H5
Nakuru 110 F4
Nal'chik 98 K2
Nallihan 76 P4
Nālūt 106 H2
Namagan 82 N9
Namakzar-e Shadad 101 G1
Namanga 110 F4
Namapa 112 F2
Namasagali 110 E3
Nam Can 90 C5
Nam Co 94 F2
Namdalen 56 G4
Nam Dinh 90 D2
Namib Desert 112 A4
Namibe 112 A3
Namibia 112 B4
Namlea 92 (2)C3
Namo 92 (2)A3
Nampa 38 C2
Nam Ping 90 B3
Namp'o 88 C4
Nampula 112 F3
Namsos 56 F4
Namtsy 84 M4
Namur 62 G4
Namwala 112 D3
Namwŏn 88 D6
Nan 90 C3
Nanaimo 38 B1
Nanao 88 J5
Nanchang 86 F5
Nanchong 86 D4
Nancy 70 B2
Nanda Devi 94 C2
Nānded 94 C5
Nandurbar 94 B4
Nangalala 116 G2
Nangapinoh 92 (1)E3
Nangatayap 92 (1)E3
Nangis 66 J5
Nangong 86 F3
Nang Xian 94 F3
Nanjing 86 F4
Nankoku 88 G7
Nannine 116 C5
Nanning 90 D2
Nanortalik 34 X4
Nanpan 90 D2
Nanping 86 F5
Nansei-shotō 86 H5
Nantes 66 D6
Nanton 36 D1
Nantong 86 G4
Nanumea 114 H6
Nanuque 50 J7
Nanyang 86 E4
Napa 38 B3
Napalkovo 82 N3
Napamute 44 (1)F3
Napas 84 C4
Napasoq 34 W3
Napier 118 F4
Naples = Napoli 72 J8
Naples 42 E4
Napo 50 C4
Napoli 72 J8
Naqb Ashtar 100 C6
Nara, *Japan* 88 H6
Nara, *Mali* 106 D5
Narathiwat 90 C5
Narbonne 66 H10
Nardò 72 N8
Nares Strait 32 J2
Narev 58 N5
Narew 58 L5
Narmada 94 C4
Narnaul 94 C3
Narni 72 G6
Narok 110 F4
Närpes 56 L5
Narrabi 116 J6
Narrandera 116 J6
Narsimhapur 94 C4
Nart 86 F2
Narva 56 P7
Narva 56 Q7
Narva Bay 56 P7
Narvik 56 J2
Nar'yan Mar 78 K1
Naryn 84 F6
Năsăud 74 M2
Nashua 40 F2
Nashville 42 D2
Našice 74 F4
Nasik 94 B4
Nasir 110 E2
Nassarawa 108 F3
Nassau 42 F4
Nässjö 56 H8
Nastapoka Islands 34 R5
Nasugbu 90 G4
Naswá 101 G5
Nata 112 D4
Natal 50 K5
Natara 84 L3
Natashquan 34 U6
Natchez 42 C3
Natchitoches 42 C3
National Park 118 E4
Natitingou 108 E2
Natuna Besar 92 (1)D2
Naujoji Akmenė 58 M1
Naumburg 60 G5
Na'ūr 100 C5
Nauru 114 G6
Nauta 50 C4
Nautonwa 94 D3
Navahermosa 68 F5
Navahrudak 56 N10
Navajo Reservoir 38 E3
Navalmoral de la Mata 68 E5
Navalvillar de Pela 68 E5
Navapolatsk 78 E3
Navlya 78 F4
Navoi 82 M9
Navojoa 36 E6
Navrongo 108 D2
Navsari 94 B4
Nawabshah 96 J4
Nāwah 96 J3
Naxçıvan 98 L4
Naxos 76 H7
Naxos 76 H7
Nayakhan 84 T4
Nāy Band, *Iran* 96 G3
Nāy Band, *Iran* 101 E3
Nayoro 88 M1
Nazaré 68 A5
Nazareth 100 C4
Nazarovo 82 S6
Nazca 50 C6
Nazca Ridge 52 E3
Naze 86 H5
Nazilli 76 L7
Nazino 82 P6
Nazran' 98 L2
Nazrēt 110 F2
Nazwá 96 G5
Nazyvayevsk 78 P3
Ndélé 110 C2
Ndjamena 104 B5
Ndjolé 108 G5
Ndola 112 D2
Neale Junction 116 E5
Neapoli 76 F8
Nea Zichni 76 F3
Nebbi 110 E3
Nebitdag 96 F2
Nebo 116 J4
Nebraska 38 G2
Neckar 60 D7
Neckar 60 D8
Neckarsulm 60 E7
Necker Island 114 K3
Necochea 52 K6
Nédély 104 C4
Needles 44 D2
Nefedovo 78 P3
Nefta 106 G2
Neftçala 98 N4
Neftekamsk 78 K3
Neftekumsk 98 L1
Nefteyugansk 78 P2
Nefza 72 D12
Negage 110 B5
Negār 101 G2
Negēlē 110 F2
Negele 110 F2
Negev 100 B6
Negomane 112 F2
Negombo 94 C7
Negotin 74 K5
Negotino 76 E3
Négrine 106 G2
Negro, *Argentina* 52 J7
Negro, *Brazil* 50 E4
Negros 90 G5
Negru Vodă 74 R6
Nehbandān 96 G3
Nehe 84 M7
Nehoiu 74 P4

Neijiang 86 C5
Nei Mongol 86 E2
Neiva 50 B3
Neixiang 86 E4
Nejanilini Lake 34 M5
Nek'emtē 110 F2
Nelidovo 78 F3
Neligh 38 G2
Nellore 94 C6
Nel'ma 84 P7
Nelson 34 N5
Nelson, *Canada* 38 C1
Nelson, *New Zealand* 118 D5
Nelspruit 112 E5
Nēma 106 D5
Nēman 56 N10
Neman 58 M2
Nemours 66 H5
Nemperola 92 (2)B5
Nemunas 58 P3
Nemuro 88 N2
Nen 84 L7
Nenagh 64 D9
Nenana 44 (1)H3
Nene 62 B2
Nenjiang 84 M7
Neosho 40 B3
Nepa 84 H5
Nepal 94 D3
Nepalganj 94 D3
Nepean 40 E1
Nepomuk 60 J7
Ner 58 H5
Nera 72 G6
Neratovice 60 K6
Neris 58 P2
Nerja 68 G8
Neryungri 84 L5
Nesebŭr 74 Q7
Ness City 42 B2
Netanya 100 B4
Netherlands 62 H2
Netherlands Antilles 46 L6
Nettilling Lake 34 S3
Neubrandenburg 60 J3
Neuburg 60 G8
Neuchâtel 70 B3
Neuenhagen 60 J4
Neufchâteau, *Belgium* 62 H5
Neufchâteau, *France* 66 L5
Neufchâtel-en-Bray 62 D5
Neuhof 60 E6
Neumarkt 60 G7
Neumünster 60 F2
Neunkirchen, *Austria* 70 M3
Neunkirchen, *Germany* 60 C7
Neuquén 52 H6
Neuruppin 60 H4
Neusiedler 58 F10
Neusiedler See 70 M3
Neuss 62 J3
Neustadt, *Germany* 62 L5
Neustadt, *Germany* 60 F2
Neustadt, *Germany* 60 F7
Neustadt, *Germany* 60 G6
Neustadt, *Germany* 60 G8
Neustadt, *Germany* 60 H7
Neustrelitz 60 J3
Neu-Ulm 60 F8
Neuwerk 60 D3
Neuwied 62 K4
Nevada 38 C3
Nevada 40 B3
Nevado Auzangate 50 C6
Nevado de Colima 46 D5
Nevado de Cumbal 50 B3
Nevado de Huascaran 50 B5
Nevado de Illampu 50 D7
Nevado Sajama 50 D7
Nevados de Cachi 52 H4
Never 84 L6
Nevers 66 J7
Nevesinje 74 F6
Nevėžis 56 M9
Nevinnomyssk 98 J1
Nevşehir 76 S6
Newala 110 F6
New Albany, *Ind.*, *United States* 40 C3
New Albany, *Miss.*, *United States* 42 D3
New Amsterdam 50 F2
Newark, *N.J.*, *United States* 40 F2
Newark, *Oh.*, *United States* 40 D3
Newark-on-Trent 62 B1
New Bedford 40 F2
Newberg 38 B1
New Bern 42 F2
Newberry 42 E3
New Braunfels 42 B4
New Britain 114 F6
New Brunswick 34 T7
Newburgh 40 F2
Newbury 62 A3
New Bussa 108 E3
Newcastle, *Australia* 116 K6
Newcastle, *United States* 38 F2
Newcastle-under-Lyme 64 K8
Newcastle-upon-Tyne 64 L6
Newcastle Waters 116 F3
New Delhi 94 C3
New England 38 F1
Newe Zohars 100 C5
Newfoundland 34 V5
Newfoundland 34 V7
New Georgia Island 114 F6
New Glasgow 34 U7
New Guinea 80 S10
New Hampshire 40 F2
New Hampton 40 B2
New Hanover 114 F6
Newhaven 62 C4
New Haven 40 F2
New Iberia 42 C3
New Ireland 114 F6
New Jersey 40 F2
New Liskeard 40 E1
New London 40 F2
Newman 116 C4
Newmarket 62 C2
New Meadows 38 C2
New Mexico 44 E2
Newnan 42 E3
New Orleans 42 D4
New Plymouth 118 E4
Newport, *Eng.*, *United Kingdom* 62 A4
Newport, *Wales*, *United Kingdom* 64 K10
Newport, *Ark.*, *United States* 42 C2
Newport, *Oreg.*, *United States* 38 B2
Newport, *R.I.*, *United States* 40 F2
Newport, *Vt.*, *United States* 40 F2
Newport, *Wash.*, *United States* 38 C1
New Providence 42 F5
Newquay 64 G11
Newry 64 F7
New Siberia Islands = Novosibirskiye Ostrova 84 P1
New Smyrna Beach 42 E4
New South Wales 116 H6
Newton, *Ia.*, *United States* 40 B2
Newton, *Kans.*, *United States* 42 B2
Newtownards 64 G7
New Ulm 40 B2
New York 40 E2
New York 40 F2
New Zealand 118 B5
Neya 78 H3
Neyrīz 101 F2
Neyshābūr 96 G2
Ngabang 92 (1)D2
Ngalu 92 (2)B5
Ngaoundéré 108 G3
Ngara 110 E4
Ngawihi 118 E5
Ngo 108 H5
Ngoura 104 C5
Ngozi 110 D4
Nguigmi 108 G2
Nguru 108 G2
Nha Trang 90 D4
Nhulunbuy 116 G2
Niafounké 106 E5
Niagara Falls 40 E2
Niamey 108 E2
Niangara 110 D3
Nia-Nia 110 D3
Nias 92 (1)B2
Nicaragua 46 G6
Nicastro 72 L10
Nice 70 C7
Nicholls Town 42 F4
Nicobar Islands 90 A5
Nicosia = Lefkosia 76 R9
Nida 58 K7
Nidym 84 F4
Nidzica 58 K4
Niebüll 60 D2
Niedere Tauern 70 J3
Niefang 108 G4
Nienburg 60 E4
Niesky 60 K5
Nieuw Amsterdam 50 F2
Nieuw Nickerie 50 F2
Nieuwpoort 62 E3
Niğde 76 S7
Niger 106 G5
Niger 108 E2
Nigeria 108 F2
Nigoring Hu 86 B3
Niigata 88 K5
Niihau 44 (2)A2
Nii-jima 88 K6
Nijar 68 H8
Nijmegen 62 H3
Nikolayevsk-na-Amure 84 Q6
Nikol'sk 78 J3
Nikopol' 78 F5
Nik Pey 98 N5
Nikšić 74 F7
Nilande Atoll 94 B8
Nile 104 F3
Niles 40 C2
Nimach 94 B4
Nîmes 66 K10
Nimule 110 E3
Nin 70 L6
Nine Degree Channel 94 B7
9 de Julio 52 J6
Ning'an 88 E1
Ningbo 86 G5
Ningde 86 F5
Ninghai 86 G5
Ninh Hoa 90 D4
Ninohoe 88 L3
Niobrara 38 F2
Niobrara 38 G2
Nioro 106 D5
Nioro du Sahel 108 C1
Niort 66 E7
Nipigon 40 C1
Niquelândia 50 H6
Nirmal 94 C5
Niš 74 J6
Nisa 68 C5
Niscemi 72 J11
Nishinoomote 88 F8
Nisyros 76 K8
Niterói 52 N3
Nitra 58 H9
Nitra 58 H9
Nitsa 78 M3
Niue 114 K7
Nivelles 62 G4
Nizamabad 94 C5
Nizhnekamsk 78 K3
Nizhnekamskoye Vodokhranilishche 78 K3
Nizhneudinsk 84 F5
Nizhnevartovsk 78 Q2
Nizhneyansk 84 P2
Nizhniy Lomov 78 H4
Nizhniy Novgorod 78 H3
Nizhniy Tagil 78 M3
Nizhnyaya Tunguska 84 H4
Nizhyn 78 F4
Nizip 98 G5
Nizza Monferrato 70 D6
Njazidja 112 G2
Njombe 110 E5
Njombe 110 E5
Nkambe 108 G3
Nkhotakota 112 E2
Nkongsamba 108 F4
Noatak 44 (1)F2
Nobeoka 88 F7
Noci 72 M8
Nogales, *Mexico* 44 D2
Nogales, *United States* 44 D2
Nogat 58 J3
Nogent-le-Rotrou 66 F5
Noginsk 78 G3
Noginskiy 82 S5
Nogliki 84 Q6
Noheji 88 L3
Noia 68 B2
Noire 90 C2
Nojima-zaki 88 K6
Nok Kundi 96 H4
Nola, *Central African Republic* 110 B3
Nola, *Italy* 72 J8
Nolinsk 78 J3
Noma-misaki 88 F8
Nome 44 (1)D3
Nomoi Islands 114 F5
Nomo-saki 88 E7
Nong'an 88 C1
Nong Khai 90 C3
Noord-Beveland 62 F3
Noord-Oost-Polder 62 H2
Noordwijk aan Zee 62 G2
Norak 96 J2
Noranda 40 E1
Nordaustlandet 120 (1)L1
Norden 60 C3
Nordenham 60 D3
Norderney 60 C3
Norderstedt 60 F3
Nordfriesische Inseln 60 D2
Nordhausen 60 F5
Nordhorn 62 K2
Nordkapp 56 N1
Nordkinn 56 P1
Nordkinnhalvøya 56 P1
Nordkvaløya 56 J1
Nordli 56 G4
Nördlingen 60 F8
Nord-Ostsee-Kanal 60 E2
Nordstrand 60 D2
Nordvik 82 W3
Nore 64 E9
Norfolk, *Nebr.*, *United States* 38 G2
Norfolk, *Va.*, *United States* 40 E3
Norfolk Island 114 G8
Noril'sk 82 R4
Norman 42 B2
Normanton 116 H3
Norman Wells 34 F3
Nørre Åby 60 E1
Nørre Alslev 60 G2
Norristown 40 E2
Norrköping 56 J7
Norrtälje 56 K7
Norseman 116 D6
Norsk 84 N6
Northallerton 64 L7
Northam 116 C6
Northampton 62 B2
North Andaman 90 A4
North Battleford 34 K6
North Bay 40 E1
North Cape 118 D2
North Carolina 42 F2
North Channel 64 G6
North Charleston 42 F3
North Dakota 38 F1
Northeast Providence Channel 42 F4
Northeim 60 F5
Northern Cape 112 C5
Northern Ireland 64 E7
Northern Mariana Islands 114 E4
Northern Province 112 D4
Northern Territory 116 F4
North Foreland 62 D3
North Horr 110 F3
North Iberia 46 F2
North Island 118 D3
North Korea 88 C4
North Little Rock 42 C3
North Platte 36 F3
North Platte 38 F2
North Ronaldsay 64 K2
North Sea 64 N4
North Stradbroke Island 116 K5
North Taranaki Bight 118 D4
North Uist 64 E4
Northumberland Strait 34 U7
North Vancouver 38 B1
North West 112 C5
North West Basin 116 C4
North West Cape 116 B4
North West Christmas Island Ridge 114 K4
North West Highlands 64 G4
Northwest Territories 34 G4
Norton 42 B2
Norton Sound 44 (1)E3
Norway 56 F5
Norwegian Sea 56 B4
Norwich, *United Kingdom* 62 D2
Norwich, *United States* 40 F2
Nos 78 H1
Nos Emine 74 Q7
Nosevaya 78 K1
Noshiro 88 K3
Nos Kaliakra 74 R6
Noşratābād 96 G4
Nosy Barren 112 G3
Nosy Bé 112 H2
Nosy Boraha 112 J3
Nosy Mitsio 112 H2
Nosy Radama 112 H2
Nosy-Varika 112 H4
Notec 58 G4
Notia Pindos 76 D5
Notios Evvoïkos Kolpos 76 F6
Notre Dame Bay 34 V7
Notsé 108 E3
Nottingham 62 A2
Nottingham Island 34 R4
Nouâdhibou 106 B4
Nouakchott 106 B5

Nouméa 14 G8
Nouvelle Calédonie 114 G8
Nova Gorica 70 J5
Nova Gradiška 74 E4
Nova Iguaçu 52 N3
Nova Mambone 112 F4
Nova Pazova 74 H5
Novara 70 D5
Nova Scotia 34 T8
Novaya Igirma 84 G5
Novaya Karymkary 78 N2
Novaya Kasanka 78 J5
Novaya Lyalya 78 M3
Novaya Zemlya 82 J3
Nova Zagora 74 P7
Novelda 68 K6
Nové Město 58 F8
Nové Mesto 58 G9
Nové Zámky 58 H10
Novgorod 78 F3
Novi Bečej 74 H4
Novi Iskŭr 74 L7
Novi Ligure 70 D6
Novi Marof 70 M4
Novi Pazar, *Bulgaria* 74 Q6
Novi Pazar, *Yugoslavia* 74 H6
Novi Sad 74 G4
Novi Vinodolski 70 K5
Novoaleksandrovsk 78 H5
Novoalekseyevka 78 L4
Novoanninsky 78 H4
Novocheboksarsk 78 J3
Novocherkassk 78 H5
Novodvinsk 78 H2
Novo Hamburgo 52 L4
Novohrad-Volyns'kyy 78 E4
Novokazalinsk 78 M5
Novokutznetsk 82 R7
Novokuybyshevsk 78 J4
Novo Mesto 70 L5
Novomikhaylovskiy 98 H1
Novomoskovsk 78 G4
Novonazimovo 84 E5
Novorossiysk 98 G1
Novorybnoye 84 H2
Novoselivka 74 S2
Novosergiyevka 78 K4
Novosibirsk 82 Q6
Novosibirskiye Ostrova 84 P1
Novosil' 78 G4
Novotroitsk 78 L4
Novouzensk 78 J4
Novozybkov 78 F4
Nový Bor 60 K6
Nový Jičín 58 H8
Novyy Port 82 N4
Novyy Uoyan 84 J5
Novyy Urengoy 82 P4
Novyy Uzen' 82 J9
Nowa Ruda 58 F7
Nowata 42 B2
Nowogard 58 E4
Nowo Warpno 60 K3
Nowra 116 K6
Now Shahr 96 F2
Nowy Dwór Mazowiecki 58 K5
Nowy Sącz 58 K8
Nowy Targ 58 K8
Nowy Tomyśl 58 F5
Noyabr'sk 82 P5
Noyon 62 E5
Nsombo 112 D2
Ntem 108 G4
Ntwetwe Pan 112 C4
Nu 94 G2
Nuasjärvi 56 Q4
Nubian Desert 104 F3
Nudo Coropuna 50 C7
Nueltin Lake 34 M4
Nueva Rosita 44 F3
Nueva San Salvador 46 G6
Nuevo Casas Grandes 44 E2
Nuevo Laredo 44 G3
Nugget Point 118 B8
Nuhaka 118 F4
Nuku'alofa 114 J8
Nuku Hiva 114 M6
Nukumanu Islands 114 F6
Nukunonu 114 J6
Nukus 82 K9
Nullarbor Plain 116 E6
Numan 108 G3
Numazu 88 K6
Numbulwar 116 G2
Numfor 92 (2)E3
Numto 78 P2
Nunarsuit 34 X4
Nunavut 34 M3
Nuneaton 62 A2
Nunivak Island 44 (1)D3
Nunligram 84 Y3
Núoro 72 D8
Nuquí 50 B2
Nura 78 P4
Nurābād 101 D1
Nurata 96 J1
Nurmes 56 Q5
Nürnberg 60 G7
Nürtingen 70 E2
Nurzec 58 M5
Nushki 96 J4
Nutak 34 U5
Nuuk 34 W4
Nuussuaq 34 W2
Nyagan' 78 N2
Nyahururu 110 F3
Nyala 104 D5
Nyalam 94 E3
Nyamlell 110 D2
Nyamtumbo 110 F6
Nyandoma 78 H2
Nyantakara 110 E4
Nyborg 60 F1
Nybro 56 H8
Nyda 82 N4
Nyima 94 E2
Nyingchi 94 F3
Nyírbátor 74 K2
Nyíregyháza 58 L10
Nykarleby 56 M5
Nykøbing 60 G2
Nyköping 56 J7
Nylstroom 112 D4
Nymburk 58 E7
Nynäshamn 56 J7
Nyngan 116 J6
Nyon 70 B4
Nysa 58 D6
Nysa 58 G7
Nyukhcha 78 J2
Nyunzu 110 D5
Nyurba 84 K4
Nyuya 84 K4
Nzega 110 E4
Nzérékoré 108 C3
N'zeto 110 A5
Nzwami 112 G2

O

Oaho 44 (2)D2
Oahu 114 L3
Oakdale 42 C3
Oakham 62 B2
Oak Lake 38 F1
Oakland 38 B3
Oak Lawn 40 C2
Oakley 42 A2
Oak Ridge 40 D3
Oamaru 118 C7
Oaxaca 46 E5
Ob' 78 N2
Obama 88 H6
Oban 64 G5
O Barco 68 D2
Oberdrauburg 70 H4
Oberhausen 62 J3
Oberkirch 60 D8
Oberlin 42 A2
Oberndorf 70 H3
Oberstdorf 70 F3
Oberursel 60 D6
Obervellach 58 C11
Oberwart 70 M3
Obi 92 (2)C3
Obidos 50 F4
Obigarm 96 K2
Obihiro 88 M2
Obluch'ye 84 N7
Obninsk 78 G3
Obo, *Central African Republic* 110 D2
Obo, *China* 86 C3
Oborniki 58 F5
Obouya 108 H5
Oboyan' 78 G4
Obskaya Guba 82 N4
Obuasi 108 D3
Ob'yachevo 78 J2
Ocala 42 E4
Ocaña, *Colombia* 50 C2
Ocaña, *Spain* 68 G5
Ocean City 40 E3
Ocean Falls 34 F6
Oceanside 44 C2
Och'amch'ire 98 J2
Ochsenfurt 60 E7
Oconto 40 C2
Oda 108 D3
Ōda 88 G6
Ōdate 88 L3
Odda 56 D6
Odemira 68 B7
Ödemiş 76 L6
Odense 60 F1
Oder = Odra 58 F6
Oderzo 70 H5
Odesa 78 F5
Odessa = Odesa, *Ukraine* 78 F5
Odessa, *United States* 44 F2
Odienné 108 C3
Odorheiu Secuiesc 74 N3
Odra 58 F6
Odžaci 74 G4
Oeiras 50 J5
Oelrichs 38 F2
Oelsnitz 60 H6
Oeno 114 N8
Oestev 52 H7
Ofaqim 100 B5
Offenbach 60 D6
Offenburg 70 C2
Ōgaki 88 J6
Ogasawara-shotō 80 T7
Ogbomosho 108 E3
Ogden 38 D2
Ogdensburg 34 R8
Ogilvie Mountains 34 C4
Oglio 70 E5
Ogosta 74 L6
Ogre 56 N8
Ogre 56 N8
O Grove 68 B2
Ogulin 70 L5
Ohai 118 A7
Ohio 40 C3
Ohio 40 D2
Ohre 60 J6
Ohrid 76 C3
Ohura 118 E4
Oiapoque 50 G3
Oil City 40 E2
Oise 62 E5
Ōita 88 F7
Ojinaga 44 F3
Ojos del Salado 52 H4
Oka 84 G6
Okaba 92 (2)E4
Okahandja 112 B4
Okanagan Lake 36 C2
Okano 108 G4
Okanogan 38 C1
Okara 94 B2
Okarem 96 F2
Okato 118 D4
Okavango Delta 112 C3
Okaya 88 K5
Okayama 88 G6
Okene 108 F3
Oker 60 F4
Okha, *India* 96 J5
Okha, *Russia* 84 Q6
Okhansk 78 L3
Okhotsk 84 Q5
Okhtyrka 78 F4
Okinawa 86 H5
Okinawa 86 H5
Oki-shotō 88 G5
Okitipupa 108 E3
Oklahoma 42 B2
Oklahoma City 42 B2
Okoppe 88 M1
Okoyo 108 H5
Okranger 56 E5
Oksino 78 K1
Oktinden 56 H4
Oktyabr'sk 78 L5
Oktyabr'skiy 78 K4
Okurchan 84 S5
Okushiri-tō 88 K2
Olancha 38 C3
Öland 56 J8
Olanga 56 Q3
Olathe 42 C2
Olava 60 J7
Olavarría 52 J6
Oława 58 G7
Olbia 72 D8
Olching 70 G2
Old Crow 44 (1)K2
Oldenburg, *Germany* 60 D3
Oldenburg, *Germany* 60 F2
Oldenzaal 62 J2
Oldham 64 L8
Old Head of Kinsale 64 D10
Olean 40 E2
Olekma 84 L5
Olekminsk 84 L4
Oleksandriya 78 F5
Olenegorsk 56 S2
Olenek 84 J3
Olenëk 84 L2
Olenëkskiy Zaliv 84 L2
Olhão 68 C7
Olib 70 K6
Olinda 50 L5
Oliva 68 K6
Olivet 38 G2
Olivia 40 B2
Olmos 50 B5
Olney 42 B3
Olochi 84 K6
Olonets 78 F2
Olongapo 90 G4
Oloron-Ste-Marie 66 E10
Olot 68 N2
Olovyannaya 84 K6
Olpe 62 K3
Olsztyn 58 K4
Olt 74 M4
Olten 70 C3
Olteniţa 74 P5
Oltu 98 K3
Oluan-pi 90 G2
Olvera 68 E8
Olympia 38 B1
Olympos 76 E4
Olympus 76 Q10
Olyutorskiy 84 W4
Olyutorskiy Zaliv 84 V4
Om' 82 N6
Oma 94 D2
Omae-saki 88 K6
Omagh 64 E7
Omaha 38 G2
Omak 38 C1
Omakau 118 B7
Oman 96 G5
Omapere 118 D2
Omarama 118 B7
Omaruru 112 B4
Omba 94 E2
Ombrone 72 F6
Omdurman = Umm Durman 104 F4
Omegna 70 D5
Omeo 116 J7
Om Hajer 104 G5
Omīdeyeh 101 C1
Omis 70 M7
Ommen 62 J2
Omolon 84 T3
Omoloy 84 N3
Omo Wenz 110 F2
Omsk 82 N6
Omsukchan 84 S4
Ōmū 88 M1
Omulew 58 L4
Omuta 88 F7
Onda 68 K5
Ondangwa 112 B3
Ondjiva 112 B3
Ondo 108 E3
Ondörhaan 86 E1
One and a Half Degree Channel 94 B8
Onega 78 G2
O'Neill 38 G2
Oneonta 40 F2
Oneşti 74 P3
Onezhskoye Ozero 78 F2
Ongjin 88 C5
Ongole 94 D5
Onguday 82 R7
Oni 98 K2
Onilahy 112 G4
Onitsha 108 F3
Ono 88 J6
Onon 84 J7
Onon 84 J7
Onslow Bay 46 J2
Onsong 88 E2
Ontario 34 N6
Ontinyent 68 K6
Ontonagon 40 C1
Onyx 44 C1
Oodnadatta 116 G5
Oologah Lake 42 B2
Oostburg 62 F3
Oostelijk-Flevoland 62 H2
Oostende 62 E3
Oosterhout 62 G3
Oosterschelde 62 F3
Ootsa Lake 34 F6
Opala 110 C4
Oparino 78 J3
Opava 58 G8
Opelika 42 D3
Opelousas 42 C3
Opheim 38 E1
Opochka 78 E3
Opoczno 58 K6
Opole 58 G7
Opornyy 82 J8
Opotiki 118 F4
Opp 42 D3
Opunake 118 D4

Opuwo 112 A3
Oradea 74 J2
Orahovac 74 H7
Orai 94 C3
Oran 68 K9
Orán 52 J3
Orange 112 C5
Orange, *Australia* 116 J6
Orange, *France* 66 K9
Orange, *United States* 42 C3
Orangeburg 42 E3
Orangeville 40 D2
Orango 108 A2
Oranienburg 60 J4
Orapa 112 D4
Orăştie 74 L4
Oraviţa 74 J4
Orbetello 72 F6
Orco 70 C5
Ordes 68 B1
Ordes Santa Comba 68 B1
Ordu 98 G3
Ordway 38 F3
Öreälven 56 K4
Örebro 56 H7
Oregon 38 B2
Oregon 40 A3
Orekhovo-Zuyevo 78 G3
Orel 78 G4
Orem 38 D2
Orenburg 78 L4
Orestiada 76 J3
Orford Ness 62 D2
Orhei 74 R2
Orihuela 68 K6
Orillia 40 E2
Orinoco 50 D2
Orinoco Delta = Delta del Orinoco 50 E2
Orissaare 56 M7
Oristano 72 C9
Orivesi 56 Q5
Orkla 56 F5
Orkney Islands 64 K3
Orlando 42 E4
Orléans 66 G6
Orlik 84 F6
Orly 62 E6
Ormara 96 H4
Ormoc 90 G4
Ormos Almyrou 76 G9
Ormos Mesara 76 G9
Ornans 66 M6
Ornö 56 K7
Örnsköldsvik 56 K5
Orocué 50 C3
Orofino 38 C1
Oromocto 40 G1
Orona 114 J6
Oronoque 50 F3
Oroqen Zizhiqi 84 L6
Orosei 72 D8
Orosháza 74 H3
Oroszlany 58 H10
Orotukan 84 S4
Oroville 38 B3
Orroroo 116 G6
Orsay 66 H5
Orsha 78 F4
Orsk 78 L4
Orşova 74 K5
Ørsta 56 D5
Ortaklar 76 K7
Orthez 66 E10
Ortigueira 68 C1
Ortisei 70 G4
Ortles 70 F4
Ortona 72 J6
Ortonville 40 A1
Orūmīyeh 98 L5
Oruro 50 D7
Orvieto 72 G6
Orville 66 L6
Ōsaka 88 H6
Osăm 74 M6
Osceola 40 B2
Oschatz 60 J5
Oschersleben 60 G4
Osh 82 N9
Oshamambe 88 L2
Oshawa 40 E2
Oshkosh, *Nebr., United States* 38 F2
Oshkosh, *Wis., United States* 40 C2
Oshogbo 108 E3
Osijek 74 F4
Ōsimo 70 J7
Oskaloosa 40 B2
Oskarshamn 56 J8
Oslo 56 F7
Oslofjorden 56 F7
Osmancık 98 F3
Osmaniye 98 G5
Osnabrück 62 L2
Osor 70 K6
Osorno 52 G7
Osprey Reef 116 J2
Oss 62 H3
Osseo 40 B2
Ossora 84 U5
Ostashkov 78 F3
Oste 60 E3
Osterburg 60 G4
Østerdalen 56 F6
Osterholz-Scharmbeck 60 D3
Osterode 60 F5
Östersund 56 H5
Ostfriesische Inseln 60 C3
Ostiglia 70 G5
Ostrava 58 H8
Ostróda 58 K4
Ostrołęka 58 L4
Ostrov, *Czech Republic* 60 H6
Ostrov, *Russia* 78 E3
Ostrova Medvezh'i 84 T2
Ostrov Atlasova 84 S6
Ostrova Vrangelya 32 V4
Ostrov Ayon 84 V2
Ostrov Belyy 82 N3
Ostrov Beringa 84 V6
Ostrov Bol'shevik 82 V2
Ostrov Bol'shoy Begichev 84 J2
Ostrov Bol'shoy Lyakhovskiy 84 Q2
Ostrov Bol'shoy Shantar 84 P6
Ostrov Chechen' 98 M2
Ostrov Iturup 88 P1
Ostrov Kil'din 56 T2
Ostrov Kolguyev 82 H4
Ostrov Komsomolets 82 T1
Ostrov Kotel'nyy 84 P1
Ostrov Kunashir 88 P1
Ostrov Mednyy 84 V6
Ostrov Mezhdusharskiy 82 H3
Ostrov Novaya Sibir' 84 S2
Ostrov Ogurchinskiy 96 F2
Ostrov Oktyabr'skoy 82 S2
Ostrov Onekotan 84 S7
Ostrov Paramushir 84 T6
Ostrov Rasshua 84 S7
Ostrov Shiashkotan 84 S7
Ostrov Shumshu 84 T6
Ostrov Simushir 84 S7
Ostrov Urup 84 S7
Ostrov Ushakova 82 Q1
Ostrov Vaygach 82 K3
Ostrov Vise 82 P2
Ostrov Vosrozhdeniya 82 K9
Ostrov Vrangelya 84 W2
Ostrowiec Świętokrzyski 58 L7
Ostrów Mazowiecka 58 L5
Ostrów Wielkopolski 58 G6
Ostuni 72 M8
Osum 76 C4
Ōsumi-shotō 88 F8
Osuna 68 E7
Oswego 40 E2
Oświęcim 58 J7
Otago Peninsula 118 C7
Otaki 118 E5
Otaru 88 L2
Oţelu Roşu 74 K4
Othonoi 76 B5
Oti 108 E3
Otjiwarongo 112 B4
Otočac 70 L6
Otog Qi 86 D3
Otoineppu 88 M1
Otorohanga 118 E4
Otranto 72 N8
Otrøy 56 D5
Ōtsu 88 H6
Otta 56 E6
Ottawa 40 E1
Ottawa, *Canada* 40 E1
Ottawa, *Ill., United States* 40 C2
Ottawa, *Kans., United States* 42 B2
Ottawa Islands 34 Q5
Otterøy 56 F4
Ottobrunn 70 G2
Ottumwa 40 B2
Otukpo 108 F3
Ouachita Mountains 42 C3
Ouadâne 106 C4
Ouadda 110 C2
Ouagadougou 108 D2
Oualàta 106 D5
Ouargla 106 G2
Ouarzazate 106 D2
Oudenaarde 62 F4
Oudenbosch 62 G3
Oudtshoorn 112 C6
Oued Medjerda 72 D12
Oued Meliane 72 D12
Oued Tiélat 68 K9
Oued Zem 106 D2
Ouésso 108 H4
Ouezzane 106 D2
Oujda 106 E2
Oulainen 56 N4
Oulu 56 N4
Oulujärvi 56 P4
Oulujoki 56 P4
Oulx 70 B5
Oum-Chalouba 104 D4
Oum-Hadjer 104 C5
Ounarjoki 56 N3
Our 62 J4
Ouray 38 E3
Ourense 68 C2
Ouricurí 50 J5
Ourthe 62 H4
Oustreham 62 B5
Outer Hebrides 64 D4
Outjo 112 B4
Outokumpu 56 Q5
Out Skerries 64 M1
Ouyen 116 H7
Ovacık 76 R8
Ovada 70 D6
Ovalle 52 G5
Ovareli 98 L3
Overflakkee 62 G3
Overlander Roadhouse 116 B5
Overland Park 42 C2
Overton 38 D3
Övertorneå 56 M3
Ovidiopol' 74 T3
Oviedo 68 E1
Owaka 118 B8
Owando 108 H5
Owase 88 J6
Owatonna 40 B2
Owensboro 40 C3
Owens Lake 38 C3
Owen Sound 40 D2
Owerri 108 F3
Owo 108 F3
Owosso 40 D2
Owyhee 38 C2
Owyhee 38 C2
Oxford, *New Zealand* 118 D6
Oxford, *United Kingdom* 62 A3
Oxnard 44 C2
Oyama 88 K5
Oyapock 50 G3
Oyem 108 G4
Oyen 36 D1
Oyonnax 70 A4
Özd 58 K9
Ozernovskiy 84 T6
Ozero Alakol' 82 Q8
Ozero Aralsor 78 J5
Ozero Aydarkul' 82 M9
Ozero Balkhash 82 N8
Ozero Baykal 84 H6
Ozero Beloye 78 G2
Ozero Chany 82 P7
Ozero Chernoye 78 N3
Ozero Il'men' 78 F3
Ozero-Imandra 56 R2
Ozero Inder 82 J8
Ozero Janis'jarvi 56 R5
Ozero Kamennoje 56 R4
Ozero Kanozero 56 T3
Ozero Karaginskiy 84 U5
Ozero Khanka 88 G1
Ozero Kolvitskoye 56 S3
Ozero Kovdozero 56 S3
Ozero Kulundinskoye 82 P7
Ozero Kushmurun 78 N4
Ozero Lama 84 D2
Ozero Leksozero 56 R5
Ozero Lovozero 56 T2
Ozero Morzhovets 78 H1
Ozero Njuk 56 R4
Ozero Ozhogino 84 R3
Ozero Pirenga 56 R3
Ozero Pyaozero 56 R3
Ozero Saltaim 78 P3
Ozero Sarpa 78 J5
Ozero Segozeroskoye 78 F2
Ozero Seletyteniz 82 N7
Ozero Sredneye Kuyto 56 R4
Ozero Taymyr 82 U3
Ozero Teletskoye 82 R7
Ozero Tengiz 78 N4
Ozero Topozero 56 R4
Ozero Umbozero 56 T3
Ozero Vygozero 78 G2
Ozero Yalpug 74 R4
Ozero Zaysan 82 Q8
Ozero Zhaltyr 78 K5
Ozero Zhamanakkol' 78 M5
Ozersk 58 M3
Ozhogina 84 R3
Ozhogino 84 R3
Ozieri 72 C8
Ozinki 78 J4
Ozona 44 F2
Ozurget'i 98 J3

P

Paamiut 34 X4
Paar 60 G8
Paarl 112 B6
Pabbay 64 E4
Pabianice 58 J6
Pabna 94 E4
Pacasmayo 50 B5
Pachino 72 K12
Pachuca 46 E4
Pacific Ocean 114 M3
Pacitan 92 (1)E4
Packwood 38 B1
Padalere 92 (2)B3
Padang 92 (1)C3
Padangpanjang 92 (1)C3
Padangsidempuan 92 (1)B2
Paderborn 60 D5
Pádova 70 G5
Padre Island 42 B4
Padrón 68 B2
Paducah, *Ky., United States* 40 C3
Paducah, *Tex., United States* 44 F2
Padum 94 C2
Paekdu San 88 D3
Paeroa 118 E3
Pafos 76 Q10
Pag 70 K6
Pag 70 L6
Pagadian 90 G5
Pagai Selatan 92 (1)B3
Pagai Utara 92 (1)B3
Pagalu = Annobón 108 F5
Pagan 114 E4
Pagatan 92 (1)F3
Page, *Ariz., United States* 44 D1
Page, *Okla., United States* 42 C3
Pagosa Springs 38 E3
Pagri 94 E3
Pahiatua 118 E5
Paia 44 (2)E3
Paide 56 N7
Päijänne 56 N6
Painan 92 (1)C3
Painesville 40 D2
Paisley 64 H6
Paita 50 A5
Pakaraima Mountains 50 E2
Pakch'ŏn 88 C4
Paki 108 F2
Pakistan 96 J4
Pakokku 90 A2
Pakotai 118 D2
Pakrac 70 N5
Paks 74 F3
Pakxé 90 D3
Pala 104 B6
Palafrugell 68 P3
Palagónia 72 J11
Palagruža 72 L6
Palamós 68 P3
Palana 84 U5
Palanga 58 L2
Palangkaraya 92 (1)E3
Palanpur 94 B4
Palantak 96 H4
Palatka, *Russia* 84 S4
Palatka, *United States* 42 E4
Palau 72 D7
Palau 114 D5
Palau 114 D5
Palawan 90 F5
Palazzolo Arcéide 72 J11
Palembang 92 (1)C3
Palencia 68 F2
Paleokastritsa 76 B5
Palermo 72 H10
Palestine 42 B3
Palestrina 72 G7
Paletwa 90 A2
Palghat 94 C6
Pali 94 B3
Palikir 114 F5
Palimbang 90 G5
Palk Strait 94 C7
Palma 68 N5
Palma del Rio 68 E7
Palma di Montechiaro 72 H11
Palmanova 70 J5

Palmares	**50**	K5
Palmarola	**72**	G8
Palmas	**50**	H6
Palmas	**52**	L4
Palm Bay	**42**	E4
Palmdale	**44**	C2
Palmerston	**118**	C7
Palmerston Island	**114**	K7
Palmerston North	**118**	E5
Palm Harbor	**42**	E4
Palmi	**72**	K10
Palmira	**50**	B3
Palmyra Island	**114**	K5
Palojärvi	**56**	M2
Palopo	**92**	(2)B3
Palu, *Indonesia*	**92**	(2)A3
Palu, *Turkey*	**98**	J4
Paluostrov Taymyr	**82**	R3
Palyavaam	**84**	W3
Pama	**108**	E2
Pamhagen	**70**	M3
Pamiers	**66**	G10
Pamlico Sound	**42**	F2
Pampa	**44**	F1
Pampas	**52**	J6
Pamplona, *Colombia*	**46**	K7
Pamplona, *Spain*	**68**	J2
Pana	**40**	C3
Panagyurishte	**74**	M7
Panaji	**94**	B5
Panama	**46**	H7
Panamá	**50**	B2
Panama Canal = Canal de Panamá	**46**	J7
Panama City	**42**	D3
Panara	**70**	G6
Panaria	**72**	K10
Panarik	**92**	(1)D2
Panay	**90**	G4
Pančevo	**74**	H5
Panciu	**74**	Q4
Pandharpur	**94**	C5
Panevėžys	**58**	P2
Pangin	**94**	F3
Pangkajene	**92**	(2)A3
Pangkalpinang	**92**	(1)D3
Pangnirtung	**34**	T3
Panguitch	**38**	D3
Pangutaran Group	**90**	G5
Panhandle	**44**	F1
Panipat	**94**	C3
Panjāb	**96**	J3
Panjgur	**96**	H4
Pankshin	**108**	F3
Pantanal	**50**	F7
Pantar	**92**	(2)B4
Pantelleria	**106**	H1
Páola	**72**	L9
Paoua	**110**	B2
Pápa	**74**	E2
Papa	**44**	(2)F4
Papakura	**118**	E3
Papantla	**46**	E4
Paparoa	**118**	E3
Papa Stour	**64**	L1
Papa Westray	**64**	K2
Papenburg	**60**	C3
Papey	**56**	(1)F2
Papua New Guinea	**114**	E6
Papun	**90**	B3
Pará	**50**	G5
Para	**50**	H4
Parabel'	**82**	Q6
Paracatu	**50**	H7
Paracel Islands	**90**	E3
Paraćin	**74**	J6
Pará de Minas	**50**	J7
Paragould	**42**	C2
Paragua, *Bolivia*	**50**	E6
Paragua, *Venezuela*	**50**	E2
Paraguay	**48**	F6
Paraguay	**52**	J3
Paraíba	**50**	K5
Parakou	**108**	E3
Paralimni	**100**	A1
Paramaribo	**50**	F2
Paranã	**50**	H6
Paranã	**50**	H6
Paraná	**52**	J5
Paraná	**52**	K4
Paraná	**52**	L3
Paranaguá	**52**	M4
Paranaíba	**50**	G7
Paranaíba	**50**	G7
Paranavaí	**52**	L3
Paranestio	**76**	G3
Paraparaumu	**118**	E5
Paray-le Monial	**66**	K7
Parbhani	**94**	C5
Parchim	**60**	G3
Pardo	**50**	J7
Pardubice	**58**	E7
Pareh	**98**	L4
Parepare	**92**	(2)A3
Parga	**76**	C5
Parigi	**92**	(2)B3
Parika	**50**	F2
Parintins	**50**	F4
Paris, *France*	**66**	H5
Paris, *Tenn., United States*	**42**	D2
Paris, *Tex., United States*	**42**	B3
Parkersburg	**40**	D3
Park Rapids	**40**	A1
Parla	**68**	G4
Parma	**70**	F6
Parma, *Italy*	**70**	F6
Parma, *United States*	**40**	D2
Parnaíba	**50**	J4
Parnassus	**118**	D6
Pärnu	**56**	N7
Pärnu	**56**	N7
Paros	**76**	H7
Paros	**76**	H7
Parry Bay	**34**	Q3
Parry Islands	**34**	L1
Parry Sound	**40**	D2
Parsons	**42**	B2
Parthenay	**66**	E7
Partinico	**72**	H10
Partizansk	**88**	G2
Paru	**50**	G4
Parvatipuram	**94**	D5
Paryang	**94**	D2
Pasadena, *Calif., United States*	**44**	C2
Pasadena, *Tex., United States*	**42**	B4
Paşalimani Adası	**76**	K4
Pasawng	**90**	B3
Paşcani	**74**	P2
Pasco	**38**	C1
Pasewalk	**60**	K3
Pasig	**90**	G4
Pasinler	**98**	J3
Pasłęk	**58**	J3
Pasłek	**58**	J3
Pasleka	**56**	L9
Pašman	**70**	L7
Pasni	**96**	H4
Paso de Hachado	**52**	G6
Paso de Indios	**52**	H7
Paso de la Cumbre	**52**	H5
Paso de San Francisco	**52**	H4
Paso Río Mayo	**52**	G8
Paso Robles	**44**	B1
Passau	**60**	J8
Passo Fundo	**52**	L4
Passos	**50**	H8
Pastavy	**56**	P9
Pasto	**50**	B3
Pastos Bons	**50**	J5
Pásztó	**74**	G2
Patagonia	**52**	G8
Patan, *India*	**94**	B4
Patan, *Nepal*	**94**	E3
Patea	**118**	E4
Pate Island	**110**	G4
Paterna	**68**	K5
Paterno	**72**	J11
Paterson	**40**	F2
Pathankot	**94**	C2
Pathein	**90**	A3
Pathfinder Reservoir	**38**	E2
Patia	**50**	B3
Patiala	**94**	C2
Patmos	**76**	J7
Patna	**94**	E3
Patnos	**98**	K4
Patos de Minas	**50**	H7
Patra	**76**	D6
Patraikis Kolpos	**76**	D6
Patreksfjörður	**56**	(1)B2
Pattani	**90**	C5
Pattaya	**90**	C4
Patti	**72**	J10
Paturau River	**118**	D5
Pau	**68**	K1
Pauini	**50**	D5
Pauini	**50**	D5
Paulatuk	**44**	(1)N2
Paulo Afonso	**50**	K5
Paul's Valley	**42**	B3
Päveh	**98**	M6
Pavia	**70**	E5
Pävilosta	**56**	L8
Pavlikeni	**74**	N6
Pavlodar	**82**	P7
Pavlohrad	**78**	G5
Pavlovsk	**78**	H4
Pavlovskaya	**78**	G5
Pavullo nel Frignano	**70**	F6
Paxoi	**76**	C5
Paxson	**44**	(1)H3
Payerne	**70**	B4
Payette	**38**	C2
Payne's Find	**116**	C5
Paysandu	**52**	K5
Payson	**44**	D2
Payturma	**82**	S3
Pazar	**98**	J3
Pazardzhik	**74**	M7
Pazin	**70**	J5
Peace	**34**	H5
Peace River	**34**	H5
Peach Springs	**44**	D1
Pearsall	**42**	B4
Pebane	**112**	F3
Pebas	**50**	C5
Peć	**74**	H7
Pecan Island	**42**	C4
Pechora	**78**	K1
Pechora	**78**	L1
Pechorskoye More	**82**	J4
Pechory	**56**	P8
Pecos	**44**	F2
Pecos	**44**	F2
Pécs	**74**	F3
Pedja	**56**	P7
Pedra Azul	**50**	J7
Pedra Lume	**108**	(1)B1
Pedreiras	**50**	J4
Pedro Afonso	**50**	H5
Pedro Juan Caballero	**52**	K3
Pedro Luro	**52**	J6
Peel Sound	**34**	M2
Peene	**60**	J3
Peenemünde	**60**	J2
Pegasus Bay	**118**	D6
Pegnitz	**60**	G7
Pegu	**90**	B3
Pegunungan Barisan	**92**	(1)B2
Pegunungan Iban	**92**	(1)F2
Pegunungan Maoke	**92**	(2)E3
Pegunungan Meratus	**92**	(1)F3
Pegunungan Schwaner	**92**	(1)E3
Pegunungan Van Rees	**92**	(2)E3
Pehuajó	**52**	J6
Peine	**60**	F4
Peißenberg	**70**	G3
Peixe	**50**	H6
Pekalongan	**92**	(1)D4
Pekanbaru	**92**	(1)C2
Peking = Beijing	**86**	F3
Peleduy	**84**	J5
Peleng	**92**	(2)B3
Pelhřimov	**58**	E8
Pelješac	**72**	M6
Pello	**56**	N3
Pellworm	**60**	D2
Pelly Bay	**34**	P3
Peloponnisos	**76**	D7
Pelotas	**52**	L5
Pelym	**78**	M2
Pemangkat	**92**	(1)D2
Pematangsiantar	**92**	(1)B2
Pemba	**112**	G2
Pemba Island	**110**	F5
Pembina	**38**	G1
Pembine	**40**	C1
Pembroke, *Canada*	**40**	E1
Pembroke, *United Kingdom*	**64**	H10
Pembroke, *United States*	**42**	E3
Peñafiel	**68**	F3
Peñaranda de Bracamonte	**68**	E4
Peñarroya-Pueblonuevo	**68**	E6
Pendleton	**38**	C1
Pendolo	**92**	(1)G3
Pend Oreille Lake	**38**	C1
Pen Hills	**40**	E2
Peniche	**68**	A5
Península de Azuero	**46**	H7
Peninsula de Guajira	**46**	K6
Península Valdés	**52**	J7
Péninsule de Gaspé	**34**	T7
Péninsule d'Ungava	**34**	R4
Penmarch	**66**	A6
Penne	**72**	H6
Pennines	**64**	K7
Pennsylvania	**40**	E2
Penrith	**64**	K7
Pensacola	**46**	G2
Penticton	**38**	C1
Penza	**78**	J4
Penzance	**64**	G11
Penzhina	**84**	V4
Penzhinskaya Guba	**84**	U4
Penzhinskiy Khrebet	**84**	V4
Peoria, *Ariz., United States*	**44**	D2
Peoria, *Ill., United States*	**40**	C2
Percival Lakes	**116**	D4
Peregrebnoye	**78**	N2
Pereira	**50**	B3
Pergamino	**52**	J5
Périgueux	**66**	F8
Peristera	**76**	G5
Perito Moreno	**52**	G8
Perleberg	**60**	G3
Perm'	**78**	L3
Përmet	**76**	C4
Pernambuco	**50**	K5
Pernik	**74**	L7
Péronne	**62**	E5
Perpignan	**66**	H11
Perrine	**42**	E4
Perry, *Fla., United States*	**42**	E3
Perry, *Ga., United States*	**42**	E3
Persepolis	**101**	E2
Persian Gulf	**101**	C2
Perth, *Australia*	**116**	C6
Perth, *United Kingdom*	**64**	J5
Pertuis Breton	**66**	D7
Peru	**40**	C2
Peru	**50**	C6
Peru-Chile Trench	**48**	D5
Perúgia	**72**	G5
Pervomays'k	**78**	F5
Pervoural'sk	**78**	L3
Pésaro	**70**	H7
Pescara	**72**	J6
Pescia	**70**	F7
Peshawar	**94**	B2
Peshkopi	**76**	C3
Peshtera	**76**	G2
Peski Karakumy	**96**	G2
Peski Kzyylkum	**82**	L9
Peski Priaral'skiye Karakumy	**82**	L8
Pesnica	**70**	L4
Pessac	**66**	E9
Petah Tiqwa	**100**	B4
Petalioi	**76**	G7
Petaluma	**38**	B3
Pétange	**62**	H5
Petare	**46**	L6
Petauke	**112**	E2
Peterborough, *Canada*	**40**	E2
Peterborough, *United Kingdom*	**64**	M9
Peterhead	**64**	L4
Peter I Øy	**120**	(2)JJ3
Petersburg	**40**	E3
Petersfield	**62**	B3
Petershagen	**60**	D4
Petilia	**72**	L9
Petit Mécatina	**34**	U6
Peto	**46**	G4
Petre Bay	**118**	(1)B1
Petrich	**76**	F3
Petrila	**74**	L4
Petrinja	**70**	M5
Petrolina	**50**	J5
Petropavlovka	**84**	H6
Petropavlovsk	**78**	N4
Petropavlovsk-Kamchatskiy	**84**	T6
Petrópolis	**52**	N3
Petroşani	**74**	L4
Petrovac	**74**	J5
Petrovsk-Zabaykal'skiy	**84**	H6
Petrozavodsk	**78**	F2
Petrun	**78**	M1
Petukhovo	**78**	N3
Pevek	**84**	W3
Pezinok	**58**	G9
Pfaffenhofen	**60**	G8
Pfarrkirchen	**60**	H8
Pflach	**70**	F3
Pforzheim	**60**	D8
Pfunds	**70**	F4
Pfungstadt	**60**	D7
Phalaborwa	**112**	E4
Phalodi	**94**	B3
Phan Rang	**90**	D4
Phan Thiêt	**90**	D4
Phatthalung	**90**	C5
Phet Buri	**90**	B4
Phichit	**90**	C3
Philadelphia, *Miss., United States*	**42**	D3
Philadelphia, *Pa., United States*	**42**	F2
Philippeville	**62**	G4
Philippines	**90**	G5
Philippine Trench	**80**	R8
Philips	**34**	K7
Phillipsburg	**38**	G3
Phitsanulok	**90**	C3
Phnum Penh	**90**	C4
Phoenix	**44**	D2
Phoenix Islands	**114**	J6
Phôngsali	**90**	C2
Phuket	**90**	B5
Piacenza	**70**	E5
Piádena	**70**	F5
Pianosa	**72**	E6

Piatra-Neamţ	**74**	P3
Piauí	**50**	J5
Piazza Armerina	**72**	J11
Pibor Post	**110**	E2
Picacho del Centinela	**44**	F3
Picayune	**42**	D3
Pichilemu	**52**	G5
Pico	**106**	(1)B2
Pico Almanzor	**68**	E4
Pico Cristóbal Colón	**46**	K6
Pico da Bandeira	**52**	N3
Pico da Neblina	**50**	D3
Pico de Itambé	**52**	N2
Pico de Teide	**106**	B3
Pico Duarte	**46**	K5
Picos	**50**	J5
Picton, *New Zealand*	**118**	D5
Picton, *United States*	**40**	E2
Pic Tousside	**104**	C3
Piedras Negras	**44**	F3
Pieksämäki	**56**	P5
Pielinen	**56**	Q5
Pierre	**38**	F2
Pierrelatte	**66**	K9
Piers do Rio	**50**	H7
Piešťany	**58**	G9
Pietermaritzburg	**112**	E5
Pietersburg	**112**	D4
Pietrasanta	**70**	F6
Piet Retief	**112**	E5
Pieve di Cadore	**70**	H4
Pihlájavesi	**56**	P6
Pik Aborigen	**84**	R4
Piketberg	**112**	B6
Pik Kommunizma	**96**	K2
Pik Pobedy	**82**	P9
Piła	**58**	F4
Pilaya	**52**	H3
Pilcomayo	**50**	E8
Pilibhit	**94**	C3
Pilica	**58**	J7
Pimba	**116**	G6
Pimenta Bueno	**50**	E6
Pinamalayan	**90**	G4
Pinamar	**52**	K6
Pinang	**90**	B5
Pınarbaşı	**98**	G4
Pinar del Río	**46**	H4
Pinarhisar	**76**	K3
Pińczów	**58**	K7
Pindaré Mirim	**50**	H4
Pine Bluff	**40**	B4
Pine Bluffs	**38**	F2
Pine City	**40**	B1
Pine Creek	**116**	F2
Pine Creek Reservoir	**40**	A4
Pinega	**78**	H2
Pineios	**76**	E5
Pine Island Bay	**120**	(2)GG3
Pineland	**42**	C3
Pinerolo	**70**	C6
Pineville, *Ky., United States*	**40**	D3
Pineville, *La., United States*	**42**	C3
Pingdingshan	**86**	E4
Pingguo	**90**	D2
Pingle	**90**	E2
Pingliang	**86**	D3
P'ing-tung	**90**	G2
Pingxiang, *China*	**90**	D2
Pingxiang, *China*	**90**	E1
Pinhel	**68**	C4
Pini	**92**	(1)B2
Pinka	**70**	M3
Pink Mountain	**34**	G5
Pinneberg	**60**	E3
Pinsk	**78**	E4
Pioche	**38**	D3
Piombino	**72**	E6
Pioneer	**44**	D2
Pioneer Mountains	**38**	D1
Pionerskii	**58**	K3
Pionerskiy	**78**	M2
Piotrków Trybunalski	**58**	J6
Piove di Sacco	**70**	H5
Piperi	**76**	G5
Pipestone	**40**	A2
Pipiriki	**118**	E4
Piqua	**40**	D2
Piracicaba	**52**	M3
Pireas	**76**	F7
Pirin	**76**	F3
Piripiri	**50**	J4
Pirmasens	**60**	C7
Pirna	**60**	J6
Pirot	**74**	K6
Piru	**92**	(2)C3
Pisa	**58**	L4
Pisa	**70**	F7
Pisco	**50**	B6
Písek	**58**	D8
Pīshīn	**96**	H4
Pishin	**96**	J3
Piska	**58**	L4
Pisticci	**72**	L8
Pistóia	**70**	F7
Pisz	**58**	L4
Pitcairn Islands	**114**	P8
Piteå	**56**	L4
Piteälven	**78**	C1
Piteşti	**74**	M5
Pithara	**116**	C6
Pithiviers	**66**	H5
Pitkyaranta	**78**	F2
Pitlochry	**64**	J5
Pitlyar	**78**	N1
Pitt Island	**118**	(1)B2
Pittsburg	**42**	C2
Pittsburgh	**40**	D2
Pitt Strait	**118**	(1)B2
Piura	**50**	A5
Pivka	**70**	K5
Placer	**90**	G4
Placerville	**44**	B1
Plaiamonas	**76**	E5
Plains	**44**	F2
Plainview	**44**	F2
Planalto Central	**50**	H6
Planalto da Borborema	**50**	K5
Planalto do Mato Grosso	**50**	G6
Plankinton	**38**	G2
Plano	**42**	B3
Plasencia	**68**	D5
Plast	**78**	M4
Plateau Batéké	**108**	G5
Plateau du Djado	**106**	H4
Plateau du Limousin	**66**	F8
Plateau du Tademaït	**106**	F3
Plateau of Tibet = Xizang Gaoyuan	**94**	D2
Plateaux Batéké	**110**	A4
Platinum	**44**	(1)E4
Plato	**46**	K7
Plato Ustyurt	**82**	J9
Platte	**42**	B1
Platteville	**40**	B2
Plattling	**60**	H8
Plattsburgh	**40**	F2
Plattsmouth	**42**	B1
Plau	**60**	H3
Plauen	**60**	H6
Plavnik	**70**	K6
Plavsk	**78**	G4
Playas	**50**	A4
Plây Cu	**90**	D4
Pleasanton	**44**	G3
Pleiße	**60**	H5
Plentywood	**38**	F1
Plesetsk	**78**	H2
Pleven	**74**	M6
Pljevlja	**74**	G6
Płock	**58**	J5
Pločno	**74**	E6
Ploieşti	**74**	P5
Plomari	**76**	J6
Plön	**60**	F2
Płońsk	**58**	L5
Plovdiv	**74**	M7
Plumtree	**112**	D4
Plungė	**58**	L2
Plymouth, *United Kingdom*	**64**	H11
Plymouth, *United States*	**40**	C2
Plyussa	**56**	Q7
Plyussa	**78**	E3
Plzeň	**58**	C8
Po	**70**	E5
Pocahontas	**46**	F1
Pocatello	**38**	D2
Pochet	**84**	F5
Pochinok	**78**	F4
Pocking	**70**	J2
Pocomoke City	**40**	E3
Podgorica	**74**	G7
Podkamennaya Tunguska	**84**	F4
Podol'sk	**78**	G3
Podravska Slatina	**74**	E4
Poel	**60**	G2
Pofadder	**112**	B5
Poggibonsi	**70**	G7
Pogradec	**76**	C4
P'ohang	**88**	E5
Pohnpei	**114**	F5
Pohokura	**118**	F4
Pohořelice	**70**	M2
Point Arena	**36**	B4
Point Barrow	**44**	(1)F1
Point Conception	**44**	B2
Point Culver	**116**	D6
Point d'Entrecasteaux	**116**	B6
Pointe-Noire	**108**	G5
Point Hope	**44**	(1)D2
Point Hope	**44**	(1)D2
Point Pedro	**94**	D7
Point Sur	**38**	B3
Poitiers	**66**	F7
Pokaran	**94**	B3
Pokhara	**94**	D3
Poko	**110**	D3
Pokrovsk	**84**	M4
Pola de Siero	**68**	E1
Poland	**58**	G6
Polar Bluff	**46**	F1
Polatlı	**76**	Q5
Polatsk	**78**	E3
Police	**60**	K3
Polichnitos	**76**	J5
Poligny	**66**	L7
Poligus	**82**	S5
Polillo Islands	**90**	G4
Polis	**76**	Q9
Polistena	**72**	L10
Pollachi	**94**	C6
Pollença	**68**	P5
Polohy	**78**	G5
Polomoloc	**90**	H5
Polonnaruwa	**94**	D7
Poltava	**78**	F5
Poltavka	**88**	F1
Põltsana	**56**	N7
Poluostrov Shmidta	**84**	Q6
Poluostrov Yamal	**82**	M3
Poluy	**82**	M4
Põlva	**56**	P7
Polyaigos	**76**	G8
Polyarnye Zori	**56**	S3
Polyarnyy	**84**	X3
Polykastro	**76**	E4
Polynesia	**114**	J6
Pombal	**68**	B5
Pomeranian Bay	**58**	D3
Pomeroy	**38**	C1
Pomorie	**74**	Q7
Pompano Beach	**42**	E4
Pompei	**72**	J8
Ponca City	**42**	B2
Ponce	**46**	L5
Pondicherry	**94**	C6
Pond Inlet	**34**	R2
Ponferrada	**68**	D2
Poniatowa	**58**	M6
Ponoy	**78**	H1
Pons	**66**	E8
Ponta Delgada	**106**	(1)B2
Ponta do Podrão	**108**	G6
Ponta do Sol	**108**	(1)B1
Ponta Grossa	**52**	L4
Ponta Khehuene	**112**	E5
Pont-à-Mousson	**66**	M5
Ponta Porã	**52**	K3
Pontarlier	**66**	M7
Pontassieve	**70**	G7
Ponta Zavora	**112**	F4
Pont-d'Alin	**66**	L7
Ponteareas	**68**	B2
Ponte da Barca	**68**	B3
Pontedera	**70**	F7
Ponte de Sor	**68**	C5
Pontevedra	**68**	B2
Pontiac	**40**	C2
Pontianak	**92**	(1)D3
Pontivy	**66**	C5
Pontoise	**62**	E5
Pontorson	**66**	D5
Pontrémoli	**70**	E6
Ponza	**72**	G8
Poogau	**70**	J3
Poole	**64**	L11
Poole Bay	**64**	L11
Pooncarie	**116**	H6
Poopó	**50**	D7
Poopó Challapata	**52**	H2
Popayán	**46**	J8
Poperinge	**62**	E4
Popigay	**82**	W3
Poplar Bluff	**40**	B3
Poplarville	**42**	D3
Popocatépetl	**46**	E5
Popokabaka	**108**	H6
Popovača	**70**	M5
Popovo	**74**	P6
Poprad	**58**	K8
Poprad	**58**	K8
Porangatu	**50**	H6
Porbandar	**96**	J5
Porcupine	**44**	(1)K2
Pordenone	**70**	H5
Poreč	**70**	J5
Poret	**72**	H3
Pori	**56**	L6
Porirua	**118**	E5
Porlamar	**46**	M6
Poronaysk	**84**	Q7
Poros	**76**	F7
Porosozero	**78**	F2
Porozina	**70**	K5
Porpoise Bay	**120**	(2)T3
Porriño	**68**	B2
Porsangen	**56**	N1
Porsgrunn	**56**	E7
Portadown	**64**	F7
Portage	**40**	C2
Portage la Prairie	**38**	G1
Port Alberni	**38**	B1
Port Albert	**116**	J7
Portalegre	**68**	C5
Portales	**44**	F2
Port Arthur, *Australia*	**116**	J8
Port Arthur, *United States*	**42**	C4
Port Augusta	**116**	G6
Port-au-Prince	**46**	K5
Port Austin	**40**	D2
Port Burwell	**34**	U4
Port Charlotte	**42**	E4
Port Douglas	**116**	J3
Portel, *Brazil*	**50**	G4
Portel, *Portugal*	**68**	C6
Port Elizabeth	**112**	D6
Port Ellen	**64**	F6
Porterville	**44**	C1
Port Fitzroy	**118**	E3
Port-Gentil	**108**	F5
Port Harcourt	**108**	F4
Port Hardy	**34**	F6
Port Hawkesbury	**34**	U7
Port Hedland	**116**	C4
Port Hope Simpson	**34**	V6
Port Huron	**40**	D2
Pórtici	**72**	J8
Portimão	**68**	B7
Port Jefferson	**40**	F2
Portland, *Australia*	**116**	H7
Portland, *Ind., United States*	**40**	D2
Portland, *Me., United States*	**40**	F2
Portland, *Oreg., United States*	**38**	B1
Portland Island	**118**	F4
Port Laoise	**64**	E8
Port Lavaca	**42**	B4
Port Lincoln	**116**	G6
Port Loko	**108**	B3
Port Louis	**112**	(1)B2
Port Macquarie	**116**	K6
Port-Menier	**34**	U7
Port Moresby	**116**	J1
Port Nolloth	**112**	B5
Porto, *Corsica*	**72**	C6
Porto, *Portugal*	**68**	B3
Porto Alegre	**52**	L5
Porto Amboim	**112**	A2
Portocheli	**76**	F7
Porto do Son	**68**	A2
Pôrto Esperidião	**50**	F7
Portoferraio	**72**	E6
Pôrto Franco	**50**	H5
Port of Spain	**50**	E1
Pôrto Grande	**50**	G3
Portogruaro	**70**	H5
Porto Inglês	**108**	(1)B1
Portomaggiore	**70**	G6
Pôrto Murtinho	**52**	K3
Pôrto Nacional	**50**	H6
Porto-Novo	**108**	E3
Port Orford	**38**	B2
Porto San Giórgio	**72**	H5
Pôrto Santana	**50**	G3
Porto Santo	**106**	B2
Pôrto Seguro	**50**	K7
Porto Tolle	**70**	H6
Porto Tórres	**72**	C8
Porto-Vecchio	**72**	D7
Pôrto Velho	**50**	E5
Portoviejo	**50**	A4
Port Pire	**116**	G6
Portree	**64**	F4
Port Renfrew	**38**	B1
Port Said = Bûr Sa'îd	**104**	F1
Port St. Johns	**112**	D6
Port Shepstone	**112**	E6
Portsmouth, *United Kingdom*	**62**	A4
Portsmouth, *N.H., United States*	**40**	F2
Portsmouth, *Oh., United States*	**40**	D3
Portsmouth, *Va., United States*	**40**	E3
Port Sudan = Bur Sudan	**104**	G4
Port Sulphur	**42**	D4
Port Talbot	**64**	J10
Portugal	**68**	B5
Viseu, *Portugal*	**68**	C4
Portugalete	**68**	G1
Port-Vendres	**66**	J11

Port-Vila 114 G7
Port Warrender 116 E2
Posadas 52 K4
Poschiavo 70 F4
Poshekhon'ye 78 G3
Poso 92 (2)B3
Posŏng 88 D6
Posse 50 H6
Pößneck 60 G6
Post 44 F2
Postmasburg 112 C5
Postojna 70 K5
Posušje 74 E6
Potapovo 82 R4
Poteau 42 C2
Potenza 72 K8
P'ot'i 98 J2
Potiskum 108 G2
Potlatch 38 C1
Potosi 50 D7
Potsdam, *Germany* 60 J4
Potsdam, *United States* 40 F2
Pottuvil 94 D7
Poughkeepsie 40 F2
Pourerere 118 F5
Pouto 118 E3
Póvoa de Varzim 68 B3
Povorino 78 H4
Powder 38 E1
Powder River 38 E2
Powell River 34 G7
Poyang Hu 86 F5
Požarevac 74 J5
Poza Rica 46 E4
Požega 74 H6
Poznań 58 F5
Pozoblanco 68 F6
Prabumulih 92 (1)C3
Prachatice 58 D8
Prachuap Khiri Khan 90 B4
Prado 50 K7
Præstø 60 H1
Prague = Praha 58 D7
Praha 58 D7
Praia 108 (1)B2
Prainha 50 G4
Prairie du Chien 40 B2
Prapat 92 (1)B2
Praslin Island 112 (2)B1
Pratas = Dongsha Qundao 90 F2
Prato 70 G7
Pratt 38 G3
Prattville 42 D3
Praya 92 (1)F4
Preetz 60 F2
Preiļi 56 P8
Premnitz 60 H4
Premuda 70 K6
Prentice 40 B1
Prenzlau 58 C4
Preobrazhenka 84 H4
Preparis Island 90 A4
Preparis North Channel 90 A3
Preparis South Channel 90 A4
Přerov 58 G8
Presa de la Boquilla 44 E3
Presa de las Adjuntas 44 G4
Presa Obregón 44 E3
Prescott 38 D4
Preševo 74 J7
Presho 38 G2
Presidencia Roque Sáenz Peña 52 J4
Presidente Prudente 52 L3
Presidio 44 F3
Preslav 74 P6
Presnogorkovka 78 N4
Prešov 58 L9
Presque Isle 40 G1
Přeštice 60 J7
Preston, *United Kingdom* 64 K8
Preston, *Minn., United States* 40 B2
Preston, *Mo., United States* 40 B3
Pretoria 112 D5
Preveza 76 C6
Priargunsk 84 K6
Pribilof Islands 44 (1)D4
Priboj 74 G6
Příbram 58 D8
Price 38 D3
Prichard 42 D3
Priego de Córdoba 68 F7
Priekule 56 L8
Prienai 58 N3
Prieska 112 C5
Priest Lake 38 C1
Prievidza 58 H9
Prijedor 74 D5
Prijepolje 74 G6
Prikaspiyskaya Nizmennost' 78 K5
Prilep 76 D3
Primorsk 56 Q6
Primorsko Akhtarsk 78 G5
Prince Albert 34 K6
Prince Albert Peninsula 34 H2
Prince Albert Sound 34 H2
Prince Charles Island 34 R3
Prince Edward Island 102 G10
Prince Edward Island 34 U7
Prince George 34 G6
Prince of Wales Island, *Australia* 116 H2
Prince of Wales Island, *Canada* 34 L2
Prince of Wales Island, *United States* 34 E5
Prince of Wales Strait 34 H2
Prince Patrick Island 32 Q2
Prince Regent Inlet 34 N2
Prince Rupert 34 E6
Princess Charlotte Bay 116 H2
Princeton, *Canada* 38 B1
Princeton, *Ill., United States* 40 C2
Princeton, *Ky., United States* 40 C3
Princeton, *Mo., United States* 40 B2
Prince William Sound 34 B4
Príncipe 108 F4
Prineville 38 B2
Priozersk 56 R6
Priština 74 J7
Pritzwalk 60 H3
Privas 66 K9
Privolzhskaya Vozvyshennost 78 H4
Prizren 74 H7
Probolinggo 92 (1)E4
Proddatur 94 C6
Progreso 46 G4
Prokhladnyy 98 L2
Prokop'yevsk 82 R7
Prokuplje 74 J6
Proletarsk 78 H5
Proliv Longa 84 X2
Proliv Vil'kitskogo 82 U2
Prophet 34 G5
Propriano 72 C7
Prorer Wiek 60 J2
Proserpine 116 J4
Prosna 58 G6
Prosperidad 90 H5
Prostojov 58 G8
Proti 76 D7
Provadiya 74 Q6
Prøven = Kangersuatsiaq 34 W2
Providence 40 F2
Providence Island 112 (2)B2
Provideniya 84 Z4
Provincetown 40 F2
Provins 66 J5
Provo 38 D2
Provost 34 J6
Prudhoe Bay 44 (1)H1
Prudnik 58 G7
Prüm 62 J4
Pruszków 58 K5
Prut 74 R4
Pružany 58 P5
Prvić 70 K6
Pryluky 78 F4
Prypyats' 54 G2
Przasnysz 58 K4
Przemyśl 58 M8
Przeworsk 58 M7
Psara 76 H6
Psebay 98 J1
Pskov 78 E3
Ptolemaïda 76 D4
Ptuj 70 L4
Pucallpa 50 C5
Pucheng 86 F5
Puch'ŏn 88 D5
Púchov 58 H8
Pucioasa 74 N4
Puck 58 H3
Pudasjärvi 56 P4
Pudozh 78 G2
Puebla 46 E5
Pueblo 38 F3
Puelches 52 H6
Puelén 52 H6
Puente-Genil 68 F7
Puerto Acosta 50 D7
Puerto Aisén 52 G8
Puerto Alegre 50 E6
Puerto Angel 46 E5
Puerto Ayacucho 46 L7
Puerto Barrios 46 G5
Puerto Berrío 50 C2
Puerto Cabezas 46 H6
Puerto Carreño 46 L7
Puerto del Rosario 106 C3
Puerto de Navacerrada 68 G4
Puerto Guarini 50 F8
Puerto Heath 50 D6
Puerto Inírida 50 D3
Puerto Leguízamo 50 C4
Puerto Libertad 44 D3
Puerto Limón 50 B3
Puertollano 68 F6
Puerto Maldonado 50 D6
Puerto Montt 52 G7
Puerto Nuevo 46 K7
Puerto Peñasco 44 D2
Puerto Princesa 90 F5
Puerto Real 68 D8
Puerto Rico 46 L5
Puerto Rico 50 D6
Puerto Rico Trench 48 E1
Puerto Santa Cruz 52 H9
Puerto Suárez 50 F7
Pukapuka 114 N7
Pukatawagen 34 L5
Pukch'ŏng 88 E3
Pukë 74 G7
Pula 70 J6
Pulaski 40 E2
Puławy 58 M6
Pullman 38 C1
Pułtusk 56 L10
Pulu 82 Q10
Pülümür 98 H4
Puncak Jaya 92 (2)E3
Puncak Mandala 92 (2)F3
Pune 94 B5
Punia 110 D4
Puno 50 C7
Punta Albina 112 A3
Punta Alice 72 M9
Punta Angamos 52 G3
Punta Arena 38 B3
Punta Arenas 52 G9
Punta Ballena 52 G4
Punta Dungeness 52 H9
Punta Eugenia 46 A3
Punta Galera 52 G6
Punta Gallinas 46 K6
Punta Gorda 42 E4
Punta La Marmora 72 D8
Punta Lavapié 52 G6
Punta Lengua de Vaca 52 G5
Punta Mala 50 B2
Punta Mariato 46 H7
Punta Medanosa 52 H8
Punta Negra 50 A5
Punta Norte, *Argentina* 52 J7
Punta Norte, *Argentina* 52 K6
Punta Pariñas 50 A5
Punta Rasa 52 J7
Puntarenas 46 H6
Punta San Gabriel 44 D3
Punta San Telmo 46 D5
Punta Sarga 106 B4
Puponga 118 D5
Puqi 86 E5
Puri 94 E5
Purmerend 62 G2
Purpe 84 B4
Purukcahu 92 (1)E3
Purus 50 E5
Puruvesi 56 Q6
Pusan 88 E6
Pushkin 78 F3
Püspökladany 58 L10
Putao 90 B1
Putaruru 118 E3
Putian 86 F5
Putna 74 P4
Puttalami 94 C7
Putten 62 G3
Puttgarden 60 G2
Putumayo 50 C4
Puuwai 44 (2)A2
Puy de Dôme 66 H8
Puy de Sancy 66 H8
Puysegur Point 118 A8
Pweto 110 D5
Pwllheli 64 H9
Pyal'ma 78 G2
Pyatigorsk 98 K1
Pyè 90 B3
Pyhäjärvi 56 M6
Pylos 76 D8
Pyŏktong 88 C3
P'yŏnggang 88 D4
P'yŏngyang 88 C4
Pyramid Island 118 (1)B2
Pyramid Lake 38 C2/3
Pyrenees 66 E11
Pyrgos 76 D7
Pyrzyce 58 D4
Pyshchug 78 J3
Pytalovo 56 P8

Q

Qadīmah 96 C5
Qādub 96 F7
Qagan Nur 86 F2
Qal'aikhum 96 K2
Qalamat Nadqān 101 D5
Qalāt 96 J3
Qal'at Bīshah 96 D5
Qal'eh-ye Now 96 H3
Qamdo 86 B4
Qamīnīs 104 C1
Qaraaoun 98 F7
Qardho 110 H2
Qartaba 100 C2
Qasr Farafra 104 E2
Qaṭanā 100 D3
Qatar 101 D4
Qatrāna 100 D5
Qattâra Depression 104 E2
Qāyen 96 G3
Qazangöldag 98 M4
Qazax 98 L3
Qazımämmäd 98 N3
Qazvīn 96 E2
Qena 104 F2
Qeqertarsuatsiaat 34 W4
Qeqertarsuatsiaq 34 V2
Qeqertarsuup Tunua 34 V3
Qeshm 101 F3
Qeshm 101 G3
Qeys 101 E3
Qezel Owzan 98 N5
Qezi'ot 100 B6
Qianshanlaoba 82 Q8
Qiaowan 86 B2
Qidukou 94 G2
Qiemo 82 R10
Qijiang 86 D5
Qijiaojing 82 S9
Qila Saifullah 96 J3
Qilian 86 C3
Qilian Shan 86 B3
Qingdao 86 G3
Qinghai Hu 86 B3
Qinghai Nanshan 86 B3
Qingjiang 86 F4
Qingshuihe 86 E3
Qingyang 86 D3
Qingyuan, *China* 86 E6
Qingyuan, *China* 86 G2
Qinhuangdao 86 F3
Qinzhou 90 D2
Qionghai 90 E3
Qiqian 84 L6
Qiqihar 84 L7
Qīr 101 E2
Qira 82 Q10
Qiryat Ata 100 C4
Qiryat Motzkin 100 C4
Qiryat Shemona 100 C3
Qishn 96 F6
Qolleh-ye Damāvand 96 F2
Qom 96 F3
Qomishēh 96 F3
Qornet es Saouda 100 D2
Qorveh 98 M6
Qotūr 98 L4
Quang Ngai' 90 D3
Quangolodougou 108 C3
Quang Tri 90 D3
Quanzhou 90 F2
Quaqtaq 34 T4
Quarto Sant'Elena 72 D9
Quba 98 N3
Quchan 96 G2
Québec 40 F1
Quedlinburg 60 G5
Queen Charlotte 34 E6
Queen Charlotte Islands 34 E6
Queen Charlotte Sound 34 E6
Queen Charlotte Strait 34 F6
Queen Elizabeth Islands 32 M2
Queen Maud Gulf 34 L3
Queensland 116 G4
Queenstown, *Australia* 116 J8
Queenstown, *New Zealand* 118 B7
Queenstown, *South Africa* 112 D6
Queets 38 B1
Quelimane 112 F3
Quemado 44 E2
Querétaro 46 D4
Quesnel 34 G6
Quetta 96 J3

Quezaltenango 46 F6
Quezon 90 F5
Quezon City 90 G4
Qufu 86 F3
Quibala 112 A2
Quibdó 46 J7
Quijotoa 44 D2
Quilmes 52 K5
Quilpie 116 H5
Quimbele 110 B5
Quimilí 52 J4
Quimper 66 A5
Quimperlé 66 B6
Quincy 40 B3
Qui Nhon 90 D4
Quionga 110 G6
Quirindi 116 K6
Quito 50 B4
Qujing 90 C1
Qumar He 94 F1
Qumaryan 94 F1
Qurayyāt 96 G5
Qurghonteppa 96 J2
Qurlurtuuq 34 H3
Qus 104 F2
Quseir 104 F2
Quzhou 86 F5

R

Raab 70 L3
Raahe 56 N4
Raalte 62 J2
Raasay 64 G4
Raas Caseyr 110 J1
Raas Xaafuun 110 J1
Rab 70 K6
Rab 70 K6
Rába 74 E2
Raba 92 (2)A4
Rabak 104 F5
Rabat 72 J13
Rabat 106 D2
Rabca 70 N3
Rābigh 96 C5
Rabka 58 K8
Rach Gia 90 D5
Racine 40 C2
Ráckeve 74 F2
Rădăuţi 74 N2
Radbuza 60 H7
Radeberg 60 J5
Radebeul 60 J5
Radhanpur 94 B4
Radnevo 74 N7
Radom 58 L6
Radomir 74 K7
Radomsko 58 J6
Radoviš 76 E3
Radstadt 58 C10
Raduznny 82 P5
Radviliškis 58 N2
Rae-Edzo 34 H4
Raetihi 118 E4
Raevavae 114 M8
Rafaela 52 J4
Rafah 100 B5
Rafaï 110 C3
Rafḩā 96 D4
Rafsanjān 101 G1
Raglan 118 E3
Ragusa 72 J12
Raha 92 (2)B3
Rahad el Berdi 104 D5
Rahimyar Khan 96 K4
Raichur 94 C5
Raiganj 94 E3
Raigarh 94 D4
Rainach 70 L4
Rainbow Lake 34 H5
Rainier 38 B1
Rainy Lake 40 B1
Rainy River 40 B1
Raipur 94 D4
Rai Valley 118 D5
Rajahmundry 94 D5
Raja-Jooseppi 56 Q2
Rajapalaiyam 94 C7
Rajgarh 94 C3
Rajkot 96 K5
Raj Nangaon 94 D4
Rajshahi 94 E4
Rakhiv 74 M1
Rakovica 70 L6
Rakovník 58 C7
Rakovski 74 M7
Rakvere 56 P7
Raleigh 42 F2
Ralik Chain 114 G5
Ram 100 C7
Rama 46 H6
Ramallah 100 C5
Rambouillet 66 G5
Rameswaram 94 C7
Rāmhormoz 101 C1
Ramla 100 B5
Ramlat Rabyānah 104 C3
Râmnicu Sărat 74 Q4
Râmnicu Vâlcea 74 M4
Rampur, *India* 94 C2
Rampur, *India* 94 C3
Ramree Island 90 A3
Ramsgate 64 P10
Ramtha 100 D4
Ranau 92 (1)F1
Rancagua 52 G5
Ranchi 94 E4
Randazzo 72 J11
Randers 56 F8
Randijaure 56 K3
Randolph 38 G2
Rånes 62 B6
Rangamati 94 F4
Rangiora 118 D6
Rangoon = Yangon 90 B3
Rankin 44 F2
Rankin Inlet 34 N4
Ranong 90 B5
Ransiki 92 (2)D3
Rānya 98 L5
Rapa 114 M8
Rapalla 72 D4
Rapallo 70 E6
Rapar 96 K5
Raperswil 70 D3
Rapid City 38 F2
Rapid River 40 C1
Rapla 56 N7
Rapur 96 J5
Raroia 114 N7
Rarotonga 114 K8
Râs Abu Shagara 104 G3
Ra's al Ḩadd 96 G5
Ra's al Ḩazrah 101 D4
Ra's al Hilāl 104 D1
Ra's al Khajī 101 C2
Ra's al Khaymah 101 F4
Ra's al Kūh 101 G4
Ra's al Muraysah 104 E1
Ra's al 'Udayd 101 D4
Ra's az Zawr 101 C3
Râs Banâs 104 G3
Ras Beddouza 106 C1
Ras Bir 104 H5
Ras Dashen Terara 104 G5
Ra's-e Barkan 101 C2
Raseiniai 56 M9
Râs el Nafas 100 B7
Ra's Fartak 96 F6
Râs Ghârib 104 F2
Rasht 98 N5
Rāsk 96 H4
Raška 74 H6
Ras Kasar 104 G4
Ra's Madrakah 96 G6
Râs Nouâdhibou 106 B4
Rason Lake 116 D5
Rass Jebel 72 E11
Rass Mostefa 72 F12
Rassokha 84 H2
Rast 74 L6
Ras Tannūrah 101 D3
Rastatt 62 L6
Rastede 60 D3
Ratak Chain 114 H4
Ratangarh 96 K4
Rat Buri 90 B4
Rath 94 C3
Rathenow 60 H4
Rathlin Island 64 F6
Ratlam 94 C4
Ratnagiri 96 K6
Raton 38 F3
Ratta 84 C4
Ratten 70 D4
Ratzeburg 60 F3
Raudhatain 101 B1
Raukumara Range 118 F4
Rauma 56 L6
Rausu 88 N1
Răut 74 R2
Ravalli 38 D1
Ravānsar 98 M6
Rāvar 101 G1
Ravenna 70 H6
Ravensburg 70 E3
Ravensthorpe 116 D6
Ravnina 96 H2
Rāwah 98 J6
Rawaki 114 J6
Rawalpindi 96 K3
Rawa Mazowiecka 58 K6
Rawāndiz 98 L5
Rawicz 58 F6
Rawlinna 116 E6
Rawlins 38 E2
Rawson 52 J7
Rawu 94 G3
Raychikhinsk 84 M7
Raymond 38 B1
Raymondville 44 G3
Rayong 90 C4
Razdol'noye 88 F2
Razgrad 74 P6
Razlog 74 L8
Reading, *United Kingdom* 64 M10
Reading, *United States* 40 E2
Realicó 52 J6
Rebbenesøya 56 J1
Rebun-tō 86 L1
Rechytsa 78 F4
Recife 50 L5
Recklinghausen 62 K3
Recknitz 60 H3
Reconquista 52 K4
Recreo 52 H4
Red, *Canada/ United States* 38 G1
Red, *United States* 42 B3
Reda 58 H3
Red Bluff 44 B1
Red Cloud 42 B1
Red Deer 34 J6
Redding 38 B2
Redditch 62 A2
Redfield 38 G2
Red Lake 34 N6
Red Lakes 36 H2
Red Lodge 38 E1
Red Oak 40 A2
Redon 66 C6
Redondela 68 B2
Red River = Song Hông 90 C2
Red Sea 104 G3
Redwater 34 J6
Red Wing 40 B2
Redwood City 38 B3
Redwood Falls 40 A2
Reed City 40 C2
Reedsport 38 B2
Reefton 118 C6
Rega 58 E4
Regen 60 H7
Regen 60 J8
Regensburg 60 H7
Regenstauf 60 H7
Reggane 106 F3
Réggio di Calabria 72 K10
Réggio nell'Emilia 70 F6
Reghin 74 M3
Regina 36 F1
Rehau 60 H6
Rehoboth 112 B4
Rehovot 100 B5
Reichenbach 60 H6
Reigate 64 M10
Reims 62 G5
Reinach Bad 70 C3
Reindeer Lake 34 L5
Reinosa 68 F1
Reisi 72 J11
Reliance 34 K4
Relizane 106 F1
Remada 106 H2
Remagen 62 K4
Rembang 92 (1)E4
Remeshk 101 H3
Remiremont 66 M6
Remscheid 62 K3
Rena 56 F6
Rendina 76 F4
Rendsburg 60 E2
Rengat 92 (1)C3
Reni 74 R4
Renmark 116 H6
Rennes 66 D5
Reno 70 G6
Reno 38 C3
Rentería 68 J1
Renton 38 B1
Renukut 94 D4
Reo 92 (2)B4
Replot 56 L5
Reprêsa de Balbina 50 F4
Represa de Samuel 50 E5
Represa de Sao Simao 50 G7
Represa Ilha Solteíra 50 G7
Represa Tucuruí 50 H4
Republic 38 C1
Republic of Ireland 64 D8
Repulse Bay 116 J4
Requena 50 C5
Reşadiye 98 G3
Resen 74 J8
Réservoir Cabonga 40 E1
Réservoir Caniapiscau 34 T6
Réservoir de La Grande 2 34 R6
Réservoir de La Grande 3 34 R6
Réservoir de La Grande 4 34 S6
Réservoir Gouin 40 F
Réservoir Manicouagan 34 T6
Réservoir Opinaca 34 R6
Réservoir Pipmuacan 40 G
Reshteh-ye Kūhhā-ye Alborz 96 F2
Resistencia 52 K4
Reşiţa 74 J4
Resolute 34 N2
Resolution Island, *Canada* 34 U4
Resolution Island, *New Zealand* 118 A7
Resovo 76 K3
Rethel 62 G5
Rethymno 76 G9
Réunion 112 (1)B2
Reus 68 M3
Reutlingen 60 E8
Revda 78 L3
Revillagigedo Island 44 (1)L4
Revin 62 G5
Revivim 100 B5
Revúca 58 K9
Rewa 94 D4
Rexburg 38 D2
Reykjanes 56 (1)B3
Reykjavík 56 (1)C2
Reynosa 42 B4
Rezat 60 F7
Rezé 66 D6
Rēzekne 56 P8
Rezina 74 R2
Rezovo 74 R8
Rheda-Wiedenbrück 60 D5
Rhein = Rhine 70 C2
Rheinbach 62 K4
Rheine 62 K2
Rheinfelden 70 C3
Rhin = Rhine 70 C2
Rhine 70 C2
Rhinelander 40 C1
Rho 70 E5
Rhode Island 40 F2
Rhodes = Rodos 76 L8
Rhondda 64 J10
Rhône 66 K9
Rhyl 64 J8
Ribadeo 68 C1
Ribas do Rio Pardo 52 L3
Ribe 56 E9
Ribeauville 66 N5
Ribeirão Prêto 52 M3
Ribeiria = Santa Eugenia 68 A2
Ribera 72 H11
Riberalta 50 D6
Ribnica 72 J3
Rîbniţa 74 S2
Ribnitz-Damgarten 60 H2
Říčany 60 K6
Riccione 70 H7
Richardson Mountains 44 (1)K2
Richfield 38 D3
Richland 38 C1
Richlands 40 D3
Richmond, *Australia* 116 H4
Richmond, *New Zealand* 118 D5
Richmond, *Ky., United States* 40 D3
Richmond, *Va., United States* 40 E3
Ridgecrest 44 C1
Ridgway 40 E2
Ried 70 J2
Riesa 60 J5
Rieti 72 G6
Rifle 38 E3
Rīga 56 N8
Riggins 38 C1
Rigolet 34 V6
Rijeka 70 K5
Riley 38 C2
Rimava 58 J9
Rimavská Sobota 58 K9
Rímini 70 H6
Rimouski 40 G1
Rineia 76 H7
Ringe 60 F1
Ringkøbing 56 E8
Ringkøbing Fjord 56 D9
Ringsted 60 G1
Ringvassøya 56 J1
Rinteln 60 E4
Rio Branco 50 D5
Río Colorado 52 J6
Río Cuarto 52 J5
Rio de Janeiro 52 N3
Rio de Janeiro 52 N3

Río de la Plata 52 K6
Río Gallegos 52 H9
Rio Grande 44 E2
Río Grande, *Argentina* 52 H9
Río Grande, *Mexico* 44 F4
Rio Grande 52 L5
Rio Grande City 42 B4
Rio Grande do Norte 50 K5
Rio Grande do Sul 52 L4
Ríohacha 46 K6
Río Largartos 46 G4
Riom 66 J8
Río Mulatos 50 D7
Rionero 72 K8
Rionero in Vulture 74 C9
Río Tigre 50 B4
Rio Verde 50 G7
Rio Verde de Mato Grosso 50 G7
Ripley, *Oh., United States* 40 D3
Ripley, *Tenn., United States* 40 C3
Ripley, *W.Va., United States* 40 D3
Ripoll 68 N2
Ripon 64 L7
Rishiri-tō 84 Q7
Rishon le Ziyyon 100 B5
Ritchie's Archipelago 90 A4
Ritzville 38 C1
Rivadavia 52 G4
Riva del Garda 70 F5
Rivarolo 70 C5
Rivas 46 G6
Rivera, *Argentina* 52 J6
Rivera, *Uruguay* 52 K5
Riversdale 112 C6
Riversdale Beach 118 E5
Riverton, *Canada* 34 M6
Riverton, *New Zealand* 118 A8
Rivesaltes 66 H11
Rivière-du-Loup 40 G1
Rivne 78 E4
Rivoli 70 C5
Riwoqê 94 G2
Riyadh = Ar Riyāḍ 101 B4
Rize 98 J3
Rizhao 86 F3
Roanne 66 K7
Roanoke 40 D3
Roanoke Rapids 42 F2
Robe 116 G7
Robertsfors 56 L4
Robertval 40 F1
Roboré 50 F7
Robstown 42 B4
Roccastrada 72 F6
Rochefort, *Belgium* 62 H4
Rochefort, *France* 66 E8
Rochelle 40 C2
Rocher River 34 J4
Rochester, *United Kingdom* 62 C3
Rochester, *Minn., United States* 40 B2
Rochester, *N.H., United States* 40 F2
Rochester, *N.Y., United States* 40 E2
Rockall 54 C2
Rockefeller Plateau 120 (2)EE2
Rockford 40 C2
Rockhampton 116 K4
Rock Hill 40 D4
Rock Island 40 B2
Rocklake 38 G1
Rockport 38 B1
Rock Rapids 40 A2
Rock Springs 38 E2
Rocksprings 44 F3
Rocky Mount 40 E3
Rocky Mountains 34 F5
Rødby Havn 60 G2
Roddickton 34 V6
Rodez 66 H9
Rodi Gargánico 72 K7
Roding 60 H7
Rodney 40 D2
Rodopi Planina 74 M7
Rodos 76 L8
Rodos 76 L8
Roebourne 116 C4
Roermond 62 J3
Roeselare 62 F4
Roes Welcome Sound 34 P4
Rogers City 40 D1
Rogerson 38 D2
Rogliano 72 D6
Rogue 38 B2
Rohrbach 70 K2
Rohtak 94 C3
Roi Et 90 C3
Roja 56 M8
Rokiškis 56 N9
Rokycany 58 C8
Rolla 40 B3
Rolleston 118 D6
Rolvsøya 56 M1
Roma 92 (2)C4
Roma, *Australia* 116 J5
Roma, *Italy* 72 G7
Roman 74 P3
Romania 74 L4
Romans-sur-Isère 66 L8
Rombas 62 J5
Rome = Roma 72 G7
Rome, *Ga., United States* 42 D3
Rome, *N.Y., United States* 40 E2
Romney 40 E3
Romny 78 F4
Rømø 60 D1
Romorantin-Lanthenay 66 G6
Rona 64 G2
Ronan 36 D2
Roncesvalles 68 J2
Ronda 68 E8
Rondônia 50 E6
Rondônia 50 E6
Rondonópolis 50 G7
Rondu 96 L2
Rongcheng 86 G3
Rønne 58 D2
Ronneby 56 H8
Ronne Entrance 120 (2)JJ3
Ronne Ice Shelf 120 (2)MM2
Ronse 62 F4
Roosendaal 62 G3
Roper Bar 116 F2
Roraima 50 E3
Røros 56 F5
Rosário 50 J4
Rosario, *Argentina* 52 J5
Rosario, *Mexico* 36 D6
Rosario, *Mexico* 36 E7
Rosario, *Paraguay* 52 K3
Rosário Oeste 50 F6
Rosarito 36 C6
Rosarno 72 K10
Roscommon 64 D8
Roseau 46 M5
Roseburg 38 B2
Roseires Reservoir 104 F5
Rose Island 114 K7
Rosenburg 44 G3
Rosenheim 70 H3
Roses 68 P2
Rosetown 34 K6
Rosica 74 N6
Rosignano Solvay 70 F7
Roşiori de Vede 74 N5
Roskilde 56 G9
Roslavl' 78 F4
Rossano 72 L9
Ross Ice Shelf 120 (2)Z1
Ross Lake 38 B1
Roßlau 60 H5
Rosso 106 B5
Rossosh' 78 G4
Ross River 34 E4
Ross Sea 120 (2)AA2
Røssvatnet 56 G4
Røst 56 G3
Rostāq 101 E3
Rosthern 34 K6
Rostock 60 H2
Rostov 78 G3
Rostov-na-Donu 78 G5
Rostrenen 66 B5
Roswell 44 F2
Rota 114 E4
Rotarua 118 F4
Rote 92 (2)B5
Rotenburg, *Germany* 60 E3
Rotenburg, *Germany* 60 E5
Roth 60 G7
Rothenburg 60 F7
Roto 116 J6
Rott 70 H2
Rotterdam 66 K2
Rottnen 58 E1
Rottumeroog 62 J1
Rottumerplaat 62 J1
Rottweil 70 D2
Rotuma 114 H7
Roubaix 62 F4
Rouen 62 D5
Rouiba 68 P8
Round Mountain 116 K6
Round Rock 42 B3
Roundup 38 E1
Rousay 64 J2
Rouyn 40 E1
Rovaniemi 56 N3
Rovereto 70 G5
Rovigo 70 G5
Rovinj 70 J5
Rovuma 110 F6
Rowley Island 34 R3
Rowley Shoals 116 C3
Roxas 90 G4
Roxburgh 118 B7
Royal Leamington Spa 62 A2
Royal Tunbridge Wells 62 C3
Royan 66 D8
Roye 62 E5
Royston 62 C2
Rozdil'na 74 T3
Rožňava 58 K9
Rrëshen 76 B3
Rtishchevo 78 H4
Ruacana 112 A3
Ruahine Range 118 E5
Ruapehu 118 E4
Ruapuke Island 118 B8
Ruarkela 94 D4
Ruatahuna 118 F4
Ruatoria 118 G3
Ruawai 118 D3
Rub' al Khālī 96 E6
Rubi 110 C3
Rubtsovsk 82 Q7
Ruby 44 (1)F3
Rudan 101 G3
Ruda Śląska 58 H7
Rudbar 96 H3
Rüdersdorf 60 J4
Rudkøbing 60 F2
Rudnaya Pristan' 88 H2
Rudnyy 78 M4
Rudolstadt 60 G6
Rūdsar 98 P5
Rue 62 D4
Ruffec 66 F7
Rufiji 110 F5
Rugby, *United Kingdom* 62 A2
Rugby, *United States* 36 G2
Rügen 58 C3
Ruhnu 56 M8
Ruhr 62 L3
Rum 64 F5
Ruma 74 G4
Rumāh 101 B4
Rumaylah 101 B1
Rumbek 110 D2
Rum Cay 46 K4
Rumigny 62 G5
Rumoi 88 L2
Runanaga 118 C6
Rundu 112 B3
Ruoqiang 82 R10
Ruo Shui 86 C2
Rupa 70 K5
Rupat 92 (1)C2
Rupert 34 R6
Rupert 38 D2
Rurutu 114 L8
Ruse 74 N6
Rushon 94 G3
Rushville, *Ill., United States* 40 B2
Rushville, *Ind., United States* 40 C3
Rushville, *Nebr., United States* 38 F2
Russell 38 G3
Russellville, *Ark., United States* 42 C2
Russellville, *Ky., United States* 42 D2
Rüsselsheim 60 D7
Russia 56 L9
Russia 80 M3
Rust'avi 98 L3
Ruston 42 C3
Rutana 110 E4
Rute 68 F7
Ruteng 92 (2)E4
Rutland 40 F2
Rutog 94 C2
Ruvo di Puglia 72 L7
Ruvuma 110 F6
Ruzayevka 78 H4
Ružomberok 58 J8
Rwanda 110 D4
R-Warnemünde 60 H2
Ryazan' 78 G4
Ryazhsk 78 H4
Rybinsk 78 G3
Rybinskoye Vodokhranilishche 78 G3
Rybnik 58 H7
Rychnov 58 F7
Ryde 62 A4
Rye Patch Reservoir 38 C2
Ryki 58 L3
Ryl'sk 78 F4
Ryn-Peski 78 J5
Ryōtsu 88 K4
Rypin 58 J4
Ryukyu Islands = Nansei-shotō 86 H5
Rzeszów 58 M7
Rzhev 78 F3

S

Sa'ādatābād, *Iran* 101 E1
Sa'ādatābād, *Iran* 101 F2
Saale 60 G6
Saalfeld 60 G6
Saalfelden 70 H3
Saanen 72 B2
Saar 62 J5
Saarbrücken 62 J5
Saarburg 62 J5
Saaremaa 56 L7
Saarlouis 62 J5
Saatli 98 N4
Saatly 96 E2
Saba 46 M5
Şab' Ābār 100 E3
Šabac 74 G5
Sabadell 68 N3
Sabah 92 (1)F1
Sabang 90 B5
Sabhā 106 H3
Sabiñánigo 68 K2
Sabinas 44 F3
Sabinas Hidalgo 44 F3
Sabine 42 E3
Sabine Lake 42 C3
Sabinov 58 L8
Sabkhet el Bardawîl 100 A5
Sable Island 34 V8
Sablé-sur-Sarthe 66 E6
Sabôr 68 C3
Sabun 82 C5
Sabzevār 96 G2
Săcele 74 N4
Sachanga 112 B2
Sachs Harbour 34 G2
Säckingen 70 C3
Sacramento 38 B3
Sacramento 38 B3
Şad'ah 96 D6
Sadiqabad 96 K4
Sadiya 94 G3
Sado 68 B6
Sadoga-shima 88 K4
Sadon 98 K2
Sado-shima 86 K3
Sa Dragonera 68 N5
Säffle 56 G7
Safford 44 E2
Safi, *Jordan* 100 C5
Safi, *Morocco* 106 D2
Safonovo, *Russia* 78 F3
Safonovo, *Russia* 78 J1
Safranbolu 76 Q3
Saga, *China* 94 E3
Saga, *Japan* 88 F7
Sagami-nada 88 K6
Sagar 94 C4
Sagastyr 82 Z3
Sage 38 D2
Saginaw 40 D2
Sagiz 78 K5
Sagiz 78 K5
Saguache 38 E3
Sagua la Grande 46 H4
Sagunt 68 K5
Sahāb 100 D5
Sahagún 68 E2
Sahara 102 C3
Saharah el Gharbîya 104 E2
Saharanpur 94 C3
Saharsa 94 E3
Şahbuz 98 L4
Sahel 102 C4
Sahiwal 96 K3
Sahuaripa 44 E3
Šahy 74 F1
Saïda, *Algeria* 106 F2
Saïda, *Lebanon* 100 C3
Sa'īdābād 101 F2
Saidpur 94 E3
Saigo 88 G5
Saigon = Hô Chi Minh 90 D4
Saiha 94 F4
Saihan Toroi 86 C2
Saiki 88 F7
Saimaa 56 P6
Saimbeyli 98 G4
Sā'in 101 F1
Saindak 96 H4
St. Albans 62 B3

St-Amand-Montrond 66 H7
St. Andrä 70 K4
St. Andrews 64 K5
St. Anthony 34 V6
St. Arnaud 118 D5
St. Augustin 62 K4
St. Augustine 42 E4
St. Austell 64 H11
St-Avold 62 J5
St. Barthélémy 46 M5
St-Brieuc 66 C5
St. Catharines 36 L3
St-Chamond 66 K8
St-Claude 66 L7
St. Cloud 40 B1
St. David's 64 G10
St-Denis, *France* 62 E6
St-Denis, *Réunion* 112 (1)B2
St-Dié 70 B2
St-Dizier 66 K5
Ste-Anne-de-Beaupré 40 F1
Ste-Menehould 62 G5
Saintes 66 E8
Stes-Maries-de-la-Mer 66 K10
St-Étienne 66 K8
St-Étienne-du-Rouvray 62 D5
St-Félicien 40 F1
St-Florentin 66 J5
St-Flour 66 J8
St. Francis 38 F3
St. Gallen 70 E3
St-Gaudens 66 F10
St. George, *Australia* 116 J5
St. George, *United States* 38 D3
St. Georgen 70 D2
St. Georges 40 F1
St. George's 46 M6
St. George's Channel 64 F10
St-Germain-en-Laye 62 E6
St-Girons 66 G11
St. Helena 102 C7
St. Helena Bay 112 B6
St. Helens, *United Kingdom* 64 K8
St. Helens, *United States* 38 B1
St. Helier 66 C4
St-Hubert 62 H4
St. Ignace 40 D1
St. Ives 64 G11
St-Jean-d'Angely 66 E8
St-Jean-de-Luz 66 D10
St-Jean-de-Maurienne 70 B5
St-Jean-sur-Richelieu 40 F1
St. John 34 T7
St. John's 34 W7
St. Johnsbury 40 F2
St. Joseph 40 B3
St-Jovité 40 F1
St. Kilda 64 D4
St. Kitts-Nevis 46 M5
St. Laurent 50 G2
St-Laurent-en-Grandvaux 70 A4
St. Lawrence 40 G1
St. Lawrence Island 44 (1)C3
St-Léonard 40 G1
St-Lô 62 A5
St. Louis, *Senegal* 106 B5
St. Louis, *United States* 40 B3
St. Lucia 46 M6
St. Maarten 46 M5
St-Malo 66 D5
St. Marys 40 D2
St. Matthew Island 44 (1)C3
St-Mihiel 62 H6
St. Moritz 70 E4
St-Nazaire 66 C6
St-Nicolas-de-Port 70 B2
St. Niklaas 62 G3
St-Omer 62 E4
St-Palais 66 D10
St-Pamphile 40 G1
St-Paul 70 B6
St. Paul 38 G2
St. Paul 40 B2
St. Peter 40 B2
St. Peter Ording 60 D2
St. Peter-Port 66 C4
St. Petersburg = Sankt-Peterburg 78 F3
St. Petersburg 42 E4
St-Pierre-et-Miquelon 34 V7
St. Pierre Island 112 (2)A2
St-Pol-de-Léon 66 A5
St-Pol-sur-Ternoise 62 E4
St. Pölten 70 L2
St-Quentin 62 F5
St-Raphaël 70 B7
St. Siméon 40 G1
St. Stephen 40 G1
St. Thomas 40 D2
St-Tropez 70 B7
St. Truiden 62 H4
St-Valéry-sur-Somme 62 D4
St. Veit 70 K4
St. Veit an der Glan 74 B3
St. Vincent and the Grenadines 46 M6
St-Vincent-les-Forts 70 B6
St-Vith 62 J4
Saipan 114 E4
Sajószentpéter 58 K9
Säkäkah 96 D4
Sakaraha 112 G4
Sakarya 76 N4
Sakarya 76 N4
Sakata 88 K4
Sakchu 88 C3
Sakha 84 N3
Sakhalin 84 Q6
Sakhalinskiy Zaliv 84 Q6
Sakhon Nakhon 90 C3
Šäki 98 M3
Sakishima-shotō 86 H6
Sakskøbing 60 G2
Sal 78 H5
Sal 108 (1)B1
Sala 56 J7
Šal'a 58 G9
Salacgrīva 56 N8
Sala Consilina 72 K8
Saladillo 52 K6
Salado 52 J4
Salālah 96 F6
Salamanca, *Mexico* 46 D4
Salamanca, *Spain* 68 E4
Salamanca, *United States* 40 E2
Salamina 76 F7
Salamīyah 100 E1
Salar de Uyuni 52 H3
Salawati 92 (2)D3
Salayar 92 (2)B4
Salbris 66 H6
Saldus 56 M8
Sale 116 J7
Salekhard 82 M4
Salem 38 B2
Salem, *India* 94 C6
Salem, *United States* 40 C3
Salerno 72 J8
Salgótarján 58 J9
Salida 38 E3
Salihli 76 L6
Salihorsk 78 E4
Salima 112 E2
Salina 72 J10
Salina, *Kans., United States* 38 G3
Salina, *Ut., United States* 38 D3
Salinas, *Brazil* 50 J7
Salinas, *Ecuador* 50 A4
Salinas, *Mexico* 44 F4
Salinas, *United States* 44 B1
Salinas Grandes 52 J4
Salinópolis 50 H4
Salisbury, *United Kingdom* 62 A3
Salisbury, *Md., United States* 40 E3
Salisbury, *N.C., United States* 40 D3
Salisbury Island 34 R4
Şalkhad 100 D4
Salla 56 Q3
Salluit 34 R4
Salmās 98 L4
Salmon 38 C1/D1
Salmon 38 D1
Salmon Arm 34 H6
Salmon River Mountains 38 C1
Salo 56 M6
Salon-de-Provence 66 L10
Salonta 74 J3
Sal'sk 78 H5
Salsomaggiore Terme 70 E6
Salt 100 C4
Salta 52 H3
Saltee Islands 64 F9
Saltillo 44 F3
Salt Lake City 38 D2
Salto 52 K5
Salton Sea 44 C2
Saluda 42 E3
Salûm 104 E1
Saluzzo 70 C6
Salvador 50 K6
Salvadore 48 F5
Salween 90 B2
Salyan 98 N4
Salyersville 40 D3
Salym 78 P3
Salzach 70 H2
Salzburg 70 J3
Salzgitter 60 F4
Salzwedel 60 G4
Samaipata 50 E7
Samar 90 H4
Samara 78 K4
Samarinda 92 (1)F3
Samarkand 96 J2
Sāmarrā' 98 K6
Şamaxı 98 N3
Sambalpur 94 D4
Sambas 92 (1)D2
Sambava 112 J2
Sambhal 94 C3
Sambir 58 N8
Sambre 62 F4
Same 110 F4
Sami 76 C6
Sāmkir 98 M3
Samoa 114 J7
Samobor 70 L5
Samoded 78 H2
Samokov 74 L7
Šamorín 58 G9
Samos 76 J7
Samos 76 J7
Samothraki 76 H4
Samothraki 76 H4
Sam Rayburn Reservoir 42 C3
Samsang 94 D2
Samsø 56 F9
Samsun 98 G3
Samtredia 98 K2
Samut Songkhram 90 B4
San 58 L7
San 108 D2
Şan'ā 104 H4
Sanaga 108 G4
San Ambrosio 52 F4
Sanana 92 (2)C3
Sanana 92 (2)C3
Sanandaj 98 M6
San Angelo 44 F2
San Antonia Abad 68 M6
San Antonio, *Chile* 52 G5
San Antonio, *United States* 46 E3
San Antonio de los Cobres 52 H3
San Antonio-Oeste 52 H7
Sanāw 96 F6
San Benedetto del Tronto 72 H6
San Bernardino 44 C2
San Bernardo 52 H5
San Borja 50 D6
San Carlos, *Chile* 52 G6
San Carlos, *Philippines* 90 G3
San Carlos, *Venezuela* 50 D3
San Carlos de Bolivár 52 J6
San Carlos del Zulia 50 C2
San Carlos Lake 44 D2
San Cataldo 72 H11
Sanchahe 88 C1
Sanchakou 82 P10
Sanchor 94 B4
Sanchursk 78 J3
San Clemente Island 44 C2
San Cristóbal 114 G7
San Cristóbal, *Argentina* 52 J5
San Cristóbal, *Venezuela* 50 C2
San Cristóbal de las Casas 46 F5
Sancti Spíritus 46 J4
Sandakan 92 (1)F1
Sandane 56 D6
Sandanski 76 F3
Sanday 64 K2
Sandefjord 56 F7
Sanders 44 E1
Sanderson 44 F2
Sandfire Flat Roadhouse 116 D3
San Diego 44 C2
Sandıklı 76 N6
Sandnes 56 C7
Sandnessjøen 56 G4
Sandoa 110 C5
Sandomierz 58 L7
San Donà di Piave 70 H5
Sandoway 94 F5
Sandpoint 38 C1
Sandray 64 E5
Sandviken 56 J6
Sandy 38 D2
Sandy Cape 116 K4
Sandy Island 116 D2
Sandy Lake 34 N6
Sandy Lake 34 N6
Sandy Springs 42 E3
San Felipe 36 D5
San Félix 52 E4
San Fernando, *Chile* 52 G5
San Fernando, *Mexico* 42 B5
San Fernando, *Philippines* 90 G3
San Fernando, *Spain* 68 D8
San Fernando de Apure 50 D2
Sanford, *Fla., United States* 42 E4
Sanford, *N.C., United States* 42 F2
San Francis 42 A2
San Francisco, *Argentina* 52 J5
San Francisco, *United States* 38 B3
Sangamner 94 B5
Sangān 96 H3
Sangar 84 M4
Sangāreddi 94 C5
Sângeorz-Băi 74 M2
Sangerhausen 60 G5
Sangha 108 H4
Sanghar 96 J4
San Gimignano 70 G7
San Giovanni in Fiore 72 L9
San Giovanni Valdarno 70 G7
Sangir 92 (2)C2
Sangkhla Buri 90 B3
Sangkulirang 92 (1)F2
Sangli 94 B5
Sangmélima 108 G4
Sangre de Cristo Range 44 E1
Sangsang 94 E3
Sangue 50 F6
Sangüesa 68 J2
Sanjō 88 K5
San Joaquin Valley 38 B3
San Jose 38 B3
San José 46 H7
San Jose de Buenavista 90 G4
San José de Chiquitos 50 E7
San Jose de Jáchal 52 H5
San José del Cabo 46 C4
San José de Ocuné 50 C3
San Juan 46 H5
San Juan, *Argentina* 52 H5
San Juan, *Costa Rica* 46 H6
San Juan, *Puerto Rico* 46 L5
San Juan, *United States* 44 E1
San Juan Bautista 52 K4
San Juan de los Cayos 50 D1
San Juan de los Morros 50 D2
San Juan Mountains 38 E3
San Julián 52 H8
Sankt-Peterburg 78 F3
Sankuru 110 C4
Sanlıurfa 98 H5
San Lorenzo 44 D3
Sanlúcar de Barrameda 68 D8
San Lucas 46 C4
San Luis 52 H5
San Luis Obispo 44 B1
San Luis Potosí 46 D4
San Luis Rio Colorado 44 D2
San Marcos 42 E4
San Marino 70 H7
San Marino 70 H7
San Martín 50 E6
Sanmenxia 86 E4
San Miguel 46 G6
San Miguel 50 E7
San Miguel de Tucumán 52 H4
San Miguel Island 44 E2
San Miniato 70 F7
San Nicolas de los Arroyos 52 J5
San Nicolás de los Garzas 42 A4
San Nicolas Island 44 C2
Sânnicolau Mare 74 H3
Sanok 58 M8
San Pedro, *Philippines* 90 G4
San-Pédro 108 C4
San Pablo 90 G4
San Pedro, *Argentina* 52 J3
San Pedro, *Bolivia* 50 E7
San Pedro de las Colonias 44 F3
San Pedro Sula 46 G5
San Pellegrino Terme 70 E5
San Pietro 72 C9
Sanqaçal 98 N3
San Rafael 52 H5
San Remo 70 C7
San Roque 68 E8
San Salvador 42 G5
San Salvador 46 G6
San Salvador de Jujuy 52 H3
Sansar 94 C4
San Sebastián = Donostia 68 I1
San Sebastian de los Reyes 68 G4
Sansepolcro 70 H7
San Sévero 72 K7
Sanski Most 70 M6
San Stéfano 72 H8
Santa Ana, *Bolivia* 50 D7
Santa Ana, *El Salvador* 46 G6
Santa Ana, *Mexico* 44 D2

Santa Ana, *United States* 44 C2
Santa Bárbara 36 E6
Santa Barbara 44 C2
Santa Barbara Island 44 C2
Santa Catalina 52 H4
Santa Catalina Island 44 C2
Santa Catarina 52 L4
Santa Clara, *Columbia* 50 D4
Santa Clara, *Cuba* 36 K7
Santa Clarita 44 C2
Santa Comba Dão 68 B4
Santa Cruz 52 G9
Santa Cruz, *Bolivia* 50 E7
Santa Cruz, *United States* 44 B1
Santa Cruz de Tenerife 106 B3
Santa Cruz Island 44 B2
Santa Cruz Islands 114 G7
Santa Eugenia 68 A2
Santa Fe 38 E3
Santa Fé 52 J5
Sant'Agata di Militello 72 J10
Santa Isabel 114 F6
Santa Isabel 52 H6
Santa la Grande 36 K7
Santa Margarita 36 D7
Santa Maria 106 (1)B2
Santa Maria, *Brazil* 52 L4
Santa Maria, *United States* 44 B2
Santa Maria das Barreiras 50 H5
Santa Marta 46 K6
Santana do Livramento 52 K5
Santander 68 G1
Sant'Antioco 72 C9
Santa Pola 68 K6
Santarém, *Brazil* 50 G4
Santarém, *Spain* 68 B5
Santa Rosa, *Argentina* 52 J6
Santa Rosa, *Acre, Brazil* 50 C5
Santa Rosa, *R.G.S., Brazil* 52 L4
Santa Rosa, *Calif., United States* 38 B3
Santa Rosa, *N.Mex., United States* 44 F2
Santa Rosa Island 44 B2
Santa Vitória do Palmar 52 L5
Sant Boi 68 N3
Sant Carlos de la Ràpita 68 L4
Sant Celoni 68 N3
Sant Feliu de Guixols 68 P3
Santiago 52 G5
Santiago, *Brazil* 52 L4
Santiago, *Dominican Republic* 46 K5
Santiago, *Philippines* 90 G3
Santiago, *Spain* 68 B2
Santiago de Cuba 46 J5
Santiago del Estero 52 J4
Santo André 52 M3
Santo Antão 108 (1)A1
Santo Antônio de Jesus 50 K6
Santo Antônio do Içá 50 D4
Santo Domingo 46 L5
Santo Domingo de los Colorados 50 B4
Santoña 68 G1
Santos 52 M3
San Vicente 90 G3
San Vincenzo 72 E5
Sanya 90 D3
Sao Bernardo do Campo 50 E4
São Borja 52 K4
São Carlos 52 M3
São Félix, *M.G., Brazil* 50 G6
São Félix, *Pará, Brazil* 50 G5
São Filipe 108 (1)B2
São Francisco 50 J6
São João de Madeira 68 B4
São Jorge 106 (1)B2
São José do Rio Prêto 52 L3
São Luís 50 J4
São Miguel 106 (1)B2
Saône 66 K7
São Nicolau 108 (1)B1
São Paulo 52 L3
São Paulo 52 M3
São Paulo de Olivença 50 D4
São Raimundo Nonato 50 J5
São Tiago 108 (1)B1
São Tomé 108 F4
São Tomé 108 F4
São Tomé and Príncipe 108 F4
São Vicente 108 (1)A1
São Vicente 52 M3
Saparua 92 (2)C3
Sapele 108 F3
Sapes 76 H4
Sapientza 76 D8
Sa Pobla 68 P5
Sapporo 88 L2
Sapri 72 K8
Sapudi 92 (1)E4
Sapulpa 42 B2
Saqqez 98 M5
Sarāb 98 M5
Sara Buri 90 C4
Sarajevo 74 F6
Sarakhs 96 H2
Saraktash 78 L4
Saramati 94 G3
Saran 82 N8
Saranac Lake 40 F2
Sarandë 76 C5
Sarangani Islands 92 (2)C1
Saranpul 78 M2
Saransk 78 J4
Sarapul 78 K3
Sarapul'skoye 84 P7
Sarasota 42 E4
Sarata 74 S3
Saratoga 38 E2
Saratoga Springs 40 F2
Saratov 78 J4
Saravan 96 H4
Sarawak 92 (1)E2
Saray 76 K3
Sarayköy 76 L7
Sarayönü 76 Q6
Sarbāz 96 H4
Sarbīsheh 96 G3
Sárbogárd 74 F3
Sar Dasht 98 L5
Sardegna 72 E8
Sardinia = Sardegna 72 E8
Sardis Lake 42 B3
Sar-e Pol 96 J2
Sargodha 96 K3
Sarh 108 H3
Sārī 96 F2
Saria 76 K9
Sarıkamış 98 K3
Sarıkaya 98 F4
Sarikei 92 (1)E2
Sarina 116 J4
Sariñena 68 K3
Sarīr Tibesti 104 C3
Sariwŏn 88 C4
Sark 66 C4
Sarkad 74 J3
Sarkand 82 P8
Sarkikaraağaç 76 P6
Şarkişla 98 G4
Şarköy 76 K4
Sarmi 92 (2)E3
Särna 56 G6
Sarnia 40 D2
Sarny 78 E4
Sarolangun 92 (1)C3
Saronno 70 E5
Saros Körfezi 76 J4
Sárospatak 58 L9
Sarre 66 M5
Sarrebourg 66 N5
Sarreguemines 66 N4
Sarria 68 C2
Sartène 72 C7
Sartyn'ya 78 M2
Saruhanli 76 K6
Sārur 98 L4
Sárvár 70 M3
Sarvestān 101 E2
Sarviz 74 F2
Sarykamyshkoye Ozero 82 K9
Saryozek 82 P9
Saryshagan 82 N8
Sarysu 82 M8
Sary-Tash 96 K2
Sarzana 70 E6
Sasaram 94 D4
Sasebo 88 E7
Saskatchewan 34 K6
Saskatchewan 34 L6
Saskatoon 34 K6
Saskylakh 82 W3
Sassandra 108 C4
Sassari 72 C8
Sassnitz 60 J2
Sassuolo 70 F6
Satadougou 108 B2
Satara 94 B5
Satna 94 D4
Sátoraljaújhely 58 L9
Satti 94 C2
Sättna 56 J5
Satu Mare 74 K2
Satun 92 (1)B1
Sauce 52 K5
Saudi Arabia 96 D4
Sauk Center 40 B1
Saulgau 70 E2
Saulieu 66 K6
Sault Ste. Marie, *Canada* 40 D1
Sault Ste. Marie, *United States* 40 D1
Saumlakki 92 (2)D4
Saumur 66 E6
Saunders Island 48 J9
Saurimo 110 C5
Sauðarkrókur 56 (1)D2
Sava 70 L5
Savaii 114 J7
Savalou 108 E3
Savannah 32 K6
Savannah, *Ga., United States* 42 E3
Savannah, *Tenn., United States* 42 D2
Savannakhet 90 C3
Savaştepe 76 K5
Savè 108 E3
Save 112 E4
Sāveh 96 F2
Saverne 60 C8
Savigliano 70 C6
Savona 70 D6
Savonlinna 56 Q6
Savu 92 (2)B5
Sawahlunto 92 (1)C3
Sawai Madhopur 94 C3
Sawqirah 96 G6
Sawu Sea 92 (2)B4
Sayanogorsk 82 S7
Sayansk 84 G6
Sayhūt 96 F6
Säylac 104 H5
Saynshand 86 E2
Sayram Hu 82 Q9
Say'ūn 96 E6
Say-Utes 82 J9
Sazan 76 B4
Sazin 96 K2
Scafell Pike 64 J7
Scalea 72 K9
Scarborough 64 M7
Scarp 64 E3
Schaalsee 60 F3
Schaffhausen 70 D3
Schagen 62 G2
Scharbeutz 60 F2
Schärding 70 J2
Scharhörn 60 D3
Scheeßel 60 E3
Schefferville 34 T6
Scheibbs 70 L3
Schelde 62 F3
Schenectady 40 F2
Scheveningen 62 G2
Schiedam 62 G3
Schiermonnikoog 62 H1
Schio 70 G5
Schiza 76 D8
Schkeuditz 60 H5
Schlei 60 E2
Schleiden 62 J4
Schleswig 60 E2
Schlieben 60 J5
Schlüchtern 60 E6
Schneeberg 60 G6
Schneeberg 60 H6
Schönebeck 60 G4
Schongau 70 F3
Schöningen 60 F4
Schouwen 62 F3
Schramberg 70 D2
Schreiber 40 C1
Schrems 70 L2
Schull 64 C10
Schwabach 60 G7
Schwäbische Alb 70 E2
Schwäbisch-Gmünd 70 E2
Schwäbisch-Hall 60 E7
Schwalmstadt 60 E6
Schwandorf 60 H7
Schwarzenbek 60 F3
Schwarzenberg 60 H6
Schwarzwald 70 D3
Schwaz 70 G3
Schwechat 58 F9
Schwedt 58 D4
Schweich 62 J5
Schweinfurt 60 F6
Schwenningen 70 D2
Schwerin 60 G3
Schweriner See 60 G3
Schwetzingen 60 D7
Schwyz 70 D3
Sciacca 72 H11
Scicli 72 J12
Scobey 38 E1
Scotia Ridge 52 K9
Scotia Sea 120 (2)A4
Scotland 64 H5
Scott City 38 F3
Scott Inlet 34 T2
Scott Island 120 (2)Z3
Scott Reef 116 D2
Scottsbluff 38 F2
Scottsboro 40 C4
Scotty's Junction 44 C1
Scranton 40 E2
Scunthorpe 64 M8
Seal 34 M5
Sea of Azov 78 G5
Sea of Galilee 100 C4
Sea of Japan 88 G3
Sea of Marmara = Marmara Denizi 76 L4
Sea of Okhotsk 84 Q5
Sea of the Hebrides 64 E4
Searchlight 44 D1
Searcy 40 B3
Seaside 38 B1
Seattle 38 B1
Sebeş 74 L4
Sebkha Azzel Matti 106 F3
Sebkha de Timimoun 106 E3
Sebkha de Tindouf 106 D3
Sebkha Mekerrhane 106 F3
Sebkha Oum el Drouss Telli 106 C4
Sebkhet de Chemchâm 106 C4
Sebnitz 60 K6
Sebring 42 E4
Secchia 70 F6
Sechura 50 A5
Secretary Island 118 A7
Secunderabad 94 C5
Sécure 50 D7
Sedalia 40 B3
Sedan 62 G5
Sedano 68 G2
Seddonville 118 C5
Sede Boqer 100 B6
Sedeh 96 G3
Sederot 100 B5
Sédico 70 H4
Sedom 100 C5
Seeheim 112 E5
Seelow 60 K4
Seesen 60 F5
Seevetal 60 E3
Séez 70 E5
Seferihisar 76 J6
Segamat 92 (1)C2
Segezha 78 F2
Seghnān 96 K2
Ségou 108 C2
Segovia 68 F4
Segré 66 E6
Séguédine 106 H4
Seguin 42 B4
Segura 68 H6
Sehithwa 112 C4
Sehnde 60 E4
Seiland 56 M1
Seiling 42 B2
Seinäjoki 56 M5
Seine 66 F4
Sekondi 108 D3
Selassi 92 (2)D3
Selat Bangka 92 (1)D3
Selat Berhala 92 (1)C3
Selat Dampir 92 (2)D3
Selat Karimata 92 (1)D3
Selat Makassar 92 (1)F3
Selat Mentawai 92 (1)B3
Selat Sunda 92 (1)D4
Selawik 44 (1)F2
Selb 60 H6
Selby 38 G1
Selçuk 76 K7
Selebi-Phikwe 112 D4
Sélestat 70 C2
Selfoss 56 (1)C3
Seligman 44 D1
Seljord 56 E7
Selkirk 36 G1
Selkirk Mountains 36 C1
Sells 44 D2
Selm 62 K3
Selmer 40 C3
Selpele 92 (2)D3
Selvas 50 C5
Selwyn Lake 34 L5
Selwyn Mountains 44 (1)L3
Semanit 76 B4
Semarang 92 (1)E4
Sematan 92 (1)D2
Sembé 108 G4
Seminoe Reservoir 38 E2
Seminole, *Okla., United States* 38 G3
Seminole, *Tex., United States* 44 F2
Semiozernoye 82 L7
Semipalatinsk 82 Q7
Semiyarka 82 P7
Semois 62 H5

Semporna	92	(1)F2
Sena Madureira	50	D5
Senanga	112	C3
Senatobia	42	D3
Sendai	88	L4
Senec	70	N2
Seneca	42	E3
Senegal	108	A2
Sénégal	108	B1
Senftenberg	60	J5
Senhor do Bonfim	50	J6
Senica	58	G9
Senigallia	70	J7
Senj	70	K6
Senja	56	J2
Senlis	62	E5
Sennar	96	B7
Senneterre	40	E1
Sens	66	J5
Senta	74	H4
Seoni	94	C4
Seoul = Sŏul	88	D5
Separation Point	118	D5
Sept-Îles	34	T6
Seraing	62	H4
Serakhs	96	H2
Seram	92	(2)D3
Seram Sea	92	(2)C3
Serang	92	(1)D4
Serbia = Srbija	74	H6
Serdobsk	78	H4
Serebryansk	82	Q8
Sered'	74	E1
Şereflikoçhisar	76	R6
Seregno	70	E5
Serein	66	J6
Seremban	92	(1)C2
Serenje	112	E2
Sergelen	86	E1
Sergeyevka	78	N4
Sergipe	50	K6
Sergiyev Posad	78	G3
Seria	92	(1)E2
Serifos	76	G7
Serik	76	P8
Seringapatam Reef	116	D2
Sermata	92	(2)C4
Seronga	112	C3
Serov	78	M3
Serowe	112	D4
Serpa	68	C7
Serpukhov	78	G4
Serra Acari	50	F3
Serra Curupira	50	E3
Serra da Chela	112	A3
Serra da Espinhaço	50	J7
Serra da Ibiapaba	50	J4
Serra da Mantiqueira	52	M3
Serra de Maracaju	52	K3
Serra do Cachimbo	50	F5
Serra do Caiapó	50	G7
Serra do Roncador	50	G6
Serra dos Carajás	50	G5
Serra dos Dois Irmãos	50	J5
Serra dos Parecis	50	E6
Serra do Tiracambu	50	H4
Serra Estrondo	50	H5
Serra Formosa	50	F6
Serra Geral de Goiás	50	H6
Serra Geral do Paranã	50	H7
Serra Lombarda	50	G3
Serra Pacaraima	50	E3
Serra Parima	50	E3
Serra Tumucumaque	50	F3
Serre da Estrela	68	C4
Serres, *France*	66	L9
Serres, *Greece*	76	F3
Serrinha	50	K6
Sertã	68	B5
Serui	92	(2)E3
Servia	76	D4
Sêrxü	86	B4
Sese Islands	110	E4
Sesfontein	112	A3
Sesheke	112	C3
Sessa Aurunca	72	H7
Sestri Levante	70	E6
Sestroretsk	56	Q6
Sestrunj	70	K6
Sesvete	70	M5
Setana	88	K2
Sète	66	J10
Sete Lagoas	50	J7
Setesdal	56	D7
Sétif	106	G1
Settat	106	D2
Setúbal	68	B6
Sŏul	114	C2
Seurre	66	L7
Sevana Lich	98	L3
Sevastopol'	98	E1
Seven Lakes	44	E1
Sevenoaks	62	C3
Severn, *Canada*	34	P5
Severn, *United Kingdom*	64	K10
Severnaya Dvina	78	H2
Severnaya Osetiya	98	L2
Severnaya Zemlya	82	U1
Severn Estuary	64	J10
Severnoye	78	K4
Severnyy	82	L4
Severobaykal'sk	84	H5
Severodvinsk	78	G2
Severomorsk	56	S2
Severoural'sk	78	M2
Severo-Yeniseyskiy	82	S5
Sevier Lake	38	D3
Sevilla	68	E7
Sevlievo	74	N7
Seward Peninsula	44	(1)E2
Seyakha	82	N3
Seychelles	112	(2)B2
Seychelles Islands	102	J6
Seydişehir	76	P7
Seydisfjörður	56	(1)G2
Seyhan	98	F5
Seymchan	84	S4
Seymour, *Australia*	116	J7
Seymour, *Ind., United States*	42	D2
Seymour, *Tex., United States*	42	B3
Sézanne	66	J5
Sezze	72	H7
Sfakia	76	G9
Sfântu Gheorghe	74	N4
Sfax	106	H2
's-Gravenhage	62	G2
Sha'am	101	G3
Shabunda	110	D4
Shabwah	96	E6
Shache	82	P10
Shādegān	101	C1
Shadehill Reservoir	38	F1
Shagamu	108	E3
Shagonar	82	S7
Shag Rocks	52	N9
Shahbā'	100	D4
Shahdāb	101	G1
Shahdol	94	D4
Shah Fuladi	96	J3
Shahjahanpur	94	C3
Shahrak	96	H3
Shahr-e Bābāk	101	F1
Shahrtuz	96	J2
Shakhrisabz	96	J2
Shakhtërsk	84	Q7
Shakhty	78	H5
Shakhun'ya	78	J3
Shaki	108	E3
Shakotan-misaki	88	L2
Shama	110	E5
Shamattawa	34	N5
Shamrock	44	F1
Shand	96	H3
Shandong Bandao	86	G3
Shangani	112	D3
Shangdu	86	E2
Shanghai	86	G4
Shangqui	86	F4
Shangrao	86	F5
Shangzhi	86	H1
Shangzhou	86	D4
Shantarskiye Ostrova	84	P5
Shantou	86	F6
Shanwei	90	F2
Shanyin	86	E3
Shaoguan	86	E6
Shaoxing	86	G5
Shaoyang	86	E5
Shapkina	78	K1
Shaqrā'	101	A4
Sharga	82	T8
Sharjah = Ash Shāriqah	101	F4
Shark Bay	114	E8
Shark Reef	116	L2
Sharm el Sheikh	104	F2
Sharūrah	96	E6
Shashe	112	D4
Shashi	86	E4
Shasta Lake	38	B2
Shatsk	78	H4
Shats'k	58	N6
Shaubak	100	C6
Shawano	40	C2
Shcherbakove	84	U3
Shchigry	78	G4
Shchuch'ye	82	L6
Shchuchyn	56	N10
Sheberghān	96	J2
Sheboygan	40	C2
Sheffield, *New Zealand*	118	D6
Sheffield, *United Kingdom*	64	L8
Sheffield, *Al., United States*	40	C4
Sheffield, *Tex., United States*	44	F2
Shegmas	78	J2
Shelburne	34	T8
Shelby	38	D1
Shelbyville	40	C3
Shelikof Strait	44	(1)F4
Shenandoah	40	A2
Shendam	108	F3
Shendi	104	F4
Shenkursk	78	H2
Shenyang	88	B3
Shenzhen	86	E6
Shepetivka	78	E4
Shepparton	116	J7
Sherbro Island	108	B3
Sherbrooke	40	F1
Sheridan	38	E2
Sherkaly	78	N2
Sherlovaya Gora	84	K6
Sherman	42	B3
's-Hertogenbosch	62	H3
Shetland Islands	64	M1
Shetpe	82	J9
Sheyenne	38	G1
Sheykh Sho'eyb	101	E3
Shiant Islands	64	F4
Shibata	88	K5
Shibetsu, *Japan*	88	M1
Shibetsu, *Japan*	88	N2
Shibotsu-jima	88	P2
Shiderty	82	N7
Shihezi	82	R9
Shijiazhuang	86	E3
Shikarpur	96	J4
Shikoku	88	G7
Shikoku-sanchi	88	G7
Shikotan-tō	88	P2
Shikotsu-ko	88	L2
Shiliguri	94	E3
Shilka	84	K6
Shilka	84	K6
Shillong	94	F3
Shilovo	78	H4
Shimabara	88	F7
Shimla	94	C2
Shimoda	88	K6
Shimoga	94	C6
Shimo-Koshiki-jima	88	E8
Shimoni	110	F4
Shimonoseki	88	F7
Shināş	101	G4
Shīndan	96	H3
Shingū	88	H7
Shinjō	88	L4
Shinyanga	110	E4
Shiono-misaki	88	H7
Shiprock	38	E3
Shiquan	86	D4
Shirakawa	88	L5
Shīrāz	101	E2
Shire	112	E3
Shiretoko-misaki	88	N1
Shiriya-zaki	88	L3
Shīr Kūh	96	F3
Shivpuri	94	C3
Shiyan	86	E4
Shizuishan	86	D3
Shizuoka	88	K6
Shkodër	74	G7
Shomishko	82	K8
Shorap	96	J4
Shoreham	62	B4
Shoshone, *Calif., United States*	38	C3
Shoshone, *Id., United States*	38	D2
Shoshoni	38	E2
Shostka	78	F4
Show Low	44	E2
Shoyna	78	H1
Shreveport	42	C3
Shrewsbury	64	K9
Shuangliao	88	B2
Shuangyashan	84	N7
Shubarkuduk	82	K8
Shulan	88	D1
Shumagin Islands	44	(1)E5
Shumen	74	P6
Shumikha	78	M3
Shuqrah	96	E7
Shurchi	96	J2
Shūr Gaz	101	H2
Shurinda	84	J5
Shuryshkary	78	N1
Shuya	78	H3
Shuyang	86	F4
Shwebo	90	B2
Shymkent	82	M9
Sialkot	96	K3
Siatista	76	D4
Šiauliai	58	N2
Sibay	78	L4
Šibenik	74	C6
Siberia = Sibir	80	N3
Siberut	92	(1)B3
Sibi	96	J4
Sibigo	92	(1)B2
Sibir	80	N3
Sibiu	74	M4
Sibolga	92	(1)B2
Sibu	92	(1)E2
Sibuco	90	G5
Sibut	110	B2
Sicilia	72	G11
Sicilian Channel	72	F11
Sicily = Sicilia	72	G11
Šid	74	G4
Siddipet	94	C5
Siderno	72	L10
Sidi Barrani	104	E
Sidi Bel Abbès	106	E
Sidi Kacem	106	D
Sidirokastro	76	F
Sidney	38	F
Sidoan	92	(2)B
Sidorovsk	82	Q
Sieburg	62	K
Siedlce	58	M5
Sieg	62	K
Siegen	62	L
Siemiatycze	58	M
Siĕmréab	90	C4
Siena	70	G
Sierpc	58	J
Sierra Blanca	44	E
Sierra Colorada	52	H
Sierra de Calalasteo	52	H4
Sierra de Córdoba	52	H5
Sierra de Gata	68	D4
Sierra de Gúdar	68	K4
Sierra del Nevado	52	H6
Sierra de Perija	46	K7
Sierra Grande	52	H7
Sierra Leone	108	B3
Sierra Madre	46	F5
Sierra Madre del Sur	46	E5
Sierra Madre Occidental	36	E5
Sierra Madre Oriental	44	F3
Sierra Morena	68	E6
Sierra Nevada, *Spain*	68	G7
Sierra Nevada, *United States*	44	B1
Sierra Vizcaino	36	D5
Sierre	70	C4
Sifnos	76	G8
Sig	68	K9
Sigean	66	H10
Sighetu Marmaţiei	74	L2
Sighişoara	74	M3
Siglufjörður	56	(1)C1
Sigmaringen	70	E2
Signal Mountain	40	C3
Siguiri	108	C2
Sihanoukville	90	C4
Siilinjärvi	56	P5
Siirt	98	J5
Sikar	94	C3
Sikasso	108	C2
Sikea	76	F4
Sikeston	40	C3
Sikhote Alin	88	H1
Sikinos	76	C8
Siklós	74	F4
Siktyakh	84	L3
Sil	68	C2
Šilalė	58	M2
Silandro	70	F4
Silba	70	K6
Silchar	94	F4
Şile	76	M3
Silhouette Island	112	(2)B1
Siliana	72	D12
Silifke	98	E5
Siling Co	94	E2
Silistra	74	Q5
Silivri	76	L3
Siljan	56	H6
Sillamäe	56	P7
Silsbee	42	C3
Siluas	92	(1)D2
Šilutė	58	L2
Silvan	98	J4
Silver Bay	40	B1
Silver City	44	E2
Silver Lake	38	B2
Silver Plains	116	H2
Simanggang	92	(1)E2
Simao	86	C6
Simav	98	C4
Simcoe	40	D2
Simeonovgrad	74	N7

Simeria	58	N12
Simeulue	92	(1)A2
Simferopol'	98	F1
Şimleu Silvaniei	74	K2
Simmerath	62	J4
Simojärvi	56	P3
Simpang	92	(1)C3
Simpson Desert	116	G4
Sinabang	92	(1)B2
Sinai	104	F2
Sinaia	74	N4
Şinak	98	K5
Sinalunga	72	F5
Sinanju	88	C4
Sincelejo	50	B2
Sinclair's Bay	64	J3
Sindangbarang	92	(1)D4
Sindelfingen	60	E8
Sines	68	B7
Singa	104	F5
Singapore	92	(1)C2
Singapore	92	(1)C2
Singaraja	92	(1)E4
Singen	70	D3
Sîngerei	74	R2
Singida	110	E4
Singkawang	92	(1)D2
Singkep	92	(1)C3
Singkilbaru	92	(1)B2
Singleton	116	K6
Siniscóla	72	D8
Sinj	74	D6
Sinjār	98	J5
Sinkat	104	G4
Sinni	72	L8
Sinop	98	F2
Sinsheim	60	D7
Sinton	42	B4
Sinŭiju	88	C3
Sinyaya	84	L4
Sió	74	F3
Siófok	74	F3
Sion	70	C4
Sioux City	40	A2
Sioux Falls	40	A2
Sioux Lookout	36	H2
Siping	88	C2
Sipiwesk	34	M5
Sipura	92	(1)B3
Sira	56	D7
Siracusa	72	K11
Sir Banī 'Yās	101	E4
Sir Edward Pellew Group	116	G3
Siret	74	P2
Siret	74	Q4
Sîrgān	96	H4
Şiria	58	L11
Siri Kit Dam	90	B3
Sirk	101	G3
Sirohi	94	B4
Sirsa	94	C3
Sirsi	94	B6
Sisak	74	D4
Sisian	98	L4
Sisimiut	34	W3
Sisŏphŏn	90	C4
Sisseton	38	G1
Sistema Central	68	E4
Sistema Iberico	68	H3
Sisteron	70	A6
Sitapur	94	D3
Sitasjaure	56	J3
Siteia	76	J9
Sitges	68	M3
Sithonia	76	F4
Sitka	34	D5
Sittard	62	H4
Sittwe	94	F4
Sivand	101	E1
Sivas	98	G4
Siverek	98	H5
Sivrihisar	76	P5
Siwa	104	E1
Siyäzän	98	N3
Sjælland	56	F9
Sjenica	74	H6
Sjenica Jezero	74	G6
Sjöbo	58	C2
Skädlderviken	58	B1
Skaerbaek	60	D1
Skagen	56	F8
Skagerrak	56	D8
Skantzoura	76	G5
Skardu	96	L2
Skaulo	56	L3
Skawina	58	J8
Skegness	62	C1
Skellefteå	56	L4
Ski	56	F7
Skiathos	76	F5
Skidal'	58	P4
Skien	56	E7
Skikda	106	G1
Skipton	64	L8
Skjern	56	E9
Škofja Loka	70	K4
Skopelos	76	F5
Skopje	74	J7
Skövde	56	G7
Skovorodino	84	L6
Skowhegan	40	G2
Skuodas	56	L8
Skye	64	F4
Skyros	76	G6
Skyros	76	G6
Slagelse	60	G1
Slaney	64	F9
Slano	74	E7
Slantsy	56	Q7
Slaný	60	K6
Slatina	74	M5
Slave	32	N3
Slave Lake	34	J5
Slavonska Požega	74	E4
Slavonski Brod	74	F4
Slavyanka	88	F2
Slavyansk-na-Kubani	98	H1
Sławno	58	F3
Sleaford	62	B1
Sleeper Islands	34	Q5
Slidell	42	D3
Sligo	64	D7
Sligo Bay	64	D7
Sliven	74	P7
Slobozia, *Moldova*	74	S3
Slobozia, *Romania*	74	Q5
Slonim	56	N10
Slough	62	B3
Slovakia	58	H9
Slovenia	70	K4
Slovenj Gradec	70	L4
Slovenska Bistrica	70	L4
Slov"yans'k	78	G5
Słubice	58	D5
Slunj	70	L5
Słupca	58	G5
Słupsk	58	G3
Slutsk	78	E4
Slyudyanka	84	G6
Smålandsfarvandet	60	G1
Smallwood Reservoir	34	U6
Smargon'	56	P9
Smederevo	74	H5
Smila	78	F5
Smirnykh	84	Q7
Smiths Falls	40	E2
Smokey Hills	42	B2
Smoky	34	H6
Smøla	56	D5
Smolensk	78	F4
Smolyan	76	G3
Smooth Rock Falls	40	D1
Smyrna	42	E3
Snæfell	56	(1)F2
Snake	38	C1
Snake River Plain	38	D2
Snåsavatnet	56	F4
Sneek	62	H1
Snezhnogorsk	82	R4
Snežnik	70	K5
Snina	58	M9
Snøhetta	56	E5
Snøtinden	56	G3
Snowdon	64	H8
Snowdrift	34	J4
Snowville	38	D2
Snyder	44	F2
Soalala	112	H3
Soanierana-Ivongo	112	H3
Soa-Siu	92	(2)C2
Sobral	50	J4
Sochaczew	58	K5
Sochaux	70	B3
Sochi	98	H2
Socorro	44	E2
Socotra = Suquṭrā	96	F7
Socuéllamos	68	H5
Sodankylä	56	P3
Söderhamn	56	J6
Södertälje	56	J7
Sodo	110	F2
Soe	92	(2)B4
Soest	62	L3
Sofia = Sofiya	74	L7
Sofiya	74	L7
Sofiysk, *Russia*	84	N6
Sofiysk, *Russia*	84	P6
Sofporog	56	R4
Sōfu-gan	86	L5
Sogamoso	50	C2
Sognefjorden	56	C6
Sogod	90	G4
Sog Xian	94	F2
Sohâg	104	F2
Soignies	62	G4
Soissons	62	F5
Sokch'o	88	E4
Söke	76	K7
Sokhumi	98	J2
Sokode	108	E3
Sokol	78	H3
Sokółka	56	M10
Sokolo	108	C2
Sokolov	60	H6
Sokołów Podlaski	58	M5
Sokoto	108	F2
Sokoto	108	F2
Sokyryany	74	Q1
Solander Island	118	A8
Solapur	94	C5
Sölden	70	F4
Solenzara	72	D7
Solikamsk	78	L3
Sol'-Iletsk	78	L4
Soliman	72	E12
Solingen	62	K3
Sollefteå	56	J5
Soller	68	N5
Solna	56	J7
Solomon Islands	114	F6
Solothurn	70	C3
Solov'yevsk	84	K6
Šolta	74	D6
Soltau	60	E4
Sol'tsy	78	F3
Solway Firth	64	J7
Solwezi	112	D2
Soma	76	K5
Sōma	88	L5
Somalia	110	H2
Sombor	74	G4
Sombrerete	44	F4
Somerset, *Australia*	116	H2
Somerset, *Ky., United States*	40	C3
Somerset, *Pa., United States*	40	E2
Somerset Island	34	N2
Someş	74	K2
Somme	62	E4
Sommen	56	H8
Sömmerda	60	G5
Sømna	56	F4
Sondags	112	D6
Sønderborg Ærø	60	E2
Sondershausen	60	F5
Sóndrio	70	E4
Songavatn	56	D7
Songea	110	F6
Song Hông	90	C2
Songhua	86	H1
Songhua Hu	88	D2
Songhua Jiang	88	D1
Songkan	86	D5
Songkhla	90	C5
Songnam	88	D5
Songnim	88	C4
Songo	112	E3
Songololo	108	G6
Songpan	86	C4
Sonid Yuoqi	86	E2
Sonid Zuoqi	86	E2
Son La	90	C2
Sonneberg	60	G6
Sono	50	H6
Sonora	44	B1
Sonora	44	D3
Sonoyta	44	D2
Sonsorol Islands	92	(2)D1
Sonthofen	70	F3
Sopot	56	K9
Sopron	70	M3
Sora	72	H7
Soracaba	52	M3
Sorel	40	F1
Sorgun	98	F4
Soria	68	H3
Sorø	60	G1
Soroca	74	R1
Sorochinsk	78	K4
Sorong	92	(2)D3
Soroti	110	E3
Sørøya	56	L1
Sorrentó	72	J8
Sorsele	56	J4
Sorso	72	C8
Sort	68	M2
Sortavala	56	R6
Sørvagen	56	G3
Sosnogorsk	82	J5
Sosnovo	56	R6
Sosnowiec	58	J7
Sos'va	78	M3
Sos'vinskaya	78	M2
Soto la Marina	44	G4
Soubré	108	C3
Soufli	76	J3
Souilly	62	H5
Souk Ahras	72	B12
Sŏul	88	D5
Soulac-sur-Mer	66	D8
Soumussalmi	56	Q4
Soûr	100	C3
Soure	68	B5
Sour el Ghozlane	68	P8
Souris	36	F2
Souris	36	G2
Sousa	50	K5
Sousse	106	H1
South Africa	112	C6
Southampton, *Canada*	40	D2
Southampton, *United Kingdom*	62	A4
Southampton Island	34	Q4
South Andaman	94	F6
South Atlantic Ocean	52	P6
South Australia	116	F5
South Baymouth	40	D1
South Bend	40	C2
South Boston	40	E3
South Carolina	42	E3
South Charleston	42	E2
South China Sea	90	E4
South Dakota	38	F2
South Downs	62	B4
South East Cape	116	J8
South East Point	116	J7
Southend-on-Sea	62	C3
Southern Alps	118	B6
Southern Cross	116	C6
Southern Indian Lake	34	M5
South Georgia	52	P9
South Harris	64	F4
South Haven	40	C2
South Hill	40	E3
South Island	118	B6
South Korea	88	D5
South Lake Tahoe	38	B3
South Orkney Islands	120	(2)A3
South Pacific Ocean	52	P6
South Platte	38	F2
Southport	64	J8
South Ronaldsay	64	K3
South Sandwich Islands	120	(2)C4
South Sandwich Trench	48	H9
South Saskatchewan	36	D1
South Shetland Islands	120	(2)MM4
South Shields	64	L7
South Taranaki Bight	118	D4
South Uist	64	E4
South West Cape, *Auckland Island*	118	(2)A1
South West Cape, *Australia*	116	H8
Southwest Cape	118	A8
South West Pacific Basin	114	L9
Southwold	62	D2
Sovata	74	N3
Sovetsk, *Russia*	56	L9
Sovetsk, *Russia*	78	J3
Soweto	112	D5
Sōya-misaki	88	L1
Sozopol	74	Q7
Spa	62	H4
Spain	68	F5
Spalding	62	B2
Sparks	44	C1
Spartanburg	42	E3
Sparti	76	E7
Sparwood	38	D1
Spassk-Dal'niy	88	G1
Spearfish	38	F2
Spencer	40	A2
Spencer Gulf	116	G6
Spetses	76	F7
Spey	64	J4
Speyer	62	L5
Spiekeroog	60	C3
Spiez	70	C4
Spišska Nová Ves	58	K9
Spitsbergen	120	(1)P2
Spittal	70	J4
Split	74	D6
Spokane	38	C1
Spoleto	72	G6
Spooner	40	B1
Sprague	38	C1
Spratly Islands	90	E4
Spray	38	C2
Spree	60	K4
Spremberg	60	K5
Spring	42	B3
Springbok	112	B5
Springe	60	E4
Springer	44	F1

Springerville 44 E2
Springfield, *Colo., United States* 44 F1
Springfield, *Ill., United States* 40 C3
Springfield, *Mass., United States* 40 F2
Springfield, *Mo., United States* 40 B3
Springfield, *Oh., United States* 40 D3
Springfield, *Oreg., United States* 38 B2
Springfield, *Vt., United States* 40 F2
Spring Hill 42 E4
Springs 112 D5
Springs Junction 118 D6
Springsure 116 J4
Springville, *Al., United States* 42 D3
Springville, *N.Y., United States* 40 E2
Squamish 38 B1
Squinzano 72 N8
Srbija 74 H6
Srbobran 74 G4
Sredenekolymsk 84 S3
Sredinnyy Khrebet 84 T6
Srednesibirskoye Ploskogor'ye 84 F3
Srednogorie 76 G2
Śrem 58 G5
Sretensk 84 K6
Srikakulam 94 D5
Sri Lanka 94 D7
Srinagar 94 B2
Stack Skerry 64 H2
Stade 56 E10
Stadlandet 56 C5
Stadskanaal 62 J2
Stadtallendorf 60 E6
Stadthagen 60 E4
Staffa 64 F5
Staffelstien 60 F6
Stafford 64 K9
Staines 62 B3
Stainz 70 L4
Stakhanov 78 G5
Stalowa Wola 58 M7
Stambolijski 76 G2
Stamford, *United Kingdom* 62 B2
Stamford, *United States* 40 F2
Standish 40 D2
Stanford 40 D3
Stanke Dimitrov 76 F2
Stanley, *Australia* 116 J8
Stanley, *Falkland Islands* 52 K9
Stanley, *United States* 38 F1
Stanovaya 84 T3
Stanovoye Nagor'ye 84 J5
Stanovoy Khrebet 84 L5
Staphorst 62 J2
Stapleton 38 F2
Starachowice 58 L6
Stara L'ubovňa 58 K8
Stara Pazova 74 H5
Stara Planina 76 F1
Staraya Russa 78 F3
Stara Zagora 74 N7
Starbuck Island 114 L6
Stargard Szczeciński 56 H10
Starkville 42 D3
Starnberg 70 G2
Starnberger See 70 G3
Start Point 66 B3
Staryy Oskol 78 G4
Staszów 58 L7
Statesboro 42 E3
Statesville 42 E2
Staunton 42 F2
Stavanger 56 C7
Stavoron 62 H2
Stavropol' 98 J1
Stavropol'skaya Vovyshennost' 78 H5
Steamboat Springs 38 E2
Steens Mountains 38 C2
Stefansson Island 34 L2
Stege 60 H1
Ştei 74 K3
Stein 60 G7
Steinach 70 G3
Steinfurt 62 K2
Steinjker 56 F4
Stenay 62 H5
Stendal 60 G4
Steno Antikythiro 76 F9
Stephenville 42 B3
Sterling 38 F2
Sterling City 44 F2
Sterling Heights 40 D2
Sterlitamak 78 L4
Sternberk 58 G8
Stettiner Haff 56 G10
Stevenage 62 B3
Stevens Point 40 C2
Stevens Village 44 (1)H2
Stewart 34 F5
Stewart 44 (1)K3
Stewart Island 118 A8
Steyr 70 K2
Stillwater 42 B2
Stinnett 44 F1
Štip 76 E3
Stirling 64 J5
Stjørdal 56 F5
Stockach 70 E3
Stockerau 70 M2
Stockholm 56 K7
Stockport 64 K8
Stockton, *Calif., United States* 44 B1
Stockton, *Kans., United States* 44 G1
Stockton-on-Tees 64 L7
Stœng Trêng 90 D4
Stoke-on-Trent 64 K8
Stokksnes 56 (1)F2
Stolac 74 F6
Stolberg 62 J4
Stolin 78 E4
Stollberg 60 H6
Stonehaven 64 K5
Stony Rapids 34 K5
Stör 60 E2
Stora Lulevatten 56 K3
Stord 56 C7
Store Bælt 60 F1
Støren 56 F5
Store Sotra 56 B6
Storlien 56 G5
Storm Bay 116 J8
Storm Lake 40 A2
Stornoway 64 F3
Storozhevsk 78 K2
Storozhynets' 74 N1
Storsjøen 56 F6
Storsjön, *Sweden* 56 G5
Storsjön, *Sweden* 56 J6
Storuman 56 J4
Storuman 56 J4
Stour 62 C2
Stowmarket 62 D2
Strabane 64 E7
Stradella 70 E5
Strait of Belle Isle 34 V6
Strait of Bonifacio 72 D7
Strait of Dover 62 D4
Strait of Georgia 38 B1
Strait of Gibraltar 68 E9
Strait of Hormuz 101 G3
Strait of Juan de Fuca 38 B1
Strait of Malacca 92 (1)C2
Straits of Florida 42 E5
Strakonice 60 J7
Stralsund 56 G9
Strand 112 B6
Stranda 56 D5
Strandavatn 56 D6
Stranraer 64 H7
Strasbourg 70 C2
Strasburg 44 F1
Străşeni 74 R2
Stratford, *Canada* 40 D2
Stratford, *United States* 38 F3
Stratford-upon-Avon 62 A2
Strathroy 40 D2
Stratoni 76 F4
Stratton 40 F1
Straubing 70 H2
Straumnes 56 (1)B1
Strausberg 60 J4
Streaky Bay 116 F6
Streator 40 C2
Strehaia 74 L5
Strelka, *Russia* 84 E5
Strelka, *Russia* 84 S4
Strezhevoy 78 Q2
Strimonas 76 F4
Strofades 76 C7
Strómboli 72 K10
Strömsund 56 H5
Stronsay 64 K2
Stroud 64 K10
Struga 76 C3
Strugi-Krasnyye 56 Q7
Strumica 76 E3
Stryjama 74 M7
Stryy 58 N8
Stryy 58 N8
Strzegom 58 F7
Strzelce Opolskie 58 H7
Strzelin 58 G7
Sturgeon Bay 40 C2
Sturgeon Falls 40 E1
Sturgis, *Ky., United States* 40 C3
Sturgis, *S.D., United States* 38 F2
Šturkö 58 E1
Štúrova 58 H10
Sturt Stony Desert 116 G5
Stuttgart, *Germany* 70 E2
Stuttgart, *United States* 42 C3
Stykkishólmur 56 (1)B2
Suai 92 (2)C4
Suakin 104 G4
Subcule 104 H5
Subi Besar 92 (1)D2
Sublette 44 F1
Subotica 74 G3
Suceava 74 P2
Suck 64 D8
Sucre 50 D7
Sudak 98 F1
Sudan 104 E5
Sudan 108 D2
Suday 78 H3
Sudbury, *Canada* 40 D1
Sudbury, *United Kingdom* 62 C2
Sudd 110 E2
Sudová Vyshnya 58 N8
Suez = El Suweis 104 F2
Suez Canal 104 F1
Suffolk 42 F2
Sugun 96 L2
Suḥār 101 G4
Suhl 60 F6
Suide 86 E3
Suifenhe 88 F1
Suihua 84 M7
Suippes 62 G5
Suir 64 E9
Suixi 86 E6
Suizhong 86 G2
Suizhou 86 E4
Sukabumi 92 (1)D4
Sukadana 92 (1)D3
Sukhinichi 78 G4
Sukhona 78 H3
Sukkertoppen = Maniitsoq 34 W3
Sukkur 96 J4
Sula 78 K1
Sula 78 K1
Sula Sgeir 64 F2
Sulawesi 92 (2)A3
Sulejówek 58 L5
Sule Skerry 64 H2
Sulgachi 84 N4
Sulina 74 S4
Sulingen 62 L2
Sullana 50 A4
Sullivan 42 C2
Sulmona 72 H6
Sulphur Springs 42 B3
Sultanhanı 76 R6
Sultanpur 94 D3
Sulu Archipelago 90 G5
Sulu Sea 90 F5
Sulzbach 62 K5
Sulzbach-Rosenberg 60 G7
Sulzberger Bay 120 (2)CC2
Sumatera 92 (1)C2
Sumatra = Sumatera 92 (1)C2
Sumba 92 (2)A5
Sumbawa 92 (2)A4
Sumbawabesar 92 (2)A4
Sumbawanga 110 E5
Sumbe 112 A2
Šumen 98 B2
Sumenep 92 (1)E4
Sumisu-jima 88 L8
Sumkino 78 N3
Summer Lake 38 B2
Summerville 42 E3
Summit 34 B4
Šumperk 58 G8
Sumqayıt 98 N3
Sumter 42 E3
Sumy 78 F4
Sunbury 40 E2
Sunch'ŏn 88 D6
Sun City 112 D5
Sundance 38 F2
Sundarbans 94 E4
Sunday Strait 116 D3
Sunderland 64 L7
Sundridge 40 E1
Sundsvall 56 J5
Sundsvallsbukten 56 J5
Sungaipenuh 92 (1)C3
Sungei Petani 90 C5
Sunnyvale 38 B3
Sun Prairie 40 C2
Suntar 84 K4
Suntsar 96 H4
Sunwu 84 M7
Sunyani 108 D3
Suomussalmi 78 E2
Suō-nada 88 F7
Suonenjoki 56 P5
Suordakh 84 P3
Suoyarvi 78 F2
Superior 36 H2
Supetar 74 D6
Süphan Daği 98 K4
Sūqash Shuyūkh 101 B1
Suqian 86 F4
Suquţrā 96 F7
Sūr 96 G5
Sura 78 J4
Surab 96 J4
Surabaya 92 (1)E4
Sūrak 101 H4
Surakarta 92 (1)E4
Šurany 74 F1
Surat 94 B4
Surat Thani 90 B5
Surdulica 74 K7
Sûre 62 H5
Surfers Paradise 116 K5
Surgut 82 N5
Surgutikha 82 R5
Surigao 90 H5
Surin 90 C4
Surinam 50 F3
Surkhet 94 D3
Sūrmaq 101 E1
Surovikino 78 H5
Surskoye 78 J4
Surt 106 J2
Surtsey 56 (1)C3
Susa 70 C5
Şuşa 98 M4
Sušac 74 D7
Susak 70 K6
Susanville 38 B2
Suşehri 98 H3
Sušice 60 J7
Susitma 44 (1)G3
Susuman 84 R4
Susurluk 76 L5
Sutherland 112 C6
Sutlej 94 B3
Suusamyr 82 N9
Suva 114 H7
Suvorov Island 114 K7
Suwałki 58 M3
Suwannaphum 90 C3
Suweilih 100 C4
Suweima 100 C5
Suwŏn 88 D5
Suzak 78 N6
Suzhou, *China* 86 F4
Suzhou, *China* 86 G4
Suzuka 88 J6
Suzu-misaki 88 J5
Svalbard 120 (1)Q2
Svalyaya 74 L1
Svartenhuk Halvø 34 V2
Svatove 78 G5
Sveg 56 H5
Svendborg 56 F9
Šventoji 56 N9
Sverdrup Islands 120 (1)DD2
Svetac 74 C6
Sveti Nikole 76 D3
Svetlaya 84 P7
Svetlogorsk 58 K3
Svetlograd 98 K1
Svetlyy, *Russia* 58 K3
Svetlyy, *Russia* 82 L7
Svidník 58 L8
Svilengrad 76 J3
Svishtov 74 N6
Svitava 58 F8
Svitovy 58 F8
Svobodnyy 84 M6
Svratka 58 F8
Svyetlahorsk 78 E4
Swain Reefs 116 K4
Swains Island 114 J7
Swakopmund 112 A4
Swale 64 K7
Swan 48 C2
Swan Hill 116 H7
Swan Islands 46 H5
Swan River 34 L6
Swansea, *Australia* 116 J8
Swansea, *United Kingdom* 64 J10
Swaziland 112 E5
Sweden 56 H6
Sweetwater 44 F2
Swider 58 L5

Świdnica 58 F7
Świdnik 58 M6
Świdwin 58 E4
Świebodzin 58 E5
Swift Current 36 E1
Swindon 62 A3
Świnoujście 56 H10
Switzerland 70 C4
Syalakh 84 L3
Syamzha 78 H2
Sydney, *Australia* 116 K6
Sydney, *Canada* 34 U7
Syke 62 L2
Syktyvkar 78 K2
Sylacauga 42 D3
Sylhet 94 F4
Sylt 56 E9
Sylvania 40 D2
Sym 82 R5
Sym 82 R5
Symi 76 K8
Synya 78 L1
Syracuse, *Kans., United States* 44 F1
Syracuse, *N.Y., United States* 40 E2
Syrdar'ya 96 J1
Syrdar'ya 82 L8
Syria 96 C3
Syrian Desert = Bādiyat ash Shām 100 D4
Syrna 76 J8
Syros 76 G7
Sytomino 78 P2
Syzran' 78 J4
Szamos 74 K1
Szamotuły 58 F5
Szarvas 58 K11
Szczecin 58 D4
Szczecinek 58 F4
Szczytno 58 K4
Szeged 74 H3
Szeghalom 74 J2
Székesfehérvár 74 F2
Szekszárd 74 F3
Szentendre 74 G2
Szentes 74 H3
Szerencs 58 L9
Szigetvár 74 E3
Szolnok 74 H2
Szombathely 74 D2
Szprotawa 58 E6

T

Tab 74 F3
Tabarka 72 C12
Tabas 96 G3
Taber 38 D1
Table Cape 118 G4
Tabong 94 G3
Tábor 58 D8
Tabor 84 R2
Tabora 110 E5
Tabou 108 C4
Tabrīz 98 M4
Tabuaeran 114 K5
Tabūk 96 C4
Tacheng 82 Q8
Tachov 60 H7
Tacloban 90 H4
Tacna 50 C7
Tacoma 36 B2
Tacuarembó 52 K5
Tacurong 92 (2)B1
Tadjoura 104 H5
Tadmur 98 H6
Tadoussac 40 G1
Taech'ŏn 88 D5
Taegu 88 E6
Taejŏn 86 H3
Tafahi 114 J7
Tafalla 68 J2
Tafila 100 C6
Tafi Viejo 52 H4
Taganrog 78 G5
Taganrogskiy Zaliv 78 G5
Tagul 84 F6
Tagum 90 H5
Tagus 68 B5
Taharoa 118 E4
Tahiti 114 M7
Tahoe Lake 34 K2
Tahoka 44 F2
Tahoua 108 F2
Tahrūd 101 G2
Tai'an 86 F3
T'ai-chung 86 G6
Taihape 118 E4
Taihe 86 E5
Taikeng 86 E4
Tailem Bend 116 G7
Tain 64 H4
T'ai-nan 86 G6
T'ai-Pei 86 G6
Taiping 92 (1)C1
Taipingchuan 88 B1
T'ai-tung 90 G2
Taivalkoski 56 Q4
Taiwan 90 G2
Taiwan Strait 90 F2
Taiyuan 86 E3
Taizhou 86 F4
Ta'izz 96 D7
Tajikistan 96 J2
Tajima 88 K5
Tajo 54 D3
Tak 90 B3
Takaka 118 D5
Takamatsu 88 H6
Takaoka 88 J5
Takapuna 118 E3
Takasaki 88 K5
Takayama 88 J5
Takefui 88 J6
Takengon 92 (1)B2
Takestān 96 E2
Takht 84 P6
Takhta-Bazar 96 H2
Takhtabrod 82 M7
Takhtakupyr 82 L9
Takijuq Lake 34 J3
Takikawa 88 L2
Takoradi 108 D4
Taksimo 84 J5
Takua Pa 90 B5
Takum 108 G3
Talak 106 F5
Talara 50 A4
Talas 82 N9
Tal'at Mūsá 98 G6
Talavera de la Reina 68 F5
Talaya 84 S4
Talbotton 42 E3
Talca 52 G6
Talcahuano 52 G6
Taldykorgan 82 P9
Tālesh 96 E2
Taliabu 92 (2)B3
Talibon 90 G4
Talitsa 78 M3
Tall 'Afar 98 K5
Tallahassee 42 E3
Tallaimannar 94 C7
Tall al Laḥm 101 B1
Tallinn 56 N7
Tall Kalakh 100 D2
Tallulah 36 H5
Tall 'Uwaynāt 98 K5
Tălmaciu 74 M4
Tal'menka 82 Q7
Talon 84 R5
Tāloqān 82 N10
Taloyoak 34 N3
Talsi 56 M8
Taltal 52 G4
Tama 40 B2
Tamale 108 D3
Tamanrasset 106 G4
Tamanthi 94 G3
Tamási 74 F3
Tamazunchale 36 G7
Tambacounda 108 B2
Tambey 82 N3
Tambo 116 J4
Tambov 78 H4
Tambu 92 (2)A3
Tambura 110 D2
Tampa 42 E4
Tampere 56 M6
Tampico 46 E4
Tamsagbulag 86 F1
Tamsweg 70 J3
Tamworth, *Australia* 116 K6
Tamworth, *United Kingdom* 62 A2
Tana, *Kenya* 110 G4
Tana, *Norway* 56 P2
Tanabe 88 H7
Tanacross 44 (1)J3
Tanafjorden 56 Q1
Tanaga Island 44 (3)C1
T'ana Hāyk' 104 G5
Tanahgrogot 92 (1)F3
Tanahjampea 92 (2)A4
Tanahmerah 92 (2)F4
Tanami 116 E4
Tanami Desert 116 F3
Tánaro 70 C6
Tandag 90 H5
Tăndărei 74 Q5
Tandil 52 K6
Tanega-shima 88 F8
Tanew 58 M7
Tanezrouft 106 E4
Tanga, *Russia* 84 J6
Tanga, *Tanzania* 110 F5
Tanger 106 D1
Tangermünde 60 G4
Tanggu 86 F3
Tangmai 94 G2
Tangra Yumco 94 E2
Tangshan 86 F3
Tanimbar 114 D6
Tanjona Ankaboa 112 G4
Tanjona Bobaomby 112 H2
Tanjona Masoala 112 J3
Tanjona Vilanandro 112 G3
Tanjona Vohimena 112 H5
Tanjung 92 (1)F3
Tanjungbalai 92 (1)B2
Tanjung Cangkuang 92 (1)C4
Tanjung Datu 92 (1)D2
Tanjung d'Urville 92 (2)E3
Tanjungkarang Telukbetung 92 (1)D4
Tanjung Libobo 92 (2)C3
Tanjung Mengkalihat 92 (1)F2
Tanjungpandan 92 (1)D3
Tanjung Puting 92 (1)E3
Tanjungredeb 92 (1)F2
Tanjung Selatan 92 (1)E3
Tanjungselor 92 (1)F2
Tanjung Vals 92 (2)E4
Tankovo 82 R5
Tankse 94 C2
Tanlovo 78 P1
Tanney 62 G5
Tanout 108 F2
Tanta 104 F1
Tan-Tan 106 C3
Tanzania 110 E5
Tao'an 86 G1
Taomasina 112 H3
Taongi 114 J4
Taormina 72 K11
Taos 44 E1
Taoudenni 106 E5
Taourirt 106 E2
T'ao-yuan 90 G2
Tapa 56 N7
Tapachula 46 F6
Tapajós 50 F4
Tapauá 50 E5
Tapolca 74 E3
Tappahannock 42 F2
Tapsuy 78 M2
Tapuaenuku 118 D6
Taquarí 50 F7
Tara 78 Q3
Tara 82 N6
Tarābulus 106 H2
Taracua 50 D3
Tarāghin 106 H3
Tarakan 90 F6
Taran 82 N3
Taranaki = Mount Egmont 118 E4
Tarancón 68 H5
Taranto 72 M8
Tarapoto 50 B5
Tarare 66 K8
Tarascon 66 K10
Tarauacá 50 C5
Tarauacá 50 C5
Tarawa 114 H5
Tarawera Lake 118 F4
Tarazona 68 J3
Tarbes 66 F10
Tarbet 64 F4
Tarcoola 116 F6
Taree 116 K6
Tarfaya 106 C3
Târgovişte 74 N5
Târgu Frumos 74 Q2
Târgu Jiu 74 L4
Târgu Lăpuş 74 L2
Târgu Mureş 74 M3
Târgu-Neamţ 74 P2
Târgu Ocna 74 P3
Târgu Secuiesc 74 P3
Tarhunah 106 H2
Tarif 101 E4
Tarifa 68 E8
Tarija 52 J3
Tarīm 96 E6
Tarim 82 Q9
Tarim Pendi 82 Q10
Tarīn Kowt 96 J3
Tariskay Shan 82 Q9
Taritatu 92 (2)E3
Tarkio 42 B1
Tarko Sale 82 P5
Tarlac 90 G3
Tarn 66 H10
Tarna 58 K10
Tärnaby 56 H4
Târnăveni 74 M3
Tarnogskiy Gorodok 78 H2
Tărnovo 76 K2
Tarnów 58 K7
Tarnowskie Góry 58 H7
Taro 70 E6
Taroom 116 J5
Taroudannt 106 D2
Tarquínia 72 F6
Tarragona 68 M3
Tarras 118 B7
Tàrrega 68 M3
Tarso Emissi 104 C3
Tarsus 98 F5
Tartagal 52 J3
Tartu 56 P7
Ţarţūs 100 C2
Tarutyne 74 S3
Tarvisio 70 J4
Tasbuget 78 N6
Tashigang 94 F3
Tashir 98 L3
Tashkent 82 M9
Tash-Kömür 82 N9
Tashtagol 82 R7
Tasiilaq 34 Z3
Tasikmalaya 92 (1)D4
Taskesken 82 Q8
Tasman Bay 118 D5
Tasmania 114 E10
Tasmania 116 H8
Tasman Mountains 118 D5
Tasman Sea 118 B3
Tăşnad 74 K2
Taşova 98 G3
Tassili du Hoggar 106 F4
Tassili-n'-Ajjer 106 G3
Tasty 82 M9
Tata, *Hungary* 74 F2
Tata, *Morocco* 106 D3
Tatabánya 74 F2
Tatarbunary 74 S4
Tatariya 78 J3
Tatarsk 82 P6
Tatarskiy Proliv 84 P7
Tateyama 88 K6
Tathlina Lake 34 H4
Tatta 96 J5
Tatvan 98 K4
Tauá 50 J5
Tauberbischofsheim 60 E7
Tauern 70 J4
Taumarunui 118 E4
Taungdwingyi 90 B2
Taung-gyi 94 G4
Taungup 94 F5
Taunsa 94 B2
Taunton, *United Kingdom* 64 J10
Taunton, *United States* 40 F2
Taunus 62 L4
Taunusstein 62 L4
Taupo 118 F4
Tauragė 58 M2
Tauranga 118 F3
Tauroa Point 118 D2
Tavda 78 N3
Tavda 78 N3
Tavira 68 C7
Tavoy 90 B4
Tavşanli 98 C4
Taw 64 J11
Tawas City 40 D2
Tawau 92 (1)F2
Tawitawi 92 (1)F1
Taxkorgan 82 P10
Tay 64 J5
Tayga 82 R6
Taylorville 42 D2
Taym 96 C4
Taymā' 104 G2
Taymura 84 F4
Taymylyr 84 L2
Tay Ninh 90 D4
Tayshet 84 F5
Tayuan 84 L6
Tayyebād 96 H3
Taza 106 E2
Tazeh Kand 98 M4
Tazenakht 106 D2
Tāzirbū 104 D2
Tazovskiy 82 P4
Tazovskiy Poluostrov 82 N4
Tazungdam 90 B1
T'bilisi 98 L3
Tchamba 108 G3
Tchibanga 108 G5
Tchin Tabaradene 106 G5
Tczew 58 H3
Te Anau 118 A7
Te Araroa 118 G3
Te Aroha 118 E3

Te Awamutu	118	E4
Teberda	98	J2
Tébessa	106	G1
Tebingtinggi	92	(1)B2
Téboursouk	72	D12
Techa	78	M3
Techiman	108	D3
Tecuala	44	D4
Tecuci	74	Q4
Tedzhen	96	H2
Tees	64	L7
Tegal	92	(1)D4
Tegernsee	70	G3
Tegina	108	F2
Tegucigalpa	46	G6
Tegul'det	82	R6
Te Hapua	118	D2
Te Haroto	118	F4
Tehek Lake	34	M3
Teheran = Tehrān	96	F2
Tehrān	96	F2
Teignmouth	64	J11
Tejo = Tagus	68	B5
Te Kaha	118	F3
Tekirda	76	K4
Tekirdağ	98	B3
Teknaf	94	F4
Teku	92	(2)B3
Te Kuiti	118	E4
T'elavi	98	L3
Tel Aviv-Yafo	100	B4
Telegraph Creek	44	(1)L4
Telén	52	H6
Teles Pires	50	F5
Telford	64	K9
Telfs	70	G3
Teller	44	(1)D2
Telsen	52	H7
Telšiai	58	M2
Teltow	60	J4
Teluk Berau	92	(2)D3
Teluk Bone	92	(2)B3
Teluk Cenderawasih	92	(2)E3
Telukdalem	92	(1)B2
Teluk Kumai	92	(1)E3
Teluk Sampit	92	(1)E3
Teluk Sukadana	92	(1)D3
Teluk Tomini	92	(2)B2
Tema	108	D3
Tembenchi	82	T4
Temerin	74	G4
Temerloh	90	C6
Teminabuan	92	(2)D3
Temochic	44	E3
Tempe	44	D2
Témpio Pausária	72	D8
Temple	44	G2
Temryuk	98	G1
Temuco	52	G6
Tenali	94	D5
Tendaho	104	H5
Ten Degree Channel	94	F7
Tendrara	106	E2
Ténéré	106	G5
Ténéré du Tafassasset	106	G4
Tenerife	106	B3
Ténès	106	F1
Tenggarong	92	(1)F3
Tenke	112	D2
Tenkodogo	108	D2
Tennant Creek	116	F3
Tennessee	32	K6
Tennessee	36	J4
Tenojoki	56	P2
Tenteno	92	(2)B3
Tenterfield	116	K5
Teo	68	B2
Teófilo Otoni	50	J7
Tepehuanes	36	E6
Tepic	36	F7
Teplice	58	C7
Ter	68	N2
Terceira	106	(1)B2
Terek	98	L2
Teresina	50	J5
Tergnier	62	F5
Termez	96	J2
Términi Imerese	72	H11
Termirtau	82	N7
Térmoli	74	C8
Ternate	92	(2)C2
Terneuzen	62	F3
Terni	72	G6
Ternitz	70	M3
Ternopil'	78	E5
Ternuka	118	C7
Terracina	72	H7
Terrassa	68	N3
Terre Haute	42	D2
Terry	38	E1
Tersa	78	H4
Terschelling	62	H1
Teruel	68	J4
Tervel	98	B2
Tervola	56	N3
Teseney	104	G4
Teshekpuk Lake	44	(1)F1
Teshio	88	L1
Teslin	44	(1)L3
Teslin	44	(1)L3
Tessalit	106	F4
Têt	66	H11
Tete	112	E3
Teterow	60	H3
Teteven	76	G2
Tétouan	106	D1
Tetovo	74	H8
Teuco	52	J3
Teulada	72	C10
Tevere	72	G6
Teverya	100	C4
Tevriz	78	P3
Te Waewae Bay	118	A8
Texarkana	42	C3
Texas	36	F5
Texel	62	G1
Teya	82	S5
Teykovo	78	H3
Thaba Putsoa	112	D5
Thabazimbi	112	D4
Thailand	90	C4
Thai Nguyên	90	D2
Thal	94	B2
Thale Luang	90	C5
Thamarīt	96	F6
Thames	64	L10
Thamūd	96	E6
Thane	94	B5
Thanh Hoa	90	D3
Thanjavur	94	C6
Thann	70	C3
Tharad	94	B4
Thar Desert	94	B3
Thargomindah	116	H5
Tharwāniyyah	101	E5
Thasos	76	G4
Thasos	76	G4
Thaton	90	B3
Thaya	58	E9
The Bahamas	42	F4
The Bluff	42	F4
The Dalles	38	B1
Thedford	38	F2
The Fens	62	B2
The Gambia	108	A2
The Granites	116	E4
Thelon	34	L4
The Minch	64	F3
The Naze	62	D3
Thenia	68	P8
Theniet el Had	68	N9
Theodore Roosevelt	50	E5
Theodore Roosevelt Lake	44	D2
The Pas	34	L6
Thermaikos Kolpos	76	E4
Thermopolis	38	E2
The Sisters	118	(1)B1
The Solent	62	A4
Thessalon	40	D1
Thessaloniki	76	E4
Thetford	64	N9
Thetford Mines	40	F1
The Twins	118	D5
The Wash	64	N9
The Weald	62	B3
The Whitsundays	116	J4
Thief River Falls	40	A1
Thiers	66	J8
Thiès	108	A2
Thika	110	F4
Thimphu	94	E3
Þingvallavatn	56	(1)C2
Thionville	62	J5
Thira	76	H8
Thira	76	H8
Thirasia	76	H8
Thiruvananthapuram	94	C7
Thisted	56	E8
Þistilfjöður	56	(1)F1
Thiva	76	F6
Thiviers	66	F8
Þjórsá	56	(1)D2
Tholen	62	G3
Thomasville	42	E3
Thompson	34	H6
Thompson	34	M5
Thompson Falls	38	C1
Thomson	42	E3
Thonon-les-Bains	70	B4
Þórisvatn	56	(1)D2
Þorlákshöfn	56	(1)C3
Þorshöfn	56	(1)F1
Thouars	66	E7
Thrakiko Pelagos	76	H4
Three Forks	38	D1
Three Kings Island	118	C2
Three Rivers	40	C2
Throckmorton	42	B3
Thuin	62	G4
Thun	70	C4
Thunder Bay	40	C1
Thuner See	70	C4
Thung Song	90	B5
Thüringer Wald	60	F6
Thurso	64	J3
Tīāb	101	G3
Tianjin	86	F3
Tianmen	86	E4
Tianqiaoling	88	E2
Tianshifu	88	C3
Tianshui	86	D4
Tianshuihai	96	L2
Tiaret	106	F1
Tibati	108	G3
Tibooburra	116	H5
Tibesti	104	C3
Tibet = Xizang	94	E2
Tiburón	46	B3
Tîchît	106	D5
Tichla	106	C4
Ticino	70	D4
Ticul	46	G4
Tidjikdja	106	C5
Tieling	88	B2
Tielongtan	94	C1
Tielt	62	F3
Tienen	62	G4
Tien Shan	82	Q9
Tien Yen	90	D2
Tierra Amarilla	38	E3
Tiétar	68	E4
Tiflis = T'bilisi	102	H1
Tifton	42	E3
Tifu	92	(2)C3
Tighina	74	S3
Tignère	108	G3
Tigre	50	B4
Tigris	98	K6
Tijuana	36	C5
Tikanlik	82	R9
Tikhoretsk	78	H5
Tikhvin	78	F3
Tikrīt	98	K6
Tiksi	84	M2
Tilburg	62	H3
Tilichiki	84	V4
Tillabéri	108	E2
Tillamook	38	B1
Tilos	76	K8
Timanskiy Kryazh	78	K2
Timaru	118	C7
Timashevsk	78	G5
Timber Creek	116	F3
Timerloh	92	(1)C2
Timimoun	106	F3
Timişoara	74	J4
Timmins	40	D1
Timon	50	J5
Timor	92	(2)C4
Timor Sea	116	E2
Tinaca Point	114	C5
Tindivanam	94	C6
Tindouf	106	D3
Tineo	68	D1
Tinglev	60	E2
Tingo Maria	50	B5
Tingri	94	E3
Tingsryd	58	E1
Tiniroto	118	F4
Tinnsjø	56	E7
Tinogasta	52	H4
Tinos	76	H7
Tinos	76	H7
Tinsukia	94	G3
T'i'o	104	H5
Tipperary	64	D9
Tirana = Tiranë	76	B3
Tiranë	76	B3
Tirari Desert	116	G5
Tiraspol	74	S3
Tire	76	K6
Tiree	64	F5
Tirschenreuth	60	H7
Tirso	72	C9
Tiruchchirāppalli	94	C6
Tirunelveli	94	C7
Tirupati	94	C6
Tiruppur	94	C6
Tiruvannamalai	94	C6
Tisa	74	H4
Tišnov	58	F8
Tisza	58	M9
Tiszafóldvár	74	H3
Tiszafüred	74	H2
Tiszaújváros	58	L10
Tit-Ary	82	Z3
Titel	74	H4
Titova Korenica	70	L6
Titovo Velenje	72	K2
Titu	74	N5
Titusville	42	E4
Tivaouane	106	B6
Tiverton	64	J11
Tivoli	72	G7
Tiyās	100	E2
Tizi Ouzou	106	F1
Tiznit	106	D3
Tjeldøya	56	H2
Tjørkolm	56	D7
Tlemcen	106	E2
Tmassah	104	C2
Toad River	34	F5
Tobago	46	M6
Tobelo	92	(2)C2
Tobermorey	116	G4
Tobermory, *United Kingdom*	64	F5
Tobermory, *United States*	40	D1
Tobi	92	(2)D2
Toblach	70	H4
Toboali	92	(1)D3
Tobol	78	M4
Tobol	78	M4
Tobol'sk	78	N3
Tobseda	78	K1
Tocantins	50	H5
Tocantins	50	H5
Tocee	70	D4
Tocopilla	52	G3
Todi	72	G6
Tofino	38	A1
Togo	108	E3
Toimin	72	H2
Toi-misaki	88	F8
Tōjō	88	G6
Tok	44	(1)J3
Tokar	104	G4
Tokat, *Sudan*	96	C6
Tokat, *Turkey*	96	C1
Tokelau	114	J6
Tokmak	82	P9
Tokoroa	118	E4
Toksun	82	R9
Tok-tō	86	J3
Toktogul	82	N9
Tokushima	88	H6
Tokuyama	88	F6
Tōkyō	88	K6
Tolaga Bay	118	G4
Tôlañaro	112	H4
Tolbo	82	S8
Toledo, *Brazil*	52	L3
Toledo, *Spain*	68	F5
Toledo, *United States*	40	D2
Toliara	112	G4
Tolitoli	92	(2)B2
Tol'ka	82	Q5
Tol'ka	82	Q5
Tollense	60	J3
Tolmezzo	70	J4
Tolmin	70	J4
Tolna	74	F3
Tolosa	68	H1
Tol'yatti	78	J4
Tolybay	82	L7
Tom'	82	R6
Tomah	40	B2
Tomakomai	88	L2
Tomar	68	B5
Tomari	84	Q7
Tomaszów Lubelski	58	N7
Tomaszów Mazowiecki	58	K6
Tombouctou	106	E5
Tombua	112	A3
Tomé	52	G6
Tomelloso	68	H5
Tomini	92	(2)B2
Tommot	84	M5
Tomo	50	D2
Tompo	84	P4
Tom Price	116	C4
Tomra	94	E2
Tomsk	82	Q6
Tomtor	84	Q4
Tomu	92	(2)D3
Tonalá	46	F5
Tondano	92	(2)B2
Tønder	60	D2
Tonga	110	E2
Tonga	114	J7
Tonga Islands	114	J8
Tongareva	114	K6
Tonga Trench	114	J8
Tongbai	86	E4
Tongchuan	86	D4
Tongduch'ŏn	88	D5
Tongeren	62	H4
Tonghae	88	E5

Tonghua 88 C3
Tongliao 86 G2
Tongling 86 F4
Tongshi 90 D3
Tongue 38 E1
Tongyu 86 G2
Tónichi 36 E6
Tonj 110 D2
Tonk 94 C3
Tonkābon 96 F2
Tônlé Sab 90 C4
Tonnay-Charente 66 E8
Tönning 60 D2
Tonopah 38 C3
Tooele 38 D2
Toora-Khem 82 T7
Toowoomba 116 K5
Topeka 36 G4
Topki 82 R6
Toplița 74 N3
Topock 44 D2
Topol'čany 58 H9
Topolobampo 36 E6
Torbali 76 K6
Torbat-e Heydarīyeh 96 G2
Torbat-e Jām 96 H2
Tordesillas 68 F3
Torells 68 N2
Torgau 60 H5
Torgelow 58 C4
Torhout 62 F3
Torino 70 C5
Tori-shima 88 L8
Torneälven 56 L3
Torneträsk 56 K2
Tornio 56 N4
Toro 68 E3
Toronto 40 E2
Tororo 110 E3
Toros Dağları 98 E5
Torquay 64 J11
Torrance 44 C2
Torreblanca 68 L4
Torre de Moncorvo 68 C3
Torrejón de Ardoz 68 G4
Torrelavega 68 F1
Torremolinos 68 F8
Torrent 68 K5
Torreón 44 F3
Torres Strait 116 H2
Torres Vedras 68 A5
Torrevieja 68 K6
Torrington 38 F2
Tortol 72 D9
Tortona 70 D6
Tortosa 68 L4
Tortum 98 J3
Torūd 96 G2
Toruń 58 H4
Tory Island 64 D6
Torzhok 78 G3
Tosa-wan 88 G7
Tostedt 60 E3
Tosya 76 S3
Totaranui 118 D5
Tôtes 62 D5
Tot'ma 78 H3
Totora 50 D7
Tottori 88 H6
Touba, *Ivory Coast* 108 C3
Touba, *Senegal* 108 A2
Tougan 108 D2
Touggourt 106 G2
Toul 66 L5
Toulépleu 108 C3
Toulon 66 L10
Toulouse 66 G10
Toummo 106 H4
Toungoo 90 B3
Tourcoing 62 F4
Tournai 62 F4
Tours 66 F6
Touws River 112 C6
Tovuz 98 L3
Towanda 40 E2
Towari 92 (2)B3
Towcester 62 B2
Towner 38 F1
Townsend 38 D1
Townshend Island 116 K4
Townsville 116 J3
Toxkan 82 P9
Toyama 88 J5
Toyohashi 88 J6
Toyooka 88 H6
Toyota 88 J6
Tozeur 106 G2
Trâblous 100 C2
Trabzon 98 H3
Tracy 40 A2
Trail 38 C1
Traiskirchen 70 M2
Trakai 56 N9
Tralee 64 C9
Tralee Bay 64 B9
Tramán Tepuí 50 E2
Tranås 56 H7
Trancoso 68 C4
Trang 90 B5
Trangan 92 (2)D4
Transantarctic Mountains 120 (2)B1
Trapani 72 G11
Trappes 62 E6
Traun 70 K2
Traunreut 70 H3
Traunsee 70 J3
Traversay Islands 48 H9
Traverse City 40 C2
Travnik 74 E5
Trbovlje 70 L4
Trébbia 70 E6
Třebíč 58 E8
Trebinje 74 F7
Trebišov 74 J1
Trebnje 70 L5
Trebon 70 K1
Tregosse Islets 116 K3
Trelew 52 H7
Trelleborg 56 G9
Tremonton 38 D2
Tremp 68 L2
Trenčín 58 H9
Trent 64 M8
Trento 70 G4
Trenton, *Canada* 40 E2
Trenton, *United States* 40 F2
Trepassey 34 W7
Tres Arroyos 52 J6
Três Corações 50 H8
Tres Esquinas 50 B3
Tres Lagos 52 G8
Trespaderne 68 G2
Treuchtlingen 70 F2
Treviglio 70 E5
Treviso 70 H5
Triangle 112 E4
Tricase 72 N9
Trichur 94 C6
Trier 62 J5
Trieste 70 J5
Triglav 70 J4
Trikala 76 D5
Trikomon 100 A1
Trilj 70 M7
Trincomalee 94 D7
Trinidad 50 E1
Trinidad, *Bolivia* 50 E6
Trinidad, *United States* 44 F1
Trinidad, *Uruguay* 52 K5
Trinidad and Tobago 50 E1
Trinity Islands 44 (1)G4
Trino 70 D5
Trion 42 D3
Tripoli, 76 E7
Tripoli = Trâblous 100 C2
Tripoli = Tarābulus 106 H2
Trischen 60 D2
Tristan da Cunha 102 B9
Trivandrum = Thiruvananthapuram 94 C7
Trjavna 98 A2
Trnava 74 E1
Trogir 74 D6
Troina 72 J11
Troisdorf 60 C6
Trois Rivières 40 F1
Troitsk 78 M4
Troitsko-Pechorsk 78 L2
Trojan 76 G2
Trollhättan 56 G7
Trombetas 50 F4
Tromsø 56 K2
Trona 38 C3
Trondheim 56 F5
Trondheimsfjörden 56 E5
Troodos 98 E6
Trotuș 74 P3
Trout Lake, *N.W.T., Canada* 34 G4
Trout Lake, *Ont., Canada* 34 N6
Troy, *Al., United States* 42 D3
Troy, *N.Y., United States* 40 F2
Troyan 74 M7
Troyes 66 K5
Trstenik 74 J6
Trudovoye 88 G2
Trujillo, *Peru* 50 B5
Trujillo, *Spain* 68 E5
Truro, *Canada* 34 U7
Truro, *United Kingdom* 64 G11
Trusovo 82 J4
Truth or Consequences 44 E2
Trutnov 58 E7
Tryavana 76 H2
Trzcianka 58 F4
Trzebnica 58 G6
Tsetserleg 84 G7
Tshabong 112 C5
Tshane 112 C4
Tshikapa 110 C5
Tshuapa 110 C4
Tsiafajavona 112 H3
Tsimlyanskoy Vodokhranilishche 78 H5
Tsiroanomandidy 112 H3
Ts'khinvali 98 K2
Tsuchiura 88 L5
Tsugaru-kaikyō 88 L3
Tsumeb 112 B3
Tsumkwe 112 C3
Tsuruga 88 J6
Tsuruoka 88 K4
Tsushima 88 E6
Tsuyama 88 H6
Tua 68 C3
Tual 92 (2)D4
Tuân Giao 90 C2
Tuapse 98 H1
Tubarão 52 M4
Tübingen 70 E2
Tubize 62 G4
Tubruq 104 D1
Tubuai 114 M8
Tubuai Islands 114 L8
Tucano 50 K6
Tuchola 58 G4
Tucson 44 D2
Tucumcari 44 F1
Tucupita 50 E2
Tucuruí 50 H4
Tudela 68 J2
Tuguegarao 90 G3
Tugur 84 P6
Tui 68 B2
Tuktoyaktuk 44 (1)L2
Tula, *Mexico* 44 G4
Tula, *Russia* 78 G4
Tulare 38 C3
Tulcea 74 R4
Tulkarm 100 B4
Tullamore 64 E8
Tulle 66 G8
Tulln 70 M2
Tuloma 56 S2
Tulsa 36 G4
Tulsequah 44 (1)L4
Tulun 84 G6
Tulung La 94 F3
Tulu Weiel 110 E2
Tumaco 50 B3
Tumān 96 H2
Tumen 88 E2
Tumereng 50 E2
Tumkur 94 C6
Tumut 116 J7
Tunca 76 J3
Tunceli 98 H4
Tunduru 112 F2
Tundzha 74 P8
Tungir 84 L5
Tungku 92 (1)F1
Tungsten 44 (1)M3
Tungusk 82 S5
Tunis 106 H1
Tunisia 106 E2
Tunja 50 C2
Tupelo 42 D3
Tupik 84 L6
Tupiza 52 H3
Tupper Lake 40 F2
Tuquan 86 G1
Tura, *India* 94 F3
Tura, *Russia* 84 G4
Turan 82 S7
Turangi 118 E4
Turayf 104 G1
Turbat 96 H4
Turbo 50 B2
Turda 74 L3
Turek 58 H5
Turgay 82 L8
Turgay 82 L8
Turgayskaya Stolovaya Strana 82 L7
Tŭrgovishte 74 P6
Turgutlu 76 K6
Turhal 98 G3
Turin = Torino 70 C5
Turinsk 78 M3
Turiy Rog 88 F1
Turka 84 H6
Türkeli Adası 76 K4
Turkestan 82 M9
Turkey 98 D4
Turkmenbashi 96 F1
Turkmenistan 96 G2
Turks and Caicos Islands 46 K4
Turks Islands 46 K4
Turku 56 M6
Turma 84 N6
Turnhout 62 G3
Turnov 58 E7
Turnu Măgurele 74 M6
Turpan 82 R9
Turpan Pendi 82 S9
Turquino 48 D2
Turtas 78 N3
Turtkul' 96 H1
Turtle Island 116 K3
Turu 82 J5
Turugart Pass 82 P9
Turukhan 84 C3
Turukhansk 82 R4
Turukta 84 K4
Tuscaloosa 42 D3
Tuscola 42 D2
Tuticorin 94 C7
Tutonchany 84 E4
Tutrakan 74 P5
Tuttle Creek Reservoir 42 B2
Tuttlingen 70 D3
Tutuila 114 K7
Tuvalu 114 H6
Tuxpan, *Mexico* 36 E7
Tuxpan, *Mexico* 36 G7
Tuxtla Gutiérrez 46 F5
Tuyên Quang 90 D2
Tuy Hoa 90 D4
Tuymazy 78 K4
Tuz Gölü 98 E4
Tuz Khurmātū 98 L6
Tuzla 74 F5
Tver' 78 G3
Tweed 64 K6
Twentynine Palms 44 C2
Twilight Cove 116 E6
Twin Buttes Reservoir 44 F2
Twin Falls 38 D2
Twizel 118 C7
Two Harbors 40 B1
Tyachiv 74 L1
Tygda 84 M6
Tyler 36 G5
Tylkhoy 84 U4
Tym 82 Q6
Tynda 84 L5
Tyne 64 K6
Tynemouth 64 L6
Tynset 56 F5
Tyra 82 S7
Tyrifjorden 56 F6
Tyrnavos 76 E5
Tyrrhenian Sea 72 F8
Tyry 84 P4
Tysa 58 M9
Tyukyan 84 K4
Tyumen' 82 M6
Tyung 84 K3
Tyva 84 F6

U

Uaupés 50 D3
Ubá 50 J8
Ubaitaba 50 K6
Ubangi 110 B3
Ube 88 F7
Úbeda 68 G6
Uberaba 50 H7
Uberlândia 50 H7
Überlingen 70 E3
Ubon Ratchathani 90 C3
Ubrique 68 E8
Ucayali 50 B5
Uchami 82 T5
Ucharal 82 Q8
Uchiura-wan 88 L2
Uchkuduk 82 L9
Uckermark 60 J3
Ucluelet 38 A1
Uda, *Russia* 84 F5
Uda, *Russia* 84 N6
Udachnyy 84 J3
Udagamandalam 94 C6
Udaipur 94 B4
Uddevalla 56 F7
Uddjaure 78 C1
Uddjaure Storavan 56 K4
Udine 70 J4
Udmurtiya 78 K3
Udon Thani 90 C3
Udupi 94 B6
Uecker 60 J3
Ueckermünde 60 J3
Ueda 88 K5
Uele 110 C3
Uelen 84 AA3

Uel'kal 84 Y3
Uelzen 60 F4
Ufa 78 L3
Ufa 78 L4
Uganda 110 E3
Ugep 108 F3
Ugine 70 B5
Uglegorsk 84 Q7
Uglich 78 G3
Ugljan 70 L6
Ugol'nyye Kopi 84 X4
Ugulan 84 S4
Uh 74 K1
Uherské Hradiště 58 G8
Uherský Brod 58 G8
Uiju 88 C3
Uil 78 K5
Uil 78 K5
Uinta Mountains 38 D2
Uitenhage 112 D6
Újfehértó 74 J2
Ujiji 110 D4
Ujjain 94 C4
Ujung Pandang 92 (2)A4
Ukerewe Island 110 E4
Ukhta 82 J5
Ukiah 38 B3
Ukkusissat 34 W2
Ukmergė 58 P2
Ukraine 54 G3
Ulaanbaatar 84 H7
Ulaangom 82 S8
Ulan 86 B3
Ulan Bator = Ulaanbaatar 86 D1
Ulan-Ude 84 H6
Ulchin 88 E5
Uldz 84 J7
Ulety 84 J6
Ulhasnagar 94 B5
Uliastay 82 T8
Ulindi 110 D4
Ullapool 64 G4
Ullŭng do 88 F5
Ulm 70 F2
Ulog 74 F6
Ulongue 112 E2
Ulsan 88 E6
Ulu 84 M4
Ulubat Gölü 76 L4
Ulugqat 96 K2
Ulukışla 98 F5
Ulungur Hu 82 R8
Ulunkhan 84 J5
Uluru 116 F5
Ulu-Yul 84 D5
Ulva 64 F5
Ulverston 64 J7
Ulya 84 Q5
Ul'yanovsk 78 J4
Ulytau 82 M8
Uman' 78 F5
Umarkot 96 J4
Umba 78 F1
Umeå 56 L5
Umeälven 56 J4
Umfolozi 112 E5
Ummal Arānib 106 H3
Umm al Jamājim 101 A3
Umm Durman 104 F4
Umm Keddada 104 E5
Umm Lajj 104 G3
Umm Qaşr 101 B1
Umm Ruwaba 104 F5
Umnak Island 44 (1)E5
Umtata 112 D6
Umuarama 52 L3
Unalakleet 44 (1)E3
Unalaska Island 44 (1)E5
'Unayzah 100 C6
Underberg 112 D5
Ungava Bay 34 T5
Ungheni 74 Q2
Ungwana Bay 110 G4
União da Vitória 52 L4
Unije 70 K6
Unimak Island 44 (1)D5
Unim Bāb 101 D4
Unini 50 E4
Union 40 B3
Union City 46 G1
Union Springs 42 D3
United Arab Emirates 96 F5
United Kingdom 64 G6
United States 32 M5
Unna 62 K3
Unraven 44 E1
Unst 64 M1
Unstrut 60 G5
Unzha 78 H3
Upernavik 34 W2
Upernavik Kujalleq 34 V2
Upington 112 C5
Upolu 114 J7
Upper Hutt 118 E5
Upper Klamath Lake 38 B2
Upper Lake 38 C2
Upper Lough Erne 64 E7
Upper Sandusky 40 D2
Uppsala 56 J7
Upsala 40 B1
'Uqlat al 'Udhaybah 101 B2
Urad Houqi 86 D2
Urakawa 88 M2
Ural 78 K5
Ural Mountains = Ural'skiy Khrebet 54 L1
Ural'sk 78 K4
Ural'skiy Khrebet 54 L1
Urambo 110 E5
Uranium City 34 K5
Uraricoera 50 E3
Uray 78 M2
Urbana, *Ill., United States* 40 C2
Urbana, *Oh., United States* 40 D2
Urbania 70 H7
Urbino 70 H7
Urdzhar 82 Q8
Uren' 78 J3
Urengoy 82 P4
Urgench 96 H1
Urho 82 R8
Uritskiy 78 N4
Urla 76 J6
Urlaţi 74 P5
Uroševac 74 J7
Uro-teppa 96 J2
Urt 86 C2
Uruaçu 50 H6
Uruapan 46 D5
Urucurituba 50 F4
Uruguaiana 52 K4
Uruguay 52 K5
Uruguay 52 K5
Ürümqi 82 R9
Urus Martan 98 L2
Uryupino 84 L6
Uryupinsk 78 H4
Urzhum 78 K3
Urziceni 74 P5
Usa 82 L4
Uşak 98 C4
Usedom 60 J3
Useless Loop 116 B5
Usfān 96 C5
Ushtobe 82 P8
Usingen 60 D6
Usk 64 J10
Usman' 78 G4
Usol'ye Sibirskoye 84 G6
Ussel 66 H8
Ussuri 88 G1
Ussuriysk 86 J2
Usta 78 J3
Ust'-Alekseyevo 78 J2
Ust'-Barguzin 84 H6
Ust' Chaun 84 W3
Ústí 58 F8
Ústica 72 H10
Ust'-Ilimsk 84 G5
Ústí nad Labem 58 D7
Ust'-Ishim 82 N6
Ustka 58 F3
Ust'-Kamchatsk 84 U5
Ust'-Kamenogorsk 82 Q8
Ust'-Kamo 82 T5
Ust'-Karenga 84 K6
Ust'-Khayryuzovo 84 T5
Ust'-Kulom 78 K2
Ust'-Kut 84 G5
Ust'-Kuyga 84 P3
Ust'-Labinsk 98 H1
Ust'-Maya 84 N4
Ust'-Mukduyka 82 R4
Ust'-Muya 84 K5
Ust' Nem 78 K2
Ust'-Nera 84 Q4
Ust'-Nyukzha 84 L5
Ust'-Olenek 84 K2
Ust'-Omchug 84 R4
Ust' Ozernoye 84 D5
Ust' Penzhino 84 V4
Ust'-Pit 84 E5
Ustrem 78 N2
Ust'-Sopochnoye 84 T5
Ust' Tapsuy 78 M2
Ust'-Tarka 82 P6
Ust'-Tatta 84 N4
Ust'-Tsil'ma 82 J4
Ust' Un'ya 78 L2
Ust'-Urkima 84 L5
Ust' Usa 78 L1
Ust'-Uyskoye 82 L7
Usu 82 Q9
Usuki 88 F7
Utah 36 D4
Utah Lake 38 D2
Utata 84 G6
Utena 56 N9
Uthal 96 J4
Utica 40 E2
Utiel 68 J5
Utrecht 62 H2
Utrera 68 E7
Utsjoki 56 P2
Utsunomiya 88 K5
Uttaradit 90 C3
Utva 78 K4
Uummannaq Fjord 34 V2
Uummannarsuaq 34 Y5
Uusikaupunki 56 L6
Uvalde 46 E3
Uvargin 84 X3
Uvat 78 N3
Uvinza 110 E5
Uvira 110 D4
Uvs Nuur 82 S7
Uwajima 88 G7
Uy 78 M4
Uyar 82 S6
Uyuk 82 N9
Uyuni 52 H3
Uzbekistan 82 L9
Uzhhorod 74 K1
Užice 74 G6
Uzunköprü 74 P8

V

Vaal 112 D5
Vaasa 56 L5
Vác 74 G2
Vacaria 52 M4
Vachi 96 E1
Vadodara 94 B4
Vado Ligure 70 D6
Vadsø 56 Q1
Vaduz 70 E3
Værøy 56 G3
Vaganski Vhr 70 L6
Vagay 78 N3
Váh 58 H8
Vakh 78 Q2
Valbonnais 70 A6
Valcheta 52 H7
Valdagno 70 G5
Valday 78 F3
Val-de-Meuse 70 A2
Valdemoro 68 G4
Valdepeñas 68 G6
Valdez 34 B4
Valdivia 52 G6
Val-d'Or 40 E1
Valdosta 36 K5
Valdres 56 E6
Valea lui Mihai 74 K2
Valence 66 K9
Valencia, *Spain* 68 K5
Valencia, *Venezuela* 50 D1
Valencia de Alcántara 68 C5
Valenciennes 62 F4
Vălenii de Munte 74 P4
Valentia Island 64 B10
Valentine 38 F2
Valenza 70 D5
Valera 50 C2
Valga 78 E3
Val Horn 36 F5
Valjevo 74 G5
Valka 56 N8
Val'karay 84 X3
Valkeakoski 56 N6
Valkenswaard 62 H3
Valladolid, *Mexico* 46 G4
Valladolid, *Spain* 68 F3
Valledupar 50 C1
Vallée de Azaouagh 106 F5
Vallée du Tîlemsi 106 F5
Vallée-Jonction 40 F1
Vallejo 38 B3
Vallentuna 56 K7
Valletta 72 J13
Valley City 38 G1
Valley Falls 38 B2
Valley of the Kings 104 F2
Valli di Comacchio 70 H6
Vallorbe 70 B4
Valls 68 M3
Valmiera 56 N8
Valognes 62 A5
Val-Paradis 40 E1
Valparai 94 C6
Valparaíso, *Chile* 52 G5
Valparaíso, *Mexico* 44 F4
Valsad 94 B4
Val'tevo 78 H2
Valuyki 78 G4
Valverde del Camino 68 D7
Vammala 56 M6
Van 98 K4
Vanadzor 98 L3
Vanavara 84 G4
Van Buren 40 G1
Vancouver, *Canada* 38 B1
Vancouver, *United States* 38 B1
Vancouver Island 34 F7
Vandalia 42 D2
Vanderbijlpark 112 D5
Vanderhoof 34 G6
Van Diemen Gulf 116 F2
Vänern 56 G7
Vangaindrano 112 H4
Van Gölü 98 K4
Van Horn 44 F2
Vanimo 92 (2)F3
Vanino 84 Q7
Vankarem 84 Y3
Vanna 56 K1
Vännäs 56 K5
Vannes 66 C6
Vanrhynsdorp 112 B6
Vantaa 56 N6
Vanua Levu 114 H7
Vanuatu 114 G7
Van Wert 40 D2
Vanzevat 78 N2
Vanzhil'kynak 84 C4
Varāmīn 96 F2
Varanasi 94 D3
Varangerfjorden 56 R2
Varaždin 74 D3
Varazze 70 D6
Varberg 56 G8
Vardar 76 E3
Varde 56 E9
Vardenis 98 L3
Vardø 56 R1
Varel 60 D3
Varėna 58 P3
Varese 70 D5
Vârful Moldoveanu 74 M4
Vârfurile 74 K3
Varginha 52 M3
Varkaus 56 P5
Varna 98 B2
Värnamo 56 H8
Varnsdorf 60 K6
Várpalota 74 F2
Varto 98 J4
Varzi 70 E6
Varzy 66 J6
Vásárosnamény 74 K1
Vasilikos 100 A2
Vaslui 74 Q3
Västerås 56 J7
Västervik 56 J8
Vasto 72 J6
Vasvár 70 M3
Vatan 66 G6
Vathia 76 E8
Vatican City 72 F7
Vatnajökull 56 (1)E2
Vatomandry 112 H3
Vatra Dornei 74 N2
Vättern 56 H7
Vaughn 44 E2
Vawkavysk 58 P4
Växjö 56 H8
Vayuniya 94 D7
Vazhgort 78 J2
Vecht 62 J2
Vechta 62 L2
Vecsés 74 G2
Vedaranniyam 94 C6
Vedea 74 N6
Veendam 62 J1
Veenendaal 62 H2
Vega 56 F4
Vega 44 F1
Vegreville 34 J6
Vejen 60 E1
Vejer de la Frontera 68 E8
Vejle 56 E9
Vel' 82 G5
Vela Luka 74 D7
Velenje 70 L4
Veles 76 D3
Vélez-Málaga 68 F8
Velika Gorica 70 M5
Velika Plana 74 J5
Velikaya 84 W4
Velikiye Luki 78 F3
Velikiy Ustyug 78 J2
Veliko Tŭrnovo 74 N6
Vélingara 108 E2
Velingrad 74 L7
Velita Kladuša 70 L5

Velké Meziříčí 58 F8
Velký Krtíš 58 J9
Velletri 72 G7
Vellinge 58 C2
Vellore 94 C6
Velopoula 76 F8
Vel'sk 78 H2
Velten 60 J4
Velva 38 F1
Venaria 70 C5
Vence 70 C7
Venda Nova 68 C3
Vendôme 66 G6
Venev 78 G4
Venézia 70 H5
Venezuela 50 D2
Vengurla 94 B5
Veniaminof Volcano 44 (1)F4
Venice = Venézia 70 H5
Venice 42 D4
Venlo 62 J3
Venray 62 H3
Venta 78 D3
Ventimiglia 70 C7
Ventotene 72 H8
Ventspils 56 L8
Vera, *Argentina* 52 J4
Vera, *Spain* 68 J7
Veracruz 46 E5
Veraval 94 B4
Verbania 70 D5
Vercelli 70 D5
Verdalsøra 56 F5
Verde 50 G8
Verden 60 E4
Verdun 62 H5
Vereeniging 112 D5
Vereshchagino 84 D4
Verín 68 C3
Verkhneimbatsk 84 D4
Verkhnetulomskoe
Vodokhranilishche 56 R2
Verkhneural'sk 78 L4
Verkhniy Baskunchak 78 J5
Verkhnyaya Amga 84 M5
Verkhnyaya Toyma 78 J2
Verkhnyaya Tura 78 L3
Verkhovyna 74 M1
Verkhoyansk 84 N3
Verkhoyanskiy Khrebet 84 M3
Vermillion 38 G2
Vermont 36 M3
Vernal 38 E2
Verneuil 62 C6
Vernon, *France* 62 D5
Vernon, *United States* 42 B3
Vero Beach 42 E4
Veroia 76 E4
Verona 70 F5
Versailles 62 E6
Verviers 62 H4
Veselí 70 N2
Vesijarvi 56 N6
Vesoul 60 B9
Vesterålen 56 G2
Vestfjorden 56 G3
Vestmannaeyjar 56 (1)C3
Vestvagøy 56 G2
Vesuvio 72 J8
Veszprém 74 E2
Vet 112 D5
Vetluga 78 J3
Vetluga 78 J3
Veurne 62 E3
Vevey 70 B4
Vezirköprü 98 F3
Viana do Castelo 68 B3
Vianden 62 J5
Viangchan 90 C3
Viaréggio 70 F7
Viaréggio 72 E5
Viborg 56 E8
Vibraye 66 F5
Vic 68 N3
Vicenza 70 G5
Vichuga 78 H3
Vichy 66 J7
Vicksburg 42 C3
Victor Harbor 116 G7
Victoria 80 J10
Victoria 116 H7
Victoria, *Argentina* 52 J5
Victoria, *Canada* 38 B1
Victoria, *Malta* 72 J12
Victoria, *Romania* 74 M4
Victoria, *Seychelles* 112 (2)C1
Victoria, *United States* 42 B4
Victoria de las Tunas 46 J4
Victoria Falls 112 D3
Victoria Island 34 J2
Victoria Land 120 (2)W2
Victoria Strait 34 M3
Victoriaville 40 F1
Victoria West 112 C6
Vidalia 36 K5
Vidamlja 58 N5
Videle 74 N5
Vidin 74 K6
Viedma 52 J7
Vienna = Wien 70 M2
Vienna 40 C3
Vienne 66 F7
Vienne 66 K8
Vientiane = Viangchan 90 C3
Vierzon 66 H6
Vieste 72 L7
Vietnam 90 D3
Viêt Tri 90 D2
Vigan 90 G3
Vigévano 70 D5
Vigia 50 H4
Vigo 68 B2
Viho Valentia 72 L10
Vijaywada 94 D5
Vik 56 (1)D3
Vikna 56 E4
Vila de Conde 68 B3
Vilafranca del Penedàs 68 M3
Vila Franca de Xira 68 A6
Vila Nova de Gaia 68 B3
Vilanova y la Geltru 68 M3
Vila Real 68 C3
Vila-real 68 K5
Vilhelmina 56 J4
Vilhena 50 E6
Vilija 56 N9
Viljandi 56 N7
Vilkaviškis 58 N3
Villa Ahumada 46 C2
Villablino 68 D2
Villacarrillo 68 G6
Villach 70 J4
Villacidro 72 C9
Villa Constitución 36 D7
Villa de Cos 46 D4
Villafranca 70 F5
Villafranca de los Barros 68 D6
Villagarcia 68 B2
Villagrán 44 G4
Villahermosa 46 F5
Villa Huidobro 52 J5
Villalba 68 C1
Villaldama 44 F3
Villalpando 68 E3
Villamartín 68 E8
Villa Montes 52 J3
Villanueva 44 F4
Villanueva de Cordoba 68 F6
Villa Ocampo 44 E3
Villaputzu 72 D9
Villarrobledo 68 H5
Villa San Giovanni 72 K10
Villavelayo 68 H2
Villavicencio 50 C3
Villaviciosa 68 E1
Villedieu-les-Poêles 62 A6
Villefranche-de-Rouergue 66 H9
Villefranche-sur-Saône 66 K8
Villena 68 K6
Villeneuve-sur-Lot 66 F9
Villers-Bocage 62 B5
Villers-Cotterêts 62 F5
Villerupt 62 H5
Villeurbanne 66 K8
Villingen 70 D2
Vilnius 56 N9
Vilsbiburg 70 H2
Vilshofen 70 J2
Vilvoorde 62 G4
Vilyuy 84 L4
Vilyuysk 84 L4
Vilyuyskoye
Vodokhranilishche 84 J4
Vimoutiers 62 C6
Vimperk 70 J1
Viña del Mar 52 G5
Vinaròs 68 L4
Vincennes 42 D2
Vineland 40 F3
Vinh 90 D3
Vinkovci 74 F4
Vinnytsya 78 E5
Vinson Massif 120 (2)JJ2
Vinstri 56 E6
Vinzili 78 N3
Vioolsdrift 112 B5
Vipava 70 J5
Vipiteno 70 G4
Vir 70 L6
Virac 90 G4
Viranşehir 98 H5
Virawah 94 B4
Virden 38 F1
Vire 62 B6
Virginia 36 L4
Virginia 40 B1
Virginia Beach 40 E3
Virgin Islands,
United Kingdom 48 E2
Virgin Islands,
United States 48 E2
Virihaure 56 J3
Virôchey 90 D4
Virovitica 74 E4
Virton 62 H5
Virtsu 56 M7
Virudunagar 94 C7
Vis 74 D6
Visalia 38 C3
Visby 56 K8
Viscount Melville Sound 34 J2
Viseu, *Brazil* 50 H4
Viseu, *Portugal* 68 C4
Vişeu de Sus 74 M2
Vishakhapatnam 94 D5
Vishera 82 K5
Vishnevka 82 N7
Visoko 74 F6
Visp 70 C4
Visselhövede 60 E4
Vistula = Wisła 54 F2
Viterbo 72 G6
Viti Levu 114 H7
Vitim 84 J5
Vitolište 76 D3
Vitória 52 N3
Vitória da Conquista 50 J6
Vitoria-Gasteiz 68 H2
Vitré 66 D5
Vitry-le-François 62 G6
Vitsyebsk 78 F3
Vitteaux 66 K6
Vittel 70 A2
Vittória 72 J12
Vittório Véneto 70 H5
Viveiro 68 C1
Vivi 82 T4
Vize 76 K3
Vizhas 78 J1
Vizianagaram 94 D5
Vizinga 82 H5
Vizzini 72 J11
Vjosë 76 C4
Vladikavkaz 98 L2
Vladimir 78 H3
Vladivostok 88 F2
Vlasotince 74 K7
Vlasovo 84 N2
Vlieland 62 G1
Vlissingen 62 F3
Vlorë 76 B4
Vltava 58 D8
Vöcklabruck 70 J2
Vodice 70 L7
Vodnjan 70 J6
Vogelsberg 60 E6
Voghera 70 D6
Vohipeno 112 H4
Vöhringen 70 F2
Voi 110 F4
Voinjama 108 C3
Voiron 66 L8
Voitsberg 70 L3
Vojens 60 E1
Vojmsjön 56 J4
Vojvodina 74 G4
Volary 60 J8
Volcán Antofalla 52 H4
Volcán Barú 46 H7
Volcán Cayambe 50 B3
Volcán Citlaltépetl 32 L7
Volcán Corcovado 52 G7
Volcán Cotopaxi 50 B4
Volcán Domuyo 52 G6
Volcán Lanin 52 G6
Volcán Llullaillaco 52 H3
Volcán San Pedro 52 H3
Volcán Tajumulco 46 F5
Volga 78 J5
Volgodonsk 78 H5
Volgograd 78 H5
Völkermarkt 70 K4
Volkhov 78 F3
Völklingen 62 J5
Volksrust 112 D5
Volochanka 82 S3
Volodarskoye 78 N4
Vologda 78 H3
Volonga 78 J1
Volos 76 E5
Volosovo 56 Q7
Volta Redonda 50 J8
Volterra 70 F7
Volti 70 D6
Volzhskiy 78 H5
Voorne 62 F3
Voranava 56 N9
Vorderrhein 70 E4
Vordingborg 60 G1
Voreios Evvoïkos Kolpos 76 E6
Voreria Pindos 76 C4
Vorkuta 78 M1
Vormsi 56 M7
Vorona 78 H4
Voronezh 78 G4
Vorstershoop 112 C5
Võru 56 P8
Vosges 70 C2
Voss 56 D6
Vostochno-Sibirskoye
More 84 U2
Vostochnyy Sayan 82 T7
Vostok Island 114 L6
Votkinsk 82 J6
Vozhgora 78 J2
Vranje 74 J7
Vranov 58 L9
Vranov nad Toplau 74 J1
Vratsa 74 L6
Vrbas 74 E5
Vrbas 74 G4
Vrbovsko 70 L5
Vrendenburg 112 B6
Vršac 74 J4
Vryburg 112 C5
Vryheid 112 E5
Vsetín 58 G8
Vučitrn 74 J7
Vukovar 74 G4
Vuktyl' 78 L2
Vulcăneşti 74 R4
Vulcano 72 J10
Vung Tau 90 D4
Vuollerim 56 L3
Vuotso 56 P2
Vyatka 78 K3
Vyazemskiy 84 N7
Vyaz'ma 78 F3
Vyborg 56 Q6
Vychegda 78 K2
Vyksa 78 H3
Vylkove 74 S4
Vynohradiv 58 N9
Vyshniy Volochek 78 F3
Vyškov 58 G8
Vytegra 78 G2

W

Wa 108 D3
Waal 62 H3
Waalwijk 62 H3
Wabē Shebelē Wenz 110 G2
Waco 42 B3
Wad Banda 104 E5
Waddān 104 C2
Waddeneilanden 62 G1
Waddenzee 62 H1
Wadena 40 A1
Wādī al Fārigh 104 C1
Wādī al Hamīm 104 D1
Wadi Halfa 104 F3
Wādi Mūsā 100 C6
Wad Medani 104 F5
Wadsworth 44 C1
Wafangdian 86 G3
Wafangdian 88 A4
Wagga Wagga 116 J7
Wahai 92 (2)C3
Wahiawa 44 (2)C2
Wahpeton 38 G1
Waiau 118 D6
Waiblingen 70 E2
Waidhofen 70 K3
Waidhofen an der Ybbs 74 B2
Waigeo 92 (2)D3
Waiheke Island 118 E3
Waihi 118 E3
Waikabubak 92 (2)A4
Waikaia 118 B7
Waikaremoana 118 F4
Waikato 118 E4
Waikawa 118 B8
Wailuku 44 (2)E3
Waimate 118 C7
Waingapu 116 B1
Wainwright 44 (1)F1
Waiouru 118 E4
Waipara 118 D6
Waipawa 118 F4
Waipiro 118 G4
Waipukurau 118 F5
Wairoa 118 F4
Waitakaruru 118 E3
Waitaki 118 C7
Waitangi 118 (1)B1
Waitara 118 E4

Waiuku 118 E3
Wajima 88 J5
Wajir 110 G3
Wakasa-wan 88 H6
Wakayama 88 H6
Wakeeney 44 G1
Wakefield 64 L8
Wake Island 114 G4
Wakkanai 88 L1
Waku-Kungo 112 B2
Wałbrzych 58 F7
Walcheren 62 F3
Wałcz 58 F4
Waldmünchen 60 H7
Waldshut-Tiengen 70 D3
Walen See 70 E3
Wales 64 J9
Wales Island 34 P3
Walgett 116 J6
Walker Lake 44 C1
Walkerville 116 J7
Wall 38 F2
Wallaceburg 40 D2
Walla Walla 38 C1
Wallis et Futuna 114 J7
Walpole 116 C6
Walsall 64 L9
Walsenburg 38 F3
Walsrode 60 E4
Waltershausen 60 F6
Walvis Bay 112 A4
Wamba 110 D3
Wana 96 J3
Wanaaring 116 H5
Wanaka 118 B7
Wandel Sea 32 A1
Wandingzhen 90 B2
Wanganui 118 E4
Wanganui 118 E4
Wangen 70 E3
Wangerooge 60 D3
Wangiwangi 92 (2)B4
Wan Hsa-la 90 B2
Wanxian 86 D4
Wanyuan 86 D4
Warangal 94 C5
Warburg 60 D5
Ward 118 E5
Wardha 94 C4
Waregem 62 F4
Waremme 62 H4
Waren 60 H3
Warendorf 62 K3
Warka 58 L6
Warla 58 H6
Warmandi 92 (2)D3
Warminster 64 K10
Warm Springs 38 C3
Warren, *Mich.*, *United States* 40 D2
Warren, *Oh.*, *United States* 40 D2
Warren, *Pa.*, *United States* 40 E2
Warrensburg 40 B3
Warrenton 112 C5
Warri 108 F3
Warrington, *United Kingdom* 64 K8
Warrington, *United States* 42 D3
Warrnambool 116 H7
Warroad 40 A1
Warsaw = Warszawa 58 K5
Warstein 60 D5
Warszawa 58 K5
Warta 58 F5
Warwick 64 L9
Wasatch Range 44 D1
Wasco 44 C1
Washap 96 H4
Washburn Lake 34 K2
Washington 38 B1
Washington, *N.C.*, *United States* 40 E3
Washington, *Pa.*, *United States* 40 D2
Washington, *Ut.*, *United States* 38 D3
Washington D.C. 32 J6
Wassenaar 62 G2
Wasserburg 70 H2
Watampone 92 (2)B3
Waterbury 40 F2
Waterford 64 E9
Waterloo 40 B2
Watersmeet 40 C1
Watertown, *N.Y.*, *United States* 40 E2
Watertown, *S.D.*, *United States* 38 G1
Watertown, *Wis.*, *United States* 40 C2
Waterville 40 G2
Watford 62 B3
Watford City 38 F1
Watmuri 92 (2)D4
Watrous 34 K6
Watsa 110 D3
Watseka 42 D1
Watson Lake 44 (1)M3
Wau 110 D2
Waubay Lake 38 G1
Waukegan 40 C2
Waukesha 40 C2
Waurika 42 B3
Wausau 36 J3
Waverly 40 C3
Wavre 62 G4
Wawa 40 D1
Wāw al Kabīr 104 C2
Waxxari 82 R10
Waycross 42 E3
Waynesboro, *Ga.*, *United States* 42 E3
Waynesboro, *Miss.*, *United States* 42 D3
Waynesville 40 D3
Weaverville 38 B2
Weber 118 F5
Webi Shaabeelle 110 G3
Webster 38 G1
Weddell Island 52 J9
Weddell Sea 120 (2)A2
Wedel 60 E3
Weed 38 B2
Weert 62 H3
Wei 86 D4
Weichang 86 F2
Weida 60 H6
Weiden 60 H7
Weifang 86 F3
Weihai 86 G3
Weilburg 60 D6
Weilheim 70 G3
Weimar 60 G6
Weinan 86 D4
Weinheim 60 D7
Weining 86 C5
Weipa 116 H2
Weiser 38 C2
Weißenburg 60 F7
Weißenfels 60 G5
Weißwasser 60 K5
Weixi 90 B1
Wejherowo 58 H3
Welkom 112 D5
Welland 62 B2
Wellesley Islands 116 G3
Wellingborough 66 E1
Wellington, *New Zealand* 118 E5
Wellington, *Colo.*, *United States* 38 F2
Wellington, *Kans.*, *United States* 42 B2
Wells 38 C2
Wellsboro 40 E2
Wellsford 118 E3
Wellton 44 D2
Wels 70 K2
Welwyn Garden City 62 B3
Wenatchee 38 B1
Wenchang 90 E3
Wenga 110 B3
Wenman 50 (1)A1
Wentworth 116 H6
Wen Xian 86 C4
Wenzhou 86 G5
Werder 60 H4
Werdēr 110 H2
Werl 62 K3
Werneck 60 F7
Wernigerode 60 F5
Werra 60 F6
Wertheim 60 E7
Wesel 62 J3
Wesel Dorsten 60 B5
Weser 60 E4
Wessel Islands 116 G2
West Antarctica 120 (2)GG2
West Bank 100 C4
West Branch 40 D2
West Cape 114 G10
West End 42 F4
Western Australia 116 D5
Western Cape 112 B6
Western Ghats 94 B5
Western Reef 118 (1)B1
Western Sahara 106 C4
Wester Ross 64 G4
Westerschelde 62 F3
Westerstede 62 K1
Westerwald 62 K4
West Falkland 52 J9
West Frankfort 42 D2
West Glacier 38 D1
West Lunga 112 C2
West Memphis 42 C2
Weston 40 D3
Weston-super-Mare 64 K10
West Palm Beach 42 E4
West Plains 40 B3
Westport, *New Zealand* 118 C5
Westport, *Republic of Ireland* 64 C8
Westray 64 J2
West Siberian Plain = Zapadno-Sibirskaya Ravnina 80 L3
West Virginia 40 D3
West Wendover 38 D2
West Yellowstone 38 D2
Wetar 92 (2)C4
Wetaskiwin 34 J6
Wete 110 F5
Wetumpka 42 D3
Wetzlar 60 D6
Wewak 92 (2)F3
Wexford 64 F9
Wexford Harbour 64 F9
Weyburn 36 F2
Weymouth 64 K11
Whakatane 118 F3
Whale Cove 34 N4
Whalsay 64 M1
Whangarei 118 E2
Wharfe 64 L7
Wheeler Peak 44 E1
Wheeler Ridge 44 C2
Wheeling 42 E1
Whitby 64 M7
White, *Nev.*, *United States* 38 C3
White, *S.D.*, *United States* 34 L8
White Bay 34 V6
White Cliffs 116 H6
Whitecourt 34 H6
Whitefish Point 40 C1
Whitehaven 64 J7
Whitehorse 44 (1)L3
White Island 118 F3
Whitemark 116 J8
White Mountain Peak 38 C3
White Mountains 34 S8
Whitemouth 38 G1
White Nile = Bahr el Abiad 104 F5
White River, *Canada* 40 C1
White River, *United States* 38 F2
White Sea = Beloye More 78 G1
White Sulphur Springs 38 D1
Whiteville 42 F3
White Volta 108 D3
Whitney 40 E1
Whyalla 116 G6
Wichita 42 B2
Wichita Falls 42 B3
Wick 64 J3
Wickenburg 44 D2
Wicklow Mountains 64 F8
Widawka 58 J6
Wieluń 58 H6
Wien 70 M2
Wiener Neustadt 70 M3
Wieringermeer Polder 62 G2
Wiesbaden 60 D6
Wiesloch 60 D7
Wiesmoor 60 C3
Wigan 64 K8
Wiggins 38 F2
Wil 70 E3
Wilbur 38 C1
Wilcannia 116 H6
Wildeshausen 60 D4
Wilhelmshaven 60 D3
Wilkes-Barre 40 E2
Wilkes Land 120 (2)U2
Willapa Bay 38 B1
Willemstad 50 D1
Williams, *Australia* 116 C6
Williams, *Ariz.*, *United States* 38 D3
Williams, *Calif.*, *United States* 38 B3
Williamsburg 40 E3
Williams Lake 34 G6
Williamson 42 E2
Williamsport 40 E2
Willis Group 116 K3
Williston, *Fla.*, *United States* 42 E4
Williston, *N.D.*, *United States* 38 F1
Williston Lake 34 G5
Willmar 40 A
Willow 44 (1)H
Willowmore 112 C
Willow River 40 B
Willow Springs 40 B
Wilmington, *Del.*, *United States* 40 E
Wilmington, *N.C.*, *United States* 42 F
Wilson 40 E
Wilson Reservoir 42 B
Wilson's Promontory 116 J
Wiluna 116 D
Winamac 40 C
Winchester, *United Kingdom* 64 L1
Winchester, *Ky.*, *United States* 40 D
Winchester, *Va.*, *United States* 40 E
Windhoek 112 B
Windischgarsten 70 K
Windom 40 A
Windorah 116 H
Windsor, *Canada* 40 D
Windsor, *United Kingdom* 62 B
Windsor, *United States* 42 F
Windward Islands 46 N
Windward Passage 48 D
Winfield, *Al.*, *United States* 42 D
Winfield, *Kans.*, *United States* 44 G
Wingate Mountains 116 E
Winisk 34 P
Winisk 34 P
Winisk Lake 34 P
Winnemucca 38 C
Winner 38 G
Winnfield 36 H
Winnipeg 34 M
Winona, *Minn.*, *United States* 40 B
Winona, *Miss.*, *United States* 42 D
Winschoten 62 K
Winsen 60 F
Winslow 44 D
Winston-Salem 40 D
Winterberg 60 D
Winter Harbour 34 J
Winterswijk 62 J
Winterthur 70 D
Winton, *Australia* 116 H
Winton, *New Zealand* 118 B
Wisbech 62 C
Wisconsin 36 H
Wisconsin 40 B
Wisconsin Dells 40 C
Wisconsin Rapids 40 C
Wisła 58 H
Wisła 58 H
Wisłoka 58 L
Wismar 60 G
Wissembourg 60 C
Witney 62 A
Witten 62 K
Wittenberge 60 G
Wittenoom 116 C
Wittingen 60 F
Wittlich 62 J
Wittmund 60 C
Wittstock 60 H
Witzenhausen 60 E
W. J. van Blommesteinmeer 50 G
Wkra 58 K
Władysławowo 58 H
Włocławek 58 J
Włodawa 58 N
Wodzisław Śląski 58 H
Wohlen 70 D
Wokam 92 (2)D
Woking 64 M1
Wolf Creek 38 D
Wolfen 60 H
Wolfenbüttel 60 F
Wolf Point 38 E
Wolfratshausen 70 G
Wolfsberg 70 K
Wolfsburg 60 F
Wolgast 60 J
Wollaston Lake 34 K
Wollaston Peninsula 34 H
Wollongong 116 K
Wołomin 58 L
Wolsztyn 58 F
Wolverhampton 64 K
Wŏnju 88 D
Wŏnsan 88 D
Woodbridge 62 D

Woodburn 38 B1
Woodland 38 B3
Woodstock, *Canada* 40 G1
Woodstock, *United Kingdom* 62 A3
Woodstock, *United States* 40 C2
Woodville, *New Zealand* 118 E5
Woodville, *Miss., United States* 42 C3
Woodville, *Tex., United States* 42 C3
Woodward 38 G3
Woody Head 118 E3
Woonsocket, *R.I., United States* 40 F2
Woonsocket, *S.D., United States* 38 G2
Worcester, *South Africa* 112 B6
Worcester, *United Kingdom* 64 K9
Worcester, *United States* 36 M3
Wörgl 70 H3
Workington 64 J7
Worksop 62 A1
Worland 38 E2
Worms 60 D7
Wörth 60 D7
Worthing 64 M11
Worthington 36 G3
Wosu 92 (2)B3
Wotu 92 (2)B3
Wowoni 92 (2)B3
Wrangell 34 E5
Wrangell Mountains 34 C4
Wray 36 F3
Wrexham 64 K8
Wrigley 34 G4
Wrocław 58 G6
Września 58 G5
Wu 86 D5
Wubin 116 C6
Wubu 86 E3
Wuchang 86 H2
Wuchuan 86 E2
Wuday'ah 96 E6
Wudu 86 C4
Wuhai 86 D3
Wuhan 86 E4
Wuhu 86 F4
Wüjang 94 C2
Wukari 108 F3
Wuli 94 F2
Wunsiedel 60 G6
Wunstorf 60 E4
Wuppertal 60 C5
Würzburg 60 E7
Wurzen 60 H5
Wushi 82 P9
Wusuli 86 J1
Wutach 70 D3
Wuwei 86 C3
Wuxi 86 G4
Wuxu 90 D2
Wuyuan 86 D2
Wuzhong 86 D3
Wuzhou 90 E2
Wye 64 J9
Wyndham 116 E3
Wynniatt Bay 34 J2
Wyoming 36 E3
Wyszków 58 L5
Wytheville 42 E2

X

Xaafuun 110 J1
Xàbia 68 L6
Xaçmaz 98 N3
Xaidulla 82 P10
Xainza 94 E2
Xai-Xai 112 E4
Xam Nua 90 C2
Xankändi 98 M4
Xanten 62 J3
Xanthi 76 G3
Xapuri 50 D6
Xar Moron 84 K8
Xàtiva 68 K6
Xiahe 86 C3
Xiamen 90 F2
Xi'an 86 D4
Xiangcheng 86 E4
Xiangfan 86 E4
Xianghoang 90 C3
Xianghuang Qi 86 E2
Xiangtan 86 E5
Xianning 86 E5
Xianyang 86 D4
Xiaogan 86 E4
Xiao Hinggan Ling 84 M7
Xiaonanchuan 94 F1
Xichang 90 C1
Xigazê 94 E3
Xi Jiang 86 E6
Xilinhot 86 F2
Xincai 86 E4
Xingcheng 86 G2
Xinghua 86 F4
Xingtai 86 F3
Xingu 50 G5
Xingyi 90 C1
Xinhe 82 Q9
Xining 86 C3
Xinjin 86 G3
Xinmin 88 B2
Xintai 86 E3
Xinxiang 86 E3
Xinyang 86 E4
Xinyu 86 F5
Xinyuan 82 Q9
Xinzhou 86 E3
Xinzo de Limia 68 C2
Xique Xique 50 J6
Xi Ujimqin Qi 86 F2
Xiushu 86 E5
Xiwu 94 G2
Xixia 86 E4
Xi Xiang 86 D4
Xizang 94 E2
Xizang Gaoyuan 94 D2
Xuanhua 86 E2
Xuchang 86 E4
Xuddur 110 G3
Xuwen 90 E2
Xuzhou 86 F4

Y

Ya'an 86 D3
Yabassi 108 F4
Yabēlo 110 F3
Yablonovyy Khrebet 84 J6
Yabrūd 100 D3
Yabuli 88 E1
Yacuma 50 D6
Yadgir 94 D5
Yagodnyy 78 N3
Yahk 34 H7
Yakima 38 B1
Yako 108 D2
Yakoma 110 C3
Yaksha 78 L2
Yakumo 88 L2
Yaku-shima 88 F8
Yakutat 44 (1)K4
Yakutsk 84 M4
Yala 90 C5
Yalova 76 M4
Yalta 98 F1
Yalu 88 D3
Yalutorovsk 78 N3
Yamagata 88 L4
Yamaguchi 88 F6
Yamarovka 84 J6
Yambio 110 D3
Yambol 74 P7
Yamburg 82 P4
Yamdena 92 (2)D4
Yamoussoukro 108 C3
Yampa 38 E2
Yampil' 74 R1
Yamsk 84 S5
Yan'an 86 D3
Yanbu'al Baḩr 96 C5
Yancheng 86 G4
Yandun 86 A2
Yangambi 110 C3
Yangbajain 94 F2
Yangdok 88 D4
Yangi Kand 98 N5
Yangjiang 90 E2
Yangon 90 B3
Yangquan 86 E3
Yangshuo 90 E2
Yangtze = Chang Jiang 86 D4
Yangzhou 86 F4
Yanhuqu 94 D2
Yani-Kurgan 82 M9
Yanji 88 E2
Yankton 38 G2
Yano-Indigirskaya Nizmennost' 84 N2
Yanqi 82 R9
Yanqing 86 F2
Yanshan 90 C2
Yanskiy Zaliv 84 N2
Yantai 86 G3
Yaoundé 108 G4
Yap 114 D5
Yapen 92 (2)E3
Yaqui 36 E6
Yaransk 78 J3
Yardımcı Burnu 76 E8
Yare 62 D2
Yaren 114 G6
Yarensk 78 J2
Yari 50 C3
Yarkant 96 L2
Yarkovo 78 N3
Yarlung Zangbo 94 F3
Yarmouth 34 T8
Yaroslavl' 78 G3
Yar Sale 78 P1
Yartsevo 78 F3
Yashkul' 78 J5
Yasnyy 78 L4
Yāsūj 101 D1
Yatağan 76 L7
Yathkyed Lake 34 M4
Yatsushiro 88 F7
Yavari 50 C5
Yawatongguzlangar 82 Q10
Yaya 82 R6
Yayladaği 98 F6
Yazd 96 F3
Yazdān 96 H3
Yazd-e Khvāst 101 E1
Yazoo City 42 C3
Ydra 76 F7
Ye 90 B3
Yea 116 J7
Yecheng 96 L2
Yecla 68 J6
Yefremov 78 G4
Yegendybulak 82 P8
Yei 110 E3
Yekaterinburg 78 M3
Yelets 78 G4
Yell 64 L1
Yellowknife 34 J4
Yellow River = Huang He 86 C3
Yellow Sea 86 G3
Yellowstone 38 E1
Yellowstone Lake 38 D2
Yeloten 96 H2
Yelva 82 J5
Yelwa 108 E2
Yemen 96 E7
Yemetsk 78 H2
Yenakiyeve 78 G5
Yengisar 96 L2
Yenihisar 76 K7
Yenisey 82 S6
Yeniseysk 82 S6
Yeniseyskiy Kryazh 82 S5
Yeo Lake 116 D5
Yeovil 64 K11
Yeppoon 116 K4
Yeraliyev 82 J9
Yerbogachen 84 H4
Yerevan 98 L3
Yerington 38 C3
Yerkov 76 S5
Yerkoy 98 F4
Yermak 82 P7
Yermitsa 78 K1
Yernva 82 J5
Yershov 78 J4
Yerupaja 50 B6
Yerushalayim 100 C5
Yesil' 78 N4
Yeşilhisar 98 F4
Yeşilköy 76 L4
Yessey 82 U4
Yevlax 98 M3
Yevpatoriya 78 F5
Yeyik 82 Q10
Yeysk 78 G5
Yibin 86 C5
Yichang 86 E4
Yichun, *China* 86 E5
Yichun, *China* 86 H1
Yilan 86 H1
Yıldız Dağları 76 K3
Yıldızeli 98 G4
Yinchuan 86 D3
Yingcheng 86 E4
Yingkou 86 G2
Yining 82 Q9
Yirga Alem 110 F2
Yitomio 56 M3
Yitulihe 84 L6
Yiyang 86 E5
Yli-Kitka 56 Q3
Ylivieska 56 N4
Ylöjärvi 56 M6
Yoakum 42 B4
Yoboki 104 H5
Yogyakarta 92 (1)E4
Yokadouma 108 G4
Yoko 108 G3
Yokohama, *Japan* 88 K6
Yokohama, *Japan* 88 L3
Yokosuka 88 K6
Yokote 88 L4
Yola 108 G3
Yonago 88 G6
Yonezawa 88 L5
Yong'an 90 F1
Yongdeng 86 C3
Yŏnghŭng 88 D4
Yongren 90 C1
Yongxiu 86 F5
Yonkers 40 F2
York, *United Kingdom* 64 L8
York, *Nebr., United States* 38 G2
York, *Pa., United States* 40 E3
Yorkton 34 L6
Yoshkar Ola 78 J3
Yŏsu 88 D6
Yotvata 100 C7
You 90 D2
Youghal 64 E10
Youghal Bay 64 E10
Youngstown 40 D2
Yozgat 98 F4
Yreka 38 B2
Ystad 58 C2
Ysyk-Köl 82 P9
Ytre Sula 56 B6
Ytyk-Kyuyel' 84 N4
Yu 90 D2
Yuan 90 C2
Yuanjiang 90 C2
Yuanmou 90 C1
Yuanping 86 E3
Yucatán 46 F5
Yucatan Channel 46 G4
Yuci 86 E3
Yudoma 84 Q4
Yuendumu 116 F4
Yueyang 86 E5
Yugorenok 84 P5
Yugoslavia 74 H6
Yugo-Tala 84 S3
Yukagirskoye Ploskogor'ye 84 S3
Yukon 44 (1)E3
Yukon Territory 44 (1)K2
Yukorskiy Poluostrov 82 L4
Yüksekova 98 L5
Yukta 84 H4
Yuli 82 R9
Yulin, *China* 90 E2
Yulin, *China* 86 D3
Yuma 44 C2
Yumen 86 B3
Yumin 82 Q8
Yuncheng 86 E3
Yun Xian 90 C2
Yuogi Feng 82 R8
Yurga 82 Q6
Yurimaguas 50 B5
Yurla 78 K3
Yuroma 78 J1
Yur'yevets 78 H3
Yu Shan 90 G2
Yushkozero 56 S4
Yushu, *China* 86 B4
Yushu, *China* 86 H2
Yusufeli 98 J3
Yutian 82 Q10
Yuyao 86 G4
Yuzhno Kuril'sk 88 N1
Yuzhno-Sakhalinsk 84 Q7
Yuzhno-Sukhokumsk 98 L1
Yuzhnoural'sk 78 M4
Yverdon-les-Bains 70 B4
Yvetot 62 C5

Z

Zaanstad 62 G2
Ząbkowice Śląskie 58 F7
Zabok 70 L4
Zābol 96 H3
Zabrze 58 H7
Zacatecas 44 F4
Zadar 70 L6
Zadonsk 78 G4
Zafora 76 J8
Zafra 68 D6
Zāgheh-ye-Bālā 98 M6
Zagora 106 D2
Zagreb 70 L5
Zagyva 58 K10
Zāhedān 96 H4
Zahirabad 94 C5
Zahlé 100 C3
Zahrān 96 D6
Zaječar 74 K6
Zakamensk 84 G6

Zākhō	98	K5
Zakopane	58	J8
Zakynthos	76	C7
Zakynthos	76	C7
Zala	70	M4
Zalaegerszeg	70	M4
Zalari	84	G6
Zalaszentgrót	70	N4
Zalău	74	L2
Ẓalim	96	D5
Zaliv Aniva	84	Q7
Zaliv Kara-Bogaz Gol	96	F1
Zaliv Kresta	84	Y3
Zaliv Paskevicha	78	L5
Zaliv Shelikhova	84	T5
Zaliv Terpeniya	84	Q7
Zamakh	96	E6
Zambezi	112	C2
Zambezi	112	E3
Zambia	112	D2
Zamboanga	90	G5
Zambrów	58	M5
Zamora	68	E3
Zamość	58	N7
Zanda	94	C2
Zandvoort	62	G2
Zanesville	42	E2
Zangguy	96	L2
Zanjān	98	N5
Zannone	72	H8
Zanzibar	110	F5
Zanzibar Island	110	F5
Zaozernyy	82	S6
Zapadnaya Dvina	78	E3
Zapadno-Sibirskaya Ravnina	82	L5
Zapadnyy Sayan	82	S7
Zapata	44	G3
Zaporizhzhya	78	G5
Zaprešić	70	L5
Zaqatala	98	M3
Zara	98	G4
Zarafshan	82	L9
Zaragoza	68	K3
Zarand	101	G1
Zaranj	96	H3
Zarasai	56	P9
Zaraza	50	D2
Zarechensk	56	R3
Zaria	108	F2
Zărneşti	74	N4
Zarqā'	100	D4
Zarqān	101	E2
Żary	58	E6
Zarzadilla de Totana	68	J7
Žatec	58	C7
Zavetnoye	78	H5
Zavidoviči	74	F5
Zavitinsk	84	M6
Zayarsk	82	U6
Zaysan	82	Q8
Zayü	90	B?
Zbraslav	58	D?
Zēbāk	96	K2
Zēbār	98	L5
Zeebrugge	62	F3
Ẓefat	100	C4
Żeilona Góra	58	E6
Zeist	62	H2
Zeitz	60	H5
Zelenoborskiy	56	S3
Zelenograd	78	G3
Zelenogradsk	58	K3
Zelenokumsk	98	K1
Zella-Mehlis	60	F5
Zell am See	70	H3
Zémio	110	D2
Zemlya Alexsandry	82	G1
Zemlya Frantsa-Iosifa	82	J2
Zemlya Vil'cheka	82	L1
Zempoalteptl	46	E5
Zenica	74	E5
Zerbst	60	H5
Zermatt	70	C4
Zeta Lake	34	K2
Zeulenroda	60	G6
Zeven	60	E3
Zevenaar	62	J3?
Zeya	84	M6
Zeya	84	M6
Zeydābād	101	F2
Zeyskoye Vodokhranilishche	84	M5
Zgharta	100	C2
Zgierz	58	J6
Zgorzelec	58	E6
Zhailma	78	M4
Zhaksy	78	M4
Zhaksykon	78	M5
Zhaltyr	78	M4
Zhambyl	82	M9
Zhanatas	82	M9
Zhangbei	86	E2
Zhangguangcai Ling	86	H2
Zhangjiakou	86	E2
Zhangling	84	L6
Zhangwu	86	G2
Zhangye	86	B3
Zhangzhou	90	F2
Zhanjiang	90	E2
Zhaodong	84	M7
Zhaoqing	90	E2
Zhaosu	82	Q9
Zhaoyuan	86	H1
Zharkamys	82	K8
Zharkent	82	P9
Zharma	82	Q8
Zharyk	82	N8
Zhaxigang	94	C2
Zheleznogorsk	78	G4
Zhengzhou	86	E4
Zhenjiang	86	F4
Zherdevka	78	H4
Zhetybay	82	J9
Zhezkazgan	82	M8
Zhigalovo	84	H5
Zhigansk	84	L3
Zhilinda	84	J2
Zhob	96	J3
Zholymbet	82	N7
Zhongba	94	D3
Zhongdian	86	B5
Zhongning	86	D3
Zhongshan	90	E2
Zhongze	86	G5
Zhoukou	86	E4
Zhuanghe	86	G3
Zhucheng	86	F3
Zhumadian	86	E4
Zhuo Xian	86	F3
Zhytomyr	78	E4
Žiar	58	H9
Zibo	86	F3
Zichang	86	D3
Zieriksee	62	F3
Ziesar	60	H4
Zigong	86	C5
Ziguinchor	106	B6
Zikhron Ya'aqov	100	B4
Žilina	58	H8
Zillah	104	C2
Zima	84	G6
Zimbabwe	112	D3
Zimmi	108	B3
Zimnicea	74	N6
Zinder	108	F2
Zinjibār	104	J
Zirc	58	G1
Žirje	72	K
Zistersdorf	70	M
Zitava	58	H
Zittau	60	K
Ziway Hāyk'	110	F
Zixing	90	E
Zlaté Moravce	58	H
Zlatoust	78	L
Zlín	58	G
Zlīţan	106	H
Złotów	58	G
Zmeinogorsk	82	Q
Znamenskoye	82	N
Żnin	58	G
Znojmo	70	M
Zoigê	86	C
Zomba	112	F
Zongo	110	E
Zonguldak	76	F
Zouar	104	C
Zouérat	106	C
Żovka	58	M
Zrenjanin	74	H
Zschopau	60	J
Zug	70	D
Zugdidi	98	J
Zuger See	70	D
Zugspitze	60	I
Zuid-Beveland	62	I
Zuni	44	I
Zunyi	86	D
Županja	74	F
Zürich	70	D
Zuru	108	F
Žut	72	E
Zutphen	62	[illegible]
Zuwārah	104	[illegible]
Zuyevka	82	[illegible]
Zvishavane	112	E
Zvolen	58	[illegible]
Zvornik	74	G
Zwedru	108	C
Zweibrücken	62	[illegible]
Zwettl	70	L
Zwickau	60	H
Zwiesel	60	J
Zwolle	62	J
Zyryanka	84	S
Zyryanovsk	82	Q
Żywiec	58	J